# HEALING JC
## WITH TI

# BLACK MADONNA

"In her book *Healing Journeys with the Black Madonna,* master musician, dance and music historian, and imaginative storyteller Alessandra Belloni captures the magic of the feminine soul of Southern Italy. She explores the origins of the Black Madonna from the ancient goddesses of Greece and North Africa to the syncretism with Catholicism in Italy. With brilliant storytelling, she shares of the spirit of the Black Madonna as she is experienced in modern Italy. Most importantly, this book transports readers on an inner journey in which they experience the archetype of the Black Madonna within, so they may continue to keep her mystery and healing alive in today's world. Read this book and be transformed!"

DR. GABRIELLE FRANCIS, AUTHOR OF *THE ROCKSTAR REMEDY*

"*Healing Journeys with the Black Madonna* is an emotional tour de force that will leave you astonished by its power. But I warn you, this is not a book for those who are not ready to reflect deeply on their wounds, how they were created, and the path of recovery. The honesty within these pages is rare and appreciated in a world that often thrives off of gilded artifice and the excuses it often births. Do yourself a favor and purchase two copies of this book, one for yourself and one for someone else. The Black Madonna will let you know who is in need."

TAYANNAH LEE MCQUILLAR, AUTHOR OF *THE SIBYLS ORACULUM*

"Alessandra Belloni weaves a magical web, enabling readers to feel as if they are traveling alongside her. We share her profound experiences as she visits Black Madonnas and communes with goddesses. Packed with music and art, *Healing Journeys with the Black Madonna* is simultaneously memoir, spiritual guide, travelogue, and a shamanic document that serves as a reminder that rhythm is the cure. This is a book to read not once but again and again. "

JUDIKA ILLES, AUTHOR OF *ENCYCLOPEDIA OF SPIRITS*
AND *ENCYCLOPEDIA OF 5000 SPELLS*

"Alessandra Belloni is an international living treasure. Her deep and profound knowledge of the Black Madonna is unsurpassed, and her sacred performances are literal transmissions of numinous truth to the audience. She brings us all gems of timeless spiritual knowing. Those passionate about the Black Madonna and the eternal Goddess can find no better guide to the inner esoteric awareness and hidden secrets than Belloni. She is the carrier of magic, which she shares generously with us all."

AVA PARK, FOUNDER AND DIRECTOR OF THE MUSEUM OF WOMAN AND PRESIDING PRIESTESS OF THE GODDESS TEMPLE OF ORANGE COUNTY

"Alessandra's superb book is a surprising revelation and a powerful reminder to many of us who lost touch with the rich shamanic heritage of the Old World. She is a real passionate pioneer in the revival of this universal divine Earth Goddess archetype, a tradition from the remote villages of Southern Italy. This personal and illuminating book is an essential addition to the modern shamanic renaissance."

ITZHAK BEERY, AUTHOR OF *THE GIFT OF SHAMANISM*, *SHAMANIC TRANSFORMATIONS*, AND *SHAMANIC HEALING* AND PUBLISHER OF SHAMANPORTAL.ORG

"As a drumming and dancing shaman, Alessandra Belloni embodies everything that the Black Madonna represents: entering the depths of self for healing and transformation, honoring the earth and the rhythm of life, finding balance and wholeness, interconnection, reclaiming the power of the Divine Feminine, embracing the mysterious to find awe and wonder. She guides us to enlightenment."

AMI BELLI, VICE PRESIDENT AND INTERNATIONAL LIAISON FOR HEALTH RHYTHMS AT REMO, INC.

"People have been trying to find a cure for their anxiety and depression since the dawn of time. Today we might consider psychoanalysis, psychotherapy, or psychopharmacology, but in Southern Italy they have been using erotic dance, chants, sensual shamanic drumming, and songs for centuries to accomplish a cure. Alessandra takes us on a journey back in time to Southern Italy to reveal the rituals of the Black Madonna where she experienced the cure firsthand. This book is a must-read for anyone interested in learning alternative ways to relieving anxiety and depression."

JOSEPH V. SCELSA, ED.D., LMHC, FOUNDER AND DIRECTOR OF THE ITALIAN AMERICAN MUSEUM IN NEW YORK CITY

# HEALING JOURNEYS
## WITH THE
# BLACK MADONNA

### CHANTS, MUSIC, AND SACRED PRACTICES
### OF THE GREAT GODDESS

## ALESSANDRA BELLONI

Bear & Company
Rochester, Vermont

Bear & Company
One Park Street
Rochester, Vermont 05767
www.BearandCompanyBooks.com

Text stock is SFI certified

Bear & Company is a division of Inner Traditions International

**Library of Congress Cataloging-in-Publication Data**
Names: Belloni, Alessandra, author.
Title: Healing journeys with the black madonna : chants, music, and sacred practices of the great goddess / Alessandra Belloni.
Description: Rochester, Vermont : Bear & Company, [2019] | Includes bibliographical references and index.
Identifiers: LCCN 2018035507 (print) | LCCN 2018051801 (ebook) | ISBN 9781591433422 (pbk.) | ISBN 9781591433439 (ebook)
Subjects: LCSH: Black Virgins. | Goddesses. | Mary, Blessed Virgin, Saint—Devotion to.
Classification: LCC BT670.B55 B45 2019 (print) | LCC BT670.B55 (ebook) | DDC 202/.114—dc23
LC record available at https://lccn.loc.gov/2018035507

Printed and bound in the United States by Lake Book Manufacturing, Inc. The text stock is SFI certified. The Sustainable Forestry Initiative® program promotes sustainable forest management.

10   9   8   7   6   5   4   3   2   1

Text design and layout by Virginia Scott Bowman
This book was typeset in Garamond Premier Pro, Avenir, and Gill Sans with Jensen, Gill Sans, and Avenir used as display typefaces

To send correspondence to the author of this book, mail a first-class letter to the author c/o Inner Traditions • Bear & Company, One Park Street, Rochester, VT 05767, and we will forward the communication, or contact the author directly at **www.alessandrabelloni.com.**

*This book is dedicated to the memory of my
dear mother, Elvira Rossetti, a true, living example
of compassion and unconditional love.
She encouraged me to be an artist and follow my dreams.
She was an empowered woman from a generation
when there was no women's liberation.
She was truly nonjudgmental and accepted
everyone, no matter what color, sexual preference,
or gender. She embodied the unwavering love of the
Great Mother—the Black Madonna.
Grazie, Mamma Elvira!*

# Contents

# The Return of the Archetype in Times of Need

## By Matthew Fox

I HAVE LONG BEEN INTERESTED in the Black Madonna ever since—back in my first year of my doctoral studies in France—I stood in Chartres Cathedral and saw Her statue for the first time. I was amazed. Even though I had been a Roman Catholic for twenty-seven years and had studied within the Dominican Order for ten years and was a newly minted priest, I had never once heard of Her.

After gazing at Her for some time, I approached a French woman in the cathedral and asked her about this icon. She replied, "Oh, that is the result of so many candles being lit here over the centuries; the statue has turned black." I took another look at the statue and concluded that the woman, here in her own special cathedral from the twelfth century, had lost touch entirely with her own tradition and did not have a clue about the Black Madonna. I resolved to learn more about the Black Madonna, and ever since then I have had my antennae up to learn more about Her, having read a number of books, listened to the experiences of many people including their dreams, lectured on Her, and written quite a bit about Her.*

But this book by Alessandra Belloni and her presentation of this ancient archetype is special. It is special because the author comes from the land that holds the oldest shrines we know of that honor the Black Madonna. Although the Black Madonna can be found in Russia, Czechoslovakia, Germany, Switzerland, Spain, France, Poland, Brazil, and Portugal, the oldest shrines are in Sicily and date to at least the third century; Sicily is, after all, only a hop, skip, and jump from Africa. This book is special too, because, though the author has read about and researched the Black Madonna, much of her experience and knowledge comes from her pilgrimages to the Madonna's shrines and from learning the ancient traditions, stories, rituals, songs, and dances of her Sicilian ancestors.

The approach in this book is both biographical and instructional because the encounters with the Black Madonna altered the author's life on several occasions and, eventually, the lives of many she has connected with through pilgrimages, rituals, music, and dance and in healing sessions. The author's experience with the Black Madonna and with the healings of those she has led in ceremony to the Black Madonna are recounted with verve and imagination—it is an adventure to read this book just as it has been an adventure to live it, I'm sure. This book is a memoir of the author's journey of interactions with the Black Madonna. Carl Jung says that archetypes return when we need them. From listening to people's dreams and experiences of the Black Madonna for years, it is clear to me that She is returning at this time, this critical time, in human and planetary history.

Why is the Black Madonna returning in such force today? Might it be because Mother Earth is struggling for her own survival? I am writing this as the volcanoes in Hawaii are belching smoke, gases, and fire thirty thousand feet into the air, and I am reminded how, a few years

*See Matthew Fox, *The Hidden Spirituality of Men: Ten Metaphors for Awakening the Sacred Masculine* (Novato, Calif.: New World Library, 2008, 231–44), in which I discuss the needed marriage of the Black Madonna and the Green Man today.

ago, I was invited to do a dialogue in Hawaii with a Pele expert on Pele and the Black Madonna. In addition to the dialogue, at a retreat center on the island of Maui we each blessed a new statue to the Black Madonna that a local artist was commissioned to render. It was a moving event and a sweet pairing of the Black Madonna and Pele. One thing they both have in common, in addition to their gender, is a fierceness and wildness that has often gotten covered up or tamed by patriarchy. (Kali in India has this same fierceness and reminds us that with creativity comes destruction. And the word *kali* means "black" in the Hindi language; thus Kali is a Black Madonna of the East.) Belloni also makes a connection between Pele and the Black Madonna in this book.

It takes a certain fierceness to face climate change, the extinction of countless species, the disappearance of rain forests and trees and soil and animals in our times. There is, as the Sufi mystic Hafiz put it, a "fierce battle" going on, and people need to be awakened and aroused. This is one reason the Black Madonna is returning in our time—to wake us up from our anthropocentric (Pope Francis calls it our "narcissistic") slumber. This is one reason why the African goddess Isis was often pictured wearing a headdress with rattles—to wake people up and to rattle our institutions, to awaken us from slumber. This awakening is at the essence of all spirituality, isn't it? As Kabir, the fifteenth-century Indian mystic put it, "You have been sleeping for millions and millions of years. Why not wake up this morning?"

This is a wake-up book.

Another reason the archetype of the Black Madonna is reaching out to us today is that more people are recognizing that *black lives matter* and *women's lives matter* and *gay and transgender lives matter*. It is time to challenge the oppression of people of color, of women, of gays and lesbians, and of transgender people the world over. Blacks, whites, Hispanics, Asians, and indigenous peoples everywhere are being called to stand up to the racism, sexism, and homophobia that have ruled for so many centuries. The Black Madonna leads the way, for She is the Universal Mother, fully accepting of the immense and praiseworthy diversity of our species in all its marvelous wonderfulness. The MeToo movement, which has empowered many women to speak out and tell the truth of their abuse in workplaces and at home, the Black Lives Matter movement, the LGBTQ movement—all these trends are signs of the times. And the Black Madonna is both listening and urging with renewed energy and passion for justice and balance. The Black Madonna is a symbol of the return of the Divine Feminine that is so needed to inspire and empower girls and women and men also. People of all colors and backgrounds are invited to this dance of humanity in all its diversity.

Deep Ecumenism is about celebrating the diversity of religious traditions, and this too is a sign of our times, and it is very precious to the Black Madonna. After all, we are all descendants of Mother Africa and the African Mother who mothered our species. Why should religion fight against religion when at the heart of all religion there lies a zeal to connect to the Sacred, to the One, to the All, to the Mother? It is no accident, as Belloni indicates in this book, that the Black Madonna is to be found in sundry cultures and religions, from Asia to Africa, from Judeo-Christian religions to the ancient goddess religions that fermented in the towns of southern Italy, which were more Greek than Italian, and that to this day celebrate the Black Madonna feasts each year. I thank Alessandra for making so many and often daring journeys and pilgrimages to these many sites and for allowing us to accompany her there in these pages.

The Black Madonna is cosmic, an aspect that is explored thoroughly in the pages of this book—from the ancient story of a meteorite that struck the Earth and birthed the original Black Madonna; to the story in Islam of the holy shrine made of black stone in Mecca, also thought to have originated from a meteorite called the Kaaba that fell from the heavens, wherein a black Mariam, Mother of Jesus, is carved; to the twelve stars representing the twelve signs of the zodiac and therefore cosmic universality. Many are the stories that underscore the *cosmic sense,* the sense of the Cosmic Mother and the Cosmic Mary (a companion to the Cosmic Christ), that the Black Madonna awakens us to.

And how important and timely is it that, at this moment in history, we are receiving from science a new story of the Cosmos, a new creation story therefore, that is universal and transcends cultural and religious boundaries? The Cosmic Mother invites us to move beyond our Earth-destroying anthropocentrism as a species to realizing anew that we are part of and completely dependent on and interdependent with a vast universe, one that is 13.8 billion years in its unfolding up to our time and, as we learned just two summers ago, contains two trillion galaxies, each with hundreds of billions of stars. And here we are—small, modest, imaginative, wonder-filled, destructive-prone human beings. It is important to put our species in context. A new cosmology and a renewed appreciation of the Cosmic Black Madonna assist in that essential task. The Black Madonna archetype personalizes this vast universe for us for She is an active and engaged mother who cares and grieves for Her children.

The return of the Black Madonna incites us to personalize the universe once again: the universe is not out there someplace but rather within us. It is everything we know and yearn to know; everything we feel and yearn to feel. It is all our music, passions, dreams, and silence, and it can be profoundly dark. It is in us, and we are in it. Many astronauts and cosmonauts launched into the heavens came back mystics, and they told us why: there in the silence of the black Cosmos, Earth—lit up and glistening with her oceans, snowcapped mountains, green continents, and rivers—beckoned them home like a mother.

We do not live just in the Cosmos but in this special local neighborhood of the Cosmos, the Earth. The Black Madonna is returning because She is representative of Mother Earth. After all, as Thomas Berry puts it, "ecology is functional cosmology"; so if the Earth is in trouble, the Cosmos is in trouble. Belloni points out how black the soil is in Sicily where so many Black Madonna statues and remembrances abound. The great mystic Meister Eckhart used to say that "the ground of the soul is dark." Yes, it is. So too are the depths of the soil and the depths of space and the depths of the oceans. Darkness is depth, and depth is darkness. We need to cease being afraid of the dark and instead awaken the courage to explore the caves and caverns of not only the Earth but also of our own selves, our own souls. Quit living on the surface of life and dig down deeper to where the mysteries and the darkness lie. The womb is dark also, and we were all content there for nine good months. From the darkness emerges new life.

And so the Black Madonna represents the return to mysticism, to the mysteries, to the depths of our lives and souls, and to rituals that will take us to these depths, depths of joy and depths of silence and grief, what the mystics call the *via positiva* and the *via negativa*. This book is rich with practices and songs, chants, and dances that can assist our journey into the depths. "Launch out into the deep," advised Saint John of the Cross, a mystic-activist of the sixteenth century.

This book assists us in that important journey, a journey back to Mother Earth, to Stella Maris, to *la mer* (the sea and also mother), where all life began—the fetal waters of the womb, the fetal waters of Mother Earth, our oneness, our origins, our Source. This book invites us to cease standing safely on the shore, to enter the depths, to launch into the deep. And it gives us tools for doing so. For the Black Madonna is doing the beckoning.

I once had a dream of the Divine Feminine returning. In the dream the feminist poet Adrienne Rich, dressed in a silver wet suit, emerged from the ocean in the middle of the night with a full moon illuminating the waters of the sea. She pointed to her knee, suggesting genuflection, reverence, adoration, humility, a return to the Earth as sacred. It was a powerful and transcendent dream and remains with me to this day, and it came from the realm of the mothers, like this book.

There is great healing in this return to the Source, and this book is all about healing. Instead of covering up the wounds of Mother Earth with denial and distractions, we are asked to look deep inside ourselves and our cultures for the truth and for the true self—wounds and all—and to look at the wounds, not cover them up with happy talk and with flight into addictions but instead to develop the courage to make the journey inward.

"Wisdom today," the late and martyred monk Thomas Merton

wrote, "begins with sorrow." (Significantly, Merton underwent a conversion experience to Christianity at the Shrine of the Black Madonna in Cobre, Cuba, as a young man and dedicated his first mass as a priest to the Black Madonna.) The Black Madonna is a sorrowful mother, one who has tasted grief and feels grief over the abuse of Mother Earth and her suffering creatures but also feels grief for women, who are victims of abuse under patriarchy; people of color, who are victims of racism; and gays and transgender persons, who are victims of abuse under heterosexism. The Black Madonna is with the oppressed, but She does not abandon the oppressor either—for She wants universal healing. We can all move from victimhood to empowerment and from oppressor to being with others. We can all learn to let go.

This is the path of compassion, and that is what Jesus teaches and Muhammad teaches and the Dali Lama teaches and all spiritual traditions teach: our godlike powers of compassion. Rather, it is our goddesslike powers of compassion, for it is not coincidence that the words for *compassion* in both Hebrew and Arabic derive from the word for *womb*. Compassion is about interdependence, and what is more interdependent than mother and fetus in the womb? And as Belloni point out, the Earth herself harbors a womb and is the birthplace of all mothering and fathering.

So the Black Madonna calls us to newer expressions of compassion. This is what waking up is about; this is what enlightenment means: that we become active instruments for compassion. We become the hands of the Compassionate One. The Black Madonna is all about compassion for She celebrates interdependence, which is the basis of all compassion. We are all part of one another and involved in one another, whether that be our common joy and celebration or our common suffering.

All these lessons of the Return of the Black Madonna at this time are to be found in this rich book, this wild ride, with a devotee of the Black Madonna who has learned from the ancients, done her homework and her heart work, danced the dance, drummed the drums and tambourines, and bled while doing so in a shamanistic gift for our times.

The late Thomas Berry, who called himself a "geo-logian" rather than a theologian, used to say that at our time in history "we do not need more professors; we do not need more priests. What we need are more shamans." This book is a special book also because it is shared by a person who is part scholar, part ritual maker, part story listener and story sharer, part pilgrim, part wild woman. But she is fully a healer and fully a shaman. It comes through clearly in these pages where she shares her hard-earned wisdom and that of her ancestors who from ancient times danced with the Black Madonna first as Isis and Cybele and who invite us to do the same in our times.

It has been my privilege to have worked and prayed deeply with indigenous people of my land, and there were a number of moments when reading this book that I was struck by how indigenous the stories told and the practices enacted in the villages of the author's homeland echoed those among the First Peoples of the Americas. This book contributes to a necessary and long-overdue healing between European cultures and indigenous cultures. It might begin with a healing that Thomas Merton called for in a myth he wrote about indigenous history where he writes: "The spirits have held out toward us in their hands in silence, and in their hands their orchids and oranges . . . they have sung to us, they have followed us, friendly. . . . We have not understood their playful modes. We have fought Eros."* This fighting of Eros is addressed head on in this book. The Black Madonna is not ashamed or regretful for Eros. She invites us there. In the Bible, the Book of Wisdom declares: "This is wisdom: To love life." Isn't that what Eros is about? Why be afraid of it? (Unless, of course, we lack the spirituality to sustain it.)

There are ways to heal, for example, that the author tells about near the end of her book that take us beyond the limits of Western medicine as we know it and therefore beyond the drugging of victims of abuse by medical professionals. In reading this section on healing deep abuse I was led to think that maybe the many victims of priestly abuse for example might derive considerable support from the kinds of rituals

---

*Thomas Merton, *Raids on the Unspeakable* (New York: New Directions, 1966), 137.

and ceremonies that are shared in this book. Such people should all be gifted with a copy of this book and invitations to dance the ceremonies of the Black Madonna.

Reading this book we learn of the often thrilling adventures of the author in pursuit of the Black Madonna—indeed, to read this book *is* an adventure—and reading it is to be invited to further initiations into shamanhood. For these many reasons it is a great gift for our time. The return of the Black Madonna is a great and needed gift for our time. Thank you to Alessandra Belloni for being the wild woman she is and the generous recipient of the mysteries of the past, the return of the oppressed, the bold defender of the mysteries of the Divine Feminine incarnated here as the Black Madonna.

MATTHEW FOX is a spiritual theologian who draws inspiration from the Creation Spirituality lineage about which he has written, taught, and spoken about for forty-five years. When Cardinal Ratzinger dismissed him from the Dominican Order after 34 years, he became an Episcopalian priest. He holds a doctorate from the Institut Catholique de Paris and founded the University of Creation Spirituality in Oakland, California. Fox is a recipient of the Abbey Courage of Conscience Peace Award (other recipients being the Dalai Lama, Mother Teresa, Ernesto Cardenal, and Rosa Parks); the Ghandi King Ikeda Award; the Tikkun National Ethics Award; and other awards. His work has been honored by theologians, artists, healers, and thought leaders around the world. He is the author of thirty-five books, including *Original Blessing, Passion for Creation: The Earth-Honoring Spirituality of Meister Eckhart; A Spirituality Named Compassion; The Hidden Spirituality of Men; Naming the Unnameable: 89 Wonderful & Useful Names for God . . . Including the Unnameable God;* and *Order of the Sacred Earth.*

# Four Mystical Experiences That Led Me to the Black Madonna

*I am fascinated and inspired by the Black Madonna. She is the female embodiment of God. Her power hails from the fact that She influences all of humanity in a very global and inclusive way. She embraces everyone, and everyone has access to Her divine spirit and power. She also represents the cradle of humanity, which began in Africa.*

ALESSANDRA BELLONI

I FELL IN LOVE WITH SOUTHERN ITALIAN FOLK MUSIC in the late 1970s and began performing professionally in 1980. At that time I decided to start deep field research on the folk music, theater, and dance of Southern Italy. As part of this research, I participated in many religious festivals held in the regions of Lazio, Abruzzo, Campania, Naples, Calabria, Puglia, and Sicily.

During this time I discovered the rich and colorful folklore that is still alive and thriving in these remote villages, especially around the

Fig. P.1. Alessandra Belloni with the Black Madonna of Moiano;
photo montage by Armando Mei

times of the feasts dedicated to the Madonna. These were not your typical blond-haired, blue-eyed versions of Mother Mary. In most cases, they were black statues or paintings known as Madonna Nera (Black Madonna) or Madonna Bruna (Brown Madonna), and they had dark skin.

Often by chance, I came upon beautiful, white Romanesque or Baroque churches situated near the sea, in fields, near caves, or perched on high mountains. In these locations I discovered the most amazing, mysterious Black Madonnas. I felt a powerful energy coming from them—from their faces and eyes full of tenderness, forgiveness, austerity, compassion, sorrow, and universal love.

When I participated in the feasts and processions, I witnessed thousands of people taking vows, lifting the heavy statues, and running uphill effortlessly with them. They walked barefoot for hours, singing and chanting, crying, praying, and asking for miracles.

In the beginning, I did not know that the Black Madonna was a Christian tradition with deep roots in the pre-Christian worship of Mother Earth. I also did not know why the Madonna was black. When I first asked the priests the question *"Perche la Madonna è nera?"* (Why is the Madonna black?), the answer was curious. The priest responded, *"È nera perche è nera."* (She is black because She is black.) I took this to mean that it was a mystery and should be respected as a mystery. But still, I wanted to know more.

Another typical answer to my question was, "It is the candle smoke." It was obvious this was not the truth. These statues often have white and red dresses and cloaks, blue mantels and golden stars, none of which have turned black from the candle smoke. Just as there are many black Christs around the world (a large number in Italy), there are also a proliferation of Black Madonnas. I was sure there was a sound, symbolic reason for the blackness of the Madonnas' skin. I was determined to find out the truth. Although it took several years, the Black Madonna manifested Herself to me, opening a portal that transformed my life.

## THE HEALING VISION OF
## THE BLACK MADONNA OVER MY HOSPITAL BED

There are times in our lives when things happen so fast and so unexpectedly, especially when you are young and feel that the world is in the palm of your hand.

For me, the year 1986 was one of those times. I was enjoying a successful artistic career in New York City with my music and theater company, I Giullari di Piazza (The Jesters of the Square), which I founded with the brilliant musician, guitarist, and composer John La Barbera. The company was a result of our falling in love, a musical and creative love, which brought us a great deal of recognition onstage. The troupe was performing a new folk opera at Carnegie Music Hall in Pittsburgh to excellent reviews.

Unfortunately, the artistic success and the stress of the grueling performance schedule brought deep conflicts between John and me. With a great deal of pain, we decided to separate that year. I admit that emotionally I was a wreck. When we entered Carnegie Music Hall for dress rehearsal, I fainted. But the show must go on! Somehow, I managed to find my strength again and performed the opera *Don Giovanni and His Servant Pulcinella,* which I wrote and directed.

Yet I couldn't fully enjoy its success because I had suddenly become very ill with heavy irregular bleeding. I was young and extremely scared. When I finally went for routine testing, I was diagnosed with cervical dysplasia, a serious precancerous condition. I had to undergo surgery immediately. Cervical conization is a terrifying experience, and it affected me deeply, on many levels. I felt powerless at the thought of my womb being cut and was very worried about the consequences it would have on me later, both emotionally and physically.

My wonderful mother, Elvira, came from Italy to support me with her unconditional love, as she had always done. I knew that she would be praying for me as I went in for surgery at Mount Sinai Hospital. But something happened that was more intensely spiritual than I ever could have imagined. It was as though a magical portal opened for me that changed my life forever. Was it my mother's fervent prayers, or something more?

When I woke up in the recovery room, I had a crystal-clear vision of the Black Madonna embracing me and protecting me. She was standing over my bed with Her benevolent black face beaming down at me. She wore a blue cape and a gold crown, holding Her arms wide open and Her hands straight in front of Her as if sending me powerful rays of healing energy. There was a bright white light emanating from them.

Full of compassion, the Black Madonna told me that I was to follow Her path, which was to feel other people's pain. I knew that my heart had suddenly opened to understand the suffering of the world and of the Earth herself. I immediately turned to my right in the recovery room and knew clearly that someone nearby was dying. But it wasn't frightening; it was just part of life's circle. I don't recall how much time passed in this blissful moment of spiritual awakening initiated by the Black Madonna, but it was so real, and I felt so protected that I did not want it to end.

I told the doctors who came to check on me that I felt fine and that I knew the woman on my right was dying. I told them that I felt an immense sadness for her. The medical team was in disbelief seeing that I was no longer bleeding, that I had absolutely no pain and was so awake and aware, and that I had also sensed death in the room.

This was the beginning of a spiritual awakening that has transformed my personal and artistic life. When I was brought back to my room, my mother was waiting for me. The fact that my musical partner, John La Barbera, was also there showed me that he still loved me. I felt so much joy in seeing them both, even though I could see the anxiety and fear in their faces.

I told my mother about my vision of the Black Madonna. She understood immediately that I had inherited the gift from her: the ability to communicate with the Virgin Mary and receive Her grace. It was a vision of the Madonna that literally saved my mother's life during a bombing in World War II in Rome, a story I will tell in greater detail later in this book.

I was released from the hospital the next day feeling completely different and knowing that I was being guided after my healing vision of the Black Madonna. It still remained a mystery to me, but I was ready to follow Her path, wherever it led.

## THE BLACK MADONNA AS MOTHER EARTH: SHE IS ALIVE!

In January 1987, one month after my surgery, I decided to take a rest and leave New York so I could fully recover. I went to visit my sister, Gabriella, in Los Angeles. I was so happy to be in the sun and the heat and go to the beach in the middle of the winter. At the time, Gabriella was working in film production and writing scripts. She enjoyed a typical Hollywood lifestyle with parties and celebrities.

Gabriella did not have a strong spiritual life, however. In the years to come, she often told me, "It is very difficult to be the sister of the Black Madonna!" This came out of an incredible mystical experience I had during this visit with her. It happened when Gabriella's film-producer boyfriend offered to take us for a ride in his private airplane. I love flying and had always wanted to go up in a small aircraft.

There I was in a small, three-seater airplane, sitting alone in the backseat. Gabriella's boyfriend took us on a wonderful ride up along the Pacific Coast to Santa Barbara. Soon we were gliding over the ocean, and I gazed in amazement at the gorgeous mountains and the desert. Suddenly, I heard a powerful voice speaking to me, a beautiful, haunting woman's voice coming from the ocean and the Earth. It told me that She was the voice of Mother Earth. She was the voice of the beginning of life, the primordial waters. She said that She was alive—breathing, thinking, nurturing, and, at times, destroying. In a whisper, She told me that She was also in great pain and that human beings were not respecting Her. She said that because of this we did not have much time left. Finally, She announced that She was the voice of the Black Madonna.

Held in the arms of Father Sky, the Great Spirit, God, I began to understand the mystery of this connection. It was so overwhelming that I began to cry. As big tears rolled down my face, I wondered if my sister and her boyfriend had heard this voice too, but I was afraid to ask. What if they hadn't? Was I crazy?

As I wrote this book in February 2017, I realized that a powerful dream of the Earth Mother had guided me here to Hawaii twenty years earlier. In this dream I was flying over the Earth, over the ocean, but I was in the form of a rare bird. I could see that the greed of human beings had destroyed much of the Earth. I was in pain and felt desperate. Suddenly, floating over the ocean, I saw an island shaped like the stylized profile of a woman. Then I saw that the woman was crying a tear of lava. When I heard her voice, I knew that it was the voice of the Earth crying out, asking me for help. I woke up sobbing, not knowing what this dream really meant, not knowing where this place was; yet I knew it existed.

A few months later I found myself using a mileage ticket to take my first trip to Hawaii. I had been invited by an Italian American man who wanted to bring my music group to perform at the University of Hawaii. He told me that I could stay in a lovely house on the beach in Lanikai. The home was owned by his good friend Shayla. When I arrived in Lanikai, which means "sacred waters" in Hawaiian, I really felt I had found paradise.

As I put down my bags and met Shayla, I had a strong sense of déjà vu. I felt that I had known her before and that I had been here before. Even her house seemed familiar. Then I looked across the ocean and saw the lava island of which I had dreamed! I told Shayla, "I have been here before in my dreams, flying as a special bird."

Shayla didn't think my dream vision was strange at all. (I knew that she was a spiritual being since she had many statues of goddesses and Madonnas throughout her home.) She hugged me and said, "Then you are definitely in the right place." I asked her about the island across the water from her house and learned that it was a sacred place called Mokulua. Right then and there, I decided that I had to learn how to kayak so I could visit the island before I returned to New York.

When I did go kayaking, together with my friend Tom, I discovered the lava tear as I approached the shore of the little island. I was greeted by a dozen giant turtles and amazing rare birds who were nesting there. They all started singing to me, as if they had been waiting for me. I sat beside Tom on the lava rocks in shock. He looked at me in amazement and said, "You were guided here, Alessandra. The birds and turtles are happy that you have returned."

Later, Shayla told me that these rare birds were called shearwater birds and were almost extinct. This was the bird I had become in my dream as I was flying over Mokulua! To Shayla's amazement, during a full moon, a few of these birds flew over her backyard on the beach as I was doing a ritual prayer to the moon, chanting and drumming using a ring. Did I call them with my songs? How could the Hawaiian birds or elements respond to my Italian ritual musical tradition?

The day Tom and I kayaked to Mokulua had started out as rainy and stormy. It seemed impossible to go out onto the sea. But I felt a sudden inspiration to take out my ocean drum and chant "Jesce Sole" (Come Out Sun). "Jesce Sole" is an ancient Neapolitan chant invoking the healing energy of the sun (which I will teach you later in this book). I went right into the ocean, chanting in the storm. Within an hour not only did it stop raining but the sun came out in all its glory.

These two powerful experiences led me to realize even more that the Black Madonna and the Earth Mother guided me to Hawaii, showing me clearly that the Earth is alive, that the Dark Mother is alive. In Hawaii, She is known as Pele, the black female goddess of the volcano. I also knew that the sun was alive and that the endangered species had a clear message for me: we must care for Her as ancient indigenous people have done for thousands of years, respecting Her as a living being.

It was this essential truth—the endangered state of our beautiful planet and of humankind as well—that motivated me to create a musical production dedicated to Mother Earth and Her possible salvation. My opera *The Voyage of the Black Madonna* premiered at the Cathedral of Saint John the Divine and is the embodiment of my devotion.

I will now guide you through this mystical journey of awakening and discovery through an ancient beautiful myth of creation so that you too can experience the mysteries of the Black Madonna, the Earth, and the African Mother, the womb from which we all came.

# Acknowledgments

I KNOW THAT I HAVE BEEN BLESSED with a special lifestyle, both as an artist and as a woman. I chose a difficult path, combining spirituality and devotion to the Black Madonna and the ancient Earth Mother Goddess with music, theater, dance, and ritual drumming, an art form that is not commercial, particularly in New York City, where I live—a place that is extremely competitive and difficult on many levels. I think it is a miracle that I have been able to live my dream, perform, and teach around the world. Writing this book about my life's work and my personal healing story has also been a dream, and I am very grateful to many people around the world; without their support, I would have never been able to achieve this goal.

I am honored and proud to be part of Inner Traditions • Bear and Company Publishers and their family of authors. I am especially grateful to the great writer and visionary Matthew Fox, who is one of my mentors and a source of inspiration.

I have been blessed with other amazing mentors, and I thank the Very Reverend Dean James Parks Morton and his wife, Pamela, whom I consider my spiritual parents and who gave me the possibility of being artist in residence at the Cathedral of Saint John the Divine. I also want to honor the memory of Remo Belli, founder of Remo, Inc., who believed in me as a percussionist and teacher and opened the doors to the world; thank you to his wife, Ami, and the entire Remo family.

Special thanks to New York City's Mayor Bill de Blasio and his wife, First Lady Chirlane McCray, for their support, endorsement, and belief in my work and mission. And for their hard work to make New York a place of equality and justice that embraces artists like me.

A special thank-you to my sister, Gabriella, for being a role model in women's right to freedom and for bringing me to New York, and to my brother, Muzio. To my friends and family in Hawaii: Shayla Spencer, for giving me a place to write in paradise; Father Phil Harmon and Jésus Puerto of Kahumana Farm and Retreat Center; and Professor Apela Colorado in Maui with the Indigenous Mind Science Program. Thank you to Mel Bay Publications and William Bay for letting me use the *tammorriata* drumming lesson from my *Rhythm is the Cure* book and DVD published with them in 2007.

My special gratitude to my musical partner and collaborator John La Barbera, a wonderful guitarist, composer, and great friend since 1976. Thank you, dear John, I could not have accomplished all these musical achievements without you. Our music together is a true act of love.

And special gratitude to my late ex-husband Dario Bollini, who shared with me, for fourteen years, the passion and devotion for the Black Madonna, supporting my research and performances. We shared a great love: happy, intense, and challenging. He passed away too young in 2009. His smile and gentle soul are greatly missed, but he is around us when we play the chants that he wrote to the Black Madonna. *Grazie, Dario, riposa in pace!* Thanks to his daughter, Daphne Bollini.

To my New York collaborators: Arden H. Mason, for the beautiful painting used on the cover; Mara Gerety, Mark Mindek, Joe Deninzon, Cathy Brown, Ray Wu, Mallorie Vaudoise, Vincenza Dante, Carla E. Huelsenbeck, Bethany Morgan, Amara Hillary Posey, Summer Minerva, Steve Gorn, Scotty Brancher, Daniella Courvoisier, Andrea Nehesi, Gerborg, Esmerelda, Zuzu, Sara, and Dragata.

To the writers: Itzhak Beery, Tayahanna Lee McQuillar, Lucia Chiavola Birnbaum, Lee Hawkins, Angelo Tonelli, and Luisa del Giudice and Armando Mei.

My friends and inspiration: Tara Johanson, Joseph Giannini (Gypsy Joe), Greg Friedman, Ava Park, Phila Hoops, Amaya, and Manex Ibar. To all the actors and dancers of my company, I Giullari di Piazza, especially Giuseppe de Falco, Ivan Thomas, Francesca Silvano and Susan Eberene.

I am grateful to all the women who have been part of my life through the years, for giving me the inspiration to continue this work and to write this book—I know that they all inspire others with their survivors' force—Tara from San Diego, Stephanie from California and Hawaii, and Lorena and Susan from New York.

To my supporters and members of my board of directors: Dr. Joseph Scelsa, Michael Connolly, John Lauro, Joan Marchi Migliori, Josephine Maietta, and Professor Dolores de Louise.

To everyone at the Cathedral of Saint John the Divine, especially Lisa Schubert, Kent Tritle, and Paul Winter. To Stefano Albertini and Kostja Kostic, professors at NYU Casa Italiana.

My immense gratitude is to all the people in Italy, especially in Southern Italy, where I have learned this tradition: writer-composer Roberto De Simone, anthropologist Luigi Lombardi Satriani, author-archaeologist Armando Mei, Raffaele Inserra, Vittorio De Paola, Francesco Braccio, Salvo Salvatore Evalto, Don Mino from the Basilica of Seminara, all the people of Parco Jalari, Sebastiano Pietrini and Federico Chiofalo in Sicily, and Gaia and Antonio Pescetti of La Chiara di Prumiano, Tuscany, for hosting my healing workshop, Rhythm is the Cure, for eighteen years with true love and compassion.

I thank the churches and towns of Moiano, Seminara, Torre Annunziata, Viggiano, Montevergine, Foggia, Positano, and Tindari. In Brazil: Carminha Levy, Maurizio Longobardi, Siba, and Magda Pucci and Paulo Dias.

Grazie!

# Mamma Elvira's Miracle

I BELIEVE THAT EVERYTHING THAT HAPPENS to us is inter-connected and leads us to our destinies: even things that seem small and inconsequential, things that seem impossibly large, things that occurred before we were born. An ordeal my mother survived years before my birth helped shape me. Events that took place when I was a child—when I was too young to comprehend them and make choices—also shaped my fate.

To truly understand me and the unconventional path my life took, I must bring you back to the beginning. Like pieces of a puzzle, these events will seamlessly fit together and make perfect sense. They begin with the bombing of Rome in 1943.

My mother is the true source of inspiration for this book. I began writing it when my mother was still alive; then circumstances in my life as an artist, a performer, and a woman struggling with the pain of divorce and lost loved ones led me to finish this book many years later. But perhaps the delay happened for a reason. I believe that this is a time where transformation and women's empowerment is greatly needed to make the world a better place. And I strongly feel that this book can be a stepping-stone to achieve this.

Fig. I.1. Mamma Elvira in California;
photo by Gabriella Belloni

## LA NOTTE DI SAN LORENZO, AUGUST 10, 2003

My mother, Elvira Rossetti, was born in a Roman neighborhood called San Lorenzo. It was the only part of the city that was bombed during World War II. Tonight, in San Lorenzo, six decades after the bombing, there will be a feast of commemoration for the sixty years since the bombing, a celebration, and fireworks. The time between sunset on August 10 and dawn on August 11 is known as "The Night of the Shooting Stars," or *La Notte di San Lorenzo.* This year it is a magical, hot, and steamy summer night, which one can only know in Italy in the summertime. August 10 is the evening when we look up into the skies, watching for shooting stars to wish upon. Legend has it that those shooting-star wishes come true, and I believe it.

Back in 1943, there was no time to observe the feast since Rome had been bombed less than a month earlier by the Americans on July 19. Now, more than sixty years later, there is a memorial ceremony to commemorate that day with photographs and books. But I don't need a memorial ceremony to remind me what happened, for my family history is steeped in its events.

My mother, then twenty-five years old, was living in Rome with her family when her neighborhood was bombed. Elvira had inherited psychic powers from her mother's lineage, people who were originally from Spain and were most likely Sephardic Jews or Gypsies. On July 18, 1943, the night before Rome was bombed, my mother had a premonition that San Lorenzo would be attacked. Her premonition came in the form of a powerful dream. In it, she saw bombs dropping from the skies. The building she lived in exploded, and she was buried in its ruins. As she struggled to catch her breath in this dream, my mother had an intense vision of the Madonna hovering above her, pulling her free, rescuing her from beneath the crumbled remains of what was once her home. The Madonna in my mother's dream resembled the Madonna della Strada, the Madonna of the Street, who was depicted in a large painting in my mother's home.

This is why, when Mamma heard the warning sirens before the bombs were dropped the following day, she took the painting of the Madonna della Strada with her. Just as in the dream, the house exploded. My grandmother, mother, and her two younger sisters were violently hurled down three stories. By some miracle, my mother found herself alive and on her knees, clutching the portrait of the Madonna della Strada, with her sisters grabbing on to her.

Although my mother and her sisters were safe, my grandmother wasn't so lucky. No one could find her, and it was feared that she was buried beneath the ruins under cement and dust and the bodies of other tenants. Frantic, my mother ran through the rubble shouting her mother's name, searching for her. She found my grandmother by chance when she noticed a hand sticking out from under the wreckage and recognized the family ring on her finger. Alone, Elvira dug through the rubble with an uncommon strength that seemed to come from a heavenly force. The Madonna! Not only did the Madonna lead my mother to *find* my grandmother but She also gave my mother the might to singlehandedly rescue my grandmother from being buried alive. My mother was so touched by divine intervention that she didn't even realize that she was hurt and bleeding from the head. Without thinking of her own safety, my mother mustered all of her strength and compassion in an act of true, unconditional love, which saved my grandmother's life.

As soon as she dug Grandmother free, Mamma Elvira called for the firemen, who put my grandmother onto a truck full of Nazi soldiers. It was headed to the best hospital in the area, San Giacomo, which had been taken over by the Germans. My mother jumped onto the truck with my grandmother, unafraid of the Nazis, praying fervently to the Madonna to save my nonna Rosa. Nonna was still breathing but not moving. She came close to losing her legs and was paralyzed at the age of forty-two.

My grandfather and my father (who was engaged to Elvira at the time) were at work when the bombing began. Arriving at the house, they found only destruction. In desperation, they searched for the family among the rubble. It was total chaos, with frightened people running about screaming. Corpses littered the ruins. Amid the confusion they heard stories of a brave young woman who had been miraculously found alive clutching the Madonna della Strada and had saved her own mother. Somehow they knew this young woman was Elvira and managed to locate her and Nonna Rosa at San Giacomo Hospital.

A few days later, Regina Elena, the queen of Italy, came to visit the people who were wounded in the bombing of San Lorenzo. She'd heard about Elvira's courage and awarded my mother the Medal of Honor. The queen also gave my mother money, because the family had lost everything they owned in the bombing. All of the newspapers wrote about this courageous young woman who saved her mother's life. They even published photos of her with the queen. For a short time, Elvira Rossetti was a heroine of the war.

Elvira's World War II experience was indeed a miracle. I feel that it's important that her story be told, for it is a tale of empowerment and courage for women who, like me, are on a spiritual journey in search of the true essence of feminine energy and healing power. I have no doubt that it was the Madonna of the Street who touched my mother with grace and enabled her to pull her own mother out from the rubble.

This is why I dedicated my book to my mother, Mamma Elvira,

Fig. I.2. Elvira Rossetti by
the Tiber, Rome, 1942

and to the unwavering love of the Great Mother—to Mother Earth and
to Mamma Roma, the She-Wolf of Rome. My vow to the Madonna is
to tell my story in Her honor and praise and to bring to the world my
personal journey, the one that guides me to Her and Her infinite compassion, and one that leads others to Her as well. I am pleased that you
have joined me on this pilgrimage.

## THE JOURNEY BEGINS

From 1943 Rome, fast-forward to the year 2003. I had just left Mamma
Elvira to travel to the south of Italy, and I missed her so much already.
Although eighty-six years old and blind from diabetes, she was still
strong and powerful in her own way. At one point, when I helped
Mamma sit up in a chair, I had a revelation. It happened when I looked
at the small antique painting of the Madonna and Child, painted on a
piece of wood that unfolded into three parts, by her bed. (Mamma had
the painting for years; I remembered it from my childhood.) Suddenly,

I realized that the Madonna in the center was flanked by two female angels playing tambourines (see plate 1).

"How perfect," I thought. "They are playing the instrument I learned to master, the instrument that heals and is connected to rituals for the Madonna." This is the exact same instrument played by my maternal grandfather, Nonno Rodolfo Rossetti.

I asked my mother if she remembered the painting and how she came to have it. Sightless, she smiled, recalling very well the Madonna and the Angels with the tambourines. I could almost see her picturing them in her mind. Then Mamma told me that she thought the painting was the perfect connection between her, the Madonna, and me. Chills covered my body when Mamma said that she had bought this old painting before I was even born, to keep it by her side always, for protection.

For more than fifty years my mother had been praying to this painting of the Madonna and the angels—in times of despair, desolation, and loneliness, when my father betrayed her, insulted her, and humiliated her. For more than fifty years, she found compassion, refuge, and mercy in the Madonna's sweet beneficence. What a powerful image!

I looked at my mother, blind, sitting placidly in the chair where she now spent most of her time, and I wondered if she was becoming like the Madonna herself, sitting on her throne, always there for me, offering me guidance and unconditional love. I felt sad because I had to leave her to start my performance tour in Southern Italy. I asked Mamma for her blessing, kissed her, and hugged her, then went out the door. It broke my heart to leave her side, but I had no choice.

As I went out into the heat, I heard my mother's lyrical, still-young voice calling, "*Sta attenta con la macchina, va piano, non ti stancare troppo, mangia, riposa, chiamami quando arrivi, mi raccomando!*" (Be careful on the road, go slow, don't get too tired, eat, rest, and call me when you arrive!) I took the Autostrada del Sole (Highway of the Sun) to Naples, the beautiful city that has inspired so much of my work over the years, the cradle of this amazing *cultura popolare* (popular culture) and the heart of the folk music, dance, and drumming that honors the Black Madonna.

The sunset was an amazingly vivid red and orange, perhaps due to the unbearable heat. I breathed the stifling air and looked at the familiar surroundings, trying to imagine how many times I must have driven down this highway over the past twenty-three years during my field trips to discover more and more about the mysteries of the Black Madonna.

I love this land: the dry mountains, the small villages with their medieval towers half destroyed, their old churches full of dark Madonna icons, their cafés and bars where old men sit all day playing cards, where women pick tomatoes, singing as they work, then go to their rustic kitchens to make pungent sauces with those juicy, sun-ripened tomatoes. These lovely villages are full of peasant women whose ancient faces are reminiscent of Mother Earth herself. These same women chant behind statues of the Virgin Mary during feast day processions and play the tammorra with such fervent passion. Deep in my soul, I feel that I am one of them.

Exiting the highway at Castellammare di Stabia, which sits on the Bay of Naples, I passed the ruins of Pompeii and the ancient Roman thermal baths, where, for thousands of years, people have come to be cured by the healing mud and curative waters. Many memories flooded back to me as I sat alone by the pool at the Hotel delle Terme in the shadow of Mount Vesuvius, the sleeping volcano. On this eve of San Lorenzo, I gazed at the huge full moon and waited for a shooting star upon which to make my special wish.

As I bathed in the thermal waters that night, in the ancient land of the Black Madonna, I stared at the moon through my hands, which I held in a triangle shape. This was my secret ritual of praying and receiving energy from the Goddess of the Moon, Diana, but in no way did I invent it. This unique method of prayer dated back to age-old women's rituals in which they held a great iron ring, called *l'anellone piceno,* between their hands, raised it high above their heads, and gazed at the moon through its center. When done just right, the moon's rays shine perfectly through the ring, touch the iron, and pulsate along the hand's lifeline, giving the ring bearer immense power and infinite energy.

I actually own one of these rare rings. It was given to me by Dario, a very important man in my life—he had the ring made especially for me (see plate 18). I have used it many times in different powerful points on the Earth, praying to the mysterious Goddess of the Moon—Stella Diana, Dea della Luna, Artemis of Ephesus. This moon deity is a black goddess who represents the dark side of the moon, the blackness of the Cosmos, the immense universe, and the mystery of the life-giving woman. She is one of the many aspects of the Black Madonna. I will share my knowledge of this secret magical ring and moon ritual later on in this book (see page 274).

That night, in the shadow of Mount Vesuvius, on the eve of San Lorenzo, I gazed up into the evening sky. I held my hands toward the moon as though my fingers were the ring, for I have learned how to receive the moon's magic even without the ring. *La Luna* looked down upon me, smiling, benevolent yet mysterious. I felt her intensity and again recalled Dario and our connection to the moon. I remembered falling in love with him under the full moon many years earlier in 1975. He and I were also deeply joined by our devotion and connection to the Black Madonna—She guided our mutual journey.

In fact, Dario and I came to this very hotel on our way to the *tammorriata* festival, with its ritual drumming in honor of the Madonna. Returning to the hotel at sunrise, after a night of wild, erotic dancing, Dario and I drank the Dionysian sparkling wine and felt the energy simmer between us as we made love, tasting the sensuality of the volcanic earth and breathing in the pungent aroma of the thermal waters.

In this magical place, Mother Earth is forever alive, inhaling and exhaling, as though the dark volcanic soil itself is moving with seismic shocks, peppered with the strong perfume of lava, offering us Her primordial healing mud from Her womb. The ancient Greeks and Romans venerated Her as Cybele, black goddess of the Earth. The Neapolitans worship Her as la Madonna Nera di Montevergine—the Black Madonna of Montevergine (Virgin Mountain), the sacred mountain where the Roman poet Virgil kept his garden of magical healing herbs.

In the sultry heat on the Night of the Shooting Stars, I looked around and felt the potency of the towering volcano that stood to my left. I saw the sacred mountain protecting me, embracing me from behind, and the full moon shining directly onto me. It was enchanting, dreamlike. And finally, I saw a shooting star! In this land abundant with the Black Madonnas, I made my wish: I want to write about Her, to intertwine my story and Hers as one, to tell my journey of self-discovery and how I came to write the folk opera *The Voyage of the Black Madonna*.

I vowed to empower and inspire others around the world to follow Her sacred path, beginning with my own personal story of healing and redemption. This was my wish as the shooting star arched across the sky, then disappeared—and now I am seeing this realized by the publication of this book.

## BAPTIZED IN THE TIBER

Let's go back again to the beginning, to my beginning. My father, Eugenio Belloni, was robust, commanding, and very handsome. Dark complexioned, he looked as though he were of mixed blood, possibly of African origins.

His family was from the republic of San Marino, and his grandparents joined Giuseppe Garibaldi, the hero who was responsible for unifying Italy. Garibaldi and his followers traveled around the world, so I always wondered if my great-grandparents were indeed from an exotic place, somewhere besides Italy.

Some thought my father even looked Native American. Eugenio was a true free spirit with unusual ways. He worked with his hands, carving marble, all his life. He also was a champion in sports, especially cross-country skiing, horseback riding, rowing, running, and gymnastics, and won many competitions in these areas. In addition, Eugenio worshipped Mother Nature, the spirits of the mountains, the rivers, and the sea. He prayed ardently to the Sun God but never went to church. He hated Catholicism and the priests with as much passion as he loved Nature.

My parents had three children: my sister, Gabriella, my brother, Muzio, and me, the youngest. I had the distinction of being the only one baptized in the River Tiber. My father believed that I was the daughter of the river, to which he was strongly connected. One day, when I was an infant, my parents went out on the Tiber in the little boat my father used for his rowing competitions and dipped me under a small waterfall called La Pimpinella. It was an unusual but beautiful initiation to Nature.

My parents didn't know that this was a common initiation ritual among the Yoruba religion, which comprises the traditional religious and spiritual concepts and practices of the Yoruba people. Its homeland is in present-day southwestern Nigeria and the adjoining parts of Benin and Togo, commonly known as Yorubaland. Yoruba is now one of the three largest ethnic groups in Nigeria, concentrated in the southwestern part of the country; African studies cited their population to be around ten million.

So, unwittingly, they also made me a Daughter of the orisha Ochun. An orisha is a spirit or goddess, in the Yoruba tradition, and Ochun is the goddess of love, rivers, waterfalls and sweet waters, eros, dance, and music. In Brazil, Ochun is strongly connected to the Black Madonna, called Nossa Senhora Aparecida (Our Lady of the Apparition). This might explain my strong link to the Black Madonna as an adult—I was unintentionally baptized as a daughter of Ochun.

Yoruba religion is formed of diverse traditions. It has influenced a host of thriving traditions such as Santería in Puerto Rico and Cuba, and Umbanda and Candomblé in Brazil. I discovered this interesting information about Ochun in the 1980s, first in New York, in Central Park, performing with Puerto Rican and Cuban drummers, and years later in the magical land of Brazil, when I went through a difficult initiation rite, which I describe later in this book.

Even as a child I knew that I had an unusual family. There was no one quite like us in Rome. My father, Eugenio, would often go around the house naked or with nothing but a fig leaf covering his genitals. My mother, on the other hand, was reserved and never showed her body to us. Although my father was a precursor of the hippie generation, he was domineering and hard on us, especially on my sister, Gabriella, and my mother.

Fig. I.3. Elvira Rossetti and Eugenio Belloni
by the Tiber, Rome, 1942

My parents certainly made a stunning couple for they were both dark and exotic, but honestly, they didn't have much in common. They had a happy marriage for a few years, but by the time I was five, they had already begun to have terrible fights. At times Eugenio was violent and extremely frightening. He was, in a way, the stereotype of an Italian male, very seductive and unfaithful. He had many affairs; he cheated and lied to my beautiful mother, who was a loyal, honest, and devoted wife.

At that time, in Italy in the 1960s, Catholic women couldn't get legally separated from their husbands; divorce was not yet legal, due to the power of the Vatican. My poor mother suffered a great deal and was consumed by my father's betrayals. Subdued by a patriarchal society, even her own mother would tell her, "This is your husband, and you must keep him until you die." My mother found support in her prayers and in the endless Hail Marys she whispered. I remember my mother always saying, *"Devi avere fede"* (You must have faith).

By the time I was nine, my parents told my siblings and me that they were thinking of splitting up, and it broke my heart. But when they finally did get a separation, I knew it was the only way my mother would survive. In many ways it saved her wounded spirit and restored her dignity and pride. She was one of the few women at that time (1966) to actually get a legal separation in Rome, proving her great strength and courage. Elvira was a role model for all women struggling with domestic violence and abuse by their husbands.

## MY FIRST COMMUNION AND INITIATION TO THE BLESSED MOTHER

At the age of eight or nine, many young Catholic girls become excited about receiving their First Holy Communion because they get to wear a pretty white dress. But for me, my communion was a landmark event as it commemorated my personal initiation to the Blessed Mother as well as my first retreat with Her. In a sense, my communion paved the way for my devotion to the Black Madonna.

When it came time for me to take the sacrament of First Holy Communion, we followed my mother's family tradition. The sacrament was to take place in an elite ancient stone convent in the center of Rome called Santa Teresa del Bambin Gesù. Although it was a joyous sacrament, my first communion came at the worst possible time for my parents. After a horrible fight, my father decided to leave the house. Like my mother and my siblings, I was devastated, but as the youngest, I was probably the most desperate. So as to make my communion, I knew that I had to go into the *ritiro spirituale* (spiritual retreat) for one week at the convent. With all of the fighting going on at home, I knew that I would find peace and comfort at Santa Teresa, but I was reluctant to leave my mother. It would mark my first time away from home.

Before she left me at the convent, my mother hugged me and whis-

Fig. I.4. Alessandra Belloni's Holy Communion,
Church of Saint Teresa, Rome

pered that she knew I was in the right place at the right time. Then
I was shown to the retreat house where girls like me would live for a
week, not allowed to see anyone but one another and the nuns. Not
only would we have no outside contact but also we were to remain
in silence unless we were singing, praying, or chanting. To some, this
might sound horrible, but to me it was pure heaven.

The first time I entered the chapel I saw the most exquisite painting of the Madonna della Vittoria. I knelt down before Her and cried,
thinking about my parents and their possible separation. I asked the
beneficent Madonna for a miracle: to bring my father back home and to
keep our family together. This was to be the first of many strong mystical experiences I would have in my life.

In the chapel I remember seeing the Madonna's sweet face weep with
me. Then she smiled kindly, nodded, and told me that my father would
be back home by the time I left the convent after my communion.

Even though I was only a child, the retreat at Santa Teresa was a deep, transcendent experience for me. I felt so peaceful there that I didn't want to leave. I prayed every day at the feet of my dear friend la Madonna, nurtured and protected.

The day of my First Holy Communion arrived. There were many girls, a long line of us, all dressed in white vestments with white wimples on our heads, similar to what the nuns wore. It was a spectacular ceremony. We were not permitted to see anyone until we went out into the church. To my surprise, both my father *and* my mother were there together, smiling warmly, finally reunited and in harmony. I felt that the Madonna had listened to my prayers and performed the miracle I had pleaded for, even though my parents' reunion would be short-lived.

A long time afterward, I realized that the painting of the Madonna I had prayed so ardently under in the convent was believed by many to be Maria Maddalena, Mary Magdalene, another aspect of the Black Madonna. I was being led to Her, even as a young girl of eight.

## PRELUDE: A CHILD ACTRESS DISCOVERED BY ANNA MAGNANI, THE FIRST BITE OF LOVE, AND ESCAPING TO NEW YORK

In many ways I had a tough childhood, watching my parents constantly fight and witnessing domestic violence firsthand in a time when that expression wasn't even used yet. I lived in the typical Italian patriarchal society in which women were supposed to receive abuse and accept it. I knew at once that this wasn't the type of life I wanted for myself when I grew up, and I would do everything in my power to avoid it.

One of my worst childhood memories was being molested when I was only twelve. I was on my way home from school to have lunch. A tall, distinguished-looking man wearing dark sunglasses entered the building with me and came into the elevator. Polite and innocent, I thought he was going to visit someone in our building. I had no idea that he had followed me from school and that he was what we called a *maniaco sessuale,* a pedophile sex maniac.

As soon as the elevator took off, the man began saying obscene words to me. He touched my breasts, which were already quite large for my age. I was terrified, but I did the right thing. I didn't scream but calmly stopped the elevator and sent it back down to the ground floor. (I didn't want him to find out where I lived.) That was the longest five minutes in my life.

As soon as we reached the ground floor, I began yelling for help. My attacker quickly ran out of the elevator. The concierge immediately came out, and we called the police and then my parents, but he was gone. My father was determined to catch this maniaco sessuale and probably would have killed him if he had found him. I went to the police station, and unlike many other girls who were victims of child molestation, I filed a complete report with an accurate description of my attacker. A few months later, he was caught and was put in jail.

To this day I am proud of my courage as a little girl—I fought for women's rights and stood up against sexual abuse, even as a twelve-year-old. This incident, though horrible, was a blessing, in a sense. Although it left a deep scar in my life, it would later help me in my healing work with other women, especially victims of sexual abuse.

Despite these sad incidents, there were also good times with my family. What redeemed me most was being a child performer. I loved the attention I got—thrived on it, even. I sang and acted in front of a mirror, changing outfits constantly. Everyone told me I had a good singing voice. Soon I became the soloist of my school choir. For fun, I even started a small underground theater group.

My mother was always very supportive of my artistic inclinations, probably because she had wanted to be an actress herself but was denied permission by her parents. Mamma even resembled the great Italian actress Anna Magnani. Magnani is perhaps best known for her portrayal of a Sicilian widow in the film *The Rose Tattoo,* which earned her an Academy Award for Best Actress and for her memorable role in the Roberto Rossellini film *Open City.*

When I was fourteen, I had the immense blessing of being cast by the legendary Anna Magnani to play her niece in the play

*La Lupa* (The She-Wolf). It was written by the esteemed Sicilian author Giovanni Verga and was directed by Franco Zeffirelli. I was over the moon with delight at my good fortune.

This incredible career opportunity occurred at the same time I experienced my first love—my first kiss with a beautiful boy named Piero. It was magical as my classmate and I kissed after school in Villa Borghese Park at dusk, surrounded by fireflies.

Piero was handsome, wild, and tall, with dark-blond hair, amazing piercing dark almond eyes, and beautiful features. He dressed very cool and played the electric guitar. I was a budding singer, so it was a perfect combination. We both wanted to be artists and musicians. My dream was about to begin with the once-in-a-lifetime role, being part of the cast in Anna Magnani's play.

But unfortunately, that dream was never realized. My tyrannical father denied permission for me to go on tour with the production to London. He had the power to sign the consent documents and passport, which he refused to do. So I never made it to the big stage with my mother's idol, Anna Magnani. Both Mamma and I cried for a long time afterward, and we swore revenge on my father.

Around the same time, my first love, Piero, and his family moved from Rome to Florence. Though less than two hundred miles, it seemed a world away for us. My heart was broken as Piero and I separated. We still loved each other deeply. I even promised him that he would be my first lover when I turned eighteen.

After losing both Piero and *La Lupa,* I continued to cry for months, missing my sweet lover, as he missed me. I was suffering from what I would later find out to be the "bite of love," which causes women to become *tarantate.* It is a form of depression attributed to the mythical bite of the spider, the tarantula, which usually begins at puberty. I now realize that it was during this time that I became a *tarantata,* feeling trapped by the spiderweb of the patriarchal society and the loss of my first love.

It was this feeling of anguish, mixed with anger, sadness, and a deep longing for love and freedom that later drew me to escape to New York.

Fifteen years later, this key, traumatic episode of my life inspired me to write my own version of the play *La Lupa* and to portray her as a tarantata. As I had promised myself, this dream came true many years later in New York's Greenwich Village. But first, I had to get there.

## 1971: A REBELLIOUS ITALIAN TEENAGER ESCAPES TO NEW YORK

In the summer of 1971, my mother had the brilliant idea to take me to New York City. We would visit my sister, Gabriella, who had gone there a year earlier to study film. My hippie brother, Muzio, who bore an uncanny resemblance to Jimi Hendrix, had followed Gabriella to New York, so we would get to see him too. Thrilled, I left for a month-long vacation with ten dollars, a small suitcase of summer clothes, an immense curiosity, and a desire for freedom. I was pursuing my American dream.

When I said good-bye to my father at Rome's Fiumicino Airport, I somehow knew I wouldn't be coming back. On July 20, 1971, a Pan Am flight from Rome to JFK International Airport took me to my destiny. I was just a teenager, mature in some ways but still very innocent and naive about life, especially in a city as fast paced and dangerous as New York City in the 1970s.

But I instantly fell in love with this wild, perilous place. So did my mother. We went sightseeing through the entire city on foot: Greenwich Village, Times Square, and Central Park. There seemed to be music on every street corner and an incredible energy in the air. Mamma and I felt like we were actresses in a movie. We remembered a film we saw together (and loved) a couple of years earlier, *Midnight Cowboy,* much of which took place on these very streets.

One day I decided to spend the afternoon exploring the city by myself. I had never felt such liberation! I decided right then and there that I would not be returning to Rome with my mother. I wanted time to be free, to be myself, to be on my own, to find a way to express my artistic inspiration without asking anybody's permission. I wasn't sure

Fig. I.5. Alessandra Belloni
acting in Greenwich Village, 1975

how Mamma would take this—and forget about my domineering father. I walked to the West Side and threw the keys to our Roman home into the Hudson River shouting, *"Liberta!"* (Freedom!)

When my mother started to pack her suitcase for the flight back to Rome, she noticed that I wasn't packing mine. Mamma understood immediately. She began crying even before I said, "I'm not coming home with you. I'm staying in New York with my brother and sister." I know this broke her heart, but Mamma Elvira never let on. She was always an intelligent, strong woman full of love and compassion, and so she accepted my decision. Even though I was a minor, she didn't force me to leave with her. Mamma said that she would come back in six months to see how I was doing, and if she saw anything wrong, she would take

Fig. I.6. Gabriella Belloni at NYU Film School

me back to Rome to finish school and get back to my regular life. What an amazing thing my mother did for me! It changed the path of my life.

## LIVING IN THE MYTHICAL 1970S
## IN GREENWICH VILLAGE

The years that unfolded in New York after my drastic life-changing decision to stay there were intense, especially for someone so young. They left a deep impression on my soul for the rest of my life. I went from the repressed, patriarchal society of Italy to living in wanton, sur-real Greenwich Village. It was a stewpot of creativity, and famous artists were part of the movement.

All of my important rites of passage happened in New York: falling in love, losing my virginity and being intiated into womanhood, getting my first job, being independent, even acting in NYU films and singing in cabarets. But my time in New York was not always easy; a great deal of drama went with it and some tragic events as well. One in particular left me with deep emotional scars.

Two months after my arrival in Manhattan, a terrible thing happened: my sweet sister, Gabriella, was raped! Someone followed her to the apartment we shared in the Village and attacked her at gunpoint. By some miracle, I was spared, simply because I wanted to go to a different shop for groceries while Gabriella returned home alone. Although by some divine intervention I was spared, I was still traumatized by the experience.

I came home with a bagful of food to an empty apartment as four detectives arrived, looking for my sister. Where was Gabriella? After calling the police and reporting the rape, she was all alone and in shock. Instead of waiting for the police to get there, Gabriella ran to my brother for support and protection and then went to the hospital.

More than forty years after she was raped, Gabriella still says that it was better it happened to her instead of me. Can you imagine such self-sacrifice? In time, Gabriella learned to accept this terrible experience as simply being part of life in those crazy days. She has written about it in her book, *My American Dream,* which we hope will become a film.

I deeply felt my sister's pain—and still do.

About ten years ago, during a session with one of my students who was also a victim of rape, I realized that it was my sister Gabriella's violent attack that led me to the healing work I do today. Although I wasn't aware of this at the beginning of my work as a healer, my realization was a pivotal moment.

Even after Gabriella's sexual assault, my brother, sister, and I decided to stay in New York. For more than a year, I lived in a SoHo loft with other artists, including my second love, a golden-haired Dutch film student named Joan. He took great care of me during my first year in the city. Unfortunately, the angelic Joan was an illegal immigrant and was deported in 1972. My young heart was broken again as Joan suddenly disappeared from my life.

Even if I felt alone at times living in the big, wild city in the '70s, I wasn't lonely. I knew that I was in the right place at the right time. I wanted to be an artist, and struggling with the unbalanced schedules and financial instability was part of an artist's life. I was happy to do what I loved most—sing and act. I worked as a waitress in Greenwich Village's Caffé Reggio to pay for my studies at HB (Herbert Berghof) acting studio, took voice and music lessons, and studied pantomime.

I now believe that the invisible hand of the Madonna was the driving force behind my mother, which fueled my own devotion to the Madonna. I also believe that I was fully protected by Her. Even though I took many risks in those times, I was always safe. This also gave me the energy and courage to begin my own spiritual quest.

My quest is far from over, and it is still full of adventure, romance, music, passion, and mysterious supernatural events, all leading to the Black Madonna.

CHAPTER 1

# Who Is
# the Black Madonna?

*O splendid star on the serrated mountain,*
*with miracles shining like a sunbeam, hear the people.*
*From all around they rally, rejoicing,*
*rich and poor, young and old,*
*they assemble here to see with their own eyes,*
*and return from it filled with grace.*
*Rulers and magnates of royal stripes,*
*the mighty of the world, having obtained indulgence*
*for their sin, they cry out and beating their breast*
*they kneel and cry here: Ave Maria.*

"Stella Splendens in Monte" (Splendid Star
on the Mountain ) from *Llibre Vermell de
Montserrat* (Red Book of Montserrat)

WE LIVE IN A DANGEROUS TIME in which both women and men need to connect to the true knowledge and healing aspect of the Divine Feminine. In many ways I believe that this is the only thing that will save us. I feel the calling now more than ever to awaken the true power of women and to help men become aware of the ancient spirituality of the Divine Feminine, which can heal our relationships.

In this time of world turmoil and paradigm shifts, I feel that there is a great need to acknowledge that God is a woman and She is black. In this book, I hope to convince you that the Black Madonna is indeed alive and that She has the power to heal and transform. In this age when racism against people of color is still a raging disease infecting our society, it is my wish to bring attention to the serious situation in which we are living. With this book as the catalyst, I will make a deep connection to sacred black images, which are popular all over the world yet suppressed in much of the traditional-thinking, white-dominated, male-governed world. It is my humble hope that the images, myths, and beliefs provided in this book will help heal our society.

The Black Madonna is a Christian tradition with origins in pre-Christian devotion to the Earth Mother Goddess and the African Mother. The Black Virgin also represents the womb of the Earth, the dark side of the moon, the universe, the Cosmos, and the mystery of the life-giving woman. Like the Earth's womb, women's wombs have often been broken through different types of abuse and unhealthy relationships. As the Earth continues to regenerate herself, she nourishes us, even if we are abusing her with pollution, mining, and global warming. It is my wish that women who have also suffered abuse can take a cue from Mother Nature and learn self-healing techniques, like those described in this book.

In these pages, I will shed a new light on the ancient tradition of the Black Madonna for all people from all walks of life to utilize, especially women. It will make the Black Madonna as accessible to others as She has been to me, making Her come alive, transform, and help those in pain.

## A MYTH OF CREATION:
## THE BLACK METEORITE THAT FELL FROM THE STARS

During my thirty years of research, I discovered many fascinating myths and legends relating to the Black Madonna. The oldest myths in the

Mediterranean culture say that a black meteorite fell from the stars and was adored as a divinity in Anatolia (Turkey).* It was then brought to Rome during the wars with Hannibal and made into a statue of the earth goddess Cybele under the prophecy of the Sibilla Cumana (Cumaean Sibyl), prophetess of the underworld. She foretold that Rome would win the war with Hannibal—but only if they carved a statue of Cybele in the temple that is now the Church of the Black Madonna of Ara Coeli. The sybil also foretold the birth of the Messiah from a virgin and the return to a new Golden Age.

Most of the churches and sanctuaries devoted to Black Madonnas in Italy and around the world are actually built on the ruins of temples dedicated to different goddesses, including Isis (Egypt), Cybele (Anatolia, Turkey), Diana Efesina or Artemis (Ephesus, Turkey), Aphrodite Venus from Erice Sicily, Demeter or Ceres, Persephone (Enna Sicily), Hecate (Pompei), Naples Tanit (Phoenicia, Carthage) , and Gaia. In some places, as in Tindari, Sicily, the Black Madonna's church stands today beside an ancient archaeological site and temple of the goddess Demeter.

I was especially fascinated by the inscriptions found on the statues in Tindari and in the village of Montevergine (near Naples), which boldly proclaim: *Nigra Sum Sed Formosa,* meaning "I am black but beautiful." The phrase is also translated as "I am black and beautiful" and "I am black but comely" from the Bible's Song of Solomon 1:5. It references the Queen of Sheba, who is believed to have been from Ethiopia, thus affirming the African origin.†

One of the first representations of the Black Madonna is indeed the Queen of Sheba. She is the treasured lover of King Solomon, known to be either a Shulamite or from Ethiopia. Her name can also be translated

---

*Many of the goddesses are also from Sicily (and Naples, Pompei), which was a great part of Greece. To this day the most important and largest temples to the goddesses are indeed in Sicily, known as the Island of Demeter and Persephone (see Mary Taylor Simetti's, *On Persephone's Island*). It is most important that I emphasize the goddesses' origins and worship in Sicily and Pompei, as you will find in many classical texts. I am including here a few quick references regarding the Greek goddesses.

†See *Solomon and Sheba* by Barbara Black Koltuv, page 128, www.amazon.com/Solomon -Sheba-Inner-Marriage-Individuation/dp/0892540249.

Fig. 1.1. *Nigra Sum Sed Formosa* (I am black but beautiful),
Black Madonna of Tindari, Sicily; photo by A. Belloni

to mean "seven," which ties in neatly to the southern Italian legend of
the Seven Black Madonnas. This beautiful legend about the Seven Sisters
(which I will recount later in the book) is also intertwined with the Roman
poet Virgil, who was initiated in the mysteries of the goddess Cybele.

Some of the rituals performed today in Southern Italy are the same as they were in pre-Christian times. They use ecstatic dances, haunting chants, and ritual drumming with tambourines and frame drums as devotional instruments. Worshippers reenact ancient fertility rites through the sensual dances in honor of the earth goddesses Cybele and Demeter and the moon goddess Diana.

American archaeologist, author, and scholar Marija Gimbutas says that the first statues of Mother Earth were actually made from dark soil, and it is known among farmers that the darkest soil is the most fertile. The connection between dark, fertile soil and the dark skin of the Black Madonnas, many of whom women pray to to help them bear children, is unmistakable.

The Black Virgin also has a deep esoteric meaning and has been an important part of Christianity: Her worship flourished in the Middle Ages among the Knights Templar. In some places, as in Southern France, Mary Magdalene is another aspect of the Dark Mother, as seen with the powerful statue of Santa Sarah la Kali in Saintes-Maries-de-la-Mer, capital of Camargue, Southern France, and a place of pilgrimage for the Gypsies, or Romani.

The Black Madonna is seen also as Mary, the mother of Jesus. She is worshipped by Christians all over the world and is often crowned. In addition, She is recognized by the pope and the Vatican as the Mother of God and for Her many miracles. As explained by Ean Begg in his book, *The Cult of the Black Virgin,* there are more theories about the Black Madonna. Begg explained that Mary was Jewish. She was from North Africa, lived in a hot climate, and had dark skin.

The Byzantine portraits of the Blessed Mother attributed to Saint Luke show Mary as brown skinned and because of this are referred to as Madonna Bruna. Black Virgins were also crafted by the dark-skinned peoples of the Middle East. Artists used dusky wood, such as ebony or wood from olive, oak, apple, and pear trees, and the volcanic rock basalt, which is black. The numerous black and dark Jesus icons found worldwide, but especially in Southern Italy, are crafted from similar materials.

In early Christianity, people still worshipped the ancient Greek and Roman goddesses. The dominant religion of the Holy Roman Empire involved many goddesses melting into one another. Eventually, the older statues of the goddesses and pagan deities were destroyed, but many of these smaller statues survived, hidden in the earth or in the hollows of trees, especially in remote rural locations, just like the Black Madonnas that are found throughout Southern Italy.

The Divine Feminine principle was represented by Black Virgins who depicted Mary, the mother of Jesus. Side by side with Christianity, the ancient goddess religion survived into the Christian era. The most popular cults were devoted to three black goddesses: Artemis (of Ephesus), Cybele, and Isis. (I will delve into more about these important figures later in the book.)

In the year 431 CE, the Virgin Mary was proclaimed as the Mother of God in Ephesus, Turkey, where it is believed that She spent Her last years and made Her Assumption into heaven. To this day, the most important feast in Italy is Ferragosto, the Feast of the Assumption, on August 15, when the whole country, especially the south, celebrates Mary, the Mother of God, rising miraculously into heaven.

The most passionate and powerful feasts celebrating the Black Madonnas stretch long into the night. These are ceremonies that incorporate ritual drumming, ancient chants, and trance dances. Countless miracles and supernatural phenomenon occur during these celebrations with no logical explanation. But I believe that if you trust in the Universal Mother's unconditional love, anything is possible.

## DISCOVERING SOUTHERN ITALIAN FOLK MUSIC, TRAVELING TO ITALY, AND UNVEILING THE BLACK MADONNA

I did not consciously begin my quest for the Black Madonna but instead was found by Her. It all began in 1979, during a summer full of passion, music, and transformation. I fell in love with Southern Italian folk music and with the wonderful guitarist who reintroduced me to it, John La Barbera. I had met John a couple of years earlier at Greenwich Village's Caffé Dante on McDougal Street (across from Bob Dylan's house). John had just returned from his musical tour in Italy with the Southern Italian folk music group Pupi e Fresedde, who also worked in America with the Bread and Puppet Theater group.

John missed Italy immensely, and when he walked into Caffé Dante with his guitar, he was hoping to meet some Italian artists. When we met we liked each other immediately. John was tall and handsome, with curly black hair and a mustache. He always dressed in dark clothes, smoked a pipe, like me, and really had his own style. He was humorous when speaking English, but he was even funnier when he spoke in his imperfect Italian because sometimes he said inappropriate words that left the Italians howling. I fell in love with John's guitar playing. I thought he embodied the god Bacchus with his ecstatic music and laughter, and I was swept into John's arms like a Bacchante in a trance.

I sang Italian folk songs with John, and he accompanied me as if he had done so all of his life. We both felt that we had past lives together. Many times when we were in Italy together, we felt that we had lives intertwined there as musicians during the Renaissance—performing, traveling around, and living intricate love stories.

I was completely bewitched by the unbridled, powerful music John had learned from the Italian musicians, especially the healing dance of the tarantella. The music's unique, passionate style of tambourine playing touched something deep and familiar in my heart. As I watched John master the obsessive 6/8 rhythms, I decided that I just *had* to learn how to play the tambourine so that I could accompany him.

It was some time later, after I'd mastered the *tamburello*, an Italian tambourine, that I realized I was continuing my paternal grandfather's tradition. He also played the tamburello, as well as the mandolin. Perhaps this was the reason the intense 6/8 rhythm seemed so familiar to me in the beginning. It truly *was* in my blood.

Fig. 1.2. A photo from 1985 of I Giullari

The fruit of John's and my romance is the group we founded in 1980, called I Giullari di Piazza (The Jesters of the Square). We dedicated it to the revival of Southern Italian folk music and dance and the theater of the commedia dell'arte, and we are still performing to this day, thirty-seven years later—a real act of love!

Back in 1980, John and I knew that the only way to be authentic in this style of music and theater, to fully understand the culture and interpret it for the New York audience, we had to go back to Southern Italy as often as possible to do field research, in addition to our extensive library research in New York and Rome. We were so young, so in love, so poor, and so happy, playing inspiring music together, traveling from town to town across Southern Italy, experiencing crazy situations, many times risking our lives in dangerous and remote areas where the Mafia still ruled over everything and everyone. Despite these perils, John and I were always safe and always found hospitality with wonderful people. Perhaps it was once again the Black Madonna, always looking out for me.

## COAST OF THE GODS, TROPEA, CALABRIA

While traveling through remote areas of Southern Italy, I often ended up in stunning places, which I believe was not by chance but by destiny: atop a sacred mountain, near the turquoise Mediterranean Sea, beside rivers and waterfalls, in green valleys and small canyons with gorgeous, white Romanesque or Baroque churches. I noticed something about each of these places that was always the same: on a high altar or in a small chapel, a mysterious, beautiful figure of the Black Madonna also stood. I was intrigued, drawn to Her.

I saw beautiful and enigmatic Byzantine paintings showing Her with dark or black skin and many totemlike statues that depicted a beautiful, dark-skinned woman sitting on a majestic throne holding a black baby Jesus. She called to me in silence, staring at me with Her great inky black or hazel eyes, which followed me into every corner of the church. She seemed to know what I was feeling. She seemed to know all my secrets. I felt an intense energy coming from the Madonnas' faces and eyes, full of tenderness, forgiveness, austerity, compassion, sorrow, and universal love.

When I participated in feasts and processions, I witnessed thousands of people making vows, lifting the heavy statues, running uphill, walking barefoot for hours, singing and chanting, crying, praying, and asking for miracles, which still happen. As I continued my research, I discovered that the Black Madonna is a Christian tradition that has roots in the pre-Christian worship of the Earth and the African Mother. I needed to know more.

One of the most amazing experiences I had regarding trance and shamanic power was that first year in Calabria. It was after the Feast of the Madonna of the Sea in Vibo Marina on August 21. The men, mainly local fishermen and new friends whom I'd met there, had a rowdy party on the beach at night. They roasted the fish they'd caught on a homemade coal grill. They drank a great deal of wine, sang, and danced nonstop to the frantic 6/8 rhythm of the tarantella Calabrese. This is a martial arts type of dance known as *la scherma,* which was originally done with knives.

They clearly entered a trance and shifted into the role of shaman. I honestly became afraid and watched with John La Barbera, worried about what might happen next. Suddenly, the dark-faced, blue-eyed men took off most of their clothes and began dancing intricate tarantella steps on burning hot coals. They danced for several minutes, without stopping, with no pain or burns. As they danced, they made the sign of the cross, looking out into the sea where the boat carrying Mary was still lit, and shouted "*Evviva Maria!*" (Long live Mary!). The men ended with a haunting Arabic-sounding chant to Our Lady, which I will share with you later (see pages 360–61).

## CALABRIA, 1980: DISCOVERING THE FIRST BLACK MADONNA

In the summer of 1980, John and I went to Calabria for the first time, looking for musicians specializing in the music for the *tarantelle calabresi,* playing the *chitarra battente,* which is a ten-string Renaissance folk guitar. We were also on a quest to meet Professor Luigi Lombardi Satriani, the famous writer and anthropologist. Satriani was also a great scholar and collector of folk music and legends.

On a hot summer day, John and I took a long, eight-hour train ride from Rome to Tropea, Calabria. We carried his guitar, my first tambourine, a tape recorder, and a camera, plus lots of curiosity and delight—we were about to learn more about the infectious music of this remote region, a culture that has been uncontaminated by outside influences: the true authentic cultura popolare.

The train station at Tropea was hot and deserted. It seemed that we had gone back in time. The few people we saw looked at us suspiciously because we were obviously outsiders. John and I agreed not to speak English so we wouldn't attract too much attention as American tourists. Unfortunately, it didn't work. I had a knack for attracting attention—I was young, dark complexioned, and exotic looking, so men often stared at me and at times followed us. It made John scared, and he felt very uncomfortable; still, we pressed on with our research.

When our host came to pick us up in a Mercedes, we immediately understood that he was a big shot in this small town. Our "room" in his house was more like the presidential suite in a paradise resort: beautifully appointed with a huge veranda. We sat there at sunset gazing at the sea and the smoking island of Vulcano, which is part of Sicily. As we soaked in the beauty around us, John and I played music, inspired by the magic of the land. He stroked his sensuous guitar, and I sang erotic songs in dialect. Everything around us was mysterious, including the Black Madonnas whom we would soon meet.

John and I were treated like a king and queen. We ate amazing food and received a level of hospitality we had never experienced before. The people of Calabria were honored that we had come all the way from New York to learn more about their traditions. They couldn't believe that we were going to bring their rich traditions back to America.

Our host hired John and me to play in his hometown of Parghelia. (Its name in Greek is Para Elios, which means "in front of the sun.") We were to perform for the feast of their beautiful Madonna Bruna, a Byzantine icon with brown skin and soulful, merciful eyes. In the role of the masked character Pulcinella from the Neapolitan commedia dell'arte, I sang and played tambourine, as John accompanied me on guitar. The people of Parghelia loved it.

The procession for Madonna Bruna, after our performance, was extremely powerful. I felt oddly moved and drawn to the Dark Mother of Jesus. I asked if there were more Madonnas, Bruna or Nera, in the area and was told that there indeed were.

The next day, John and I were taken to the beautiful town of Tropea itself, which was very different from its dusty train station. Tropea was a jewel of art and magnificent scenery perched above the turquoise Tyrrhenian Sea (see plate 2). I was in awe when I came face-to-face with the well-known Black Madonna in Tropea's stunning cathedral. La Madonna di Romania (Madonna of Romania) is a dark icon believed to be from the Orient.

I stared at Her rich, dark skin, Her beautiful face with its enor-

Fig. 1.3. Black Madonna dei Poveri, Calabria; photo by A. Belloni

mous, melancholic, deep onyx eyes. She held Her sweet, dark baby Jesus to Her left cheek as He looked up at Her. But it was as though Her thoughts were elsewhere as She stared into the infinite, into us, into our hearts and our souls. She was staring at me and the world.

Her style of dress was not traditional Italian. Instead, She wore a beautiful golden crown of stars and a Byzantine-inspired dark cape and tunic decorated with symbols and jewelry. (Later, in my studies, I realized that the crown symbolized that She was Mary, Mother of God and Queen of Heaven.) Baby Jesus wore a red tunic and also wore a crown. With His left hand He held on to His mother's veil, as if asking for Her protection. This is, by far, one of the most affectionate icons of Mary and Jesus. The love and compassion emanating from Them was palpable.

A childhood memory of seeing another Black Madonna flooded

back to me. I suddenly remembered seeing a similar, very dark Madonna in one of my mother's favorite churches near our home, Santa Maria Maggiore. In Rome they did not call Her la Madonna Nera but rather la Madonna della Neve (Our Lady of the Snow).

According to the legend, in the early years of Christianity, when Mary was officially recognized by the church, a nobleman from Rome named Giovanni and his wife had a strange dream. This dream occurred between the night of August 4 and 5, in the year 352 CE. In it, he saw the Virgin Mary asking to build a church honoring Her where the next morning they would find fresh snow (in August when it is so hot in Rome!). The nobleman told this to Pope Liberio, who had the exact same dream. The following morning, a miraculous snow fell on Esquiline Hill, and Pope Liberio ordered a great church, Maggiore, to be built on that spot. The huge beautiful basilica, financed by the nobleman Giovanni, became known as Basilica di Santa Maria della Neve or ad Nives.

In Tropea, I asked about la Madonna di Romania's legend and history. This Madonna icon dates back to 1330 and is the protector of Tropea. She reputedly stopped the plague from coming to their town in the Middle Ages and saved them from several earthquakes. Her last miracle was performed during World War II. The story goes that when American airplanes were flying low to drop bombs on the town, a strange mist covered Tropea. Because the pilots couldn't see, they didn't drop the bombs, and Tropea was spared. The one bomb that fell nearby incredibly did not explode but landed intact in the sea, causing no damage whatsoever to this idyllic place.

Immediately, I recalled the miracle my mother received from the Madonna during the bombing of Rome during the same war and was moved even more by the story. I felt very connected to Tropea—to the stunning Madonnas, the breathtaking landscape, the turquoise sea, the beautiful beaches, and the wonderful people. So much so that I return to Tropea almost every summer and still lead pilgrimages there today.

The beautiful medieval town was sculpted into the rocks in ancient times, dating back even before the Greeks. The name Tropea itself is Greek and is believed to mean "trophies," referring to the prizes that were won during the Grecian age and later during the Roman Empire. These trophies were hung on a specific tree in a specific way as a sign of victory. One of the celebrated trophies was won by the Roman emperor Scipione l'Africano, a Roman citizen who was actually African.

The original settlement of Tropea dates from the ninth century CE, during the Bronze Age. The Greeks settled in Tropea by the sixth century BCE, and the Romans in the third century. Tropea has narrow cobblestone streets and is full of old arches, as well as steps hewn from ancient stones, which lead straight down to the sea. Tropea's beach has fine, white sand, as soft as talcum powder, and clear water. At low tide, you can walk to the beautiful Madonna dell'Isola (Madonna of the Island). She is another lovely Madonna del Mare (Madonna of the Sea), protectress of the sea, the fishermen, and all the people who live on the coast.

Once a year, on August 15, during the Feast of the Assumption of Mary, the fishermen dress in white and blue and carry the huge statue down the steep rocks into a boat decorated with flowers and lights (see fig. 1.4, on p. 37, and plate 3). An explosion of fireworks begins a procession of colorful boats along the coast, filled with local fishermen and residents. The festival symbolizes their devotion to the Madonna del Mare. Still more fireworks accompany the procession, which lasts until sunset. As the sun descends, the Madonna returns to the church of Santa Maria dell'Isola, built on a rocky promontory. The fishermen again take Her on their shoulders and climb the steep stone steps as the women of the town chant behind them, carrying long candles. It's a spectacle of sight and sound—and deep piety.

Up until thirty years ago, this Madonna had deep brown skin, but Her restoration left Her with white skin. This is something the Vatican has been doing systematically over the years, with obvious racist motivations: they don't want people worshipping black sacred images. Yet it is undeniable that dark-skinned icons are at our pre-Christian roots.

Despite Her now lily-white complexion, Madonna del Mare is dressed in blue and white, just like Yemanja, the Afro-Brazilian goddess of love and water. She is also the Greek Aphrodite or the Roman Venus, born out of the foam of the sea. The first time I saw Her, She reminded me of a mermaid who enchanted fishermen. Although I did not know much about the background of this devotion, I found myself overwhelmed with emotion and weeping at the beginning and end of the procession. I wanted to be blessed by the Madonna del Mare, who is also called Stella Maris (Star of the Sea). I wanted to be purified in the water of the sea, so crystal clear that it seemed more miraculous than the holy water in church.

Because I kept asking why the Madonna was black, several local people suggested that if I wanted to find out anything about the old folklore, myths, and legends, I should go to the expert, Professor Satriani, who had written many books on the culture of Calabria and the south of Italy. Eventually, I did.

When I visited Satriani in his palace, I quickly realized that he was the nobleman of the area. I found Satriani to be a truly wonderful human being, loving and caring.

I knocked on his door as a complete stranger, yet he was still welcoming. He was intrigued by the fact that I had come all the way from New York to study *musica popolare* and traditional dances. Extremely helpful, he suggested texts and recordings I should study. After I thanked him, I couldn't resist asking my burning questions: Why is the Madonna of Romania dark skinned? And why are there so many dark and black Madonnas around here?

Satriani responded, "Well, young lady, you are asking too much. The Black Madonna is a mystery, and as such, you must accept Her. We all worship Her here as Mary, the Mother of God. She is the most miraculous of all since the beginning of time." Then he continued with an even more intriguing proposition: "If you want to see a powerful

Fig. 1.4. Procession of the Madonna of the Sea;
photo by Alessandra Belloni

Black Madonna, you must go to the Feast of la Madonna dei Poveri [the Madonna of the Poor] in Seminara. It honors the most beautiful and powerful Black Madonna of all."

Knowing that I was intrigued, Satriani added, "You will find the feast very interesting, I am sure. You should read the book *Le feste dei poveri* [The Feasts of the Poor] by Annabella Rossi. She has done great work on the feasts of the saints and the Black Madonna from a sociological approach. But her book is hard to find." He showed me some of the books in his impressive collection, wished me good luck, and told me to stay in touch, which I have done throughout the years.

I did not know that one day I would be very grateful to Professor Satriani for taking me to his estate on the beach, when on September 11, 2001, following a premonition, I changed my return ticket to New York and decided to take a vacation in my beloved Tropea!

## HISTORY OF THE BLACK MADONNA DI ROMANIA, TROPEA

As I mentioned, Tropea's icon of the dark Madonna was discovered around the year 1330, and at the time, it was assumed that She came from the Orient. The beautiful Byzantine icon attributed to Saint Luke mysteriously turned up on a shore that was a popular place for Tropean fishermen to sell and trade their catch.

La Madonna di Romania was the maker of many miracles. In addition to those mentioned previously, a miracle occurred in 1638 when She appeared in several dreams to Spanish Monsignor Ambrogio Corduba. In these night visions, She warned the monsignor of a big earthquake that would strike Calabria. She told the monsignor that if he brought Her image through the streets of Tropea in a procession, She would protect the town. On March 27, he led a procession of devotees following Her painting through the streets. At that moment, a huge earthquake struck the area, but the town of Tropea was spared. The same miracle occurred in 1783 during a much larger, more disastrous earthquake, which changed the shape of the region of Calabria. Once again, Tropea was spared as they processed through the town with the Black Madonna protecting them. Her feast day is September 8, celebrated with a powerful procession through the town of Tropea and ending always with folk music and the passionate tarantella calabrese.

# HISTORY OF
# THE MADONNA DELL'ISOLA

In my research, I discovered that the church dedicated to the Madonna dell'Isola was most likely built between the sixth and seventh centuries. At first, it welcomed a community of Basilian monks. In the eleventh century, it was passed on to the Benedictines, who still own it today, under the Abbey of Montecassino.

The origins of this diocesan sanctuary are tied to a prodigious event that occurred during Byzantine Iconoclasm, when a wooden statue of the Madonna miraculously drifted to Tropea's beaches from the Orient. Many noted that it was as if She were trying to escape the destruction of sacred images that was carried out in the Byzantine Empire between the eighth and ninth centuries. Unfortunately, that dark wooden statue of Mary has vanished, but the sanctuary is still there, looking out to the same sea that gave this Madonna Her millenary roots.

I became completely fascinated by the fact that all the Black Virgins seemed to come to life during the Middle Ages, thus beginning Her strong devotions in Italy, France, Spain, Turkey, and Greece. Much of the folklore describes Her as appearing mysteriously by boat, specifically in shipwrecks, and saving the people onboard ships that had originated from the Orient or Africa.

During the Byzantine Empire and the time of the Crusades, Christian traditions mixed with those of the Moors, primarily through music and dance. People lived in fear that the end of the world was near, and the Black Madonna quelled these fears. She protected them. During the Middle Ages and the time of the Black Death, people carried the Madonna, drumming and dancing in a trance in the streets, to expel their fears of death by the Plague. Although the Plague is a thing of the past, this tradition is still alive today, and the Black Madonna's powers live on, as does She. My personal experiences with Her have shown me this time and time again. Without a doubt, I firmly believe that the Black Madonna possesses the power to protect us from ongoing wars, disease, and political crisis.

## THE QUEST BEGINS:
## THE EARTH IS ALIVE AND DARK

The entire Calabrian coast is so spectacular that it is often called the Coast of the Gods, extending all the way from Pizzo Calabro to Capo Vaticano, Tropea, and on to Scilla. This part of Italy is filled with ancient Greek ruins since the south of Italy was once part of Greece and, in fact, was called Magna Grecia. The lush palette of the coastline is breathtaking, with the sea in shades varying from turquoise to green, blue, and even purple at sunset. The beaches are filled with soft, fine sand, and the rock formations create amazing sculptures. Because of all of this, the ancient land of Calabria seems magically alive; it is one of Mother Earth's true power centers.

Climbing down the mountains into the sea on my first visit, I felt a powerful energy that I could not explain. It was as mysterious and sensual as the Black Madonnas who watched me silently from the white Romanesque and Baroque churches. I felt an immense sense of peace and healing, especially at la Rocca del Leone, the "rock of the lion," near the town of Zambrone (perhaps because I am a Leo!). This is where I found my first power spot.

I swam around the huge rock and sat on "the head of the lion," feeling its dark strength. It was as though the rock were alive, infusing me with its magical powers and wisdom of the ages, telepathically communicating its ancient knowledge. I felt like a sea priestess without knowing exactly what it meant. It was all so natural and familiar.

At the time, I followed my own personal initiation ceremony, bathing in the clear waters, performing cleansing rituals that no one had taught me before, yet I instinctively knew. Today, after decades of research, I know exactly what they meant: they were for Yemanja and Ochun, goddesses of the sea, river, waterfalls, love, and eros, from the Yoruba religion. But back then, I followed an inner voice that was guiding me to remember the past. It was the same voice that was guiding me to the ancient sites of the Black Madonna: the voice of the African Mother and Her drums.

Through those first years of my research, traveling through Calabria and the volcanic areas around Naples, a revelation came to me stronger and stronger, especially in my dreams. The revelation was this: it was no accident that all these mysterious statues and paintings of la Madonna Nera are located near incredible power points of the Earth. In caves, by the sea, atop sacred mountains, beside the healing waters of rivers and lakes, on great, dark oak trees—these are the places where the Black Madonna's mysteries are found. It was clear to me that the ancient settlements of pre-Christian cultures chose gorgeous places like Tropea, where the earth is dark and fertile, where the mountains meet the most beautiful ocean, knowing they were power points. The ancient Greeks were especially knowledgeable about this power and were initiated in the mysteries of the goddess of the Earth, as evidenced by the Eleusinian mysteries.

For centuries, on the Madonnas' feast days, pilgrims visited these sacred sites, honoring the Earth, touching the healing soil or stones, drinking the miraculous water, bringing branches from the trees, and asking and receiving miracles. In numerous locales, part of the devotion was to chant for hours or to drum and dance the tarantella all night long in an altered state of mind, similar to a shamanic trance. Naturally, the priests never took part in these wild, orgiastic rituals. Seeing this type of pagan devotion to a Christian deity made me wonder: What was there before the Christian churches were built? Why were these African rhythms being played during these ceremonies, complete with frenzied drumming and sensual dances, in front of a church?

Slowly I began to understand why the priests were hiding the true meaning of the Black Madonna, often sanctioning that the skin of the Madonnas in these paintings be made lighter during restoration. Perhaps the church could change the color of Her skin, but they could not repress the fervor of Her devotees. Her healing power was too strong and so was Her compassion—as was the passion of Her followers.

As I continued my field and scholarly research on the pre-Christian origins of Southern Italian folk music and dance, I began a parallel research on the cult of the Black Virgin, without really knowing where it would lead me. The main goal was to write and direct folk operas with John La Barbera. We wanted to perform these works in New York, mainly to educate Italian Americans about their heritage and authentic folkloric traditions, since these had been lost due to assimilation into the American culture. For a long time, I didn't know how I would portray the Black Madonna tradition in my shows. It took many years of personal healing journeys to figure this out, but I never gave up.

Every summer for thirty years I returned to Calabria, Campania, Puglia, Lazio, Abruzzi, and Sicily, traveling through remote areas to become immersed in the unbridled drumming and dance rituals in honor of the Madonna. This was not dry, dusty research in libraries—I got down and dirty with the peasants. I learned to play the tambourine all night long until sunrise without tiring, my hands bleeding onto the skin of the drum without pain, dancing barefoot on sharp rocks and cobblestones without feeling discomfort. The more I played and danced, the more energy I felt. This was the miracle of devotion to the Black Madonna.

Often I slept on the beach, diving into the sea at sunrise, feeling blessed, free, chanting, and drumming and at times making love in the sea, in the arms of Aphrodite. Lying down on the warm rocks after an entire night of ritualistic singing, dancing, and tambourine playing, I felt as though I were inside the womb of Mother Earth. I felt safe and protected, as if the Dark Mother Herself were looking down upon me from Her throne.

I believe it is very important for our well-being and for our own empowerment to find our own power spots in Nature and to build our altars in our homes, where we can go and recharge our energies, meditate, sleep, dream, and ask for healing.

After I began this journey unveiling the Black Madonnas in Southern Italy, I was able to learn how to feel the energy and power of the Earth, of Her rivers and seas. I also understood the power of the Black Madonna images, of the altars and the rituals done in devotion.

## ✴ Finding Your Own Power Spots in Nature, Building an Altar, and Chanting to the Mother

I will now guide you through a simple ritual, which can be done either in Nature or indoors, where you can build your altar. No matter where you live, you should be able to find a secluded place in a park, by a big, old tree, or by water, such as a river, lake, or the sea. This is the best way to begin your connection with the Earth Mother or to tune in with Her if you already have a deep connection. It's important to isolate yourself from the daily routine, to let go completely of cell phones and electronics, to find your secluded spot in Nature, and just be with Her.

- Sit on the grass by a tree with your back against the trunk. If you sit still and quiet, you will feel the energy coming from the tree and from the ground below. If appropriate, you can also lie down on the earth or grass or sit on a rock and breathe deeply, feeling the energy radiating from the womb of the Earth. Also tune in with the sun above, making the connection between our Mother and our Father.
- Make the tree or rock into an altar and bring offerings such as special flowers (usually white or yellow roses) or fruit (like an orange or apple).
- Take at least three deep breaths and ask for the cosmic energy and the Great Mother to come to you as you hold your breath. I guarantee that you will soon feel the energy vibrating through your body from head to toe. The prayer I often use is "I ask the cosmic energy to connect me to the great Dark Mother."
- As you receive the life force from the Mother and the light from the Father, surround yourself with an image of the Black Madonna embracing you. Keep that protective energy around you, sealing the energy and life force that was sent to you.
- Thank Her, the Dark Mother, the womb of the Earth, for Her protection.
- You can then begin to pray and chant using your voice as loud as is comfortable, opening your throat chakra. I am including the haunting chant from Calabria (see pages 355–56), which I first heard when

the men entered a trance state and danced on hot coals, a prayer I have heard many times, especially from my teacher Vittorio de Paola. I also arranged the chant for the drum.

- Normally, the ritual is done barefoot, on the earth or on the stone floor of a church in front of an image of the Black Madonna. You can kneel, sit, or stand. If you build your own altar at home, using one of the images of the Black Madonna in this book, you can light white candles for Her and burn frankincense. You will find the chant at the end of the book in the appendix to chapter 1 (see pages 355–56). Release this chant and prayer to Her as many times as you feel you need to, usually seven times. You can sing closing your eyes, using the resonance of your voice to enter an altered state of mind.

- Most likely you will have a vision of Mary, the Mother of God, blessing you and protecting you. Remember to pray for Her as the Earth Mother, the Dark Mother, the beginning of life that we come from and return to, the sacred womb of the Divine Feminine. She will grant you the grace.

# CHAPTER 2

# Drumming in Honor of the Black Madonna

*Oh beautiful girl, your name is Rose. What a beautiful name your mother has given you! She has given you the name of the most beautiful flower up in heaven.*

FROM "CANTO A' FIGLIOLA"
(CHANT TO THE WOMAN)

MY ARTISTIC TRANSFORMATION and spiritual initiation began during that unforgettable summer of 1980. I fell in love with Southern Italian folk music, with the wildness of the land and the earthiness of the people.

At times I took great risks, traveling through Southern Italy, researching the music and the culture with my boyfriend, John. Together, we shared many crazy, dangerous adventures, especially in Calabria, where we ended up being chased by the local Mafia. John and I really were strangers in a strange land!

Unfortunately, I attracted too much attention in our travels. Some of the tough guys hanging out around town nicknamed me Marrakesh. (I suppose because I looked like I came from Morocco rather than Rome.) I had to learn how difficult it was to be a free woman in the south of Italy, where the attitudes are very patriarchal. I hoped that this wouldn't hinder my research and stand in the way of me being considered a serious musician, but sometimes I suppose it did.

I learned that in the ancient times there were matriarchs in the region, in Greek settlements, which included very important cities like Sibari and Crotone, where the famous Pythagoras lived. Nowadays, due to the Catholic Church and Arabic influence, women don't enjoy the freedom and power they did during pre-Christian times, when the mysteries of women (and the Black Madonna) were revered, even worshipped.

In 1980 in Calabria, I discovered that the local Mafia, known as 'Ndràngheta, also contributed to the oppression of women. Because of my undeniable power—drumming with the men in these towns, dancing wildly nonstop, challenging their strength with my tireless tamburello playing—I became an easy target. I was blessed to meet wonderful people who became my family and embraced me, making me part of their tribe, protecting me so that no one—not even the Mafia—would touch me. Perhaps this was the divine hand of the Black Madonna reaching out to me again.

That first year my mother used her social connections to pave the way for John and me to meet local folk musicians in a very strange town called Torretta di Crucoli on the Ionian Sea. There I met the very talented Neapolitan tambourine player Nando Citarella. I ran into Nando by chance walking along the beach. I stopped him and asked, "*Ciao, che suoni il tamburello? E le Tarantelle? Io voglio imparare a suonare!*"

Nando was taken by surprise by me, a young woman who was clearly not a local, suddenly asking him if he played the tambourine and if she could learn from him. This was the beginning of a lifelong friendship among John, Nando, and me. That summer the three of us spent endless nights drumming, dancing, drinking, and eating under the stars, in the mountains, and on the beach. Nando eventually led me to another Black Madonna.

Our new friend Nando invited John and me to travel with him to a campground called Kursaal near Tropea on the Tyrrhenian side of

Calabria. Surrounded by fragrant lemon trees, the camp was extremely rustic, quite uncomfortable, and infested with the largest, toughest mosquitoes I have ever encountered anywhere in the world. Nevertheless, Kursaal became a popular hangout for all the best players of musica popolare, so John and I endured the conditions. For many years to come, a group of us would meet there in the summer, jamming, playing all night long, drinking lots of wine, eating fantastic food, partying, laughing, creating new songs, and dancing the wild, sensual tarantella Calabrese.

This rustic campground became my "school" to learn the intricacies of Southern Italian folk music and dance, because, at the time, there was no formal school. I met some of my most important teachers at Kursaal who also became lifelong friends. One was Vittorio De Paola, a wonderful local folk musician who ended up being one of my most influential mentors. (You'll hear more about Vittorio in chapter 6.) Another was Raffaele Inserra, who hailed from a town near Naples and played the large tambourine or frame drum called the *tammorra*. Raffaele had a vast knowledge of the beautiful, distinctive rhythm called *tammorriata,* usually played at the feasts in honor of la Madonna Nera and providing the music for the folk dance of the same name. The word *tammorriata* is derived from *tammorra,* the principal instrument used for the dance and festival or ritual. The word *tammurriata* is also commonly used.

Raffaele was only nineteen years old when I met him, but he was a big, impressive-looking guy with huge arms and hands. His physique helped him develop the stamina needed to master the large tammorra frame drum he played for the night rituals of the tammorriata. This traditional drumming in honor of the Madonna usually lasted at least six hours, sometimes more.

Raffaele told me with pride that he made his own tambourines. I was determined to visit him in his hometown of Gragnano, near Naples, to learn more about his drumming tradition. I also longed to see firsthand the feasts of the Madonna around Raffaele's hometown. Until that point, I had only read about them in the books by Neapolitan writer Roberto De Simone.

To do authentic research, I needed to see these feasts revering the

Fig. 2.1. Nando Citarella drumming the tammorriata rhythm
at Raffaele Inserra's house

Fig. 2.2. Master drummer Raffaele Inserra showing his tambourines

Black Madonna as a participant and devotee, not as an observer.

Although I did not yet know how to play the tammorriata rhythms, when I heard this powerful 4/4 beat with its strong, complicated accents, it pulsated within my heart and pierced deep into my soul. It was as if I were experiencing a muscle memory of my ancient past. I didn't understand a word they sang in this odd dialect, but having read De Simone's books, I knew that the lyrics were about sex and love and praised women.

When Raffaele played, I could feel those sharp accents and slaps on the center of the drumskin resonating inside my womb, reaching down into my very essence, making me move up and down and to the side, trying to follow this sensual dance that Raffaele played so expertly on the tammorra.

The tammorra is a large frame drum, sixteen inches in diameter, and quite heavy. It is studded with a double row of metal jingles called *ciceri, cimbali,* or *piattini.* Today, they are made with the tops of tomato cans, and the frame itself is fashioned from the strainers used by peasant women to plant seeds in the earth. So, it's a very "earthy" instrument.

The drumming technique requires great strength and stamina. I knew from the books I had studied that this drumming style had been a women's tradition in Southern Italy, but most recently only a few elderly ladies played it. In De Simone's writing, I was fascinated to learn that back in ancient times the drummers were female priestesses initiated in the mysteries of the goddesses Cybele, Isis, Inanna, and Artemis. These goddesses were unfamiliar to me in the summer of 1980, but I was eager to learn all I could about them.

At some point, the drummers shifted from being women to being men. At ceremonial events honoring the Blessed Mother, men generally perform the ritual drumming.

## TAMMORRIATA DRUMMING RITUAL FOR THE MADONNA AND MASTER DRUMMER RAFFAELE

Besides being famous for drumming, Gragnano is also famous for its pasta, tomatoes, tomato sauce, and a special sparkling wine that is

Fig. 2.3. Woman playing the tammorra; photo by A. Belloni

considered by many to be the best in the world (and difficult to find in the United States). Its flavor seems to have the volcanic essence of the area; I decided that it must be a secret recipe that Bacchus himself had passed down.

Fed by volcanoes, the land surrounding Naples is extremely fertile, dark, and rich with nutrients from centuries of volcanic flow. The color of the soil might also explain why there are so many Black Madonnas in the area. Naples itself is one of the most beautiful cities in the world; it lounges above the sea like a sensuous woman. In fact, its original Greek name was Partenope, which means "the virgin." Protected by the famous Madonna of Piedigrotta, Naples was and still is a strong esoteric center in Italy with a complex tradition of magic.

My friend Raffaele spoke in a very thick Neapolitan dialect. Since he didn't finish high school, he never learned much traditional Italian. He worked in the fields picking tomatoes and making wine. Because of this, Raffaele was deeply connected to the land. He knew everything about the plants and animals of the region. But since Raffaele spoke a cryptic Neapolitan dialect, I had a difficult time understanding him—and John didn't understand a word he said. Yet, between the music and the wine, the three of us managed to communicate. I remember laughing for hours watching John and Raffaele having absurd conversations after many glasses of strong red *vino*. Sometimes they fell asleep as they talked or played music together.

Raffaele and I became fast friends. He had a generous heart in addition to his enormous talent. When he invited John and me to visit him in Gragnano, we immediately accepted his special invitation. I asked Raffaele to make me a couple of tammorra. He happily complied, honored that I would be taking a piece of him back to America. Raffaele said, *"Alessà, nu juorno ce ne jimme tutte n'ammerica!"* (Alessa, one day you must take us all to America!)

When John and I visited Raffaele in Gragnano, I saw for myself that he was truly from poor peasant stock. His people all worked the land, picking tomatoes and lemons and working in pasta factories. It was a real shock for me, having come from affluent Rome, to witness firsthand the abject poverty of the people in Southern Italy. Yet I was moved at how giving and openhearted they were. In fact, one of the most abundant (and longest) meals I ever enjoyed was at the home of Raffaele's mamma the first time I was a guest there. John and I were treated like royalty, like long-lost family.

The Inserra home was humble and small. The building itself dated back to the eighteenth century. Although their home was simple, it was beautifully decorated with altars and lovely images of the Black Madonna, mainly the Black Madonna of Montevergine. In local dialect, the affectionate title for Her was Mamma Schiavona—the Serving, or Slave, Mother. This colloquial name refers to our Blessed Mother always being there to serve us and to attend to our needs, granting us Her graces and giving us unconditional love. I loved these old paintings and the colorful altars decorated with plastic flowers, candles, and jewelry. It strongly resembled the *botanicas* (shops that sell herbs, charms, and other religious or spiritual items associated with Santeria, an Afro-Cuban religious tradition) I knew back in New York City.

Raffaele told me that Mamma Schiavona's feast began on May 8 and continued until September 16. During that time, his entire family—including his mother and all of the relatives—went on a pilgrimage to Her shrine. They traveled by bus or on foot, because they couldn't afford a car. The true sign of devotion was to climb barefoot up the mountain, chanting and praying to the Black Madonna, asking Her for miracles and healing. Pilgrims like Raffaele and his family entered the church at sunrise, walking on their knees to the altar, crying and feeling the joy of being close to the Blessed Mother of God.

After singing beautiful ancient chants inside the church in four-part harmonies in the Lydian mode,* they exited the church to start the actual feast. Outside, they began playing the powerful tammorriata rhythm and performed the alluring tammorriata dance for many hours. It included sensual arm movements and was complemented by the sound of Neapolitan castanets. All the while they ate sumptuous food and drank fantastic wine from the region's distinctive volcanic earth. The way Raffaele described the experience to me, I couldn't wait to experience it myself. I longed to get up close and personal with the Black Madonna at Her feast.

Raffaele had grown up in this tradition and had learned how to play the tammorra drum as a teenager, following his ancestoral tradition from hundreds of years ago. Today, he's considered one of the best players of this complicated drumming style. He is, by far, the best builder of tammorra instruments and isn't bashful about telling you that he's well known all over Italy. I'm proud to call him my friend and teacher. Every year, I make a special stop during my pilgrimage to the Black Madonna to visit Raffaele. I bring him my students and followers, who are always taken and touched by his talent and generosity. Many of them have had life-changing experiences with Raffaele in Gragnano, which I will share in the last chapter.

---

*The mode represented by the natural diatonic scale F–F (containing an augmented fourth).

## MY FIRST TAMMORRIATA RITUALS

I was very excited when Raffaele invited me to participate in the tammorriata festival in Lettere, which was near his hometown. The feast was in honor of Saint Anne, the Blessed Virgin's mother and, according to legend, the mother of all the Seven Sisters. It was an experience that changed my life. Her feast day is July 26, and the nightlong festival takes place in a church atop a mountain not far from Mount Vesuvius.

Part of Saint Anne's ritual involves walking up along the dark

Fig. 2.4. Devotional altar for the Madonna of Montevergine;
photo by A. Belloni

mountain road in pitch-black darkness. I followed Raffaele on foot, carrying my instruments and tape recorder. Almost immediately, one of my sandals broke. Instead of helping me, Raffaele began laughing. In his heavy Neapolitan dialect, he suggested that I might as well take off both shoes since the tradition was for hard-core peasants to go barefoot. This symbolized their devotion to Saint Anne. I realized that this was going to be a sacrifice, a vow to the Mother of Mary, the Madonna. So I took off my other sandal.

Raffaele knew that my brother, Muzio, was very sick at the time, physically and emotionally, struggling with his dark side. My good friend encouraged me to pray intensely during the tammorriata and to dance all night for my brother's healing. I did the best I could since this was all new to me. I was shocked to discover the next day that the ceremony really did work—my brother suddenly and miraculously got better. This was just the beginning of the many healing experiences I had while drumming, dancing, and chanting during processions of the Madonna.

Outside the beautiful Neapolitan Baroque church, there was a big carnival-like feast in full swing, with many vendors selling delicious food and their exhilarating homemade wine. Raffaele guided me through the crowd and into the church to light candles for Sant'Anna. The brown-skinned statue was truly stunning and appeared to be real—She looked like a living woman staring at you with Her hand pointing toward you. The statue is thought to date back to the year 1503. The church in Lettere was built almost a hundred years later, in 1600, and is now a place of strong devotion with great celebrations that include the tammorriata ritual.

One of the traditions from the Middle Ages is for pregnant women to take the blessed water in the baptistry and touch their belly. Another is to take a white handkerchief and place the dust left behind when the statue is moved (for the procession) within the handkerchief. This serves as protection against disease.

When Raffaele and I came out of the church at around ten thirty that night, we ate wonderful food and drank some of that incredible wine, which was so connected to the drumming. That's when I heard the powerful rhythms of the drums. The sound seemed to penetrate the very walls of my chest. Five tammorra players, all men, appeared. They formed circles around the singers. The dancers who swirled inside these circles played castanets and performed a very sensual couples' dance. I was astonished at the erotic passion that charged the air. I thought this was a religious feast! As I listened to the lyrics in the heavy Neapolitan dialect, I was shocked—they were the most sexually explicit words I had ever heard in a song.

The tambourines that they played were decorated with colorful ribbons, symbols, and figures to bring good luck and banish the evil eye. The colors they chose—red, yellow, blue, green, and white—were particularly powerful in chasing away bad spirits.

The men playing the drums looked very strong. They had enormous arms and hands and weathered, dark-skinned faces from working in the surrounding hot, sunny fields when they weren't drumming.

Fig. 2.5. Couple dancing the tammorriata; photo by A. Belloni

When the elder women joined them to play, it was very moving. They were also of solid, peasant stock, with beautifully gnarled faces that recalled the old matriarchal society of Southern Italy. These were women who had known nothing but hard work their entire lives. They had given birth to many children and gone right back to toiling in the fields, never complaining, ruling the household, and working closely with the land. Their drumming tradition, like those of the men, emanated directly from that fertile, dark, volcanic soil from which they drew their sustenance—and their very lives.

Today, as in ancient times, the beauty of the tammorriata dance is the way the energies of male and female come together in a primordial celebration of life, fertility, and love. The complementary male and female ways of playing the drum, the male-and-female castanets, the male-and-female movements of the arms, as in an act of love, and the singing style explain it all. The men and women freely express their sexuality through words, drumming, and movement, which reveals a primal balance and harmony between them, a balance that, unfortunately, has been totally lost in today's Western society. The sensuous tammorriata is an attempt to restore that balance.

I will never forget my first tammorriata ritual with Raffaele. As I watched the beautiful fluid movements of the dancers' arms and hands (usually a male and female couple) playing the Neapolitan castanets, I understood more and more that it was a hedonistic ancient fertility dance that symbolized lovemaking, further enhanced by the erotic lyrics.

Totally drawn to the dance, I was suddenly invited inside the magic circle by a man I didn't know. Raffaele nodded, signifying that I should let go of my inhibitions, join in, and follow my dance partner. Seeking the unspoken rule of synchronicity in the tammorriata is similar to finding the perfect rhythm when you are making love. I did as Raffaele encouraged. I followed the strange man into the mysteries of the tammorriata and continued to dance, exchanging partners, exhilarated by my moving, spiritual initiation into the dance, until the sun rose.

# THE SENSUAL TAMMORRIATA DANCE
# FOR ARTEMIS AND CYBELE

The tammorriata ritual dance represents a moment when everyone in the circle enters the same ecstatic dimension and feels the same heartbeat in a collective euphoria, a moment of abandonment, release, and liberation. Everything that happens during the dance could not happen in real life.

During the tammorriata, the dancers open their arms as if embracing their partners and lean back and forth toward each other as though making love. Through the years, at each tammorriata ritual, I witnessed astounding moments of ecstasy among the dancers, some young but usually older people, all extremely lascivious in their movements. Once I saw two very heavyset women come together and dance as light as air. First they were smiling, then they let go like madwomen. It was as though they were showing off their sexual prowess to each other. I have also seen dancers intertwine their legs in an embrace similar to copulation. The passion and abandon is always breathtaking to behold.

Another time, two men danced together, first staring at each other from afar, then drawing nearer with their arms open, bobbing up and down, their bodies moving closer and farther from each other in a kind of challenge. It was as though they were about to fight or become lovers. Then they drew apart and showed off their dancing skills, vying to be proclaimed the best.

In another tammorriata, I saw a very alluring woman using her castanets with abandon, making peculiar sounds with them. She was closely followed by a man who was courting her in a sort of mating dance. The woman moved nearer to the man as the tammorra player got louder and faster, the musician perfectly tuned in to the passionate dance that his music inspired. At one point, it seemed as though the dancers' bodies were becoming one. It was so erotic! At the height of their fervor, the woman suddenly moved away, leaving the man silently begging for her to return to him. It was exquisite.

◆◆◆

In performing this dance myself, I learned (often at my own expense) that you must really give and sometimes take from your partner, who is usually a complete stranger. But regardless, you must be prepared to surrender yourself completely to the dance. You must be willing to look him straight in the eye, to trust and follow his magical, sensual movements, and to lose yourself in them. I must admit that even dancing with old men can be an exhilarating, ecstatic experience when doing the tammorriata.

I have participated in various tammorriata rituals and have experienced some unexpected carnal reactions that really took me by surprise. Even though I'd been a free-spirited teenager in Greenwich Village in the 1970s, nothing quite prepared me for the abandon with which many danced the tammorriata. I was still shocked by the behavior of the old and young alike in these gatherings, which were supposed to be religious. In a sense, they *were* religious, but in an uninhibited, hedonistic sense.

As I deepened my research and studied texts, which described the ancient orgiastic rituals performed in and around Naples for the goddess Cybele and the god Dionysus, I had a revelation. I realized that my assumptions that these so-called peasants from the south were burdened with sexual taboos or that women weren't permitted to express themselves carnally in front of a crowd were wrong.

One example is an elderly man who approached me during the tammorriata and asked me to dance with him: he had a salami in his mouth and a flask of wine on his head. This old gentleman couldn't have been more Dionysian. I accepted his invitation and as we danced realized that he was spouting obscenities at me, which were mainly fantasies, detailing what he wanted to do with me. I smiled politely and pretended not to understand his dialect. At the end of our thrilling dance, I found out that this horny grandpa was eighty-six years old. He didn't need to take Viagra; he had the tammorriata instead, not to mention his potent homemade wine that he carried around in barrels on his tricycle.

## DANCING WITH SATURNA

One of my most significant tammorriata teachers was a woman named Saturna. Her name, which is derived from the legendary Saturnalia rituals in which riotous music and ecstatic dances were performed, perfectly matched her personality. Saturna and I only met at the tammorriata festivals, and she always approached me smiling and hinting in a very seductive way that if I *really* wanted to discover the essence of the tammorriata, I had to dance with her. So, I did.

Saturna had large, voluptuous hips, blond hair, and pendulous, prominent breasts, which she showed off with pride. Although she was missing a couple of teeth, her smile was provocative. Saturna danced with her entire body, and even her face got into the act. She made incredible expressions of pleasure and uttered strange, alluring sounds, which often made me think that she was having an orgasm as she danced. Perhaps she was.

Doing the tammorriata at Saturna's side, I understood the sexual symbolism of all the gestures, each move representing a lovemaking position. Saturna took total pleasure in showing me "how it was really done by the local women." It was an unforgettable initiation into the tammorriata for which I am very grateful.

One of the instruments used to accompany the dance is the *putipu* or friction drum. Traditionally, this unique drum was played only by men since the act of playing it resembles a man masturbating. The hand moves quickly up and down a bamboo stick, which must be wet, creating loud bass sounds. Saturna would break the rules and often played the putipu herself. With abandon, pleasure, and joy, Saturna's enticing smile would heighten the eroticism of the act as she made guttural sounds and humorous comments.

To me, Saturna represented the ancient matriarchal society of Naples and the region of Campania. Her role was to challenge the men who tried to stop her from having fun. I never knew whether she was married. I always saw her with different dance partners and sometimes watched her disappear with them into the darkness of the surrounding fields. To this day, Saturna remains an enigma to me but a key person in my initiation to the tammorriata.

Perhaps my most shocking tammorriata moment came one night as the ritual was ending and the sun was about to rise. Saturna approached me, sweaty and drunk, accompanied by a few men and women. In dialect, she asked me if I wanted to join them to do the *rint'e e for a* (the in-and-out) on the beach beside the mountain that hugged the Amalfi Coast. I quickly responded that she must be joking. But Saturna wasn't. Quite seriously, she pulled me closer, saying, "This is how we do it here."

I treated Saturna's lewd invitation as a joke, responding, "Yes, sure, I read about this in a book: the ancient orgies for Dionysus!" Saturna was insistent. She called to her companions, who were also very eager for me and Dario to join them in this orgiastic ritual. I kept putting them off, saying, "It is the feast of the Madonna! Come on, you must be kidding." But they were very serious, explaining, "*La Madonna è la Signora, la Mamma di tutti.*" (The Madonna is the Lady, the Mother of us all.) Saturna was referring to la Madonna di Materdomi, the Mother of God, very important among the famous Seven Sisters, who bestowed Her blessing upon this act. To remind me of this, Saturna kept singing seductively, "*Ue Marò, ue Marò! Chillo vo fa, sott'u lietto ncopp'u lietto chillo vo fa!*" (Oh Madonna, oh Madonna! He wants to do it, over the bed, under the bed, he wants to do it!) This was a typical improvised verse of the tammorriata. Then Saturna sang the beautiful verse, "*Uoi Signò, uoi Signò, a rosa d'argento, è a rosa d'amore!*" (Our Lady, the silver rose, is the rose of love!) Suddenly, I understood the deep magical and religious meaning of those lyrics, and I felt as if the sensuality of the dance was imprinted in the depth of our souls and in the very eyes of the enigmatic Nostra Signora (Our Lady), the Madonna.

But what could I say? As a researcher, I was intrigued by Saturna's unexpected invitation, but as a married woman, I felt frightened and uneasy. This is why my response to Saturna was ultimately, "Thank you so much for inviting me, but I really am too tired. It's been a long night. The sun is coming up, and we must rest before we drive back to

Fig. 2.6. Saturna playing the friction drum during the feast
for the Madonna of Materdomini

Rome. Maybe another time." She and her friends laughed, calling me
l'Americana. Then they hugged me and left, singing and dancing their
way down the road.

At the time, I didn't realize that this experience would vividly
influence my imagination later as I choreographed for the stage the
"Orgiastic Rites of Dionysus and the Bacchae" for my show *Tarantella:
Spider Dance,* to the beat of our Techno-Tammorriata.

## THE FEAST OF THE MADONNA OF MATERDOMINI AND THE ANCIENT RITUAL OF TAMMORRIATA DRUMMING

During the night of August 14, if you go to Nocera Inferiore, a small town near Salerno, south of Naples, you can still follow a big crowd up a narrow, dark road to arrive in front of a beautiful church where there are many lights and decorations in celebration of Mary the Dark Mother of God, la Madonna di Materdomini. You will hear singing and drumming, as in the old times. Nothing has changed for hundreds of years.

In the past, people traveled in carriages covered with tents and blankets. The women would dress in black because they had to be most respectful in front of the dark Madonna of Materdomini, who was also venerated by the Turks. It was easy to get lost in the huge crowd, among the various carts selling delicious and unusual local food, such as pigs noses and feet, which are boiled and eaten with a lemon, and huge baguettes filled with eggplant, garlic, and other ingredients called *impupata* or *panuozzo*.

This sacred celebration had ancient origins, dating back to the pagan cults of the Goddess of the Moon—Diana or Artemis of Ephesus in Turkey. The Byzantine-style icon of the beautiful Brown Madonna is believed to have come from Turkey on a ship. The devotion is said to have originated in 1041, when a young peasant woman named Caramari (Cara a Maria) had a vision while resting under an oak tree. Mary told her to dig under the tree and there she would find a beautiful icon of Mary, Mother of God. Just as her vision instructed her, Caramari excavated the icon from the earth. According to legend, the image was positioned between two marble tablets. She was astounded by the beautiful image of the Brown Madonna, which had been buried during the iconoclastic persecution. Its artist is unknown.

Twenty years later, in the same spot where Caramari found the icon, an ex-soldier named Pietro de Regina decided to build a church. With help from various kings and popes, it became a well-known sanctuary, protected by King Ruggero the Norman, Federico the II, and the French kings of the D'Anjou family. Devotion to this beautiful icon grew stronger because of the many miracles that happened here.

The Feast of the Madonna of Materdomini begins with the novena (a form of worship consisting of special prayers recited on nine successive days), with chanting and reciting the rosary. The nine days of prayers occur before the worshippers reach the big central door of the church, which is closed. They chant a devotional prayer to the Madonna in dialect in front of the door in high, haunting harmonies. Then they ask for the door to be opened. In the dark, the singers and devotees walk into the church. Some head straight to the icon on the altar, while others hold large candles.

Before exiting the church, those who have come to ask for healing

Fig. 2.7. Our Lady of Materdomini; photo by A. Belloni

and miracles walk behind the painting on the altar. With their left hand, they touch the sacred stone behind the Madonna's shoulder and then touch their faces, necks, and heads. Part of a pre-Christian and also Byzantine ritual, this is such a heartfelt ceremony that it made me and others cry when we witnessed it.

As the pilgrims and singers come out of the church, drummers are waiting to begin the typical beat of the tammorriata, that stirring African 4/4 rhythm that makes everyone dance. Castanets are also part of this sensual dance in honor of the Great Mother. The chanting over the drums overtakes the whole square as the dancers get wilder and more erotic. The pagan celebration continues until sunrise, with the celebrants drinking homemade wine and eating throughout the night. This festival seems to be a continuation of those ancient Dionysian ecstatic rites so popular during the height of Pompeii, as seen in the frescos on the walls of the famous Villa dei Misteri (Villa of the Mysteries), on the outskirts of Pompeii (see plate 5), and in artifacts housed in the National Archaeological Museum, Naples.

The Festa di Sant'Anna (Feast of Saint Anne) on July 26 was my initiation to the tammorriata ritual, followed by Materdomini, Madonna delle Galline, dei Bagni, and Montevergine. While learning the tammorriata, I discovered that these ancient orgiastic dances done for Diana or Artemis were not something of the past. They still exist in Naples and are known as the *mbrecciata* or *tarantella compricata*.

## THE ANCIENT
## ORGIASTIC TARANTELLA COMPRICATA

In my research I learned that the tarantella dance was originally one of liberation, and it certainly liberated men and women sexually, even hundreds of years ago. Described in Abele De Blasio's text from the late 1800s, he attested that the erotic tarantella was performed as a reenactment of pre-Christian orgiastic rituals done by "savages." Back then, the dance was referred to as *semplice* (simple) if performed by only women and *complicata* or *compricata* (complicated) if performed by men and women together. However, no matter who was performing it, it was usually performed naked.

De Blasio, a doctor, scientist, and anthropologist, described this dance in his writings as obscene and sinful. He said that the tarantella was popular in the poorest areas of Naples, where people, mainly men, would ask an old witch to participate in the *tarantella semplice o compricata*. Running into stinking, filthy alleyways, the old hag would quickly gather a group of women, who would come out into the darkness hidden by their shawls as they walked on the stones, their clogs keeping the rhythm of the tarantella.

After entering an old tavern, the women suddenly took off all their clothes and began the wild, ribald dance—screaming, pulling their hair, rolling on the ground, dancing, jumping, doing acrobatics, and reaching a climax on their own. This was known as the simple tarantella. They were reenacting the dance of the tarantate, women who had been bitten by the mythical tarantula, and also recalling the Bacchae, female followers or priestesses possessed by Bacchus, the Roman god of wine (counterpart to the Greek god Dionysus). *Tarantella* means "little spider." (I describe more about the Bacchae in chapter 11 in connection to the healing trance ritual of the tarantella, known as *pizzica*.)

The erotic complicated tarantella traditionally took place in a large room, a dormitory, separated by a thin curtain from the kitchen and the toilet. In this room hung a painting of the Madonna of Pompeii with a lit candle beneath it. The old woman who initiated the orgiastic dance took the painting from the wall and placed it upside down, just in case the Madonna did not like what was about to happen. Next, young, naked ladies and their lovers came from behind the sheer curtain as the old woman began to play the tammorra, singing lewd lyrics as the dancers played their castanets and simulated the movements of sexual intercourse. Suddenly, two young men would appear, completely naked. They jumped on the women and pulled them behind the curtain, beginning the orgy. De Blasio then reported that what happened behind the curtain was so obscene and sinful that he and his friends ran away. Although I appreciate De Blasio's work, still I find this part difficult to believe.

## THE ORIGIN OF THE TARANTELLA

My research indicates that the tarantella originated in Southern Italy, in Naples, and in regions like Puglia and Calabria. As noted earlier, the tarantella was an ancient dance of possession performed by women known as Bacchae. It symbolized the liberation of female sexuality, which was repressed by patriarchal society and was also part of an orgiastic ritual performed by men and women in honor of Cybele and Artemis, later for the ecstatic rites of Dionysus or Bacchus.

It is known that the tarantella was still enacted in 1969 as described by the *femminielli* (men who became women, literally "little women"). It is also practiced among homosexual or transgender men on February 2, during Candlemas for the Black Madonna of Montevergine. Amazingly, this tarantella compricata was also done during World War II and in postwar times. The Neapolitans tell fascinating stories of Americans (including African American soldiers) who found out about this uninhibited tradition of orgiastic dance and paid the men and women to show them how the tarantella was *really* done.

I had read about this unusual sexual dance before I was enticed at the tammorriata feast by Saturna and her companions. When she invited me to participate in that orgiastic ritual on the beach, I realized that this was not something of the past to be read about in books but rather that the tarantella compricata was alive and well and still being enacted in Naples. And I had the honor of being invited to participate. I was astonished! The ancient frescoes that I had admired at the Villa of the Mysteries, depicting women's sexual initiation into the rites of Dionysus, suddenly came alive before my eyes.

## SINGING TO "A' FIGLIOLA"

Onstage, I often sing a beautiful chant called "A' Figliola" (To the Woman), which I had learned in these wild tammorriata rituals. It was traditionally sung for the Black Madonna, mainly the Black Madonna of Galline. The lyrics describe the *figliola,* the woman, as being simultaneously mother, virgin, sister, and bride. She is a castle, a rose, a garden, a fountain, and a well. She is the Sun, Moon, Earth, and Sea. She is called the water into which men want to dive and drown and, finally, enter the cave from where we are born and wish to return. It doesn't take much imagination to realize that the cave symbolizes the womb and the act of birth from the Black Virgin Mountain.

This Black Virgin Mountain is itself connected to devotion to the Black Madonna and is the symbolic womb of the Earth, which can be considered a virgin, because each spring the Earth gives birth to new life without assistance. In the song, the men express the desire to climb the mountain and enter the garden. The women, in turn, invite the men to go across the waters, to climb higher, to be unified in an act of universal love, where anguish and fear disappear. The magical symbolism of mother, sex, death, and rebirth is explained in very few words wrapped in mystery of the darkness.

I knew that I had to make a pilgrimage to the most important of the Seven Sisters, the Black Madonna of Montevergine, called Mamma Schiavona by her devotees. At Montevergine, I knew that I would reach another dimension of devotion: the spiritual Christian tradition of the Blessed Mother combined with the pre-Christian worship of the goddess Cybele or Mother Earth.

### The Seven Sisters

- Madonna dell'Arco (Pomigliano d'Arco)
- Madonna Pacchiana di Castello Somma Vesuviana
- Madonna delle Galline (Pagani)
- Madonna dei Bagni (Scafati)
- Madonna dell'Avvocata di Maiori
- Madonna of Materdomini
- Madonna of Montevergine

This sacred high mountain of Montevergine used to be called Mount Partenio, or Virgin, and it is known that Virgil used to climb it to find inspiration for his poems. On this sacred mountain stood the temple of the goddess Cybele, in whose mysteries Virgil was initiated. There, in the temple, he passed his seven-stage journey of initiation and became *il mago poeta* (the magician poet). Virgil stayed on the mountain, where he gave knowledge to those who came seeking it and planted a garden of magical herbs that could heal the sick. The Neapolitans believed that Virgil was the sun god and for centuries have sung the powerful "Jesce Sole" chant in his honor. Today, the Neapolitans still believe in Virgil's powers as the sun god and call on him for the healing energy of the sun. I also found a link between Virgil and some of the myths referenced in the traditional songs I was studying.

## THE MYTH OF CUPID, VIRGIL, AND THE SYBILS IN TRADITIONAL SOUTHERN ITALIAN SONGS

As I furthered my research in the region of Campania, I found that there were wonderful myths about the origins of these sensuous songs. Some people claim that the author of the works was Cupid himself. Though a gifted poet and the messenger of love, Cupid was also a very naughty boy, and so the lyrics are about sex. Cupid was obscene and mischievous, and the church condemned him to hell.

The legend goes on to say that the song's other author was the poet Virgil. Known to be a magus or shaman, Virgil often visited the sacred mountain Montevergine, where he composed these songs, and was said to be inspired by a skull, which he always kept nearby. It is believed that this skull was from the head of an old woman who had predicted that if Virgil ever went to sea, he would die. Despite her warnings, Virgil went out to sea anyway and died of sunstroke as he sang what would be his last song, *"Vurria addeventare pesce d'oro"* (I Would Like to Become a Golden Fish). These and other songs are believed to be in an old book that was lost in the depths of the sea near Naples. According to the legend, the fishermen learned the songs as they held their ears to large seashells. The legend also tells the myth of the Sybilla Cumana.

Living on the shore of Cuma near the Temple of Apollo and the volcanic lake Averno was a priestess called the Cumaean Sybil. She was a very beautiful virgin who had a book that contained all of the songs from all over the world. The sybil's book also included prophecies from which she saw the past and the future. She even foretold the birth of Christ from a virgin. But since the Cumaean Sybil was arrogant, she assumed that *she* would be the one to give birth to the Messiah. As she heard the angels sing in heaven, she followed the chants all the way to Bethlehem, where, to her surprise, she saw the Virgin Mary cradling Baby Jesus in her arms. As the sybil touched the Blessed Mother, she was immediately transformed into an ugly old crone. Her magical book was taken from her, and she was condemned to repeat all its songs by heart forever.

These legends are symbolic of the nature of these powerful primeval songs.

Cupid gives them their amatory power; Virgil their magical qualities, their connections to the afterlife and other dimensions; and the Cumaean Sybil gives music the ability to prophesize the future and see the past.

Meanwhile, the Neapolitan legend of the Seven Sisters (recounted in chapter 3) is also connected to the sybils. Traditionally, the number seven is considered a magical number. This is true in pre-Christian culture and in Eastern traditions: there are seven chakras or energy points in the Hindu tradition and seven levels of initiation in the ancient mysteries. With the arrival of Christianity, the method in which the pre-Christian goddesses were worshipped by peasants of the agricultural society was transformed into the cult of the Madonna. The feast days of the Madonna also follow the ancient calendar of pagan rites, beginning the Monday after Easter (Madonna dell'Arco) and going until September 16.

## THE MAGICAL SHAMANIC POWER OF THE FRAME DRUM AND THE TAMMORRIATA

The frame drum has a great deal of mystical symbolism and serves many functions. It can be used to welcome good spirits, send away evil ones, or facilitate the journey of a shaman entering the spirit world. Some of the oldest known images, paintings, mosaics, and statues of frame drummers date back to around 3000 BCE. The earliest depiction of a player is that of a woman, the niece of the Sumerian king in Ur, drumming for the goddess Inanna.

In Southern Italy, when the peasants play the frame drum for healing ceremonies, they often go beneath a tree, since many magical rituals are connected to the sacred tree of life. Interestingly enough, in Siberia, a tree used for this purpose is also known as the shamanic tree, and the word *shaman* originates in Siberia. Both the tree and the drum represent the passage between the Earth and the supernatural, giving the healer or shaman a means to journey through other dimensions. Between these two worlds, the shaman performs healing rituals that can cure the sick.

In the Southern Italian tradition the tammorra or tambourine player has the power to lead people into a trance, which allows them to release their disease or trauma and resurface from it cured. In some rituals for the Black Madonna delle Galline (Black Madonna of the Hens), an old woman touches the forehead of a supplicant with a chicken feather dipped in a special oil, just before this person attends the tammorriata ceremony for the Madonna, hoping to be healed.

I was to discover many more fascinating myths and legends surrounding the tammorriata as my quest and my research continued. I truly felt a calling and became obsessed with learning how to use the frame drum for healing ceremonies and as a devotional instrument to accompany my voice and prayers, but I had no idea yet how this would happen.

In my quest to learn, I spent a great deal of time out in the field. I stood shoulder to shoulder with pilgrims and devotees in these mysterious nightlong ceremonies. I continued to practice and to try to understand why the frame drum was such a female-fueled instrument in the past. I had to prove my strength many times in Italy, challenged by men who thought I would give up and not be able to play for as many hours as they did. But they were wrong, because I always kept going, even if my playing thumb became bloody. I developed the stamina and an inner strength to drum with the best of the men, a skill I now teach around the world, especially to women.

## THE HISTORY OF
## THE TAMMORRIATA FRAME DRUM

The Italian frame drum is a musical instrument connected to women's rituals dating back to ancient Egypt and Sumerian culture, honoring Isis and Inanna. It was also adopted by the Greeks and Romans to honor the moon goddess Artemis or Diana, Dionysus or Bacchus, god of the vine, and Cybele. In Islamic regions, the large tambourine called the *mazhar* is the closest to the Italian tamburello, sporting five groups of jingles. In the South of Italy women use the circular frame of the strainers or sifts that they use when they plant seeds in the earth and construct the drum using goat skins and the tops of tomato cans for the jingles.

In Italy's Puglia region, the instrument is used for a music and trance dance therapy called *pizzica tarantata* (from which the tarantella originated). The word *pizzica* literally means "bite." Beginning in the early Renaissance in Southern Italy and other parts of the Mediterranean, this fast and sensual dance was used to treat *tarantismo,* an affliction attributed to the mythical bite of the tarantula or the bite of unrequited love (*morso d'amore*). This mental disorder was often caused by sexual abuse, anxiety, repressed sexuality, and the feeling of being caught in a web that binds. In this musical exorcism, women used the tambourine for the healing ceremonies, guiding the trance and curing the tarantate. (In chapter 11, I go into depth about the history and origins of tarantismo, the tarantate, and the tarantella.)

In Campania during the tammorriata, the drum accompanies the singers who sing in *endecasillabi* form (the principal meter in Italian poetry). The variations are improvised, and therefore the drumming is also improvised. It takes great skill for the drummer to follow the singers and for the dancers to follow the rhythm of the drums with their feet.

The dancers use the Neapolitan castanets, which differ from the Spanish castanets with which most people are familiar. They were probably introduced in Italy by the Gypsies during the Renaissance. Neapolitan castanets are hand carved from the wood of olive trees. Because of their shape, one half is called male and the other female. The dancers' beautiful arm and hand movements show a strong African influence and are again symbolic of lovemaking. But the gestures made with the castanets also symbolize exorcisms and expelling the evil eye.

When I first started learning how to play the tammora and the castanets, I noticed that young women no longer have the physical strength to play the drum for many hours. Perhaps this is because they no longer work in the fields or knead bread but now have regular jobs and have become more "civilized." I find this very unfortunate. But I encourage everyone, especially women, to pick up the tammorra, play it, and start developing your strength, even though your hands may sometimes bleed. Bleeding is part of the initiation ritual. The challenges I overcame by drumming actually helped me a great deal with the flow of energy both onstage and in life.

With the drumming techniques I describe here I hope to inspire other women to work hard to find the inner strength that all women possess and to develop the necessary stamina. Drumming for hours with men and women is absolutely exhilarating. I believe that it helps bring back our lost harmony and balance.

## ⚶ The Tammorriata Drumming Style and Technique

The tammorriata style of drumming has deep roots in Africa. The rhythm of the drumming is essentially in 4/4 time with different accents, according to the singing. As I explained earlier, the tammorra is a large frame drum, sixteen inches wide, with a double row of jingles. The most difficult part of playing is balancing the instrument between two hands so that the movement of the drum will not tire the arm.

The wrist of the hand holding the drum moves continuously, allowing the jingles to make a rhythmic sound according to the beats tapped out by the playing hand. The playing hand hits the skin alternating between palm, fingertips, and thumb. When the drumskin is hit in the center, it gives a low-pitched sound. When it is hit on the edges near the frame, it brings forth a thinner, clear sound. (Also see appendix to chapter 2, page 356.)

To be honest, there are many ways of playing the tammorra, and each player develops his or her own technique, using the movement of the whole body in a sort of drumming dance. I encourage you to do the same: move with your frame drum, holding it close to your heart and feeling the vibrations through your heart and lower chakras (energy points).

Holding the drum with the left hand and playing with the right is called the male style of playing. In the female style of playing, the drum is held with the right hand and played with the left hand. Strangely enough, this is the way I naturally started playing, even though I am normally right-handed. I didn't realize that I was continuing an ancient women's tradition! It just came very naturally for me.

This drum has a hypnotic effect for me, personally. I encourage you to begin a new musical journey with this powerful, ancient style of drumming. Keep it close to your heart and solar plexus, and you will feel a shift in your energy points, releasing emotional and sexual blockages.

Once you learn the basic patterns, I encourage you to improve your technique and chant your own lyrics, composing new prayers to the Great Mother, thus evolving this tradition into a form of sacred ceremony that can be used today.

A frame drum is easy to carry and portable. You can play it outside—by a tree, in a field, by the sea, or anywhere you are moved to play. You can also play it inside your house, in front of the altar you create in honor of the Black Madonna using the images in this book.

Another powerful option is to create a circle and play with other people. As you play the simple patterns described below—slap-dum or jingle-jingle, slap-dum, slap-dum—you can incorporate some simple but powerful movement, such as moving your arms around above your head. You can move your arms up and down with your knees, bending them, while feeling the one and two pulsations in your solar plexus. This helps to release sexual energy blockages and to let go of trauma held inside the womb. It also is a conduit to receive erotic empowerment—almost as if you were making love with the frame drum.

If you practice this beautiful and ancient style of drumming, I assure you that you will feel empowered. I hope that you will make it a practice until one day you make a pilgrimage to the Black Madonna's sacred sites and offer Her the gift of your drumming as a sign of your devotion, just as the ancient priests and priestesses did.

# CHAPTER 3

# The Prophetess, the Poet, and the Pagan Goddesses

*The day of wrath, that day*
*will dissolve the world in ashes,*
*David being witness along with the sibyl.*

From "Dies Irae" (Day of Wrath),
Gregorian chant by Tomaso of Celano

THE YEAR 1987 WAS A TIME of spiritual awakening for me. Years later I discovered that this occurred to many people around the world, as described in the brilliant book *The Mayan Factor* by Jose Arguillez. He states—through incredibly complex calculations—that the Mayan calendar in 1987 was going to be the beginning of a new cycle of consciousness following the New Age movement.

This new awakening for me came after my healing experience at Mount Sinai Hospital, with the vision of the Black Madonna over my bed, and when I heard Her voice during my flight up the California coast. I carefully studied *The Cult of the Black Virgin* by Ean Begg, a book that was given to me by Elisa, a close friend and performer in my group. I still consider this book one of my bibles to this day. It was extremely illuminating and guided me in finding places and legends of the Black Madonna connected to the ancient worship of the various goddesses.

In the summer of 1987, fully recovered and in great spirits, I returned to Italy. I had broken up with John the year before, after struggling for a long time. However, our musical love remained strong and has kept alive our special friendship and musical collaboration for many years.

As fate would have it, when I returned to Rome, I reconnected with a very important lost love, Dario Bollini, whom I had met in 1975, the same year I worked with director Federico Fellini on his film *Casanova*. Dario was a handsome and sexy, dark Italian man and extremely romantic. He was also smart and well educated—an avid reader—and he spoke several languages. I asked him to help me with my research on the Black Madonna, Her history and legends, and to help me write the story for the opera that later I would present in New York. I knew that Dario was an excellent writer, was very poetic, and could create rhymes with a beautiful style, so he was a perfect collaborator. Unfortunately, in addition to being brilliant, Dario was also plagued by addiction. With immense compassion, I decided to help him out of his own shadow and into the light by sharing with him my devotion and research on the Black Madonna.

Once a world traveler employed by Alitalia Airlines, Dario was now under house arrest and sold books in the square near his home to earn a living. One day someone sold Dario *Il segno di Virgilio* (The Sign of Virgil), a very rare book, written by one of my favorite writers in this field, the Neapolitan director and composer Roberto De Simone. This huge book resembles a tome of prophecies from the sibyl herself. Dario gave me the book, one of only a few editions, and I was very lucky to get it.

De Simone was also the founder of the fantastic Neapolitan music and theater company Nuova Compagnia di Canto Popolare, which had inspired John and me to start our group, I Giullari di Piazza.

# VIRGIL AND THE
# CAVE OF THE SIBYL IN CUMA

I was thrilled to receive that magical book about Virgil. *Il segno di Virgilio* was the beginning of a long period of research for us. It explored the connection between the Roman poet Virgil and the Black Madonna of Montevergine, the goddess Cybele, and the Sibilla Cumana (Cumaean Sibyl), plus many more Madonnas, goddesses, and intricate symbols. The book is full of wonderful images and portrays Virgil as no one had ever done before.

I have been fascinated by the sybil since I was a child. I was born in Rome, in the San Giovanni area, not far from the Colosseum, where there is a beautiful church dedicated to Saint John the Baptist. In the past, this area was known as the area of the witches who performed magical rituals during the summer solstice. (The solstice later became the Feast of Saint John the Baptist, celebrated on June 24, honoring his death at the hands of Salome, Herodias, and King Herod.) Many Roman pagan festivals and cult practices were absorbed in this way by the Vatican and the Roman Catholic Church, and the Feast of Saint John is one of the major festivals of this sort. This part of Rome, near the Aventine Hill, is also one of the Bacchae's favorite places.

As a child, I remember my sister calling me Cassandra and la sibilla for my strange psychic powers and clairvoyance, which I inherited from my mother. I was always drawn to mythology and Greek studies, adored studying Latin, and loved reading Virgil's *Aeneid*.

My fascination with the Cumaean Sibyl began from reading and translating Virgil's poems from Latin into Italian. The sibyl was so mysterious as she spoke from under the earth itself, telling prophecies that changed the fate of the Roman Empire. I grew up surrounded by these stories and the places nearby, in the mountains known as the Monti Sibillini (Mountains of the Sibyl), or the Sibylline Mountains.

The Cumaean Sibyl is also connected to the Black Madonna. In one of her prophecies she stated that a black meteorite had fallen from the stars and was being kept in Anatolia, Turkey. She went on to say

Fig. 3.1. The Cumaean Sybil, floor of Siena Cathedral;
photo by D. Bollini

that the stone had to be brought to Rome and must be carved into a statue of the goddess Cybele, black goddess of the Earth. Only in this way could Rome win the wars against Hannibal in Carthage in the years 205–203 BCE.

So it was done, and Rome defeated Hannibal, thanks to paying heed to the sibyl's prophecy. Where once the temple to the goddess Cybele stood in Rome we now find the Black Madonna in the Church of Santa Maria in Aracoeli (which means "altar of heaven" in Latin) in Piazza Venezia, close to where I was born.

## VIRGIL, THE MAGICIAN POET

In *Il segno di Virgilio,* I read that Publius Vergilius Maro, known to us as Virgil (70–19 BCE), born in Mantua, is best remembered for his masterpiece the *Aeneid.* In this work he presents the emperor Augustus as a descendant of the half-divine Aeneas, a refugee from the fall of Troy and legendary founder of Rome. On his deathbed, Virgil claimed that the *Aeneid* was unfinished and expressed a desire to have it burned, but it became the national epic of ancient Rome, a monument of Latin literature, and has been regarded as one of the great classics of Western literature ever since. Virgil's other works include the *Eclogues* and the *Georgics,* which are also considered masterpieces.

Virgil lived in Naples for many years, a city then known as Partenope after the Greek name for the Virgin and later renamed Neapolis, which means "new city." It was a city that already had a powerful esoteric tradition. Virgil is considered an initiate of this type of ancient esoteric magico-religious tradition. Three centuries after his death, he was considered a sun god and a magician.

De Simone stated that Virgil is still alive in Neapolitan legends and myth and is worshipped as a mago poeta. Together with the sibyl, he is considered to have prophesied the birth of Christ using his powers of clairvoyance.

The acclaimed poet also had vast knowledge of religious esoteric studies, medicine, and astrology. These elements are crystal clear in

Fig. 3.2. Mosaic depicting the Roman poet Virgil;
photo from the Bardo Museum in Tunisia

his writings. This part of Virgil's life, with its intricate symbolism, alchemy, magic, and superstitious traditions, became more widely known in the Middle Ages (500–1500 CE). In the fourth century, Virgil was also an integral part of the Christian religion as he foretold the birth of Christ. In the past hundred years, many philosophers and writers have studied the numerous aspects of Virgil the poet magician and necromancer.

Through the centuries, Virgil became the strongest connection between the pagan and the Christian world, especially in Naples, where people still believe in the magic power of *il segno di Virgilio* (the magic sign of Virgil), which was the result of Virgil's extensive esoteric studies and knowledge and the belief that he could also heal the sick.

It is known that Virgil used to climb the mountain Partenio

(now known as Montevergine, near Avellino) to find inspiration for his poems. On that sacred mountain stood the temple of the goddess Cybele, in whose mysteries Virgil was initiated. There, in the temple, he passed his seven-stage journey of initiation and became a healer/poet. Virgil stayed on the mountain, where he gave knowledge to those who came seeking it and planted a garden of magical herbs that could heal the sick. The Neapolitans believed that Virgil was the sun god and for centuries have sung the powerful "Jesce Sole" chant in his honor and to call for the healing energy of the sun.

The Neapolitans still believe in Virgil's power as one of the greatest healers who ever lived. His mythical tomb, la Tomba di Virgilio, is still a place of devotion, and the Neapolitans bring offerings there during the night of the feast of the Black Madonna of Mount Carmel, which falls between September 7 and 8.

As noted earlier, Virgil was initiated into the mysteries of Cybele on Montevergine. Part of Virgil's initiation also occurred in the famous cave in Cuma, where he evoked the response of the Cumaean Sibyl there. He obviously knew the state of trance and possession, which he describes in his poems. As he describes in his *Aeneid,* Virgil entered the underworld guided by the sibyl through a tunnel under the earth, which led to the ancient Lake of Averno, where he met Hecate, the triple goddess of the underworld, at the very spot believed to be the entrance to Hades by way of the River Styx. This journey into the underworld would later inspire the brilliant Italian poet Dante Alighieri's *Divine Comedy,* especially the first section, known as the *Inferno.*

Lake Averno was also sacred to the goddess Melfi. It is a very powerful volcanic site where the earth is constantly moving, and the exhalation of the sulfuric waters can have a trance-inducing effect. This area must have had a profound effect on Virgil's initiation, and he describes it in Book VII of the *Aeneid.*

De Simone explained that Virgil brought forth his magical powers and made a special sign with his hands, arms, and a special tree branch with a serpent around it. The sign was also the letter *Y.*

Legend has it that Virgil's mother gave birth to him after dreaming that she would give birth to a laurel branch, the sacred plant of poets and philosophers. In the morning, as she was walking in the countryside, she went into labor and had Virgil right on the soil of their land. It is believed that the baby came out without crying and had an extremely sweet expression on his face that gave a sense of peace and joy.

The legend also says that in the same spot where Virgil came to life, a tree mysteriously sprang from the earth. This tree became known as the Tree of Virgil. Women thought that the tree had magical powers and went to touch it before and after they gave birth. A similar tradition now exists with Mary and the Black Madonna.

As I immersed myself in this book, I realized that De Simone had delved deeply into an ancient esoteric Neapolitan tradition. I felt that if I wanted to really understand the meaning and symbolism of the Black Madonna, Her devotion, and musical tradition, I had to experience a form of initiation myself and expect the unexpected.

De Simone explained that men who wanted to be initiated into the mysteries of the goddess Cybele had to reenact the rite of Attis, which meant castration on a tree trunk, thereby becoming women and priestesses of the goddess. These priestesses, including transgender ones, used the large tammorra frame drum and tambourines in devotional chants and orgiastic dances of fertility in honor of the Earth Mother, Cybele. I also discovered that the tradition is still alive in the tammorriata festival in honor of Mamma Schiavona, the Black Madonna of Montevergine, and the Madonnas known as the Seven Sisters. Femminielli, men dressed as women, lead the procession up the mountain, chanting and drumming.

De Simone, who is gay, concluded that Virgil himself was homosexual, as he was never married nor had a fiancée and because he reportedly had the nickname Parthenias (a Greek word meaning "maiden"). What is certain is that Virgil represents a connection between the ancient goddesses and the Black Madonna, as he was initiated in the mysteries of Cybele, Hecate, and Isis, who were portrayed as black.

This story also connects to the Neapolitan legend of the seven

Fig. 3.3. Cave of the Sybil, prophetess of the underworld;
photo by A. Belloni

Madonnas as seven sisters. In the legend, the last of the sisters was considered the ugliest, so She ran away to a high mountain to make pilgrims search hard to find Her. When they arrived, they discovered that this so-called homeliest sister was, in fact, the most beautiful of all the Madonnas, and She was black. (I describe this Madonna of Montevergine and Her tradition in depth in chapter 4.)

Inspired by De Simone's book, I decided that to write my opera, like Virgil, I had to begin my journey from the Cave of the Sibyl. In a sense, I needed to travel from the underworld up to the sacred mountain of Montevergine and the ancient temple of Cybele. Interestingly enough, this is the same location that, centuries later in the 1300s, inspired Dante Alighieri's *Divine Comedy*, which begins with the descent into the inferno.

# MY FIRST JOURNEY
# TO THE CAVE OF THE SIBYL

It was a hot summer day in July 1987, at least 100 degrees, when I decided to take Dario's old Fiat 126 down to Cuma, about two hours south of Rome. The road, which leads there, is still the ancient Roman Domitian Way. Although it is a narrow, treacherous road, when you drive on something built more than two thousand years ago, it does not really matter. It just feels wonderful to know that something so old still exists—and on which Virgil himself quite possibly traveled. The road circles the famous Lake Averno, which I found very powerful. I thought, "There it is, the entrance to hell. . . . How did the Romans know that? How did they go in and come out of it? Or, at least, how did Virgil? The first mystery . . ."

Then, I saw the sign for Antro della Sibilla, or Cave of the Sibyl, just like I had read in De Simone's book. The road ends there. I still remember feeling very excited and frightened. I had no idea what was there or what I was going to do except maybe take photos with my fancy Pentax camera.

As I entered the cave (see plate 6), the guards probably thought that I was crazy since it was during the hottest part of the day, around two in the afternoon. No one in their right mind was there. No doubt everyone was at the beach across the way, swimming in the blue waters of the Mediterranean Sea instead of exploring a stifling cave.

As I made my way inside, I suddenly felt completely at home. It was as though I recognized something familiar yet totally mysterious. Walking down the ancient cobblestones, I turned left into what are called the chambers. I found myself in a stunning, haunting place with architecture I'd never seen before, impressive even to Romans like me who grew up practically in the shadow of the Colosseum.

The Cave of the Sibyl is a trapezoid-shaped corridor cut out of tufo stone. Along the corridor are seven chambers running parallel to the side of the hill. The corridor leads to an innermost chamber, where the sibyl was thought to have prophesied. I walked very slowly and entered every chamber, each with a stone altar, and sat, touching the stones to feel their energy. Sunlight streamed in from a hole cut in the stones on the opposite side of the cave, creating a magical effect. It was unbelievably powerful and humbling.

It all seemed unreal. These chambers were cut perfectly into a trapezoidal form by the ancient Cumani who lived there like cliff dwellers before the Romans came. The Cumani built it for her, la sibilla. But who was she? Did she really exist? The legend said that she lived for hundreds of years and that her voice emanated from under the earth when evoked to give prophecies.

When I finally arrived at the last chamber, I realized that this was the mythical place where the Cumaean Sibyl sat and spoke her prophecies. I felt her presence and heard a voice in my head. Since I am a singer, the first thing that came naturally to me was to sing in the cave. To my astonishment the sound and the reverberations were beyond human power. I knew that the cave was intentionally built to have this resonance. I could feel that thousands of years ago initiated priests and priestesses came there to chant and evoke the sibyl. But when she spoke to them, she actually sang!

Inspired, I kept singing, feeling that the sibyl might answer me. Then I sat on her throne and for some time was caught between worlds. I had never experienced an altered state of mind, and as I looked at the stone walls, I could see so many figures, faces, and symbols. The cave was alive! The echo of my voice may have caused my altered state of mind, yet the Earth itself also had a haunting power that I had never felt before. All around and underneath the cave, the black soil is volcanic. Close by, there is a place where the earth keeps moving and steam comes out from the underworld. It was indeed alive, always changing, always moving.

I closed my eyes and asked who the sibyl is, and the answer came to me that she is the voice of the Earth. I immediately recalled the mystical experiences I had had a few months earlier, flying over the Pacific Ocean along the California coast. The voice I heard then was similar to the voice I heard now. The voice, which had spoken to me above the Pacific, said that she could see the past, present, and future. This reminded me of Hecate, the triple goddess of the underworld.

I don't know how much time I spent there; I was completely alone the whole time. The heat and sweltering temperature made it seem almost like a sweat lodge. For all that time, I was not really there but rather somewhere else in the past, remembering and honoring the sibyl, a wisewoman priestess, the Sophia who embodied the voice of the Earth. Through inhalations of the volcanic soil and smoke, the sibyl guided Virgil to enter the underworld. She foretold the destruction of the world, the birth of the Messiah, and the return to a new golden age.

I knew that I had received incredible information from this ancient place and had to write it down. I was certain that this would be the beginning of my opera *The Voyage of the Black Madonna*. As I read Virgil's poetry inscribed in Latin on the stone tablets all around the cave, I realized that Virgil would be the lead character in the opera and that he would come back to save humanity from self-destruction and help save the Earth from the dangerous ecological situation that was slowly killing it. Like Virgil, I was being guided to write my new story of enlightenment by the sibyl.

## GOD IS A WOMAN, AND SHE IS BLACK

After visiting the cave, I became obsessed with the legends of the Black Madonna, Virgil, and especially the sibyl. I discovered through my research that most sybils were African; they were not white as we were often taught in school. That meant that the Cumaean Sybil was also black like the Madonna.

I felt connected to her, since I'd always had clairvoyant powers, and I had premonitions through my dreams. In my research, I discovered that the Duomo di Siena (Siena Cathedral), a stunning work of art and architecture, has a famous inlaid mosaic floor, crafted by some of the most well-known artisans of the Renaissance, that includes a representation of the sibyls of the ancient world.

There are believed to be ten sibyls, including the Cumaean Sibyl.

The Egyptians speak of the Libyan Sibyl, said to be the daughter of Noah, who traveled with him on the ark during the Great Flood. She wrote twenty-four books, including a prediction of the end of the world. There is the Delphic Sibyl, also called Daphne, daughter of the blind seer Tiresias and beloved by Apollo. Others are the Hellespontine, Tiburtine, Phrygian, Erythraean, Cimmerian, Persian, and Samian Sibyls, all powerful oracles and priestesses throughout the classical world.

Each sibyl, including the Cumaean Sibyl, is depicted holding a book of prophecies. As part of my research, I decided to go to Siena, to visit the cathedral, accompanied by my musical partner John La Barbera, who would compose the music for the opera. I knew that we would both find more inspiration there. Also, John used to live in Siena, and this was the place he first met the group of folk musicians from Puglia, Pupi e Fresedde, who changed his life, and therefore mine, forever.

As we entered the spectacular, immense cathedral, built in 1236, we stared at the floor in wonder, astonished to realize that we were practically walking on top of the sibyls. The mosaics were made from marble, mainly in shades of white, rose, and black. To our amazement, the Lybian Sybil was black like the Madonna (see plate 7). These oracles were life size, depicted in artistic, sensual positions, at times with enigmatic expressions on their faces, each holding their respective book of prophecies. John and I walked around slowly, our eyes fixed on these beautiful women priestesses, trying to imagine what the architects of that era were trying to tell us by carving these mythical oracles on the floor of the cathedral.

The artists and architects of the Renaissance were alchemists and knew about magic. They achieved the highest of the art forms through esoteric initiations. In the Duomo di Siena, they showed their knowledge and powers in all the splendor and beauty that human beings could possibly achieve. And by choosing the symbolism of the sibyls, they dedicated their masterpiece cathedral to the Divine Feminine.

John and I continued exploring, following the path indicated by the church. Soon we arrived at the intimate chapel of the Madonna known as la Madonna del Voto (Madonna of the Vow). She is the one who blesses and protects horses and their riders during the Palio di Siena, the famous horse race ridden for centuries in Siena's Piazza del Campo. The moment we entered the chapel, we saw her: la Madonna del Voto, the Black Madonna (see plate 8).

"The Madonna del Voto is a Black Madonna!" I said to John, who had not realized this before. Both of us became very emotional, and I began to cry. Right beside Her, on the floor below Her and on Her right, I noticed another lovely, perfectly sculpted life-size of a dark-skinned woman. She was holding up a flame to the Madonna and had long, sumptuous hair. She also carried an oil lamp, as if to illuminate Her. To our surprise, John and I read that this was Mary Magdalene in adoration of Mary, Mother of Jesus. (Later on in my research, I would discover a deep connection between Mary Magdalene and the Black Madonna when I visited Southern France.)

Once again, I felt that I had been guided to this point, and She, the Great Mother, the Dark Goddess, was telling John and me to write the opera in Her honor. I felt an immense inspiration overcome me. John said he that felt it as well. Immediately, we shared our feelings with some friends who were visiting from New York. I described how I was going to write *The Voyage of the Black Madonna,* explaining that She was the beginning of life, the archetype of the African Mother, and, indeed, the Universal Mother of us all. In disbelief, one of the women said to me, "You mean to tell me that God is a woman, and She is black?"

"Yes!" I replied. "God is a woman, and She is black!"

## HISTORY AND MYTHS
## OF THE SIBYL AND VIRGIL

The century before the coming of the Christian era was a time of great political turmoil. There were civil wars throughout the Roman Empire, dictatorship took hold, and much blood was shed to change the political leaders.

At the same time, the old religion was losing power and, as a consequence, was practiced under the sign of Fortuna, the goddess of fortune. She was depicted blindfolded, spinning cloth on the wheel of fortune. This was followed by an increase in the belief of astrology and divination. In this time of fear and insecurity, many apocalyptic disasters occurred, including the volcanic eruption of Mount Vesuvius, which destroyed Pompeii, as the oracles and sibyls announced the tragic end of an era.

In Rome they followed the Etruscan mathematical school established by Pythagoras. The mathematicians calculated that during certain cycles (120 and 365 years after the founding of Rome) a cosmic cycle would end, and all the constellations would realign in their original positions. In the Orient and everywhere in the Roman Empire, oracles announced that at this time of alignment of the stars, a time of calamity would arrive.

Indeed, during the difficult times of the civil wars, especially in the year 88 BCE, many strange natural phenomena occurred. Powerful earthquakes opened the earth, and fire appeared in the sky, accompanied by the sound of haunting trumpets and the shadows of armies, not unlike the myth of the Four Horsemen of the Apocalypse from the New Testament who are said to have appeared in 1000 BCE.

The *libri Sibyllini* (Sibylline books) contained sacred verses by a mythical priestess of Apollo, the Cumaean Sibyl, among other prophecies. The Phrygian Sibyl even had a vision of the end of the world, proclaiming: "*Tuba de coelo vocem luctuosam emitet, tartareum chaos ostendet dehiscens terra.*" (A trumpet from heaven shall release a mourning sound, and the earth shall open and show hell's abyss.) The books were popular in ancient Rome, when rituals based in the Etruscan tradition were performed to intrepet the will of the gods and divine the future and were consulted to seek the prophecies of the sibyls. Stored in the Temple of Jupiter in Rome, they were destroyed in a fire in 83 BCE.

The Cumaean Sibyl was the most important among the Romans. During Virgil's time, she was already a legend, and her cult was considered *mago religioso,* magical and religious at the same time. Her many names included Amaltea, Demofile, and Erifile. The Cumaean Sibyl is closely related to the prophetess Cassandra. Both foretold the fall of Troy and the new powerful city that would be founded by Aeneas: Rome. One popular belief suggests that Cassandra and the sibyl are the same prophetess.

It is believed that the sibyl was originally from Babylonia and came to Cuma, in Campania, where she was the oracle in a cave near the Temple of Apollo. She foretold the Trojan War and Aeneas's journey to Italy, in Lazio, where Rome would be built. She did not speak her prophecies verbally. Instead, the sibyl proclaimed them by "singing the Fates" and writing on oak leaves. These would be arranged inside the entrance of her cave, but if the wind blew and scattered them, she would not help to reassemble the leaves to form the original prophecy again.

The poet Ovid writes about the sibyl in his *Metamorphosis*. In it, the sibyl says, "I would have had the gift of immortality and eternal youth if I had sacrificed my virginity to Apollo. He wished to kidnap me and rape me; he was dying of desire to seduce me." Apollo said, "Oh, Cumaean Virgin, tell me your wish, and you will have it." In response, the sibyl says, "So, I picked up a handful of dust and showed it to him and asked to live as many years as there were grains of sand. I did not think to ask for eternal youth." And so she remained forever old.

The Cumean Sibyl's prophecies foretold the destruction of Carthage, the fall of the Roman Empire, the return of a golden age, and the coming of the Messiah after the destruction of the world. She also foretold the terrible eruption of Vesuvius, which destroyed Pompeii in 79 BCE. Her exact prophecy was, "But the flame that comes after, stoked by the fury of all Italy, blazing with terrible force will burst forth toward the sky and burn many cities and kill many men, and the air will be filled with smoke and cinders."

The sibyl and her prophecies were a bridge between the worlds of the living and the dead. In Virgil's *Aeneid*, he writes of Aeneas's journey to the underworld to visit his dead father, but the sibyl warned him:

*Trojan, Anchises' son, the descent of Avernus is easy.*
*All night long, all day, the doors of Hades stand open.*
*But, to retrace the path, to come up to the sweet air of*
*   heaven,*
*That is labour indeed.*

*AENEID* 6.126–129

My first trip to the Cave of the Sibyl, followed by my transformational visit to Siena's Cathedral, made me realize that I had to tell the Black Madonna's story, but I still didn't know how it would unfold. But in that first summer the inspiration for the beginning of the opera came to me. I will share with you all the traveling adventures that guided me to write the opera with beautiful music by John La Barbera and lyrics written by Dario and myself, thus connecting our lives forever.

## PROLOGUE OF
## *THE VOYAGE OF THE BLACK MADONNA*
## AND THE HEALING CHANT TO THE SUN

In this chant, which opens the opera, Virgil, a poet and a healer, is searching for the true knowledge to save the world from self-destruction. He meets the Cumaean Sibyl, prophetess of the underworld, who foresees the destruction of the Earth and the return to a new Golden Age. The sibyl tells Virgil that the only way to find true knowledge is through purification and to call on the Universal Mother to help him through his voyage of initiation. Virgil makes his powerful magical sign and chants to the sun god, the haunting Neapolitan chant "Jesce Sole," to receive his fire of immortality. We follow Virgil as he unveils the Seven Sisters, the Seven Black Madonnas, and goddesses in a spiritual quest to save the world from self-destruction and to heal our Mother Earth. During his journey Virgil encounters the goddesses Isis, Artemis, Hecate, Aphrodite, Yemanja, and Cybele, and each one brings him to unveil one of the Black Madonnas (explained in chapter 10).

## ✳ How to Use the Chant "Jesce Sole" to Invoke Healing and Meditation

As John, Dario, and I wrote and performed the opera, I realized the true strength and healing power of the Neapolitan chant "Jesce Sole," which is sung to make the sun rise and invoke its curative abilities. This chant uses the haunting Lydian scale, also called the Neapolitan scale, which was known in pre-Christian times for having the power to calm the mind. When this chant is done in canon, with the melody overlapping with a vocal drone, the healing effect is very clear. You will find the melody, lyrics, and audio links in the appendix for chapter 3 (page 358).

In the past eighteen years that I have been using this powerful chant in my healing workshops, together with the sound of the ocean drum, which creates the calming effect of the waves, to bring people into a calm state of mind after experiencing the trance dances. This helps them feel embraced by the mother of waters, the beginning of life, and receive the light from above from the sun god. I want to share the healing power of this ancient chant with you.

I normally sing it in C, but you can find the key that best suits you, according to your vocal range. The most important part of this chant is to let out your voice freely, opening your throat chakra. In Italy, especially in Naples, we do this naturally—it really helps release energy and gives us great strength to speak up.

I first read about this chant in a Renaissance Neapolitan collection of fairy tales, Giambattista Basile's *Pentamerone*, which is considered a masterpiece of Renaissance literature, all written in Neapolitan dialect and later translated into Italian by Italo Calvino in his famous *Italian Folktales*.

This means that "Jesce Sole" has been sung for centuries. People believed that it had the power to invoke the sun to rise—a great power given to our voices. I encourage you to find that power by using the strength and clarity of the open vowels *je* (like "yea") and *so*.

You can sing it slowly and then pick up the rhythm if it feels appropriate. It can be done a cappella (only voices, unaccompanied) or with the sounds of the waves created by the ocean drum, recalling the way it was often sung by the sea at dawn.

"Jesce Sole" is also beautiful to sing with other people in canon. This way there is a constant drone. You can also use a drone instrument such as a harmonium, or the song can be accompanied by a string instrument like the violin. This hypnotic drone effect, together with the Lydian mode, has very strong healing powers.

If you want to connect to the haunting voice of the sibyl, find a special cave or chamber under the earth where the echo is natural and there is a delay and chant "Jesce Sole." As you sing, think of Virgil leaving the underworld and going into the Temple of Apollo.

You can sing this chant in the morning, as I have done many times, when you really want the sun to come up. Sing it to send away clouds, sometimes even rain. I have witnesses in Hawaii, Brazil, and Italy who can vouch for the powers of "Jesce Sole." This chant has really made all these things happen. I hope that it will help you to find your inner power and bring you into the divine light of God (or the sun god).

# CHAPTER 4

# The Throne of the Madonna in Montevergine and the Legend of the Seven Sisters

*O Madonna, you are so beautiful! We find you all the way
up this mountain!*
*O please, beautiful Child, open this gate to us, this gate to
Paradise.*
*We have come here many times and we have always
received your grace.*
FROM "CANTO DELLA MADONNA DI MONTEVERGINE"
(CHANT TO THE MADONNA OF MONTEVERGINE)

AFTER MY MYSTICAL EXPERIENCE at the Cave of the Sybil in Cuma near Naples, I felt like the poet Virgil myself: I was on my own quest for true knowledge and enlightenment. As my inspiration to write the opera about the Black Madonna grew stronger, I let myself be guided. I knew that the next stop of my journey had to be Virgil's second sacred place: the high mountain of Montevergine, near Avellino, not far from Naples.

For several years I had been blessed to attend the powerful tammorriata rituals, the sensual drumming and dancing in honor of the Black Madonna and wild celebrations through the night into the sunrise. With each ceremony I felt the erotic power of this tradition more deeply and made a vow to master the tammorra so I could become a modern-day priestess initiated into the ancient rites of the Goddess and the Black Madonna.

I knew that I needed to reach the sacred mountain of Montevergine to visit the most important of the Seven Sisters, the Black Madonna called Mamma Schiavona. In my research, I learned that she had the most beautiful, haunting, healing chant.

Years earlier, my friend and drum teacher Raffaele (see chapter 1) had told me that the feast days for this beautiful Madonna Nera were from May 8 to September 16. I knew that the people who worshipped Her climbed the breathtakingly high mountain on foot, usually barefoot, chanting haunting melodies and beating the wonderful, sensual rhythm of the tammorriata on large frame drums. I needed to see Her ceremony with my own eyes.

I was beginning to understand that the Italian frame drum, the tammorra, was the ancient devotional instrument of the Black Madonna, just as in pre-Christian times, when it had been the sacred instrument of the goddess Cybele. Priestesses in ancient Greece and Rome honored the Goddess during fertility ceremonies, playing frame drums, singing, dancing wildly, and inviting men to join them in ecstatic rites in forests, woods, and sacred mountains.

According to ancient mythology, Cybele discovered that her handsome, youthful lover Attis had been unfaithful to her and planned to marry the nymph Sagaris. In an uncontrollable fit of anger and jealousy, Cybele burst into the wedding feast. The terrified Attis became afflicted with a wild, temporary madness and fled to the mountains. He fell under a pine tree and castrated himself, bleeding to death beneath the tree. Immediately regretting that her actions had caused Attis such distress, Cybele mourned her loss. In turn, Zeus promised her that from that day on, the pine tree would remain sacred forever in memory of Attis.

Historically, men who wanted to be initiated in the mysteries of Cybele became women through a ritual castration reenacting the myth of Attis. They were known as Galli, and as priestesses they played the frame drums and danced in ecstasy.

Interestingly enough, I discovered that all of these erotic musical and dance traditions were still alive and well in Montevergine. They were very similar to those traditions initiated thousands of years ago. As I mentioned, to this day, in Naples, gay and transgender men known as femminielli celebrate the feast of the Madonna known as Candlemas, or La Candelora, on February 2. In the Christian tradition, this name derives from the Latin *candela* and *candelario*. The feast's name loosely translates to "feast of candles, candle, twine, and waxed cord." The femminielli, dressed like women, perform chanting, ritual drumming, and dancing and also play the castanets.

I was extremely fascinated by the Galli, the men who became women to honor the goddess Cybele. At the time, I didn't know that in later years, in my workshops, I would meet young men who had decided to become women because they always felt that they were female. They came to my workshops when they found out about the ancient tradition of the Galli and the tammorriata dance to honor the Madonna of Montevergine.

Shortly after my visit to the Cave of the Sybil, I decided to drive my old Fiat to visit my gay friend Guido. He lived in the area near Benevento, a town that had become famous in the Middle Ages as a favorite place for witches to perform their nocturnal dances and magical rituals around a mythical walnut tree. (Benevento is also an area sacred to the goddess Isis, where I will take you in chapter 5.)

A devotee of the Black Madonna, my friend Guido was a singer of Neapolitan folk music. I asked him to take me up the sacred mountain of Montevergine to show me the true devotion and tradition associated with the pilgrimage. Guido had gone there many times with his mother (who also knew the sacred chants), so he was the perfect guide.

My friend and I set out on a beautiful summer day, driving up from the city of Avellino to the gorgeous mountainous area known as Irpinia. Contrary to my experience visiting the sibyl's cave, the air became cold

Fig. 4.1. Black Madonna of Montevergine, also known as Mamma Schiavona;
photo by A. Belloni

and fresh, giving us a sense of being high on the pure, clean oxygen that
we were breathing. The road was narrow and winding, eleven kilometers all the way up to the top. Between the extremely crisp, clear air and
the twisting road, I felt a sense of dizziness and lightness, as though I
were flying.

As we drove the steep, twisting road, I couldn't believe that, to
demonstrate true devotion, pilgrims to this day hike up the hallowed
mountain on foot, often without shoes, at times coming from distances
of a hundred kilometers away. To scale the mountain on foot, it takes
at least twelve hours through wooded trails from the bottom of the
mountain near the town of Ospedaletto. The pilgrims usually leave at
night or in the early evening to arrive at sunrise, chanting the beautiful

"Canto della Madonna di Montevergine" in the Lydian scale. They enter an altered state of mind through the chanting, not feeling tired at all but rather energized.

The first line of the traditional chant is *E saglimmo stu muntagnone, e jammo a truva' Mamma Schiavona* (Let's climb up this mountain, let's go visit Mamma Schiavona, our Servant Mother). The ascent of this high peak represents a genuine journey of initiation in the mystery of the Black Madonna, a sacrifice made with great faith to ask for healing and miracles. (I will share some sections of this ancient healing chant at the end of this chapter.)

The most powerful part of this initiation is the stop made at the ancient Throne of the Madonna, called, in dialect, la Seggia ra Maronna (the Madonna's Chair). My friend, who knew this was the oldest and most powerful part of the pilgrimage, showed me the way through the woods to the mythical place where it was believed that Mamma Schiavona herself had stopped to rest when she tired during her climb.

Guido and I arrived at this "throne," following other pilgrims. This section of the pilgrimage had to be made on foot. The place we sought was difficult to find since it was hidden by huge trees: oaks and walnuts. Magically, a large rock appeared on the side of the mountain. Instantly, I felt as though everything shifted and that I was in an enchanted forest. Guido and I truly entered another dimension. Today, looking back, I am sure that this was a portal into the Divine Feminine energy of the ancient Great Mother.

At the Madonna's Chair, I was told that the tradition was to pray while sitting on the throne, which appeared as a round excavation in the rock. It was customary to also bring a small, personal offering, sometimes a flower or even a lock of your own hair, tie it with leaves, and place it there with a branch and a written prayer.

The magic of this rock is that anyone can fit inside perfectly, no matter how big you are. As you sit there to pray, you see the imprint of the Madonna's feet on the stone facing you; this is the place where She rested. As I gazed at the imprint of the Madonna's feet in the rock, I

Fig. 4.2. The sacred mountain Montevergine, seen from Avellino;
photo by A. Belloni

felt powerless meditating on this mystery and became lost in the mists of time.

Seated on the throne, I leaned back, pressing my head against the ancient rock, my hands on the arms of the throne, staring at the "feet" of the Madonna. I sobbed deeply and closed my eyes. The next thing I remember is that I either passed out or entered an altered state. Whatever it was, it's difficult to explain, but I felt something I had never experienced before: it was the rock's own vibration. This tremor was so strong that it seemed to come from beneath the earth. It coursed through my body, like the essence of the Earth's core itself . . . the soul of the Universal Mother.

This was similar to the experience I had had at the Cave of the Sybil, just as haunting but somehow more nurturing. In the cave I had felt close to the underworld; but on the mountain, I felt close to heaven. I have no idea how much time passed. I started communicating with the Divine Mother telepathically. (I still had not seen Her painting.) Something deep within me realized that this was the ancient site of the temple of Cybele, possibly even where Virgil himself had his own garden of healing herbs and where he became the mago poeta.

It was clear to me that this was the very spot where the poet Virgil had been initiated in these mysteries and received heavenly inspiration to write his *Eclogues*. One medieval legend asserts that Virgil experienced his revelation about the birth of the messiah to a virgin on this same very sacred Virgin Mountain. It is probably for this reason that this peaceful place was part of early Christianity. This powerful site of devotion has been here for thousands of years and is indeed alive. Much like the Earth herself, like the dark, rich, fertile earth, black like Mamma Schiavona. I heard an echo in my mind telling me, "Yes, God is a woman . . . and She is black."

Like Virgil, I believed that the ancient people knew that the Earth was a living being, and they respected her and honored her with sacrifices and magic rituals, with chanting, drumming, and dancing in a trance.

This throne was the proof. There, at this sacred place, you asked her for miracles and healing. This I did, while weeping. I prayed for the health of my mother and for the health of my brother and my boyfriend, Dario, who were both struggling from addictions. I asked for them to be released from the dark side and to finally be free from their self-destructive personalities.

All around me, I saw beautiful braids made from the long, lush branches of the bright green juniper trees, which were so abundant on that sacred mountain. Juniper foliage slightly resembles pine needles but is scalelike instead of needlelike as pine branches are. These lovely woven pieces resembled crowns of flowers, which were braided and tied with a knot.

Following an old legend, or propitiatory rite, unmarried women had been coming up the mountain for centuries to ask the Madonna to grant them a husband. These were the offerings they left for Her. The braid and the knot symbolized the knot that you tie on the wedding day. Young women would make the pilgrimage, walking up the forest path. When they arrived at the Madonna's powerful throne, they presented the braided, knotted juniper while chanting or reciting:

Fig. 4.3. Praying at the Throne of the Madonna of Montevergine

Fig. 4.4. Offerings by the pilgrims at
the Throne of the Madonna of Montevergine

*Colo Nodo che so legato so trovato lo fidanzato.*
*(With the knot that I tied I will find a fiancé, or a*
*boyfriend.)*
*Co lo Nodo che so' legato quest'anno ci vengo sola*
*l'anno chi bene co no bello guaglione.*
*(With the knot that I tied this year, I come alone and*
*next year with a beautiful man.)*
*Co sto nodo che so legato quest'anno ci vengo zita l'anno*
*chi bene co no bello marito.*
*(With the knot that I tied this year, I come as a maiden*
*and next year with a beautiful husband.)*

Some people may think that this is just an old superstition, but I assure you, it is much more than that. While I was sitting in the supernatural throne looking at the imprint of the Madonna's feet, taking in all the signs of magic around me, I had no doubt that these women knew a secret formula, an enchantment, to bring love and a husband into their lives. If the magic didn't work, they would have stopped doing it, right? But instead, they have come for hundreds of years, and their wishes have been granted.

At that moment, I understood that I needed to ask the Madonna to bring true love back into my life. I prayed that one day I would even marry Dario and return there with him as my husband. I stood, left the throne, and picked up some juniper branches, working hard to make a braid. I tied a knot with my scarf, which I left there as a sign of my devotion. I recited the enchantment, asking for a miracle, as the chances of being with Dario in a serious, committed relationship were extremely slim. Yet I strongly believed in the power of the Black Virgin of Montevergine.

It is extremely interesting to note that ancient sanctuaries were all built in symbolic positions of sacred power: inside caves, making devotees immediately feel connected to the underworld and the womb of the Earth; on top of high mountains, making pilgrims climb high to feel close to heaven; or beside the sea, bringing worshippers to the primordial waters and the beginning of life. Montevergine, associated with the symbolic ascent into heaven, is an important energy point for three reasons: because of its great height, its close proximity to the Mediterranean Sea, and its location opposite the great volcano Vesuvius, the mountain of fire and transformation. Montevergine is extremely powerful, encompassing three potent elemental attributes in one sacred site.

The Madonna is also identified with the mountain as Montevergine. She becomes the mountain, and the devoted sing to Her, embraced by Her nurturing love. In English, the chant translates as follows: "We came and left many times, and we have always received your graces, and we promise that we will come back every year, and if we don't see you here, we will see you in eternity and in Paradise."

From afar, I heard pilgrims chanting. I came out of my trance on the Throne of the Madonna. It was time for me to go see Her, our Mamma Schiavona. I walked up the trail to the car, listening to the haunting chants and the lovely voices of the devotees. I had heard recordings of this chant in Roberto De Simone's collection, yet nothing was quite like hearing it in person. Hearing these women chant loudly in perfect harmony seemed to penetrate my very being.

As a singer, I couldn't figure out how they could keep chanting without losing their voices. My friend explained that when you are devoted, a miracle occurs that keeps your voice true and strong. De Simone described the same phenomena in his book *Chi è devoto* (Who Is Devoted).

As we climbed higher, the air seemed even lighter, and I was surprised to see cars and some small buses completely covered with decorations of flowers and ribbons (see fig. 4.5). On their roofs were paintings of the Madonna of Montevergine. Some even had small shrines on their car tops. What an unusual devotional scene it was, seeing these striking automobile shrines as the chant's music blasted out of their stereos. It was so typically Neapolitan!

When Guido and I arrived at the summit a beautiful and enormous white marble sanctuary appeared. I again felt a high level of energy and excitement. I was consumed with an eagerness to visit Her, the Blessed

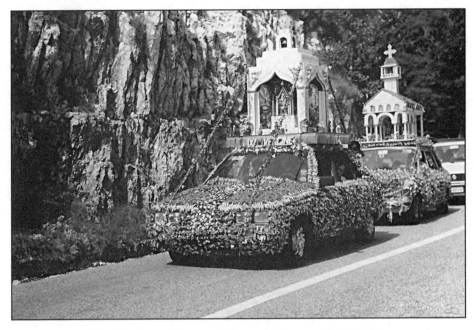

Fig. 4.5. Decorated cars of devotees going up Montevergine

Mother, in Her shrine. I knew that a very important part of the ritual was to crawl up the ancient steps of the sanctuary on your hands and knees, often kissing or licking the ground, even though this practice was forbidden by the Catholic Church. To deter this sort of paganistic devotion, a new sanctuary had been built, and the shrine's original direction was changed. But this didn't stop the faithful. I noticed that the devotees who had walked dozens of miles barefoot went into the church's old section instead of the new one. There, they repeated the ancient ritual, chanting, entering into trance states.

Unlike them, I didn't enter the shrine on my knees. Instead, I approached it from the main entrance. And there She was! The Madonna was depicted in an enormous Byzantine painting, one of the most magnificent examples of this style of painting in the world. Her skin was brown, no longer black, since the Vatican decided to make Her complexion lighter in Her most recent restoration, a practice that the Catholic Church has been doing systematically to many black or dark Madonna icons.

Majestic, with dark, olive skin, the Madonna of Montevergine has beautiful, benevolent hazel eyes that follow you to every corner of the church. It is as if She is telling you, "I am protecting you, wherever you go." She has a seductive, extremely enigmatic smile, like several other Madonna figures. Her head is turned to the left, and Her throne is held up by two black angels. Her dark baby Jesus sits on Her lap, staring up at Her, grasping Her dark-brown dress. She wears an exquisite golden crown and is bedecked with earrings and necklaces, which make Her resemble a Gypsy queen.

The painting is believed to date back to the eleventh century, although the original one (now not visible) probably is from much earlier. No one is sure who the artist was, but like most other Byzantine paintings of the dark Madonna, this one is also attributed to Saint Luke (but it is unlikely). The painter was most definitely a spiritually enlightened artist with a skilled technique as he made the painting appear alive. The effect of Her haunting eyes following you throughout the church is breathtaking (see plate 9).

Once more I began to weep, full of overwhelming emotions. Falling on my knees in front of the altar, I felt loved and nurtured by Her benevolent expression, cradled in her protection. I honestly felt as though She had been waiting for me for many years and was saying to me, *"Quanto tempo, figlia mia!"* (Such a long time, my daughter!) I immediately felt as though I were being held in Her arms. This feeling would come repeatedly when I visited Black Madonnas in other locations, but at Montevergine, it was astounding.

I prayed for the Earth, for peace, for the healing of women. Again, I prayed for my mother, for my brother, and for Dario. I knew that I had to bring Dario to Her someday, but since he was still under house arrest, I had no idea how and when this would happen. But I knew that it *had* to happen to save him. I kept my faith in the Blessed Mother, confident that it would come to be. I knew that people with a dark side, oppressed by addictions, felt embraced by the Dark Mother as they say, *"La Mamma Schiavona 'tutto accoglie e tutto perdona."* (Our Mother welcomes all of us and forgives us all.) The gorgeous chant of the pilgrims outside haunted me, even though I could not see them. But it didn't seem to matter, because their voices permeated me.

I discovered a very interesting fact about these ancient rituals. The Catholic Church accepted the rituals and traditions, which date back to ancient times, even pre-Christian practices. However, often the church made drastic changes, which infuriated the peasants and pilgrims who visited from all over the country, knowing only the devotion they had learned from the oral tradition of their ancestors. As mentioned before, the church authorities changed the direction of the entrance of the sanctuaries and suddenly forbid the pilgrims to sleep inside the church or to sing and drum inside the sanctuary.

In the old tradition, the pilgrims climbed the mountain all night long and arrived at the sanctuary at dawn, facing the sun. They entered the old church by ascending the old steps, which had been carved more than a thousand years ago, on their knees. On each step they chanted one verse of the old prayer to Mamma Schiavona, invoking Her healing power. The stairway represented the sacrifice of their devotion, even the mountain itself. The chant says *E saglimmo lu primmo grado la Maronna ce dace la mano* (As we go up the first step, the Madonna gives us Her hand). This chant continues for eleven steps with eleven verses.

The stair-step chant, in the Lydian mode, is done by groups of thirty or more people, in harmony, as they kneel—some bleeding on the stones—asking for miracles. The sound is so haunting that it pierces your very soul, awakening a primordial healing force. As people pray to Her, the Blessed Mother, the Mother of Christ, they also pray to Her son: *E Bambino e Bambiniello e apritece stu cancello* (Oh, little Baby Jesus, please open this gate for us).

A particularly astonishing miracle occurred in Montevergine's shrine not so long ago. A man in a wheelchair was brought to the Madonna by others, who lifted him up on each step as they chanted. The reporter who described the incident wrote that the man was lame and was asking for grace. Suddenly, the man stood, walked normally, kissed the painting, and thanked the Madonna. Just as he promised Mamma Schiavona, every year he returns to reenact the miracle in front of Her devotees.

Fig. 4.6. Women chanting to the Black Madonna at Montevergine

Miracles and healings like these are not a thing of the past but still occur today. As I walked inside the sanctuary, I entered the side of the *ex-votos* (the vows made by people who had received Her grace). This chapel was literally covered with hundreds of artifacts made of gold and silver, as well as some paintings. Each was created by a person who had received the Madonna's grace. These objects represented the body part that was healed: the heart, brain, leg, arm, hand, or stomach. Others depicted a scene of the miracle, such as being saved in a tempest at sea, from a mountain storm, or at the scene of a car accident. The style of this unique, sacred art is extremely special, primitive, and poetic. They are testimonials of both the old devotion and the modern-day miracles, as you can see from the dates inscribed on the ex-voto.

Traditionally, devotees leave the chapel at sunrise, after the kneeling on the steps. They face the sun and sing the ancient healing chant "Jesce Sole" and the "A' Figliola," a chant in praise of the woman. (I described "A' Figliola" in greater detail in chapter 2.) When the chanting is over, they begin the feast, which dates back to the orgiastic rituals

Fig. 4.7. Women processing and drumming the tammorriata in Montevergine;
photo by D. Bollini

for Cybele and Diana. Besides gorging on food and drink, there is also drumming while dancing the powerful tammorriata.

## THE BLACK MADONNA OF MONTEVERGINE AS MARY, MOTHER OF JESUS

I returned to Montevergine many times, and later with Dario, who came along to assist me with my research. From my studies, I discovered how the Southern Italian devotion to the Black Madonna was unique compared with Spain, France, or Poland. In Italy the people had kept alive the ancient pre-Christian musical and dance traditions that the Vatican had tried to repress by forbidding them. The Vatican did not succeed in Magna Grecia, the coastal areas of Southern Italy, and the favorite land of Dionysus, Cybele, Artemis, and Isis.

As I continued traveling to remote areas in search of the Black Madonna, a number of facts surfaced about how the Vatican tried to whiten the skin of Madonnas depicted in these paintings, sometimes even changing the appearance of the statues. In the thirteenth century we know that in Montevergine there was originally a painting of a Black Madonna with very dark skin, which bore the inscription *Nigra Sum Sed Formosa*. (For more about this, see chapter 7, page 194.)

To me, tampering with important historic artifacts is inexcusable. Most of these sacred dark images date from the year 700 CE to the fourteenth century. Many churches were built over or around temples where there were busts of ancient goddesses. Most of these legends tell us that the statue or painting arrived on a Turkish ship from Asia or North Africa, or else it appeared magically in a cave or tree, atop a mountain, washed ashore on a beach, or on the banks of a river.

As stated by other researchers, including Ean Begg, it is clear that both Mary and Jesus were dark skinned and that only in the Renaissance did painters hired by the church (such as Botticelli and Raphael) begin painting them light skinned with blue eyes and blond hair. This white European image of Mary is what the Vatican wanted to spread around the world. For the most part, the Catholic Church succeeded, but not entirely.

We know there are thousands of Black Madonnas throughout the world, and they are the true patron saints of most Catholic countries. Some of these include the Madonna di Loreto (Italy), Our Lady of Czestochowa (Poland), the Black Madonna of Chartres (France), the Black Madonna of Montserrat (Spain), Our Lady of Einsiedeln (Switzerland), Nossa Senhora Aparecida (Brazil), Morenita de Guadalupe (Mexico), Virjen de la Regla (Cuba), and many others, including those in Russia, Germany, Ireland, and England.

## MAMMA SCHIAVONA: PATRON OF GAY AND TRANSGENDER PEOPLE

The true power of the Black Madonna and Her tradition is that everyone is accepted by Her, especially outcasts and those who have experienced trauma and loneliness. Because of this, the Madonna of

Montevergine is also known as the patron of gays. She is celebrated with a unique, uninhibited feast every year on February 2, which is Candlemas. The name derives from the Latin Candelora, "Feast of Candles, Feast of Light."

The presentation of Jesus at the temple celebrates an early episode in the life of Jesus in which he is brought to the temple as an infant and offered as a sacrifice to God. Other traditional names of this feast day include Candlemas, the Feast of the Purification of the Virgin, and the Meeting of the Lord.

Interestingly enough, in Brazil, February 2 is the festival of Yemanja, goddess of the sea (comparable to Greece's Aphrodite). It is celebrated with ritual drumming, trance dances, and processions along the ocean by the fishermen with thousands of people participating.

A beautiful legend explains why Mamma Schiavona is the patron saint of gays. In the year 1256, two homosexual men provoked a scandal among the local people and were tied by the locals to a tree, destined to die on the cold mountain. It was the Blessed Mother, Mamma Schiavona, who saved the two young men, restoring them to life and giving them the freedom to be who they were. This miracle was a sign of supernatural compassion, and because of it, many homosexuals became her devotees.

To this day, every February 2, challenging the freezing weather of the high mountain, the femminielli and transgender men and women climb the mountain in a procession, drumming, chanting, and dancing the erotic dance of the tammorriata. It is believed that Mamma Schiavona gives everything and forgives everything.

Today, well-known singer and drummer Marcello Colasurdo is the most important leader of this movement and one of the best singers and masters of the tammorriata tradition. Far from being an invention of the modern era, the LGBTQ community is actually the descendant of an ancient tradition and devotion that dates back to the ancient rites of the goddess Cybele, the myth of Attis, and the celebrations of the Corybantes, priests who worshipped Cybele through ecstatic drumming and dancing.

This very ritual by the femminielli and the priests initiated in the mysteries of Cybele inspired me later to write and stage the last scene in our opera *The Voyage of the Black Madonna,* featuring the actors dressed as women, telling the legends of the Seven Sisters and of Mamma Schiavona, and dancing an orgiastic tammorriata.

## HISTORY OF CYBELE: THE MYTH OF ATTIS AND TRANSGENDERISM

In Rome, Cybele was known as Magna Mater (Great Mother). During the Punic Wars, as I mentioned before, the Roman commander, Scipio Africanus, on the advice of the Sibylline books, introduced Cybele from Pessinos and established Her worship in Rome. As a goddess of fertility, she personified the Earth and its abundant benefits. She was also regarded as the Great Mother and the producer of all plant life. In addition, Cybele was believed to protect wild animals, especially the lion. Her exotic cult also introduced the orgiastic rites performed by priests. Cybele is usually represented wearing a high, cylindrical hat, seated on a throne or on a chariot drawn by lions, and holding a frame drum (see fig. 4.8).

The symbol of Cybele was the pinecone, which stems from the myth (and tragic love story) of Cybele and Attis. Told in greater detail earlier in this chapter, Cybele's jealousy caused Attis to go mad and castrate himself. Zeus took pity upon Cybele's grief and proclaimed the pine tree sacred in Attis's memory. Some of the rituals performed by the priests of Cybele are related to ancient myths about the goddess, in particular the myth of Cybele and Attis. The practice of self-mutilations was adopted by the priests of Cybele, the notorious Galli.

## THE PRIESTS OF CYBELE: THE GALLI / CORYBANTES

The eunuch priests of Cybele were called Galli (singular, Gallus) and practiced a variety of masochistic rituals and ceremonies. In Greece, the Galli of Cybele were also known as Corybantes.

The notorious transgender Galli were known for their

Fig. 4.8. The goddess Cybele playing a frame drum, 4th century BCE;
Thessaloniki Museum, Greece

self-inflicted castrations, loud music, use of hallucinogenic plants, and frenetic dancing, although it is believed that Roman citizens were forbidden to become Galli priests, join in the frenzied celebrations, or undergo ritual castration. The Galli priests of Cybele practiced transvestism and made every effort to appear and behave as women. Their linen-and-silk clothing was a combination of fashionable feminine and priestly dress. They wore their hair long, arranged in elaborate hairstyles, which were complemented by various wreaths, ribbons, and other adornments. They also wore the high, cylindrical hat called the *polos*. In addition, the Galli adopted female mannerisms and speech patterns and applied an extensive range of cosmetics to enhance their feminine appearance. They participated in orgiastic rituals and ceremonies accompanied by loud, ecstatic cries and the frenzied music of flutes, drums, and cymbals.

As seen in the mosaics and frescoes in Pompeii, these are the exact same movements, appearances, and instruments still used today in the area of Naples among the first inhabitants of the region of Campania known as Oschi, and especially in Montevergine, honoring the Black Madonna. This tradition has remained alive for thousands of years, despite the challenge of the Vatican.

During the festival in honor of Cybele, elements of the Cybele and Attis myth were reenacted. Some of these ceremonies and rituals involved cutting down a pine tree, which represented the dead Attis. The tree was honored, wrapped in bandages, and taken to the temple of Cybele. The pine was then decorated with violets, which were believed to be the flowers that had sprung from the blood of Attis. As part of this religious ceremony, the priests of Cybele cut their arms so that their blood fell on Cybele's altar and on the sacred pine tree.

## THE MEGALESIA:
## THE FESTIVAL OF CYBELE

The Megalesia was the festival of the Magna Mater, or Cybele, celebrated between April 4 and 20, with games and theatrical performances. Sumptuous feasts were held on the first day of the Megalesia, and it ended with chariot races at the Circus Maximus in ancient Rome. The eunuch priests of Cybele carried Her image through Rome to the sound of tambourines, horns, flutes, and cymbals. As they danced through the Roman streets, they beat themselves bloody in an ecstatic ritual. Some Romans became *archigalli* (chiefs of the Galli), who sacrificed bulls' genitals to the goddess Cybele instead of their own. This led to the rite of the *taurobolium*, which involved the blood sacrifice of a bull to Cybele and Venus. The blood of the sacrificial animal poured through the platform onto the face and body of a priest standing below. After the bloody baptism, the priest would present himself before his fellow worshippers of Cybele, purified and regenerated. We find remnants of this bloody ritual and symbolic priesthood alive today in the Spanish tradition of the *corrida* and the *toreador,* commonly known as bullfighting. A similar tradition is also popular in the Basque regions of France, in Bayonne, and in San Sebastiano, Spain.

I personally took part in one of these mad and bloody celebrations in Bayonne. It was a three-day and three-night ritual in which the whole town (everyone extremely drunk) is chased by a horned and angry *vachette* (young bovine). I saw many people get gored and bleed all over the place. Of course, I witnessed this from a safe distance since I ran in the opposite direction from the vachette. Bull chasing and sacrifice were definitely not for me! No, I could not have been a Corybant.

## HISTORY OF THE
## SANCTUARY OF MONTEVERGINE

This peaceful, remote place on Montevergine, which the Romans called Partenio, became a refuge for the early Christians who went there to escape from the Roman persecutions. We know that Saint Felix, Saint Maximus, and Saint Modestinus were on Partenio before the seventh century BCE.

Then, in the seventh century, Saint Vitalinus arrived in Montevergine to live as a hermit. He also built the first small church there, which was later destroyed by the Saracens. Undaunted, the Christian devotion continued, and mystics went to Montevergine to find peace, to pray, and to live in harmony with Nature.

Saint Guillemin of Vercelli arrived as a hermit in the year 1118, following a white dove who guided him there. He built the first official church on the site in 1124. There, the saint had a mystical, miraculous experience involving the unusual painting of the Madonna in the church, which was similar to other renditions in medieval times. It depicted a beautiful, sensual Mary breastfeeding Baby Jesus. During prayer, Saint Guillemin witnessed milk dripping from the Madonna's breast. This supernatural experience was a sign from the Virgin, asking him to build a church in Her name. That he did, in the year 1135, with a clerical community, which embraced both men and women—a woman served as abbott. This church and monastery became a very important place of devotion in the Middle Ages.

It's important to note that Saint Guillemin came from a noble family. At a very young age, he renounced the wealth of his upbringing and decided to become a wandering monk, as many did in those days of mystical enlightenment. The time of the Crusades was also the age of the pilgrimages to Santiago de Compostela and Jerusalem. Saint Guillemin walked the long road to Compostela, through the Alps, then back down to the south of Italy. He walked mostly barefoot, as other monks did at that time. He wore the traditional white tunic with a red cross on the back and brought back with him the famous shell of Compostela, a Galician scallop shell, as proof that he completed his journey.

Saint Guillemin became a crucial part of the transition between the Byzantine Greek Orthodox Church, which ruled over the south of Italy at that time, and the Roman Catholic Church, which wanted to take over Southern Italy. The Catholic Church aimed to eliminate the Greek influence in Magna Grecia, which carried pre-Christian devotion mixed with elements of Arab culture. For many years the city of Naples and the surrounding region kept the ancient Hellenic culture of the Byzantine Empire from Constantinople.

At that time, Southern Italy was invaded and dominated by the Normans from northern Europe. Around the year 1000 CE, Pope John XIII claimed the victory of the Roman Catholic Church over the Greek Orthodox Church, thus replacing the Greek language previously used in the liturgy with Latin. The Catholic Church created an entirely new document, which stated that Constantine himself had given to the pope the city of Rome and the West. The Catholics clearly preferred Norman rule over Southern Italy to the old Greek and Arab culture. At that exact same time, Saint Guillemin succeeded in winning the support of Ruggeri, the Norman king, and with his help he founded one of the strongest congregations in the south of Italy, which endures to this day—the Sanctuary of Montevergine.

⚜

I will never forget my first visit to Mamma Schiavona and the incredible emotions I felt as I visited Her throne in the woods; I was overwhelmed by the strong sense of never wanting to leave. When I have returned over the years and brought people with me (including pilgrims from America), most people have felt the same way. When they are close to the Black Madonna, they don't want to leave Her side. It is as though time stops, and we regress inside a portal where everything is peaceful, embraced by Her love and compassion.

I later discovered that this phenomenon was the remnant of a memory from a time when people slept inside the sanctuary, as they did inside the temples of the goddesses. At night, they would receive Her vision and messages through dreams. Another way in which the Vatican tried to thwart the old traditional devotions was to forbid the pilgrims to sleep inside the church. Understandably, this created enormous conflicts. We are blessed, though, that we are still able to honor the Holy Mother with chanting, drumming, and dancing, a tradition that is at least three thousand years old.

As my friend Guido and I left the sanctuary that summer in 1987, I felt the eyes of Mamma Schiavona following me and a voice saying, "I will see you again, my daughter!" I promised Her that I would come back to see Her every year, learn Her songs, and bring them to New York. Divine inspiration overwhelmed me to open *The Voyage of the Black Madonna* with the processional chant to the Madonna of Montevergine.

## LYRICS AND MEANING OF
## THE CHANT OF THE
## MADONNA OF MONTEVERGINE

This haunting chant, like others from the Neapolitan tradition, uses the Lydian scale. I learned from Steve Gorn—an outstanding musician and master of the *bansuri,* an Indian flute—that this scale is identical to the Indian evening raga. (One of the inexplicable connections between Southern Italy and the Eastern Hemisphere is that Dionysus is also thought to be Shiva.)

I have sung the hypnotic melody of its powerful chant and prayer for Mamma Schiavona in moments of joy as well as sadness, fear, and desperation. I've always found a deep healing emanating from the ancient Lydian scale and from the lyrics, which invoke Her help, in a very familiar, colloquial way. I'm confident that you will too. You will find the melody, lyrics, and audio links in the appendix to chapter 4, page 359.

During my healing workshops, I have seen many people sob as they chant, even if they don't speak Italian or Neapolitan. I believe this reaction releases the profound feelings they hold for their mothers. Over and over during my tours, I have watched friends, students, and participants break down, cry, and fall to their knees, either at the feet of the Black Madonna or while singing the chant. It always moves me.

This is the chant I sang when my beloved mother, Elvira, passed away on February 24, 2007. I was in Rome at that time, and I am thankful for that. I had dreamed in 2002 that my mother would pass in February, the dates that came in my dream were February 14 and 24, but not the year. Mamma Elvira got sick on February 14 and was hospitalized. She passed on February 24.

Just a few minutes after she made the transition, I asked the Madonna, who had protected Mamma all of her life, to accompany her into heaven and hold her in Her arms. I sang this, along with another prayer, to Mother Mary at my mother's funeral, knowing that my voice could reach the heavens. Her soul was now free to fly into the arms of God and Mother Mary.

On many occasions I have felt that this chant must have originated in ancient Greece. Sometimes my voice goes into a space that opens a spiritual portal into another time. I envision myself in a procession, as a priestess initiated in the mysteries of Cybele, holding the frame drum and chanting into it, entering a temple at night.

Other people who have worked with me have had similar experiences. I've met several great musicians who enter into an altered state with this chant, including Steve Gorn and Siba, a famous Brazilian musician who has played with me on the rebec, a medieval folk violin. John La Barbera made a magnificent arrangement for flute, violin, strings, and *oud* (a pear-shaped stringed instrument) as part of the opera.

## ✡ How to Receive the Chant of the Madonna of Montevergine

I entreat you, the reader, to listen to this chant, read the lyrics, and feel it resonate within you. Contemplate the thousands of years that this melody has been passed down, always in devotion and with the hope of healing and receiving grace from the Madonna. You must delve deeply inside your heart and search for the grace you would like the Blessed Mother to grant you. Visualize that you are on the sacred mountain as you follow the chant. Montevergine emanates healing energy all around and to this day remains one of the most important mystical places in Europe.

I suggest that before you sing you light a candle, smudge with incense, breathe, and relax. If you are inspired, walk with purpose, especially in Nature, since this is a processional chant. Try to find a pine branch or cone or even violets, sacred to Cybele and Mamma Schiavona. Feel free to carry the lyrics with you if you find them difficult to memorize. What's important is that your heart is in the prayer, and at each line you let your voice come out stronger, as if reaching for the top of the mountain or paradise.

This is an excellent chant to sing with a chorus since one person can do the solo part and the others can do the response—and each person can take turns singing the lead. It is especially moving done as a procession in front of candles that are lit beneath a painting or image of the Black Madonna. So great is its strength that you will actually see Her come alive. In addition, you can kneel at Her feet and leave the candle there for Her. But when you leave, don't turn your back on Her. Instead, walk backward while staring at Her face and chanting. I perform this ceremony every year at my retreat Rhythm is the Cure in Tuscany before I lead the healing trance dances. It is extremely moving to observe each person's reaction and how his or her emotions emerge as we keep the chant going.

Alternately, you can build an altar using some of the images in this book or using a Black Madonna statue you might find in your travels to Italy, France, or even in the United States.*

Singing the chant in front of a homemade altar is especially powerful. You can also play this simple, beautiful melody on the flute and strings or have others accompany you on any of these instruments.

At the end of this ceremonial chant and procession, it is preferable to sit in silence, or to lie down and let Her image or vision come to you. Have no doubt that she, the Black Madonna, usually does come. She even appears in our dreams, always with a symbolic message. It is up to us to recognize it and apply it to our lives. Know that if you let Her, she will come to you.

---

*There are many Black Madonnas in America. In New York, the Madonna from Montevergine is found at Our Lady of Mount Carmel Church in the Bronx. The Madonna from Montserrat, Spain, is in Manhattan's Saint Ignatius of Loyola Church. In Miami, there is Our Lady of Regla. In many cities, including New York, you will find the Madonna of Guadalupe from Mexico, the Madonna of Czestochowa from Poland, and Nossa Senhora Aparecida from Brazil, just to name a few.

# CHAPTER 5

# Unveiling the Powerful Black Madonna of Freedom and the Egyptian Goddess Isis

*Grant me this grace, Madonna Brunettella,*
*Grant me this grace with your mercy,*
*as you granted me the miracle of your star!*
*When I saw your beautiful face, your beautiful black face,*
*I understood where true love lies, and I understood that*
  *you are Eternity.*
  "Canto della Madonna Brunetella" (Song to
  the Madonna known as the Little Dark One);
  lyrics by Alessandra Belloni, music by John La
  Barbera, dedicated to Dario Bollini

I WAS IMMENSELY FASCINATED BY the mountain region around Montevergine, that ancient, sacred mountain of Mamma Schiavona and the goddess Cybele. This beautiful province of Avellino and Benevento, now known as Irpinia, had been part of the focus of my research. Later in 1986, I decided to write my own version of the Sicilian tragedy *La*

*Lupa* by Giovanni Verga, with music by J. La Barbera. It's about a woman believed to be a witch because of her erotic powers over men.

I felt drawn to learn more about this fascinating culture and decided that to do in-depth research on the tradition of Southern Italian witchcraft, I had to spend time in this beautiful but spooky area. The whole area has a very mystical feel, with haunting medieval castles, wild Nature, forests, rivers, and huge trees. The famous Fiume Sabato, or Sabbath River, runs near Benevento, a town known for centuries for its witches' dance around the mythical walnut tree.

An aura of history permeates the ancient land of the Samnites, which was named Beneventum (a Latin word meaning "good wind") by the Romans who first colonized it. An inner province of Campania, bordering the regions of Molise and Puglia, it is a mountainous, rugged territory with an average elevation of nine hundred meters. There are also a number of large river basins—such as the Fortore and the Volturno—and the Valle del Calore, once occupied by a vast lake.

In the fifth century BCE the area was called Samnium and was part of Magna Grecia. The Samnites were seminomadic people who used guerrilla combat techniques. They managed to hold the Romans at bay until 290 BCE. The Samnites were always proud of their roots, and as Cicero remarked, they never wanted to speak Latin.

Driven by great curiosity, I went once more to visit my good friend Guido in Montesarchio, a town near Benevento. I asked Guido if he could help me look for the mythical walnut tree so I could deepen my research on witchcraft and find my inspiration for my interpretation of *La Lupa*.

You might recall that at age fourteen, I had the great blessing of being cast by the legendary Italian actress Anna Magnani to play her niece in *La Lupa*. So I felt a special affinity to the story, even though my father ultimately didn't let me accept the role. Losing the role and losing a young love at the same time inspired me to write my own version and portray the lead character as a tarantata, a woman bitten by love, trapped in a patriarchal society.

The great Sicilian writer Giovanni Verga's play is about a woman in her late forties, called Pina, who is accused of being a witch because she expresses her sexuality freely. No one can resist Pina, not even the local priest. They called her La Lupa, the She-Wolf, because she could not get enough—of anything. The townspeople also think Pina killed her husband with a magic spell.

One day Pina falls madly in love with a young man named Nanni who cannot resist her and is taken by a great passion for her. They become lovers, and the whole town knows it. Then Pina—La Lupa— offers Nanni her innocent and pure daughter in marriage, as long as they stay together in the same house. It is then that the sinful love triangle begins, to her daughter's great shame and pain. The sinful Pina is banned from the town. Her lover is forced to go through penance by the church authorities and is sent away, which causes Pina to go completely mad without her lover. Haunted and bewitched by La Lupa, Nanni decides to kill her as they make love one last time.

I remember watching *La Lupa* in the theater with my mother when I was a kid, before I had met Anna Magnani. I was bewitched by Magnani's powerful stage presence, especially during that last scene. She opened her blouse and offered her breasts to her lover (an actor who was also her lover in real life, a man much younger than she) so he could stab her and end her misery. To me, La Lupa was a martyr, not a witch.

When I decided to rewrite and perform *La Lupa* in New York, I had to do deep research on the magic of Southern Italy and the history of the tarantate, the women who suffered from tarantismo. To create my own story, I felt that I had to begin in Benevento's famous area of the witches, where they performed their magic rituals around the mythical walnut tree for centuries.

In my research, I discovered that Southern Italians attribute the beginning of witchcraft to Salome and Herodias, after the beheading of Saint John the Baptist. Legend says that both women craved the unattainable holy man and then demanded his death from King Herod. When John the Baptist's head was brought to them on a silver platter, it magically began to speak and cursed them, condemning them to roam in darkness forever.

Fig. 5.1. Tarantata scene from *La Lupa*—Alessandra Belloni and I Giullari di Piazza

During the rites of the summer solstice, which later became the Feast of Saint John the Baptist, the witches symbolically invoke the two sinful women—Salome and Herodias—as they dance wild erotic dances around the walnut tree of Benevento.

In my adaptation of the play, La Lupa and her daughter are reincarnations of Salome and Herodias. La Lupa was born on the night of the summer solstice, during one of those magic rituals around the walnut tree. In the last part of the play, I portray her as a tarantata, a woman suffering from the "bite of love," which ultimately makes her go completely mad, driving her to her own death.

Before I began the writing process, I wanted to understand who these witches of Benevento were. I wanted to discover if they were falsely accused and burned because the priests were afraid of women's power just like in the play *La Lupa*. I was also curious about the dances performed during these rituals. I found books with great drawings of the tarantella performed around the walnut tree. This depicted the tradition during the Middle Ages of men and women wearing masks and outrageous costumes, dancing, spinning, and playing tambourines.

I discovered that the area surrounding Benevento was an ancient sacred site of the goddess Isis, known also as the queen of the dead. This is why so many Black Madonnas are found in these powerful sites, often located in the middle of Nature. To fully understand the relationship of the cult of Isis to the Black Madonna, one must know her myth.

## THE CULT OF ISIS

During Roman times, the cult of Isis, the Egyptian goddess of the moon, proliferated in Benevento, so much so that the emperor Domitian had a temple erected in her honor. Within this cult, Isis was a sort of *trimurti,* a triad; she became identified with Hecate, goddess of the underworld, and Diana, goddess of the moon and the hunt. These deities were also connected with magic.

The cult of Isis probably stands on the basis of some elements of paganism that survived in succeeding centuries. For instance, the characteristics of some witches can be connected with those of Hecate. *Janara,* the same term used for witches in Benevento, arguably could be derived from the name of Diana, the black moon goddess with many breasts. To this day there is a statue of the goddess Isis hidden in Benevento Cathedral.

One of the most frightening experiences of my life happened during a powerful night of the full moon, in the middle of the forest surrounding Benevento. I had convinced Guido to take Dario and me to meet Guido's friend, a violinist virtuoso who claimed that he knew exactly where the mythical walnut tree was. Although I have blocked out his name (probably on purpose), I shall never forget his face, his eerie smile, and the magical, unexpected powers he had when he played the violin.

The violinist agreed to take us to this secret legendary place, which he knew because his grandmother had shown it to him. When we met him at his house, he told us to pick white roses and to wear them as protection against evil powers. I was a little scared, I will admit, yet I did not take him too seriously. Dario, who did not believe in much, thought that it was all a joke. The four of us—the violinist, Dario, Guido, and me—drove to a secret spot in the forest, in a valley surrounded by mountains, near the famed Sabbath River, from which the rites of the Sabbath derive.

The violinist told us to descend a hill after we stopped the car on a flat part of the road. With his violin in his hands, he said, "Follow me. I will take you to the secret meeting place. I know how to play and conjure the witches to dance around the tree and who will invoke the queen of the dead . . . Hecate. But only if they accept you will they appear. You must play the tambourine with me."

As we followed the violinist down the path through the giant trees in the forest, with no clue of where we were going, I could hear the river in the distance. When we stopped close to the Sabbath River, the violinist laughed as he began to play a haunting, piercing melody with ferocity. He blurted out that he could bring back the witches. Playing the fast tarantella triplets with him on the violin I kept praying that we would be protected.

In what seemed like a moment, everything shifted. The trees around us were not trees anymore but giant dark figures, moving silhouettes undulating in the darkness. At times they were illuminated by the light of the full moon. I could see women with long hair and flowing skirts. I could hear laughter and cries, cries of happiness not of sorrow. The whole forest had transformed as the mad violinist played in a fury and I accompanied him with my tambourine.

Dario stared at me in shock, pointing at my hands. He said, *"Alessandra, le tue mani sono diventate verdi!"* (Your hands have turned green!) In complete surprise, I stared at my playing hands. A strong, green light emanated from my fingers as I played the fast tarantella rhythm.

"Yes, my hands are green! *Aiuto!* Help!" I cried. I stopped playing and looked at the evil violinist, who was still laughing, looking menacing and otherworldly. I laid my tambourine down flat. Then, as I tried to ask him what the hell was going on, my tambourine suddenly flipped up by itself and started rolling toward the river. Again, I heard laughter and saw dark silhouettes, who seemed to be inviting us to go to the Sabbath River.

The violinist yelled, "They are waiting for you, Alessandra. They want you to go down to the river by the walnut tree, the witches and the queen of the dead. Aha, aha!" I jumped in terror, managed to get hold of my tambourine, and told Dario and Guido, "Let's get out of here now!" That's when I noticed that the white roses we had worn for protection from the spirits had vanished.

The violinist did not want to leave, however. He said, "You asked for this. Now you have to stay."

But I didn't. Without hesitation, I started running toward the car, chanting the chant to the Black Madonna of Montevergine at full volume, asking for Her protection. Dario was running ahead of me. I had never seen him run so fast! He turned to ask me to please stop tapping his shoulders. Since I was holding the drum, I was obviously not tapping his shoulders. Some invisible being was doing so! When he realized this, Dario turned white and ran even faster toward his car, which, when we arrived, began magically to move all by itself. The car was physically rolling away from us.

Working together, Dario, Guido, and I were able to slow the car and bring it to a stop. Thank God, it was a small Fiat and not very heavy. By this time, the violinist had stopped playing. He looked almost like his normal self again. Only, he did not say much. He was amused but also upset that we had interrupted the ritual he had successfully begun in our honor to invoke the power of the witches of Benevento.

I never saw him again.

## THE WITCHES OF BENEVENTO

It seems that the legend of the witches of Benevento dates back to the Samnite peoples and the Roman classical period. In the fourth century BCE, the ancient colonists of Magna Grecia, transplanted to the Samnium, practiced the orgiastic worship of Cybele (this is when Ovid sang of the horrendous Styx yearning for children's blood). By 1600, the saga had spread rapidly throughout Europe.

Unlike other towns, where the witches had an evil reputation, Benevento's mythology suggests that they have inspired poets and artists for centuries. Legend has it that belief in the existence of the witches mixed with echoes of the mysterious orgiastic rites of the Lombards who had settled in Benevento, the capital of their vast southern duchy. Benevento's chief physician, Pietro Piperno, tells this in his 1639 essay, *De Nuce Maga Beneventana* (On the Magical Walnut Tree of Benevento).

It is told that on the night between Saturday and Sunday, the witches had the custom to meet around a big walnut tree to give birth to their demonic Sabbath. They arrived at the meeting place by flying on the handles of their brooms and after having rubbed themselves with a miraculous unguent, which gave them not only the ability to fly but also to become invisible to indiscreet eyes. This is what they chanted: "Unguent, unguent, carry me to the walnut tree of Benevento, above the water and above the wind, and above all other bad weather."

Around the great walnut tree, a savage jumble would begin. People feared these women and believed that they had the ability to pass under doors during the night. According to the testimony of the presumed witches, the walnut tree must have been tall, an evergreen, and of a "noxious nature." There are various hypotheses about where on the riverbank of the Sabbath the walnut tree was located. The legend does not rule out that there could have been more than one tree.

The popular belief that Benevento was the Italian witches' gathering place has abundant implications, blurring the border between reality and imagination. Many hypotheses on the birth of the witches' legend exist. Likely, the synergy of several elements has given Benevento its lasting fame as the "City of the Witches."

In his essay, Pietro Piperno traced the roots of the witch legend back to the seventh century when Benevento was the capital of a Lombard duchy. The invaders, although they had formally converted to Catholicism, did not renounce their traditional pagan religion. Instead, they worshipped a golden viper (perhaps winged or with two heads). This may have had a connection to the cult of Isis as the goddess was able to control serpents. The Lombards developed a singular ritual of hanging the hide of a goat on a tree near the Sabbath River in honor of their god Wotan, father of the gods.

The Christians of Benevento intrepreted these frenzied rites based on their existing beliefs about witches: in their eyes the Lombard warriors were witches, the goat was the incarnation of the devil, and the cries suggested orgiastic rites. It's likely the gatherings under the walnut tree, one of the main features of the witch legend, probably derived from Lombard customs. However, these practices are also found in the cult of the moon goddess Artemis, who is similar to Isis.

The first centuries of the diffusion of Christianity were characterized by a harsh battle against the pagan, rural, and traditional *culti,* which resulted in the demonization of rituals like those of the women in Benevento. They became "witches" in popular culture. Instead of archetypal mother figures, these women were dedicated to orgiastic rites and knew how to induce infertility and abortions.

It became clear to me that the magic rituals in this area, along with the cults in honor of the Black Madonna, were part of the medieval religious history of Southern Italy. These rites embodied deep connections to pre-Christian mythology with expressions of Christianity. They were practiced in agricultural settlements by subcultures of the peasants. This pre-Christian history became part of the folk culture, expressed through the local music and social customs.

Although I was traumatized by the experience with the mad violinist in the forest, I also realized that I had underestimated the power of the so-called witches of Benevento, the walnut tree, and the Sabbath River. It was clear that this was not merely a myth; they truly existed. They had supernatural powers that came from centuries of highly trained priestesses initiated in the mysteries of the goddesses Isis, Cybele, and Diana. They used ecstatic music and dances, tambourines, and, later, the tarantella. They also utilized the energy that was still surrounding the forest and traditional gathering places. To summon their spirits, you only had to play the right music with certain vibrations, and they would magically appear.

This supernatural experience in the forest near Benevento helped me bring to the stage the dance of the witches around the walnut tree of Benevento in my play *La Lupa*. I also called upon those frightening memories to help me get into my role as a woman with magical powers who later became a tarantata.

I am convinced that many of these supposed witches were wrongly accused of their sins. At the same time, I saw clearly that over time, some of them began to perform their rituals in the darkness and not in the light, perhaps to protect themselves from their accusers.

Although I was fascinated by the witches of Benevento and the sacred walnut tree, I chose not to find out more, to keep a distance, and to stay in the light of Our Blessed Mother, the Black Madonna, who is true wisdom and manifests herself in these places of occult powers to remind us that we are indeed protected by Her love.

## BEING GUIDED TO THE BEAUTIFUL MADONNA BRUNETTELLA

There are times in our lives when things seem to happen all at once, creating a vortex of energy from which it is hard to escape, times when people who have crossed our paths and have made an impact on our heart and soul reappear for specific reasons, often when we are going through difficult experiences and transitions. This is exactly what happened to me between 1986 and 1987, on a physical, spiritual, and emotional level.

As I shared with you in my preface, at that time I had been diagnosed with cervical dysplasia. The surgery I had to have, cervical conization, affected me deeply on many levels. I felt powerless at the thought of my womb being cut, and I was very worried about the consequences it would have on me, emotionally and physically, especially since I was told that I would probably never be able to get pregnant or bear children. When I woke up in the hospital recovery room, I had a crystal-clear vision of the Black Madonna embracing me and protecting me. I don't recall how much time had passed in this blissful moment of spiritual awakening by the Black Madonna, but it was so real, and I felt so protected that I never wanted it to end. I did not know which Black Madonna had appeared to me at that time, but I always had a clear picture in my mind of Her face and gold crown. I wondered if I would ever find Her.

Two years after my miraculous vision in Mount Sinai Hospital, this powerful Black Madonna came to me again in an extraordinary way, in the magical area near Benevento, showing Her light and compassion. At the same time, I reconnected with Dario (my lost love!) and made up my mind to help him out of his drug addiction and change his life, both with my unconditional love and by bringing him to the Black Madonna.

After my transcendent experiences at the Cave of the Sybil and with the Black Madonna of Montevergine, I really wanted Dario to be my partner: to take photos, shoot videos, and drive with me to remote, deserted areas. Although Dario was intrigued, he was powerless. The conditions of his house arrest stipulated that he couldn't leave his home. After some research, I discovered that in Italy it was possible to get special permission from a judge to get a work release if you were under house arrest. On Dario's behalf, I wrote to the court stating that his work with me was crucial, citing his specialized education in classical studies and his writing skills. I prayed, and by some miracle, the prayers I had offered to the Madonna of Montevergine were effective. Once again, la Madonna granted me grace. Dario was given permission to travel with me as a research assistant. Our first journey together was a pilgrimage to Montevergine, the magical mountain of the Black Madonna, Mamma Schiavona, in Irpinia. In addition to doing research, I wanted to thank the Madonna in person.

Our visit to the sacred mountain was followed by the haunting, frightening experience near Benevento, with the mad violinist summoning the witches in the forest. To our surprise we had gone from being high on the sacred mountain, near heaven and blessed by the light of the benevolent Black Madonna, to the darkness of the valley below, in the midst of thick forests in the Samnio, by the spooky Sabbath River

Fig. 5.2. Our Lady of Freedom inside the church of Moiano;
photo by A. Belloni

and the walnut tree of the witches. Dario and I continued our search for the Seven Sisters in the province of Benevento, knowing that we would find more powerful Black Madonnas in that area.

One day, in our quest for another Black Madonna, Dario and I got lost in the mountains of that beautiful region. Up to this point, it had been something of a wild goose chase, but I hadn't lost hope. By chance, we ended up in a beautiful church in the town of Moiano, thinking that we were still lost. But instead, we were found—by the Madonna.

It was early afternoon, and no one else was there, just Dario, me, and the church's caretaker. The man welcomed us to the Church of Brunettella, which means "the Little Dark One." The caretaker seemed to read us like a book as he told us, "If you need a miracle, She will do it. Just pray and ask Her. She will free anyone who believes in Her. She is la Madonna della Libera [Our Lady of Freedom]!"

And there She was! The most beautiful statue I have ever seen. A majestic, life-size figure fashioned of ebony, totally black, with huge hazel eyes. Her captivating gaze was both austere and benevolent. As I looked at Her, the tone of Her gaze constantly changed. She wore a bright red dress and was wrapped in a thick blue cape covered with golden stars. On Her lap, a black baby Jesus faced out with His right arm raised and His left hand holding His Blessed Mother's hand. She sat on her throne regally, like the queen She is. On Her head was a red veil covered by a spectacular gold crown inlaid with precious jewels and topped with twelve shining stars. I meditated and prayed and suddenly recognized Her. This was the Black Madonna who had appeared to me at my hospital bed! I was overcome by emotion: speechless.

When Dario and I looked at Brunettella, we both felt an overwhelming love and compassion radiating from Her. We stood there in silence and prayed for a long time. At the exact same moment, he and I saw the center star on Her solid gold crown move and salute us as if silently telling us, "Come to me!"

Dario and I looked at each other and then exclaimed in unison, "*La stella si muove!*" (The star is moving!) Then we both began sobbing, understanding that this was indeed a miracle, unexplainable—it simply was. We felt something inside of us shift, making us comprehend that we were protected by Her. I heard a voice saying, "You must believe in me. Have faith. You will make it. Always come back to me." She ended each statement with the words *figlia mia,* which means "my daughter."

Dario, who had come from a very different world until then, one that was superficial and self-destructive, received a real miracle of awakening. We were both shaken when we left the church and thanked the caretaker for his illuminating words and advice. The sacristan told us to

Fig. 5.3. Dario and Alessandra on the mountain over the sea
traveling through Southern Italy

come back for Her feast day on September 8, adding with a smile, "*La Madonna vi aspetta.*" (The Madonna will wait for you.)

Dario's addictions stopped immediately, and he stayed sober for many years, touched by la Madonna della Libera, who freed him from his dark side. We had asked Her for transformation, and from Her, Dario received the light, Her blessing, and God's blessing. He became religious and spiritual and was very grateful to me for bringing him to the light.

After this miraculous experience at the Church of Brunettella, Dario and I felt a deeper love for each other and also felt more connected to the Earth. We both felt that this Madonna was extremely sensual, resembling Isis in Her enigmatic face. That same day we took a ride in the stunning mountains of the Benevento region, breathing its fresh, stimulating air. Dario and I lay down near the ruins of an ancient castle and made passionate love, right on the ground, as if going back thousands of years to perform the sacred marriage as an ancient rite of initiation to Mother Earth. In ancient times, this was known as *hieros gamos*.

This magical erotic experience would remain inside us forever and created a strong bond very hard to break. It seemed that we both went back into some ancient time. I felt that we had lived together in a past life. We had been a priest and a priestess initiated in the mysteries of the Goddess and had been magically brought back together by the Black Madonna to continue our karma, following a sacred path.

Later, I wrote a love song for Dario about our miracle of the star titled "Canto della Madonna di Brunettella," which became a beautiful part of the opera *The Voyage of the Black Madonna*. I wrote the lyrics, and John La Barbera wrote the music. It is the song I shared in the beginning of this chapter.

## THE PROCESSION OF
## LA MADONNA DELLA LIBERA

After receiving the miracle from la Madonna Brunettella, I knew that Dario and I must keep our promise to become part of the procession on Her feast day on September 8. I was told that in this particular procession, the older women had kept alive an ancient tradition of archaic chants to the Madonna that was unique to their town. Anthropologists and ethnomusicologists have noted that these haunting chants—with their unique harmonies, melodies, dissonance, and vocal production—are remarkably similar to the singing of the famous Bulgarian women's choirs. I could never imagine the power and impact these women and their voices would have on me.

When Dario and I arrived on the morning of September 8, the procession had already begun. From experience, I had learned that the fastest way to catch up with the Madonna and Her celebratory band and singers who moved through the entire town was to ask the local police.

"*Dov'è la Madonna?*" They all knew where She was because they had to block the roads as the procession passed. Dario and I ran in the

Fig. 5.4. Procession of Our Lady of Freedom

direction they indicated, he with the video camera and me with my tape recorder.

When we first laid eyes on the procession, Dario and I were startled by the huge crowd. The band played strange, out-of-tune melodies, which seemed otherworldly, and followed the Queen of Heaven. The statue of the Black Madonna was even more striking in daylight than it had been in the semidarkened church. La Brunettella was indeed the queen. Adorned with exquisite jewelry, Her shining blue cape studded with stars, She seemed like Egyptian royalty. Her dark skin glowed as though She were alive. Upon seeing Her, I burst into tears and couldn't figure out how to work my tape recorder or how to take photographs. It was strange how I was completely overcome.

The others in the procession realized that Dario and I weren't locals. They were curious about us, wondering where we were from and why we were there. As we trailed behind the statue, some came right out and asked. I told them that I had come from New York as a devotion to the Black Madonna and was studying Her tradition, adding that I was a musician and wanted to write an opera for Her. They told me that I must wait for the women singers, since they possessed the true knowledge of the songs in the old dialect.

From a distance, I heard a very odd melody and what seemed like many voices in a dissonant song. As the singers drew closer, I was completely bewitched, practically hypnotized by a group of fifteen older women, hugging one another other tightly and chanting loudly with their mouths wide open. They produced the most unusual, haunting, discordant harmonies in an ancient Neapolitan dialect that I could not understand. Yet, somewhere in the depth of my being, *I understood,* and it moved me to the core. The women saw me and understood that I was completely drawn to them. They permitted me to follow them closely, which was a great honor. I knew that they didn't let everyone do this.

Dario was also extremely moved, but thank God, he was able to film this remarkable occurrence. I was too awestruck to take photographs or record it. Thanks to Dario, I have this incredible research material on tape. The women's faces are spectacular, with their distinctive, Old World features and fervent expressions.

These women chanted for at least eight hours without getting tired. They took turns singing solo and answering in harmony. Although the chant was to the Madonna della Libera, the melody was totally archaic, using the Lydian scale found in most ancient Neapolitan music. The women walked barefoot as they sang. Their dark-brown faces, hands, and legs reminded me of the Earth herself. These were the peasant women of the ancient Greek matriarchal society who carried the wisdom and knowledge of the priestesses of the Goddess. I wondered if they knew this. Their leader was a woman named Rosetta, who to this

Fig. 5.5. Women chanting to Our Lady of Freedom during the procession

day at age eighty-six has the most powerful voice I have ever heard. She claims that her voice is the gift of the Madonna Brunettella, who has appeared in her dreams many times. In the dreams the Madonna revealed to her that She has blessed her with this beautiful voice so she can sing Her praise until the day she dies.

All I wanted was to walk beside them, to feel the healing energy coming from those incredibly powerful voices that never tired. I moved beside them, following the statue until the evening, when they entered the church. This is probably the most moving part of the feast, when the Madonna returns to the church, and everyone is screaming, "Evviva Maria!" while clapping, crying out, and sobbing uncontrollably.

It was then that I witnessed something very unusual, something I thought didn't occur anymore since it had been forbidden by the Vatican. As the statue was brought back to the altar, the women chanted and a group of devotees got down on their knees. Each man or woman had one person leading him or her with a handkerchief tied to the wrist, pulling the devotee along the floor with the head down. The devotees, crawling on their knees, proceeded to lick the ground where the statue had passed. I had never seen anything like it! I almost fainted as I realized what was happening. This was real! Incredibly real! The crowd began whispering. Someone told me that the people licking the ground had received miracles, and their vow was to do the *strascino* ("licking of the floor") as a sign of their commitment and to thank the Madonna for Her miracle.

The chanting of the women continued until everyone had performed the ritual of the strascino. Later, when Dario and I looked back at the video, we could see that the people seemed to be in a collective trance. When the chanting ended, we clearly watched them wake up and come out of it. For me, this will always remain the most moving experience I've had at the feet of the Black Madonna. Later, I re-created it on stage, together with the legend of la Madonna Brunettella.

After the procession, I was told of several miracles that had taken place during previous processions. Not too long ago a mother had brought her daughter, who was mute and had never spoken a word. During the women's chanting, at the feet of the statue, the girl began talking for the very first time and was healed by la Madonna della Libera, finally free to speak. Another recent miracle happened to a young teenage boy I met who had fallen under a tractor while working in the fields. Pinned under the tractor, he would certainly have died, but he had a vision of the Madonna della Libera and was miraculously saved, only losing part of his right arm.

After witnessing our first procession, Dario and I returned to Moiano every year for ten years. We became friends with everyone in the town, including the priest in charge of the church; the choir director; the local folk music group, Musicalia; and, of course, with the old women singers. Every year on September 8, they patiently waited for Dario and me to arrive at the procession. The women generously let me become part of their group, which was always a very moving experience. Dario, who was kind and giving by nature, always brought gifts for all the people we knew in the town. They appreciated this immensely as the presents came all the way from America. To this day people in

Fig. 5.6. Ritual of licking the floor inside the church in Moiano

Moiano still ask me about Dario, and it is very emotional for me to return there; I feel his spirit around me.

## HISTORY AND TRADITION OF THE BLACK MADONNA OF MOIANO

There is great mystery surrounding this beautiful and miraculous statue, Our Lady of Freedom. Over the years, I learned many interesting stories and legends from my friend, musician Amerigo Ciervo, a native of Moiano.

This Black Madonna in particular is a centuries-old enigma. The statue has always been at the Church of Brunettella, but no one knows for certain where She came from. She was originally in another church that was destroyed by a fire. We know from accounts dating back to 1641 and 1707 that many bishops visited the town, including Bishop Filippo Albini, who wrote: "There is in Moiano a statue of the Blessed Virgin Mother, and through Her, God works powerful miracles, as shown by the numerous golden offerings that are exhibited by Her image. She is known as Our Lady of Freedom, and Her statue is made of dark wood. The native people of the town worship Her with great devotion."

As I researched Santa Maria della Libera, I discovered that according to legend She arrived mysteriously on a Turkish ship. Starting in the ninth or tenth century, pilgrims began visiting Her shrine in Moiano and experienced numerous miracles and cures. It was often said that people had a distinct feeling of serenity after visiting Her shrine. Understandably, their extraordinary devotion to Her and Her miracles haven't waned over the centuries; they've only grown stronger.

The church of Moiano itself is very old and was destroyed during a terrible earthquake in 1514. The church and statue were restored in 1550. During this restoration, they found ninth- and tenth-century Byzantine coins buried around the statue. On the coins were inscriptions of Constantine the Seventh and Our Lady of the Sign, a Greek icon brought from the Orient. The Madonna of Moiano was restored to the likeness of Our Lady of the Sign.

According to the Catholic Church, the Turks invaded Italy in 1571 and would not allow the local people to practice Catholicism in the areas they occupied. In Moiano, victory over the Turks was attributed to the many individuals who prayed to Our Lady of Moiano. She was thereafter called Madonna della Libera (Our Lady of Freedom).

Moiano is located in a beautiful natural setting, near the well-known medieval town Sant'Agata dei Goti, a magical village first founded by the ancient Samnites and later taken over by the Romans, and then the Goths. The town has a haunting appearance as it ends abruptly at the edge of the river gorge.

The people who inhabited both these villages have been known to struggle to earn a living. Extreme poverty forced many to immigrate to

America, including the family of New York City mayor Bill de Blasio. Those who stayed lived off the land in an agricultural society, very close to the earth. It is a town without much history but rich with devotion to Our Lady of Freedom.

## THE TRADITION OF THE DEVOTION AND VIGIL ON SEPTEMBER 7

The celebration in honor of the Black Madonna Brunettella begins on August 15 with the Feast of the Assumption. On that day, a flag showing Her beautiful image hangs high between two balconies. From this moment, they begin the harvest of wheat and oil, blessed by the Black Virgin.

August 30 marks the beginning of the Novena, with devotional prayers, as the statue of the Madonna is then taken up to the main altar. The crowd of devotees gets bigger every day until the feast day, which is more celebrated than Christmas.

September 7 is the vigil of the feast, with powerful rituals typical of the south of Italy. In the afternoon, the devotees bring the statue of the Black Madonna down from the altar and begin to dress Her with two solid gold crowns (one is for Baby Jesus). The crowns were made in 1914 with gold that was taken from all the church offerings. Brunettella is then covered with a shining blue cape decorated with golden stars. She is also adorned with golden earrings, necklaces, and bracelets. A black velvet cloth is pinned at the feet of the statue, onto which many golden objects are sewn. In the chapel, there is an amazing exhibit of the "treasure," a gazebo covered with golden and silver ex-votos of people who have been healed, representing arms, legs, feet, hands, and hearts.

At the same time, the ritual dress of the women devotees is blessed by the priest. Until forty years ago, women actually wore a different type of ceremonial dress, which was white with a blue sash, just as it is done for the other dark Madonna known as la Madonna dell'Arco, near Naples. Outside the church, a carriage goes around receiving gifts of food, pasta, chickens, cakes, cookies, and flowers, which are auctioned off the next day at the feast.

## SEPTEMBER 8, THE FEAST DAY

The feast begins at five in the morning inside the church with great commotion as pilgrims begin coming from nearby villages. There is a morning service at eight o'clock, and as more pilgrims arrive, the crowd moves down the middle aisle of the church on their knees—crying, sobbing, and asking the Madonna for grace and a miracle.

The procession officially begins as the beautiful statue of Brunettella is carried out of the church on the shoulders of men, usually about a dozen. There is normally an auction outside the church among groups of men who challenge each other to carry the Madonna. During this auction, people bring offerings of money and gold to pin to the Madonna's decorations, which are pinned to the arch and throne made of wood that is built around Her statue and carried through the streets.

The procession goes all over town, even venturing inside tiny alleyways. In every neighboring village there is an explosion of fireworks in honor of the Blessed Mother. As the people in Moiano say, "*La Madonna deve vedere il fuoco.*" (The Madonna has to see the fire!) This is also an ancient ritual.

The procession is led by the town's band and the women singers with their amazing, haunting voices and melodies. It usually ends around eight o'clock at night, when Our Lady of Freedom is taken inside the church, carried backward toward the altar. A huge crowd of devotees follows the statue, chanting, crying, going down on their knees, and licking the floor as a sign of devotion in acknowledgment of having received Her grace. The women's haunting chant leads the entire ceremony and ritual. Inside the church, the singing becomes more desperate and yearning.

The lyrics sung in the old dialect express a feeling of sadness and anguish, which comes from saying good-bye to the Black Madonna, expressing the great pain of leaving Her side. Gradually, the church empties. The women who have been chanting and following the procession barefoot are now tired, dirty, sweaty, and hungry. They return home for the ritual dinner.

Outside, many lights remain burning, keeping the feeling of the feast alive. The band begins to play traditional tunes. The feast truly ends when the last mother comes out of the church with her little boy or girl and gives a last kiss to the statue of the beautiful Madonna Nera della Libera.

This ritual and cult of the Black Virgin can be connected with other more ancient ceremonies of pre-Christian origins, typical of the end of summer and dedicated to a goddess of the underworld. The journey into the other world begins in the month of September with the feasts of many Black Madonnas. They seem to express the pain and mourning of the Divine Feminine over the death of Mother Nature, who is preparing for winter.

In many folk legends and traditions, the villagers reenact the mythical death of Mother Nature as plants begin to shed their fruit and abundance and plant their seeds in the ground, in the Earth's womb. The ancient ritual connected to the feast in Moiano is the rite of Persephone, the Tesmoforie Attiche (festivals from Attica), a fall ritual celebrated only by women between September and October. The ritual reenacts the descent of Persephone into the underworld, with death rites and great celebrations honoring her return to the Earth. Persephone was depicted with a black face. This is one of the symbols of the Black Madonna of Moiano, also known as the queen of the dead.

The early agricultural civilization of Southern Italy was mainly a matriarchal society that worshipped the goddesses Demeter, Cybele, and Isis. In the beginning of Christianity, it is clear that the Madonna replaced these female deities, becoming the Divine Feminine.

## TRADITIONAL RITUALS FOR
## THE BLACK MADONNA OF MOIANO*

**The tradition of the chickens:** During the feast, many chickens are gathered as a strong symbol of the Black Madonna. As in other places, like Pagani, for the Feast of the Madonna delle Galline and different cultures in general, chickens and other birds are associated with the

---

*Also known as death rites = *riti dei morti.*

goddesses of the underworld and have the shamanic power to lead us into the underworld and meet our shadows.

**Gold:** Gold also connects us to a kingdom that is far away, a heaven that is golden and shiny. It is also connected to fire. Gold is an element traditionally used for burial ceremonies and in cemeteries. It is common in Moiano to bury a person with an image of the Black Madonna. This tradition likely comes from the ancient Egyptians, since the cult of Isis and Osiris had a strong presence in this area.

**The palms:** These are wooden objects shaped like palm leaves and covered with black velvet. On the day of the feast, all the gold and silver offerings are placed on them, and they are carried in procession by women dressed in black and blue.

**The prayers:** The *litanie*, or prayers, are chanted during the feast day on September 8, usually by priests, for monetary compensation. The same ritual is used during the Feast of the Dead near the tombs.

**The chart (chariot):** During the vigil, a chart carried by bulls is taken to a cave to pick up specific stones, which symbolize the mysterious journey into the cave, inside the Great Mother's womb.

**The ritual dress:** Not too long ago, the dress was white with a blue sash for women. Men used to wear these colors when they were chosen to carry the statue in the procession. The color white is also associated with death. In folk mythology, dead people come back to Earth to see us during the Feast of the Dead wearing a white tunic.

## THE MEANING AND SYMBOLISM OF THE STRASCINO RITUAL

The licking of the floor in the church of our Lady of Freedom is without a doubt the most powerful and emotional part of the ritual. It has obvious ancient origins and is similar to other forms of devotion and magic rituals in Southern Italy. This archaic form of devotion in Moiano has a strong symbolism of death, a connection to the underworld as well as Dante's *Inferno*. It symbolizes the descent into the subterranean grotto, the mysterious and hypothetical journey of Persephone going into the underworld, symbolically representing death as with the coming of winter the Earth seems to die. When Persephone comes back from Hades she brings rebirth to all life on Earth. To lick the floor of the church means to enter the sacred space, to be part of the mysterious initiation to the divinity, to ask for Her protection, and to ensure a direct connection with Her without mediation.

The strascino also represents a magical exorcism from death, and it is often done by peasants and agricultural societies. Flagellation and sacrifice, such as shedding your own blood, represent accepting death, the assumption of death, but a controlled and limited death. In the context of the magic ritual, it is known to bring back life. It is also believed that after the shedding of one's blood, we can celebrate a new, protected rebirth and life.

As described by Carlo Levi in his book *Christ Stopped at Eboli,* the Madonna with a black face, associated with wheat and animals, was no longer the Mother of God but rather a divinity from the underworld. She was the peasant Persephone, Isis, queen of the dead, in the shadows of the womb of the Earth, the infernal goddess of wheat.

## THE CULT OF
## ISIS IRPINIA AND BENEVENTO

As I learned more about the history of Benevento and its surrounding areas, it became clear that the connection between Brunettella and Isis wasn't merely a myth. In my research I discovered that near Moiano, in Sant'Agata dei Goti and Benevento, there existed temples of Isis. The esoteric folk tradition in the region was directly connected to the cult of Isis, the most important and complex of all the black goddesses, the African Egyptian mother. As a matter of fact, even renowned author and historian Ean Begg stated that the Black Virgins, either called Diana or Cybele, are all one: Isis.

Born in Africa in 125 CE, the great Roman writer Lucius Apuleius mentioned Isis in his classic book *The Golden Ass*. In it he refers to Isis as the Universal Goddess, incorporating the attributes of all the other goddesses: "I am Nature, the universal Mother, mistress of all the elements, primordial child of time, sovereign of all things spiritual, queen of the dead, queen also of the immortals, the single manifestation of all gods and goddesses that are."

In art, Isis is usually depicted as a black African queen goddess, spreading her wings of love. Often, she is shown nursing the infant Horus on her lap—and herein lies the origin of the iconography of the Madonna and Child. Even the scepter used by Isis is similar to that of the Black Virgins, as well as the colors of the capes and dresses many of the Madonnas wear. Isis's priests often offer her a ship, which is also a symbol of Aphrodite—all of which recall legends like that of Brunettella, of her mysterious arrival on a ship like many other Black Madonnas.

The high priests of Isis also eat the roses that are attached to their *sistrum* (an ancient Egyptian percussion instrument consisting of a metal frame with transverse metal rods used in the initiation rituals). Isis is associated with the rose blossom as a sacred feminine symbol, just as Mary the Blessed Mother is. We see traces of this today in the chants people still do for the Madonna during the tammorriata rituals, which proclaim, *"Bella figliola ca te chiamme Rosa,"* which translates roughly to "Oh beautiful Woman, your name is Rose, the most beautiful flower found in Paradise" (this "rose" symbolically refers to the woman's vulva).

## THE MYTH OF ISIS

One of the many myths of Isis, and perhaps the most famous, is the story of her great love for Osiris. Isis cares for her dead husband, Osiris, and brings him back to life with her love. (She also tends the dead.) The power and patience of love is the gift Isis brings from thousands of years ago. Inscribed in stunning hieroglyphs, the great Hymn to Isis is found in the pyramid texts, which date back to 2491 BCE. Later the myth was recorded by Plutarch, the Greek historian and philosopher.

The goddess Isis was the first daughter of Geb, god of the Earth, and Nut, the goddess of the overarching sky. Isis was born on the first day between the first years of creation and was adored by her human followers.

Isis was the goddess of the Earth in ancient Egypt and loved her brother Osiris.

When they married, Osiris became the first king of the Earth. Their brother Set, immensely jealous of their powers, murdered Osiris so he could usurp the throne.

Set did this by tricking Osiris into stepping into a beautiful box made of cedar, ebony, and ivory that he had ordered built to fit only Osiris. Set then sealed it up to become a coffin and threw it into the river. The river carried the box out to sea. It washed up in another country, resting in the upper boughs of a tamarisk tree when the waters receded. As time passed, the branches covered the box, encapsulating the god in his coffin in the trunk of the tree.

In a state of inconsolable grief, Isis tore her robes to shreds and cut off her beautiful black hair. When she finally regained her emotional balance, Isis set out to search for the body of her beloved Osiris so that she might bury him properly. The search took Isis to Phoenicia, where she met Queen Astarte. Astarte didn't recognize the goddess and hired her as a nursemaid to the infant prince.

Fond of the young boy, Isis decided to bestow immortality on him. As she was holding the royal infant over the fire as part of the ritual, the queen entered the room. Seeing her son smoldering in the middle of the fire, Astarte instinctively (but naively) grabbed the child out of the flames, undoing Isis's magic, which would have made her son a god.

When the queen demanded an explanation, Isis revealed her identity and told Astarte of her quest to recover her husband's body. As she listened to the story, Astarte realized that the body was hidden in the fragrant tree in the center of the palace, and she told Isis where to find it.

Sheltering his broken body in her arms, Isis carried the body of Osiris back to Egypt for proper burial. There she hid it in the swamps on the delta of the Nile River.

Unfortunately, Set came across the box one night when he was out hunting. Infuriated by this turn of events and determined not to be outdone, he murdered Osiris once again, this time hacking his body into fourteen pieces and throwing them in different directions, knowing that they would be eaten by the crocodiles.

Isis searched and searched, accompanied by seven scorpions who assisted and protected her. Each time she found new pieces she rejoined them to reform his body. But Isis could only recover thirteen of the pieces. The fourteenth, his penis, had been swallowed by a crab, so she fashioned one from gold and wax. Inventing the rites of embalming and speaking some words of magic, Isis brought her husband back to life.

Magically, Isis then conceived a child with Osiris and gave birth to Horus, who later became the sun god. Assured that having the infant would now relieve Isis's grief, Osiris was free to descend to become the king of the underworld, ruling over the dead and the sleeping. Osiris's spirit, however, frequently returned to be with Isis and the young Horus, who both remained under his watchful and loving eye.

Isis was worshipped throughout the Greco-Roman world. During the fourth century, when Christianity was gaining a foothold in the Roman Empire, her worshippers founded the first Madonna cults so as to keep her influence alive. Some early Christians even called themselves *pastophori,* meaning the shepherds or servants of Isis, which may be where the word *pastor* originated. Author Ean Begg found in his research that the city of Paris was indeed built as a center for Isis, explaining that it is the original meaning of its name, Par-Is. Paris is also another place with great devotion to the Black Madonna. The original name was "Lutetia of the Parisii." It was named after a tribe of Celts known as the Parisii during the Roman era of the first to the fourth century. The Pariasians were the followers of Isis, who was known as the chief goddess of the Greco-Egyptian empire.

## ISIS APPEARING TO LUCIUS APULEIUS AT HIS FINAL INITIATION

The following passage from *The Golden Ass,* which recounts Isis appearing to Lucius Apuleius, was put to haunting music by composer John La Barbera for our opera *The Voyage of the Black Madonna,* which I sang with great passion in the Italian translation.

Behold, I am in your presence, having been stirred by your prayers, O Lucius, I, the parent of the things of Nature, mistress of the elements, firstborn of the ages, highest divinity, queen of the dead, first among the Gods, single appearance of gods and goddesses; I who dispense by my commands the bright summit of the sky, the healing winds of the sea, the mournful silences of the world below. I whose single divinity as whole of the world is venerated in the form of many shapes, various rites, and under many a name. Thence, first-born Phrygians call me Pessununtia, Mother of God, from there, the autochtones of Attica call me Cecropeian Minerva, the floating Cyprians call me Paphian Venus, arrow-carrying Cretans call me Diana Dictynna, the trilingual Sicilians call me Stygian Proserpina, the Eleusians call me the ancient goddess Ceres, some call me Juno, others Bellona, those men of yours call me Hecate, and those men there call me Rhamnusia. And the Ethiopians, who are illuminated by the nascent rays of the dawning sun god, and the Africans and the Egyptians, being strong in ancient doctrines, and honoring me with the proper rites, call me by my true name, Queen Isis.

Another interesting quote from Egyptologist Armando Mei discusses the relationship between Isis and the theological and cosmological traditions of Southern Italy.

In archaeological terms, it is now clear that after the fall of Egypt, all theological traditions and rituals were preserved by Isis's priests, who went on to found the so-called Theological School of Alexandria of Egypt (or Didaskaleion) during the second century BC. Its followers crossed over the Mediterranean Sea, heading for Italy and its islands, such as Sicily. During the Greeks' domination in Southern Italy, also known as Magna Grecia, the school had a strong influence on customs and traditions and progressively changed all religious beliefs. For the first time in ages, the populations of Southern Italy began to worship a new Goddess, coming from the mysterious land of Egypt, known as the black land, or El Khemé, from which the term Alchimy comes. The Black Goddess, the alchemist deity, She who turns visible into invisible, the whore and the saint, the bride and the virgin, slowly became the most worshipped deity in Southern Italy, influencing also the Roman's theological traditions.

Archaeologists unearthed many artifacts and found several of Isis's temples, particularly in the Region of Campania, in the ancient towns of Pompeii, Herculaneum, and Oplontis (actually known as Torre Annunziata, where the emperor Nero's wife's impressive villa was found). Archaeologists found in Beneventum Isis's greatest temple in Southern Italy, which testifies to the vital importance of the Goddess in the popular religion of that time. In Pompeii and Herculaneum ruins, many frescoes are witness of the Egyptian Goddess influence in daily life. Many scenes of mysterious rituals show the devotion of the Southern Italian population for the black goddess.

How did the rituals work? What were the purposes?

Observing the Egyptians paintings and bas-reliefs, we can assume that the core of Isis's function was to convey energy to enable the pharaoh's soul to be reborn, using particular tools such as the Uadji, the stick of power generally used by goddesses and characterized by a lotus flower at the top. That flower symbolized the lifeblood, the cosmic energy for rebirth. Temple of Dendera bas-reliefs clearly reveal the goal, showing Isis—appearing as the Hathor goddess—giving life to a dead pharaoh.

Relationship between Isis and Energy was preserved during the Roman period, and the tradition has spread even to the 1800s. Therefore, since ancient times, the black goddess changed relationship between Man and Nature, to the eyes of mankind introducing a unitary model based on Cosmological Energies implemented through specific rituals. That is why the Isis Hymn of Nag Hammadi is essential to understand the core of the new cosmological theology coming from Egypt; it is crucial to take a careful approach to deeply understand the meaning of its duality and the Goddess's evolution as Madonna Nera of Christianity.

I'm confident that the love story between Dario and me is deeply connected to the Black Madonna and in a way, also, to Isis. Dario and I resonated with the myth of Isis and Osiris in a big way, and we studied it avidly in various texts. We felt that there was a strong affinity between Isis's myth and our unusual love story. In some ways, I felt like Isis—so in love and full of compassion for her lover, using her magical powers and flying to bring Osiris (who had been symbolically killed and dismembered) back to life.

Yes, I felt like Isis because I "flew" back and forth to Italy many times for several years to be in the arms of my beloved Dario/Osiris, each time restoring back to life a piece of his lost soul. Dario's beautiful soul—and heart—had been shattered when he was a child by abuse from his father and by an overprotective, controlling mother. To self-medicate, Dario became part of the superficial aspect of his generation's "sex, drugs, and rock 'n' roll" credo. His shadow and his dark side grew stronger with his drug use, and his self-esteem diminished. I became Dario's goddess, his Isis, restoring him into a whole person, celebrating his full resurrection. This was especially true after the miracle of the moving star on the crown of the Madonna della

Libera. I learned about magic during that time and, like Isis, would have done anything to keep my soul mate and me together.

Dario and I were married right after performing *The Voyage of the Black Madonna* at the Cathedral of Saint John the Divine. We were happy for many years, and in my dreams, I still see Dario smiling and thanking me for the love I gave him.

The women who serve the Goddess and the Black Madonna as healers always want to nourish and transform the weaknesses and wounds of the men they love, just like Isis restored the dead Osiris. I spent years working on this aspect of my devotion. At times I felt that I had to protect myself both emotionally and physically to be able to continue my work. My experience healing Dario from drug addiction through the Black Madonna also taught me that I can be the vehicle of the miracle, but I cannot accomplish that transformation unless the person (the man) is willing to shed the dark side and walk into the light.

I often see Brunettella or hear her speak to me. When I take other people to see her on the pilgrimages I lead to Moiano, they have had similar experiences. They break down in tears as we chant together to la Madonna della Libera, who has the power to free us all from our sadness, troubles, addictions, and disease. All you must do is believe.

## CHANTS AND PRAYERS TO MADONNA BRUNETTELLA, MADONNA DELLA LIBERA, AND ISIS

I learned these chants, which you will find in the appendix to chapter 5 on page 360, from the wise old women in the procession following the statue of Our Lady of Freedom. The women had an immense power when they were chanting, and I felt as if their voices came from the womb of the Earth herself.

Their faces reminded me of the matriarchal society of ancient Magna Grecia. Most of these women lived hard lives, working in the fields and giving birth to many children. They were skilled midwives and knew how to cure the sick, using special herbs. The women learned this healing through an oral tradition. The area of Moiano from which this chant comes is also known for the female healers who can take away *il malocchio,* the evil eye. (I learned how to do this too and share it in chapter 6, when I describe my journey in Calabria.)

Most of these folk healers were originally known as *guaritrici.* These were not the female healers who later, in the Middle Ages and during the Renaissance, became known as *streghe,* or "witches," "who were persecuted by the Catholic Church during the Inquisition. However, at that time, the church also tried to repress the practices of these herbal healers.

This past summer, for the first time in fifteen years, I was blessed to hear the voice of the lead singer from Moiano, Rosetta, whom I mentioned before. She saw me singing in the chapel together with the group of women whom I had brought with me during my pilgrimage to the sacred sites of the Black Madonna. Even if we had not seen each other in a very long time, we recognized each other immediately from the years when I followed Brunettella's procession with her. Showing great affection, she hugged me and all the women in my group and took us to the feet of the statue of Our Lady of Freedom and began to sing for us, asking me to harmonize with her.

I was honored and did my best to follow her powerful voice, even though I was crying and was overcome with emotions. I was amazed to see that her voice is just as strong as before and understood that it is indeed a miracle of the Black Madonna who wants Rosetta at age eighty-six to sing for Her and teach others until her last day on this Earth.

You can use these prayers to heal others, also invoking the healing power of the goddess Isis, the mother and queen of all healers. If you have loved ones who suffer from addiction, direct this chant at them. You can chant alone or with a chorus but remember to really open the vowels when you say, "Evviva Maria" and "Madonna della Libera." There is no need to use instruments, as these chants are traditionally done a cappella.

You can also make an altar with the image of Our Lady of Freedom. Near Her, remember to keep a flower or candle or photos of the people who are in need of help. I suggest carrying a small picture of Her with you when you are traveling as protection.

I invite you to use these prayers to invoke the healing power of the Earth and of Mother Mary in times of sadness, despair, disease, and loneliness, as well as in gratitude for all graces received.

CHAPTER 6

# The Devotion to the Black Madonna of the Poor

*We hurry toward death, let us desist from sin.*
*I have resolved to write about the contempt of the world,*
*that the now living will not bide their time in vain things.*
*Now is the hour to rise from the evil sleep of death.*
*Life is short, and shortly it will end;*
*Death arrives faster than anyone fears.*
*Death annihilates all and has mercy with no one.*

FROM *LLIBRE VERMELL:*
*AD MORTEM FESTINĀMUS PECCARE DESISTAMUS*

## THE MIDDLE AGES AND MUSICAL EXORCISMS

I strongly believe that today we are living in a time similar to the Middle Ages, and for the past few years I have felt the urge to convey this message on stage by performing the musical I wrote in 2006 titled *Tarantella: Spider Dance*. It includes a scene dedicated to the Black Madonna from Calabria, la Madonna dei Poveri (Our Lady of the Poor), and Her trance-drumming rituals dating back to medieval times of the Plague, rituals still practiced today on Her feast day.

In the Middle Ages, people in Europe and especially in parts of Italy believed that the end of the world was coming, and they lived with a great fear of death by war, natural disaster, or contagious disease. They believed that the Black Madonna protected them. I am fascinated by the fact that it was during the so-called Dark Ages that all the Black Virgins came to life with strong devotions in Italy, France, Spain, Turkey, and Greece. It is important to note that during the Byzantine Empire and at the time of the Crusades, our Christian traditions mixed with those of the Moors through music and dance.

When the Plague spread all over Europe, decimating the population, people carried statues of the Black Madonna in powerful processions. They drummed and danced in circles and in a trance state and paraded through the streets to expel the fear of death and to stop the Plague from coming to their villages. Through musical exorcisms, which used the obsessive 6/8 of the tarantella rhythms, identical to African drumming rituals, entire villages celebrated the miracles of the Black Madonna—protecting their towns from the Plague as well as from earthquakes and foreign invasions.

This tradition is alive today, especially in the region of Calabria, and I firmly believe from my own experiences that the Black Madonna is alive today with the same power to protect us from the ongoing wars, disease, and political crises we experience.

## TROPEA, AUGUST 14, 2016:
## THE FEAST OF LA MADONNA DEI POVERI

It was a beautiful summer night in Calabria, warm with a seductive breeze. I was listening to the relaxing sound of the waves of the Mediterranean Sea as I sat on a terrace at the Hotel Terrazzo sul Mare in my beloved Tropea. This is a very intimate and charming small hotel built right on a cliff overlooking the beautiful turquoise sea, with ancient rock formations all around. Owned by a strong, attractive Calabrese woman, Maria, darkskinned with piercing, wide black eyes, is one of the best chefs I have ever met, and she runs the whole place—

Fig. 6.1. Madonna dei Poveri being carried during a procession;
photo by A. Belloni

and the kitchen—like a matriarch. Her husband obeys her and follows her like a student following a guru. Every year she gives me my favorite room, which opens onto a white-and-blue terrace, where I can watch the breathtaking sunsets (see plate 4), say my prayers, and meditate as I stare at the island of Stromboli with its active volcano.

I have done many rituals on these beaches at sunset facing the volcano and will never forget that once, together with John and Dario, as I was chanting and drumming to Xango, the African Yoruba god of fire and thunder—lightning, thunder, and heavy rain arrived—and we had to run for our lives! Another time, to my great surprise, the volcano started smoking and shaking.

Stromboli is one of the seven Aeolian Islands of Sicily, known also as the Seven Sisters. The volcano has been erupting for as long as records exist—some two thousand years. The Romans called it the Lighthouse of the Mediterranean. Locals refer to the volcano as *iddu,* a dialect word meaning simply "him." The volcano gives its name to a category of eruption: strombolian. Tourists flock to watch from a safe distance as lava and gas are ejected from craters just below the summit at intervals of roughly twenty minutes. In the daytime this is visible as a plume of gas that looks like smoke. At night, you can see fiery red fountains shooting upward. Stromboli has been inhabited for thousands of years. It has great similarities with the Big Island in Hawaii, which also has an active volcano, where they worship the black goddess Pele, another aspect of the Black Madonna.

Tropea is my favorite little town, and I am even more attached to it than to my native Rome. I have been coming here since 1980, when I was young and curious to learn everything about this ancient folk music and dance tradition, secretly being guided to the Black Madonnas in this town. Only now, thirty-seven years later, do I realize that she called me here. Here, in this beautiful white medieval town carved in tufo stone, I have learned powerful rituals, rhythms, and dances, received the wisdom of the elders, and honestly had some of the best parties of my life, which often ended with sensual and romantic love.

I was in Calabria to celebrate on August 14, the Feast of the Madonna of the Poor, the Black Madonna of Seminara. I have been devoted to this Madonna since the first time I visited Her in 1987, and I was especially looking forward to the festivities that honor Her ascension into heaven. That first ritual of the Feast of la Madonna dei Poveri was a real initiation! Trying to convince someone to go with me was quite difficult as this town is known not only for the Black Madonna but also for its strong Mafia. So I had come back to Calabria alone to continue my research. I knew from Professor Satriani and various anthropology books I had read that on this day the feast of the Black

Madonna was celebrated with giant puppets reenacting an ancient fertility rite and wild drumming—a ritual that affirmed our connection with Africa, so close to Calabria, at the end of the Italian boot.

Only a few months before I had had the amazing experience awakening from anesthesia with the vision of the Black Madonna over my bed, followed by the mystical experience of flying over the Pacific Ocean near the California coast and hearing the voice of Mother Earth. My perception and sensitivity were completely transformed. I felt clear and ready, a portal had now been opened, and so I had decided to write an opera dedicated to the Black Madonna and Her healing power. Acting on that decision, I hopped into Dario's Fiat and drove all the way down to Calabria from Rome, 740 kilometers, which was quite dangerous at that time as the highway, the Salerno-Reggio, had the highest death tolls due to accidents in all of Europe. Ultimately, the road was never completed because of the power of the local Mafia, which controlled even the highway, with no intervention by the Italian government.

After a ten-hour drive alone, literally risking my life and praying to arrive in one piece, I made it to Calabria. With me were images of the Black Madonna. I made little altars in the Fiat! My poor mother was terrified and had asked Dario not to give me his car, but he knew that this trip was very important, so I promised to call both my mother and him as often as possible from the only working phones on the broken-down highway.

When I finally got to Vibo Marina near Tropea, I went to visit my good friends at the infamous campground Kursaal (described in earlier chapters), where all the folk musicians would come to hang out and play for fun and sometimes for money, food, or wine and where every year I learned incredible amounts of material—folk legends, folk songs and chants, intricate rhythms, tamburello styles, and the fast tarantella Calabrese. We always stayed up until sunrise and slept little. Because the cabins were full of mosquitoes and the bunk beds were so uncomfortable, we often slept on the white sand beaches. Those were some of most beautiful times of my life, which I cherish deeply and which inspired me to grow as an artist.

I was extremely happy to see my good Calabrese friend Vittorio de Paola, the master folk musician who became my "life guru" through the years and whom I consider one of my teachers to this day, together with Raffaele Inserra, the tammorriata master from Gragnano. We all met in that memorable summer of 1980, and they became my real tribe. Vittorio and I shared many adventures as well as field research on the folk traditions and various processions for saints, like San Rocco and the Madonnas, always accompanied by ritual drumming and dances.

I begged him and his family to go with me to see and take part in the Feast of la Madonna dei Poveri in the town of Seminara, province of Reggio Calabria.

I was surprised to see that my Calabrese friends laughed at me, telling me that I was *pazza* (crazy). Recently there had been a heavy *faida,* a dangerous fight between local Mafia families, and many people had died.

No one really wanted to go there, not even for the feast. Because I was not born in Calabria, I could not really comprehend what my friends meant in their attempts to warn me. All I knew was that I felt guided by the Madonna to go see Her on such an important day and celebration in her honor. I kept telling everyone that on Her feast day She would protect us. The only one who had the courage to go with me was a young man from Rome named Lucio, a student of anthropology and a folk musician. He was very dark, quite handsome, and looked Calabrese, which was a good thing. We knew no outsiders would dare go to this town due to the latest news, and we had to find a way to blend in with the locals.

Lucio drove the Fiat for me and warned me to change clothes and look less conspicuous, to avoid attracting attention as a foreigner, especially after such a series of shootings. I followed his advice and hid my camera in my bag, but I openly carried my tambourine, which became my passport everywhere I went. When the locals saw that I could play their tarantella Calabrese, all suspicion vanished.

We drove down the road, wrongly called a highway, toward Reggio Calabria. It had only two lanes and it was pitch dark at night with no roadway illumination. As we approached the exit for Seminara, I was astonished to see giant olive trees around us. They seemed to be thousands of years old.

I thought that here is the Earth at her best, so rich in her gifts to us! The word *seminara* comes from *semen* (Latin for "seed"). *Seminare* in Italian means "to plant seeds in the earth." From the trees and the name of the town it was very clear to me how this Black Madonna must be connected to the Earth.

We had to park far from town since the whole town was closed for the procession. As we walked on the narrow cobblestone streets, people looked at us a little cautiously, but when I asked about the feast, la Madonna Nera, and showed them my tamburello, they all laughed and said, "*Benvenuta figghia! A Madonna t'accumpagna.*" (Welcome, daughter! The Madonna accompanies you.)

I was intrigued by the many ceramic stores displaying beautiful folk art, which included statues of la Madonna dei Poveri, as well as devil masks, gargoyles, goddesses such as Demeter and Persephone, and naturally our favorite god—Bacchus. I knew that I had to get one of the Madonna statues but also knew that I had to see Her, the real one, first.

As we were getting closer to the church, the street decorations and local crafts sold by vendors were extremely attractive and festive, as was the local food being cooked in the street. The air was filled with strong smells of goat meat, sausages, and sweet almond pastries. There were also tambourine makers selling beautiful handcrafted goat-skin tambourines. I tried them, playing their fast rhythms, making quite an impression as a woman and not a local. I decided that at the end of the feast I had to get one of those special tambourines blessed by the Madonna Nera.

Then suddenly, I heard drumming, very powerful loud drumming. Snare drums. As the sound got closer, I started running up the hill and shouting to Lucio, "Let's find the drummers!"

So taken by the music, we both felt that we were in Africa and not in Italy any longer. At the top of the hill we found a group of about twenty snare drummers, along with a bass drummer and a cymbalist,

Fig. 6.2. Leader of the drummers processing, followed by giant dancing puppets, Seminara Calabria; photo by A. Belloni

marching and playing at an obsessive loud and fast 6/8 rhythm. It was a tarantella beat but felt African and tribal. The leader of the team was a tiny man with a thick mustache who was playing super-fast with his drumsticks, making intricate patterns. He had a beautiful, proud face as he directed the group of drummers.

It was there that I also saw the most beautiful giant puppets, called I Giganti, dancing toward us in a sensuous tarantella, processing behind the drummers, who stopped to make a circle so that the puppeteers could take center stage. One of the puppets was a stunning black African king, the mythological Grifone. Dressed in green, red, and gold, he wore a crown and was courting in a dance the beautiful white Italian queen, the mythical Mata, smiling in a gold cape and a red and blue dress (see plate 12). In this dancing courtship, Mata and Grifone fall in love, and their union represents the coming together of African and Southern Italian cultures.

I had been using puppets in our theater group for a few years and always wanted to find more information about this tradition, which I knew was very old, dating back to the Middle Ages. I was fascinated by the art of the puppeteers who were hidden inside the giant puppets and had such a beautiful, elegant way of dancing the tarantella and re-creating a sensual courtship between the African king and the Italian queen. The historic roots of the dance of the giganti are probably Aragonese. During Spanish rule and in the time of the Turkish invasions, these influences came to Calabria with the Moors.

It is interesting that this tradition is found not only in Calabria but also is popular in Messina, Sicily, for the Feast of the Assumption of Mary on August 15, and even in Spain, Malta, and Belgium, although always slightly altered and with other myths as the background. (Later, I found this same tradition during Carnival in Recife, in Northeast Brazil.)

The ritual dance of the giants is a true triumph of the love between the white queen Mata and the black African king Grifone. Spurred on by the rhythmic beat of drums, the dance is then sealed with an embrace and a kiss symbolizing peace among our cultures and races. I was curious about this "pagan" sensual ritual and did not know another surprise was coming—a more erotic fertility ritual.

The drums got louder, and I saw a dark-skinned man, dressed in white and blue, dancing with a *palio* (large flag) in a very unusual way. He looked very proud as he held the huge blue flag with golden stars between his legs and performed an extremely phallic dance with the pole tied to his arm. He danced in a circle and also dropped down on his knees in a circular motion, whirling, as if caressing the earth, to the loud 6/8 rhythm of the tarantella played on the snare drums. I jumped up and decided to follow this wild man and the drummers. They all smiled at me, and I noticed that they all had large mustaches like the leader. Even the flag bearer sported a big mustache. He had a lovely, benevolent smile and nodded to me to follow him through the streets toward the procession of la Madonna Nera.

I realized that this ritual, rich in symbolism, was probably older than the Middle Ages. No wonder so many anthropologists had studied it through the years. Feeling the fast rhythm inside my bones and pulsating in my heart, I began dancing in a circular motion, following the

Fig. 6.3. Flag bearer processing during the Feast of la Madonna dei Poveri.

steps of the flag bearer and the I Giganti through the winding streets, up and down, not thinking at all that I could break an ankle or fall on the cobblestones. I was feeling deliriously happy and light as I spun around in circles.

As I danced to this African-accented rhythm, I arrived in front of the beautiful Basilica, where a huge crowd was screaming "Evviva Maria!" as the stunning statue of the Black Madonna dei Poveri was, at that moment, coming out of the church. The Madonna of the Poor. There She was, unbelievably powerful and mysterious.

At the sight of Her, I felt completely ecstatic. Finally, I saw a beautiful black statue, which looked very ancient, with a strange enigmatic smile and face that seemed so alive, staring at all of us, with no real eyes, yet looking *alive*.

Dressed in a simple ancient-looking, earth-colored tunic, Her face was the color of the Earth herself, dark brown. And astonishingly to me, she had blond hair. Wearing beautiful silver jewelry, large earrings, and necklaces, She looked North African and even Gypsy. Her black son, Jesus, stood on Her lap, holding a globe in His hands. A group of twelve men dressed in white and blue carried Her out of the church. It was clear that the statue was very heavy, as the Queen of Heaven's incredible throne is made of solid silver and gold. Two golden angels, perched above Her on each side, were holding an oriental-looking canopy with elaborate decorations.

I stared at Her and wondered why it is that this Black Madonna, who has blond hair, wears a very simple earth-colored tunic with no other colors on Her but is surrounded by a heavily decorated and precious throne, Her own altar. She was an unusual, ancient-looking, mysterious, and enigmatic statue, almost one meter tall; yet She looked bigger. She seemed to be staring at me from above Her throne, smiling as if she were happy that I had finally arrived. . . . This was my feeling, again to be welcomed by Her as Her daughter.

## THE DEVOTION OF
## THE BLACK MADONNA OF THE POOR

As they started the procession from the church through the town, the huge crowd followed, with the local band playing out-of-tune, weird-sounding music, similar to the famous Fellini's film scores, and everyone showing deep emotions, screaming "Evviva Maria!" I decided to follow, not knowing how long it would be. I began to cry, my voice joining with the crowd.

The drumming in the back sounded like ta-ta, ta-ra-ta, ta-ta, ta-ra-ta, and the bass drum sounded boom-boom-boom. Cymbals crashed loudly at the accents of the tarantella. My heart was with the drums, my soul with the Madonna, and my mind—seemed to be gone. Somewhere lost in the mists of time, returned to the Middle Ages.

I joined in the prayers, saying the Hail Marys of the rosary, while an invisible force pushed me through the crowds. I didn't know what had happened to my friend Lucio, who had come with me; we had decided that if we got separated we would meet at the church at the end of the ceremony. But I had no idea when that would be! The procession had started at five o'clock. When would it end? No one could tell. Some people said it usually went on until around midnight.

I knew from the book by Annabella Rossi, *Le feste dei poveri* (The Feasts of the Poor), that this Madonna was called Our Lady of the Poor because when She was found in the year 951 under the ruins of a burned temple, only the poor people could lift Her up. When rich people tried to do it, the statue became too heavy and could not be moved. A beautiful legend!

According to my research, the statue probably originated in the year 700, when it is said that She arrived in the town of Taureana (an ancient Greek settlement) from the Orient. The Saracens invaded Calabria that year, destroyed the town, and burned the church, so the beautiful Black Madonna vanished. But in the year 951, some peasants one night saw a strong shining light, like lightning, coming out of the Earth up toward the sky. They were frightened and went to the authorities, describing what they saw. The authorities went to the spot where the peasants had seen the light and dug into the ground, unearthing the mysterious statue of the Black Madonna. They realized that She was the same statue from the church that had burned, yet She was miraculously intact 251 years later.

When the authorities tried to lift Her, She became heavy; no one could bring Her up. Then the poor peasants tried to lift Her, and She instantly became light. Ever since then, She was called la Madonna dei Poveri, Our Lady of the Poor.

That August 14, I felt that I had stepped back in time as I continued to walk along the procession following the Madonna Nera dei Poveri. Feeling so protected by Her, with so much compassion coming from Her enigmatic face, I could not leave Her side and could not stop weeping at times.

As the sun went down, Her beautiful throne lit up and made Her even more regal, powerful, and full of light. I knew She would grant us all graces and make miracles as She had done for so many centuries.

Fig. 6.4. Flag bearer whirling his flag during the procession
for la Madonna dei Poveri

Praying and feeling the healing energy of this enormous devotion, we walked up and down the hill on winding country roads, some of them not even paved. Often the carriers had to stop and rest, at times even in front of the Mafia bosses, who kneeled by the Blessed Mother, some even weeping and asking for grace. Their tough macho attitude and arrogance completely gone, without embarrassment they offered their naked soul to the Madonna and asked for forgiveness. That's when I understood that the Black Madonna embraces all with Her compassion.

Many hours later we arrived back at the church, and I heard the drummers playing stronger and faster, the 6/8 even more obsessive and powerful.

The flag bearer came dancing toward Her, the Great Mother of us all. In a final erotic circular dance, he looked as if he were about to impregnate the Black Madonna, spinning around on his knees with his flag and finally running toward Her as if with an erect phallus. The crowd shouted, "Evviva Maria!" and applauded as he got close to Her, where She was waiting, almost embracing him. He ran toward Her to kiss Her face. I felt that the fertility rite had once again been completed. The Earth will continue to nourish us as She has done for thousands of years.

There we were again, even my missing, almost-lost friend Lucio, and hundreds of people in front of the church, everyone looking up into the sky, waiting for the fireworks to start. The boom-boom-boom signal came, and in astonishment I watched the most elaborate fireworks I have ever seen. More emotions overcame me. I've loved fireworks since I was a child and celebrated New Year's Eve at home with my father, who threw fireworks off our balcony in Rome. It was extremely dangerous, but we all loved it. To this day, fireworks bring back special childhood memories, as well as the joy of celebrating feast days of Mary, Mother of God.

That night, in the summer of 1987, I made a promise that I would come back to see Her, Our Lady of the Poor, every year that I was in Calabria. I knew that I had to stage this dramatic musical tradition for our opera. I felt very inspired, but I knew the task I was taking on would not be easy.

Through the years, I have come back to this very place and visited many others in Calabria, accompanied by John and my husband, Dario. We also traveled with other musicians from all over—New York, California, and Italy—sharing incredible experiences with our good Calabrese friend Vittorio de Paola, one of my teachers and mentors. I will share now for the first time some of these surreal experiences that include seers, healers, apparitions, miracles, and even werewolves.

## HISTORY, MYTHOLOGY, AND LEGENDS OF THE MADONNA DEI POVERI

In my research on this stunning Black Madonna I found that She was connected to Her sisters in Spain (Our Lady of Montserrat) and to Madonnas at various locations in Italy—Tindari, Viggiano, and Foggia.

People also believe Her to be one of the Seven Sisters. Another sister exists in Montserrat, Spain, where She was also worshipped in the Middle Ages, at the time of the Crusades, with music and powerful rituals.

This part of the history made a lot of sense to me, given that Southern Italy was so indelibly mixed with the Spanish. Later in the Renaissance—following the domination and invasions of the Moors, the Byzantine Empire, the Turkish Empire, and the Normans who took over during the Middle Ages—Spain dominated the land known as the Kingdom of the Two Sicilies for three hundred years. The influence of these cultures is very clear when you hear the Calabrese folk music. It has Arabic scales, intricate rhythms, and syncopations with beautiful instruments such as the *chitarra battente* (Renaissance folk guitar) and the *lira calabrese,* which is like the North African *vielle.* (Similar instruments found in Pernabuco, in northeastern Brazil, are the *chitarra nortestina* and the *rebec.*)

Other Black Madonna researchers have connected Her to an ancient mysterious devotion of the pagan cult of the Great Mother. She was worshipped for a few thousand years in different parts of the Mediterranean with many different names: Gea, Isis, Demeter, Artemis, Diana, Epona. She was the Myrionyme (which in Greek means "the goddess with ten thousand names"), and it seems easy to connect the name Myrion to Mary and Gea or Gaia, Mother Earth goddess.

Also known to have two different aspects of the Madonna are Isis and Demeter, as well as other female deities connected to the eternal cycle of life. As I explained in the previous chapter, Isis especially was portrayed as black while holding her son Horus in her arms, just like our Madonna and Child. Demeter too suffered from the loss of her adored daughter, Persephone. This shows us that there was a primordial matriarchal religion that was substituted by the patriarchal religion in more recent times but which is still alive inside Catholicism with its syncretism and special legends that were derived from the pagan world.

## HISTORY OF THE GIGANTI (GIANT PUPPETS)

The legend of the giganti says that a gigantic Moor, whose name was Hassan Ibn Hammar, landed, with about fifty pirates, near the city of Messina and Reggio Calabria in 970 CE and sacked the area. One day, during a raid, he saw a girl named Mata, who was the daughter of the nobleman Cosimo II di Castellaccio. The Moor suddenly fell in love with her. She was tall and beautiful and also a devoted and chaste Christian. Hassan Ibn Hammar proposed to her, and when she refused, he went into a rage. According to some historical accounts, the Moor beat her father in a tournament, thus winning her hand in marriage. He did his best to make her love him. A Saracen, he converted to Christianity and changed his name to Grifo (but later was known as Grifone because of his height) and received baptism. He became a farmer and lived in peace with everyone. The chaste Mata, struck by his repentance, fell in love with him and agreed to marry him.

The truth is that the giganti have an ancient origin, from the myths of the giants. Like the Eleusinian mysteries, the mysteries of the Theoi Megaloi (Greek meaning "great gods") of Samothrace (an island in the northern Aegean Sea) were highly respected in the ancient Mediterranean, particularly during Hellenistic and Roman times. There is evidence of the existence of these Samothracian gods and their mysteries, both in literature and archaeology. Some Greek and Roman authors identify these gods with non-Samothracian deities, including, most commonly, Demeter, Persephone, Hades, and Hermes, as well as with the Dioscuri (from the Greek Dioskouroi, meaning "sons of Zeus") and Corybantes.

## LA MADONNA DEI POVERI BECOMES ALIVE ON STAGE

My main intention for my extensive research was to find a way to bring to the stage these archaic forms of devotion through music, theater, and dance, thus conveying to the audience the true power of the Black Madonna, giving them a transformational experience like the one I had had during the processions.

I have been greatly inspired by most of the Black Madonna's rituals everywhere, but I must admit that the one that has come alive through me as a director and performer is la Madonna dei Poveri and Her wild celebration in Seminara. When I first staged *The Voyage of the Black Madonna*, I re-created the scene of finding Her under the earth with peasants digging and lifting Her up. I played the statue of the Black Madonna that came alive, wearing a beautiful mask. We chanted some of the prayers from Calabria and staged the procession of the flag and the giant puppets using the drumming of the 6/8 beat of the tarantella. The audience loved it.

It was many years later, though, in 2006, that the true essence and meaning of this Madonna from Calabria, sister of the one in Montserrat, Spain, came to me in haunting visions. At the time, I had begun writing a new production, *Tarantella: Spider Dance*. I was obsessed with telling the true history of this powerful healing dance through the trance rituals I had been part of in the south of Italy and in other parts of the world.

I felt as if I had lived in the Middle Ages when the worship of the Black Madonna was very popular in Europe. During that time, pilgrims traveled far to visit Madonnas housed in monasteries. They performed penance, walked for months, and arrived at the monasteries chanting, drumming, and re-creating circular dances. The most famous pilgrimage was and still is Santiago de Compostela.

It was during the Crusades, the time of wars between faiths, that killed so many innocent people, the time when the Black Death came and decimated one-third of the population in Europe, when people were overcome by fear and their devotion to the Black Madonna saved them, healed them, and brought light into the darkness of their oppressed lives. They took the beautiful statues, such as the one from Seminara, in procession, asking Her to stop the Plague and the wars and bring healing to the town. The people from Calabria performed musical exorcisms playing the fast 6/8 rhythm of the tarantella on their drums, dancing wildly, spinning and turning until they fell, to get rid of the evil energies that tried to attack them.

I felt very strong emotions, sensing the parallels between then and now. I watched as AIDS decimated the population of New York, and I still see how many other contagious diseases, such as hepatitis C, continue to claim lives. Cancer has become an epidemic, and we are again living through our own version of the crusades with all the violence among Christians, Jews, and Muslims and repeated terrorist attacks, often guided by greed and the desire to invade fertile lands rich in oil.

The beauty of this time of turmoil is that, as in the Renaissance, people across the planet have been awakening to a new age and looking for another way to connect to Mother Earth, to the Divine Feminine, to God, and the Christ. This new movement has created wonderful artists, musicians, writers, visionaries, spiritual leaders, and healers, all who seem to be in search of the same answer—connecting to our higher selves.

I deeply feel that one way to come out of the darkness of oppression and depression caused by fear, which has been put inside many of us by the power of governments and leading corporations, is to understand that we are indeed loved and protected by the Great Mother, the Black Madonna, the female aspect of God, who loves us all, regardless of race, religion, or economic class.

To make this statement, She has guided me to stage probably the most powerful scene I ever directed: "The Procession of the Black Madonna." With the music to *Cuncti Simus Concanentes* (Let Us All Sing Together), a medieval Latin hymn or chant in honor of Our Lady of Montserrat, from the *Llibre Vermell de Montserrat,* I choreographed a powerful spinning dance to release fear of death, using the rhythms I'd heard from the drummers in Calabria.

During the performance, as we begin the chant with a haunting and powerful violin solo by violinist Joe Deninzon, Death comes out in the form of a fantastic stilt dancer (played by the talented Mark Mindek) wearing a death mask and a long black costume with flowing veils; he goes among the audience members, scaring them, representing the Black Death and evil.

When the rhythm of the tarantella begins, I come out as the priestess of the Black Madonna, singing *Cuncti Simus Concanentes.* I sing *Ave Maria* (the first line of the chant) and play a very fast, accented 6/8 on my large frame drum. I keep singing and lead a procession of dancers dressed in black robes, their faces covered with red veils symbolizing blood, one of them carrying a painting of the Black Madonna. This particular image is a painting by my friend Arden H. Mason, whom I have known for forty-three years and who made this painting when he was almost between worlds—very ill with heart disease and waiting for a heart transplant. It is the same beautiful image used on the cover of this book, and I will describe it more later. He is also a great stilt dancer, and when he got his new heart, which was in and of itself a miracle from the Black Madonna, he again was part of our production.

The dancers and I circle around Death, and I fight Death back and forth using my drum as a shield. The veiled dancers then fall in desperation at the feet of the Black Madonna, throwing themselves on the floor as they ask for a miracle. The drums get faster, louder, playing the authentic 6/8 rhythm from the Madonna dei Poveri and San Rocco in Calabria, and we begin a fast spinning dance in a spiral and then in a circle. Narrowing in on Death, empowered by this musical exorcism, we chase away Death. Our black robes twirling, veils flying, we release all fear and toxins out of the body. We spin faster and faster, finally falling at the feet of the Black Madonna to receive Her enlightenment. The dance and drumming end abruptly as we kneel down, bending forward so that our foreheads touch the floor.

Feeling connected to the Earth, thanking her for transforming our pain and grief, we end this collective ceremony by rising up to thank the Black Madonna and chanting "Ave Maria." The lights go down in a blackout as we slowly whirl to the left, the direction of the heart, as done by the Sufis, thus bringing our Christian tradition together with Islam in a beautiful ritual of peace. The audience is left breathless and breaks into a loud, powerful applause. And so ends Act 1.

## SUPERNATURAL EXPERIENCES IN CALABRIA

### Apparitions and Visions of Mary and Jesus, the Evil Eye Healer, the Werewolf

During our thirty years of traveling in Calabria, we spent most of the time with a group of local Calabrese folk musicians led by the maestro Vittorio de Paola, one of the best singers and tarantella dancers I have ever seen. He also impressed me with his in-depth knowledge of the region's old folk traditions. I met him at the same time that I met Raffaele, in 1980, and felt an instant affection for him and his family, particularly his beautiful little daughter, Anna, who sang haunting duets with him in the Calabrese dialect.

I knew that I could learn a lot from this self-taught man. His philosophy of life bewitched me, and together with Dario and John, we became a close tribe. Meeting every summer for twenty years, we lived through the most wonderful and amazing experiences, always led by our love for folk music.

After the Black Madonna had granted us a miracle, and Dario was healed from drug addictions, he was finally free to travel with me to do extensive research in the south of Italy. In 1990 we began renting a very old country house from a woman named Nicolina. She was a healer and shared her ancient Earth wisdom with me. She was a robust, tall woman with dark eyes, dark hair, and a great smile. A hardworking peasant woman, she had three handsome sons and a very strange husband who never spoke a word with any one—he seemed to mainly communicate with animals.

Nicolina had a simple farmhouse in the country right above the beautiful coast on the sea of Parghelia. The land was surrounded by animals and had a rich garden with all kinds of plants, fruit, and herbs. Nicolina liked me right away and told me many stories of magic and local folklore. She knew that I was devoted to the Madonna, and every year when I returned she had new accounts of apparitions of Mary in Calabria. She shared with me that she was a healer, that her grandmother had taught her the ancient craft to heal diseases of the skin and bones and to take away *il malocchio*, the Evil Eye. She showed me the rite to see if a person has the Evil Eye, which is part of the old Italian witchcraft tradition.

A couple of times she performed a ritual that determined whether I had the Evil Eye. She filled a bowl with water and blessed the water by saying certain prayers. She then spilled a drop of olive oil in the water. If I did not have the Evil Eye, she said that the drop of oil would float and slowly enlarge without breaking. If I did have it, the drop would break into many tiny drops. When this happened, Nicolina would repeat the ritual, saying many prayers and formulas until the oil drop no longer broke apart. Usually she volunteered to do this magic ritual if she felt that someone had given me "Eye" out of jealousy.

She felt that I also had the gift and that I too could heal and take the malocchio away, so she taught me how to do the ritual and told me that it had to be done on Christmas Eve. I cannot share the information that she gave me, but I am extremely grateful to her for this teaching, as it proved to be helpful a few times. Dario and I became very attached to Nicolina, and every year we visited we brought friends from America with us—mainly musicians, like John and our flutist, Susan; our singer, Ivan; and other artist friends who shared in our wild adventures. It was through Nicolina and her devotion to the Madonna that we would find the most amazing, magical places where both Jesus and Mary appeared and where women could talk to the dead to heal others.

One of the most vivid experiences came on a night of the full moon. We were staying at Nicolina's when we found ourselves unable to sleep due to strange sounds of heavy breathing and chains being pulled, as if a big animal was desperately trying to free itself. We heard loud howling, and it sounded to us as if we were surrounded by a pack of wild dogs—it was terrifying!

Thanks to my good friend and teacher Vittorio de Paola, we found out that, unfortunately, Nicolina was married to a werewolf! Vittorio explained how he, as a teenager, would go out during full moon nights with his friends to "catch" the werewolves who he knew were out in the countryside, howling to the moon. They suffered from what we call in Italy *mal di luna* (moon sickness), possibly a form of hysteria or even a self-destructive depression that during full moon nights afflicts both men and women. The afflicted would feel anguish, had a strong pain in their stomach, and crawled on four legs, screaming and howling and strangely communicating with dogs who came around as their protectors.

When my friend Vittorio went out hunting for the werewolves, he realized that these people were suffering. They were not dangerous; the wild dogs around them were the real danger. The dogs could feel their pain, and if anyone got close to the "werewolf," the dogs would attack them and possibly kill them.

The myth of the *lycanthropes* growing hair and being aggressive and attacking people is, indeed, only a legend. But the people afflicted by the werewolf condition did exist in Italy, even in cities like Rome, as my father used to tell me.

One of the most beautiful stories about this suffering of people diagnosed with mal di luna is in the film *Kaos* by the Taviani brothers, based on the novel *Moon Sickness* by renowned Sicilian writer Luigi Pirandello. In the novel a lonely young bride, Sidora, has been living only briefly with her new husband, Bata, when the first full moon of their marriage occurs. Bata warns her to bar the doors and windows, and then goes outside and howls so horribly that he leaves his wife petrified.

I know to you this may sound completely made up, but I assure you that these tragic events were actually part of poor Nicolina's life. When my friend Vittorio came over to the house under the excuse of playing some tarantella and having a party, he showed us all the signs of her husband's disease. The man was extremely introverted, hardly ever spoke, and when he did, no one understood him, only the animals. He often used his hands like paws, and if he saw meat, even raw, he grabbed it like a dog. Other than that, he was perfectly normal and never caused trouble or was dangerous.

However, he was in great pain during the full moon, compelled to howl and whine like a dog. I will never forget when one morning dear Nicolina, who had not slept during the full moon because of all the dogs howling, looked at me in despair and said, *"Ah, Alessandra, che vita da cani!"* (Ah, Alessanda, it's a dog's life!) To this day, I am still grateful to this wise peasant woman who showed me the unconditional love she had for her husband and taught me Earth wisdom from Calabria.

One year when I was visiting her, Nicolina told us to look for a specific olive tree in a garden where an apparition of Jesus had been seen.

So on a hot summer day, John, Susan, Dario, and I ventured out into the fields, up the hills above Tropea, to look for the olive tree where Jesus's face had appeared. We were skeptical but of course eager and curious to see for ourselves.

The story of the sighting begins on Easter Monday, that same year, when a nearby woman who owned a farmhouse with an olive tree had a dream that it would snow and that a miracle would happen. Since it never snows there, especially around Easter, the woman knew that this dream was a premonition. After the traditional great meal for the feast, which in Italy is called La Pasquetta (Little Easter), the woman fell asleep.

While she slept, a powerful storm started up, full of snow and thunder. Lightning struck the tree, breaking it in half, one burned half lying on the ground. In the center of the tree, clear enough to be seen, appeared the face of Jesus, a crown of thorns on his head. Afterward the place became a shrine of devotion where people came to ask for healing. It was not a church, just someone's house that became a place of devotion.

Typical to traveling in Calabria, since there are no signs anywhere, we were lost for a while on our way to the farmhouse but arrived at the site at high noon, in the heat of the lunch hour. Venturing toward the miraculous olive tree, protected by a little fence with some flowers at its feet, we stopped and stared for a while, but try as we might, we were unable to see the face of Jesus. We walked around the tree, looked at each other with a shrug indicating that we were giving up, and began to turn away from the tree as if to leave. But then, as we took one last look at the tree before going, we all saw the face of Christ at exactly the same moment. There it was, the face of Jesus, in agony on the cross, His eyes, eyebrows, hair, nose, chin tilted down, the thorns crowning his head.

With tears in our eyes we looked at each other, feeling amazed and a little frightened. It was profound to see the face look so alive! We knelt and said some prayers. This was not a painting: it was *Jesus appearing to us* on an olive tree trunk, showing his agony and suffering for the world. We stayed there in silence for a long time, then sat by the tree praying, realizing that this was not something to explain. It just was.

We felt truly blessed by receiving this miracle of Jesus appearing only for the four of us. There was no one else there, and no one from the house even came out. I remember driving down the hill to the sea, feeling that the apparition of Jesus's face on the tree had a deeper meaning than we thought. My sense was that he wanted to be recognized and acknowledged by us. Firsthand knowledge of his blessed face definitely put me in an ecstatic state, and John and Susan told me that they felt the same way, that this experience was life transforming for them too. It became our inspiration for our Passion play.

We thanked Nicolina for having shared this information with us and told her to please tell us of any other unusual visions or apparitions she might hear about in the area. And so, she did.

Another extraordinary moment was witnessing the apparition of Mary in the middle of the day, over an oak tree, in the midst of lightning and thunder, in a location that became a shrine but was not a church.

Following Nicolina's advice, we drove farther north in Calabria, toward the city of Cosenza, and by chance (or miracle?) found the place she indicated and followed a crowd who gathered every weekend in this oak grove high up on a mountain. There was a young woman who had a recurrent mystical experience and supernatural powers: every Sunday at noon she would go into a trance, fall on her knees by a large oak tree, pray to the sky or heaven, and invoke the help of Mary to heal the sick and help the poor.

Most of the time a miracle happened. We were there for a couple of hours, watching the crowd prepare by bringing pitchers of water, holding white handkerchiefs, praying, and otherwise attending to the young woman who seemed weak and was helped by her husband.

Dario and I were there, waiting for this strange phenomenon to happen; as the only outsiders, we wondered what was really going on— nothing was happening yet. But then we saw everyone look up into the sky, and at that moment, we saw it! The blue summer sky grew dark, thunder and lightning came, and the silhouette of the Blessed Mother, the Virgin Mary, with her hands open and down toward us, appeared high on top of the oak tree in a deep purple color.

At the sight of Our Lady, the woman passed out and fell on the ground, and as she touched the earth, water came out from the spring that was underneath. We couldn't believe it, but it was occurring right in front of our eyes. The sick people in the crowd came forward to be touched by the woman in trance.

Dario and I were in shock and in disbelief. It was too much to figure out what was going on around us. It was just inexplicable!

We went closer to the young woman and got some of the miraculous water that was coming out of the ground, drank it, and prayed with the rest of the devotees, some saying that they were already feeling relieved from their illness.

Dario and I took the healing water back to Nicolina and our mothers, feeling that its sacred properties could always help us in times of need.

Looking back, it's hard to explain how it felt to be a part of these supernatural and miraculous events in these sacred locations in the middle of Nature, Mother Nature, Mother Earth. We felt blessed to be shown again and again that everything was connected to the Black Madonna, with Her expression of being *alive,* sharing Her son Jesus's pain as He appeared on a tree trunk, revealing to us how the Earth is alive with all kinds of signs and gifts of love. Every time I had a mystical experience, I felt that I was becoming more of a healer myself, that I could see things in a psychic way that I did not know I could and was in possession of magical powers.

Dario said many times, "*Ho sposato una maga, una streghetta, una curandera.*" (I married a maga, a little witch healer.)

We shared so many wonderful magical experiences that one book will never be enough to tell the stories. All I can say is that after all these years I am grateful and bless Dario's soul for always being ready to go with me to these places in search of the Great Mother, Her miracles, and truth.

## A REVELATION AT THE FEAST OF
## LA MADONNA DEI POVERI:
## THE BLACK MADONNA IS ALIVE!

On August 14, 2016, I had an amazing revelation at the Feast of Our Lady of the Poor, where I led my third pilgrimage of the Black Madonna with a wonderful group from America, travelers mainly from New York and California.

I have been blessed to be able to lead this pilgrimage to the sacred sites of the Black Madonna in Southern Italy and felt from the beginning that I was guided by Her, in dreams and in my daily reality, to create this pilgrimage and make Her known to the world, to bring her to people who normally would have never known Her the way I do.

On the last day of the tour, I chose the Madonna dei Poveri from Seminara Calabria to close the pilgrimage in a powerful way. After coming here for so many years I had a shocking revelation. When I arrived with the group, the feast had begun with the procession of the giant puppets and the drummers playing the fast 6/8 rhythm of the tarantella on snare drums, bass drums, and cymbals. I felt the usual energy and adrenaline running fast inside me and ran toward the drummers to be part once more of this astonishing drumming and dance ritual in honor of the Black Madonna.

As I got closer I was excited to see again the *capo banda,* the lead drummer I had known since 1987. He was still of small stature but super strong. He kept an incredibly fast rhythm on the snare drums with many variations of accents and great mastery and pride. In 2016, he was very proud to tell me that he had won the golden drum award in Palmi, Calabria. I stayed with him and his group and watched with great admiration the beautiful dance of the giant puppets.

After the wild drumming and dance celebration I felt la Madonna dei Poveri call me to go inside the church and pay homage to Her, as I have done for so many years. The church was crowded with all the devotees from the town getting in line to be close to Her, to touch

Her with a white handkerchief, which is the traditional way to receive Her blessings and healing. It was emotional for me, as it had been many times before, to stand there looking at Her, as She stared back at me, following me in my movements.

I know that she could see me and everyone. Yes, this Madonna to me is one of the most mystical and mysterious with Her beautiful dark-brown face. There are no eyes painted on Her face, but at the same time, She has a clear gaze and stares at you from the depth of Her dark face.

I have always felt that She is alive, and when I followed Her in procession, I would just stare at Her, feeling an overwhelming energy of empowerment and a lot of compassion coming from Her, since She is the patron of the poor and the outcast.

Visiting Her in 2016, I looked at Her from far away and then closer, and when I finally moved near enough to touch Her, it felt too rushed. I felt that I needed more time with Her. I wondered if, indeed, she knew that I was there and that I had come from far away to show my devotion and to bring other pilgrims from other countries to Her.

Feeling sadness for leaving Her too soon, I entered the sacristy room to buy some of Her sacred images. Immediately I was drawn to a new black-and-white image that I had never seen before. The man in charge saw me go to this photo and said, "I can see you are looking at this image deeply."

In a state of awe, I stared at the unnerving, almost frightening photo.

"Yes," I said, "I can see Her now. She is alive!"

I was in total shock, as I could see the face of a woman in the photo staring at me, saying, "Here I am. See me? I am alive!"

Overcome by emotions, I said, *"E' viva la Madonna e' un essere vivente! questa e' una donna!"* (She is alive! The Madonna is a living being. She is a woman!) I was trembling! The man said, "You are definitely one special person. You are someone who knows, who deeply understood right away the true meaning of this Black Madonna. *La Madonna e' viva!* [The Madonna is alive!]"

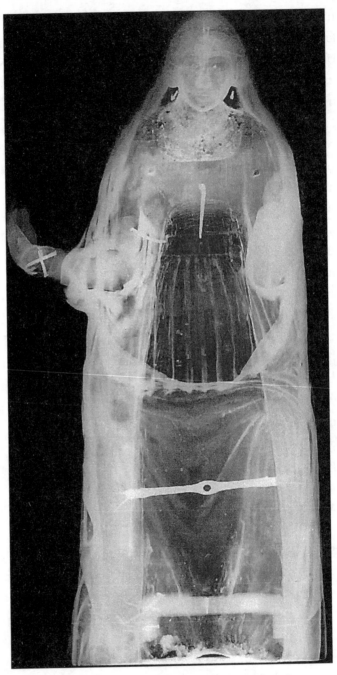

Fig. 6.5. X-rays of the Black Madonna dei Poveri:
the Madonna is alive!

The man went on to explain that I was looking at a photo of the X-rays that were taken of the statue of la Madonna dei Poveri in 2010, when She was being restored. During this restoration, the X-rays showed a miraculous image: the image of a woman alive. I could see Her! Here is a woman, alive, with eyes, nose, mouth, round face, lighter hair and black face, and beautiful jewelry. She does not hold a baby Jesus. She looks right at us, staring up from below, with a gaze that is clearly saying, "I am alive. I am here to show you that I am a living being behind the statue!"

I went rapidly through many emotions, feeling scared by Her intense look and then happy to have come to this discovery that put a light on a dilemma for all these years. This new discovery confirmed that the statues of the Black Madonna are alive, which explains why their faces constantly change expression. *E' vivente, non e'solo una sacra 'immagine!* (She lives. She is not just a sacred image!)

———◆———

*Grazie, grande Madre for revealing your true essence to me and to many people who want to see you and hear you! I pray that you protect us especially now when the evil powers are taking over in so many places, as here in America. As in the Middle Ages, we live in fear and must return to worship you and honor you as we did then, thus receiving your graces and defeating evil. Our Lady of the Poor, please grant us peace and equality on Earth! Amen.*

———◆———

I first heard this haunting and powerful prayer, a Hail Mary, from the wonderful early music group from England, the Ensemble Unicorn. The relative simplicity, dance rhythms, and strong melodies of the songs have given the music collected in the *Red Book of Montserrat* an incredible appeal to musicians who, like me, are fascinated by devotional as well as medieval music.

The melody stuck in my heart and soul, and I knew that I had to learn it, to heal myself from a broken heart, and to bring it to others. It was the time when I was feeling crushed by my difficult marriage and at the same time became known around the world as a female percussionist thanks to Remo,* with whom I was designing my instruments.

## Red Book of Montserrat

I want to share with you the lyrics and music notations of what I believe to be one of the most powerful chants or hymns to the Black Madonna: *Cuncti Simus Concanentes*. This hymn is part of the *Llibre Vermell de Montserrat* (*Red Book of Montserrat*), a manuscript collection of anonymous devotional texts to Mary, our Lady of Montserrat, containing some late-medieval songs.

The fourteenth-century manuscript was compiled at and is still located at the monastery of Montserrat, outside Barcelona, in Catalonia, Spain, where a beautiful image of the Black Madonna has been worshipped for more than fifteen hundred years. The manuscript was prepared approximately in the year 1399, and it originally contained 172 double pages, of which 32 have been lost. The title, *Red Book of Montserrat*, describes the red binding in which the collection was placed in the nineteenth century.

An anonymous monk who compiled this exquisite collection of early devotional music stated:

Because the pilgrims wish to sing and dance while they keep their watch at night in the church of the Blessed Mary of Montserrat and also in the light of day and in the church, no songs should be sung unless they are chaste and pious. For that reason these songs that appear here have been written. And these should be used modestly, and take care that no one who keeps watch in prayer and contemplation is disturbed.

---

*Remo, Inc., is the largest drum manufacturer in the world, founded in 1957 by Remo Belli.

I felt a new power overcome my whole being that connected me to the Divine Source of the Black Madonna when I played my drum. During the year 1999, I spent many nights in the dark crypt of the Cathedral of Saint John the Divine learning this song, adding the rhythm of the Madonna of the Poor from Calabria, and praying at the same time to the Black Madonna painting inside the cathedral to find strength and answers to my questions and dilemma as an unhappy wife and my pervasive fear of being alone.

Often, I felt abandoned and desperate and could only find my inner power and happiness when I played my drums and especially when I sang this song. Being inside the dark crypt of Saint John the Divine, I also imagined how it might have been in the Dark Ages, living with bigger fears of death and war and the potential end of the world. I could see how pilgrims and devotees found refuge in these powerful chants. They are full of light and praise for Her, Mary, Mother of Christ, and Universal Mother of the world.

I recorded this song with my ensemble, I Giullari di Piazza, in the year 2000 for my CD *Tarantata* (with Sounds True) in a great arrangement by my wonderful musicians, John La Barbera, violinist Joe Deninzon, bansuri flutist Steve Gorn, and percussionist Glen Velez. The melody takes you to a higher place, connects you to the higher self, and the chorus "Ave Maria" reinforces our belief in Her power of healing us all with Her benevolent compassion.

I created the rhythm to accompany the chant to help people release their inner fears and emotions as people do in the ceremonies in Southern Italy, especially by spinning and twirling like the mystical Sufis. Since Southern Italy was so inextricably mixed with the Islamic culture, it seems natural to me to bring these two beautiful traditions together with movement and rhythms.

During my workshops, many people, especially women with a history of abuse, have found immense release and healing as they entered the trance dance with this chant. During their trance, they usually have a vision of the Black Madonna extending her hand to help them come out of their pain.

I invite you to learn this beautiful and extremely healing prayer (see appendix for chapter 6, page 361) and to chant it and dance it in different forms: in unison, in harmonies, in canon; moving your body in circles, spinning to the right or left, first with your head down then lifting your head up; and at the end, falling on your knees in devotion and extending your forehead to the floor, breathing, crying, and even screaming out your pain if necessary. She, the Black Madonna, will listen and come to you as She has done for thousands of years to guide us out of the dark tunnel into the light.

# CHAPTER 7

# *Nigra Sum Sed Formosa:* "I Am Black but Comely"— The African Mother

*Nigra sum sed formosa.*
*Ave Maria,*
*Magna Mater,*
*Stella Maris,*
*Grazia plena,*
*Regina Coeli,*
*Refugium peccatorum.*

*(I am black but beautiful.*
*Hail Mary,*
*Great Mother,*
*Star of the Sea,*
*Full of grace,*
*Queen of Heaven,*
*Refuge of Sinners.)*

"Nigra Sum Sed Formosa," lyrics by
Alessandra Belloni, music by John La Barbera

MY CONTINUING TRAVELS AND ADVENTURES in Calabria led me to the beautiful land right across from Reggio Calabria, at the end of the Italian boot: the volcanic island of Sicily, also known as the island of Demeter and Persephone.

I was immersed in my research on the Black Madonna, studying the inspirational book by Ean Begg, *The Cult of the Black Virgin*, which, to me, remains the most accurate scholarly book on the history and meaning of the Black Madonna. The book was given to me by a dear friend and artist from my group, Elisa Mereghetti.

In the summer of 1988, inspired by that book, Elisa and I decided to travel to Sicily to visit the sanctuary of the Black Madonna of Tindari, a very important Black Madonna mentioned by Begg, located in a powerful, energetic spot where the mountains meet the sea on that black volcanic island. Elisa had previously traveled to Brazil and had gone to ceremonies for the orisha (goddess) Yemanja, goddess of love and the sea in the Afro-Brazilian Yoruba tradition. Together, we felt as if we were being called to go deep into the connections among the Black Madonna in Southern Italy, the Orishas in Brazil, and the African Mother.

We decided that we would go visit our friend Roberto from New York, who had invited us to the island of Pantelleria—called the Black Pearl of the Mediterranean due to its stunning black volcanic coasts. It was the beginning of many magical experiences of initiation at this spectacular location.

My first trip with Elisa was full of tests from the Black Madonna. We took a boat from Naples to Palermo and then made our way down by train, not realizing that as two young attractive women, we would draw a lot of attention.

I personally had not realized how different Sicily was from Calabria. In a way, it was more Muslim then Catholic in mentality regarding women's freedom of dress and expression. We found this out at our own expense on the way back to Rome, when we rented a car to avoid the trouble of being on trains and boats only to realize that we were being followed on the highway.

Fig. 7.1. Black Madonna of Tindari, Sicily;
photo by A. Belloni

We took a bus to the Black Madonna sanctuary from Messina, winding along the wonderful coast to go up toward the mountain of Tindari, near the coastal town of Patti and past the famous port of Milazzo. We always had men following us, and it was very difficult to get rid of them, but thank God that my experiences of living many years in New York, especially in the dangerous 1970s, proved very helpful in protecting ourselves.

We decided to begin our pilgrimage at the bottom of the mountain, by the sea, going through a cave where the Madonna was found, according to a legend, lost in the mists of time. We got off the bus in the blistering August noontime heat. When I think back, it seems obvious that we were guided to change our initial direction—to begin at the bottom of the hill, at the saltwater lakes, instead of on top where the Black Madonna now resides.

# THE SACRED SALTWATER LAKES
# OF MARINELLO

I thought that we should begin our pilgrimage there at the lakes by taking a purifying bath in the beautiful clear waters. It seemed like everything around us was enchanted. It was hot, and we were sweating as the harsh noon sun beat down on us in hundred degree heat. We then saw a grotto, a tunnel in the rocks, and decided to walk across to cool off. It was like entering the tunnel of a shamanic initiation, even though at that time I was not aware of what that meant and was simply following my intuition.

At first, we walked in silence, entering the dark narrow path under the mountain, and then I started singing and heard a strong echo. Another magical point of the Earth was embracing me. As we left the grotto we saw the shining, glimmering water of the salty lakes, and it seemed natural to go swimming in these sacred waters by the beautiful turquoise sea.

It felt as if we were doing a cleansing ritual before seeing the Madonna. No one was around; the place was deserted, and we were completely bewitched by the green, glittering water.

As we slowly entered the lakes, we felt our feet go deep into the black volcanic mud, and we saw our skin glow with the same light shining over the water. The warmth of the water seemed healing and made our bodies feel very light, and the mud under our feet felt like the Earth's womb opening to us. We felt embraced by the mother of waters, Venus, goddess of beauty, love, and sensuality—much like Yemanja and Aphrodite. The green water seemed like a mirror, the mirror of Ochun, the goddess of love and sweet water, from the Yoruba tradition from Africa.

I took my ritual bath that day without knowing that I am really a daughter of Ochun, the orisha who protects all rivers and lakes, goddess of sensuality and sexuality, Eros, and dance. She (like me) loves honey, gold, and all that shines. After all, my father had baptized me in the Tiber, the river of Rome, doing my initiation at birth.

Fig. 7.2. Lakes of Marinello, Tindari, Sicily;
photo by A. Belloni

I remember that Elisa and I laughed like little girls, entering a kind of ecstatic state, probably like women priestesses did in pre-Christian times when they led rituals of purification before the actual mysteries of the Goddess. We floated on our backs in amazement, looking up at the sacred mountain, knowing that the Black Madonna was up there in Her majestic sanctuary. We sang, in harmony, one of the Madonna songs that had been part of our Christmas show and felt an incredible resonant echo coming back to us from the mountain, as if we were amplified.

I had not seen the statue of the Madonna yet. All I had read was that the name Tindari was from an ancient Greek settlement. The Laghetti di Marinello and the surrounding beach are a natural reserve, and all around it was very quiet, even though it was peak vacation season in Italy.

We stayed in this enchanted place for several hours and then took the bus up the mountain to pay our visit to Her, the Black Madonna of Tindari, knowing that She was one of the most ancient and magical, given a powerful spot on the Earth where She was found.

I knew that one legend said that the Black Madonna had arrived in Tindari in ancient times on a ship during a tempest; She was miraculously washed ashore, saving all the fishermen who were on board. Another legend says that during the fierce storm, the ship was magically pushed toward the bay of Tindari, where the water is always calm, and the boat could not sail until the sailors left the Black Madonna statue there. Some legends say that She came from the Orient, but it is mostly believed that She came from Egypt as She resembles an African totem.

Before entering the sanctuary, we looked down at the stunning view over the sea, across from the volcanic Eolie or Aeolian Islands, also known as the Seven Sisters. We could see the beautiful shape of the strip of sand and the formation of the saltwater lakes; to our astonishment, it was a silhouette of a woman praying.

Legend says that a woman came from far away to pray to the Madonna, but when she saw that the Madonna was black, she did not believe that she was Mary, Mother of Christ. At that moment, her little daughter, playing outside the church, fell from the high cliff down to the sea. The Madonna created a miracle and made a strip of sand appear to catch and save the little girl. This miracle was the origin of the saltwater lakes. Those magical lakes change shape, but they always have the silhouette of a woman.

In my prayers I asked the Madonna Nera to please let me see Her, in all Her aspects, and to understand Her deeply and to guide me in this journey that would help me unveil Her mysteries and bring them to the world with my music. Again, I felt Her telling me that She was alive, shifting, conceiving, thinking, but that people today had forgotten and did not respect Her as they had in ancient times. In this sacred place, which is now a Nature reserve, Mother Nature is untouched, and the clarity of the sea is proof that the elements here have never been altered.

Fig. 7.3. Black Madonna of Tindari, the old statue before restoration;
photo by A. Belloni

# THE SANCTUARY OF
# THE BLACK MADONNA

I entered the beautiful sanctuary atop the mountain, overcome with emotion, and slowly walked toward the large statue of the Black Madonna, held by two black angels, suspended high up over the altar. There She was, very powerful, looking like an African queen. Her dark black face was very serious, Her eyes almost closed or looking down at us, and very peaceful. Sitting on Her throne, She was holding a black baby Jesus with the face of a grown man. She held a lily in Her right hand, the sacred flower of the Goddess. Under the statue was the beautiful inscription in Latin: *Nigra sum sed Formosa.*

The statue in 1988 was the original, made of cedar wood, before She was sent for restoration. She wore a red dress and a white cape, both embroidered in gold, and held a lily made of gold and silver. Baby Jesus had a white and gold tunic, with his right arm raised in a blessing of peace to the world.

The Black Madonna also had a crown of solid gold with many jewels. I realized later that the restoration actually brought Her back to Her ancient image, where She wears a long conical headpiece very much like the goddess Cybele.

As I walked around the church, I saw, to my astonishment, that the story and legend of the Madonna of Tindari was clearly depicted on the walls and showed that She was brought by the devotees to an existing temple of Cybele, the earth goddess, which had been there since ancient Greek and Roman times. This was a surprise in such a powerful Catholic church.

I felt something intimidating radiating from the beautiful statue, and to this day, every time I go there and stare at Her, I meditate and ask Her, "Where did you come from?" She is suspended above us, as if telling us that She has come from heaven to help us, save us, nurture us, and protect us, held by angels like an image of the Assumption of the Virgin. Yet I feel that She also represents the archetype of the African Mother.

Plate 1. Madonna with angels playing
tambourines; property of A. Belloni

Plate 2. Coast of the Gods,
Tyrrhenian Sea, Tropea, Calabria

**Plate 3.** Procession of the Madonna of the Sea, Tropea; photo by A. Belloni

**Plate 4.** Sunset in Tropea with Stromboli's volcano on the horizon; photo by A. Belloni

**Plate 5.** Reproduction of Pompeii's fresco of the tammorrita players; photo permission given by A. Belloni at restaurant GO

**Plate 6.** Cave of the Sybil, Cuma, Naples; photo by A. Belloni

**Plate 7.** Black Sybil of Lybia, floor of Siena Cathedral; photo by D. Bollini

SIBYLLA LYBICA
CVIVS MEMINIT
EVRIPIDES

INMANVS INIQVAS
VENIET. DABVNT DEO
ALAPAS MANIBVS IN
CESTIS. MISERABILIS
ET IGNOMINIOSVS
MISERABILIBVS SPEM
PRAEBEBIT.

**Plate 8.** Madonna del Voto, Siena

Plate 9. Close-up of
Mamma Schiavona,
Madonna of Montevergine;
photo by A. Belloni

Plate 10. Black Madonna
of Moiano, Our Lady of
Freedom (Brunettella);
photo by A. Belloni

Plate 11. Statue of the goddess Isis; property of A. Belloni

Plate 12. Giant puppets of Grifone and Mata; photo by A. Belloni

Plate 13. Madonna dei
Poveri procession at night

Plate 14. Black Madonna
of Viggiano inside chapel;
photo by A. Belloni

**Plate 15.** Black Madonna of Viggiano with the sun rays during procession; photo by A. Belloni

**Plate 16.** Sanctuario della Madre di Dio Incoronata, Foggia; photo by A. Belloni

Plate 17. Women carrying the Madonna del Monte Tranquillo; photo by A. Belloni

Plate 18. Anellone piceno; property of Alessandra Belloni

Plate 19. Francesca Silvano and Anthony Anderson in the dance of the Bacchae with Dionysus from the production *Tarantella: Spider Dance* by Alessandra Belloni and I Giullari di Piazza

Plate 20. Scene of the tarantate (Francesca Silvano, Danielle Hartman, Jillian Giunta); photo by Ray Wu

**Plate 21.** Scene from *Voices of the Tarantate;* photo by Ray Wu

**Plate 22.** Amara as the goddess Isis dancing with fire in *Voices of the Tarantate;* photo by Ray Wu

**Plate 23.** Ochun, by artist Luis Molina

**Plate 24.** Nossa Senhora and Ochun

Plate 25. Ending healing ritual at Rhythm is the Cure workshop held by Alessandra Belloni at La Chiara di Prumiano, Tuscany; photo property of A. Belloni

**Plate 26.** Alessandra Belloni praying at the Black Madonna's altar in San Galgano, Tuscany

The first day I saw Her my emotions were a powerful mix of veneration and respect, along with an inexplicable intimidation. I had just begun writing the opera dedicated to Her, and I knew that She would be a crucial part of the journey, as I was writing about Virgil and his initiation in the mysteries of the Goddess. I needed to acknowledge Her roots in Egypt, Africa, and the Song of Solomon. So I continued studying and going back to Tindari to see if what the books said resonated with me and my personal experiences.

Although some theories as to the Black Madonna's origin say that She came from Egypt or Ethiopia, others suggest that She came from the Orient and is a Byzantine statue from the seventh century. Being so close to Africa, I felt that the theory of Her coming from Egypt and Her connection to the Queen of Sheba was the most logical.

That first time in Tindari, in 1988, I lit candles and prayed to receive Her divine inspiration to write a beautiful opera in Her honor. I lit candles for my mother's health and for Dario's freedom. I knew that one day I would come back with him finally free. And I would return with John and other musicians to share this stunning place of devotion with other artists, to create beautiful music for Her and for devotion to Her, the sacred Earth, and the waters around Her.

## MAGICAL EXPERIENCES IN TINDARI

This spectacular place in Nature became a strong part of my devotion, as it has been for thousands of people for so many centuries. I experienced beautiful moments of awakening on the sacred earth where the Black Madonna resides and the healing waters where She was found.

In 1994, the same year that John and the flutist Susan joined me in Calabria, we traveled to Sicily to visit the Black Madonna of Tindari. Heeding my traditional ritual of purification, we first bathed in the precious Laghetti di Marinello at the bottom of the hill. We began to sing "Nigra Sum Sed Formosa," the prayer to the Madonna that we had written for Her. Susan played her flute. Suddenly, in the midst of a stiflingly hot day, the wind began blowing. We heard a voice in the distance, chanting, which then became the voice of the flute played by the wind. It came from the mountain high above, where the Madonna resides on Her throne. The flute was playing itself!

Susan was astonished but let the wind, instead of her fingers, play the melody. It was a haunting, beautiful melody that she still remembers to this day as a transformational experience that affected her life in many ways. We were all in a state of ecstasy after the experience of the face of Jesus appearing on the tree trunk; now we had the blessing of hearing the voice of Mary in the wind. Once again, we felt embraced by God and the Divine Mother.

These blissful moments expanded our creativity and inspiration and guided John and me to continue to write songs and music for the Madonna and for Jesus as featured in our Easter opera and Passion play, *Stabat Mater Donna De Paradiso*. We premiered this production in 1995 at the Cathedral of Saint John the Divine, the year after these two supernatural experiences.

## THE FEAST OF THE BLACK MADONNA OF TINDARI

In 2014, I began leading regular pilgrimages to the Black Madonna's holy sites. One day, coming out of the sanctuary in Tindari, I met a wonderful group of young Sicilian folk musicians who had been following me on the internet and wanted to get to know me as an artist and healer. I was so moved by their words of appreciation and respect that I had tears falling down my cheeks. They were surprised by my "humble reaction."

The first to become my close friend was a young, sweet, and handsome man named Federico, who I believe looks like Jesus as portrayed in the Sicilian paintings and statues. I often call him my son, as we joke about our special friendship. He introduced me to his friends Santino and Sebastiano. It was the beginning of a very special relationship and collaboration that took me to an enchanting place called Parco Museo Jalari, a park owned by the family of one of the young musicians, Sebastiano Pietrini. I then had the honor of teaching workshops at that magical park situated on the Peloritan Mountains near Barcellona Pozzo di Gotto, a town in Messina, Sicily, right across from Tindari.

I fell in love with that place, learning that Jalari was created almost forty years ago by two brothers, Mariano and Salvatore Pietrini, who had a vision to turn dry land into a huge, rich, and fertile park, museum center, and organic farm surrounded by the forest. Mariano was the artist and master who created all the giant stone sculptures found throughout the park, and Salvatore was the architect who created all the buildings and landscapes.

Mariano systematically studied the energy found in the local stones (thus the name Jalari, which means "shining stone" in Arabic) and built giant sculptures of goddesses, the Earth Mother, the Madonna and Jesus, and temples dedicated to peace and to the healing of humanity.

It was a very profound experience to connect with the ancient values that these two brothers have reawakened with Jalari. I led drumming rituals and dance ceremonies on large energetically charged stones in the mountains and by the sea and at the Megalyths of Argimusco, another stunning place way up in the mountains with huge standing stones similar to those on Easter Island.

I was also very fortunate to share the devotion to the Black Madonna with my friends, and in the summer of 2017 my friend Federico and I went for the first time to the pilgrimage on Her feast day. I was stunned by the fact that the devotion to this Madonna is spread over an area of hundreds of kilometers all over the coast and the Peloritani Mountains, and the devotees still keep their tradition of faith with pilgrimages on foot, walking up to one hundred kilometers. If they come from far away they begin on the night of September 6, but mainly they walk through the day of September 7 until the morning of September 8, usually during excruciating heat. This incredible devotion of walking along highways, roads, and trails through mountains and forests was a shock to me, as I thought it was something of the past. But it is a living tradition with thousands of people coming from all over the region to pray to Her, the Mother of God. Some people do this pilgrimage alone in a sort of meditation, others in groups singing devotional prayers. All the devotees gather about 5:00 p.m. on September 7 by the image of the Black Virgin that comes out of the church in a regal procession on top of the mountain where the sanctuary is located in Tindari. They greet Her with cries of joy, tears, and the typical Southern Italian band, following in procession behind the statue all around the mountain.

Feeling so blessed to finally take part in Her procession in a location so dear to me, I could not help but cry when the Queen of Heaven came out in all Her royalty. As the procession continued down the hill, the stunning view of the sea, the lakes, the mountains, and the coast turned purple and gold in the sunset. The whole landscape was surreal and dreamlike. As night fell, the lights around the statue were lit, adding to the supernatural power of this Madonna. All the lights of the feast decorations were so extraordinarily bright it seemed like daylight.

I was lucky to be there during the full moon, and Federico and I decided to leave the crowds, go down to the enchanted lakes, and bathe in the warm water of the sea, praying with our drums to the moon goddess (Diana) and the sea goddess (Aphrodite), sisters of the Black Madonna like the earth goddess Cybele.

As we looked up the mountain, I felt the strong female presence of the Divine Feminine sitting on Her throne. I have chanted there many times, and the echo that came back from the mountain to me seems to be Her voice. The shape of the lakes keeps changing. The saltwater of the sea comes from underneath, and in these healing waters you feel that you are embraced by Her, the goddess of the sea and love, another aspect of the Universal Mother.

## ANOTHER LEGEND OF
## THE BLACK MADONNA OF TINDARI

The following anecdote is recounted by the beautiful and accurate book by author Rev. Rosario Giordano in Tindari *una Stella per la Madre di Dio* (A Star for the Mother of God), published by Sanctuary in the year 1987 (see bibliography). In 1751, Abate Filippo Spitaleri wrote of a miraculous image of the Holy Mary who had a beautiful face and who came from Africa. She arrived at the bay of Tindari on a boat during a tempest. The boat could not move and was stuck for a long time in the bay until the people finally took the black statue ashore when they realized that She had chosen this location as Her place of worship. Given that the statue was *negrissima* (very black), it's understandable why the locals at first resisted recognizing it until they understood the power of the statue as Mary, Mother of God.

## FINDINGS FROM THE RESTORATION OF THE STATUE

Tindari's statue of the Black Madonna, sculpted from cedar wood, was sent for restoration in Palermo in 1995 on the order of the new monsignor, Ignazio Zambito, and under the supervision of an art historian and a team of specialists including two theologians. The purpose of this restoration was to bring back the original medieval characteristics of the statue. (Many theories assert that She is even older than the eleventh century.)

In this process they discovered many different layers of attempted restoration, which make it difficult to determine the actual time that the statue was carved. It was very interesting to find out that, unlike many statues of the period, the Madonna had detailed eyes, and She is not Latin or Byzantine but possibly North African, Syrian, or Egyptian, based on the shape of the eyes and presence of *kajal,* makeup used by Egyptian women. The style of the conical headpiece (similar to Cybele's) is of Greek origins, probably pre-Christian.

One fascinating theory suggests that the sculptor could have been French from the time of the Crusades and possibly was a soldier. In the restoration it was determined that the artist employed a technique used by French sculptors in the Middle Ages, carving the entire sculpture from one piece of cedar wood. It is possible that the artist was ordered to do so by a high priest, or he may have been driven by his own devotion because, while a soldier during the Crusades, he had received a miracle. In any case, with great skill the artist brought to life an eleventh-century statue that combines Middle Eastern, Byzantine, and North African styles, bringing together the West and the East in an icon that represents unity. He created a Madonna who is both Theotokos (Mother of God) and Sede Sapientae (Throne of Knowledge) and who may have navigated the sea from Africa to Sicily over what is known as *mare nostrum* (our sea), the Mediterranean, protecting the sea, the coast, and its people.

After seven months, the restoration of the Black Madonna was completed. The colors and style of the restored version were not chosen at random but are rich in medieval symbolism: Jesus is dressed in bright red and is blessing us as king and priest. The Blessed Mother is wrapped in a shiny dark-pink cloth decorated in the Italian and French style with golden stars, symbolizing the fullness of light and life. A blue-green cape, falling over Her shoulders, symbolizes the sea and the sky, and the bright green of Her skirt reminds us of spring and Mother Nature. The Middle Eastern–stylized golden jewel on Her crown is a clear symbol of the ancient sun god. All the shining gold threads on Her clothing remind us of the epiphany of the Cosmos.

## THE HISTORY OF THE ANCIENT TOWN OF TINDARI

The town of Tindari was part of greater Greece in the Classical period. It is mentioned by ancient historians and geographers under various names, the most common being Tyndaris.

According to mythology, Tyndareus was the king of Sparta, husband of Leda, and father to the mortal Castor, whose divine twin brother, Pollux, was the son of Zeus. Upon Castor's death, Pollux asked his father to let him share his immortality with his twin brother, and they were transformed into the constellation Gemini. They were called the Dioscuri or Tyndaridae and were believed to be the patrons and protectors of travelers and sailors, invoking favorable winds. Tindari is, therefore, the city of the Tyndaridae and under the protection of these brothers who watch over the sea.

Founded in 396 BCE by Dionysius I, Greek tyrant of Syracuse, Tindari was built in an important strategic location for navigation and trade. It soon became one of the major Greek centers in Sicily. In 310 BCE, the colony participated in a war against Carthage (present-day Tunisia) as an ally of Syracuse. Later, Tindari was occupied by the Carthaginians for a period of about seven years. In 254 BCE, Tindari changed hands and became a Roman outpost for several centuries. With the arrival of Christianity and the Black Madonna, it became a renowned religious location, and an abbey was built.

Around the first century CE, Tyndaris was hit by a landslide, and the inhabitants scattered to the surrounding countryside. It is believed that the landslide came at the moment that Jesus died on the cross and, the Earth shook tremendously. In the eighth century, Tindari became a bishopric seat of the early Byzantine Empire, and the first shrine to the Black Madonna was built on the ruins of the temple of Ceres, goddess of the harvest (originally Cybele).

Tindari was destroyed in 1544 by Algerian pirates, then rebuilt between 1552 and 1598. The building of the new sanctuary began in 1957 on December 8, the Feast Day of Mary, with the laying of the first stones taken from the ancient Greek and Roman temple. On September 6, 1975, the icon of the Black Madonna was taken into the new church and placed on Her new throne in the center of the temple. On May 1, 1979, the new sanctuary was solemnly consecrated and opened to devotees.

### The Tongue of Sand

Below the archaeological site and the sanctuary is the extraordinary *linguetta di sabbia* (tongue of sand), a sandbank stretching 1.5 kilometers into the Tyrrhenian Sea, resisting the destructive, relentless raids of the waves. Clearly visible from above, the tongue is raised about four meters above sea level at its highest points and creates three small saltwater lakes on its land side. The linguetta di sabbia provides an ideal home for a large variety of flora and fauna; indeed, it is now a Nature reserve. Magically, it is this sandbank that always looks like the silhouette of a woman praying (see fig. 7.4).

Fig. 7.4. Tongue of sand shaped like a woman, Tindari

## THE QUEEN OF SHEBA AND
## KING SOLOMON

Christian scriptures mention a Regina Austri (Queen of the South) who "came from the uttermost parts of the Earth," the extremities of the then known Christian world, to hear the wisdom of Solomon (Matthew 12:42; Luke 11:31).

The mystical interpretation of the Canticles or Song of Solomon makes its first appearance in Origen, who wrote a voluminous commentary in which he identified the bride of the Canticles with the Queen of the South of the Gospels—that is, the Queen of Sheba, who is assumed to have been Ethiopian. Others have suggested that the marriage of Solomon was either to the pharaoh's daughter or to an Israelite woman, the Shulamite. The bride of the Canticles is assumed to have been black due to the passage in Cant. 1:5 that translates as "I am very dark, but comely," while the New Revised Standard Version (1989) reads, "I am black and beautiful." During the Middle Ages,

Christians sometimes identified the Queen of Sheba with the prophetess the Cumaean Sibyl.

## STELLA MARIS: MOTHER OF WATERS, APHRODITE, AND THE MADONNA OF THE SEA

That first journey to Tindari in 1988 was my first experience of connecting deeply with the Black Madonna who comes from the sea and is sovereign of both the sea and the mountain above. I remember how transformational that revelation was. As we bathed in the lakes and then the sea, we felt Her true power in the primordial waters where life begins.

I was determined to learn more and find more Madonnas of the Sea, knowing that there must have been a connection to the goddesses Aphrodite and Venus. Sicily did indeed have a strong cult of Venus Erician, from Erice near Trapani, where her temple is still standing in the midst of the beautiful landscape on a hill overlooking the sea.

Back in 1988, as we continued down to the island of Pantelleria, Elisa and I immediately found another Black Madonna, la Madonna della Margana. That was only the beginning, as in truth there are hundreds, possibly thousands, all around the world.

When we got to the beautiful black volcanic island of Pantelleria, I felt a strong urge to begin writing scenes for *The Voyage of the Black Madonna*. I will never forget lying on top of the rounded white roof of a *dammuso*—a special dwelling, a roundhouse, similar to the adobes in New Mexico typical of Pantelleria, constructed from locally quarried stone—writing the first scenes of the show, sometimes even under the stars, feeling the power of the ocean coming right at me.

Seeing such a black island I instantly felt the presence of a Black Madonna, but our host, Roberto, who was very skeptical and an atheist, said that I was crazy and that I now saw Black Madonnas everywhere. He had been coming to the island for fifty years and had never seen one. I asked his maid and his house caretaker, who were locals, and they confirmed: "Yes, of course, we also have a beautiful Black Madonna here, the Madonna of the Margana. You must see Her. She is very ancient!" Roberto looked at me in astonishment, and in an apologetic way he told me that he would drive me there, since, as an architect, he also was curious about the church's history and architectural style.

We went across the island to an incredible place overlooking the sea in the middle of a field surrounded by vegetation and volcanic rocks. It is a small church, believed to have been rebuilt in the year 1123 by the Norman king Ruggero as a Basilian monastery. We walked into the church, and there She was: a painting of a beautiful, sensual, sweetly smiling Mother Mary wearing a red tunic and a dark-blue cape with golden stars. With Her right breast out of Her tunic, She feeds Her small Baby Jesus, who wears a simple brown tunic. This style of representation is known as Madonna Galaktotrophousa or, in Italian, Madonna Lattante (Madonna Breastfeeding). Their faces are brown and lighter on one side. The Madonna's hands are very dark. As in the biblical texts, Her milk is a symbol of incarnation, birth, fertility, freedom, wellness, hope, and love.

She is a nurturing dark Madonna, in the style of the ancient Byzantine icons. We were all touched by this beautiful and unique image of the Mother of God, even my atheist friend Roberto, who loved the art and style of the early Romanesque church, supposedly built in the year 551, when the Berbers from Algeria lived there.

On the back of the painting is an inscription: "This sacred image was painted in the year 852 and restored in the year 1732 to bring the old image back to its original splendor."

Once again, legend says that this dark icon was carried (in a box) on a ship coming from Egypt, Palestine, or Turkey and was thrown into the sea. She was probably found by fishermen, who took Her to the mountain to protect Her from destruction by the iconoclasts or by Arab invaders. She was carried by a donkey who suddenly decided to stop in a large field and refused to move, in a place known as Margana, from the Arabic word *marg* (fertile soil). Thus She became known as the protector of agricultural life as well as the sea.

Another legend says that one October the painting magically

Fig. 7.5. Madonna Lattante;
photo by A. Belloni

moved from the small church of Margana into the main church of Pantelleria. Six months later, the painting mysteriously went back to the Margana.

Still today, the islanders celebrate the Madonna of the Sea with two processions going up the mountain and down into the town (a common feature of the celebrations of many Black Madonnas, as I will explain later, connected to the myth of Persephone and Demeter). During the processions, people carry offerings of wheat and bread as a sign of gratitude for the abundance received from the Great Mother. The fishermen thank Her with the sign of the cross when they go out to sea and pray for Her protection from high above, overlooking the sea, singing a folk ballad, and praying in Her honor in the Sicilian dialect.

I later found out that, like other Black Madonnas, this one also has a deep esoteric meaning connected to the beginning of life itself, which is officially denied by the Catholic Church. Pantelleria was a sacred place of the cult of the black goddess Tanit, worshipped as the goddess of fertility and the earth by the Berbers, Phoenicians, and Carthaginians, with a strong connection also to Egypt and the Sumerians.

The revelation of a goddess as ancient as Tanit, popular all over the Mediterranean and North Africa, came as a surprise to me, triggering more curiosity and a desire to dig into the past and find as many connections to Africa as possible. Being so close to the spectacular Mediterranean Sea, in the midst of black volcanic rocks and forty miles from Tunisia, I felt again a strong sense of the revelation that God is a woman, and She is black. She is also the beginning of life, the primordial waters. And so I began writing my opera by opening with the first Black Madonna, la Madonna del Tindari, and Her African origins.

## SWIMMING
## IN THE ARMS OF APHRODITE

Until that time, I had been afraid of swimming in deep water and did not know how to snorkel or dive. Yet on one of the boat trips in Pantelleria, I felt protected by both the Mother of Waters and Mother Earth and conquered my fear of deep water.

I was astonished by the beauty under the deep blue sea! Swimming in these clear waters surrounded by colorful fish, I even heard sounds and thought that there were mermaids chanting somewhere deep under those black rocks rich with obsidian.

I knew that these sounds would eventually become songs, dedicated to Aphrodite, goddess of love and the sea. Later I went back to Pantelleria with Dario for our honeymoon, and I have beautiful memories of us making love in those deep blue waters, blessed by the power of Venus inside our bodies and hearts.

In my research I learned that all over Southern Italy during the summer there are countless Festa della Madonna del Mare, feasts of the Madonna of the Sea, some in honor of Black Madonnas and others in honor of white Madonnas.

Fig. 7.6. Madonna della Neve, Torre Annunziata, Naples;
photo by A. Belloni

## LA MADONNA DELLA NEVE:
## THE BLACK MADONNA OF TORRE ANNUNZIATA

This is one of my favorite feasts for its fervor and unique reenactment of the finding of the Black Madonna. I have been going to this procession for the past five years with the pilgrimage that I lead from the United States, and every time I feel more accepted and part of the local devotion.

The name, Our Lady of the Snow, is related to the Black Madonna della Neve in Santa Maria Maggiore, in Rome, right near where I was born. As a child I used pray to Her with my mother. As mentioned in chapter 1, this Madonna appeared in a dream to a wealthy patrician couple who, in a sign of gratitude and devotion, built a church in Her honor on the Esquiline Hill. This basilica is now one of the most beautiful and important churches in Rome, expanded in the year 431 CE after the Council of Ephesus.

I began my research in Torre Annunziata, thanks to the suggestion of one of my group's singers, Giuseppe de Falco, who comes from this village and introduced me to this beautiful devotion. There in the Sanctuary of Maria Santissima della Neve, a dark terracotta Greek-type image of Our Lady of the Snow is greatly venerated. Fishermen found it while at sea, near the Rovigliano rock, on August 5, 1357, and it was given the name of Santa Maria ad Nives because She was found on the same day as the Madonna della Neve in Rome.

Following a tradition that is more than five hundred years old, the great procession in Torre Annunziata starts from the church where fishermen bring a replica of the original Madonna in a box that is carefully locked and carry it to the harbor. There the box is taken out to sea on a boat, followed by the whole town, and thrown into the sea so that the fishermen can reenact the original finding of the box with the Madonna in a breath-taking simulation of the original miraculous discovery. Hundreds of people gather on the beach at dusk to watch the fishermen bring the box ashore and open it to find the stunning icon. They then reenact the fight over the icon between the people of Castellammare di Stabia and Torre Annunziata, all dressed in early Renaissance costume. At the end a judge proclaims that la Madonna Nera must stay in Torre Annunziata, and the beautiful painting is taken out on a stage on the beach, where all the devotees get a chance to ask for grace, touching Her beautiful face with the traditional white handkerchief.

I have been part of this ceremony now for years, and every time when the Neapolitan singer begins his prayer and Ave Maria, I lose control of my emotions, begin to cry, and often feel my mother's spirit next to me, as she loved the Ave Maria. After their prayers, I often guide the pilgrims who come with me from America in singing the medieval hymn *Cuncti Simus Concanentes* as we watch the fishermen take the icon back on the boat to the harbor, followed in a procession by hundreds of boats saying good-bye to the Blessed Mother of Waters. The feast ends with a Holy Mass in the square and fantastic fireworks.

Fig. 7.7. The Black Madonna of Positano;
photo by A. Belloni

## THE BLACK MADONNA OF POSITANO

Positano is probably the most exquisite small town on the Amalfi Coast, now quite famous worldwide. I used to go there in the 1970s when it was mainly a hangout for film actors, directors, and hippies. It was more charming then, but it is still beautiful.

A town of blue-and-white painted buildings that are carved into the rock, Positano has a beautiful touch of Byzantine and Moorish architecture yet is still typically Neapolitan. The origins of the town are lost in the mists of time, and it is difficult to distinguish between history and legend. One of these myths tells us that Positano was founded by the Greek god Poseidon—like the Roman Neptune, the god of the sea—for the nymph Pasitea, whom he loved. The Romans built a rich patrician villa near the great beach, including a temple of Venus, today buried by gardens and by the church devoted to Our Lady of the Assumption, where we now find the beautiful Black Madonna.

The majestic dome of the basilica dominates the whole landscape like the Great Mother herself looking over the beach and the coast. The church still includes the remains of a beautiful Byzantine mosaic floor. In the center nave stands a large Byzantine icon of a Black Madonna and Child, painted in gold on cedar wood. Again the legend says that the Madonna arrived during a tempest at sea in the eleventh century and that when the boat was in the bay of Positano the fishermen heard the Blessed Mother say, *posa, posa* (meaning "stop" or "pause"), and they interpreted that to mean that it was Her will to remain in the beautiful coastal town, where She was welcomed as a divine sign of protection.

The Benedictine monks decided to build a temple for Her in the year 1159. When She magically disappeared and reappeared over a myrtle bush, they immediately chose that site as the location of the new church. Later, it was discovered that underneath the church were the remains of the Roman villa, which had been buried in lava from the eruption of Vesuvius, while its myrtle bush survived and continued to grow.

It is no surprise that myrtle is considered a symbol of feminine power and fertility all over the Mediterranean and is used in wedding ceremonies in honor of Aphrodite, the goddess of love. Even Pliny mentions the plant's aphrodisiac power, calling it *Myrtus coniugalis* (myrtle of the wedded). Among the Romans, Venus was portrayed with a myrtle branch, confirming the relationship of that ancient cult to the great Mother of Love.

The feast day of the enchanting Black Madonna is August 15, the Feast of the Assumption of Mary, said to have taken place in Ephesus, Turkey. The actual procession happens during the evening of August 14, when the Madonna is taken out on a boat, leading a procession of hundreds of other boats, following in devotion all the way to Praiano, where there is a rock formation known as Mother and Son and where a huge ceremony offering flowers to Her, to the sea, and to the shore takes place.

This beautiful flower ritual, usually using white and red roses, is also popular in other places during the Festa della Madonna del Mare (Feast of the Madonna of the Sea), such as in Brazil for the Feast of Yemanja or Nossa Senhora da Concepcao (Our Lady of the Conception). I personally love this ceremony and have made it one of the rituals that I often share with my students.

Every summer I take my group of pilgrims to Positano during my pilgrimage to the Black Madonnas. We usually walk down the steps from the top of the mountain all the way to the beach where the Black Madonna resides. The heat is a challenge, and by the time we get down to the beach, we all feel a great need to jump in the beautiful turquoise waters. I lead the group in an offering of white flowers to the goddess of the sea and love, following the Afro-Brazilian Yoruba tradition for Yemanja, so similar to our tradition for the Madonna of the Sea. Every year when we do this ritual on the beach, magical events happen that leave everyone in the group feeling blessed by Her, the Stella Maris (Star of the Sea).

The first year was especially beautiful. After each of us offered our seven white flowers, throwing them into the water, we then dove into the sea. Afterward, I played my tambourine and chanted a Brazilian song to the mermaid, which I had learned in Northeast Brazil. No one really knew what I was singing, but suddenly three beautiful young Neapolitan girls, resembling mermaids, dove into the water. As I sang, they danced sensually in the sea, repeatedly dove and surfaced, splashing among the white flowers floating on the water. They made circles and spirals in the sea, dancing as they held the flowers, all the while looking back at us with seductive smiles. They had no idea that, in Portuguese, I was singing about exactly what they were doing.

Afterward, we stopped at the church to thank the Black Madonna. When we came out of the church, I asked all my students to join me in a final round of tammorriata drumming for Her, as is traditionally done in Naples. Suddenly, I heard my name being called, and there were two Neapolitan folk musicians and percussionists I had not seen in many years who joined in the drumming, dancing, and singing, creating a spontaneously beautiful tammorriata ritual for the Black Madonna of Positano.

Another year while we were offering flowers during the ceremony at the beach, a woman came up to me and told me that she was also devoted to the Madonna and that she was a singer who specialized in prayers to the Madonna in churches. She offered to sing for us when we went to pay homage to the Blessed Mother. We entered the church in Positano in silence, and no one else was there. As we were praying and asking for grace, the woman began to sing for us in a beautiful voice. It was one of the best Ave Marias I have ever heard, and we all broke down in tears and thanked her. She said we only had to thank Maria, *la grande Madre di Dio* (the great Mother of God), who had sent her to bless us on our journey.

The influence of Goddess rituals is still felt all over Positano. The most important remaining archetype of the pagan religions in this area is indeed the Great Mother, the Divine Feminine as Mother Earth, the queen of the sky and the mermaid who comes from the sea, often worshipped in caves along the coast. Inside these caves and the grottoes of Mother Earth, men have long searched for connection with the cosmic vital life forces.

## THE ERICIAN VENUS

The beautiful Sicilian town of Erice has had a huge influence on Sicilian history due to the strong devotion and worship practiced at the sacred *themons,* or temple, the open-air sanctuaries dedicated to the Greek Aphrodite and the Roman Venus, goddesses of love, sacred sensuality and sexuality, the sea, and fertility. This stunning location on the hills overlooking the turquoise sea and white beaches near the city of Trapani attracted ancient populations from all over the Mediterranean. Historians have found that before Venus, Potnia was worshipped there by the Elymians, the inhabitants of this flourishing site, before the arrival of the Greeks and Romans. According to legend, the city of Erice (or Eryx) was founded by Diodorus Siculus—son of Bute and the goddess Aphrodite—who built a temple there to his mother. In this sacred temple, sailors who came ashore would come to be united in sacred love-making with the *jerodulai,* priestesses of the temples regarded as sacred prostitutes who offered themselves to the sailors (and at times warriors) to share sensuality and passion. Virgil says that Aeneas, another son of Venus (Aphrodite), buried his father, Anchises, in this area before traveling to Lazio.

This cult and temple to the goddess of fertility and love dates back to the seventh or eighth century BCE, according to numerous inscriptions. The sanctuary became very well known across the Mediterranean, and in the third century BCE, the cult of Venus of Erice was brought to Rome, where two temples were built in Her honor.

It is fascinating that Christianity absorbed this name and this devotion into the cult of Santa Venere, and to my amazement I found a little temple of Santa Venere (looking exactly like Venus) in Sicily, right at the bottom of the mountain where my friends own the beautiful and magical Parco Jalari. It clearly proves that Sicily is truly the island of the Great Goddess and makes us feel protected by the sacred love and sensuality of the Divine Feminine.

## THE AFRO-BRAZILIAN RITES OF YEMANJA AND APHRODITE

I have been immensely inspired both artistically and spiritually by the ancient tradition of honoring the mother of waters with long processions in the sea, on boats, chanting, throwing flowers, and praying for Her continued protection and the renewal of life.

There is a beautiful and powerful ceremony celebrated in Brazil every year that my friend Elisa filmed for her first documentary. We both felt that there was a clear and strong connection between our Southern Italian culture and that of the African Yoruba, originally from Nigeria, which traveled to the New World during the horrifying times of slavery.

Yet most Italians who live in America are not aware of our African origins and our similarity in musical, drumming, and religious traditions. I strongly believe that this ignorance is why terrible racism has developed in the United States, and part of my mission with this book and with my performances is to make people aware of how we are all related and how many sacred rituals began in Africa.

I have been lucky to live in New York, where I have had firsthand experiences of the drumming ceremonies for the orishas, the spirits or gods of the Yoruba tradition, by participating in some tamborras led by Cuban and Puerto Rican *santeros* in Queens and the Bronx and by dancing the rumba in Central Park. I am very thankful to my friend and colleague Joseph Giannini, a musician known as Gypsy Joe, who has shone a light onto this otherwise unknown world for me. I began participating in these ceremonies in the late 1980s, discovering that because I was baptized in the Tiber, I am indeed a daughter of Ochun, who is the goddess of love and sweet waters, rivers, lakes, and dance, and is the sister of Yemanja, the mother of waters, our Aphrodite.

I dreamed that one day I would be able to go to Brazil for the amazing ceremony they hold for Yemanja every year on February 2. This dream came true in 2011, thanks to the fact that I had become well known as a percussionist and singer in the beautiful, magical land of Brazil.

In 1998, I had the immense fortune of being invited to one of Brazil's largest percussion festivals, Panorama Percussivo Mundial, mostly known as PERC PAN in Salvador, Bahia, which changed my life completely. I met many wonderful artists there who became my friends and collaborators, giving me great new inspirations: Siba, a well-known singer and composer from Recife; Helder Vasconcellos, a singer, actor, and dancer; and many others. I had the honor of sharing the stage with many more musicians, under the direction of legendary songwriter Gilberto Gil, the late master percussionist Nana Vasconcellos, and composer Hermeto Pascal. I was bewitched by their high level of artistry and talent and by how they welcomed me.

When I arrived, I did not speak a word of Portuguese. The producer, a beautiful girl named Veronica, welcomed me in English and asked me how I wanted to spend my first day in Bahia and in Brazil. I asked to be taken to the famous Yemanja shrine on the beach, as well as the church of Nossa Senhora da Concepcao. Veronica was very happy to know that I was interested in learning about their Afro-Brazilian culture and introduced me to two beautiful young black men who spoke perfect Italian because they had lived in Rome as accomplished musicians and who took me to this special place in Salvador. They told me that they were initiated in the Afro-Brazilian religion of Candomblé, and they knew the place very well. I was instantly taken by a feeling of being closer to Africa than I had ever been, with such a huge black population who still practiced African rituals.

The shrine and Nossa Senhora da Concepcao were beautiful and very familiar to me. I realized that they were almost identical to the church of la Madonna dell'Isola in Tropea, which is found on the rocks going down into the sea. Our statues of Mary and theirs are almost identical; the Madonnas have beautiful long dark hair and wear long white dresses and blue capes representing the sea and the foam of the ocean. In Salvador, though, what is most shocking and extremely powerful is that next to the Catholic Mary, Mother of Waters, is the African orisha, the sensual stunning Yemanja, the Mermaid. She is usually depicted with white skin, even though originally in Africa she was black. With her beautiful long black hair floating in the wind, wearing a very light, nearly transparent long white dress that floats as she stands on the waves of the ocean, Yemanja comes out of the sea foam like the myth of Aphrodite. She wears a beautiful headpiece, usually gold with a gold shining star on her head—the Stella Maris, Star of the Sea—and has her arms wide open as if to embrace us all with her love and sensuality. Beautiful shining stars come out of the palm of her hands as she stands proudly on a crescent moon (a symbol of many Black Madonnas) representing the Cosmic Mother from whom we all come. (See la Madonna di Loreto, Patron of Italy, page 109.) I was so happy to finally see her—the gigantic statue right in front of my eyes—that I began to weep, making my new friends cry along with me. I learned right then that Brazilians, including the men, are not afraid to show their emotions and that they can cry in public just like us Italians, especially out of devotion to the Madonna and the orishas.

My new friends guided me down to the beach to make my offering of seven white roses, counting seven waves, a ritual that I had actually learned long before with Dario, who was himself a son of Yemanja. I made a vow to return one day to celebrate Her feast day, February 2, and to go deep into the Afro-Brazilian culture to see their authentic drumming and dances.

And so I did. I began working, performing, and teaching regularly in Brazil over the next twelve years. Over the years, I have learned Portuguese and had many wild adventures—more dangerous at times than the ones I've had in Southern Italy, which I now see were only a warm-up for what was to come next.

All of this culminated in one of my most unforgettable experiences, my participation in the Feast of Yemanja in Salvador, Bahia, on February 2, 2011. I had just finished a week of teaching and performing in a resort north of Salvador and decided to stay for this feast that I had dreamed about for such a long time.

I went that morning with my good friend Veronica, producer of the first festival, all dressed in white and blue according to tradition. I brought my special tambourine painted with the image of Yemanja, and wherever I went, this became the key to my being welcomed in the circles of the priestesses, or *mães de santos* (head priestesses in Candomblé). I was shocked to see how the whole city had stopped: no one was working. The whole of Salvador was dressed in white and blue, going to pay homage to the goddess of love and the sea, with roses and praying for miracles. Thousands and thousands of people were constantly going down to the beach, first into the church to pray and light candles, then to the boats of fishermen who were taking the roses out into the ocean to where the boat with the statue of Yemanja was floating, blessing the entire coast.

All this happened to the powerful sounds of drums, *checkeres* (shakers), and loud voices singing at each *terrero*, a special shrine of Candomblé, each for a specific orisha or god. In this case, everyone

Fig. 7.8. Painting of Yemanja Ii given to Alessandra Belloni
in exchange for her drum.

was honoring only her, Yemanja, the *mãe das águas* (mother of waters).

I am glad that I had already been part of these ceremonies in New York; otherwise it would have been overwhelming to watch so many people going into a collective trance at once. Out of fifty dancers, at least twenty-five collapsed onto the sand, falling on their backs, rolling, screaming, their heads in rhythmic motion, eyes rolled back and saliva coming out of their mouths. They were in ecstasy, having visions of the saint who possessed them, and yet they kept dancing for at least twenty hours in the heat, along with everyone else on the beach.

It was an ocean of beautiful black bodies, dressed in white and blue, all moving in synchrony, all chanting to the goddess of love, freely expressing their sexuality. I was one of the few lighter-skinned people on the beach, even though all the white people in Salvador also came there to be part of the ceremony. I was astonished and extremely honored when a few people came up to me, touched my face gently, and bowed saying, *"Axé"* (a Yoruba blessing meaning "life force" or "energy") and *"Voce parece Yemanja, muito parecida a Ela! Obrigada para sua presença aqui!"* (You look like Yemanja, very similar to her! Thank you for your presence here!) I was so touched.

I went into the sea, bringing my flowers to offer to the fishermen on the boats. I thanked them and prayed to Her, the beginning of all life, where we all come from, to protect us all and to keep the flow of the waves and the tides together with the moon, caressing our Mother Earth. I prayed for Her, hoping that people on this planet would stop polluting Her and hurting Her. Otherwise, we will not survive.

## ❊ Chant and Ritual in Honor of Yemanja from Bahia, Brazil

I want to share with you the traditional chant for Yemanja as it has been done for hundreds of years in Brazil, with roots in Nigeria and Benin. I learned it before I even went to Brazil, as it has been performed for more than twenty-five years at the Cathedral of Saint John the Divine by the wonderful musician, composer, and artist-in-residence Paul Winter. He was the first to bring this sweet melody to the United States in the late 1970s, and later it became the closing song of the annual Feast of Saint Francis at the cathedral. Here we, the performers, form a procession to honor the mother of waters, the beginning of life, following the animals that have been blessed at the high altar, and onto the New York City streets, with several thousand people watching and dancing along. It is a spectacular and meaningful event.

The chant is simple and uses the voice with open sounds on vowels. The melody is joyous, and the rhythm is samba. You will find the melodic notation and lyrics in the appendix to chapter 7, page 363.

- First, you must set the intention before you begin: to acknowledge your own blessings and thank Her, the mother of waters, for all you have, and to ask Her, the goddess of love and the sea, for something very dear to you, such as your own healing, a miracle of love, or a new beginning in your work or life.

- You must dress in white and blue, bring seven white flowers (roses are the traditional flowers for Yemanja and the Madonna of the Sea) and go to a beach that is not crowded, where you will begin to offer your prayer in silence and meditation with your feet in the water.
- Afterward, count seven waves as you throw one flower at a time on each wave and watch Yemanja take your offering out into the sea. The waves represent the essence of love, giving, and receiving; as they come in they represent giving, as they go out they represent receiving.
- When you finish the ritual, you can chant as you walk backward, without turning, your back to the sea, or else Yemanja will not accept your offering and will not grant you grace.

## HISTORY OF YEMANJA

Yemoja or Yemanja is a major water deity from the Yoruba religion, which originated in Nigeria. She is an orisha, the mother of all orishas, having given birth to the fourteen Yoruba gods and goddesses. She is often syncretized with either the Black Madonna or Our Lady of Regla in the Afro-Cuban tradition (including Puerto Rico) of Santeria and the Afro-Brazilian religions of Candomblé and Umbanda. Yemanja is motherly and strongly protective and cares deeply for all her children, comforting them and taking away their sorrow. Yemanja is often depicted as a mermaid and is associated with the moon, water, and feminine mysteries. She is the protector of women: curing infertility, protection during childbirth, supporting parenting, and in general nurturing humankind with love and healing. She oversees deep secrets and the collective unconscious. According to myth, when her waters broke, it caused a great flood, creating rivers and streams, and the first mortal humans were created from her womb.

# CHAPTER 8

# The Black Madonna of the Sacred Mountain of Viggiano and the Greek Myth of Demeter and Persephone

*O our Lady of Grace, the one who carries grace in Her*
  *arms,*
*I come to you to receive your grace*
*O Mary grant us this grace*
*As God created you*
*He made you Mother of God,*
*Please Grant us this grace, O Mary.*

Traditional prayer and devotional
Tarantella titled "Madonna delle Grazie,"
from the regions of Campania and Basilicata

## THE BLACK MADONNA OF
## THE SACRED MOUNTAIN OF VIGGIANO

My passionate research on the history and legends of the Black Madonna grew stronger and stronger, and it led me to more travels to different sites in several regions of Southern Italy seeking the mysterious Black Madonnas. I fell madly in love with the land of Magna Grecia, where sanctuaries were built near temples of the ancient goddesses, surrounded by giant trees, sacred mountains, crystal-clear lakes, rivers, turquoise sea, and the dark fertile soil. I was bewitched by the beauty and majesty of Mother Nature. Sometimes you could breathe in the strong smell of earth and pasture, and I found it very erotic.

Over the years, Dario and I would drive for endless hours along narrow and often unpaved roads, where usually there were no street signs, following up on book research we had done and at times just following stories we heard from local peasants and farmers and listening to our intuition. This meant that we often got lost, and in some remote deserted places where no outsiders would go, we felt quite scared, especially if it was not a feast day. Many times I felt as if I were a character in *Christ Stopped at Eboli*—the book written by the Italian-Jewish writer Carlo Levi, published in 1945, about his exile in the remote region of Basilicata during fascism.

We often wondered if the Black Madonna was testing us. Indeed She was—She was leading us on a sacred path of initiation and sacrifices. I want to share some of those mystical experiences of being lost during our quest for the Seven Sisters, beginning with the tiny region of Basilicata between Calabria and Campania. Here, the high mountains are stunning and unspoiled, surrounded by rich vegetation, rivers, canyons, and waterfalls.

In 1990, the first time Dario and I decided to go to Basilicata (also known as Lucania), we were leaving the fragmented coast south of Salerno in Campania, coming from another spectacular Feast of the Madonna of the Sea in Agropoli on my birthday, July 24. Here, this white Madonna is very similar to Yemanja in Brazil, with a huge feast attracting thousands of people, including hundreds who follow on boats behind a ship carrying the Madonna. Dario and I had the most romantic time together, staying at a beautiful hotel by the sea and honoring the goddess of love and eros. He showered me with beautiful gifts of jewelry and special clothes, which he gave me when we were on the terrace at night watching the sea, the moon, and the fireworks, making this a birthday that I shall never forget. From Agropoli we went to the famous Greek and Roman archaeological site Paestum, where there is a giant, breathtaking temple dedicated to the Greek goddess Athena. There at sunset, in the heat of the deserted site, we walked behind the timeless stones and made passionate love, thus remembering the ancient sacred rites of the vestals, the priestesses of the goddess Venus of Erice.

Inebriated by the sensuality in the air, we decided to leave the coast and venture toward the tiny and isolated region of Basilicata, knowing that somewhere in those mountains was one of the most important Black Madonnas, la Madonna del Sacro Monte di Viggiano (the Madonna of the Sacred Mountain of Viggiano). Unfortunately, Dario insisted on driving even though he had a terrible sense of direction, made worse by the large amounts of what he always called "the elixir of Dionysus" that he had drunk. We ended up getting lost for hours, leaving behind the highway (the infamous Salerno-Reggio) to go up the narrow roads ascending the mountains on the border between Campania and Basilicata. Suddenly we were surrounded by fog, and the road began to descend. We could see the mountains all around us and had no idea how we had ended up at the bottom. We had left in the morning, and now it was late afternoon. No one was around until, out of nowhere, an old man appeared, sweeping the road with a broom that looked like one used by witches.

All I knew about Basilicata was from the book on magic and witchcraft by the famous ethnomusicologist and anthropologist Ernesto De Martino titled *Sud e magia* (The South and Magic). In this enlightening book, De Martino describes in great detail the powerful witchcraft traditions of this region, white magic spells, and the various traditions of the Evil Eye. I remember being frightened by the photos of the *megere* (sorceress), *streghe* (witches), and *stregoni* (witch doctors) and always felt that if I ever went to Basilicata I would have to have strong protection to avoid the Evil Eye. And then there I was, in the middle of a deserted road surrounded by high mountains, lost in the fog, with a weird "apparition" of an old man who looked like he had stepped out of the pages of De Martino's book to greet and welcome us to his remote land— ancient Lucania! He signaled us to stop as he swept away dust and dirt. (For what? I still wonder.) He smiled at us and looked benevolent not malicious. He said in dialect, *"Siete persi fanciulli?"* (Are you lost, kids?) "Ah-ha, ha, ha!" he laughed. We stared at each other and suddenly felt protected instead of scared and began laughing with him. "What the hell is a couple like you doing here, on this dusty road at this hour in the summer?" he asked. "Why are you not at the beach?"

"We just left the beach, a few hours ago," we replied. Then he nodded and said, "Ah, I know, you must be looking for *Her*, right?" And he pointed up high, straight ahead of us. *"Eh si, la Madonna Nera del Sacro Monte di Viggiano, chi passa di qua deve per forza andare da lei! La nostra Signora."* (Ah yes, whoever comes this way most certainly must be going to see Her, Our Lady.)

In amazement we said, "Yes, I guess you must know why we are here . . . lost in the fog and on this road."

As we got out of the car, he kindly came closer and explained the way to those mountains, saying that our little Fiat needed a miracle to make it up there. He was dressed like a peasant-shepherd, had white hair and blue eyes, and was tanned dark brown from the sun. He went on to say, "You know, She is one of the Seven Sisters." Dario and I almost fainted out of surprise, and the old man told the legend as we knew it: "They are all sisters, these Black Madonnas, and this one is the most beautiful. Hiding very high up on the sacred mountain, for such a long long time, so you have to work very hard to find Her and prove your faith and devotion to Her. She will make you get lost as a test, and only if you are worthy shall you find Her! *Ciao, buona fortuna, ca Maronna v'accumpagna!"* (Good luck, may the Madonna go with you!) He waved, helped us back into the car, closed the car doors, took his broom, walked away into the fog—and vanished! Dario and I looked at each other in disbelief, but after our miracle of the star in Moiano with Our Lady of Freedom, we knew there was no explanation: it just was.

Speechless, we started the car and followed the old man's directions, which I had written down, and began our journey up the Sacred Mountain of Viggiano. The road became narrower and steeper as we drove slowly up the winding path. The two-hour journey seemed endless, especially because we could not see the top of the mountain all the time: it was frequently shrouded in fog.

Fig. 8.1. Statue of la Madonna di Viggiano inside the church;
photo by A. Belloni

The scenery around us was spectacular, reminding me of the unspoiled mountains and Indian reservations I had seen in the American Southwest. I felt the similarity and connection between the Southern Italian indigenous people and the Native Americans. The vegetation was rich, with huge beech and oak trees, the air clean and fresh and getting cooler as we went up.

I had read that one of the majestic mountain chains in that area was called La Maddalena and wondered if they were indeed connected to the legends of Mary Magdalene, being such a mystical place.

No one told us, not even the old man, that the ride up the mountain was nine kilometers. We knew that at some point we had to park and walk the rest of the way up the mountain on foot, but no one told us it was almost two kilometers of very steep stone path (see fig. 8.2).

We parked our car and looked around. To this day, I wonder why no one else was there. Remembering the words of the ghostly old man, we realized that we had to make a sacrifice to prove to the Black Madonna that we really wanted to see Her and be with Her in this natural paradise. We had left the lowland heat behind, and the air got colder with a sharp wind as we began our pilgrimage on foot up the Sacro Monte. The mystical fog surrounded us again as we went up the winding path into the clouds, not knowing how long it would take. Every time we thought we had reached the top at the end of a curve, we saw another curve and then another, until finally the white stone path became straight, and there it was: a tiny church, more like a small chapel, built on the summit of this high mountain where we knew we would find Her, the Queen of Lucania, the Black Madonna of Viggiano. We had suddenly reached what seemed to be Shangri-la. It was the most peaceful setting, completely still but with an immense and indescribable energy in the air. We were not the least bit tired from the steep climb. Overwhelmed with emotion, Dario and I somberly entered the tiny church that reminded us of a refuge for pilgrims.

And there She was, sitting on a small throne, an amazing vision of gold in front of a dark-red background. In the presence of Her regality, we were dazzled, almost blinded in the darkness of the small chapel by

Fig. 8.2. Stone trail leading up the Sacred Mountain of Viggiano;
photo by A. Belloni

this large, majestic, beautiful, smiling Black Madonna with curly blond hair, benevolent hazel eyes, and perfect features, beaming rays of love and compassion. The statue is carved from olive wood and is covered with *real* solid gold—shining like the sun itself.

I felt breathless at this vision at first; even though I had seen Her images in books, I never expected so much regality and perfect beauty. She wore a gold crown with intricate designs and twelve stars and a gold and silver flowing cape over a gold tunic. On Her lap sat Her son Jesus, a sweet, smiling, dark-skinned child wearing a gold crown. He made a sign of peace to the world with His right hand and held a small globe in His left, while Mother Mary balanced a shining globe of the world in Her right palm. Their peaceful expressions were reassuring, protective, and welcoming. Suspended above them inside the wooden niche were two small golden angels, like cherubs, almost dancing in heaven above the Holy Mother and Child, who appeared even more radiant against the blood-red drape embroidered with golden stars (see plate 14). This was a real vision of heaven after climbing two kilometers to the top of the mountain!

I was at first overcome by many emotions, crying and smiling at the same time, yet as I knelt in prayer by the royal Black Madonna, I felt deeply at peace and very grateful to be so close to Her. In complete awe before the huge black statue, I wondered why Her hair was blond and why Her face looked so familiar. I had seen Her face in the books I had collected. I knew that She had been worshipped in this same place since early Christianity and was one of the oldest statues of the Black Madonna to be found anywhere.

I continued to pray in silence and asked Her to reveal to us why She had been hiding up here for all those centuries. I knew that Her following was strong and spread out all over the nearby regions of Calabria, Basilicata, and Campania. Yet on that day we were there all alone with Her. We felt privileged to have a private audience with the Black Madonna, similar to the one we had had in Moiano with Brunettella. Once again, I had the feeling that She was smiling at us somewhat in complicity and saying, "Now that you found Me, you must come for the feast in My honor." We promised that we would come back on Her feast day in September. After kissing Her feet, we left the chapel walking backward, with tears in our eyes, following the tradition of not turning our back on Her.

When we got outside, it was already dusk, and we had a long walk down the steep stone path. Our eyes were lost in the landscape, the spectacular view and the infinite horizon, turning purple as night approached. Again, the fog rose up, and we began our descent, which seemed to go faster at every curve in the road. We were walking down the mists of the sacred mountain, and I thought of *The Mists of Avalon*. I had just read the book by Marion Zimmer Bradley. In amazement, I suddenly understood the connection between the fog and mists and the Great Goddess. Just as in the mythical Avalon, here in Southern Italy the priestesses and priests initiated in the mysteries of the Great Goddess had to hide in Nature from the rest of civilization, to honor Her with sacred purification rituals, music, dance, and ecstasy. They could not be contaminated by the noninitiates, and the Great Goddess appeared only to them, protected by the fog. It was for their protection and Hers. We had to cross through it to be accepted by Her and show our devotion.

As we descended, the realization came to me in a flash: the Black Madonna of Viggiano is Demeter! That's why Her face seemed so familiar. I saw it clearly, like a vision.

Demeter is the goddess of the harvest, grains, and the fertility of the earth. She is the Olympian goddess of agriculture, grain, and bread who sustained humankind with Earth's richness and abundance. She presided over a mystery cult that promised its initiates the path to a blessed afterlife in the realm of Elysium. Demeter was depicted as a mature woman, often wearing a crown (like this Black Madonna) over long, curly blond hair, representing the golden wheat, and carrying a sheaf of wheat, or a cornucopia, and a torch. Demeter and Dionysus were worshipped at Eleusis, a little town near Athens. Their worship was referred to as the Eleusinian mysteries and spread through Southern Italy, then Magna Grecia.

I shared my vision of Demeter with Dario, who understood perfectly and agreed with me. We arrived back at our little Fiat, which we had now named the Madonnamobile, and it took us safely down to the bottom of the mountain to Val d'Agri (Agri Valley). We drove twelve kilometers to the outskirts of the town of Viggiano, where we found a little bed-and-breakfast to rest after our grueling climb up and down the mountain, both feeling immensely happy about our special visit with the Black Madonna.

We spent a couple of days there doing more research and enjoying the simple life of the locals. We visited the beautiful large church where the Madonna resides during the winter and bought a small statue of the Black Madonna and a book telling Her history.

## HISTORY OF THE TOWN OF VIGGIANO

The ancient Greek and Roman settlements on Sacro Monte were known as Grumentum and Venusian (from Venus). Probably the name Viggiano comes from the noble Roman family of Vibius, but others say that the name comes from the Greek word *ughinao,* meaning "a healthy place to settle." In a notary act from the year 774 CE, we find for the first time the name Bianum, Latin for Viggiano.

The initial location of the town was abandoned after the destruction of Grumentum by the Saracens in the year 878 CE. The valley became harsh and dangerous due to the invasions of the Arabs, the Byzantine domination, and later the invasions of the Lombards (Longobards)* and the Normans and the frequent flooding of the large rivers. And so the population found shelter high up in the mountains and in the thick forests.

The people found refuge in the existing monasteries and founded new ones, uniting landowners, soldiers, families of farmers, and religious people. Many brought with them icons and statues of Madonnas to save them from destruction during the iconoclastic wars. There were many Italo-Greek Basilian monks, even in the twelfth century, since Viggiano had a strong Byzantine connection and was part of the duchy or principality of Benevento. (Recall that I speak about Benevento and its Black Madonna, Our Lady of Freedom, in chapter 5.) Until the ninth century, we know that there were hermits known as the Rupi Rosse (Red Cliffs) of the ancient community of Saint Nicholas. They had an ascetic vocation, living in caves in contemplation, while the new settlements of Basilian monks took into

---

*Note that the actual name is Longobards. "The Lombards or Longobards (Latin: Langobardi; Italian: Longobardi [loŋgo'bardi]; Lombard: Longobard) were a Germanic people who ruled most of the Italian Peninsula from 568 to 774," historian Paul the Deacon wrote in the *Historia Langobardorum.*

consideration the great defensive possibilities of these locations, the favorable soil and climate, and the open attitude of the local people to the Christian religion. The Basilian monks developed the Christian teaching of Theotokos, the Mother of God, together with meditation and philosophy, and devoted great attention to the art of music. They built a rudimentary stringed instrument called a *sambuca*. Made with surprising creativity from pieces of cane from the sambuca tree with gut strings, it was similar to a small lyre. It seems clear that a great passion for music and the Madonna comes from this ancient tradition developed by the monks. Music became a crucial part of the lifestyle in Viggiano and the valley, persisting through all the periods of foreign domination by the Normans, Spanish, and French. During the flourishing of the Kingdom of Naples and the Two Sicilies, in the year 1734, Naples became a great economic power, and the arts played a strong role in this time of splendor. It was during this time that the most important Neapolitan theaters were founded, the San Carlo, Mercadante, Fiorentini, and the famous Teatro dell'Opera. Musicians and singers were paid very well, and the Viggianesi took advantage of this creative time to form orchestras similar to those in Naples, while some became traveling musicians playing the bagpipes, harp, violin, clarinet, and flute. During the eighteenth and nineteenth centuries, the small town of Viggiano was rich with woodworkers and instrument makers as well as performers.

We know from the early documentation that between the third and fourth centuries CE, the bust of this Black Madonna statue was found in a hole dug deep into the ground in the remains of a temple probably dedicated to the Greek goddess Demeter and the Roman goddess Ceres.

The veneration of this Madonna in Viggiano also echoes the myth of Demeter's daughter, Persephone, who disappears into the underworld at the beginning of winter and emerges into the light for spring and summer.

The devotion to the Black Madonna of Viggiano is still very strong today, and She is honored two times a year with colorful and powerful processions, which include chanting and great folk music, with the tarantella played by the shepherds on bagpipes and tambourines together

Fig. 8.3. Bagpipers processing down the Sacred Mountain of Viggiano
for the feast of the Black Madonna;
photo by A. Belloni

with local folk musicians. In early May the huge statue (two thousand pounds!) is carried all the way up the mountain from the church in the town of Viggiano, as if coming out from the underworld, celebrating spring, summer, and the blooming of the Earth. The Queen of Lucania, as She was named in the year 1890, stays in the small chapel on top of the sacred mountain until the first Sunday of September, when the devotees carry the heavy Black Madonna all the way back down to the valley and into the church in town, always followed by a procession of music and dance rituals.

## LEGEND AND HISTORY OF
## THE BLACK MADONNA OF VIGGIANO

I dove deep into my research about the history and legends of Viggiano and their Mary, Queen of Lucania, and found some rare books full of beautiful legends and intriguing history. One of the most fascinating books was *Lo Zodiaco di Maria* (The Zodiac of Mary), written in 1715 by Father Serafino Montorio, who had dedicated his life to the devotion of Mary and the symbolism of Her zodiac signs. In his painstaking study, he compares the twelve stars on the Madonna's crown with the twelve signs of the zodiac and the twelve regions of what was known then as the Kingdom of Naples and Sicily. He says that the Black Madonna of Viggiano represents the sign of Taurus.

He tells Her legend in a beautiful, poetic way.

There was once a very old city known as Marcelliano, right along the river Drumento, and up in the mountain there was a castle named for Janus, which was destroyed by invaders from the Orient. The people who survived built another town with a fort and a castle so strong that it could not be invaded, and they called it Viggiano. They lived in peace in the beginning of Christianity and in the year 304 AD, under the Catholic faith, with Pope Marcellus I. At that time the cruel Diocletian became the Byzantine emperor. He was a vicious persecutor of the Catholic faith and Christians. The province of Viggiano was in the region known as Campagna Felice, with the terrible Dragonzio as their governor. It is said that in only one month, 17,000 Christians were martyred.

In this difficult time of death and devastation, God sent a Divine Intervention and brought a miraculous treasure to the poor people who were afflicted by such great tragedies. During the month of July, as the shepherds went to herd their sheep high in the mountains, in the middle of the night, on the highest mountain of all, they saw a bright splendor and a flash of lightning. It seemed that a great fire was burning up toward the sky on the rocky mountaintop where there were no beech trees.

Frightened, the shepherds told the church authorities about this strange phenomenon, and they decided to go closer to the top to verify the event, as it seemed it was sent by heaven. Under the supervision of Father Omerio they agreed to climb all the way up where the light and fire seemed to be burning. When they got to the top they did not see fire, just a blinding light over a post in the earth. Both shepherds and church clergy began to dig in the dark soil, and as they dug a hole into the earth, to their amazement they found a dark wooden statue of the Blessed Mother, all shining and covered in gold that turned the sky into flames! Below Her there were many small idols, icons, and divinities made of metal, possibly of pagan origins.

Everyone felt the blessings of this miraculous finding of the statue of the Great Mother, and they began to build a small church on the high mountain, but they knew it would become very cold in the winter.

So before the winter came, they took the statue and with great care they carried the statue, descending the mountain all the way into the valley, to build a bigger church for Her in the town of Viggiano.

The Black Madonna then surprised everyone when, in May, She took flight high up into the sky, all the way to the top of the sacred mountain where She was initially found.

All the devotees followed Her there and continued building Her small chapel. They worshipped Her there until the first Sunday in September, when the Queen of Heaven showed Her power again and flew all the way down to the valley, to be venerated in the church built for Her in Viggiano.

All the townspeople and the clergy were now sure that She wanted to remain in the larger church, not in the small chapel so far up the mountain in the cold, when suddenly on the first Sunday in May, the Black Virgin showed Her will and power once more and flew back to the top of the sacred mountain.

Therefore, everyone realized that She wanted them to worship Her in both places, with a long and strenuous procession up and down the mountain to show their true devotion, thus receiving Her protection during wars, disease, and natural disasters.

Researchers say that the statue of the Black Madonna dates to between the second and fourth centuries CE and that originally they found only the head and upper torso. It was during the fourteenth and fifteenth centuries when Southern Italy was under Spanish domination that the statue was sculpted in its final form, adding the entire body and Baby Jesus. The Spanish king and queen commissioned the Catholic Church to cover the statue entirely in gold, following the model of the Black Madonna of Montserrat, as seen with Our Lady of the Poor and the Black Madonna del Tindari, of whom legend says, "They are all Sisters."

Our Lady of the Sacred Mountain of Viggiano, though, has a unique gaze that captures Her most ancient mystical origins as a Greek goddess, emanating sweetness and authority. When you are close to the statue, looking at Her intense gaze, you can feel the calling of the archaic Great Mother, Theotokos of the Greeks, and the enchantment of the primordial giver of life. Mary, Mother of Jesus, becomes a mystical pagan goddess in front of your eyes, unifying all faiths as a divinity that embodies the forces of Nature.

Another legend also tells us that the sanctuary was destroyed in the year 1050 by the Saracens and that the devotees brought the statue to the top of the mountain to hide Her in a hole in the ground, but this does not match the ancient accounts. According to the first written account, by Tomaso Bono Iurno, the sanctuary was rebuilt in the year 1393. Today, under the high altar, you can still see the hole in the dirt where the Madonna was found and where the mysterious fire and lightning originally appeared. Bono Iurno describes the beautiful statue and the sacred temple in the dioceses of Potenza and Marsico, Basilicata, as beautiful regal places of devotion dedicated to the Mother of God, Maria Santissima of the Sacred Mountain of Viggiano, the highest in the region. She was later, in 1890, proclaimed the Queen of the Region of Lucania.

Through the centuries this Black Virgin has granted many miracles to the population of the nearby regions of Basilicata, Campania, and Calabria. She has healed the sick and freed people possessed by demons or entities, restoring peace and happiness to their lives. Today the local people still describe how, during a procession, the carriers can feel the statue become suddenly very heavy, and they have to stop to put Her down. In those moments, if there is a person who is possessed by an evil spirit, he or she will go toward the statue, screaming and crying, and then in a trance will let go of the demon inside, receiving the miracle from the Black Madonna who liberates poor souls from such grief and anguish.

It is miraculous to see that the statue has never been altered by the climate and these hardcore processions. She still looks radiant in Her solemnity.

## DEVOTION AND PROCESSIONS TO THE MADONNA DEL SACRO MONTE DI VIGGIANO

This regal and solar Black Madonna has one of the strongest traditions of devotion. During the twelve- to fourteen-hour procession, groups of twelve men take turns carrying the heavy statue and at times fight for the privilege. They have eight places to stop and rest during the twelve kilometers of strenuous procession. The ritual is made even more powerful by a very intricate musical tradition.

As I mentioned, over the years devotion to the Madonna Nera di Viggiano has spread throughout the nearby regions. The pilgrims come on foot from far away, with women carrying incredible wax sculptures called *cinti* on their heads. Each group has a band of folk musicians playing the unique *zampogna,* Southern Italy's bagpipe, and the *ciaramella,* a double-reed instrument, together with tambourines and the *organetto,* or button accordion.

I had read about this special devotional folk music in books by ethnomusicologists Ernesto de Martino and Roberto Levi and heard the field recordings by American researcher Alan Lomax. The music sounded raw, timeless, North African, even Eastern Indian. I could never understand a word the people sang. It was a different dialect, actually a separate language, from an uncontaminated land protected by high mountains and wild Nature.

I was determined to go to that feast in Viggiano myself, especially after the surreal and life-changing visit to the Black Madonna, even though I admit that I was afraid I could not make the high climb for all those hours, since no cars even get close to the parking lot where we had parked that first time. The whole pilgrimage is on foot; no cars are allowed anywhere.

In 1991, Dario and I decided to honor our promise to the Madonna and went to Her feast on the first Sunday of September, which that year happened to be on my mother's birthday, September 4. I dedicated the pilgrimage to my mother and her health, praying that she would live a long time. Mamma Elvira had diabetes and was beginning to lose her sight, and I worried about her becoming blind. Thankfully, she kept her sight for another ten years.

We arrived the night before the feast and stayed at the same bed-and-breakfast on the outskirts of the town to avoid the chaos of the big festival. We got up at sunrise, knowing that since we were not able to make the entire climb, we had to meet the pilgrims halfway down the mountain. Hundreds of devotees had spent the night outside the chapel on the top of the mountain for what is called *la vigilia,* the vigil, playing music and singing all night long, drinking wine, and feasting on fantastic homegrown food.

We began walking toward the town center around 5:30 a.m., hoping to meet other pilgrims who would go up with us, so we would not feel like outsiders. I had my tamburello and was ready for anything.

To my astonishment, right by the center of the town at 6:00 a.m., I heard the familiar rhythm, drumming, and accordion melody of the tammorriata and ran in that direction to see a woman I knew from

Fig. 8.4. Old man with accordion dancing with a woman;
photo by A. Belloni

other feasts, the beautiful and wild Saturna, my tammorriata dance teacher. As you may recall, she was the one who initiated me in this powerful ceremonial dance. She was smiling at me with her toothless smile, still sensually moving her hips, and with her castanets inviting me to dance right away as if it were perfectly normal for us to both be there at 6:00 a.m. ready to party! She was with the other tammorriata player called O' Lione (the Lion), a strong and bold young albino man who was (and still is) the rival of my friend Raffaele Inserra, also an excellent player and drum maker.

Saturna and O' Lione were delighted to see me and signaled to start dancing the tammorriata right away in devotion to our beloved Blessed Mother, who had already begun Her descent from the high mountain, carried by the shepherds.

I was in ecstasy. How could I refuse such an unexpected invitation? I began to dance with Saturna to the melody played by a fabulous Gypsy player of the traditional diatonic organetto. Dario took out his camera and began to film the scene, which I still have. It is absolutely fantastic, as was the rest of that day, full of improvised dancing, drumming, and singing.

I remember at some point I mentioned that we should stop at a local café to get some breakfast before ascending the mountain, but instead of the usual cappuccino and croissant, Saturna offered us wine and *pane e salame* (bread and salami). She would not take no for an answer, and so there I was, becoming one of them: a peasant who gets up at sunrise, goes into Nature dancing, and eats the most powerful breakfast: wine, salami, cheese, and bread, all homemade and homegrown.

We danced our way to the place in the mountain, where we knew the other groups would stop, to find that the party and the tarantella feast were in full swing. Many circles of players and dancers formed, taking turns following the traditional style of *la ronda* (the circle) in devotion to the Madonna, with musicians on the outside and dancers inside.

It was then that, to my disbelief, I saw groups of older women balancing cinti on their heads—huge rectangular or circular sculptures that carried actual candles made of wax with intricate designs—each with a small statue of la Madonna di Viggiano in the center.

With great pride, they showed their devotion by dancing small intricate tarantella steps, making figure eights around each other. They were accompanied by tambourine players, including myself, singers, and a "hot" organetto player, who at the time was ninety-two years old. He began walking toward me while he played, nodding that he liked my tambourine playing and dancing around me, never missing a note.

That takes a lot of stamina for anyone—but at ninety-two? It was clear by watching the strength and energy of the players and the dancers with the cinti on their heads that these mountain people lived a very healthy life in harmony with Nature. They worked hard all their lives, every day from sunrise to sunset, but they had more energy than me. They had not slept all night, but they were tireless. I wondered if it was having wine and salami for breakfast that made them so strong. One of the women, proving my theory, invited me to carry a heavy cinto over my head. I accepted. She took a moment to help me, easily lifting it up and passing it to me to settle over my head. Wow! I could not believe the weight! I felt my head being squashed and was afraid of breaking my neck. I gestured to her after a short time (maybe a minute) that I could not keep it balanced and worried that it would fall and break. She smiled and shook her head. She knew that I was more afraid for myself than for her cinto.

The dance continued for at least another hour, and then we heard loud bagpipes and drums echoing from the mountain announcing that the procession was about to meet us. The excitement grew stronger, and we all marched up the stone path to meet the crowd and look for our beloved Black Madonna of the Sacred Mountain.

I still recall how breathtaking the moment was when She actually appeared. The big glittering gold statue was balanced on a tall wooden throne (see plate 15), creating a surreal effect as if it were coming down from heaven as it swayed sideways with the carriers making the difficult steep descent. She looked even happier and more joyous than the first time we saw Her, honored in all Her regality. Two bagpipers were leading the procession, followed by the clergy. I did not know that I was about to witness another magical event: they stopped to rest and put the statue down onto the earth and grass, and another group of devotees came, carrying a beautiful sun made of gold-painted wood with stylized rays mounted in a circle that fit perfectly around the Queen of Lucania.

We watched in amazement as "they dressed Her with the sun," as many prayers say. Everyone was crying and screaming, "Evviva Maria!" I followed the crowd as, one by one, we were motioned to get close to Her and touch Her through the glass, praying, holding a handkerchief, then touching our bodies in a quest for healing and guidance. Again, I felt that She had been waiting for me, greeting me as Her daughter, and I did not want to leave Her sight. I was drawn to the immense love and compassion I felt emanating from Her benevolent eyes. She was indeed alive.

I remembered the old man who magically appeared in the deserted road the first time we went to see Her up the mountain, when he wished us "*Ca Maronna V'accumpagna.*" (May the Madonna always be with you.) I prayed that She would always be with me.

The carriers finally shouted, "*Spalla!*" (Shoulders!), the sign to pick up the statue again, and the strong men lifted Her up, now even heavier surrounded by the wooden sculpture of the sun. We followed the majestic procession all the way down to the town, a few kilometers, to the rhythm of the tarantella alternating with the religious chants and bagpipes. As we entered the town, the official authorities appeared: the high monsignor, local priests, and other political leaders of the area, the mayor and city councilmen, all dressed up. They did the official prayers and rosary, ending the beautiful folk music of the real devotees—the peasants and shepherds. Dario and I looked at each other, nodding as we realized that none of these officials had taken part in the real ritual that honors the Madonna del Sacro Monte. They hadn't made the big physical sacrifice of climbing and descending the mountain, carrying weights, singing, playing, and dancing. They just showed up at the end, giving this ancient pagan ritual a blessing from the Catholic Church and celebrating the Holy Mass.

The procession ended with the crowd of devotees making the traditional *tre giri*—three turns around the church—a ritual observed in many feasts of the Black Madonnas. After such a powerful procession full of sounds, colors, images, and crowds, the celebration of the Holy Mass seemed out of sync. We stayed for a while but noticed that the peasants and shepherds were slowly beginning to leave. Their work was done; their devotion renewed. We followed the locals who were leaving after saluting the Madonna of the Sacred Mountain and leaving a flower or handkerchief at Her feet. We walked behind them, suddenly feeling very tired. We realized that it was past four o'clock in the afternoon. No wonder we were tired: we had been walking and processing since 5:30 in the morning! It was time to get some good rest at the bed-and-breakfast.

But once again we heard the familiar sounds of tammorras, castanets, and accordion, and we walked into another spontaneous round of tammorriata! O' Lione was there, keeping the persistent 4/4 beat, and this time the lead dancer was Lily, a beautiful young girl who

I had seen before at other rituals. She was eleven years old and an exceptionally sensual dancer for her age. She smiled at me while she was dancing with her grandfather, who moved aside and said to me, "Your turn!"

I could not believe it. Five minutes earlier I had felt so tired, ready to crash in bed at the hotel, and now suddenly I was on the spot again, asked to dance in the center of the circle. How could I refuse? Dario took out his camera again and filmed one more beautiful spontaneous magical dance moment. Around us the other players moved closer, and I noticed two funny old men: one was playing the erotic friction drum, the putipu, which I described earlier, and the other one, a very old man, had a green parakeet in an open cage. If you offered 200 lire, the bird would jump around and pick your fortune! The bird was trained in a very peculiar way: when the old man opened the cage and gave him a sign, the parakeet would jump into a small box and with his beak pick up a piece of rolled paper with a fortune inside and bring it to the old man who then gave it to the person who had paid 200 lire!

I had never seen that before, and it was very funny. He was with the Romani accordion player, and since the area has large communities of Romani, he may have been one himself.

I began to dance with young Lily, letting her lead me, following her gentle and smooth moves, our arms open as we circled around each other with our castanets. It was so different from dancing with the wild Saturna, yet equally sensual and liberating. When our dance came to an end and everyone applauded, Lily hugged me tight and asked me to come back every year to dance with her. That dance has a special place in my heart and so does Lily, who has stayed in touch with me for years and has expressed a desire to come to America, but sadly she never has.

I learned so much about these "dances of liberation": how you could let go of your sensuality dancing with another woman or with an eleven-year-old girl as a sign of devotion to the Great Mother, the Black Madonna, keeping alive the ancient tradition of the priestesses who were initiated in the mysteries. Did Saturna and Lily know this? Probably not consciously, but it did not matter, because they were continuing it and passing it on to women like me, who came from a different background. I was eager to learn these dances and pass them on to others, especially women—and later on, I did just that, helping women who came into my life in need of deep healing.

## INSPIRATIONAL MUSIC AND THE HARP OF VIGGIANO

The mystical journey to Viggiano became another great inspiration for my opera *The Voyage of the Black Madonna,* leading me to create new choreography for reenacting, on stage, the ritual in honor of Mary, Mother of God, coming out of the sun (which I describe in detail later). The image of the Black Madonna surrounded by the rays of the sun and blessing us with light became also an integral part of my healing workshops many years later.

Through my research I learned that Viggiano was famous for a specific type of harp, the *arpa viggianese,* a small portable instrument from the Renaissance and Baroque times. Street musicians who performed in the piazzas with violinists and singers carried this small folk harp on their shoulders. It was also frequently played by women. The players were all self-taught and played for the Novenas, during Christmas, and for the Madonna feasts. They were also travelers, and many eventually migrated to the United States, bringing the harp-making tradition with them. They were part of the first group of Southern Italian musicians who introduced Neapolitan songs to America. The folk harp became part of the musical arrangements made by John La Barbera for our opera, adding another dimension to the chants that he composed for each goddess: Isis, Diana, Cybele, Hecate, and Aphrodite.

## THE MYTH OF DEMETER AND PERSEPHONE

The processions in honor of the Black Madonna of Viggiano and Her stunning resemblance to the goddess Demeter have a deep connection

Fig. 8.5. The goddess Demeter in a museum in Sicily;
photo by D. Bollini

to the myth of Demeter (or Ceres in Latin) and her virgin daughter, Persephone (Proserpina), who was abducted by the god of the underworld, Hades (Pluto). The legend says that the abduction happened in Sicily, in the center of the island, by Lake Pergusa near Enna. The spot assigned by local tradition as the scene of this event was surrounded by lofty and precipitous hills. The meadows abound in flowers, and a nearby cavern or grotto was believed to be where the king of hell suddenly emerged. This lake was called Pergus by Ovid and Claudian. Demeter, deeply grieving and carrying a torch in one hand, endlessly searched for her beloved daughter. She made the seasons halt, and all plants, fruits, and trees stopped growing and died. It was Hecate, the goddess of the crossroads, underworld, and moon, who finally told Demeter that her daughter had been kidnapped by Hades.

At this point, Zeus (Demeter's husband, called Jupiter in Latin) had to intervene, sending his messenger Hermes (Mercury) to the underworld to bring Persephone back and prevent the extinction of all life on Earth. Hades agreed, to Persephone's great relief, but gave her a pomegranate as she left. When she ate the pomegranate seeds, she was bound to him for half the year—during autumn and winter—and came back to her beloved mother during the blooming spring and the dry Mediterranean summer, when plant life is threatened by drought. Pluto secretly gave her food before she left, and once one had eaten in the underworld one could not leave forever. Persephone was therefore forced to return to the underworld for four months every year. She comes out in spring and spends the time until autumn with Ceres but has to go back to the underworld in the winter.

Demeter and Persephone were also the central figures in the Eleusinian mysteries—a series of large and secretive concerts held every five years. These mysteries represented the abduction of Persephone by Hades in three phases: the descent, the search, and the ascent. The main theme is the ascent of Persephone and the reunion with her mother. Demeter and Dionysus (god of ecstasy, wine, and dance) were the two great gods of the Earth who were honored in the mysteries.

## HONORING DEMETER AND PERSEPHONE
## AND OUR LADY
## WHO SHINES IN THE SUN

I felt a deep resonance with the myth of Demeter and Persephone, the beautiful tale of love between mother and daughter and of the unconditional love of the mother, which is what I learned most from my own mother. Like Demeter, she would do anything to bring happiness to me, to support me in my work, my art, and my love stories. At times my love life, including with Dario, meant that I was taken for a while into the underworld, and she always helped me come out. She came flying to me in New York when I was ill, and she paid in full for the surgery and hospitalization, even though she was not wealthy. She behaved equally with all three of her children, always thinking of us before herself. She never stopped giving and never cared about receiving. I would not be writing this book if it was not for her teachings and her wisdom.

I now realize how blessed I am to have had such an amazing mother as a role model, and I know from the work I do, especially with women who have suffered domestic violence and abuse, that not everyone has the same experience with their mothers. Yet I always encourage everyone to connect to his or her mother on a deep soul level, and for those who did not have the best mother, to really find a way to forgive her. All mothers go through pain when they give birth. Some are even traumatized by the fact of giving birth. Some mothers have been victims of abuse themselves and were too afraid to fight back and ask for help.

During the big festive celebrations of the Black Madonna in Viggiano, I learned how important it is for a group of people to be in a circle, dancing around the Blessed Mother or Her image, and feeling protected, with a long procession, walking in Nature, chanting, and feasting. The crowning of the statue of the Madonna with the sun, its rays all around Her, is the culmination of this ecstatic celebration, and everyone touches Her and asks for healing. This inspired me to re-create a similar ceremony in my workshops, to bring healing to the students and participants who may need to reconnect with their mothers and their own inner light.

## A Circle Dance to Connect with Your Mother

I will share with you a simple circle dance choreography and a devotional tarantella that you may use for this purpose. It is best to do this outdoors in Nature, if possible, with a close group of friends. Take a walk, sing, and drum, and when you come to a beautiful spot, make a circle, holding hands, and put a sacred image of the Black Madonna in the center. You can also make a little altar where people can bring images of their own mothers. I ask everyone to set the intention of healing the relationship

Fig. 8.6. Alessandra playing frame drum
with her student Danielle in Viggiano

with their mother or just connecting with them, in the physical or spiritual world, thus invoking the unconditional love of the Universal Mother. Then to a fast rhythm (tarantella is best, of course), the group steps in unison with feet stamping front and back, alternating feet and holding hands. Each person goes into the center one by one, becoming the sun. The sun holds a red ribbon, waving it into the air to direct good energy to each person in the group, receiving the light from above, opening their heart and sharing it with every person in the group. It is amazing to watch everyone become the sun and improvise movements as they share their personal beaming rays of light.

At the end of this ceremony the circle should get closer and tighter, with everyone holding hands again and moving into the center around the image of the Black Madonna. Everyone should close their eyes, visualize their own mother, and send her beams of light, whether she is still on this plane or in the spirit world, and say, "Like Demeter who carried the torch while she was looking for her daughter, we will carry this beam of light to look for and reconnect with our mothers and the Universal Mother." I invite you to learn the prayer that I wrote for my mother one month after she passed away, titled "Requiem for Mamma Elvira," about the Unconditional Love of the Universal Mother. Together with my dancers we choreographed a powerful fire dance to this haunting prayer, which represents the fire of love that keeps burning between the mother and her children even after death (see "Requiem for Mamma Elvira," appendix 8, page 364).

# CHAPTER 9

# The Black Madonna Incoronata and the Madonna of the Seven Veils

*Let a new song of praise be sung
to the Lady crowned on high.*

*Innocent virgin maid,
Spring's first flower, new rose,
the whole world calls upon you;
the day you were born was blessed.*

*Let a new song of praise be sung
to the Lady crowned on high.*

*You are the spring of gurgling water,
Mother of the living God;
you are the light of the people,
exalted above the angels.*

FROM *LAUDARIO CORTONESE:
LAUDA ALLA MADONNA INCORONATA*

# THE BLACK MADONNA
# INCORONATA OF FOGGIA

The mystical experience on the Sacred Mountain of the Black Madonna of Viggiano out in the wilds of Nature was a true blend of ancient worship of the Earth Mother and Catholic devotion to Mary, Mother of Christ, fused into one beautiful tradition by the common people, the ones with the true wisdom.

This triggered me to go further in my quest for the Seven Sisters. For years I continued to travel from town to town, region to region, finding more legends, more fascinating histories, more Black Madonnas. I was definitely guided to find more texts and, most of all, people who were devoted to the Black Virgin in the south of Italy and who shared their knowledge with me.

I heard all kinds of mysterious legends in the regions of Basilicata and Campania. One of them was about another important sister, the Black Madonna known as Madonna Incoronata di Foggia (Our Lady Crowned of Foggia) or Madre di Dio Incoronata di Foggia (Crowned Mother of God of Foggia) in the region of Apulia or Puglia.

Puglia is the heel of the Italian boot, the region closest to Greece, and was once part of the Byzantine Empire and, earlier, Magna Grecia. In the southernmost part of Puglia, in the province of Lecce in the Salento region, people still speak a fascinating language known as Grico or Gricanico, which combines ancient Greek with the Pugliese dialect. I learned some of the songs in this beautiful language while studying the healing music of the tarantella, or pizzica tarantata. You can reach the northern part of Puglia going east from Basilicata, descending the mountains to a flat stretch of land called the *tavoliere delle Puglie* (the plateau of Puglia). After our adventures on the Sacred Mountain of Viggiano, I decided in late September to take a journey into that dry flat land of the tarantella and the bite of the tarantula, to the well-known Sanctuario della Madre di Dio Incoronata (Sanctuary of the Mother of God Crowned). Dario and I took the Madonnamobile once more, going farther east toward the Adriatic Sea. This time the ride

Fig. 9.1. Black Madonna Incoronata di Foggia;
photo by A. Belloni

was easy, about two hundred kilometers southeast of Rome on a flat, straight highway all the way to Foggia.

I had seen many pictures of this Madonna, but I knew that it would always be a different emotional experience to be right in front of Her. Each Black Virgin wears different colors, has a unique gaze, and varies in Her position on Her throne and in the way that She holds Baby Jesus.

We exited the highway, left Foggia behind for a few kilometers, and entered the countryside on another straight road that led right to the sanctuary. Beautiful pine and olive trees surrounded the large church. There were places to rest, with rustic benches and wooden tables for the pilgrims in the pine forest. Dario and I had always been fascinated by the Gypsies and their culture, and we had learned that this was a place of devotion for the Romani communities who liked to camp outside the sanctuary.

Suddenly the weather changed, adding to the strange atmosphere of the location with its large sanctuary made of white marble with an enormous pyramid in the center. The day had been clear and warm until we reached the Black Madonna's church, when suddenly clouds appeared, followed by fog, and then thunder and lightning. We parked our car and literally ran into the church to take refuge.

The inside was illuminated by dim lights and candles, which added to the somber and mysterious atmosphere. The beautiful design and architecture of the interior astonished us because it was quite modern compared to the other churches we had visited. I felt that the architect must have had an esoteric vision, making a particular statement with the pyramid outside.

The legend says that the original church was built around the year 1001, but nothing of that era was visible until I went upstairs, following the signs to *la statua dell'incoronata*. We walked along a big corridor on the side of the sanctuary, with stained-glass windows that guided us in a sort of symbolic preparation to see her: Mary, as Mother of God, and Her Son, the Christ. In the stained glass were intriguing images of flames, chalices, doves, roses, and lilies—all ancient goddess symbolism. We then reached the throne and the special stairway that led to the niche where the Madonna Incoronata resides, suspended high up, giving the effect that She is floating among the stars—a stunning and austere image.

There were a few other devotees inside the church, and I got in line behind them, waiting for my turn to go up the steps to be with Her and pray. I reached the top of the small stairway in silence, with my eyes fixed right into Her eyes. It was hard to distinguish Her face in the darkness of the large sanctuary. As soon as I got right below Her, She lit up, a blue light all around Her, the Queen of Heaven suspended in paradise surrounded by a dark-blue sky with shining gold and silver stars. I remember shaking the first time I walked up to the altar while She looked out into the infinity above me with Her great wisdom.

Unlike other Black Madonnas, Her gaze was not toward us— the devotees coming to Her for help and grace—but went straight to heaven, as if showing us that there is another dimension, beyond death,

Fig. 9.2. Black Madonna Incoronata over the oak tree;
photo by A. Belloni

that we cannot see with our eyes in this life. With Her arms and hands wide open toward the faithful, She seemed to tell us that She was there to receive us, our love and devotion, and bring us to heaven, if only we believed in Her power. She had a strong masculine face, deep black, with black eyes and hair, and wore an elaborate solid gold crown similar to the ones worn by kings and bishops, not like the other Madonnas with their crowns of twelve stars. Her baby, Jesus, also very black, stood on Her knees with his arms open, looking out into the infinite. I remember feeling that they seemed quite separate; She was not holding him as I had seen in the other statues. They both wore pure white tunics with gold embroidery in a design that seemed very Byzantine.

I was overcome with emotion, once again feeling the mystery of this sacred, huge black statue making a statement of eternal wisdom, love, and infinite healing powers. I prayed intensely to Her, tears rolling down my face, asking Her to embrace me with Her open arms and show me Her wisdom, which the ancient Greeks called *sophia*. I know that Dario felt the same emotions of intense mystery, and a somber, quiet feeling overcame both of us. This Madonna was not like the others, when you felt a wild and, at times, sensual energy; instead, She seemed to be the secret keeper of mystical knowledge. We descended the stairs and prayed quietly in front of Her. Underneath the glass-and-wooden niche, a large letter *M* for Mary is inscribed. We then walked all around the sanctuary, where we learned the beautiful legend and history of la Madonna Incoronata di Foggia.

## THE LEGEND OF
## LA MADONNA DI INCORONATA

According to legend, la Madonna Incoronata appeared miraculously on top of an oak tree on the last Saturday of April in the year 1001 in the Cervaro forest. A noble man of the area, the Count of Ariano Irpino (Irpinia, land of the Black Madonna of Montevergine and Moiano, discussed in chapters 4 and 5) had a mystical dream where he saw a beautiful deer running through a forest, followed by a beam of light. Deeply moved by curiosity the nobleman went hunting in the forest near the River Cervaro, and his dream became reality when he suddenly saw a striking light. Stunned by its splendor, the man fell to his knees under an oak tree, looked up to the shining light, and heard the voice of a woman saying, "My son, I am the Mother of God, and I want you to build a chapel for me here where the faithful shall come to venerate and worship me, to whom I shall grant many miracles." The light disappeared, and the top of the oak tree burst into flames. There he saw the statue of the Black Madonna Incoronata appear.

That same night two bulls ran away from a peasant farmer while he worked in his fields. He chased after them, and when he found them, they were kneeling before the oak tree in worship and adoration. He saw the flame and the statue of the Madonna in the tree. The farmer, named

Strazzacappa, hung a small cauldron on a branch and burned some oil in it, creating a lamp in honor of Mary, Mother of God. Strangely, this oil continued to burn for many years, never needing to be replenished. The nobleman then had a small chapel built around the tree; we can still see the original small chapel today under the high altar, together with the branch from the tree. This is a very beautiful and unique legend in which the Black Madonna appears both to a poor shepherd and to a rich landowner, revealing the universal nature of devotion to Her.

The original shrine is believed to have been built in the seventeenth century, but we know that Her apparition appeared in the eleventh century, an era known, in Italian, as the Iron Century. At that time, the Saracens dominated, and political and social confusion reigned. The common people were uneducated and ignorant, and the dominant classes suffered from poor spiritual evolution. We know that in the year 1140, the Basilian monks built a larger church with a place of rest for pilgrims and a convent used for charity for devotees, crusaders, soldiers, the sick, and the people who were wounded in the wars that were waged in the desolate surrounding area.

The same Saint Guglielmo, who built the first shrine of Montevergine and began the order of the Basiliani, lived at the site of the Madonna Incoronata for three years with some of his fellow monks, thus connecting the devotion of this Black Madonna to the one known as Mamma Schiavona in Montevergine and Our Lady of the Sacred Mountain in Viggiano.

## THE ICON AND STATUE
## OF LA MADONNA INCORONATA

Through the centuries there have been five different images, mainly paintings, representing the apparition of this Black Madonna: the main one represents the Black Madonna with Baby Jesus sitting over the oak tree surrounded by flames, and another one shows two Madonnas, one black and one white, with the rich man and the poor man at the foot of the tree.

The current beautiful statue is carved of walnut wood. Although attempts have been made to determine the date She was sculpted, it is hard to tell due to the many alterations. It seems that the statue dates to the year 1280 and is perhaps a replacement for the original one. The most significant alteration to this Madonna is that at one point, though no one knows exactly when, someone cut off the arms and took Baby Jesus away. In fact, until 1986, this Black Madonna was seen without Jesus on Her lap.

There is much mystery surrounding this strange anecdote. Some people think that the thieves wanted to steal the gold around the statue. Yet I wondered, as many did through time, why did they only steal the arms and the baby? There is no real proof that the statue originally included a Jesus, although the church authorities claim that when they decided to bring back the Madonna's arms and the baby Jesus in 1987, they found a center pole under the Madonna's tunic, indicating that another statue had probably been attached there.

The inauguration of the new statue of the Black Madonna holding Jesus was on May 24, 1987, under the blessing of Pope John Paul II, who was a great devotee of the Black Madonna. He was from Poland, a country devoted to Our Lady of Częstochowa.

To this day, la Madonna Incoronata is known for Her many miracles, including the special oil that still burns from the ancient lamp. Hundreds of sick people go to visit Her for healing year round and are often cured of their diseases.

The church that we see today was initially built by the order of Don Orione in 1950 and designed by a wonderful architect, Luigi Vagnetti. The large structure has rooms and facilities for sick pilgrims to be taken care of by priests, nuns, and family members. During one of my visits, I was startled by the arrival of an ambulance transporting a very sick woman on a stretcher. I watched as the ER nurses took the stretcher inside the church and carried the woman all the way up the stairs to the Madonna. The priest then came and asked us to leave so that the poor woman and the ER personnel could be alone in the sanctuary near the Madonna. It was very moving and shows how strongly this devotion is based on cures and miracles, like in Lourdes or Fatima.

## THE FEAST, DEVOTION, AND TRADITIONS
## OF LA MADONNA INCORONATA

Every year since the thirteenth century, a great number of devotees to this Madonna have come in pilgrimage from all over Southern Italy on the last Saturday of April to celebrate the feast commemorating Her original appearance in the year 1001.

The celebration begins on the previous Wednesday with a powerful ritual of dressing the statue of the Madonna. During the long winter months, when the old sanctuary remains closed, the statue is kept inside without Her traditional white tunic and golden jewelry. Ever since the completion of the new sanctuary, the official clergy have taken the beautiful Black Madonna out into the church and dressed Her inside the niche, covering Her with the ceremonial gold-embroidered white tunic and Byzantine jewelry. This ritual is still done today, with the participation of the faithful people of Foggia, who bow to their Blessed Mother, kneel, and beat their chests in a sign of penance and devotion.

Wednesday's somber ritual of dressing and prayer contrasts starkly with Saturday's great festive celebration in honor of the Incoronata. The procession includes a parade of colorful decorated wagons, sometimes even tractors, and people dressed in costumes portraying the apparition of the Madonna on the oak tree, as well as other religious stories, including the Annunciation, the Last Supper, the Crucifixion, and the Resurrection. Saints are also portrayed, including Saint Francis of Assisi and Mother Teresa of Calcutta. The procession goes around the sanctuary three times, a ritual known as *i tre giri,* which follows an ancient tradition popular in most feasts of la Madonna Nera, dating back to the pre-Christian rituals of various goddesses.

The most unusual feature of this feast, though, is the *Cavalcata degli Angeli,* the Cavalcade of the Angels. This is a spectacular reenactment of the heavenly scene that took place in the Cervaro forest during that marvelous night in 1001 when a storm of angels appeared to crown the head of the Black Madonna right in front of the ecstatic eyes of the Count of Ariano and the poor farmer Strazzacappa.

The powerful cavalcade takes place on the Vigil, the Friday before the actual procession, with many horses wearing colorful drapes, feathers, and crowns, mainly ridden by children and young girls dressed as angels, saints, monks, and Christian soldiers. This celebration is a great folkloric spectacle, expressing the imagination of the devotees of the Black Madonna Incoronata. No one knows when this Cavalcade of Angels began and why, but the tradition has continued for many centuries. It seems to have medieval origins, following the period's typical parade tradition using snare drums, bass drums, and long horns. It is similar to the Palio di Siena, in which the horses are the protagonists of the famous race after being blessed inside the church by the Madonna del Voto.

The tradition of walking around the sanctuary three times is observed by everyone, not only the pilgrims who come from far away on foot (often barefoot) but also the singers (men and women), the horses, and the wagons.

I have never been to this wonderful feast, but I have been going to the church of the Madonna Incoronata since the year 2014, as part of the pilgrimage that I lead every summer to the sacred sites of the Black Madonna in the south of Italy. I have watched my tour participants go into a deep state of trance as they climbed the stairway to get close to the Madonna and pray to Her. Often, as they told me afterward, they felt, like me, a suspension of time and a feeling of being lifted into the air by the Madonna Incoronata. I have watched some of them weep and tremble as they felt the spirit of their mother or grandmother who had passed away.

One of the nicest moments during the tour is seeing the copper cauldron that still contains the miraculous burning oil lit by Strazzacappa. The legend says that when the rich Count of Ariano Irpino was deathly ill, he asked to be taken to the chapel by the oak tree and to be blessed by that burning oil. He received a miracle and was cured instantly. To this day, the faithful pilgrims, especially people who are ill, ask to be touched with a silver stick dipped into the oil, often receiving a miracle. We as a group honored that beautiful ancient tradition, and I bought some of the oil to take home.

The priest told us that the year before a woman had come from

Canada to take the oil to her son who had been diagnosed with serious lung cancer; when she touched him with the oil the cancer miraculously disappeared. The priest showed us her letter, now exhibited in the small sacristy. I personally used that oil during the tour to help me with arthritis pain, and I can testify that it worked.

## LA MADONNA INCORONATA
## AND ARTEMIS OF EPHESUS

I still have a vivid memory of that first time I saw this unusual Black Madonna during my research with Dario. I had a clear revelation that the legend of this Black Virgin and Her statue were deeply connected to the goddess Diana or Artemis of Ephesus, black goddess of the forest, Nature, trees, and the moon.

The beautiful legend of the sacred deer running in the forest, receiving a beaming light, and the apparition of the Black Madonna on an oak tree over a flame recalled the ancient magic rites of the goddess Diana of the Janare (initiates of Jana Diana) in Benevento, in the area of Irpinia, when women danced around the sacred tree, invoking the goddess of the moon and forest. The count who had the vision came from the Ariano Irpino region, and flames were used during those ecstatic rites honoring the moon, for purification and to receive magical powers.

Most astonishing are the face of the Black Madonna and the open positions of Her hands. Knowing that originally She did not hold Baby Jesus, we can see that Her hand positions are similar to the famous statue of Artemis of Ephesus, which is displayed in the National Museum in Naples.

The worship of the Black Madonna by the peasants today is done on horseback. This was also popular in the Middle Ages, and it is probably connected to the Knights Templar, but there is no real evidence. Also the legend of the hunter discovering the deer full of light in the woods is directly related to the tradition of Diana, the goddess of the hunt. All animals were sacred to her, and she protected all the living beings in the forests.

Fig. 9.3. Diana Efesina in Naples National Museum;
photo by D. Bollini

These timeless legends and myths are embedded in the subconscious of the devotees and pilgrims who still reenact them without necessarily remembering the true origins, following a collective memory, a cosmic memory that shows us that indeed God is a woman, and She is black.

Taken by this revelation during that first visit to L'Incoronata, Dario and I decided to stay in Foggia and follow another intriguing and mysterious legend, the one of la Madonna dei Sette Veli, the Madonna of the Seven Veils, patron saint of the city of Foggia. We knew that She was in the beautiful Baroque cathedral in the center of the town, so we decided to stay nearby, have a calm and reflective night, and go visit Her the next day.

I must say that this one revealed Herself to be the most mysterious of all. We walked inside the cathedral, toward la Cappella della Iconavetere, and from far away we could not see a statue, only a large upright tablet covered with beautiful white drapes. As we got closer, we saw that in the center of this sacred tablet was a black oval face, supposedly the face of the Virgin Mary, but veiled—and in the shape of an egg! I remember almost fainting in surprise, realizing that this must have been an ancient esoteric center where the monks worshipped a sacred wooden tablet covered by seven white veils with an oval, veiled, black cosmic egg, which symbolized to me the beginning of life. Yet in this Catholic church, they said that the face of Mary as a young girl appeared at certain times in this featureless black oval.

The devotion to this sacred image is as strong as any devotion to a real statue, making it, in a way, more meaningful. It was inspiring to watch a large crowd of Catholics pray to a sacred tablet and a veiled, black, oval shape surrounded by white cloth. It seemed more mystical.

The legend of this apparition is one of the most haunting.

It began in the year 1062, when Foggia was not yet a city but a small village built in the marshes and swamps. Its center was a tavern known as the Taverna del Gufo (Tavern of the Owl), which attracted many hunters and cattle herders. One day a few cattle herders, who had brought their bulls to drink by the swamp, saw the bulls kneel as three flames appeared flying and floating over the water. The men went to look in the mud and found the wooden tablet wrapped in seven white veils, covering the face of the dark Madonna.

In great amazement the cattle herders took the sacred image into the Tavern of the Owl, which then became a place of devotion to the Virgin Mary until 1080, when the Norman king Robert Guiscard ordered a church built in that place in honor of the sacred tablet and

Fig. 9.4. Madonna of the Seven Veils;
photo by D. Bollini

the mysterious image of Mary, Mother of God. This small church was expanded and became known as the Church of the Holy Mary of the Seven Veils and remained a strong place of worship through the centuries, under the dominations of the Swabians, the Spanish Aragons, and the French Bourbon dynasty. The fascinating history says that the face of Mary as a young girl appeared a few times to priests or monks on March 22 (Maundy Thursday) in 1731 and again in 1745 to Saint Alfonso Maria de' Liguori, a theologian and author of important texts, including *History of Moral Theology* and *The Glories of Mary*.

Saint Alphonsus Liguori, sometimes called Alphonsus Maria

Liguori, was an Italian Catholic bishop, spiritual writer, composer, musician, philosopher, and theologian. He founded the Congregation of the Most Holy Redeemer (the Redemptorists). In 1762 he was appointed Bishop of Sant'Agata dei Goti (the special medieval town in the province of Benevento near Moiano, see chapter 5). A prolific writer, he published nine editions of his *Moral Theology* in his lifetime, and some of his best-known works are *The Glories of Mary* and *The Way of the Cross,* the latter still used in parishes during Lenten devotions. He was canonized in 1839 by Pope Gregory XVI. Alphonsus wrote 111 works on spirituality and theology with 21,500 editions and translations into seventy-two languages. His masterpiece was *The Moral Theology* (1748), only recently published in English with translation made by Ryan Grant and published in 2017 by Mediatrix Press. His best known musical work is his Christmas hymn *Quanno Nascette Ninno* (When the Baby Was Born), later translated into Italian by Pope Pius IX as *Tu scendi dalle stelle* (From Starry Skies Thou Comest).

This is one my favorite Neapolitan songs, which I have been singing since 1984 at the end of our Christmas Production "La Cantata dei Pastori (The Shepherds' Cantata) as I play Mary singing to Baby Jesus in the Nativity scene.

In his spiritual text *The Glories of Mary,* he describes his vision.

I saw many times and through different days, in the crystal image on the table, the face of the Virgin Mary as a young virgin girl, about thirteen or fourteen years old, wearing a white veil over her head. It was not as a painting but the live face of a living person, turning her face around. At the same time that I saw Her, the whole congregation witnessed the same miracle. And the devotion grew even stronger.

This vision was seen again in 1745, while there were about two thousand people in the church praying. As Mary's face appeared, a striking light touched the forehead of the saint, who was suddenly lifted a few feet above the altar. She levitated in front of the crowd of worshippers!

This church gained great fame and became the center of the whole city of Foggia. The small agricultural town had become famous through the centuries, thanks to the special church and worship of Santa Maria dei Sette Veli. The beautiful Baroque cathedral that we see today was built in 1782 and received the title of Cathedral of Foggia in the year 1855. The great festivities in Her honor are held two times a year, on March 22, to commemorate the apparitions of the eighteenth century and again during the celebration of the Assumption of Mary between August 13 and 16. The celebrations are known as the Feast of the Crowning of the Sacred Tablet of Our Holy Mary dell'Icona Vetere (of the Seven Veils).

Two days before the March 22 celebration, the sacred tablet is taken out of the chapel and covered with a silver shrine originally sculpted by the famous Neapolitan artist Giovan Domenico Vinaccia. The Madonna is then taken in procession around the center of the town. On the following day, another procession takes place with the relics of Saint Guglielmo, the patron saint of Foggia and the founder of the Basilian monk order in Montevergine and Viggiano. This is a very long procession that goes all around the town and ends back at the cathedral, where the devotees follow the relics of the saints and the sacred tablet with the Madonna of the Seven Veils. Finally, on March 22, the archbishop holds a High Mass in the cathedral to commemorate the original day of the apparition of Mary. A few days later, the silver casket is taken off the sacred tablet as it goes back into the chapel.

This powerful legend, full of symbolism and esoteric meanings, had a huge influence on my own quest for the answer to the question: Who is the Black Madonna? It showed me once more how mysterious this ancient devotion and tradition is, with so many layers of history from the different cultures and populations that mixed in the small area of Magna Grecia.

It was so fascinating for me to discover this sacred tablet covered by seven veils. Here again was the magic number seven, full of meanings in esoteric studies, its connection to our seven energy points, seven chakras of seven colors, seven musical notes in Western music, seven stages of initiation in the mysteries, and beyond to the Seven Sisters as Black Madonnas and the constellation Pleiades named for the Seven Sisters of Greek mythology. Deeper research on the number seven and its origins also brought me back to the magic and esoteric teachings of the ancient Egyptians and the goddess Isis.

In ancient times, when the Pleiades were called the Guardians of the Sky and had the mystical task of timekeeping, the Pleiadean star system was the source of the supernatural wisdom known by the high initiates of the mystery schools of Isis. I have often thought that the seven Black Madonnas and the myth that the black goddess Cybele came from a black meteorite, which fell from the stars, must be connected to the Pleiades, but there is no real evidence—just my own personal interpretation.

In Christianity the number seven appears many times. It is believed that God created the world in seven days. There are seven sacraments: baptism, penance, marriage, communion, confirmation, holy orders, and last rites. Tradition also speaks of the seven virtues, which are faith, hope, charity, fortitude, justice, prudence, and temperance, and the seven deadly sins, which are pride, envy, anger, sloth, avarice, gluttony, and lust.

The physical chakras, referred to as vortexes of power, are the vehicles of manifestation of pure cosmic energy and, in turn, designate seven different levels of the manifestation of consciousness. These seven stages of consciousness were depicted by the Egyptians, in a representation possibly originating in Atlantis, as the seven veils of the goddess Isis. In ancient times sacred dancers performed the ritual of the seven veils to gradually reveal the world beyond immediate reality. Beneath these veils are concealed all the mysteries, ageless wisdom, and learning of the past. Indeed, in *The Golden Ass* by the ancient Roman writer Apuleius, Isis declares: "I am all that has been, that is, that shall be, and none among mortals has yet dared to raise my veil." This beautiful deep revelation resonated with me and helped me understand why Foggia, this city in Southern Italy, has for thousands of years been a site of devotion to the mystical seven veils and the veiled Goddess, originating from the primordial Isis, who was dominant in all of the ancient Mediterranean cultures.

I felt immensely grateful to have had the opportunity to journey to the Cathedral of the Holy Mary of the Seven Veils in Foggia, going deeper into the secret tradition and receiving wonderful inspiration for a scene that I later staged in our opera portraying the veiled Black Madonna.

## LA MADONNA
## INCORONATA DI PESCASSEROLI

I remember leaving Foggia back in 1990 with a great feeling of new discovery and an eagerness to learn more on this sacred quest. Local worshippers at the sanctuary of the Incoronata told us that this Madonna was almost identical to the Madonna Incoronata from Pescasseroli in the region of Abruzzo.

I was startled by this new piece of information! Pescasseroli? I trembled; I used to go skiing there with my parents. My father, who was a champion cross-country skier in the 1930s and 1940s in Italy, took us there on holidays, especially for Easter, to close out the skiing season. The best memories I have of my father are along the Tiber River when we went rowing at the beach, where he would say that he honored the goddess of the sea (by posing for photos naked except for a fig leaf—no kidding!) and on the mountains where he taught me to be free in Nature, using cross-country skiing as a way to be in a peaceful setting, looking at the landscapes of the mountains, trees, and rivers. Kneeling down on the ground, he made us eat the snow and said, "This snow must remain clean. No one should ever pollute it with machines! Forget about the ski lifts. They will bring pollution!" Yes, my father was a wild man and an atheist, but I now thank him for teaching me how to honor and respect Mother Earth.

I do remember once, during our Easter skiing vacation in Pescasseroli, near the National Park of Abruzzo in the Province of L'Aquila, he made us ski all the way up a high mountain to a small chapel where there was a special mass for an ancient statue of the Madonna. I was surprised, because he was not a believer, but I followed him, of course. I had no choice; I was fourteen years old. It was a stunning location, and it was a fantastic experience to be one of the skiers who went up for devotion to the Madonna. Twenty-eight years later I realized how fortunate I was that my unusual father took me up to the remote Monte Tranquillo (Tranquil Mountain) to the small shrine of the Black Madonna, sister of la Madonna Incoronata di Foggia.

I began to look for information about this Black Madonna that I had probably visited as a teenager and asked my mother if she knew anything about this tradition in Pescasseroli. She seemed to remember that her her mother and sister, who lived all summer long in Arpino, a town south of Rome in the Ciociaria region of Lazio, had spoken about it. I then learned that, for centuries, shepherds and farmers walked with their animals through the mountains across from Lazio to Abruzzo and Puglia and back, in a form of nomadic pastoralism called transhumance, moving cattle from one grazing ground to another.

I spoke about this tradition from Lazio with Dario and John. John then realized that his mother's family had emigrated to New York from the same area, Ciociaria, from the town of Itri, where there was another Black Madonna, la Madonna della Civita, who had been honored in downtown Manhattan for many years. How amazing! We all went to do research in Southern Italy only to come full circle and rediscover that there were powerful Black Madonnas in our own grandparents' roots in the region of Lazio.

I was determined to go to all these places and honor our ancestors.

Ciociaria takes its name from a type of stringed leather shoe called *ciocie* that the people, especially women, make and wear in this mountain region. I still remember my grandmother, Nonna Rosa, singing the funny tarantella "E quando la ciociara se marita" (When a Woman from Ciociaria Gets Married), with my grandfather Nonno Rodolfo accompanying her on the mandolin during our Sunday family gatherings. The song is a fast *saltarello,* a form of tarantella from Lazio, with double meanings in the lyrics, describing how hot the women of Ciociaria are.

The region became famous in 1960 due to the success of *La Ciociara* (released in English as *Two Women*), a fantastic film that turned Sophia Loren into a star and for which she won an Oscar. Written by Alberto Moravia and directed by Vittorio De Sica, the film is about the abuse and rape of two Italian women, mother and daughter, by foreign soldiers during World War II.

## CHILDHOOD MEMORIES IN THE MOUNTAINS OF ABRUZZO AND LAZIO

I was very determined to go back to these remote places in the middle of unspoiled Nature where I used to travel as a child with my family, remembering the happy times before my parents separated. I knew it would be very emotional, but I had to do it. I was moved by the fact that the Black Madonna was around me even when I was a kid, and although I might not remember Her, I know now that She saw me.

I finally found out that every year, on the last Sunday of July, there is a long and heartfelt procession of the Black Madonna of Monte Tranquillo, which goes from Pescasseroli up to the mountain, an eleven-kilometer walk through beautiful meadows and on woodland paths along small riverbanks in one of Italy's natural treasures, the National Park of Abruzzo.

In 1993, Dario and I set out on this journey, full of excitement, remembering our experience a couple of years before on the Sacred Mountain of Viggiano. We stayed in a small bed-and-breakfast on the outskirts of Pescasseroli, which I believe was haunted, as I kept feeling spirits and hearing weird noises. Strangely, Dario got sick with a delirious fever, although he did not have a cold or any other illness, and to this day I wonder if it was the result of some sort of spell that had been cast on him.

I knew that I could not miss the opportunity for this feast of the Black Madonna, and so I took care of everything: I planned the whole day while Dario came along but felt quite numb. I felt very emotional when at around nine o'clock in the morning we arrived in the charming medieval town of Pescasseroli, remembering my beautiful times with my family and feeling my father's spirit all around. He had won many cross-country competitions in that area, as well as doing mountain climbing. He was brave and strong; nothing ever scared him, and he felt at his best "in the arms of Mother Nature," as he used to say.

I dedicated this procession to his memory, like I had dedicated the one in Viggiano for my mother. I felt that now it was time to honor him. I also dedicated the procession to my maternal grandparents, who carried on the musical traditions and had probably known about this Black Madonna.

We first went to the beautiful church of Pescasseroli to honor the Madonna Incoronata, sister of the one in Foggia. The church is called the Basilica of Saints Peter and Paul (protectors of the tarantati) and was built in the 1600s after a terrible earthquake destroyed the original church and the original town called Terra (Earth). How incredible, I thought: here is a devotion to the Black Madonna in one of the most beautiful spots on Mother Earth in a town originally called Earth!

We walked to the high altar to see this very old little statue made of dark ebony, holding a globe of the world with Her right hand and Her son, Jesus, with Her left. She had a very peaceful expression, and her eyes seemed to be closed. She had been dressed for the feast with a blue cape and a white dress with golden embroidery and wore a refined gold crown with stars and emeralds.

My research found that the first testimony and documentation of this Madonna Incoronata date back to the year 1283, when King Charles of Anjou gave orders to Christopher d'Aquino, the priest in the church of Pescasseroli, to hold a big celebration and livestock fair on the day that honors the birthday of Mary, Mother of God, September 8. It is considered a miracle that this small Madonna statue was not destroyed in the huge earthquake, which destroyed the towns of Terra and Castello in 1579. This is a common thread in the legends of all the Black Madonnas that I visited in Southern Italy: a strong earthquake came at some point in their history (including at Tindari, Seminara, and Viggiano), but the Black Madonna statues were not destroyed, thus adding to their power.

After the earthquake, the town of Pescasseroli became the beginning point of the cattle trail that ran through the mountains and down into the flat land of Puglia.

The small Black Madonna was probably brought there in the

Fig. 9.5. La Madonna Incoronata in a white dress;
photo by A. Belloni

thirteenth century by a hermit monk of the order of San Basilio, just like
the Madonna in Foggia. As seen in the Incoronata's church in Foggia,
the devotion to the Black Madonna in Pescasseroli also includes a cauldron with a special healing oil that burns inside the chapel, where the
faithful come to be anointed and cured of diseases of the body and the
spirit. I lit a candle in front of the Madonna Incoronata of Pescasseroli,
thinking that I had probably been inside this church with my family
almost thirty years before. I was deeply moved and felt that I had to
do the whole procession up the mountain for la Madonna di Monte
Tranquillo in honor of my family.

There was a big crowd gathering all around the town and into the valley where they were about to hold the Holy Mass before starting the procession through the woods and what seemed like enchanted meadows. Outside, near a small stage, there was another small statue of the Black Madonna. She had very beautiful features and a peaceful expression, holding Jesus with Her left arm as He looked up to His mother and to heaven.

She wore a bright red tunic and a blue cape and held flowers, wheat, and branches in Her right hand. People were coming from all directions, on foot and even on horseback. I had learned how to ride with my father, and later on, when I lived in Arizona, horses had been my biggest passion besides music. I felt an urge to be on a horse following the procession, and I asked around if anyone had an extra horse, but it was impossible at such late notice. Seeing that I was so eager to be part of the procession that was about to start, some women told me that I could help carry the statue if I wanted to, as in their tradition women were also carriers. I said, "Yes, of course!" thinking it would not be hard since the statue was so small. Dario looked at me in disbelief, and still feeling sick, he said that he would rather drive up the road, hoping we would find each other at the end of the day. I agreed and said good-bye, "*Ca maronna t'accumpagna*" (May the Madonna be with you), and felt a great excitement to have been chosen as one of the carriers.

We were already at 1,140 meters above sea level in Pescasseroli, and at around 11:00 a.m. the procession began on a normal paved road, only to take a completely different turn up a narrow trail full of stones and branches. The Madonna was carried first, people singing and holding candles were next, and horses came last. We kept going up this winding path, and I began to realize that this was more difficult then I thought it would be. At one point, before we stopped, up by the Crucifix of the Alpines, about 1,300 meters high, I asked if I could help carry the statue, and the women and men were happy to pass one of their spots to me. As I took hold of the left pole of the wooden stretcher, I looked at Her, the beautiful face smiling back at me, and prayed, "Please give me the strength so I can honor my father's incredible strength and power; I want him to be proud of me!" Someone shouted, *"Spalla!"* and there I was, lifting Her up with nine other people and carrying Her through a steep track in the woods surrounded by beech trees and oaks.

The view and landscape were breathtaking. I saw the famous Campo Rotondo meadow where my father used to win the cross-country skiing competitions, and tears rolled down my face. I remember entering a sort of trance, realizing how strong and focused you must be to carry Her, to keep breathing, to move your legs without making mistakes and in synchrony with the others, watching your feet to avoid stones or branches that could cause a bad fall.

I don't remember how much time passed. I know that we stopped to rest about four times and took turns carrying Her. Once we stopped by a powerful rock called il Manto della Madonna (the Cape of the Madonna). The folk legend says that the Virgin Mary stopped here on Her way up the mountain to rest from such a strenuous climb, and Her cape left an image imprinted on the rock. This legend reminded me of the one from Montevergine, the Madonna's Chair, where the imprints of Her feet are seen on the rock across the large stone that resembles Her throne.

I felt as if I were flying up the mountain, this time without skis. We reached the summit, 1,597 meters up, and only at that point did I find out that I had walked up eleven kilometers, half of the time carrying the statue! I was really in heaven, looking around remembering skiing there as a kid and thanking my father for training me to be a strong woman, teaching me how to breathe properly, how to rest and never give up. I felt his spirit again around me and forgave him for his weaknesses.

He had died suddenly on March 24, 1977, of a brain embolism at age sixty-eight, shocking everyone, as no one could imagine that the strong champion would die so young. I was the only one of his children in Rome at the time; I had just arrived from New York and did not have a chance to say good-bye. When I got to the hospital, he was already in a coma. Thank God that I was there to support my mother, who fell apart in despair, screaming that she still loved him; she always had—the only man she'd ever been with or truly loved in her entire life. I know I was in shock and traumatized by his sudden death, but at age twenty-two, I had to gather all my strength to take care of my mother and be there for her in all possible ways.

I cried for months, and now up in Monte Tranquillo, looking at the peaceful Black Madonna, I cried again. Later that day, after taking Holy Communion, as I did as a child, I was overcome by peace, feeling that there was a reason this was called the Tranquil Mountain. I understood that my father's spirit was at peace, and that even if he was not a good husband, he did love my mother truly, in his own strange way. I lay down on the grass under the hot sun, thanking the Madonna for taking me back to this special remote place to help me make peace with my father.

I fell asleep out of fatigue, enjoying the crisp air, the warmth of the sun's rays, and the feeling of resting on soft grass in unspoiled Nature. When I woke up to the sounds of fireworks announcing the beginning of the pagan-type feast, with food, wine, and folk music, I realized that I had completely lost Dario! I had really gone into another dimension for a while.

We found each other right by the small church and hugged with joy. He had slept most of the time in the car, sweating off the fever. He was a little surprised that I made the whole procession on foot while carrying the statue part of the time, forgetting that I had developed a great deal of stamina from my performances and that I was truly the daughter of a real champion. I shared that I had decided to walk all the way back too, eleven kilometers down the same path. At this point he thought either I had lost my mind or I was just possessed by the spirit of the Black Madonna, and it was Her energy that came through. I know now that this was true then, as it was true many other times in my life.

The feast continued with a great lunch of wine, homemade bread, and delicious products all freshly made in the area, which were shared by the pilgrims, just as in the old times during the transhumance—

when the shepherds and farmers walked with their sheep and cattle across the mountains during the changing of the seasons from fall to winter and back again in the spring. Around four o'clock in the afternoon, the large group who led the first procession asked the crowd to gather and begin the descent back to Pescasseroli, this time without the Black Madonna, making a line with candles and singing in Her honor. The beautiful statue was left inside the chapel to guard the mountains and protect the pilgrims who came there to visit Her and the travelers going through the cattle trail from region to region, as they had done for centuries.

I hugged Dario good-bye and followed the procession, now feeling like one of the locals, singing some of the songs and carrying a long white candle. We began to descend the mountain around five o'clock and by 8:00 p.m., we were back at the main church in Pescasseroli.

The full moon came up behind the mountains right above the church where the Black Madonna Incoronata di Pescasseroli was being honored with a final visit by the pilgrims. And there was Dario, waiting by the church, looking at the moon, our goddess Diana. He saw to his (and my own) astonishment that I was not tired but instead energized.

I believe that this was my physical initiation in finding the true inner strength that comes from the Black Madonna's healing powers. I will never forget how empowering it was to find that center of energy right in my core, in my womb and solar plexus, up through my lungs into my breath and voice. It was an incredible new feeling, a discovery of my deep life force.

I knew for the first time that I could really access the physical and spiritual power that was given to us from the Great Mother, the Magna Mater, feeling almost possessed by Her, like in ancient times when women (and sometimes men) gathered to perform rituals in the mysteries for the goddess of the earth, the sea, and the moon, thus invoking the forces of Nature and the Cosmos. This healing force has come back into my life many times, not only to help me but also to help others, especially women who have suffered trauma and abuse.

## FULL MOON RITUAL AND PRAYER
## TO THE GODDESS OF THE MOON

I shared a great devotion to the goddess of the moon with Dario. We had fallen in love during a magical full-moon night back in 1975 as we were taking a romantic walk in the countryside near his house in Rome, in Via Portuense. He was a Taurus and therefore protected by the moon, while I am a Leo, ruled by the sun. But I always felt a deep connection to the full moon, which helped open my heart to love and being loved. Dario and I spent many amazing full-moon nights together in various parts of the world. He went deep into the research of the goddess Diana and found incredible material that was, and still is, quite unknown: in particular, the women's full moon ritual of *anellone piceno* (ring of the piceni). This magic ritual was popular among women from Central Italy and the island of Cyprus. Dario bought an archaeology magazine with an article by Elisa Biancifiori, an archaeologist who explained that large rings (anellone) made of bronze with six nodes spaced evenly within the circle have been found in the women's burial grounds of the area near the province of Ascoli Piceno in Central Italy, specifically in Grottammare and Cupra Marittima in the region of Marche, dating back to between the seventh and sixth centuries BCE. These women, high priestesses, were buried with this ring placed below their navels, over their wombs. They were probably priestesses of the goddess Cupra from Cyprus, another aspect of the Great Mother. An anellone, usually made of bronze, is as wide as a regular tambourine, twelve inches, and its use still remains a mystery, even though some scholars say that it was used in honor of the goddesses Cupra and Diana as an instrument during their ceremonies.

The article was a very detailed study showing that this specific ritual ring was used by the initiated women for fertility rites and as a magic circle to draw down the power of the full moon and to enter different worlds in space.

Dario was completely bewitched by his finding, and to my immense surprise and joy, he had one of these rings made especially for me (see plate 18), following the specifications indicated in the article. We then took it to the Grand Canyon and many other places including Mexico and Southern Italy and learned how to use it to pray to the full moon. This anellone works if you grasp the ring with your hands in a specific position and hold it up to the full moon so that she shines her light through the ring.

In deep meditation and asking the moon to show me her power, I felt that I was one of the ancient priestesses and could see the moon shift, open, and become three moons. Her rays would start beaming all the way through the ring into my hands joined in prayer, going down into my veins and blood. That is the power of drawing down the moon.

After doing this ritual many times over the years, I discovered that you can achieve the same connection to the full moon and draw her power through your hands without the ring. You must focus your eyes and stare at the moon, lift your arms to the sky toward her, and join your hands by touching your wrists and veins with your thumb and index finger straight up and open, with the rest of the fingers closed. If you center the silhouette of the moon between your index and thumb, you will start feeling her power as beams of light hit your hands directly and follow your lifeline down into your veins. When that happens, concentrate on making a telepathic connection with the moon and pray to her, asking for a particular grace. She will respond with more light, a ring of bright colors like a rainbow around her shifting shape in the sky. You will probably see three moons.

I have had the most amazing results when I have done this ritual in Nature, by a river or the sea, on high mountains, and in the dark, touching the earth with my bare feet. I have shared it with very few people because I always thought it should be a secret. Now I believe that it is time that women discover how the ancient priestesses in the Mediterranean communicated with the goddess of the moon and received her power.

The transmission of this Divine Feminine ritual is dedicated to all women, especially the ones who have felt powerless as victims of abuse and need to heal their womb (see appendix 9 on page 366 for my song *Canto della Luna* "Chant to the Moon").

# CHAPTER 10

# The Haunting Image of Madonna dell'Arco

*Who is devoted to the Madonna dell'Arco, oh sister,*
*Has faith in the most beautiful name of the Madonna.*
*Oh Mary take me under your arch and protect me,*
*You have been invoked for over five centuries,*
*You show us your solemn love of the Mother,*
*Your power and Mercy as our Queen.*
*Love me as my Mother, protect me as my Queen,*
*relieve me of my pain, have mercy.*
*Santa Maria dell'Arco pray for us.*

PRAYER TO THE MADONNA DELL'ARCO

## FINDING LA MADONNA DELL'ARCO AND HECATE AND WRITING THE OPERA

I felt greatly empowered by all these fulfilling experiences, traveling to the sacred sites of the Black Madonna in so many remote towns and beautiful places in Nature that seemed forgotten by our modern civilization. As I was conceiving and writing the opera *The Voyage of the*

*Black Madonna,* which took four years, the inspiration grew stronger and stronger after each visit to each Black Madonna. My quest seemed to be endless.

I was haunted by the Black Madonna of the Seven Veils, the veiled goddess Isis, and the deep esoteric meaning of Hecate, the triple goddess of the moon. I knew that to complete the opera I had to find and visit the one Black Madonna of the Neapolitan legend of the Seven Sisters that is most identified with Hecate: La Madonna dell'Arco in Sant'Anastasia, a small village near Pomigliano d'Arco in the province of Naples. I had learned about Her first from my friend Arden Mason, who was originally from New York and also lived in Naples and Positano. Arden later painted the beautiful Black Madonna for our production titled *Tarantella: Spider Dance.* I am proud to say that this is the same beautiful image that you can see on the cover of this book. Arden showed me that the Madonna dell'Arco's devotion was probably the strongest due to the trance state of the thousands of devotees who run for miles to Her site from all over the region of Campania. They are called *fujenti,* Neapolitan for "runners."

I had seen the Madonna's image in the books by Roberto De Simone, and She looked haunting, with brown skin, a very unusual expression in Her eyes, and a bloody scar on Her left cheek. Her legends were also frightening, telling of terrible punishments inflicted on the people who disrespected Her. At the same time there are detailed accounts, with names, dates, and so on, of astonishing miracles that continue to happen today.

In my research, I found fascinating testimony that in the region of Campania, during Greek and Roman times, the cult of Hecate was very strong, especially in Rome and Naples. Her temples were usually hidden so that the priests and priestesses could hold magic rituals in secret, and her statues and images were found at crossroads. Hecate was the triple goddess of the crossroads and of the dark side of the moon.

Hecate was known for taking people into the underworld with her torch and leading the initiates from darkness into the light of true esoteric knowledge. She would protect her devotees if she was properly honored but also punish the ones who did not respect her, striking them with fire or sudden disease. Hecate was also connected to magic, witchcraft, knowledge of herbs and poisonous plants, ghosts, and necromancy. Shrines to Hecate were placed at doorways to both houses and cities in the belief that the shrine would protect them from the restless dead. Shrines were also placed at three-way crossroads where people would leave food offerings at the new moon for protection from evil spirits. (This is similar to the orisha Ylegua, who was always honored at crossroads.)

I had learned from De Simone's books that the Madonna dell'Arco's church outside Naples is built in an area that was sacred to Hecate and that her images and paintings are found at the crossroads still today, where people bring offerings to ask for protection from evil spirits and restless souls of the dead.

The first miraculous painting of the Madonna dell'Arco is believed to have appeared on a wall at a crossroad and was worshipped in a small niche where a torch was always kept lit in Her honor. It is fascinating that no one really knows how old this image is. I have never been to the Madonna's feast, but I have been to her sanctuary and have done much research on Her history and tradition, with the help of my special friend Arden, because she became an integral part of the opera I was writing.

On an early summer day in 1989, with great curiosity I went to visit Her church, which is located in the very poor, small industrial village of Sant'Anastasia, near Pomigliano d'Arco. It was also the home of one of the best groups of musica popolare, E' Zèzi, and the best singer ever devoted to the Black Madonna, Marcello Colasurdo, representative of the femminielli, the transgender and LGBTQ movement today.

The name dell'Arco comes from an ancient Roman settlement where there was a large aqueduct with many arches, and the niche was originally built under one of these big arches. I remember being overcome by a feeling of desolation in this poor and dangerous place on the outskirts of Naples. Upon entering the church, I was skeptical that this Madonna was so important and had such a strong devotion. However,

Fig. 10.1. Image of the Madonna dell'Arco;
photo by D. Bollini

that feeling changed completely as I walked around the church. The sanctuary is quite stunning and large, mainly white marble, in the Neapolitan-Baroque style.

The amazing devotion was right in front of my eyes, with thousands of ex-votos vows represented by figurines and sculptures of body parts that were healed and miracles granted by the Madonna. The air was filled with incense, adding to the mysticism of the place.

The unusual image of the Blessed Mother mesmerized me: there She was, only Her brown face visible now, with a red bloody scar on Her left cheek and looking at us with sorrow and tenderness, surrounded by beautiful inlaid marble mosaics. I admit that she was haunting but still emanated compassion. I knew that She held Her naked son, Jesus, with Her left arm, and They both hold a globe symbolizing the world, but that part of the painting was no longer visible because it is covered by precious stones, marble, and silver. The image is obviously very old and faded, and unlike other Madonnas, She was not wearing a fancy dress or elaborate cape, only an inlaid silver crown. I spent a long time sitting in prayer and also feeling a little distressed. I walked around the majestic church where devotees were constantly walking in and lighting candles. This was obviously a very active place of devotion. I asked the *sacrestano* (caretaker) about the feast on Easter Monday (Lunedi in Albis) and he told me it was impossible to get through on that day, and

I could only come if I vowed to run as a fujente for the Madonna, joining one of the teams from the different towns and neighborhoods.

Was I serious about it and ready to do that? I said that I would think about it. But after talking to my friend Arden and watching the video he filmed, I knew that there was no way I was ready for that! I bought a few images of the Madonna dell'Arco and a book of Her history and left feeling sad that I knew I could not become a fujente.

I will explain why shortly.

The book showed that this image of Mother Mary used to be much darker, back in the Renaissance. Until the year 1544, She was worshipped in a small niche at a crossroad at this same location, twelve kilometers outside Naples, where devotees would light candles, leave flowers, and touch the anointing oil that had supernatural powers for personal healing.

One day, on April 6, 1450, the Monday after Easter, two young boys were playing a ball game called *palla a maglio* right across from the small niche where the painting of the Madonna resided. In this game, the players take turns hitting a wooden ball with a stick; whoever hits the ball the farthest distance wins. One of the boys (supposedly from the town of Nola) hit a lime tree with the ball and lost the game. Infuriated, he began cursing the Madonna dell'Arco's sacred image; he picked up the ball and threw it with full force at the face of the Madonna. In that instant Her beautiful face became red, and dark red blood began to flow from Her left cheek where She was hit. All the people watching were astonished and so taken by fear that they began to cry out *miracolo!* (miracle!) and then, looking at the boy, shouted *prendetelo!* (take him!). The boy tried to escape, but the Madonna performed another miracle—he could not move his feet. As if glued to the ground, he could only sway from side to side. He was immediately bound and brought to the authority, the famous Count of Sarno, Raimondo Orsini, the Great Executioner of the Kingdom of Naples, who came to the crime scene and found the boy guilty after seeing the bleeding face of the sacred image of the Madonna. The count condemned the boy to be hanged immediately from the same lime tree, which dried up and died shortly after the hanging, showing again the supernatural power of la Madonna dell'Arco. These extraordinary events created a big uproar in the area surrounding Naples, and many people began coming to pay homage and ask for graces at the small niche with the sacred image of the Holy Mary dell'Arco, who continued to bleed for many days.

Since the people kept coming, there was a growing need to build a bigger church, and the task was undertaken by the Dominican fathers in the year 1544. And supernatural events also kept happening. In 1589 there was a forty-year-old woman living nearby who was known to be "ugly outside and inside." Mean and nasty, always cursing, her name was Aurelia del Prete. Although she was married to a decent man, Marco Cennano, people described her as demonic. One day while she was cutting wood to burn for their fire inside the house, she hurt her foot badly. Fearing she would lose her foot, she made a vow to la Madonna dell'Arco that if she got better, Aurelia would have two feet made of wax to bring to her church as a sign of thankfulness. After the woman was cured, she decided to buy the wax feet and bring them to the Blessed Mother. But on the way there, one of the wax feet fell and broke into a thousand pieces. In a fury, Aurelia threw down the other foot and stepped on it, cursing the Virgin Mary.

On Easter Monday, Aurelia's husband decided to bring to the Madonna the ex-voto he had made in wax to thank her for another grace, and he convinced his wife to go with him to the church. Aurelia went reluctantly, taking with her a small pig that she wanted to sell at the fair. But when the pig ran away, the infuriated woman grabbed the ex-voto from her husband and destroyed it, again cursing the Virgin Mary. Marco warned Aurelia not to do so, as it was well known that though this Madonna bestowed lots of miracles, she also punished those who disrespected Her. Aurelia was not moved or afraid. But almost a year later, at the beginning of Lent, she began to have great pain in her legs and feet until she could no longer walk. She called a doctor, but nothing could be done. Then on the night between Easter Sunday and Easter Monday in 1590, suddenly both her feet detached from her body. It was the anniversary of her cursing the Madonna dell'Arco, who punished Aurelia for her act of disrespect and ungratefulness. Marco and the people around her were stricken by terror and decided to bury the accursed feet underground. But when the news spread to the church authorities, they demanded to see the feet and the sick woman. The people dug up the feet and took them in a basket to the church of la Madonna dell'Arco, where they hung them by the altar for everyone to see so they would understand the supernatural powers of this exceptional Mary, Mother of God, known then as Madonna Bruna. In a sign of penance, poor Aurelia finally asked to be brought to the shrine to ask forgiveness of la Madonna dell'Arco. Aurelia died on July 28, 1590.

In a very short time this miracle and the extraordinary powers of the Madonna became known all around Naples, and hundreds of people kept coming to ask for miracles of healing and making great vows in exchange for Her grace. To this day, the feet of the nasty woman Aurelia are kept in the basket in the church. Decomposed and partially embalmed, they are indeed scary.

Many other supernatural events connected to the Madonna dell'Arco through the centuries have been blood related or foretold disasters and terrible events coming to Naples. Sometimes the Madonna would warn the faithful of oncoming danger with blood flowing from Her cheek for days on end. Once in the eighteenth century, a monsignor tried to dry the blood flowing from Her cheek, but his white handkerchief remained stainless and the blood kept flowing. There are many accounts of the Madonna keeping Her devotees, the church, and the surrounding area safe during the eruptions of Mount Vesuvius between the years 1631 and 1660. She also bled during the terrible times of the Plague that took over Naples beginning in the year 1656 and killed about four hundred thousand people. Yet there are accounts of people with the Plague going to the Madonna dell'Arco to get anointed with Her supernatural oil and being healed instantly, and others doing the same to be protected from the Plague and never getting sick. In the early 1900s the Madonna performed another miracle, the resurrection of a young girl who was almost dead, in a coma, and whose casket had been made already. The girl's father asked the Madonna to heal his daughter and bring her back to life. His grace was granted, and as promised, he brought the beautiful casket and left it in the church in remembrance of the miracle he had received. The list of miracles of la Madonna dell'Arco continues to this day.

## THE DEVOTION OF
## THE FUJENTI OR BATTENTI

The most moving and extraordinary aspect of the tradition honoring la Madonna dell'Arco is the devotion of the *battenti* (from *battere,* "to beat") or *pentintenti* (penitents), the ones who have made a vow to the Madonna to make a sacrifice for Her. As noted earlier, the penitents or fujenti run. I had first seen this incredible and shocking ritual in a film made in Naples in the early 1980s following the devotion of an extravagant and now famous Australian artist, Vali Myers, who lived in Positano and was devoted to the Madonna dell'Arco and all Black Madonnas. She passed away in 2003, at age seventy-two, but she remains a legend to this day and a role model for many women who are in search of freedom and artistic expression.

I had the honor of meeting Vali in Greenwich Village in New York, during the good old days in the late 1970s and 1980s at the Chelsea Hotel, where she lived, and at Arden's wild parties at his house in Central Park West and later in Positano. It is hard to describe my special friendship with Arden, a wonderful artist, painter, sculptor, and musician and a great stilt walker whom I had met back in the summer of 1975 in Southern France near Avignon. We were both young, kind of hippies and artists, with many interests in common. We connected right away, and he invited a group of friends and me to parties and dinners at his mother's amazing medieval villa in Menerbe. (His parents, who were both wonderful artists, loved Italy.) Although we both lived in New York, when we said good-bye then we did not think that we would meet again, as we were both so nomadic. But this is not what happened. We kept meeting again and again, by chance, in the streets of Greenwich Village, on deserted roads in the middle of the night in

Fig. 10.2. The fujenti;
photo from World News Network (wn.com)

Southern France, in Rome, and in Naples, until we realized that our friendship was indeed very special and we had to be always connected, no matter where we were in the world.

In the mid-1980s, Arden moved to an amazing penthouse in Palazzo Brancaccio in Rome and also lived in Naples. He loved the Southern Italian culture and music and became devoted to the Black Madonna, and so we shared that passion as well. Arden believed in my work and my mission and turned out to be a great supporter. To this day, I always see him as an angel. (His own father, the acclaimed painter Frank Mason, painted angels with Arden's face.) Arden ended up playing the angel on stilts in our Christmas show and our Passion play *Stabat Mater Donna de Paradiso.* He became involved in my research for the opera *The Voyage of the Black Madonna,* and we went to some of the sacred sites together, along with Dario, having very profound experiences. Arden even received a few miracles himself, which I will share.

Through Arden, I understood this trance tradition of the fujenti for the Madonna dell'Arco, as he had gone there a few times with the wild artist Vali. The history says that this intense devotion began in the Middle Ages, when only men made a vow to do penance for the

Madonna by hitting themselves (at times with chains or with leather whips) during Easter week, culminating on Easter Monday.

In the film made by Arden and his friends, we saw hundreds, possibly thousands, of men and some women, dressed all in white with blue sashes worn diagonally and carrying *stendardi* (flags) with the painting of the Madonna dell'Arco or holding small wooden crosses and running nonstop for many hours and many kilometers. The runners were divided into groups or teams called *paranza*. They began the night before Easter Monday, the teams gathering in front of the church to receive the blessing of the Madonna. Then at the sound of fireworks, they began to run without stopping, entering a trance state for eight to ten hours. By the time they arrived back at the church, most of them were in a complete deep trance, and that's when the most moving and shocking part of the ritual happened.

As if possessed by the spirit of the Madonna, many devotees began to fall to the ground in the middle of the street (where ambulances and ER people were ready to take care of them if needed), screaming and turning around and rolling all the way into the church. They moved like people possessed, as seen in the ritual of the tarantate (the bite of the tarantula), but this time possessed by the Madonna. While the ritual of the tarantati in the church in San Paolo di Galatina on June 29 is done mainly by women, this one is done mainly by men! Like Arden, I was completely overwhelmed by watching the surrender to possession, letting their bodies move wildly inside a church, crying, screaming, and asking the Madonna for help. Often receiving help and grace from Her, they vow to come back every year.

Men and women entered the church on their knees, crying, some also licking the floor all the way to the altar. This part of the ritual is closed to the public, but Arden and Vali had the amazing blessing of being allowed to film the entire ritual by a wonderful priest, Father Bernardo, who loved them very much. He had been disabled from an accident and was always at the church sweeping the floors until one day he asked the Madonna for the grace to be cured, and she healed his injuries. Thanks to this good-hearted priest, we now have incredible footage of the ritual inside the church, showing the possession of the devotees. This form of trance is practically identical to the tarantate as well as the ones initiated in Santeria and Candomblé, where the ceremonial cloths are also white and red and white and blue.

Possessed by the spirit of the Madonna (like an orisha or the tarantata, the person is called "tarantata" and is possessed by the tarantula), the fujente lets go of his or her malady, whether it is depression or hysteria, at times caused by abuse or a broken heart, or a physical disease or social condition. At the end of the ritual, the fujenti wake up completely "cured," happy and feeling purified, with no memory of what happened during the trance ritual but vowing to come back next year and repeat the same ecstatic ceremony.

I am extremely grateful to Arden for introducing me to this part of the devotion, and I was inspired to portray this ritual of possession by the Madonna in the last scene of *The Voyage of the Black Madonna*.

I mentioned that Arden himself received a few miracles. The first occurred the day after Halloween in 2001, when he literally dropped dead due to serious heart disease. He was suddenly stricken in a library near his home in Connecticut, and amazingly an ER person happened to be there returning a book and knew how to revive him. Even though Arden was dead for twenty minutes, my dear friend had no brain damage and was perfectly normal when he came back to life. He always says that, thanks to the presence of the Madonna in his life, he was saved.

A few years later, Arden became very sick again and learned that he urgently needed a heart transplant. Over the next several months he painted the most beautiful Black Madonna for me and our new production—a painting that we still use today, and which has real magical power—because She is alive. I am sure you can see Her face and expression on the beautiful cover of this book come alive for you as well. In 2008, when Arden was in the hospital and waiting for a heart, it did not look like he was going to make it. I cried and prayed every day—as did many of his friends—because we all knew that he was an angel. One night in early October, after I drove back from seeing Arden at the hospital, I took his painting of the Black Madonna out onto the balcony, lit a few candles, and lay down and prayed for Arden to receive a heart in time. Suddenly, a huge storm came, with thunder and lightning, and I felt his presence through the window. I jumped up, screaming, "Arden!" I could not figure out if this meant that he had passed away or if he had gotten a heart. Frantic, I called his closest friend, and he told me, "Yes, Alessandra, Arden just got a heart! They are flying it to him right now."

I looked at the painting of the Madonna (who you can see holds a skull) and could see Arden's soul through Her eyes. He was going to be fine. It is astonishing that at the same time, while he was in the hospital in Connecticut three hours away from me, the same thing happened there. All the lights went out in Arden's hospital room, with lamps crashing down from the ceiling, scaring all the nurses. That's when they received the call from the cardiac surgeon that they had found the right heart for him.

I thank the Black Madonna, to whom Arden is also devoted, that he is perfectly healthy today. He is painting and doing his beautiful artwork, and he remains my closest and oldest friend in America.

## WRITING AND PERFORMING
## *THE VOYAGE OF THE BLACK MADONNA*

I shared the life miracle received by Arden because I firmly believe that the healing power of the Black Madonna is not something of the past; She is as alive today as She was thousands of years ago. Arden had the same artistic vision and talent as painters did in those times, and guided by Her spirit, he made Her image come alive. When he was between worlds, I lit candles to his painting of the Black Madonna, and at that time he received the heart that saved his life.

It is this faith in Her power of transforming death into life that also motivated me to write the opera and this book. The spiritual journey that led me to write *The Voyage of the Black Madonna* is full of extraordinary adventures, supernatural experiences, funny anecdotes, and incredible moments of joy and ecstasy.

I was so blessed to have wonderful collaborators, like Dario filming and documenting, John composing fantastic scores and finding more music, Arden helping me with precious information, and many people in the south of Italy always ready to show me more places, more Black Madonnas, more apparitions, more music and dance.

The difficult task for us was to combine all this field and academic research into a powerful staged production, with modern and traditional dance choreography and folk music combined with original compositions that told a story no one had ever told before to a New York audience.

In a sense I am doing the same thing now with this book, as these stories of the Southern Italian Black Madonna traditions and Her power, music, and dance celebrations, still practiced today, have never been told before.

The process of writing the opera as a journey began in Cuma at the Cave of the Sybil, discovering the esoteric legends of the poet Virgil and the Seven Sisters, then went on to the sacred mountain of Montevergine, where the tammorriata drumming tradition for the Black Madonna Mamma Schiavona, the ancient goddess Cybele, still exists. The voyage continued to the area of Benevento and the enchanting Madonna della Libera in Moiano, down to Calabria to the drumming and giant puppet procession for la Madonna dei Poveri. Next was the island of Sicily and the spectacular site of the Black Madonna of Tindari, la Madonna del Mare, then back up the sacred mountain to the Queen of Lucania in Viggiano and down the flat land of Puglia for the mysterious Madonna Incoronata and the Madonna of the Seven Veils. Then it was up to the stunning Mountain Tranquillo for the other Madonna Incoronata in the National Park of Abruzzo.

The voyage ended with the discovery of the trance ritual for the Madonna dell'Arco on Easter Monday and the peculiar ecstatic possession of the fujenti devotees by the Holy Mother.

The true inspiration for the opera came when I received the magical book of knowledge about Virgil by Roberto De Simone, *Il segno di Virgilio*. This unique literary work led me to make the poet Virgil the principal character in the story, taking us into a mythical time through

Fig. 10.3. The three-faced mask representing the prophetess
of the underworld; photo by A. Belloni

his journey of initiation. Since he was known to be a *mago poeta*, initiated in the mysteries of the goddess Cybele, I felt that he must have gone through a great esoteric initiation to write his exquisite poetry, describing the journeys in the underworld and of the mythical Aeneas. That is why people in Naples still remember him as a poet-healer-shaman and worship him as the sun god. In a sign of devotion, they still bring offerings and flowers to his tomb near the shrine of la Madonna di Piedigrotta.

We know that Virgil's works the *Georgics* and the *Eclogues* all possessed a high esoteric knowledge. In the sixth century, the writer Fabio Planciade Fulgenzio said that Virgilio's literary works contained such mystical and profound meaning and studies that "there is no art that can explain them."

It is also fascinating that Virgil became famous as a magus in the year 1000, when people thought that the world would end and referred to him and his revelation from the sybil about the destruction of the world.

I am convinced that we are living in a similar time of fear of disasters, wars, and contagious disease. And so once again we need the protection of the Black Madonna and a new superhero like Virgil to help us through the darkness into the light.

I decided to open the production with the character of Virgil coming back to speak to the prophetess of the underworld to begin his quest to save the world from self-destruction.

My vision was to bring the audience back in time through haunting music, powerful masks, elaborate costumes, puppets, and good staging.

The beautiful music for each goddess was composed by the brilliant guitarist and now well-known composer John La Barbera, who also arranged the traditional chants that I learned during my field research. My husband, Dario, wrote the script together with me, mainly lyrics to songs, and helped with the research.

This unusual collaboration with my ex-boyfriend and husband is full of humorous anecdotes, at times with some drama, but it was the most beautiful act of love that brought the three of us very close. Therefore, the Black Madonna prevailed, and the beautiful opera dedicated to the healing of Mother Earth premiered in the crypt of the Cathedral of Saint John the Divine in May 1991.

The space was a small amphitheater built inside the original crypt of the cathedral by stonemasons in 1887, and it has the most beautiful acoustics.

We were able to perform at this sacred space all thanks to our mentors, the dean of the Cathedral, the Very Reverend Dean James Parks Morton, and his wife, Pamela Morton. We had met them a few years before while performing for various events at the majestic cathedral. I had gone there to listen to the fabulous composer and saxophone player Paul Winter. Also known as an environmentalist, he was the first to record the sounds of whales and the dolphins and created beautiful melodies imitating their voices. Back in the 1980s I used to dream of performing at this most sacred space in New York, and the dream came true thanks to Dean Morton and our special devotion to the Black Madonna.

Reverend Morton was the dean of Saint John the Divine for twenty-five years and a true visionary and spiritual leader who changed the lives of thousands of people. I am forever thankful to him and his wife, Pamela, for being my mentors and my adopted spiritual parents.

I can still recall the surreal phenomenon that happened in that magical crypt space under the earth while we rehearsed and performed. Once, as we were rehearsing, a cast member who feared being in the crypt because she thought it was spooky asked if there were any dead bodies there. I said yes, but they were good souls; they were bishops. The audience seats were right on top of their graves. At that moment John, who was sitting on stage arranging the score with other musicians, looked down at his feet and saw three small bishops from a chess game suddenly appear out of nowhere! Everyone was shocked and speechless, and it took some time before we could concentrate on our rehearsal again.

Another time during rehearsal, as we began the chants for the goddess of the sea, mother of waters, and the orisha Ochun and walked in procession from the back of the crypt, we noticed a stream of water coming out from underneath the floor of the crypt, encircling the space. We were alarmed and called the security guard, who said that there was a stream below the floor. "You must have done something to activate it, Alessandra!" he said. "Yes, we did! We chanted to the goddess of sweet waters, Ochun," we said. The supervisor of the guards, being from Trinidad, understood perfectly and just let it be.

This happened again during a performance, and we all looked at each other, feeling protected, not in danger. The small stream of water appeared for a while at the beginning of Act II and then magically disappeared under the crypt floor, which was covered with dirt and stones.

The strongest and, for me, scariest experience during the performance in the crypt was on opening night. I played the Cumaean Sybil prophetess of the underworld, wearing a brown tunic and a very spooky three-faced mask (see fig. 10.3, page 289) symbolizing seeing the past, present, and future, which (somewhat ironically) gave me no peripheral vision at all. In the scene I wanted the audience to feel that I was coming out from the earth.

I heard my musical cue, the beginning of the *Dies Irae*. I sang as I began walking slowly across a wooden platform from the back of the theater, with special effect smoke swirling around me, toward the actor playing Virgil (the wonderful singer Ivan Thomas). But because of the mask, I could not see where I was going, and suddenly my feet went through a space in the platform and I plunged through, sinking into the dirt and stones of the original crypt. I was terrified, and I know all the cast members were frozen in fear, but the show had to go on. Fortunately, I landed on my feet and was not hurt, and so as indicated in the story, I quite literally reappeared as if coming out from under the earth, climbing through stones and wood, looking like the sybil lost in the mist and dust! It was a great magical effect that looked intentional. In fact, it was so powerful that we decided to keep this "accident" by fixing the platform so it went down and then back up, and I could safely emerge, making a dramatic entrance.

Through the staging of the show, I tried to re-create the powerful visual impact of what I had experienced in the processions and rituals in Southern Italy. Following the old traditions of ritual Greek theater and Italian Renaissance street theater, all the actors and dancers were required to use masks when portraying the moon, the sun, the goddesses, and even Virgil, who also became the sacred bull honoring the goddess of the moon.

I also wanted to portray the Black Madonna as a statue that comes alive and performs miracles through sacred chants and drumming music. I had to convey what I felt during my travels in these places, seeing Her face shift, smile, and cry and feeling touched by Her grace. I played the role using special masks to express this transformation.

Inspired by the folkloric traditions in Calabria and Sicily, I decided to have a giant puppet representing the goddesses and the Earth Mother and Black Madonna, with a different color tunic and headdress according to each goddess: Isis, Artemis, Yemanja, Aphrodite, Fortuna, and Cybele.

I hired a wonderful puppeteer who made a huge Black Madonna puppet, more than eight feet tall, and to my surprise, Dario became an

Fig. 10.4. Puppet of Mother Earth, or the Black Madonna (animated by Dario Bollini), with a moon dancer, from *The Voyage of the Black Madonna;* photo property of I Giullari di Piazza, 1991

expert puppeteer, thus playing the biggest part, the Earth Mother and Black Madonna, inside the giant puppet.

We also needed paintings of the Black Madonnas, and I asked another friend, fresco painter Antonio Romano, to paint real frescos of the three most important ones: Madonna del Tindari, Madonna della Libera (Our Lady of Freedom), and Madonna dei Poveri (Our Lady of the Poor). They were stunning and looked as real as the ones in Italy since he used the old Pompeian fresco technique.

We began to assemble the cast in January 1991, and finally by early

March, we had a large company of twenty-two actors, singers, dancers, and musicians. The whole opera was sung in Italian, in different Southern Italian dialects, and Latin. A wonderful actress was the narrator, who told the stories and legends in English, following the Greek theater style of chorus and narration.

The stage direction and modern dance choreography were done by Sabatino Verlezza, while I choreographed all the folk dances. The music was arranged by John for classical guitar, mandolin, mandoloncello, harp, flute, piccolo, recorders, oboe, violin, cello, and a variety of percussion, including timpani. Three lead singers sang the score with backup vocals.

The opening of the show was the chant to Mamma Schiavona, the Black Madonna of Montevergine, sung by the fabulous Neapolitan singer Giuseppe De Falco. He grew up climbing up to Montevergine and going to Her feast as well as to la Madonna della Neve in his town, together with his mother. Whenever he sings this chant, I get very emotional. His voice is so strong, so open, coming directly from the heart, an example of typical Neapolitan natural talent.

The lead role of the opera, Virgil, was played by an amazing baritone, Ivan Thomas, who is African American and Italian. His interpretation of Virgil was "mythical," as we often say, especially in the beautiful song written by John La Barbera, "Virgil's Prayer." In this tune John created an ancient sound that transported the audience and listeners back to a pre-Christian time, and Ivan added the depth quality of his voice, which brought Earth and heaven together.

Here is the story of the opera divided in two acts.

### From *The Voyage of the Black Madonna*
### performed May 1991

The Narrator speaks: Virgil, a poet and a healer, is searching for the true knowledge to save the world from self-destruction. He evokes the Cumaean Sibyl, the prophetess of the underworld, who tells Virgil that the only way to find true knowledge is through purification and to call for the Universal Mother to help him through his voyage of initiation. Virgil prays intensely and is visited first by the Egyptian goddess Isis, the most important of all divinities, who reveals to him that she is still alive today through the traditions and devotions to the Black Madonna. She gives him the power to magically evoke the sun to rise, and the first Madonna is born: la Madonna del Tindari.

In a legend lost in the mists of time, She arrived from ancient Egypt to Sicily on a ship during a tempest. The fishermen who fell in the water with Her did not drown. They were miraculously cast safely ashore. There they found Her statue and carried it up the mountain with them, where She has been venerated ever since. She was black, and Her song in Latin says *nigra sum sed formosa*. She still protects women in childbirth and their babies.

Fig. 10.5. Black Madonna del Tindari coming out of the sun:
Alessandra Belloni, Mark Mindek, and Ivan Thomas;
photo property of I Giullari di Piazza, 1991

As his journey of initiation continues, Virgil encounters Artemis of Ephesus (the magical and mysterious goddess of the moon), who reveals to him la Madonna della Libera (Our Lady of Freedom) who is known in the town of Moiano as Brunettella (the little dark one). This beautiful Madonna arrived mysteriously on a Turkish ship in the thirteenth century and has performed many, many miracles since then. She shows Virgil Her miraculous powers by healing a mute girl of the town during the procession on Her feast day. The girl who had never spoken suddenly begins to chant "Evviva Maria" with the women at the feet of the Madonna, kissing the ground where She has passed in sign of devotion.

Virgil's journey brings him to the goddess Fortuna who spins the wheel of time and fortune. She tells him to uncover one of the most mysterious of all the Madonnas, la Madonna dei Poveri. This Black Virgin from Calabria was found under the ruins of a burned temple in the year 951 and could only be lifted by the poor. Since then She has performed many miracles, especially during the Crusades and the time of the Plague. Every year, for hundreds of years, on August 15, the whole town honors la Madonna dei Poveri with a big feast, fireworks, wild drumming, and dancing the tarantella.

One of the most powerful scenes in the show was during the miracle of la Madonna Brunettella, in which I portrayed Her statue coming to life from under the puppet of the Goddess, chanting as I brought the pilgrims to me in a procession. The actors re-created the ritual of kissing the ground, and one of the dancers played the mute girl who miraculously begins to sing as I, as the Madonna, touched her throat.

We ended Act I with an incredible explosion of drumming in insistent 6/8 tarantella rhythms while Virgil carried the symbolic flag, as in the town of Seminara, and the giant puppet danced through the audience. The audience was mesmerized!

Act II began with drumming and chanting through the audience in honor of Ochun and Yemanaja, the goddesses of love and water from the Afro-Brazilian Yoruba tradition.

Virgil continues his journey of initiation by the sea, playing his magical conch, calling for the goddess of love known in Africa as Yemanja, goddess of love and water, and to the Greeks and Romans as Aphrodite and Venus. She reveals to him that she is still alive and protects us with Her love, worshipped with the rituals for the Black Madonna of the sea. During these rituals in Italy and in Brazil, Her statue is taken on a boat to bless the sea, with people chanting, praying, throwing white flowers in the water as a blessing, to bring love and protection to the land and to the people.

We re-created this beautiful scene with an actual boat, shaking a blue cloth to mimic the waves of the sea and blessing the audience with white flowers.

After unveiling the beautiful Aphrodite, Virgil descends into the underworld. There he meets Hecate, triple goddess of the crossroads and the moon. She shows him the light that leads to true knowledge and tells him that she will punish those who don't respect her. She shows him how she is still venerated today through the devotion to la Madonna dell'Arco, where the townspeople, all dressed in white, celebrate Her by running barefoot and falling into a trance, possessed by the spirit of the Madonna, later waking up healed and receiving miracles.

The culmination of this feast of the Madonna brings purification to the devotees (fujenti), who give up their material possessions to the Virgin, taking them to the high sacred mountain and receiving spiritual enlightenment.

This was one of my favorite scenes, where I played the Madonna dell'Arco wearing a very spooky mask with a scar on the left cheek. Inspired by the Madonna of the Seven Veils, I came out as the veiled goddess, and in slow motion, the cast gathered around the veiled Madonna, bringing flower offerings. One of the actors, Giuseppe, played the arrogant boy and hit the mask, then fell down as if stricken by Her. The drums began to play the loud tammorriata ritual, and everyone fell on the floor, rolling as if they were possessed and ready to finally let go of their madness, thus receiving a miracle as the Madonna touched each one of them.

Fig. 10.6. Virgil (played by Ivan Thomas) singing to the goddess Cybele. J. La Barbera is sitting in the back (far left) with percusionists. (Puppet animated by Dario Bollini)

The final scene came out of this trance ritual of purification.

On Montevergine, Cybele, the Great Mother Earth, appears and tells Virgil that she originated from a black meteorite that fell from the stars. She tells him that his voyage has ended, and he has found the answer: she is a living being and people must return to respecting and caring for her and her sacred womb, as ancient cultures have done for thousands of years, through purification, by giving up material possessions that destroy the environment and will destroy humankind.

On the same mountain where Cybele's temple stood, the Madonna di Montevergine is alive today. Pilgrims walk for miles to see Her, chanting, drumming, and asking for miracles, which still happen and always will if one believes in the Universal Mother's unconditional love.

At the end, while I sang the "Canto di Cybele," another haunting melody written by John with lyrics by Dario, we unveiled the silhouette of a black marble pyramid, representing both the meteorite and the black stone venerated in Mecca by the Muslims, as a final message of peace.

Slowly, Virgil began to sing to Cybele, as the giant puppet came out wearing a huge white skirt, and one by one, all the actors and dancers were guided by Virgil to go inside the puppet to protect the sacred womb of the Great Mother. The lights slowly faded on the black earth goddess, leaving the audience in tears.

We performed the show in the crypt theater at the cathedral for three weeks to full houses, always receiving standing ovations and good reviews.

We went on to perform this powerful opera for a long time and in many places, including the stage outside the World Trade Center. I was always afraid of performing there, because I had had many premonitions—dreams—of the towers exploding. I knew that it would happen; I just did not know when. Dario always looked at me and asked, "When is it?" He knew by then that my powers of clairvoyance were as strong as my mother's. Later in 2001, when I was supposed to go back to New York on September 10, returning from my tour of Italy, I decided to extend my stay. I changed my ticket and took a vacation down in Calabria. I then saw the explosion of the World Trade Center on a TV screen on a beach near my beloved Tropea, exactly as I had dreamed it.

# GETTING MARRIED AT
# THE CATHEDRAL OF SAINT JOHN THE DIVINE
# DURING THE SUMMER SOLSTICE

A few weeks after the show ended, Dario and I had our wedding ceremony at the cathedral on the day of the solstice, June 22, 1991, in what Dario and I called the "wedding of the sun and the moon." It was celebrated by our mentor Dean Jim Morton. My wonderful mother, Elvira, even came from Italy; it would be her last trip to New York. My sister also came from Los Angeles, and Dario's family came from Italy.

It was a beautiful ceremony, and everyone was crying, moved by our long and troubled love story. Afterward, we had a fantastic party at Jim Morton's house, where we ate, drank, and danced the tarantella for hours—all the cast members and even the dean himself. (He still says it was one of the best weddings he ever celebrated.)

I am very grateful to have lived such a powerful love story that was blessed by both the grace of the Black Madonna, who truly bestowed a miracle by healing Dario and bringing us together, and a great spiritual leader, Jim Morton, who had a strong impact on my life. In fact, in June 1991 the dean asked us to become artists in residence at the Cathedral of Saint John the Divine, thus giving us the space to continue our spiritual and artistic work, following his vision and receiving his guidance.

## EXPERIENCING THE TRANCE
## RITUAL IN HONOR OF THE MADONNA

It was during these opera performances that I first realized the incredible power of the trance drumming ritual that we reenacted on stage for la Madonna dell'Arco, with actors and dancers throwing themselves on the floor, rolling and screaming as if possessed by the spirit of the Madonna. As I played her role, I felt that I left my body, and I know that everyone else did too. It was very real, and the audience could feel the magic in the air. At times they were even afraid that the show might stop. It was definitely a collective shamanic journey evoked by the drumming and chanting. But I did not fully realize it then.

Now I teach healing workshops around the world and have a lot of experience in leading these trance rituals where many times the participants tell me that they receive healing when they completely let their mind go and have a powerful vision of the Black Madonna touching them or laying Her hands on them. When they wake up, they usually cry, releasing their emotions of anguish or sadness and embracing total joy.

I hope to continue to inspire many people to experience this kind of release through an altered state of mind achieved with shamanic drumming, dancing, and chanting. It is an ancient tradition popular among all indigenous people around the world, and if well practiced, it is proven to be more beneficial than any conventional medicine or drugs. Before modern medicine and psychotherapy, there was shamanism, and it still exists.

## ✴ Shamanic Drumming

As a musical shaman, I invite you to take a journey of discovery and empowerment through healing rituals and deep trance states. I encourage you to find experienced healers in your community or to travel to meet ones who come from indigenous cultures.

If you have never taken a shamanic journey, you can experiment with a friend, taking turns drumming for each other. Use a regular frame drum (I recommend a drum that is sixteen inches wide) with a deep sound to tap a simple, even rhythm, like a heartbeat. As your friend drums, stand and let your body move freely, such as turning and spinning. Chanting is also very important. Invoke the protection of the Black Madonna, the archangels, or an ancestor who has guided you from the other side. Allow yourself to feel the power of a vision coming from above, while letting go of your mind.

This practice takes time, so don't rush it—let it happen naturally. When you feel that the release has happened, it is best to lie on the ground to connect to the Earth Mother, breathing deeply with your eyes

Fig. 10.7. Scene of the Madonna dell'Arco (played by Alessandra Belloni) from *The Voyage of the Black Madonna*

closed and the palms of your hands open to the sky. A final meditation is also helpful for coming back into this dimension and being grounded. When you are ready, open your eyes and wake up your body, feeling lighter with renewed energy.

This chant to Our Lady of the Hens (Madonna delle Galline), with notations and lyrics on page 367 in the appendix to chapter 10, has a haunting melody on the Lydian scale. This is the chant we used during our first production in 1991, and it made everyone leave their bodies for a while. This particular feast, honoring the Madonna of the Hens and birds in general, is of true shamanic origins. Bird feathers are used all over the world for cleansing ceremonies and to connect with the Great Spirit or Divine Feminine to ask for healing. I hope that you will find beautiful bird feathers to help in the journey and to use with the burning of sage to complete this powerful ritual of purification.

# CHAPTER 11

# Rhythm Is the Cure

## The Shamanic Power of the Tarantella

*Women women who go work in the tobacco fields,*
*you always get assaulted under the trees.*
*Who tells you to go there to pick the tobacco?*
*The landowner does not even give*
*you the right wages.*
*The sun is so strong and dries all your tobacco.*
*Women women you go in twos, come back in fours.*
*Oh Saint Paul of Galatina, please make this young*
*    lady happy.*
*Grant us a grace! To me and all the women! Oh*
*    Saint Paul of the tarantula, help us!*

"FIMMENE FIMMENE" (WOMEN WOMEN),
TRADITIONAL WOMEN'S WORK CHANT

I BELIEVE THAT LIFE HAPPENS IN GREAT CYCLES. As I am writing this book and I look back at my journey, I can see clearly the cycles in my life coming at different times, in specific years, some full of joy and others full of sadness, always leading into a new cycle and a new beginning. I deeply feel that all these cycles are part of a greater

Fig. 11.1. Healing trance dance, or tarantella, of San Rocco at Rhythm is the Cure workshop in Tuscany; photo property of A. Belloni

design, laying out our mission or reason to be here in this lifetime, and I also believe in karma. Yet, during the difficult moments in my life and facing tough decisions or losses of loved ones, I have had a hard time accepting this thought, often letting a feeling of despair or fear take over. In the end, I have always found my inner strength and positive attitude through prayers to the Madonna, through my mother's support, and often through my music. This has led me to the conclusion that *rhythm is the cure*. And I will tell you why . . .

One of the years that marked a milestone in my life is definitely 1991, the year I got married to the important love of my life, Dario, and we premiered our opera *The Voyage of the Black Madonna*.

That great joy was soon overcome by a great uneasiness, as later in the fall I became ill again with heavy irregular bleeding. My gynecologist told me that I should not take any chances since I had had cancerous cells five years earlier, and she scheduled me for another surgery. She also told me that I had to rest and could not dance. However, at that point I had an instinctive feeling that Western medicine was not the solution to my problem. I had been on my spiritual quest following the Black Madonna, I was studying various esoteric teachings, and I felt that I had to trust my strong intuition.

I have always known that I have psychic powers. As mentioned before, I have often had premonitions leading me to anticipate events like the World Trade Center attack, which stopped me from flying back to New York from Italy right before the disaster happened on September 11. Through my psychic powers I have foreseen tragedies, including the explosion of the space shuttle in Cape Canaveral in January 1986. At that time, I was in Florida to perform at Disney World. The night before the tragedy, I woke everyone up, screaming from a nightmare in which I saw a terrible explosion. The next morning I actually saw that same explosion from the Orlando airport!

These premonitions sometimes are a curse, because I see things that are frightening and I cannot do anything about it. In some cases, though, this power is a real gift. I was booked on a flight to Rome, scheduled to leave on July 17, 1996, from JFK Airport. I had a premonition that the number seventeen would bring bad luck, following an Italian superstition, so I called my travel agent to change my flight to July 20. The night of July 17, I saw the news of the explosion of flight TWA 800 to Paris and was horrified. The next morning I found out all passengers to Rome had been switched to that flight to Paris, and everyone on the flight had died. I lit a lot of candles at Saint John the Divine and got a blessing from the dean.

In the fall of 1991, as I was being told once again that I needed invasive surgery, I heard the same inner voice telling me not to do it and that I would be fine if I just trusted in my prayers to the Black Madonna, who would show me another way. Even though it seemed hard at the time, I had to trust that She was putting me through another trial for a reason. We had an important performance coming up, in which I was going to play the role of the tarantata. The doctor told me not to dance, but as you know, "the show must go on" no matter what. I told my husband—who was very worried about my health—that I had to follow my intuition and dance the healing trance dance of the pizzica tarantata, which had helped women for so many centuries.

I remember discussing my condition with a healer and Santero priest, my good friend Gypsy Joe, who had been the first one to teach me the musical and dance devotion of the Afro-Brazilian Yoruba religion and who had told me that I was a daughter of Ochun, the goddess of love, rivers, and sweet water. Joe is powerful, a real Gypsy from Calabria, with great knowledge of esoteric studies from all over the world. He is a gifted psychic healer, clairvoyant, and spiritualist initiated in the Yoruba orisha tradition. For our performance he would be playing the tambourine, the instrument that has shamanic power when played with specific accents that help induce an altered mental state and sometimes a deep trance. He told me that he would play for me like the traditional players did in Italy for so many years to cure the tarantati. He advised me to enter a meditative state and pray to the Madonna to restore my health before I entered the stage to begin the dance and to connect with the spider medicine.

I had reenacted the dance of the tarantata on stage many times before and choreographed it for my folk opera *La Lupa* in 1987. Every time I did that scene, I naturally entered an altered state of mind and felt taken back into another century when women were more repressed, oppressed, and abused by the patriarchal society in which they lived. Even though I am not from Puglia, where the dance supposedly originated, I felt that I knew the frantic rhythm and trance dance very well.

I would enter the stage all dressed in white with the traditional red scarf and begin to spin down onto a white sheet, which creates a *perimetro cerimoniale* (literally a "ceremonial perimeter," or sacred space). I would lie flat on my back with my legs open and make sensual movements that resemble those of a spider, letting the haunting melodies of the pizzica take me over, played by the violinist and tambourine player, along with the fast accents of the drum. As I heard the last musical refrain, I would jump up, and other dancers would join me as I stamped my feet and kept spinning all the way out into the audience.

For many years during my research, I had wondered who the tarantate were. Why did I identify with them? As mentioned earlier, this fast

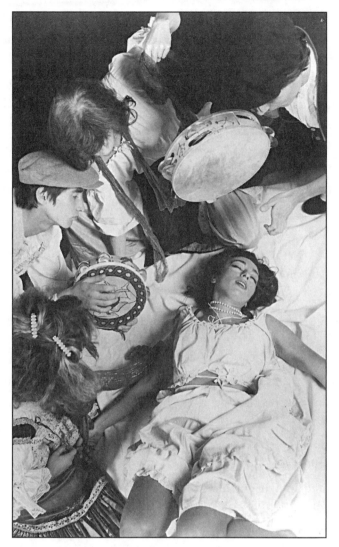

Fig. 11.2. Alessandra Belloni in tarantata scene from *La Lupa,* 1987

and sensual dance was used for centuries as a music and dance therapy to treat women and men who suffered from tarantismo. The dominant music was played on large tambourines keeping a nonstop 12/8 beat with loud accents, together with the guitar, violin, accordion, and voice. By spinning and stomping their feet, the tarantate (usually mainly women) symbolically expelled the poison of the mythical bite of the tarantula from their bodies. A double row of jingles on the tamburello accentuated the madness as the dancers moved on their backs like spiders, with very erotic movements and at times displaying acrobatic skills they did not have in their regular life.

The trancelike state that women entered proved to be beneficial for the healing of many disorders and imbalances. This energetic dance was indeed, and still is, one of the strongest forms of music and dance therapy, effective also for men who were outcast due to social status and sexual preference: for anyone, man or woman, who was homosexual and could not express their sexuality and who fell into deep depression. Their only cure was to dance the tarantella.

That night in the fall of 1991, during our performance in New York, Gypsy Joe (who is gay and part of the LGBTQ movement) reminded me, "You are one of them, Alessandra, you are also a tarantata, you must dance and receive the cure, but you must let go and slip into a trance to receive the grace." Neither the audience nor the other cast members knew what was about to happen when we began playing the pizzica.

I prayed to the Black Madonna and asked Her to lay a hand on my womb to release the poison that was stuck inside my blood and to break the web of my subconscious mind that kept me from being healthy and whole again.

As the musicians started the pizzica tarantata, I heard the haunting notes of the violin and the loud accents of the guitar and the tambourines. I spun myself down and began rolling on the floor, on the ceremonial white sheet, jumping like a spider on my back with legs up in the air, and losing control of my mind to Gypsy Joe's tambourine playing. The dance became extremely erotic, and it felt like an orgasm as I released the "venom" from my blood. I had no idea how long I danced, later realizing that it had gone on for more than twenty minutes. Other dancers from the group joined me, spinning with me in a euphoric wild finale as I was turning around the room and stamping my feet.

All I know for sure is that my bleeding stopped immediately and never came back.

I cried from happiness and hugged Gypsy Joe and my musicians. It was a real miracle! Dario was extremely happy, and from that point he accepted all the magic that came into our lives. To my amazement I realized that rhythm is the cure! I canceled my surgery, against the will of my gynecologist, and have been fine ever since. I thanked the Black Madonna of Czestochowa at Saint John the Divine and asked Her why I had been put through another ordeal with physical illness. It took some time, but the answer came a few years later. I had to experience firsthand the healing power of the authentic tarantella, connected since ancient times to the bite of the mythical spider Arachne and the goddesses Athena and Cybele, before I could bring this cure to other people, especially women who suffered from trauma due to abuse.

I will share with you the ancient myth of the Spider Woman, who is the archetype that we carry in our subconscious mind and has been part of the Mediterranean culture for thousands of years. The myth of the spider, always a female, exists throughout many indigenous cultures including Native American, African, and Maori. It is interesting that in Western patriarchal society, we instead have Spider Man!

## THE ECSTATIC RITES OF DIONYSUS

The historic dance of the tarantula originated in Puglia and Magna Grecia in pre-Christian times and was done by women taking part in the Greek Dionysian mysteries in honor of Dionysus or Bacchus, the god of ecstasy and wine. The Roman festival was called a Bacchanal, and the women, highly evolved priestesses, also initiated in the mysteries of the goddesses Cybele and Demeter, were known as Bacchae, or Baccanti in Italian. These ecstatic rites in honor of Dionysus were popular all over the Mediterranean and were particularly strong in Rome near the Aventine Hill, celebrated with music, dance, and orgiastic rituals led by the Bacchae (see plate 19).

Euripides's drama *The Bacchae* centers on Dionysus himself, a god full of dualistic symbolism (divine and mortal, Greek and foreigner, masculine and feminine). The cult of Dionysus allows women to question male supremacy but then drives them mad as punishment. At the end, it is the theater itself that gives Dionysus's worshippers their freedom as they can become, however temporarily, something other than themselves.

## THE MYTH OF ARACHNE AND ATHENA

Arachne, a beautiful young Athenian virgin and skilled weaver, is admired by everyone for her talent. Everyone asks her if she learned from Athena, goddess of weaving, wisdom, and war. Arachne proudly says that she never learned from the goddess and that she is much better than Athena at weaving. Arachne, with the arrogance typical of a young girl, then challenges Athena to a weaving contest in which they must depict a love scene. Arachne mocks the gods in her tapestry, especially Zeus and his polygamy, but her linen is the most beautiful, so she wins.

Athena, overcome by anger and jealousy, tears the linen into a thousand pieces and hits poor Arachne over the head with the spindle. Arachne, humiliated, hangs herself from a tree. Athena then feels pity for Arachne and transforms her into a spider, condemning her to weave her web forever. Thus, Arachne became the Spider Woman who never knew love, still a virgin when she died.

The myth tells us that a suicide mania overtook the women of Athens—especially virgins—who in a collective ritual hanged themselves, overcome by depression as if they were bitten by Arachne hanging from the tree.

This went on until the sybil, the oracle of Apollo from Delphi and prophetess of the underworld, ordered women to have a feast in honor of the god Dionysus and to honor the god with an initiation into his mysteries. During these ecstatic rites, women lived freely in the woods, usually wearing only deerskin, drank wine, and ate special plants that caused hallucinations. They ran and danced wildly, rocking on swings hanging from trees, celebrating lascivious orgiastic rites, and filling the air with melodies played by the lira, double flutes, sistrum, and the rhythm of the tambourines. When they evoked the god Bacchus to possess them, they would scream in chorus, *"Euoee!"*

Fig. 11.3. Villa dei Misteri in Pompeii,
young girls being initiated in the mysteries of Dionysus;
photo by A. Belloni

These initiatory rites for Dionysus were very complex, as we can observe them depicted in the majestic frescoes in the Villa dei Misteri in Pompeii. The Bacchae were not simply revelers but high priestesses with great knowledge and power, and their ecstatic rituals were, in fact, shamanic.

The Bacchae seem to be saying that it is dangerous to deny or ignore the human desire for the Dionysian experience; those who are open to the experience will find spiritual power, and those who suppress or repress the desire in themselves or others will transform it into a destructive force.

The Bacchae were very popular in ancient Rome, and Dionysus was probably the Romans' favorite god. When the Catholic Church was established, and the power of the Roman Empire became the power of the Vatican, the Dionysian rites were abolished and became unlawful. In truth, the rites died out in Greece but not in Southern

Italy. We know that during the Dark Ages there were some dances done in secret in various places, especially in the area of Benevento (the witches' dance around the walnut tree) for pagan festivals like the summer and winter solstices. The instruments used were the tambourines, various string instruments, rebec, pan pipes, and recorders. These rituals became more popular as musical exorcisms in the late Middle Ages into the early Renaissance, and the people who practiced them were often accused of witchcraft by the local church authorities.

In the Mediterranean this form of collective euphoria spread, beginning from the time of the Crusades, the Plague, and the widespread fear of the end of the world. Men and women ran wildly through the streets, dancing, holding swords, spinning, throwing themselves on the ground or in water, and saying that the tarantula bit them and that they had to get the poison out of their body. By the early Renaissance, the tarantella was already being practiced as a trance dance of purification to cure mainly women, and some men, afflicted by this mythical bite of the tarantula.

The archetype of the spider was shared through the collective unconscious as the victims felt caught in the web of their society. The musicians and percussionists were called into the streets to play the 6/8 or 12/8 rhythm that had the power to pull the poison out of the body and calm down the tarantate.

The Catholic Church, which tried over the centuries but could not stop the hidden celebrations, finally absorbed this rite, and the god Dionysus was replaced by Saint Paul. There are even historical accounts of priests who were bitten and had to "dance the poison out" inside the church and called the local musicians to perform the exorcism.

The first written account of the tarantella as an antidote was written down in 1673 by a Jesuit named Athanasius Kircher, who was the first to notate the music and the rhythm in his book *Phonurgia Nova*, with the piece called *Antidotum Tarantulae* (Antidote for the Tarantula Bite). In his study, Kircher explained how the venom from the bite of

Fig. 11.4. Scene of the tarantella ritual dance and music
from *Phonurgia Nova* by Athanasius Kircher

the *Lycosa tarantula,* or wolf spider, caused a form of madness that affected the nervous system, and the people who were bitten had to dance frantically to these special melodies, mostly in the Lydian mode, some slow and some fast, until the poison was expelled from the body through sweat, tears, and vomiting. For a long time, at least four centuries, people believed that it was indeed the poison of the spider that caused this malady, which became known as tarantismo.

## ABOUT TARANTELLA AND TARANTISMO

Unfortunately, in the United States the tarantella is known only as a silly wedding dance, and it has lost its true meaning of healing and release of sensuality. I firmly believe that it is due to the discrimination that Italian immigrants were subjected to when they came to the United States. They were often treated badly and made to feel ashamed of their heritage. To fit in with the Puritan Anglo-Saxon culture that was (and still is) dominant in the States, they had to deny their primitive yet rich folklore, which was too sensual and erotic to be accepted by the era's white supremacist society.

The true tarantella is a wild, erotic trance dance of purification. In 1961, ethnomusicologist and anthropologist Ernesto De Martino wrote a great book titled *La terra del rimorso,* now also translated into English under the title *The Land of Remorse.* This is a remarkable text, a real masterpiece of its kind in which he explained the origins of the tarantella with accurate historical and field research. He led a team of Italian psychiatrists, ethnomusicologists, anthropologists, and sociologists who went to Salento (the only place left in Italy where tarantismo still existed) to study the tarantati, live with them, and document their lives.

The researchers found specific patterns that were always repeated and similarities in all the tarantate. The women were often "bitten" at puberty, at times due to unrequited love or a lost love, and this was known as *morso d'amore* (the bite of love). Many times the first bite happened when they were working hard in the fields, often picking tobacco under the hot sun. They hallucinated and actually saw a spider coming toward them, felt a great pain in the stomach and weakness in the legs, fell to the ground in a state of hypnosis, and screamed very loudly (their cry is very similar to the Bacchantes' *euoee*), then fainted and lost consciousness for a long time. All these women lived in very poor social conditions and many times were not allowed to marry the man they wanted but were forced by their fathers to marry a man they did not love. They were often sexually abused by the landowners or their husbands and were victims of domestic violence.

At times people became tarantate due to the death of a loved one—a mother, a child, or a spouse. Men were tarantati (masculine) if they were outcasts, especially if they were homosexuals and could not freely express their desires. Their frustrations and desires came out during the dance, when they were allowed to do anything. They were not regarded as sinners but rather as people who were ill.

## TARANTELLA TRANCE RITUAL
## OR PIZZICA TARANTATA

The trance was always induced by the tambourine, usually played by older women, with a very fast 6/8 or 12/8 rhythm and a series of triplets that have specific accents. The beat and the accents, called *battute* in Italian, helped the women move in a spiderlike way to release the poison from their bodies. The women were indeed possessed by the spider, and the tarantella became known as a musical exorcism.

The exorcism took place at home. The tarantata, all dressed in white, lay on the floor on a white sheet, with colorful ribbons all around her that would be used in the dance. She began the dance on her back, moving her arms and legs like a spider, sliding, turning, and jumping off her back, performing acrobatic movements. Some women would actually hang from a rope suspended from the ceiling or from a tree, swinging in the air like a spider. When the accents on the tambourine and the music changed, the tarantata got up and started spinning, trying to free herself from an imaginary spiderweb.

The trance ritual lasted three days, and the musicians had to play the whole time with only short breaks. From time to time the tarantata would collapse, still unconscious, moaning and lamenting, and the musicians then took their rest and food breaks. These musicians were real masters, with an incredible amount of stamina, never getting tired, performing the ceremonies for three days. They were the true shamans.

The main instruments besides the tambourine were the violin or fiddle, which replaced the rebec of the Middle Ages for playing very high slurred notes and very fast triplets, classical and acoustic guitars, and the chitarra battente. The latter was used to keep the beat (the word *battente* comes from the Italian word *battere,* which means "to beat") and is a percussive guitar, playing the same accents as the tambourine and the button accordion. The musicians had to be very skilled, locking in perfectly with the triplets and accents of the tambourine without ever losing the beat, or the tarantata would have outbursts of madness and throw herself violently on the musicians. Since they were playing "the cure" and performing an exorcism, there was no room for mistakes.

The musicians were regarded and also paid as doctors, and they learned the repertoire by oral tradition since usually none of them could read music. The women who played the large tamburello often learned it from their mother or grandmother. They were true healers, with the power to induce the trance and get the poison out of the body. The voice, violin, and tambourine had the strongest effect of the cure.

The singers had to learn a huge repertoire. Some of the lyrics the singers would sing to the tarantata were *"Addo t'a pizzicao a tarantella, sott'a lu giru giru di la vunnella!"* (Where did the tarantula bite you? Under the edge of your skirt. . . . If it is the tarantula that bit you, let her dance; if it is sadness, send it off!) They also sang a prayer to Saint Paul: *"Ah ti prego Santu Paulu falla guarire ca l'ave pizzicata a tarantella."* (I beg you, Saint Paul, please heal her, as she was bitten by the tarantula.)

Until a few years ago, they would go to the Church of Saint Paul in the small town of Galatina near Lecce, where they danced to the rhythm with their hands, feet, and tambourines, jumping on the altar and all over the church, throwing themselves on the statue of the saint and asking to be healed. On the third day of the trance ritual, June 29, the tarantate were usually healed, receiving a vision of Saint Paul.

They would come out of the church graced by Saint Paul and with no memory of what had happened during the ritual of the tarantella. But the tarantate were cured for only one year, and every year, usually in June, with the heat approaching, they would fall back in the same state of mind, feel the same anguish and depression, collapse on the ground, and repeat the ritual, until on June 29 they would once again receive grace from Saint Paul. Once a tarantata, always a tarantata!

This brilliant book by De Martino became my bible and helped me in my research for many years. De Martino explained in detail the similarities of our tarantella rhythms with the trance rituals of the gnawa in Morocco, the czar in Egypt, the dervishes in Turkey and Iran, and the Afro-Brazilian Candomblé and Afro-Cuban Santeria. He also explained how the musical celebrations of the Eleusinian mysteries for the Great Mother Cybele, Persephone, and Demeter included the ecstatic orgiastic rituals of Dionysus. And then I understood why the strong devotion to the Black Madonna and the origins of the tarantella were interconnected because of Dionysus being celebrated together with the Earth Mother Goddess.

Around the time his book came out in the early 1960s, De Martino also collaborated on a wonderful documentary called *La Taranta,* by Gianfranco Mingozzi. It showed the sad and depressing conditions of the tarantate who were left in the region of Salento and told their stories with haunting images in black and white.

Unfortunately, after the book and film came out, some doctors decided to go down to Salento and help the poor tarantate by taking them to hospitals and treating them with pills and electric shock. This interference by Western medicine, together with mass media and television, contributed to the disappearance of the rituals of the pizzica tarantata and the true cure through dance therapy of people afflicted by tarantismo. By the time I was doing my field research in Puglia from the mid-1980s to the mid-1990s, looking for possible tarantate, none were left. I only met the musicians who knew and taught me the rhythm that cured. This turned out to be a real blessing for my healing work.

At the time I thought that this powerful therapy was something of the past and could not work in our modern society. Then, to my surprise in 1991, I discovered through my personal experience that the pizzica tarantata as music and dance therapy is still very effective and can help heal, especially in today's destructive social environment.

## RHYTHM IS THE CURE AND
## THE SHAMANIC POWER OF THE TAMBOURINE

The extraordinary experience of healing myself with the dance, and through the altered state of mind induced by the powerful tambourine playing of my Gypsy Santero friend, motivated me to study and learn other forms of ecstatic dances, but it mainly led me to learn more about shamanic drumming. I was drawn to all styles of drumming that were used to invoke the spirits, to bring down the god or goddess, and to induce trances through which people received a vision that brought healing to a person or community.

It became clear that the vision of the Black Madonna telling me that I had to feel other people's pain back in 1986, along with the writing of the opera to heal the Earth, allowed me to open a portal into another dimension where the ancient healing drumming and dance traditions I studied so deeply became part of my everyday life and relevant for the pain of women today. Like the Earth's womb, the wombs of women have been broken, and just as it had happened to me, my womb bleeding from past wounds, other women from all over the world shared the same pain.

As I began to study shamanism, I also began to understand my psychic powers and clairvoyance as they relate to the role of the shaman. I read many books by Rudolf Steiner, and his anthroposophy studies really resonated with me. Another author who gave me great inspiration is Matthew Fox, a real visionary who is also devoted to the Black Madonna and who used trance music and dance together with his religious training as a priest to create the amazing Cosmic Mass. He is surely one of my most relevant mentors.

I learned that we are made of not only the physical body but also the astral and ethereal bodies. The astral body is what can travel during our dreams and, through shamanic journeys guided by the drum beat, into different dimensions that exist simultaneously to our reality here on Earth. In the case of my visions and seeing the future, I can explain it as my astral body opening a window into the dimension of the near future and seeing what is about to happen as if it were happening in that exact moment. Most of the time, though, coming back into this reality when not guided by a shaman is painful and sad, and I always wake up crying and feeling exhausted. The ethereal body, I believe, is our soul and should not travel far away or our physical body would die. That is why I firmly believe that anyone who is interested in shamanism and altered states of mind should not take it lightly. This is serious work and should only be done with great and positive intentions, because when you enter the spirit world, the underworld, you can also meet negative forces. No one has ever described the journey into the underworld better then the poet Virgil in the *Aeneid* and Dante Alighieri in the *Divine Comedy*.

I knew that to be a real healer like the old women for the tarantate, I had to master the Southern Italian tambourine, and it would take years to develop the stamina to be able to play for three days. I promised myself that I had to learn to play the pizzica without stopping for at least five or six hours; so I went down to Torre Paduli in Puglia on August 15 and joined the men playing at the Feasta di San Rocco (Feast of Saint Rocco), from ten o'clock in the evening until sunrise. I went for four years in a row.

My first time at the feast, in 1984, I was really scared. There were no women participating, only men, playing the tambourine and dancing la scherma. Gathering my courage, I took out my tambourine and tried to join their ronda (circle of players). Very quickly my hands began bleeding on the tambourine due to the fast rhythm and immense strength that it required. The skin on my thumb was gone! All the players saw me and acknowledged my presence with suspicious looks, and I did not feel welcome at all. In fact, I was kicked out! The men told me to stop playing as they moved away and began another ronda. I stood there alone in the dark, holding my tambourine, feeling humiliated. I knew that it was because I was a woman and an outsider. I swore revenge and made a promise that someday I would come back, keeping the rhythm of the pizzica all night long and being accepted by the male players.

Fig. 11.5. The martial arts dance called la scherma,
during a pizzica ritual in Torre Paduli; photo by A. Belloni

When I went back in 1992, the atmosphere in Torre Paduli was very different. There were many women dancing, and it was much more open and not as scary. I was with Dario and a great musician from Puglia, Gianni De Gennaro, whom I had met in New York and who still performs with me. I admit that my drumming skills were much better, and together with Gianni, I looked at one ronda and decided to join in. I felt safe this time, especially after locking in with an old man who stared at me with great enthusiasm, so happy to have a woman in the circle. He remembered that the original players for the tarantate were women. The younger generation apparently didn't know that the tamburello had been a female instrument for hundreds of years, and they now believed that men were stronger and were the only ones who could play for a long time.

I made a commitment to change this misconception, and we began an unspoken challenge in which I was the only woman playing with at least ten men. They came directly to challenge me, playing faster and louder without stopping. Then after at least two hours, they all got tired and looked at me in shock. In dialect, one of them, Ferdinando

Bevilacqua, a man who later became my friend, said to me, "Who the hell are you, and where the hell do you come from?" "My name is Alessandra Belloni, and I come from New York, even though I am from Rome," I replied. I will never forget that moment. The news that I had come from New York to play the pizzica for San Rocco spread fast, and everyone came to check me out, still suspicious but with great curiosity. When we explained that we were all musicians, I had a theater company in America, and we had been studying folkloric traditions for a long time, everyone opened up and we made many friends. One of them invited us to stay at his trailer and to go to his tavern to continue the party after the feast was over. We all accepted this wonderful invitation, and we partied with him and his family for a week, eating lots of meat (including horse meat, which is typical of that area of Salento) and drinking very strong red wine called *niuru* (black wine).

It was there at his tavern that I met his mother, an incredibly beautiful ninety-three-year-old woman named Stella, who had been one of the tambourine players for the tarantate for most of her life. She saw that I was a stranger, but she also saw something else in me: my commitment to play the tambourine without stopping and to learn the right accents.

One night, she asked to sit next to me and spoke the magic words, "I will show you the real accents of the pizzica tarantata. I used to play nonstop, you know, when I was younger, for three days and three nights. Back then, the woman always danced nonstop, and I could not stop until she did. It was the accents of the tambourine that made her jump, then she spun around and kept spinning until she fell."

Then Stella asked her son to bring out her magic tambourine, which was at least seventy years old. She smiled, looked at me, nodded, and signaled to me to watch first. She began the strongest, loudest accents and fast triplets, with the jingles making so much sound I could not believe it was only one person and one so old. I began to cry, and she smiled, seeing that I was very moved and mesmerized by her playing, and then very seriously she kept playing the cycles and sang some of the traditional verses. With her permission, Dario filmed these precious moments. She really wanted me to learn this healing rhythm from her. She played for a while, and I felt her accents inside my womb, releasing energies, entering another dimension, feeling the pain of the tarantate that she must have cured. She was a *curandera pugliese,* a shaman from Puglia in her own way, and I am so blessed to have had that chance to sit with her for a few nights to learn and receive her gift of healing through the tambourine. Grazie, Stella! You must be a star in heaven now.

That night was my real initiation into the healing power of the tambourine. It was 1992, during one of the summers that we were traveling down to Southern Italy doing research on the Black Madonna, that I felt that everything was connected, and I was being guided. I understood later on that I did not choose to bring the healing power of the tarantella and the Black Madonna to others in need of help; it chose me. It was part of a higher design, a call that I had to follow.

I kept going back to Puglia to the feast in Torre Paduli and to see Stella to learn more, to dance more, and to develop my stamina so that I might one day be able to play for many hours straight and never feel tired but instead energized by what I call tarantella power. I knew I would write a new show about the history and legends of the tarantella, and my inspiration came from all this field research and the wild tarantella parties that we had in Puglia and Calabria, playing for entire nights until the sun came up and singing "Jesce Sole" to the dawn.

In 1996 we premiered our production *The Dance of the Ancient Spider* at Alice Tully Hall at Lincoln Center. The show was based on the myths of Arachne and Dionysus and the sad story of a tarantata. We had a sold-out audience and great reviews. In the audience were two psychiatrists from the renowned Mount Sinai Hospital who loved the story and were interested in having their psychiatric patients experience the power of the tarantella dance and rhythms. They asked me if I was interested in this work, and I was thrilled.

I began to work at Mount Sinai as a volunteer with their outpatients, many suffering from manic depression, borderline personality disorder, and hysteria, but I held my drumming and dance sessions

Fig. 11.6. Playing the pizzica with Stella,
the elder who played for the tarantate rituals

with them without knowing their cases. The doctors left me alone with
the patients so they could be free to express themselves, using drumming and movement. It was an exhilarating experience for me because,
through those months (eight sessions repeated four times over the
course of two years), people who never smiled began to smile and laugh,
people who did not talk began to communicate with others, and many
found the physical balance they had lost due to heavy medications.

In 1996 at a percussion convention and drum festival called PASIC
I met the renowned Remo Belli, the owner and founder of Remo, Inc.,
the largest drum and percussion company in the world, and the inven-
tor (in 1957) of synthetic drumheads. He watched me play my tamburello at his booth, and he was so impressed that he asked me to design
Southern Italian tambourines with his company. He proposed that I
launch a series of tambourines, which Remo, Inc., would build with
my design and my signature, based on the traditional instruments that
I played but with Remo's unique and durable synthetic skins. Remo
Belli believed that this powerful technique and great drumming style,

which strangely were largely unknown, deserved to be brought into the percussion world.

This was definitely an amazing unexpected blessing that I received, and thanks to Remo Belli and his vision and his wife, Ami, my artistic life opened to the world. He became my mentor and gave me the inspiration to pursue my path as a healer. Remo's main interest for the past twenty years had been to develop drums and drumming styles that can improve well-being and help people with physical disabilities. With him I also designed a special large tambourine with the image of the Black Madonna from Calabria and Montserrat, which I use with my students for powerful chants to the Black Madonna, such as the medieval hymn *Cuncti Simus Concanentes* (see chapter 6).

Thanks to Remo and my first percussion convention performance in 1996, I started to get a reputation and began traveling around the world as a performer and teacher. At the same time, during my travels, I studied shamanism with powerful shamans and healers whom I met in Brazil, Hawaii, Scotland, and Italy and who helped me to discover my own healing powers. I began to hold special healing dance and tambourine workshops, to use the tarantella, and to drum for the Black Madonna to heal women from around the world from various disorders—physical, emotional, and mental.

I began leading the workshops first in my studio in the crypt of the Cathedral of Saint John the Divine, which was covered with crystals that Paul Winter had left there. He gave the studio to us with this wonderful protective energy. The first groups of women to come study with me were Italian Americans who had attended my shows and were eager to discover the traditions of their ancestors. It was during those sessions that I began to see how these women transformed and changed their lives as a result of the profound awakening they received through the drumming and dance. Some even left their husbands, and others got pregnant when they thought they could not. I clearly saw that there was more power in these rhythms than I had imagined. I wanted to be a little like Stella, the old woman in Puglia, and help more women break their "webs" to find their own strength, so I decided to experiment

Fig. 11.7. Healing session using the pizzica tarantata in Calabria, 2012, with Gianni de Gennaro; photo by Manex Ibar

using the pizzica tarantata for this specific purpose, to heal women with particular emotional or physical problems.

The first woman I helped was part of the cathedral staff, a brilliant musician who had numerous cysts and could not get pregnant. I offered to do the ceremony alone with her in the crypt theater space, and she accepted, since she knew my music very well and loved it. She came dressed in white, and to my surprise, she went into a trance as I began playing and singing. I felt magically guided to play the tambourine fast and loud for a long time, at least for an hour and a half, something I had never done before in that specific setting. During the ceremony, we used the white sheet and red ribbons all around, since red has the power to cleanse the air from negative energy and bad spirits and also symbolizes women's menstrual blood.

The new tarantata spun around, fell on the sheet, and kept moving her pelvis and legs, rolling and jumping like a spider, at times screaming and completely letting go of her head in pulsating movements. She slowly released the "poison" from her womb and woke up from the trance feeling like a new person. She hugged me, and we cried and laughed together in the darkness of the crypt for a long time. About two weeks later, she came to see me to tell me that her cysts had disappeared—to the doctor's disbelief! She began to embrace her femininity and soon found a serious partner and got married. Not much later she even got pregnant, which had not been possible for her for a while. I consider this my first miracle.

After this fulfilling experience of healing my friend, I led a few more individual sessions in the crypt with women who had cysts, including my assistant from Brazil, Juliana, a young girl from New Orleans, and a couple of others. The ceremony proved to be effective and their cysts disappeared.

Through the tambourine and the dance I chose a new healing path, teaching women to find their inner power and breaking free from their subconscious spiderwebs through wild, primal, sensual dance and rhythm. I later began to use these dance ceremonies as therapy for women who have suffered sexual abuse, and I made it my mission to empower them, helping to free them from their physical and emotional traumas. These healing sessions also helped me go deep into my own "web" and helped me break free eventually from my marriage that had been going through a painful crisis. The dance helped heal my broken heart.

In August 1999 a well-known healer from New York, Ron Young, invited me to teach an intensive weekend of therapeutic drumming and dance in a secluded Renaissance villa in Tuscany called La Chiara di Prumiano. I immediately fell in love with the magic of the place, a huge estate in the middle of the Chianti region, surrounded by beautiful trees, such as Tuscan cypresses, oaks, and olive and walnut trees, and grapevines. It seemed to be full of fairies, elves, and the spirits of the mystics who lived in Tuscany during the Middle Ages and the Renaissance. My workshop with Ron was a great success, and I became friends with the owners of the villa, the wonderful Gaia and Antonio Pescetti. I planned to begin holding my own retreats there in the future.

This dream came true in August 2001 when, inspired by the healing power of the Black Madonna and the tarantella dance, I held my first intensive annual drumming and dance workshop and retreat called Rhythm is the Cure at the villa with a group of twenty-five students from the United States and Europe. It was the first of many powerful and transformational experiences that were yet to come. I am happy to say that eighteen years later, I am still leading retreats in this spectacular place. Many powerful transformations have happened during my annual retreat in Tuscany and pilgrimages to the Black Madonnas and other parts of the world, and I want to share some of these stories because I know that we can make a difference in the world—especially now, with the MeToo movement—if women speak up about their pain and abuse and bring justice to their predators.

## THE GROUP'S HEALING CEREMONY

I mainly feel guided by the Black Madonna when I am leading the ceremonies. I feel her smiling and protecting me, helping me to connect to the ancient spider medicine.

We begin with each student participating in building an altar dedicated to the Black Madonna, with an image of the Madonna Nera, candles, flowers, and offerings. Before we begin the ceremony, we chant to the Black Madonna of Montevergine, to Brunettella, to Montserrat, and la Madonna dei Poveri, singing the powerful medieval chants and chanting Hail Marys. Each person has a moment alone with Her, the Great Dark Mother, Mary, Mother of God, asking for healing. In Tuscany, we pray to the beautiful image painted by my dear friend Arden Mason; the painting hangs from a tree and seems to come alive and receive everyone's sorrow and pain, thus giving back peace and freedom.

Following the old tradition of the tarantate, we lay a white sheet on the floor, creating a sacred space. All the participants are dressed in white, holding red ribbons and sending good energy as, one by one, each person becomes the tarantata, (or tarantati) falling in a trance onto the white sheet. I begin playing the tambourine, guided by an

Fig. 11.8. Healing, spinning trance dance of San Rocco,
at La Chiara di Prumiano, Tuscany

invisible force, over the person rolling on the floor. To this day I cannot explain how I can actually play for four or five hours nonstop. As I play the fast triplets, I know that I am creating a rhythm that helps bring back the person's lost balance, and she or he breaks down, screaming and crying.

I enter the spirit world, even though I must also stay present in the moment. Around the person who is the tarantata, I see his or her ancestral spirits, who sometimes give me a message for the tarantata. If it is a woman who has been abused, I see blood pouring out of her womb, and then when the healing finally happens, I see the spider caught inside the womb jumping out. The color of the spider varies: it can be black, brown, red, white, golden. When the healing is complete, the person gets up, starts dancing in a frenzy, and spins out of the "web." Often the people being healed spin toward the painting of the Black Madonna, crying and dropping on their knees, receiving visions that they later share.

## HEALING STORIES OF WOMEN

### Glastonbury, 2001, 2002

During the summer of 2001 while teaching at the Goddess Conference in Glastonbury, England, I met one of the most important young women in my life. She was from Sweden and had just tried to commit suicide. She was in her early twenties and suffered from a severe case of bipolar disorder (she was diagnosed with manic depression and suicidal ideation). She had been in and out of psychiatric institutions. I felt immense compassion for her and asked her to follow me to Tuscany after the powerful experience she had with me in Glastonbury. I knew that she was ready for an alternative way to heal, not the conventional medications given to her by her psychiatrist and therapies that had not worked.

I knew that this girl was in great pain. She was always serious and kept a distance from everyone, but I could feel the beauty of her heart and soul. It soon became clear that she was a giving person but often felt unworthy of attention or care. I had shared with her that I used to live in Sweden with a Swedish boyfriend. After we broke up, he died, at a very young age, of a drug overdose in 1981. I told her there was still a soft spot in my heart for Sweden, and this brought us closer.

The night of the pizzica ritual came, and she went into a deep trance for many hours in a way that I had never seen before. I admit that I was frightened but feeling safe because there was a doctor and psychoanalyst also teaching with me. I could not imagine that she would go back to her traumatized birth and not come back from the trance. She kept her eyes closed, she did not breathe well, she cried, sobbed, and then became numb—until finally I was guided to tell her in Swedish, *"Jag älskar dig."* (I love you.) She then opened her eyes and smiled, hugging me as if I were her mother.

She had a breakthrough experience with the drumming and dance and released a lot of the poison inside her. After that, she came to the retreat in Tuscany every year for the next eight years. I never asked her what had happened to her. While other women shared their pain and trauma from sexual abuse, she never spoke, and I never pressured her. Finally in 2006, when for the first time I shared with my students the story of my sister's rape when I first came to New York, the Swedish girl told her horrifying story: she was abused for many years as a child by her alcoholic father. We all cried with her and hugged her. Then she smiled and said that she had broken the web of the trauma, had stopped all medications, and was writing a book, now published in Sweden, about her experiences with the tarantella and the group in Tuscany. I am proud to say that she has become an excellent tambourine player, very strong especially on the tammorriata rhythm for the Black Madonna, and has been transformed by the tarantella dance. She now has a baby daughter and is in a happy relationship, finally living a regular life. This first experience healing a woman from sexual abuse left a deep sign in my heart, as did many others that followed.

In Glastonbury at the famous annual Goddess Conference organized by the brilliant writer Kathy Jones, I met another young woman who suffered from bipolar disorder who came to me by the recommendation of her eccentric mother, a talented gay singer and musician who was worried about her daughter who had thoughts of suicide. This young British girl of about twenty years old came to my second workshop in Tuscany in 2002, and during the pizzica ritual she broke down in despair, crying, screaming, and sobbing, entering a deep trance in which I saw her abuse in a vision of blood coming out of her womb, which finally released her painful trauma.

After she woke up in a very different state, embracing her "liberation from the spiderweb," she shared her tragic story. She had been abused by her mother's lover starting at age thirteen, conceiving his child at age sixteen while they all lived together. He had obviously raped her, but with his incredible mind control, he had convinced her that she loved him. She gave birth to his daughter, with her mother knowing all about it, as well as some other women who all lived together with this one man, a monster who abused them all.

I know that I helped her heal from the trauma and gain enough strength to move out and live alone with her daughter. I was extremely happy about that—until one day four years later when, back in Glastonbury, I ended up meeting the predator monster. I was staying with one of his former lovers, and he gave me a massage, but I had no idea it was him. He tried to seduce me during the massage and kept following me afterward, and I ended up screaming at him and kicked him. He looked disgusting and had a very strange energy. When I found out that he was the abuser, I became angry and gathered all the women of the community to find a way to report him to the criminal justice system. Unfortunately, the women said that they could not do anything unless the victims themselves, including the young girl, went to the police and reported him. I was shocked and felt powerless and wished there was a way to arrest this predator. I know that he lives to this day with a harem of women who are all completely controlled by him as part of a cult. They are a hippie community of artists in England, where no one has ever thought that he was a criminal and should be put away forever.

Every time I think back, I worry about the British girl and hope that she is now strong and able to protect her beautiful daughter from the abuse of this despicable man.

## France 2011 and Calabria 2012

During my intensive healing workshop in the beautiful Basque region of France, I met a special, pretty young Basque girl through a talented young man named Manex, who was my apprentice for a while and now is a powerful shaman.

I felt a profound spiritual connection with this beautiful Basque girl, Amaya, especially during the tarantella trance ritual. When I saw images of blood and pain, I asked her about it, and she told me that she had been sexually abused from age nine to fourteen by her stepfather, who, like the man in England, had convinced her that she was madly in love with him. She had tried traditional therapeutic methods but was still feeling lost and a victim of the assault. She had gone through a long trial that finally put him in jail when her cousin, who had also been raped by the predator, reported him to the police. Three young girls came to testify about their abuse by this horrible man.

Amaya was on a personal quest to understand and heal and encountered shamanism with Manex, including my work through the tarantella trance ritual. Not only did her true healing begin, but she also awakened to a whole world of initiation, ritual, and spiritual wisdom and finally found meaning in her life. She told me that during the rituals and ceremonies with me, she kept seeing the Black Madonna offering Her hand, hugging her, and telling her to get up, free, as her pain and trauma were transformed into joy for a new life. My friend Manex decided to make a film about our connection and this beautiful story of healing, which we filmed in Calabria near Tropea. I knew that he loved her very much, and I feel that, like Dionysus, he helped heal her wounds with his care. I am extremely proud to share that they are now happily married!

### *Tuscany, Summer 2014*

I met Amara during a workshop in New York in 2013 when she was getting her master's degree in dance therapy. She was beautiful and very talented, but I sensed that she had experienced a tragedy in her life. When the details of Amara's violent history of abuse from her parents and rape from a friend came to light, I invited her to go deeper in her healing by joining my retreat in the lush hills of Tuscany to be freed from the demons of her painful past. Amara agreed and went through her profound healing and empowerment during a very intense musical exorcism.

I took Amara by the hand to the altar of the Black Madonna. While I played my shamanic tambourine in the loud 12/8 rhythm of the pizzica, she lay on the floor, crying and shaking hysterically, her body trembling violently. During the exorcism I used the drum to remove from Amara's heart a red-bladed sword that I saw in a vision while Amara simultaneously moved her arms as if removing something from her chest. After the ritual, Amara calmly testified to her powerful experience of healing. She described feeling the negative energy leave her body as she went to pay homage to the Black Madonna, first to la Madonna del Voto at Siena's Cathedral and then chanting at the medieval monastery of San Galgano, where Amara left behind her painful past once and for all.

When she came back to New York, she finished her degree and is now a licensed dance therapist and became the star of my show *Voices of the Tarantate,* about the survivors of abuse, which we performed at Theater for the New City (New York).

---

### Testimonial from Amara

Alessandra Belloni has had a profound impact on my spiritual healing and growth as a freed woman. Having suffered physical, emotional, and sexual abuse, the burdens of my past shackled me in a webbed cage of insecurities, doubts, negativity, and, most of all, immense pain. When I went to Tuscany with Alessandra in August of 2014, I knew that I would be learning the rhythms and dances of the tarantata, but I never expected to actually become one of those women. Indeed, I've suffered tremendously and have experienced poisonous wounds, and I have also danced my entire life—from classical ballet to belly dancing and fire performance—but the connection of my feminine soul to my dancing and healing process was never so influential in such a succinct way until my full evolution into a woman of the tarantata at Alessandra's workshop in Tuscany.

I was blindsided by it, to be honest, that moment I went into trance. My entire life, I've controlled, compensated, apologized for who I am, always trying to cover my wounds and minimize my damage. Although letting go has always seemed ideal, I never expected it to actually happen. I had the privilege to be surrounded by a group of loving and caring women who made me feel safe enough so that I could let go. I was in the spell of the tarantata for almost an hour, surrounded by love and a safety net that allowed me to break apart my own webs, those chains that I was tangled in. When I finally opened my eyes, the world was brighter and more beautiful. When I finally stood up, I felt ten feet taller, and my soul was as light as a feather. There was a shift in consciousness, and I suddenly knew myself, a freed woman of beauty, grace, strength, and potential.

---

## *Sicily, 2011*

I began to lead pilgrimages and tours of the Black Madonna sacred sites and one specifically to Sicily's Temples of the Goddesses. I have guided many people to these blessed lands from America and want to share one of the most powerful experiences—one that was completely unexpected, involving a woman who was a student and participant in the tour.

During this pilgrimage, I led the healing trance dance ritual of the tarantella on the beach near Agrigento. We had a group of sixteen students, and one of the women went into a deep trance and did not come back for more than twenty-four hours. I had to take care of her, together with my friend and coteacher, the philosopher-writer-shaman Angelo Tonelli.

I was extremely frightened and could not figure out what had happened or why she would not come back to our reality. She kept asking, "Where am I? What are we doing here? How did I get here?" Under Angelo's and my guidance, we all made her feel comfortable, and I had to act as if everything was perfectly normal. I prayed that she would come out of the trance with no problem and no trauma. That night she slept for a long time, and the next day when we went to the temple of Demeter in Agrigento, she had come out of the trance and was feeling well and looking quite happy. She hugged me and thanked me and then shared that the day before, when we did the trance ritual and she went into another dimension for a long time, it was actually the anniversary of her daughter's suicide! By entering the spirit world, she was able to spend that time with her daughter, which helped heal her pain. This remains one of the most powerful spiritual experiences that I have witnessed during my twenty-two years of trance dance rituals and healing workshops.

I am sharing in this book only a few stories of women's abuse and depression, things I also encountered among men, young and old, straight and gay, and they too are part of this story. I have met amazing young men, open, sensitive, and ready to do this work with me and learn the drumming, dance, and shamanic tradition. To this day, my only students who have really mastered both the drumming technique and the healing aspect of this tradition are four gay men.

I believe that as in the ancient times, now more than ever, gay and transgender men can become like high priests of the goddess Cybele and help heal our Earth and society along with the women who have been victims of sexual abuse. Statistics show that all over the world, the majority who suffer the pain and trauma of abuse and domestic violence are women. We live in a society in which men are mostly in control and where:

- Every nine seconds, a woman is assaulted or beaten in the United States.
- Worldwide, at least one in three women has been beaten, coerced into sex, or otherwise abused during her lifetime. Most often this abuse occurs at the hands of a family member.
- Domestic violence is the leading cause of injury to women, more than car accidents, muggings, and rapes combined.
- Every day in the United States, more than three women are murdered by their husbands or boyfriends.

As I feel guided by the compassion of the Black Madonna, I am more and more convinced that Western medicine and science do not have the answer for really curing the results of this abuse or helping people come out of trauma. I have seen people prescribed medications that, instead of helping them, made their conditions worse. I know that we live in a world where everything must be scientifically explained, but if you follow my journey and the journeys of the people who have come into my life, it is clear that the compassion of the Black Madonna, the understanding that She is alive, and the ancient healing trance rhythms are an antidote to the venom our society and trauma afflict upon us.

In ancient times women priestesses healed the sick, and poets like Virgil (who was homosexual) were initiated in the mysteries of the

Fig. 11.9. Ending healing ritual at Rhythm is the Cure workshop
held by Alessandra Belloni at La Chiara di Prumiano, Tuscany;
photo property of A. Belloni

Goddess and had the power to heal and to write poems that led us
into journeys of initiation. Among indigenous cultures all over the
planet, shamans (often women or two-spirited people) and elders had
the power of healing and took care of the community, using sacred
drumming and dances, connecting to the womb of the Earth, knowing that She is alive, the black Earth and African Mother from where
we come.

# The Black Madonna as Patron of All Humanity

I HAVE NOW TAKEN YOU THROUGH my spiritual journey, which began back in 1987 when I was enlightened by the need to help heal our Mother Earth and the dangerous ecological situation we have inflicted on our planet.

Now thirty-one years later, we are in a much worse situation both ecologically and politically, and the pain we have caused our Mother Earth has also been continually inflicted on women and people of color. I strongly believe that now more then ever we live in a dangerous time when both women and men need to connect to the true healing aspect of the Divine Feminine. In this time of shifting paradigms, I feel called to awaken the true power of women and to make men aware of the ancient spirituality of the Universal Dark Mother, which can help to heal our relationships and our planet. I hope that you feel the same calling.

As I reach the end of this writing journey, I look back and see that it began a long time ago. I was first inspired by my mother's life story, strength, and faith in the Madonna. Mamma Elvira was a victim of domestic violence by my father, and she fought back when many women in Italy did not because they were afraid and had to accept their husbands' supremacy. My mother taught me to always fight back and stand up to violence, especially when it is directed toward women. I suffered a great deal as a child watching scenes of violence at home, and I think my father knew that, as a man in Italy, he was protected by a patriarchal society. He felt above the law.

I cannot forget my mother's crying and swearing that one day she would leave my father, and eventually she did—she succeeded in getting a legal separation, to everyone's disbelief. I also remember her prayers, always to the Madonna, who gave her the inner strength even during the bombing of Rome, when she saved her own mother's life. Therefore, I have dedicated this book to my mother's memory. She passed away eleven years ago, when she was ninety years old. I still miss her immensely, but I do see her in my dreams, and through the writing of this book she has been very present as a guide from another dimension.

When I began my healing workshops and met so many women from all over the world with similar experiences of domestic violence and sexual abuse, it became clear that this violence against women is not just a typical issue of the Italian macho mentality but rather a virus—an infectious disease that has spread in our patriarchal societies, a dysfunction that needs to be addressed and drastically changed.

I cannot describe here all the stories of the amazing women I have met who have suffered trauma, but I want to mention some of them by name because they inspired me to continue this work and to write a production dedicated to their story of abuse, titled *Voices of the Tarantate*. I have presented this show several times in observation of Domestic Violence Month (October) with my women's ensemble, Daughters of Cybele, founded in 2009.

I chose to tell some of the strongest stories that women had shared with me, narrated by an amazing actress, Selenia Lucius, and told with powerful choreography and music featuring the very talented Francesca Silvano as the lead tarantata. We chant and drum to the Black Madonna, walk in procession to Her, invoke Her to remove our pain and heal our wombs. We end with the trance dance of the pizzica tarantata, when all the women release their trauma and embrace the fire of rebirth as blessed by the goddess Isis, played by the beautiful dancer

Amara, and an adorable little girl signifying every woman's pure innocence, played by Luisa Focella, Francesca's daughter. The audiences were always touched, and many cried during the performances.

I am grateful to all the women who have been part of my life through the years and who attended my healing workshops, giving me the inspiration to continue this work and to write this book; I know that they inspire other women survivors of violence and abuse.

I am grateful to all the women who have been part of my life through the years, for giving me the inspiration to continue this work and to write this book: I know they all inspire others with their survivors' force.

Tara from San Diego, my soul sister and fellow shamanic healer, a survivor of many years of abuse who found power through the Black Madonna and overcame the danger of suicide thanks to Her grace.

Stephanie from California and Hawaii, a victim of rape who fought back and brought justice to her attacker and now runs an organization called Surviving and Striving to help other women.

Lorena, who was afraid to release the tension in her wounds but was transformed through the trance dance. Susan from New York, a healer, yogi, and writer who has shared beautiful meditations and insights with other women through her books. And especially my sister, Gabriella, who was assaulted when we first came to New York in 1971 but always told me with amazing courage, "Better me than you!" She always fought for her freedom and wrote a book about her life story. Her traumatic experience was another motivation for me to help women who have fallen victim to abuse.

When Western medicine and conventional therapies do not have the answer to curing and helping people come out of trauma or depression, I can testify that the compassion of the Black Madonna combined with the shamanic drumming and dance traditions from Southern Italy are more effective.

This truth has also been made clear to me through the pilgrimages I have been leading to the sacred sites of the Black Madonna since 2014. For a long time, I felt that I should not bring outsiders to these remote places, afraid to interfere with the devotions of the local people. But in my dreams, I saw the Black Madonna and heard Her voice telling me that it was time for me to share with others my devotion in Her sacred locations, showing that She is a living being that can heal and transform. I know other people devoted to the Black Virgin have been following the same call, because She is manifesting Her true essence now in many different forms. Brilliant author Matthew Fox uses the name Black Madonna as the name of God, as he describes in his latest book *Naming the Unnameable: 89 Wonderful and Useful Names for God, Including the Unnameable God.*

From our first pilgrimage in Southern Italy, I felt that the locals were more than happy to receive a group of Americans or other foreigners to make them part of their tradition and devotion to the Madonna Nera. We were welcomed warmly by many, starting with drum teacher and master Raffaele Inserra near Naples and Vittorio de Paola in Calabria and new friends, such as writer and archaeologist Armando Mei from Torre, Annunziata, who shares with us his unique knowledge and esoteric studies about Egypt and the goddess Isis in relation to the cult of the Black Virgin. Armando has provided crucial information with his unique research on the Isis worship in the region of Campania, explaining the true connection of the Italian folk magic tradition with the ancient Egyptians, as seen in chapter 6. I continue to lead this intense pilgrimage inspired by the opportunity to open a portal into this ancient spiritual tradition for men and women from many different places and cultural backgrounds. When the pilgrims come to these sacred sites, they can see with their own eyes and feel with their hearts the true devotion to the Black Madonna, which has remained unchanged for thousands of years, in our precious land of Southern Italy.

## SUMMER MINERVA BRINGS THE LGBTQ MOVEMENT TO THE BLACK MADONNA IN MONTEVERGINE

One of the most fulfilling experiences for me is to have introduced a young, gay man, Summer Minerva, an actor and dancer from New York, to the femminielli devotion to the Black Madonna, Mamma Schiavona, in Montevergine, a continuation of the ancient transgender Galli that I mentioned in chapter 4.

Summer's family came to New York in the 1950s from the town right near the sacred mountain, Avellino, and even though he had visited the sanctuary in the past, he had no idea that She, the Black Madonna, was the protector of homosexuals and transgenders and that to this day the femminielli drum, sing, and dance for Her.

This discovery had a profound effect on Summer's life, helping him to understand the roots of his own identity. He is now making a film about this devotion to the Black Madonna, connecting the LGBTQ movement from New York to Naples.

## Testimonial from Summer Minerva about His Experience in Montevergine (February 2018)

In my Italian American community on the north shore of Staten Island, New York, there was never any recognition of gay people or trans people. There were no representations around me of people who reflected my sexuality or my gender identity in the community at large or in my family. At some point in my childhood, I made the insightful observation that Italians could not be gay. As a young child, this made perfect sense to me based on the sheer fact that all the men in my family and community upheld masculine behavior: competitive, boastful, entitled, and vocal about their attraction to women. It seemed like the only way to be a man was to like women and show off my athleticism and intelligence. These ways of being were not in my nature, although I did not realize until I was in my early twenties that I could be something other than a "gay guy." Through my spirituality, I began to embrace the femininity that I always felt but did not know how to name and did not know how to express.

My spiritual path, my work as a performance artist, and my curiosity about the Southern Italian folk traditions brought me to Italy on a tour of the Black Madonna sites with Alessandra Belloni. One of the Madonnas was Mamma Schiavona, or Slave Mother (Serving Mother), whose sanctuary is just a few kilometers from the small town where my grandmother migrated from in the 1950s. I had been taken to this sanctuary upon my first trip to Italy, when I met my cousins, and they wanted me to experience this amazing church on top of a tall mountain with drifting clouds creating a white, misty blanket around it. On that first trip, though, I did not know anything about the significance of this Black Madonna, particularly for the LGBTQ community. I did not know about the story of Her protecting the two gay men who were caught making love and left to die in the cold winter night. I also did not know about the third gender of the province of Campania, the femminielli.

The femminielli to me represent my gender: the body of a man, the soul of a woman. Mamma Schiavona watches over us and is there to show the world true compassion for the ways in which we are all different and therefore beautiful contributors to the mandala of diversity that is the human race. Her presence in my life teaches me about my womb—my womb of creation inside me, the incubator for the creative force that flows through me. This womb, dark and alive, needs care and attention and nourishment to bear life. Mamma Schiavona teaches me about self-love in this way and about prioritizing the parts of me that others do not see and could not see and to love all of the parts of me even if society or the people in my life find them difficult. Mamma Schiavona reminds me of the energy of my grandmother, my mother's mother, radically accepting and ready to come to the defense of those in need. In connecting with the third gender of Naples and walking this path of the Black Madonna, I have been able to confirm something that I always felt intuitively was true—that gender and spirituality can be deeply intertwined, and we have the blessings of the Mother to be who we are and do the work that we brought ourselves to the Earth to do. My scared queer younger self would have found security in meeting Mamma Schiavona sooner and knowing that in my ancestral culture, it is totally acceptable to be neither man nor woman, to know that I can honor my gods and goddesses not in spite of my gender identity but because of it, that the expression of who I am in the world is supported and blessed by Mamma Schiavona.

Fig. E.1. Summer Minerva dancing at Montevergine
for the Feast of the Femminielli

## THE BLACK MADONNA
## AS THE AFRICAN MOTHER

Through my opera and this book, I have unveiled the Black Madonna's origins from ancient devotion to the goddesses of the Earth, the sea, and the moon: devotions that enable devotees to feel the power of the Earth herself come alive and see in Her the African Mother.

At a time when racism against people of color is still a disease in our society, I intend to make a deep connection and bring awareness to the black sacred images popular all over the world, especially in America, where the majority of people are not familiar with their existence or devotion. I have taken African American friends with me to the Black Madonna sacred sites in Southern Italy and watched them weep in front of these dark statues and paintings because they were never exposed in the United States to veneration and prayer to Black Madonnas, a black Jesus, or black saints. The horror of slavery in America has wiped away their memory of the Black Mother. This knowledge could help immensely with the Black Lives Matter movement, as we can see in a very powerful speech "The Mastery of Self and the Universe," given by the Hon. Louis Farrakhan at Florida State University in 1997, when he told a huge crowd that the Madonna and Jesus were black. (Video of the speech is available online.)

> In the private chambers of the pope he has a picture of the Black Madonna and a black baby Jesus; all over the world there is a Black Madonna, but in America we have never seen it! Why is that? The Bible tells you Mary was an Egyptian woman; Jesus had hair like lamb's wool.

My quest has taken me to other sacred sites of the Black Virgin around the world. One of my favorites is in Southern France, in a stunning place known as Saintes-Maries-de-la-Mer, the capital of Camargue, where the Gypsies worship Santa Sarah la Kali, a powerful statue of the Black Madonna connected to the legend of Mary Magdalene and the goddess Kali from India who protects the Gypsies, believed to have originated in Rajastan, India.

This magical place and the regal life-size statue of the Black Madonna, with long, curly black hair and a very serious but compassionate face, have inspired me to write a beautiful song, in the medieval Dorian mode (see appendix for the epilogue, page 368). It is my first song in English and French, titled "Saint Maries de la Mer" (The Saint Marys of the Sea). The legend says that Mary Magdalene arrived there on a boat with the two other Marys: Mary of Jacob, also thought to be Mary of Clopas, and Mary Salome. It is believed that these three saints were the women who were the first witnesses to the empty tomb at the resurrection of Jesus. After the Crucifixion of Jesus, the three Marys were said to set sail from Alexandria, Egypt, with their uncle, Joseph of Arimathea.

The melody of the chant in honor of the Three Marys and the Mary Magdalen first came to me when I visited this place sacred to Santa Sarah la Kali in 2012 and was astonished at the great number of devotees coming down into the crypt where She resides and how everyone, including me and the two men who accompanied me, a filmmaker and a photographer, broke down and wept at Her feet. There I felt the presence of Mary Magdalene and could not explain why it felt so different from other Black Madonnas. The Gypsies come there from all over the world and honor Her with a big feast on May 24, during which they bring the statue into the sea, just like they do in Brazil and Southern Italy, and play music for three days. It is very interesting to me that May 24 happens to be my good friend Arden's birthday, the artist who painted the haunting Black Madonna on this book cover. He was also inspired by the Mary Magdalen. As you can see she holds the magic staff, a symbol of the Chalice Well from Glastonbury, another place where Mary Magdalen supposedly lived.

The day that I was there, I saw some Gypsies praying and chanting in low voices. Many people thought that I was a Gypsy as well, which is probably true through my mother's lineage from Spain. I spent a long time praying in the darkness of the crypt to Santa Sarah la Kali, who was dressed in white and blue, surrounded by many red candles and the smell of strong incense. I was taken back in time, during the Middle Ages, and saw myself with monks and pilgrims walking along the coast to bring offerings to Her in procession into the small and precious white church. I almost fainted and told my friends I had to go to the beach. I brought flower offerings and carried my drum. Once on the beach I felt a great desire to sing and drum for Her, the Black Madonna. I suddenly felt the pain of my favorite cousin Roberto, in Rome, who was going through a serious brain surgery as he had been diagnosed with stage-four brain cancer. As I was playing and crying, this haunting melody and North African rhythm came to me as a prayer, asking the mother of waters and Mary Magdalene to save us from disease and give us her blessings. The melody and words were flowing nonstop, given to me by the sea and the spirit of the Black Madonna. Unfortunately, when I returned to Avignon, I had completely forgotten the melody; I only remembered the words.

When I tried to sing, my mind blacked out! When I returned home, I was immensely sad at the thought of losing my favorite cousin, so young, and decided to go pray by the Hudson River where I live in New Jersey. I took my drum, and as I stared at the water, the melody of the chant and prayer came back. I now perform this song during our shows *The Voyage of the Black Madonna* and *Tarantata,* and I am very happy to share it with you, hoping that you will receive healing energy from this special prayer.

Fig. E.2. Drumming by the water

I believe that the Black Madonna embraces all the layers of the origins of humankind, the archetype of the Black African Mother and Africa as the cradle of humanity.

This revelation was very strong to me in São Paulo, Brazil, where I was studying shamanism with a powerful woman, Carminha Levy, and had the most magical trance experience of my life at the waterfalls sacred to Ochun and the Black Madonna, Nossa Senhora Aparecida, Our Lady of the Apparition.

We all remember in our collective unconscious the first Black Mother. The oldest human skeleton found on this planet is indeed an

Fig. E.3. The Holy Face in the cathedral of San Martino,
Lucca, Tuscany; photo by A. Belloni

African woman. In 1974, paleoanthropologist Donald Johanson of the
Cleveland Museum of Natural History discovered a skeleton of a female
in an excavation in Ethiopia. We know her as Lucy, but in Ethiopia her
remains are also known as Dinkinesh, which means "you are marvelous" in the Amharic language.

Wonderful African American author Tayannah Lee McQuillar in
her new book *The Sibyls Oraculum* proves that the sybils, the oracles,
were indeed African priestesses with great knowledge and wisdom.
Professor Lucia Chiavola Birnbaum in her book *The Future Has an
Ancient Heart,* with her accurate research on the Black Madonnas
in Sicily and other parts of the Mediterranean, shows us that there is
proof of African migration to Italy in 70,000 BCE, especially in Sicily,
Tuscany, and Sardinia. We can see this not only through the images of
the Black Madonna but also through the rhythms that we play in Her
ceremonies, which are exactly the same as some African rhythms: 6/8
and 12/8 for the tarantella and 4/4 for the tammorriata.

## MARY AND JESUS WERE NOT WHITE

Historically, Mary, Mariam of Nazareth, and Her son, Jesus Christ, were from the African continent. They were North African Jews and very dark skinned. In Italy, there are many paintings and statues of Black Jesus. One of the most famous is an incredibly beautiful dark wooden crucifix called the Volto Santo di Lucca, or the Holy Face of Lucca, in Tuscany. As I described before, it is also believed that Saint Luke the apostle, who had known Mary and Jesus, was the first to paint them with dark-brown skin. For the first four hundred years after the death of Christ, the early Christians acknowledged and venerated the Blessed Mother Mary and Her son the Savior as dark North Africans. This continued into the Middle Ages, when the Black Madonna statues became even more popular, blending Christian devotion with pre-Christian traditions of devotion to the ancient goddesses. Only in the latter part of the Middle Ages and the beginning of the Renaissance did the Vatican commission great painters—such as Raffaello, Michelangelo, Da Vinci, and many others—to change the appearance of the Madonna and Child, giving them white skin, blond hair, and blue eyes. These versions of Mary and Baby Jesus are now seen all over Italy and Europe. It was important that these holy images resemble the white ruling class.

But they could never repress the devotion of the Black Madonna and Her Dark Son. Even in Islam, Mary is acknowledged as dark.

For a few years I was part of the Sufi community in New York, and during a whirling ceremony, I had a strong vision of the Black Madonna in Mecca. It is then that I found out that in Islam, Mariam is very important and has many names, and in the Kaaba, the black stone of Mecca, there is only one icon that the prophet Muhammad allowed: Mariam, Mother of Jesus of Nazareth, and She is dark—a Black Madonna. The black stone of the Kaaba is also believed to have originated from a meteorite that fell from the stars, like the stone that was carved into the statue of the goddess Cybele.

My devotion to Mary is still strong, as I do believe in Christ as the

Messiah and His Mother as a powerful and holy woman. Even though Her presence in the Gospels is not as strong, we know that She was there for him in the most important moments. She was the one who initiated His first miracle at the wedding at Cana by asking Him to turn water into wine. The most important account to me—one that has touched me deeply and inspired me to later write and perform our own powerful Passion play—is Mary's presence, along with other women, at the Crucifixion.

Her suffering at the Crucifixion is described in *Stabat Mater* (Standing Mother), a thirteenth-century Catholic hymn to Mary. *Stabat Mater: Donna de Paradiso* (Lady of Paradise) was the title of the Passion play I wrote with John La Barbera. I played the Sorrowing Mother holding the dead body of Jesus and feeling deeply the pain of the Mother for Her dying son. We wrote this Passion Play four years after performing *The Voyage of the Black Madonna,* thus continuing our artistic mission showing the musical and theatrical traditions in honor of the Mother, as Mary, Mother of Christ, and as the Earth Mother.

The devotion to the Great Mother is *all one.* That's what makes this so beautiful! In a global society that puts people in boxes and behind walls, the love of the Black Madonna is unifying. The Black Madonna can impact all humanity in a very inclusive way. She embraces everyone, and everyone can have access to Her divine spirit and power. Regardless of our faith, origin, or gender, we can all benefit from this power.

She stretches out Her hands to all humankind, people in the mainstream and people on the fringes of society, especially those who have felt that there is no hope or happiness for them. I have seen people be restored to their divine original purpose, be freed to love and be loved, to grow and be empowered, and to empower others.

I feel blessed that I have been able to share my connection to the Black Madonna with many and with you and hope to have touched your heart and soul with this tradition, Her music, and Her dance.

*The Black Madonna is the female embodiment of God because God is a woman, and She is black. She embraces everyone with Her unconditional love as the Universal Mother.*

Fig. E.4. Alessandra Belloni praying at
the Black Madonna's altar in San Galgano, Tuscany

# INITIATION TO THE AFRICAN MOTHER
# AND CHANT TO OCHUN

Our journey together ends in Brazil, where there is a strong devotion to A Nossa Senhora Aparecida Do Norte, a powerful statue of the Black Madonna near São Paulo. It is the largest Marian sanctuary in the world, with millions of pilgrims going every year. Their Black Madonna is a very small statue, only a couple of feet tall, but it is truly miraculous. She was found by three fishermen in 1717 in the Rio Paraiba, broken in two parts, head and body, and was pieced together by the fishermen who built a temple for Her.

The finding of the Black Virgin in the river confirms the origins and connection of the Dark Mother with Ochun, the Yoruba orisha, the goddess and spirit of the rivers, waterfalls, and lakes. She is the veiled queen of love and sensuality, a healer and dancer who wears gold and white shining clothes during her drumming and dance ceremonies.

When I began to study shamanism with elder Carminha Levy in São Paulo, she took me into her home with great affection, because, like me, she was devoted to the Black Madonna and initiated in the Candomblé tradition as a daughter of Ochun. Carminha trained me through shamanic journeys and taught me beautiful rituals to the Black Madonna that have African origins. As part of this training, I had to go with other shamans to be blessed in the sacred waterfalls of the Black Madonna and Ochun. On an early Sunday morning, I went with her group to the waterfalls in the thick Mata Atlantica (Atlantic Forest) outside São Paulo. We had to walk a long way through mud and exotic trees. When we arrived at the waterfalls, the sight was stunning, and I felt like I had seen the place before. Yet I knew that it was the first time I was physically there.

Alexandre, the main shaman, told me that to show my devotion to Ochun and A Nossa Senhora Aparecida, I had to climb up the sacred waterfalls, which seemed crazy to me. I told him instantly, "I cannot do that; I am going to fall." But he insisted, "You must do it. It is your initiation in Her honor!" I hesitated, knowing that something would happen to me, but I had to follow the shaman.

As I put my foot on the black rock inside the waterfall, I slipped down and hit my foot on a rock, making a deep cut, which began bleeding profusely. I lost consciousness and entered a trance state. In a vision I remembered that I had seen this beautiful place during my first deep trance back in 1996 in Nashville after my debut as a Remo percussionist. During a big drum jam session, I went into a total trance, and all I remember is seeing beautiful trees, waterfalls, birds, and thinking that this must be Brazil. I realized that I was supposed to be in this sacred spot spilling my blood in the waterfalls as my initiation to Ochun and the Black Madonna as African Mother.

I suddenly saw a beautiful statue of the Brazilian Black Madonna in a niche excavated in the black rock with a lit candle. I felt Her smiling at me and saying, *"Bemvinda mea filha! Voce llego finalmente!"* (Welcome my daughter! You finally came!) I also heard the voice and power of Ochun in the water . . . something I can't quite explain except that it became a special song that I wrote a week later in Chile.

I felt great in this altered state of mind, as if traveling through a dark tunnel toward the light, where the spirits of the Indians from Brazil appeared, the Caboclos. At one point, the shaman Alexandre took me out of the water. I was still bleeding but felt no pain. He was speaking Yoruba. He took my foot, blew on it three times, and the bleeding stopped immediately. I slowly came out of the trance, looked at the statue of the Black Madonna, and felt protected. Then I realized that I could not walk back to the car through the mud, and as I chanted in Italian to the Black Madonna, praying for someone with a jeep to take me back to the car, an old man suddenly appeared through the trees. He saw me lying on the ground and said, as if he read my mind, "I do have a jeep, my dear, and I will help you."

My shaman friends were amazed, and they said that I was meant to be in this very sacred place to be initiated to the Black Madonna (Nossa Senhora) and Ochun (see plate 24), offering my blood in a sign of devotion. They carried me to the jeep, but my foot was not bleeding anymore, and I felt no pain. To this day, I have no logical explanation for what happened.

As I was sitting by the ocean in Chile a few days later, I heard a voice calling me Figlia di Ochun (Daughter of Ochun). This chant came to me in praise of the Black Madonna, the Great African Mother as Ochun, goddess of love. I am sharing it with you with the blessings of our Dark Mother and the life force of Ochun. ASHE!

### Figlia di Ochun (Italian)

*Composed by Alessandra Belloni in honor of the
Orisha goddess of love and rivers of the Yoruba African religion*

Please listen to track 12 on the accompanying audio recordings. The audio track of this chant can be downloaded at

**audio.innertraditions.com/hejobl**

*Figlia di Ochun
Figlia del fiume
Figlia del sole
E dell'amore
Torno da te come nel sogno
Nella visione che e'nel mio cuore
Nella Foresta alberi infiniti
Acqua stellata pietra dorata
La Grande Madre Madonna Nera*

#### Nossa Senhora Aparecida (Portuguese)

*Cachueras dorada agua sangrada
Sangre na agua rio de Ochun
Da Grande Mae Madonna Negra
Nossa Senhora Aparecida
Filha de Ochun, Deusa do amor*

#### Daughter of Ochun (English)

*Daughter of the River
Daughter of the sun and of love
I come back to you as in my dream, in my vision*

*Which is in my heart.*
*In the forest, infinite trees, stars in the water,*
*Golden rock, (I see) the Great Mother, Black Madonna*
*Nossa Senhora Aparecida,*
*Sacred Water Falls, sacred water, blood in the water,*
*River of Ochun, of the Great Mother, of the Black*
    *Madonna*
*Nossa Senhora Aparecida,*
*Daughter of Ochun, Goddess of Love.*

# Music and Lyrics for Chants to the Black Madonna

THE CHANTS AND EXERCISES PRESENTED in this appendix are meant to bring to life the text of the chapters listed below, allowing you to learn the melodies and techniques described. Twelve audio tracks are provided and can be downloaded at

**audio.innertraditions.com/hejobl**

The text for track 12 appears at the end of the epilogue on page 353.

### APPENDIX TO CHAPTER I
---
Vignuto il Lunga Via

*Traditional chant for the Madonna of Seminara from Calabria*

**(Track 1)**

**Chant**

Vignuto il Lunga via Canto della Madonna di Monserrato (Calabria)

**Music**

**Lyrics**

> *Vignuto il Lunga Via*
> *Pi Saluta' Maria*
> *Vignuto Sugnu ca pi sta grazia pe carita'*
> *E nu mi movo di ca si sta grazia nu ma fa*
> *Facitila O Maria*
> *Facitila Pi Carita'*

**Translation**

> *I came from far away, to greet You and to see You, Mary.*
> *I came all the way here to receive Your grace, please have pity!*
> *And I will not move from here, if You will not grant me this grace.*
> *Please grant us this grace, oh Maria, please have pity on me.*

# APPENDIX TO CHAPTER 2

## Tammorriata Technique and Teaching Method Developed by Alessandra Belloni*

### *Traditional ritual drumming for the Black Madonna from Campania*
**(Track 2 – Improvised Lyrics)**

The rhythm of the tammorriata is essentially 4/4 with different accents.

Hold the tambourine low, at waist level, putting the holding hand through the handle or holding the frame, keep the holding wrist very relaxed, moving the wrist in and the elbow out as the tambourine falls on the playing hand.

### *1st Pattern: Playing hand: slap-dum (repeated 8 times)*

Hit the center of the tambourine skin with your flat hand (slap) and the skin at the border of the frame with your fingertips, making a slap-dum sound 8 times as the tambourine bounces up and down as you lift it with your holding arm.

SLAP DUM – SLAP DUM – SLAP DUM – SLAP DUM –SLAP DUM – SLAP DUM – SLAP DUM – SLAP DUM

---

*From the book *Rhythm Is the Cure*, published by Mel Bay Publications, 2007.

## 2nd Pattern

Moving your wrist sideways, move the tambourine sideways, creating a loud jingle sound, holding the tambourine straight up in front of you.

Hit the top of the skin by the frame with a flat hand, getting a jingle sound mixed with the "dum" sound (2 times), first the outside then the inside of the drum as you're moving the tambourine sideways.

Slap the tambourine in the center of the skin and down by the edge of the frame as in the first pattern to get the slap-dum sound. (Repeat 4 times.)

**Sound:** JINGLE JINGLE SPLAP DUM SLAP DUM – JINGLE JINGLE – SLAP DUM SLAP DUM – JINGLE JINGLE SLAP DUM SLAP DUM – JINGLE JINGLE SLAP DUM SLAP DUM

**Rhythm:** TA-TA, TA-TA, TA-TA, TA-TA, TA-TA, TA-TA, TA-TA, TA-TA

## 3rd Pattern

Moving your wrist sideways hit the top of the skin (by the frame) with a flat hand getting a jingle sound mixed with the "dum" sound (2 times), first hitting the outside then the inside of the drum as you are moving the tambourine sideways. Then slap the tambourine in the center of the frame and hit the skin down by the edge of the frame as in the 1st Pattern (slap-dum) getting the sound "jingle slap dum." Repeat the same movement (jingle slap dum), then hit the center of the skin with the "slap" and go down to the edge of the frame with the "dum" sound.

**Sound:** JINGLE SLAP DUM JINGLE SLAP DUM JINGLE SLAP DUM JINGLE SLAP DUM SLAP DUM SLAP DUM (Repeat this entire sequence 4 times.)

## The Bounce Improvisation

A typical improvisation of the tammorriata is the bouncing effect, played with the palm of the hand. Cup your hand. First movement: Hit the center of the tambourine with the palm of your cupped hand. Second movement: Move the hand toward you, making two sounds (as a bouncing effect). Third movement: Go down with the fingertips to the center of the skin for the third sound (ta-ra-ta).

## 4th Pattern

This is the same as the 3rd Pattern, inserting the bounce: Moving your wrist sideways, hit the top of the skin by the frame with a flat hand, getting a jingle sound mixed with the "dum" sound (2 times), first the outside then the inside of the drum as you are moving the tambourine sideways. Then hit the center of the skin with the bounce sound (repeat 2 times), then bounce the drum 3 times hitting in the center of the skin.

**Sound:** JINGLE-BOUNCE, JINGLE-BOUNCE, JINGLE-BOUNCE, BOUNCE, BOUNCE

**Rhythm:** TA-TA- TA-RA-TA, TA-TA-TA-RA-TA, TA-TA-TA-RA-TA, TA-RA-TA, TA-RA-TA (Repeat this entire sequence 4 times.)

## 5th Pattern

Hit the center of the skin with the palm, creating the bounce effect. Then slap and go to the edge of the frame for the dum sound.

**Sound:** BOUNCE-SLAP-DUM, BOUNCE-SLAP-DUM, BOUNCE-SLAP-DUM, SLAP-DUM, SLAP-DUM, SLAP-DUM

**Rhythm:** TA-RA-TA TA-TA - TA-RA-TA, TA-TA - TA-RA-TA- TA, TA - TA-TA-TA-TA (Repeat sequence 4 times.)

# APPENDIX TO CHAPTER 3

## "Jesce Sole Chant to the Sun"

*Traditional healing chant in honor of the sun, from Campania*

**(Track 3)**

Je - sce   so   -   -   le,___   sca-glien-te im-pe-ra-to   -   re.

### Lyrics

*Jesce Sole (repeat 4 times)*
*Scagliente Imperatore (repeat 4 times)*

### Translation

*Come out sun*
*Blazing Emperor*

# APPENDIX TO CHAPTER 4

## Chant to the Madonna of Montevergine

*Traditional chant for the
Black Madonna of Montevergine, from Campania*

**(Track 4)**

## Lyrics

*E saglimmo stu muntagnone e jammo a truva' Mamma
   Schiavona*
*Jamma truva' Mamma Schiavo'*
*Che begli uocchi tene a Maronna e me parono doje stelle*
*E me parono doje ste'*
*Doje stele illuminate Mamma Mia sei incurunata*
*Mamma Mia sei incuruna'*
*E cu tutta sta cumpagnia state bona Maronna Mia*
*State bona Maronna mi'*
*State bona Maronna Mia l'anno ca bene turnammo a beni*
*L'anno ca bene turnammo a beni*
*E se nun ce verimmo mone ce verimmo all'eternita'*
*Ce verimmo all'eternita*
*E se nun ce verimmo mone Mamma aspiettace 'mparaviso*
*Mamma aspiettace 'mparavi'*
*E Maronna quante si bella staje 'ncoppa a sta muntagnella*
*Staje ncoppa a sta muntagne'*
*E Bambino e Bambiniello e apritece stu cancello*
*E apritece stu cance'*
*Simme ghiute e simme benute quante grazie c'avimmo avuto*
*Quante grazie c'avimmo avu'*

**Translation**

> Let us climb up this big mountain to visit our Mother, the
>   Slave Mother.
> The Madonna has such beautiful eyes that look like two stars,
> Two bright shining stars, shining like Her golden crown.
> Be well with all your good company, Madonna.
> Be glad for next year, we will come see You again.
> And if we don't come to You then, we'll see You in Eternity,
> If we don't come again, Mamma, wait for us in Paradise.
> Dear Madonna, how beautiful You are up on this mountain.
> O Child, O little Child, open this gate for us!
> We have come to see You so many times, how many miracles
>   we have received.

# APPENDIX TO CHAPTER 5

## Chants to the Madonna Brunettella and
## Our Lady of Freedom

### Traditional chant to the Black Madonna Our Lady of
### Freedom, from Moiano, Campania
**(Track 5)**

**Chant to la Madonna della Libera**

> *Madonna della Libera regina dell'anima mia*
> *Regina dell'anima mia*
> *Quant'e' bello a chiamare Maria!*

### Translation

*Our Lady of Freedom, You are the queen of my soul.*
*O queen of my soul,*
*It is so beautiful to call upon You, Mary!*

Ev - vi-va Ma - ri - a Ma - ri - a ev - vi-va! Ev - vi-va Ma - ri - a Ma - ri - a ev-

vi-va! A - ve, a - ve, a - ve Ma-ri - a. A - ve, a - ve, a - ve Ma-ri - a!

### Evviva Maria Chant

*Evviva Maria, Maria Evviva*
*Evviva Maria, Maria Evviva*
*Ave Ave Ave Maria, Ave Ave Ave Maria*

### Translation

*Long live Mary, long live Mary,*
*and who has created Her.*
*Hail, Hail Mary! Hail, Hail Mary!*

## APPENDIX TO CHAPTER 6

### Cuncti Simus Concanentes

*Medieval prayer to the Black Madonna of Montserrat Spain*

**(Track 6)**

**CHORUS**

CUN CTI SI MUS CON CA NEN TES  A VE MA RI___ A

**CHORUS**

CUN CTI SI MUS CON CA NEN TES  A VE MA RI___ A___

**VERSE**

## Lyrics

*Chorus: Cuncti simus concanentes; Ave Maria (repeat)*

*(1) Virgo sola existente, en affuit angelus*
*Gabriel est appelatus, atque missus caelitus*
*Clara facieque dixit; Ave Maria (repeat 2 times)*

*(2) Clara facieque dixit audite carissimi (repeat 2 times)*
*En concipies Maria; Ave Maria (repeat 2 times)*

*(3) En concipies Maria audite carissimi (repeat 2 times)*
*Pariesque filium; Ave Maria (repeat 2 times)*

*(4) Pariesque filium audite carissimi (repeat 2 times)*
*Vocabis eum Jhesum; Ave Maria (repeat 2 times)*

*Chorus: Cuncti simus concanentes; Ave Maria (repeat . . . )*

## Translation

*Chorus: Let us all sing. Hail Mary.*

*(1) As the Virgin was alone, lo an angel appeared.*
*He is called Gabriel and sent from heaven.*
*And with shining mien he said: Hail Mary.*

*(2) And with shining mien he said, hear, most beloved,
lo You shall conceive, Mary: Hail Mary.*

*(3) Lo You shall conceive, Mary, hear, most beloved,
You shall bear a son: Hail Mary.*

*(4) You shall bear a son, hear, most beloved,
You shall call him Jesus: Hail Mary.*

*Let us all sing. Hail Mary.*

## APPENDIX TO CHAPTER 7

### Chant to Yemanja

*Traditional chant to the Orisha goddess of love and sea
from the Afro-Brazilian Yoruba tradition*

**(Track 7)**

*EE EE EE EE EE E
AH ALODE YEMANJA ODOYA YEMANJA ODOJA*

# APPENDIX TO CHAPTER 8

## Requiem for Mamma Elvira

*Composed by Alessandra Belloni for her mother, arranged by Joe Deninzon*

**(Track 8)**

## Lyrics by Alessandra Belloni

*Mater dei ora pro nobis*
*Mater Amata ora pro nobis*
*Mater Eternal ora pro nobis*
*Mater Divina ora pro nobis*
*Grande Madre io ti ringrazio*
*Per il tuo amore universale*

*Grande Mater riposa in pace*
*Pace eterna a luce divina*
*(Repeat lyrics 2 times)*

*Balla votate tonna come na faccia de palomna*
*Balla votate e gira la danza della vita*
*Balla forte forte la danza della morte*
*Apri porta all' Angelo della morte*

*Ora pro nobis (repeat . . . )*

## Translation

*Mother of God pray for us*
*Beloved Mother pray for us*
*Eternal Mother pray for us*
*Divine Mother pray for us*
*Great Mother I thank you*
*For your universal love*
*Great Mother rest in peace*
*Eternal peace and divine light*

*Dance, spin around, and turn, flying like a dove*
*Dance, spin around, through the dance of life*
*Dance strong through the dance of death*
*Open the door to the Angel of Death*

*Pray for us*

# APPENDIX TO CHAPTER 9

## Chant to the Moon

*Chant to the goddess of the moon, composed by Alessandra Belloni*

**(Track 9)**

## Lyrics by Alessandra Belloni

*Dea della Luna regina del ciel, Stella Maris, Dea Della Luna Regina del cielo, famme sta grazie fammela ti prego, fammela pe carita*

**Translation**

*Oh goddess of the moon, queen of the sky, oh goddess of the moon, Star of the Sea, please grant me this grace, have mercy on me.*

## APPENDIX TO CHAPTER 10

### Chant to the Madonna delle Galline
### (Our Lady of the Hens)

*Traditional chant to the Madonna,*
*Our Lady of the Hens, Campania*

**(Track 10)**

**Lyrics**

> *Mamma de galline meje, miettece a Mano toja Figlio'*
> *Figlio' vene ca mo to sana o cannarone Figlio*
> *Figlio' chista nun se chiamma festa si nun t'accatte o sciore Figlio'*
> *A Maronna comme sa sceglie a Jurnatella soja Figlio'*

**Translation**

> *Oh Mother, Our Lady of the Hens!*
> *Please lay on me Your healing hand!*
> *Figlio*
> *Oh Figlio' Come, She will heal your throat*
> *Figlio, you can not call this a feast, unless you buy the flowers*
> *The Madonna knows how to choose Her feast Day*
> *(Oh Figliola)*

## APPENDIX TO THE EPILOGUE

### "Santa Sara, Black Madonna of the Sea"

Composed by Alessandra Belloni in honor of the Black Madonna
Santa Sarah La Kali and the Mary Magdalen from
Saint Maries de la Mer, La Camargue, France
**(Track 11)**

**Lyrics by Alessandra Belloni**

> *Saint Maries de la Mer, Vous êtes notre Mere (2 times)*
> *Saint Maries de la Mer, Reine de les Gitaines*
> *(2 times)*
> *Vous êtes la Vierge Noire*
> *Nous on chant pour toi*
> *Vous êtes la Vierge Noire*
> *Nous on dance pour toi*
> *Saint Maries de la Mer, Reine de les Gitaines*
> *Saint Maries de la Mer, Vous êtes la Magdalene*
> *Saint Maries de la Mer, Vous êtes la Magdalene.*

*Santa Sara La Kali, You are the Black Madonna*
   *(2 times)*
*Mother of the waters, we come to you for blessings*
*Mother of the waters, protect us from disease*
*You are the Black Madonna*
*We will sing for You*
*You are the Black Madonna*
*We will dance for You*
*From North Africa through Italy*
*You have come to France*
*With white horses on white sand*
*You shine over the Sea.*

*Santa Sara La Kali, You are the Black Madonna*
   *(2 times)*
*Mother of the waters, we come to You for blessings*
*Mother of the waters, protect us from disease*
*You are the Black Madonna, we will sing for You*
*You are the Black Madonna, we will dance for You*
*Santa Sarah La Kali, You are the goddess Isis*
*Santa Sarah La Kali, You are Aphrodite*
*Santa Sara la Kali, You are the Mary Magdalene*
*Santa Sara la Kali, You are the Mary Magdalene.*

## Additional Verses

*Santa Sara La Kali, Vous êtes la Vierge Noire (2 times)*
*Mere de l'eau, nous venons a vous pour des bénédictions*
*Mere de l'eau, nous protéger de la maladie*
*Vous êtes la Vierge Noire, nous on chant pour toi*
*Vous êtes la Vierge Noire, nous on dance pour toi*
*De l'Afrique du Nord à travers l'Italie*
*Vous êtes venue en France*
*Avec des chevaus blancs sur du sable blanc*
*Vous brillez sur la Mer*

*Santa Sara La Kali, Vous êtes la Vierge Noire (2 times)*
*Mere de l'eau, nous venons a vous pour des bénédictions*
*Mere de l'eau, nous protéger de la maladie*
*Vous êtes la Vierge Noire, nous on chant pour toi*
*Vous êtes la Vierge Noire, nous on dance pour toi*
*Santa Sarah La Kali, Vous êtes la déesse Isis*
*Santa Sarah La Kali, Vous êtes Aphrodite*
*Santa Sarah La Kali, Vous êtes la Marie-Madeleine*
*Santa Sarah La Kali, Vous êtes la Marie-Madeleine*

## Translations

*Holy Maries of the Sea (name of the location) You are our*
*    mother*
*Saint Maries of the Sea, You are the Queen of the Gypsies*
*You are the Black Virgin*
*We will sing for You*
*You are the Black Virgin*
*We will dance for You*
*Saint Maries of the Sea, You are Queen of the Gypsies*
*Saint Maries of the Sea, You are the Mary Magdalene*
*Saint Maries of the Sea, You are the Mary Magdalene.*

*Saint Sara, the Kali, You are the Black Virgin*
*Mother of the waters, we come to you for blessings*
*Mother of the waters, protect us from disease*
*You are the Black Madonna*
*we will sing for You*
*You are the Black Madonna*
*We will dance for You*
*From North Africa through Italy*
*You have come to France*
*With white horses on white sand*
*You shine over the sea.*

*Santa Sara La Kali, You are the Black Madonna (2 times)*
*Mother of the waters, we come to You for blessings*
*Mother of the waters, protect us from disease*
*You are the Black Madonna, we will sing for You*
*You are the Black Madonna, we will dance for You*
*Santa Sarah La Kali, You are the goddess Isis*
*Santa Sarah La Kali You are Aphrodite*
*Santa Sara la Kali You are the Mary Magdalene*
*Santa Sara la Kali You are the Mary Magdalene.*

## CREDITS FOR THE *HEALING JOURNEYS WITH THE BLACK MADONNA* AUDIO TRACKS

Copyright © 2019 by Alessandra Belloni

Artists: Alessandra Belloni: artistic director, mezzo-soprano, tambourines, frame drums, castanets, shakers

Joe Deninzon: music director, violin, mandolin, vocals

Steve Gorn: Bansuri flutes, saxophone

Wilson Montuori: classical and acoustic guitar, ukulele

Giuseppe De Falco: baritone voice

Recorded and engineered by Tom Tedesco at Tedesco Studios, Paramus, NJ

Musical arrangements by Alessandra Belloni, Joe Deninzon, in collaboration with Steve Gorn and Wilson Montuori

Joe Deninzon, Alessandra Belloni, and Steve Gorn at Tedesco Studios

# Bibliography

Allaby, Michael. *A Guide to Gaia*. New York: Dutton, 1990.

Anonymous. *Llibre Vermell de Montserrat*. Biblioteca Virtual Miguel de Cervantes. Published by Ensemble Unicorns. www.amaranthpublishing .com/LlibreVermell.htm or http://dick.wursten.be/Vermell_originaltexts _translations.htm

Apuleio, Lucio. *L'asino d'oro*. Translated by Lorenzo Scala. Milan: Sonzogno, 1987.

Apuleius, Lucius. *The Golden Ass*. Translated by Robert Graves. New York: Farrar, Strauss & Young, 1979.

Begg, Ean. *The Cult of the Black Virgin*. New York: Penguin, 1985.

Birnbaum, Lucia Chiavola. *Black Madonnas Feminism Religion & Politics in Italy*. Bloomington: iUniverse, 2000.

———. *The Future Has an Ancient Heart*. Bloomington: iUniverse, 2013.

Campbell, Joseph. *The Power of Myth*. New York: Double Day, 1988.

———. *Primitive Mythology*. New York: Penguin, 1987.

Ciervo, Amerigo. *Sancta Maria de Moiano*. Moiano: Musicalia, 1982.

Correnti, Pino Pantelleria. *La perla nera del mediterraneo*. Milano: Mursia, 1988.

De Blasio, Abele. *Inciarmatori, maghi e streghe di Benevento*. Naples: Arnaldo Forni, 1900.

de' Liguori, Alfonso Maria. *The Glories of Mary*. London: Aeterna Press 2015.

———. *History of Moral Theology*. (Originally written in 1748 in Latin.) In English, 2017. https://mediatrixpress.com/?p=1672.

De Martino, Ernesto. *Il mondo magico*. Torino: Boringhieri, 1973.

———. *The Land of Remorse*. London: Free Association Books, 2005.

———. *Sud e magia*. Milano: Feltrinelli, 1959.

De Meo D'Onorio, Giovanni. *L'Incoronata di Pescasseroli*. Foggia: The Sanctuary of la Madonna Incoronata, 1985.

De Simone, Roberto. *Canti e tradizioni popolari.* Rome: Lato Side Editore, 1979.

———. *Chi è devoto: Feste popolari in Campania.* Naples: Edizioni Scientifiche Italiane, 1974.

———. *Il segno di Virgilio.* Puteoli: Sezione Ed., 1982.

De Spirito, Angelo Michele. *Il Paese delle Streghe.* Rome: Bulzoni, 1976.

Di Nola, Alfonso. *Gli aspetti Magico Religiosi di una cultura subalterna.* Torino: Boringhieri, 1976, 1986.

Dionisio, Giuseppe, and Cinzia D'Aquino, eds. *Il volto della tradizione: Riti e tammurriate nella festa di Bagni.* Sarno: Labirinto Edizioni, 2003.

Eliade, Mircea. *Miti, sogni, misteri.* Torino: Boringhieri, 1959.

———. *Trattato di storia delle religioni.* Torino: Universale Scientifica Boringheri, 1976.

Euripide. *Alcesti, Medea, Baccanti.* Translated by Mario Vitali. Milan: Bompiani, 1993.

———. *Le tragedie.* Translated by Angelo Tonelli. Venice: Marsilio, 2007.

Farrar, Janet, and Stewart Farrar. *The Witches Goddess.* London: Phoenix Publishing, 1987.

Fox, Matthew. *Creation Spirituality.* New York: HarperCollins, 1991.

———. *Creativity.* New York: Penguin, 2004.

———. *Naming the Unnamable.* Stonington, Conn.: Homebound Publications, 2018.

Frazer, James G. *Il ramo d'oro: Studio sulla magia e sulla religione.* Torino: Boringhieri: 1965.

Gadon, Elinor. *The Once and Future Goddess.* New York: Harper & Row, 1989, 2001.

Garofalo, Salvatore. *La Madonna della bibbia.* Milan: Casa Mamma Domenica, 1958.

Getty, Adele. *Goddess Mother of Living Nature.* London: Thames & Hudson, 1990.

Gimbutas, Marija. *The Language of the Goddess.* New York: HarperCollins, 1991.

Giordano, Rosario. *Tindari una Stella per la Madre di Dio.* Naples: Edizioni del Santuario, 1987.

Harding, Esther. *Woman Mysteries: Ancient and Modern.* Boston: Shambhala, 1990.

Kircher, Athanasius. *Phonurgia.* Rome: Nova, 1673.

Koltuv, Barbara. *Black Solomon & Sheba.* York Beach, Maine: Nicholas Hays, 1993.

*Madonna dei Poveri Storia e Preghiera, Basilica e Santuario.* (Seminara Edizioni Santuario), 2016.

Markale, Jean. *Cathedral of the Black Madonna.* Rochester, Vt.: Inner Traditions, 2004.

McLean, Adam. *The Triple Goddess.* Kimball, Mich.: Phanes Press, 1989.

McQuillar, Tayannah Lee. *Sybils Oraculum.* Rochester, Vt.: Destiny Books, 2018.

*Montevergine Tradizioni e Canti Popolari Religiosi.* Naples: Edizioni del Santuario, 1974.

Montorio, Serafino. *Lo Zodiaco di Maria.* Naples: di Viggiano, 1715.

Moraldi, Luigi, ed. *I Vangeli gnostici: Vangeli di Tomaso, Maria, Verita.* Milan: Filippo a Adelphi Edizioni, 1984.

Nocera, Maurizio. *Il morso del ragno.* Colanna: Capone, 2005.

Powell, A. E. *The Astral Body.* London: Theosophical Publishing House, 1982, 1976.

Redgrove, Peter. *The Black Goddess and the Unseen Real.* New York: Grove Press, 1987.

Rossi, Annabella. *Le feste dei poveri.* Palermo: Sellerio, 1986, 1987.

Rouget. *Musica e trance.* Torino: Einaudi, 1986.

Satriani, Luigi Lombardi. *Antropologia culturale e analisi della cultura subalterna.* Milan: Rizzoli, 1980.

Sorrentino, Riamondo. *La Madonna dell'Arco.* Naples: Edizione del Santuario, 1950.

Steiner, Rudolf. *Knowledge of the Higher Worlds and Its Attainment.* New York: Antroposophic Press, 1967.

Stone, Merlin. *When God Was a Woman.* Orlando, Fla.: Harvest Books, 1976.

Streep, Pegg. *Sanctuary of the Goddesses.* New York: Little Brown & Company, 1994.

Troncarelli, Fabio. *Le streghe.* Rome: Newton Compton, 1983.

Turchi, Nicola. *Le religioni dei misteri nel mondo Antico.* Rome: Fratelli Melita Editori Dioscuri.

Vallone, Franco. *Giganti.* Vibo Valencia: Adhoc Edizioni, 2009.

Virgil (Publio Virgilio Marone). *Eneide.* Translated by Luca Canali. Milan: Mondadori, 1991.

Vitebsky, Piers. *The Shaman Voyages of the Soul Trance, Ecstasy and Healing from Siberia to the Amazon.* London: Duncan Baird, 2001.

Warner, Marina. *Alone with All Her Sex.* New York: Random House, 1983.

# Index

Numbers in *italics* preceded by *pl.* indicate color insert plate numbers.

The following study guides by Dawn Apgar are also available to assist social workers with studying for and passing the ASWB® examinations.

## Bachelors

*Social Work Licensing Bachelors Exam: A Comprehensive Study Guide,* Third Edition

Test focuses on knowledge acquired while obtaining a Baccalaureate degree in Social Work (BSW). A small number of jurisdictions license social workers in the Associate category and require the ASWB Associate examination. The Associate examination is identical to the ASWB Bachelors examination, but the Associate examination requires a lower score to pass.

## Masters

*Social Work Licensing Masters Exam: A Comprehensive Study Guide,* Third Edition

Test focuses on knowledge acquired while obtaining a Master's degree in Social Work (MSW). There is no postgraduate supervision needed.

## Clinical

*Social Work Licensing Clinical Exam: A Comprehensive Study Guide,* Third Edition

Test focuses on knowledge acquired while obtaining a Master's degree in Social Work (MSW). It is usually taken by those with postgraduate supervised experience.

## Advanced Generalist

*Social Work Licensing Advanced Generalist Exam: A Comprehensive Study Guide,* Third Edition

Test focuses on knowledge acquired while obtaining a Master's degree in Social Work (MSW). It is usually taken by those with postgraduate supervised nonclinical experience.

**Dawn Apgar, PhD, LSW, ACSW**, has helped thousands of social workers across the country pass the ASWB® examinations associated with all levels of licensure. She has consulted with many universities and professional organizations to assist with establishing licensure test preparation programs.

Dr. Apgar has done research on licensure funded by the American Foundation for Research and Consumer Education in Social Work Regulation and has served as chairperson of her state's social work licensing board. She is a past President of the New Jersey Chapter of NASW and has been on its National Board of Directors. In 2014, the Chapter presented her with a Lifetime Achievement Award. Dr. Apgar has taught in both undergraduate and graduate social work programs and has extensive direct practice, policy, and management experience in the social work field.

# Social Work Licensing Clinical Practice Test

## 170-Question Full-Length Exam

## Second Edition

Dawn Apgar, PhD, LSW, ACSW

Springer Publishing Company, LLC
11 West 42nd Street
New York, NY 10036
www.springerpub.com

*Acquisitions Editor*: Kate Dimock
*Compositor*: diacriTech

*ISBN*: 978-0-8261-8577-8
*ebook ISBN*: 978-0-8261-8578-5
*DOI*: 10.1891/9780826185785

20 21 22 23 24 / 9 8 7 6 5 4 3 2 1

The author and the publisher of this Work have made every effort to use sources believed to be reliable to provide information that is accurate and compatible with the standards generally accepted at the time of publication. The author and publisher shall not be liable for any special, consequential, or exemplary damages resulting, in whole or in part, from the readers' use of, or reliance on, the information contained in this book. The publisher has no responsibility for the persistence or accuracy of URLs for external or third-party Internet websites referred to in this publication and does not guarantee that any content on such websites is, or will remain, accurate or appropriate.

**Library of Congress Cataloging-in-Publication Data**
Names: Apgar, Dawn, author. | Association of Social Work Boards.
Title: Social work licensing clinical practice test : 170-question
   full-length exam / Dawn Apgar, PhD, LSW, ACSW.
Description: Second edition. | New York, NY : Springer Publishing Company, [2018]
Identifiers: LCCN 2017034876 | ISBN 9780826185778 | ISBN 9780826185785 (ebook)
Subjects: LCSH: Social workers—Certification—United States. | Psychiatric
   social work—United States—Examinations—Study guides. | Social
   service—United States—Examinations—Study guides. | Social
   service—United States—Examinations, questions, etc.
Classification: LCC HV40.52 .A7363 2018 | DDC 361.3076—dc23 LC record available at
https://lccn.loc.gov/2017034876

Contact us to receive discount rates on bulk purchases.
We can also customize our books to meet your needs.
For more information please contact: sales@springerpub.com

*Publisher's Note:* **New and used products purchased from third-party sellers are not guaranteed for quality, authenticity, or access to any included digital components.**

Printed in the United States of America.

*To Bill, Ryan, and Alex*

*You remind me what is important, support me so I can do it all, and always inspire me to be a better person*

# Contents

# Introduction

Despite social workers' best efforts to study for and pass the Association of Social Work Boards (ASWB®) examinations for licensure, they can encounter difficulties answering questions correctly that can ultimately lead to challenges in passing. Social workers who struggle with standardized test taking or have failed the ASWB examinations find themselves at a loss in finding resources to assist them in identifying the mistakes they made and strategies for correcting these errors. The focus of test preparation courses and guides is usually the review of the relevant content and supplying some study and test-taking tips. However, when these resources do not result in passing the ASWB examinations, social workers do not know where to turn for help.

Often, social workers will turn to taking practice tests in an effort to gauge their readiness for the ASWB examinations. In addition, they will try to use them to identify gaps in knowledge and errors in problem solving that prevent desired outcomes. Such an approach is understandable because there has been a void in available diagnostic resources. However, for several reasons, use of existing practice examinations is not usually helpful.

First, it is difficult to identify specific content that is used by test developers to formulate actual questions. For example, many practice tests do not provide the rationales for the correct and incorrect answers. In addition, they usually do not let social workers know which specific ASWB content areas were being tested (e.g., Human Development, Diversity, and Behavior in the Environment; Assessment, Diagnosis, and Treatment Planning; Psychotherapy, Clinical Intervention, and Case Management; or Professional Values and Ethics). In addition, the ASWB competencies and corresponding Knowledge, Skills, and Abilities statements (KSAs) that form the basis for question development are also not included. Thus, when questions are answered incorrectly, social workers do not know which knowledge in the ASWB content areas, competencies, and KSAs is lacking so they can go back and review relevant source materials.

Based on a practice analysis conducted by ASWB, which outlines the content to be included on the exam, content areas, competencies, and KSAs are created. Content areas are the broad knowledge areas that are measured by each exam. The content areas structure the content for exam construction and score reporting purposes. When receiving exam scores, failing candidates are given feedback on their performance on each content area of the exam. Competencies describe meaningful *sets* of abilities that are important to the job of a social worker within each content area. Finally, KSAs structure the content of the exam for item development purposes. The KSAs provide further details about the nature and range of exam content that is included in the competencies. Each KSA describes a discrete knowledge component that is the basis for individual exam questions that may be used to measure the competency.

Having ASWB content areas, competencies, and KSAs identified is critical in order to make practice tests useful for diagnosing knowledge weaknesses. The following example illustrates the usefulness of having this material explicitly stated.

## SAMPLE QUESTION

A social worker at a community mental health agency is doing a home visit to a client as he has not gotten his medication refilled as prescribed. The social worker learns that he has not been taking it for several weeks due to a belief that it is not helping alleviate his thought to "just end things." In order to assist the client, the social worker should FIRST:

A. Accompany the client to his next appointment with the psychiatrist to see if another medication can be prescribed

B. Explain to the client the importance of taking the medication as prescribed

C. Conduct a suicide risk assessment

D. Ask the client if he has suggestions for other strategies that may assist him

# ANSWER

## 1. C

### *Rationale*

Social workers have an ethical duty to respect and promote the right of clients to self-determination. However, there are times when **social workers' responsibility to the larger society** or specific legal obligations supersedes their commitment to respecting clients' decisions or wishes. These instances are when, *in the social workers' professional judgment*, clients' actions or potential actions pose a serious, foreseeable, and imminent risk to themselves (including the risk of suicide) or others (in general or aimed at identifiable third parties—duty to warn).

The client's thoughts to "just end things" may be an indicator of suicide risk. The social worker should FIRST assess the degree of risk which is present to determine whether the client is safe without use of the medication and can wait to discuss his concerns with his psychiatrist at a future appointment or needs to be treated immediately, voluntarily or involuntarily.

### *Question Assesses*

Content Area II—Assessment, Diagnosis, and Treatment Planning; Assessment and Diagnosis (Competency); The Indicators and Risk Factors of the Client's/Client System's Danger to Self and Others (KSA)

If this answer was missed, social workers need the rationale for the correct response choice in order to identify the need to review materials related to assessment, diagnosis, and treatment planning, which is the content area being assessed. Specifically, this question focused on determining competency with regard to identifying indicators of client danger to self or others (KSA). Reviewing the risk factors and signs associated with suicide would be a useful place to start. In addition, refined literature searches on behavioral, emotional, and psychological warning signs would produce more targeted information to fill this information gap.

Most practice tests will not help direct social workers toward these resources as they do not provide the ASWB content areas, competencies, and KSAs being tested. They also do not give valuable information on the topics as a way for social workers to understand the rationales for the correct answers and why the others are incorrect.

Second, practice tests rarely explicitly identify the test-taking strategies that must be used in order to select the correct answers from the others provided. Even when rationales are provided on practice tests, the test-taking strategies that should be generalized to other questions are often not explicitly stated. This void makes it difficult for social workers to see problems that they may be having in problem solving, outside of content gaps.

For example, in the sample question, social workers must be keenly aware of the client's thoughts to "just end things" as delineated by quotation marks. These thoughts may be an indication of suicide risk.

There is also a qualifying word—FIRST—used, which is capitalized in the question. The use of this qualifying word indicates that more than one of the provided response choices may be correct, but selecting the one that precedes the others is what is being asked. When clients are potentially suicidal, social workers must FIRST assess for risk.

This tool was developed to assist social workers in identifying their knowledge gaps and difficulties in problem solving by providing critical information including the content area being assessed and the test-taking strategies required in order to answer questions correctly.

Social workers should use this practice test to identify:

- Question wording that is important to selecting correct answers
- Key social work concepts that are being assessed
- Useful problem-solving strategies and themes
- Mistakes in logic
- Content areas, competencies, and/or KSAs that require additional study

This test is not intended to be a study guide, but does contain important social work content related to the KSAs. This practice test helps social workers who are struggling to find answers about what mistakes they are making and what they need to study more. It can be used in conjunction with existing study guides that provide an overview of needed social work material, *Social Work Licensing Clinical Exam: A Comprehensive Study Guide*, Third Edition by this author.

Social workers must understand their learning styles and use available resources to fill in existing content gaps through the use of visual, auditory, and/or hands-on materials. Most social work content is available for little or no cost. There is no need to purchase expensive products as there are many educational materials available for free. However, it is important that social workers make sure that these resources are rooted in the values and knowledge base of the profession, as well as produced by those providing legitimate instruction. There are no tricks or secrets associated with passing the examination that can replace learning and understanding a topic. The application of material requires being able to relate it to various scenarios or vignettes.

# Getting It Right: Understanding Multiple-Choice Tests and Applying Key Social Work Concepts

On the ASWB® examinations, social workers often struggle with application and reasoning questions which require them to take what has been learned and use it to identify correct answers given hypothetical contexts. These items require test takers to use logic or reasoning to arrive at the same response choice. Social workers are not prepared for these assessment methods as multiple-choice testing is not frequently used in social work educational programs. Often test takers are frustrated as they do not know what is being asked in questions and how to choose between answers which seem similar. Becoming more familiar with the construction of multiple-choice tests, as well as remembering concepts which are hallmarks within the social work profession, can greatly assist.

## Multiple-Choice Examinations

Many social workers do not have experience taking multiple-choice tests and are unfamiliar with the format of questions. A multiple-choice question is composed of several important parts.

> *Stem*—A stem identifies the question or problem. In ASWB examinations, stems are the KSAs or concepts to be assessed. A stem often appears at the end of a question, right before the answers. It can be a complete or incomplete sentence. A stem tells the test taker the focus of the question and how to apply the background

information provided in the question. Often questions can appear broad, but each is testing a specific KSA which is contained in the stem. The goal is to identify the stem before looking at the answers. If the stem is clearly understood, selecting the key or correct answer will be easier.

*Key*—A key is the correct answer to the question which is based on content learned in social work educational programs. The ASWB tests assess knowledge so the key is superior to the alternatives based on conceptual information that was learned in school that is not contained in the other response choices.

*Distractors*—Distractors are plausible but incorrect answers to a question. Rarely will answers appear that can be easily eliminated. ASWB does not use "all of the above" or "none of the above" response choices. Distractors are similar in length and language to the key or correct answer. Often distractors represent common mistakes made by social workers. Test takers often inappropriately select incorrect answers or distractors as they feel that they incorporate or overlap correct ones. Each answer must be assessed based on the explicit wording used and social workers must not assume redundancy between answers.

The following example will assist with identifying the parts of a sample multiple-choice question.

A client states that he has received services in the past and "it did not work out." He appears tense and angry, telling the social worker that he does not want the social worker to speak with his prior provider. In order to best assist the client, the social worker should FIRST:

A. Ask the client what did not go well in the past    ←—— *Distractor*

B. Assure the client that the prior provider will not be contacted without his permission    ←—— *Key*

C. Tell the client that services will only be focused on current problems    ←—— *Distractor*

D. Explain that effective treatment requires knowing what has been done in the past    ←—— *Distractor*

*Qualifying word*                      Stem ——

This question asks the best action to "assist" the client. The goal is to help the client. The first sentence in an ASWB vignette is often the presenting problem. In this scenario, the client is no longer receiving services from a prior provider, though the reason for the termination is unknown. The second sentence describes his current emotions, which are tense and angry, as well as his desire not to have the social worker speak to the prior provider. The stem requires the test taker to select an answer that is most helpful when confronted with an emotional client who is guarded about his past. There is a qualifying word—FIRST—which indicates that the order of these responses is important. A qualifying word may appear in or near stems of questions and should be closely attended to as they contain vital information for distinguishing between keys and distractors.

Social workers must first calm a client before asking questions. Telling or explaining does not address the emotional state of a client. Clearly his prior experience with service delivery is impacting his affect and behavior during this initial meeting. Assuring him that he has the right to make decisions about his treatment will assist with engagement, which is essential for the development of a helping relationship.

## Applying Key Social Work Concepts

There are many KSAs tested on the licensure examinations. It is very important for test takers to be familiar with the topics that will be assessed. While there are many specific KSAs, there are some important social work concepts that transcend all of them. These are principles that must be considered when distinguishing the key from distractors. While not exhaustive, these themes are consistent across questions and can be used to assist with identifying correct answers. However, the degree to which each is relevant to a particular question varies. A question to help with test-taking is listed after each relevant concept.

- Social workers have groups, organizations, and communities as clients.
  - *Does the question specifically identify an individual or family as the client or could the level of intervention be bigger (the client is a group, an organization, and/or a community)?*

- Social workers do all types of intervention including provision of concrete services, case management, policy practice, and community organization.
  - *Does the question explicitly state the type of service being provided? If not, the KSA is universal across intervention types.*

- Social workers respect client self-determination.
  - *Does the answer respect the client's right to make decisions?*

- Social workers are trained to identify the root causes of problems.
  - *Does the answer address the systematic issues rather than those impacted?*

- Social workers engage collaboratively with clients.
  - *Does the answer mention the client implicitly or explicitly as opposed to just the social worker?*

- Social workers use a systems approach to understanding functioning.
  - *Does the answer consider the interplay between biopsychosocial-cultural-spiritual functioning or the micro, mezzo, and macro levels of intervention?*

- Social workers apply their knowledge in diverse settings and with many populations.
  - *Does the answer reflect knowledge that can be generalized to all agencies, methods of practice, and client groups?*

- Social workers are committed to social justice and working with those who are oppressed.
  - *Does the answer ensure equal rights, especially for those who are poor and/or marginalized?*

Simply enhancing knowledge about multiple-choice question formatting and keeping key social work concepts in mind can greatly enhance performance. Armed with this information, test-takers are ready to take a full-length practice test to identify any further problems which may be present and can interfere with passing.

# Recommendations for Using This Practice Test

Actual ASWB® test results are based on 150 scored items and an additional 20 questions that are not scored because they are being piloted. These pilot items are intermixed with the scored ones and not distinguished in any way. Social workers never find out which ones are scored and which questions are being piloted.

In an effort to make this practice test as similar to the examination as possible, it contains 170 questions, the same number as the actual exam, proportionately distributed within the four domains—Human Development, Diversity, and Behavior in the Environment (41 questions); Assessment, Diagnosis, and Treatment Planning (51 questions); Psychotherapy, Clinical Interventions, and Case Management (46 questions); and Professional Values and Ethics (32 questions). These proportions mirror the distribution of questions across these domains on the actual ASWB examination.

The best way for social workers to use this practice test is to:

- Complete it after you have studied yet are still feeling uncertain about problem areas
- Finish it completely during a 4-hour block of time as a way of gauging fatigue and length of time it will take to complete the actual examination
- Avoid looking up the answers until after you have finished completely

■ Generate a listing of content areas in which you have experienced problems and use it as the basis of a study plan employing other source materials to further review the concepts

■ Generalize the test-taking strategies for future use on the actual examination

This practice test is to be used as a diagnostic tool, so social workers should not worry about getting incorrect answers, but should view them as learning opportunities to avoid common pitfalls and pinpoint learning needs. On the actual ASWB examination, the number of questions that social workers need to correctly answer generally varies from 93 to 106 of the 150 scored items. Since this practice test is 170 items, 20 questions would need to be randomly removed (5 from Unit I, 6 from Unit II, 6 from Unit III, and 3 from Unit IV) to determine if the overall number correct falls into this range.[1] Since many social workers who do not pass find themselves "just missing" these pass points, the value of identifying content gaps and difficulties in problem solving is tremendous because it can result in additional correct answers on the actual test.

---

[1]  Because different test takers receive different questions, raw scores on the actual exam—the actual number of correctly answered questions—go through an "equating process" to make sure that those receiving more difficult questions are not placed at a disadvantage. Equating adjusts the number of items needed to answer correctly up or down depending on the difficulty levels. This practice test has not gone through the equating process, which is why the number of correct answers needed to "pass" using ASWB standards cannot be determined.

# 170-Question Full-Length Exam

1. Grounding techniques used with clients who are experiencing flashbacks of past traumatic events primarily aim to:

   A. Connect clients with the present so that they do not have additional negative effects associated with reliving their past traumatic experiences
   B. Help clients put their past traumatic experiences into perspective by discussing them in the context of all of their significant life events
   C. Assist clients to understand the triggers for their flashbacks so that they can be reduced or avoided in the future
   D. Teach clients coping skills to reduce the emotional, physical, social, and other impacts of trauma on personal well-being

2. A client tells a social worker that she has been communicating with her recently deceased son. The client states that she has an altar in her home at which she leaves daily food offerings. She is hopeful that her son will return to the home sometime in the future to visit her. In this situation, it is MOST important for the social worker to:

   A. Determine if the client is at risk for self-harm
   B. Assess the client for psychotic symptoms
   C. Understand the mourning rituals of the client's culture
   D. Identify coping strategies which can assist the client in dealing with her loss

3. A client who has recently married undergoes genetic testing to learn if she is a carrier of a specific disease given her family history. Upon learning that she is a carrier, the client becomes very upset that the news will impact a future decision to have children. The client is nervous about telling her husband as he is not aware of the testing. In this situation, the social worker should:

   A. Arrange a joint session with the husband to support the client when she tells him
   B. Refer the client to a physician to address any medical issues associated with being a carrier
   C. Work with the client to minimize the anxiety and depression that she is experiencing
   D. Help the client understand the likelihood of her children having the disease

4. A client reports feeling very frustrated by his wife's behavior. She becomes upset when he is quiet at the dinner table, but constantly criticizes him when he speaks. The client is experiencing a:

   A. Paradoxical directive
   B. Negative feedback loop
   C. Double bind
   D. Metacommunication

5. Which is NOT a goal of treatment when working with clients who have experienced complex trauma in childhood?

   A. Removal of and protection from other sources of trauma
   B. Recognition that recovery is possible and can occur quickly
   C. Separation of residual problems from those that are uncontrollable
   D. Acknowledgement that the trauma is real and undeserved

6. A social worker who provides counseling to clients in a job training program is charged with evaluating the program's effectiveness. The social worker finds that 80% of clients get jobs and keep them for a year after graduation. The social worker is assessing an:

   A. Outcome
   B. Impact
   C. Output
   D. Input

7. A client who was briefly admitted to the hospital after a panic attack is being discharged with a prescription for a benzodiazepine. Which of the following medications has been recommended?

   A. Prolixin
   B. Lithium
   C. Prozac
   D. Ativan

8. What is the main difference between Bipolar I and Bipolar II Disorders?

   A. Bipolar I is rapid cycling while Bipolar II can have periods of sustained mania and depression.
   B. Depression is more severe in Bipolar I as compared with Bipolar II.
   C. Bipolar I must include at least one manic episode while Bipolar II includes only hypomania.
   D. Bipolar II never includes psychosis, which is always present in Bipolar I.

9. A school social worker is asked by a funder to conduct an evaluation of a youth services program. The evaluation is based on personal interviews with middle school children who are participating in the program. After explaining the nature, extent, duration, and risks of participation, what documentation will be needed in order for the social worker to ethically conduct the evaluation?

   A. Written consent from the children's guardians
   B. Written assent from the children and consent from their guardians
   C. Written consent from the children
   D. Written agency permission as the children's guardians already consented to service participation

10. Due to an agency closure, a social worker has referred a client to a new provider. With the client's consent, all relevant treatment information has been transferred. The social worker and client have also had several joint meetings with the new provider to discuss ongoing client needs. Several weeks later, the social worker learns that the client has had no contact with the new provider despite

numerous outreach attempts. The social worker feels strongly that ongoing treatment is needed. The social worker should:

A. Seek consultation to determine if steps in the referral process inhibited continuity of treatment

B. Send a termination letter with the discharge plan and contact information of the new provider

C. Meet with the client to determine whether new issues have emerged that have prevented follow through

D. Contact the client about the risks involved with not following through with the referral

11. When social workers contract with supervisors who are not employed in their agencies, all of the following documents are necessary EXCEPT:

A. Contractual agreements between social workers, supervisors, and agencies

B. Authorization by agency decision makers allowing supervisors to provide clinical supervision

C. Monthly progress reports prepared by supervisors

D. Verification from regulatory bodies that disciplinary action has not been taken against supervisors

12. When clients have co-occurring mental health and Substance Use Disorders, which statement best describes the appropriateness of taking psychotropic medications?

A. Psychotropic medications should never be taken for co-occurring disorders as they are contraindicated.

B. Psychotropic medications can only be prescribed if clients understand the side effects.

C. Psychotropic medications are part of accepted treatment protocols for co-occurring disorders.

D. Psychotropic medications have not been adequately studied in clients with co-occurring disorders, making their appropriateness questionable.

13. Who has the ultimate responsibility for selecting models of social work supervision?

A. Administrators

B. Supervisees

**C.** Supervisors

**D.** Funders

14. When making a determination of the needed level of care for an older adult client who will be moving from home into a residential setting, it is MOST helpful to assess the ability to:

   **A.** Adapt to life changes
   **B.** Manage medical problems
   **C.** Complete cognitive tasks
   **D.** Perform activities of daily living

15. During an assessment, a social worker learns that a couple spends little time apart despite having problems which have caused them to seek treatment. The wife feels lonely when her husband travels for work as she has few friends outside the marriage. The husband states that he is "smothered," but gets jealous easily, causing him to contact his wife frequently throughout the day. The husband reports that he is often unhappy as his wife seems miserable, while the wife states that she is frustrated as she is just trying to find ways to make her husband more content. In order to address the problem, treatment should focus on:

   **A.** Assisting the wife to develop a stronger sense of self-worth in the marriage
   **B.** Finding out more about past intimate relationships of both the husband and wife
   **C.** Helping the husband and wife to better understand each other's feelings
   **D.** Differentiating roles and boundaries for the husband and wife in the relationship

16. A social worker has additional information on a client situation that he would like to add to the record. It helps clarify discussions that took place with the client during the last session. In order to handle this situation properly, the social worker should:

   **A.** Ask his supervisor about agency protocol related to management of client records
   **B.** Add the material to the previous case note as it clarifies material presented in the last session
   **C.** Record the information as a new, separate entry in the record with a reason for its addition

    **D.** Refrain from documenting it in the record as it was not collected during a session with the client

17. A client is referred to a social worker as she has been repeatedly hospitalized due to medication noncompliance. During the assessment, the client admits to frequently missing doses of her prescribed medication. This behavior has resulted in numerous inpatient stays, which she complains are both costly and adversely impacting her quality of life. Which is the BEST question for the social worker to ask?

    **A.** "Why haven't you been able to take your medication as prescribed?"
    **B.** "Can you think of any advantage of having to stay in the hospital?"
    **C.** "What are some of the reasons for skipping your medication?"
    **D.** "How can I help to ensure that your medications are taken properly?"

18. When is family therapy best introduced in the treatment of clients with Substance Use Disorders?

    **A.** Concurrently with clients' acknowledgements that substance use problems exist
    **B.** When there is a recognition by clients that there is family dysfunction
    **C.** Immediately after clients complete detoxification
    **D.** Once clients are stable in their new patterns of behavior

19. During a session, a client discloses to a social worker that she was sexually abused by her father when she was an adolescent. The client has never confronted her father and does not want the social worker to disclose the information. There is no legal duty to report the abuse since the client is no longer a minor. The client reports that she sees the father regularly and he poses no current threat to children given a significant decline in functioning. In order to handle the situation ethically, the social worker should:

    **A.** Arrange to meet with the father to formally assess the risk for re-offense
    **B.** Seek supervision to determine whether to keep the information confidential

    **C.** Report the suspected abuse to the child welfare agency

    **D.** Respect the client's wishes by keeping the disclosure confidential

20. All of the following are appropriate reasons for seeking feedback from a client during the beginning phase of treatment EXCEPT:

    **A.** Ensuring an understanding of what is going to happen during treatment

    **B.** Focusing the treatment on a client's feelings and thoughts

    **C.** Emphasizing that treatment is a mutual and reciprocal process

    **D.** Conveying an interest in a client's views

21. The structured inequality of entire categories of people who have different access to social rewards as a result of their status, power, and wealth is known as:

    **A.** Social stratification

    **B.** Discrimination

    **C.** Institutional malfeasance

    **D.** Cultural difference

22. Which of the following documentation practices of supervisory sessions is MOST appropriate in social work?

    **A.** Supervisory records should solely be maintained by supervisors as they are legally responsible for the delivery of services by supervisees.

    **B.** No records should be kept by either supervisees or supervisors in order to maintain client confidentiality.

    **C.** Supervisees must maintain records of supervision sessions for licensing and other regulatory bodies.

    **D.** Supervisees and supervisors should maintain separate records of each session with both parties being able to access the other's notes as needed.

23. A newly hired social worker in an agency setting learns that he will simultaneously be supervised by more than one person. In order to minimize conflicts in this situation, the social worker should:

    **A.** Develop a memorandum of understanding with the supervisors

    **B.** Meet with the supervisors simultaneously at all times

    **C.** Review the professional code of ethics with the supervisors

    **D.** Understand the personal values and beliefs of the supervisors

24. The primary goal of court-ordered competency restoration is for clients to:

   A. Identify ways to provide restitution for actions which have harmed others
   B. Develop or regain ability to participate in legal proceedings
   C. Serve legal sentences which have been imposed, but not served due to mental impairment
   D. Identify legal standards which may apply to conduct based on mental disorders

25. Which of the following is NOT a condition often cited by courts that must be met in order for information to be considered privileged?

   A. Harm caused by disclosure of confidential information outweighs the benefits.
   B. Written records are kept documenting confidential material.
   C. Parties involved in the communication assumed that it was confidential.
   D. Confidentiality is an important element in the relationship.

26. A client tells a social worker that she is having problems with her teenage daughter's behavior. The daughter has begun to violate strict rules set in the home. The client, who is frustrated with this disobedience, states that she often does not speak to her child for days as punishment. The client does not understand why the girl questions the rules and does not behave as expected. Based on this description, which style of parenting is the client likely using?

   A. Permissive
   B. Authoritative
   C. Uninvolved
   D. Authoritarian

27. A couple seeks assistance from a social worker as they are having problems in their marriage. While they have been happily married for about 10 years, the wife complains that issues have arisen in the last year as her husband frequently telephones his mother after the couple argues. The wife states that she now feels uncomfortable around her mother-in-law and is worried that her mother-in-law has a negative opinion of her based on her husband's conversations. The husband insists that he has tried to work out issues directly with

his wife, but needs his mother's opinion to successfully resolve his feelings. This family dynamic is known as:

A. Role reversal
B. Triangulation
C. Entropy
D. Oedipal repression

28. Delusions of reference are BEST defined as:

A. Insisting assertions are correct despite contradictory evidence
B. Becoming disoriented with regard to person, place, and/or time
C. Believing neutral stimuli or communications have personal meaning or messages
D. Attributing personal failure to external factors that cannot be controlled

29. In client-centered therapy, which is NOT a core condition that must exist in order to have a climate conducive to growth and therapeutic change?

A. Congruence
B. Positive unconditional regard
C. Empathic understanding
D. Cultural competence

30. A mandated client questions the confidentiality of specific documentation that is generated as part of treatment. The social worker should:

A. Suggest the client speak to legal counsel to determine whether this material is privileged
B. Review the court order with the client to determine what documents have to be released
C. Seek supervision and/or consultation to better understand specific confidentiality standards
D. Explain that consent will be obtained prior to generating any documents to maximize client confidentiality

31. What is considered best practice in treating pregnant women who are addicted to heroin?

A. Continued use of heroin under medical supervision
B. Discontinuation of all opioids immediately

    C. Participation in intensive therapy and social support

    D. Enrollment in a methadone maintenance program

32. A social worker employed at a nursing home notices that a client with Alzheimer's disease experiences heightened delirium during the evening hours with improvement during the day. This phenomenon is referred to as:

    A. Folie à deux

    B. Dementia

    C. Sundowning

    D. Neurodegeneration

33. A social worker is assisting a client to cope with depression after a stroke. The client reports having difficulty meeting his basic needs and suggests having his daughter come to the next session to discuss his current problems as she lives nearby and is supportive. In this situation, the social worker should:

    A. Determine whether other family members or friends should be included in the meeting

    B. Explain that including her in sessions is not allowed due to confidentiality standards and their limits

    C. Ensure there is an agreement about the meeting purpose and what information will be shared

    D. Identify what specific activities of daily living the client is having problems completing

34. A hospital social worker being supervised by a professional of a different discipline finds that she is having difficulty with a social work practice issue. In this situation, the social worker should:

    A. Seek supervision from another social worker

    B. Contact the hospital administrator to request a new supervisor

    C. Consult self-help resources to identify possible solutions

    D. Determine how the issue would be handled in the supervisor's discipline

35. Performance monitoring in social work agencies does NOT aim to:

    A. Identify key aspects about how a program is operating

    B. Determine whether program objectives are being met

    C. Justify the need for service delivery to meet target problems

    D. Suggest innovations based on unachieved results

**36.** A social worker is counseling a client who suffers from depression and has recently been hospitalized for a suicide attempt. During a therapy session, the social worker notices that the client appears significantly more cheerful than she has in past weeks. The client reports that she feels better generally without citing any specific reasons for her improved affect. In this situation, the social worker should FIRST:

**A.** Document the observations in the client's file

**B.** Conduct a suicide risk assessment of the client

**C.** Ask about changes that have taken place in the client's life in the last week

**D.** Praise the client for the progress that she has made since her hospital discharge

**37.** A client who was recently promoted speaks to a social worker about how he believes that his boss does not like him and is critical of his work despite never verbally stating any dissatisfaction. The client, who has lost a previous job due to company downsizing, is nervous that he might be fired if rumors of financial troubles in the business prove accurate. After accurately reflecting the client's nervousness, the social worker can demonstrate a higher level of validation by:

**A.** Listening as the client describes further feelings about his relationship with his boss

**B.** Suggesting that the client's feelings may result from his prior job loss

**C.** Helping the client examine behavioral cues by his boss that support or dispel his claims

**D.** Explaining that his recent promotion makes it unlikely that he will be fired in the future

**38.** A social worker charged with giving a case presentation provides background and demographic information on the client, the reason for the presentation, and the interventions delivered. The supervisor would consider this case presentation to be:

**A.** Inappropriate as a case presentation should never contain demographic information

**B.** Comprehensive if the theoretical basis for the intervention modality chosen is included

**C.** Incomplete because it did not include the nature of the problem

    D. Acceptable as a basis for collaborative discussion because all of the required elements are included

39. Using a public health model, what would NOT be the resulting action from screening for substance disorders of those in emergency rooms, trauma centers, child protection settings, and other medical or behavior environments?

    A. No intervention
    B. Referral to treatment
    C. Short-term intervention
    D. Long-term intervention

40. The goal of attending behavior by social workers is to:

    A. Determine the scope and severity of client problems
    B. Assist clients to identify alternatives which result in change
    C. Encourage clients to speak openly about their concerns
    D. Explore barriers which have impeded client progress

41. What is the MOST critical factor in the selection of an appropriate intervention?

    A. Available resources
    B. Past service history
    C. Agency setting
    D. Presenting problem

42. A social worker meeting with a 10-year-old boy and his mother notices what appear to be burns on the boy's legs. After the social worker asks about the markings, the mother provides an explanation that does not seem plausible. The social worker suspects that the burns resulted from physical abuse in the home. In this situation, the social worker should:

    A. Contact authorities without disclosing the suspicions to the mother or child
    B. Question the child alone to determine who is the perpetrator of the abuse
    C. Ask the mother for evidence to support her explanation
    D. Report the suspicions to the authorities with the mother and child present

**43.** A social worker receives a referral from a high school guidance counselor for a student who has received a full scholarship to college, but decided not to attend due to family responsibilities at home. Both school officials and the social worker feel that the student is making a mistake as it is unlikely that she will be able to attend college without the current scholarship opportunity. In order to effectively work with the student, the social worker must:

   **A.** Understand the extent of the family responsibilities that prevent her attendance
   **B.** Determine the short- and long-term career goals of the student
   **C.** Acknowledge the differences in values that may exist between the student and school personnel
   **D.** Identify the natural and other supports that are available to the student and her family

**44.** Which action is BEST supported when Gender Identity Disorder, Gender Incongruence, and Gender Dysphoria are viewed using a medical model?

   **A.** Treating these disorders concurrently with medication and therapy
   **B.** Eliminating them as mental health diagnoses
   **C.** Exploring the mind–body connection associated with gender nonconformance
   **D.** Screening for physical conditions that may be comorbid

**45.** Which of the following is NOT an assessment to detect an alcohol or substance use problem?

   **A.** AUDIT
   **B.** SCOFF
   **C.** CAGE
   **D.** SDS

**46.** What is the PRIMARY distinction between defense and coping mechanisms?

   **A.** Defense mechanisms are discrete reactions to traumatic stressors while coping mechanisms are continuous unconscious actions taken to deal with everyday life events.

    **B.** Defense mechanisms fluctuate depending upon situational and personality factors while coping mechanisms are stable and rigid over time.

    **C.** Defense mechanisms are maladaptive methods of addressing threatening events while coping mechanisms are based on healthy decisions aimed toward self-preservation.

    **D.** Defense mechanisms are unconscious while coping mechanisms involve deliberate cognitive and emotional modifications.

**47.** In an initial meeting with a man who has been mandated to receive counseling due to severely beating his young son, a social worker explains the terms outlined in the court order and what can be expected in treatment. The social worker ends by asking the client, "What do you think about what we have talked about so far?" The purpose of this question is to:

    **A.** Determine the level of resistance that can be expected from the client

    **B.** Identify whether the client is aware of the legal mandates placed upon him

    **C.** Convey to the client that treatment is a mutual and reciprocal process

    **D.** Assess the presence of denial with regard to the incident in question

**48.** When marital problems are viewed as stemming from different understandings and expectations that spouses have of their marriage, social workers are using:

    **A.** Conflict theory

    **B.** Symbolic interactionism

    **C.** Functionalist perspective

    **D.** Psychodynamic models

**49.** In an initial meeting with a man who is seeking assistance after several arrests, a social worker determines that his reasoning is significantly impaired as he admits to using drugs before the meeting. The social worker wants to obtain the man's consent to find out more about his arrests and begin providing services aimed at assisting him to meet his basic needs. However, the social worker questions his ability to understand what she is asking and understand the information provided on the agency's consent form. The social worker should:

A. Waive the informed consent procedures since the man is in need of services now
B. Ask the man to sign the consent form, which will be reviewed with him at a later time
C. Use verbal informed consent procedures in lieu of written forms given his impairment
D. Arrange to meet the man at a later time when informed consent can be obtained

50. During an assessment, a client reveals a long history of substance abuse, but states that she has not used drugs in the last 15 years. She reports that she was sexually abused as both an adult and child, engaging in prostitution for many years. The client states that she has a strained relationship with her three children who she did not raise. Recent health problems have resulted in loss of ambulation, requiring her to use a wheelchair when leaving the house. The client reports that she has become isolated and unable to meet her friends due to issues with transportation. Not seeing her friends has resulted in her feeling worthless and not important to anyone. The client feels that having dinner with her friends as she did in the past would help decrease her feelings of insignificance. What will be important in establishing the measureable target for this objective?

A. Finding out the frequency of contact in her premorbid functioning
B. Identifying available resources for accessible transportation
C. Determining the impact of the poor relationships with her children on her current feelings
D. Assessing the magnitude of her hopelessness and depression

51. A social worker is treating a client with Bipolar I Disorder. When the client is in a depressive state, she feels out of control and that something terrible will happen. Which specifier should be added to this client's diagnosis to further clarify her symptoms?

A. With Catatonia
B. With anxious distress
C. With rapid cycling
D. With melancholic features

52. Which of the following is NOT associated with reductions in emotional distress due to caregiving?

    A. Transition of the person requiring care into a nursing home
    B. Death of the person requiring care
    C. Improvement in activities of daily living of the person requiring care
    D. Recovery from illness that impeded functioning of the person requiring care

53. According to the *DSM-5*, which specifier can be used with Obsessive-Compulsive and Related Disorders?

    A. With dissociative symptoms
    B. With poor insight
    C. With anxiety
    D. With adjustment problems

54. In the *DSM-5*, which is NOT a specifier for Autism Spectrum Disorder?

    A. Associated with psychosocial stressors
    B. With or without accompanying language impairment
    C. Associated with a known medical or genetic condition or environmental factor
    D. With or without accompanying intellectual impairment

55. A client who is homosexual tells a social worker that he is very distressed over his sexual attractions toward other men. His shame has prevented him from disclosing his sexual orientation to others in his family. He has low self-esteem and appears distraught. The client feels that he will not be accepted by others. In assisting the client to formulate treatment goals, the social worker should:

    A. Role model helpful methods to discuss his sexual orientation with family members and others
    B. Complete a suicide risk assessment
    C. Help the client understand the effects of internalized homophobia on his feelings
    D. Explore the client's past relationship with his family to better understand his concerns

56. A social worker receives a counseling referral for a student who is getting a social work degree at a local university. The social worker teaches a course in the program, but has not had the student in class. In order to handle the situation ethically, the social worker should:

    A. Determine how the student learned about the social worker in order to evaluate the appropriateness of the referral
    B. Meet with the student to assess whether there are any problems that could interfere with the student's ability to appropriately practice in the field
    C. Inform the student that services cannot be provided given the potential for a conflict of interest
    D. Refer the student to a colleague who has experience treating mental health professionals who are impaired

57. Which attribute is NOT a negative symptom of Schizophrenia?

    A. Diminished feelings of pleasure in everyday life
    B. Experiencing sensory experiences in the absence of a stimulus
    C. Difficulty beginning and sustaining activities
    D. Reduced speaking

58. When a social worker is meeting with a court-ordered client for the first session, the client appears apprehensive about discussing mandated services. This behavior is MOST likely an indication of the client's:

    A. Fear of having information shared with those in the criminal justice system
    B. Unwillingness to change the behavior which caused the current problems
    C. Resentment toward not being given a choice about service provision
    D. Lack of understanding about the services which must be provided

59. When doing narrative therapy, a problem must be viewed as:

    A. Commonly shared with others so that a client does not feel alone in his or her change
    B. Enmeshed with a client's sense of self which needs to be labeled so it can be addressed
    C. Pathological so that a client does not feel guilty about its existence

    **D.** Separate or external from a client so that it can be deconstructed and controlled

**60.** A social worker who is treating a client with Binge Eating Disorder asks the client to engage in self-monitoring by writing down what is eaten and any triggers of excessive food intake. Which practice method is MOST likely being used by the social worker?

    **A.** Task-centered treatment
    **B.** Cognitive behavioral therapy
    **C.** Narrative therapy
    **D.** Crisis intervention

**61.** Hegemony within our society is BEST defined as the:

    **A.** Ability of diverse cultures to work toward common goals
    **B.** Power of one group to lead and dominate other groups
    **C.** Discrimination based on gender norms that promote masculine identities
    **D.** Universal rejection of practices which do not value all people as equal

**62.** Which statement is TRUE about clients who have been diagnosed with Borderline Personality Disorder?

    **A.** They are less likely than those without the disorder to be childhood neglect or abuse victims.
    **B.** They are at greater risk of suicide as they get older.
    **C.** They usually show little improvement in social and occupational functioning over time.
    **D.** They frequently do not meet the full criteria for the disorder if assessed a decade after the first diagnosis.

**63.** A social worker is concerned about a client's alcohol use and wants to use a brief four-question screening instrument to assess for problem drinking and possible alcohol problems. First, the social worker asks the client whether she has ever wanted to cut down on her drinking. The social worker then questions whether the client ever felt bad or guilty about her drinking. Lastly, the social worker inquires about whether the client has ever had a drink first thing in the morning (an "eye opener") to steady her nerves or get rid of a hangover. In order to complete the assessment, the social worker should ask whether:

A. Alcohol consumption by the client has increased in the last year.

B. Criticism of the client's drinking has caused her to be annoyed.

C. Legal involvement has resulted from the client's drinking.

D. Medical problems that may be alcohol related have recently been diagnosed.

64. According to the professional code of ethics, a social worker who is ordered to release information without a client's consent, and such disclosure would cause harm to a client, must do all of the following actions EXCEPT:

A. Request that the court withdraw the order

B. Minimize releasing harmful information by redacting sensitive material

C. Advocate to limit the court order as narrowly as possible

D. Promote that the records be maintained under seal

65. Which statement BEST supports the need for professional development of social workers?

A. Staying well-informed of social work issues and trends makes social workers more competitive in the job market.

B. Government reforms require social workers to be knowledgeable about changes in funding and reporting requirements.

C. New research provides social workers with information that can impact the use of interventions in practice.

D. Many licensing boards require social workers to take continuing education courses in order to obtain or maintain professional credentials.

66. What is the most significant contributor to cultural convergence?

A. Education

B. Globalization

C. Marriage

D. Advocacy

67. When completing intake paperwork, a client identifies as "Latinx." The social worker should consider use of this term to mean that the client:

A. Identifies with a demographic age cohort of people who were born in the mid-1960s

    **B.** Rejects his or her ethnic heritage of origin

    **C.** Values gender identities that are not strictly binary

    **D.** Identifies with his or her Latin American origin or descent, but is not Spanish speaking

68. A social worker is terminating with an adolescent who has shown marked improvement in her anxiety. She received counseling for several months to address school absenteeism, which resulted from her excessive nervousness. During the termination process, the social worker learns that the client will be going to a new school due to redistricting. In this situation, the social worker should:

    **A.** Conduct an assessment to determine whether termination is still appropriate

    **B.** Acknowledge progress that the client has made during treatment

    **C.** Contact student services at the new school to see if follow-up services are available

    **D.** Identify relaxation techniques that can be used to reduce her anxiety in the future

69. A social worker who wants to afford a client the greatest confidentiality protections should store psychotherapy notes:

    **A.** In a section of the client's file so that they will not get disconnected from other key documents

    **B.** Separate from the rest of the client's medical or clinical record with restricted access

    **C.** At home as they are intended only for the social worker's use

    **D.** According to agency policy so that administrative standards provide additional client protections

70. A social worker believes that the client who abruptly stopped smoking cannabis after heavy, prolonged daily use may meet the criteria for Cannabis Withdrawal according to the *DSM-5*. The social worker notices that the client is anxious and restless immediately after quitting. What sign must also be present for the diagnosis to be made?

    **A.** Depressed mood

    **B.** Increased appetite or weight gain

    **C.** Hallucinations

    **D.** Denial

**71.** A social worker receives a referral for a child with a Neurodevelopmental Disorder who is having trouble in school. The social worker's goal is to identify appropriate learning opportunities within the school setting that can help address areas of delay. In order to effectively work with this child, the social worker will need knowledge of:

    **A.** Child growth
    **B.** School policy
    **C.** Past academic performance
    **D.** Family supports

**72.** In a sociogram, the intensity of interpersonal relationships is indicated by:

    **A.** Types of lines
    **B.** Arrows which may point one or both ways
    **C.** Shading of circles
    **D.** Shapes of diagrams

**73.** A client who has a stable, well-paying job tells a social worker that she plans to quit in the coming weeks. The client states that she is miserable, but she is not able to specify what she does not like about her current employment. The social worker feels that the client is making a poor decision which could have serious ramifications for her financial well-being. In order to handle this situation appropriately, the social worker must FIRST:

    **A.** Acknowledge the client's right to make her own decisions about her life
    **B.** Assess whether there have been changes in the client's life recently which are impacting on this decision
    **C.** Warn the client about the potential consequences of her decision so she has all necessary information to make an informed choice
    **D.** Assist the client with looking for another job quickly so she is able to meet her basic financial needs

**74.** A client with brain damage due to Korsakoff syndrome often tells stories based on false memories of events which never occurred. This disorder is known as:

    **A.** Hallucinations
    **B.** Denial

    **C.** False memory syndrome

    **D.** Confabulation

75. Current guidelines concerning social workers' duty to disclose confidential information without client consent to protect third parties from harm were initially established in:

    **A.** Case law

    **B.** Constitutional law

    **C.** Regulatory law

    **D.** Executive order

76. When a social worker experiences a value conflict with a client, the social worker must:

    **A.** Refer the client to another social worker

    **B.** Seek supervision to identify the reasons for the difference in beliefs

    **C.** Respect the client's right to self-determination

    **D.** Acknowledge the impact of this conflict on the problem-solving process

77. A woman seeks the help of a social worker because her son who has Schizophrenia will not take medication. She is distraught as his mental illness is causing significant problems in the functioning of the family. In an effort to help understand the son's behavior, the social worker can inform the woman that individuals with this diagnosis MOST often do not take medication due to:

    **A.** Side effects

    **B.** Anosognosia

    **C.** Comorbid physical conditions

    **D.** Denial

78. Intersectionality is BEST defined as:

    **A.** Psychological crises that result when cultural biases erode the self-image of those who are not in the majority

    **B.** Widespread negative impacts in social, emotional, psychological, and economic life domains due to discrimination

    **C.** Interdependent forms of privilege and oppression resulting from different social locations, power relations, and experiences

    **D.** Conflicting ethnic and racial values which are rooted in differences in beliefs and customs that undermine cultural pluralism

79. A social worker receives a referral for a young woman who was recently arrested after assaulting someone on the street. At intake, she reported being surprised that she got into a fight, but she admitted that she was drinking at the time of the incident. In describing her childhood, she uses a flat affect when mentioning severe physical and sexual abuse at the hands of her mother's boyfriend between ages 4 and 15. The client states that her abuse does not affect her life now, but she is unable to answer specific questions about the abuse due to being unable to remember much about the time period. The client is likely experiencing which of the following responses to trauma?

   A. Excessive guilt
   B. Intrusive thoughts and memories
   C. Depression
   D. Dissociation

80. Which behaviors would be atypical for a client with a diagnosis of Schizoid Personality Disorder?

   A. Avoiding sexual relationships
   B. Engaging in angry outbursts when criticized
   C. Declining invitations to social events
   D. Living with parents into adulthood

81. Family-centered social work practice is preferred over individual counseling when:

   A. Boundaries within the family structure are continually being violated.
   B. A family member lacks commitment to address critical issues.
   C. Violence is being perpetrated by one family member against another.
   D. Stabilization is needed for a family member in crisis due to substance abuse and/or psychosis.

82. A social worker receives a referral for a client who has been diagnosed with both Obsessive-Compulsive Disorder and Tic Disorder. The client reports regularly taking the medication prescribed by his psychiatrist, but still not being able to control his urges. He would like help to reduce his obsessive thoughts and compulsions that accompany them. In order to best assist the client, the social worker should use which of the following therapeutic models?

A. Solution-focused
B. Existential
C. Psychoanalytic
D. Behavioral

83. A social worker is conducting an assessment with a client who has been living with a chronic disease for many years. The client has been able to manage the symptoms of her illness successfully with no reported negative impact on her daily life. She has just learned that she will need to begin a complicated medication regimen in the coming weeks in order to slow the illness's progression. The client is very worried about ensuring that the drug administration does not adversely affect her current routine. The client's needs can BEST be met by the provision of:

A. Case management
B. Psychoeducation
C. Behavioral intervention
D. Psychotherapy

84. A social worker is hired by an agency to provide consultation aimed at reducing high client dropout rates. According to the funder, a greater proportion of this agency's clients leave services when compared with clients of similar providers. What is the source of the social worker's authority when making recommendations?

A. Agency employment
B. Funding mandates
C. Professional expertise
D. Organizational structure

85. A mother seeks treatment with a social worker due to her 9-year-old daughter's behavior. The child has refused to go to school due to unwillingness to be separated from her mother and is falling behind in her school work. The situation has caused stress within the family and the woman reports that she will likely be fired due to being preoccupied with her daughter's problems while at work. The mother feels hopeless and frustrated. The social worker's MOST appropriate intervention is to:

A. Suggest that the woman explain the reasons for her recent behavior to her employer

    **B.** Acknowledge that hopelessness and frustration are common in these situations

    **C.** Teach the woman ways to cope while addressing the causes of her daughter's behavior

    **D.** Recommend that the woman speak to the school about providing in-home instruction

86. Which of the following findings on social development is the BEST justification for mainstreaming children with unique learning needs?

    **A.** Peer interactions such as smiling, touching, and babbling occur at a very early age.

    **B.** Peer relationships depend on inhibiting impulses and understanding cause–effect relationships.

    **C.** Peer acceptance is affected by family support, parental interactions, and sibling relationships.

    **D.** Peer friendships are protective factors from later psychological problems and better self-image.

87. A client who has been chronically depressed is prescribed a selective serotonin reuptake inhibitor by his psychiatrist. He feels much more hopeful with many of his unhappy thoughts dissipating. The client reports that his relationship with his wife has improved, but he has recently been experiencing erectile dysfunction which has made sexual intercourse difficult. The cause of this dysfunction is MOST likely due to:

    **A.** Relationship problems that were masked by his depression

    **B.** A side effect of his antidepressant medication

    **C.** Biological changes that are typical as men age

    **D.** A mind–body connection that is trying to achieve homeostasis

88. A social worker is observing to determine if the frequency of a high rate behavior has declined due to operant conditioning. What is the MOST significant concern about using this approach?

    **A.** Observation is a very costly method of data collection.

    **B.** The client is in the presence of the social worker for part of the day.

    **C.** Some behaviors do not lend themselves to observational study.

    **D.** There are ethical issues with the use of punishment to extinguish behaviors.

89. A social worker is meeting with a third-grade boy who is struggling in school. Despite his poor grades, his parents seem disinterested in assisting him with his schoolwork. He is frustrated by his academic performance, but he does not know how to do better. What psychosocial problem is the boy MOST likely to experience if this situation is not addressed?

    A. Mistrust
    B. Isolation
    C. Guilt
    D. Inferiority

90. Which of the following consent procedures BEST informs clients of the nature and expectations of the social worker/client relationship, including confidentiality?

    A. Discussing written policies throughout the problem-solving process
    B. Providing clients with copies of all signed written consent and other forms
    C. Asking clients to sign written consent forms prior to initial meetings
    D. Ensuring that written policies are updated regularly and signed by clients

91. In object relations theory, what occurs when two contradictory thoughts or feelings cannot be tolerated simultaneously, causing only one to be recognized at a time?

    A. Isolation
    B. Resistance
    C. Splitting
    D. Rapprochement

92. A member whose behavior aims to draw attention away from addiction in the family unit is known as the:

    A. Enabler
    B. Mascot
    C. Scapegoat
    D. Lost child

93. Children with Disruptive Mood Dysregulation Disorder often meet the diagnostic criteria for:

A. Oppositional Defiant Disorder
B. Bipolar Disorder
C. Autism Spectrum Disorder
D. Histrionic Personality Disorder

94. A school social worker learns that the academic needs of a new student can be adequately met in either the regular classroom with additional supports or a separate resource room for students who require special assistance. The parents would like their child to remain with his friends in the classroom, but the guidance counselor feels strongly that the student would be better served in a resource room for at least part of the day. In this situation, the social worker should:

A. Meet with the child to determine whether there is a preference about the settings offered
B. Review the academic record to better understand the guidance counselor's recommendation
C. Suggest ways to maintain friendships while the child receives instruction in a resource room
D. Advocate for the child to receive any supports needed in the regular classroom

95. After completing an assessment, a social worker diagnoses a client with Binge Eating Disorder. In order to MOST effectively treat the client for this condition, the social worker should use:

A. Psychoanalysis
B. Ego psychology
C. Task-centered treatment
D. Cognitive behavioral therapy

96. A social worker in a hospital emergency department meets with an elderly client who demonstrates significant memory and cognitive loss. In order to differentiate whether these impairments are due to Major Neurocognitive Disorder or Delirium, the social worker should determine the:

A. Symptom progression from first onset
B. Severity of memory loss
C. Family history of neurologic or organic disorders
D. Impact on all areas of adaptive functioning

97. When completing a functional behavioral assessment, a social worker should FIRST:

    A. Determine why an intervention is needed now
    B. Identify antecedents which are hypothesized to cause the behavior
    C. Define a problem behavior in measurable terms
    D. Explain the limits of confidentiality which govern service delivery

98. Which is NOT a threat to social workers having shared power with clients?

    A. Social workers often can see issues more objectively than clients.
    B. Most services are delivered in agency-based settings.
    C. Clients may want social workers to take responsibility for change processes.
    D. Shared power challenges the claims of expert power.

99. A client is having trouble achieving a treatment goal, so the social worker breaks it down into small successive steps and rewards the client after achieving each one. This behavioral technique is known as:

    A. Biofeedback
    B. Modeling
    C. Shaping
    D. Flooding

100. During the first meeting, a client whose spouse has recently died tells the social worker that she is just now accepting the reality of the death. Understanding the needs of mourning, the social worker can expect the client to:

    A. Move sequentially through the stages of grief towards acceptance
    B. Want more time before talking about the loss
    C. Require the support of others to enhance her capacity for healing
    D. Retain her self-identity that was developed prior to the death

101. A social worker recently terminated with a client who made substantial progress in managing her anxiety. The former client has been asked by her church to facilitate a peer support group for others who have experienced similar problems. The former client is nervous about this request and asks the social worker to be a co-facilitator. The social worker feels that the former client would

benefit from this peer interaction. In this situation, the social worker should:

A. Assist with helping prepare for, but not co-facilitate, the group
B. Help co-facilitate for several sessions until the former client feels more comfortable
C. Agree to co-facilitate as the experience will be beneficial to the former client
D. Encourage participation while declining the request to co-facilitate

102. A school social worker who is facilitating a group for adolescents notices that one member who recently immigrated with her family from Japan interacts very little during most of the sessions. In order to meet this client's needs, the social worker should:

A. Suggest that meeting individually may be more appropriate to facilitate expression of feelings
B. Determine class participation to see if this behavior occurs in other settings
C. Create ongoing varied opportunities for interaction by all group members
D. Ask for input in establishing rules which govern group participation

103. During an initial session, a client appears reluctant to speak and states, "I am not sure if this is going to work out." In this situation, it is BEST for the social worker to:

A. Ignore the comment as the feelings will likely subside over time
B. Clarify what can be expected, including the roles of the social worker and client
C. Use this comment as an opening to address any hesitancy as a therapeutic issue
D. Ask about other situations in which the client has felt this way

104. A young man who has a criminal history for violent acts later becomes an acclaimed boxer. Which of the following defense mechanisms is the young man MOST likely using?

A. Introjection
B. Incorporation
C. Sublimation
D. Undoing

**105.** Conversion is BEST defined as a:

    **A.** Therapeutic process aimed at turning negative thoughts directed at others into positive ones

    **B.** Reaction to trauma which limits emotional growth and development throughout the life course

    **C.** Defense mechanism in which a repressed urge is expressed by disturbance of a body function

    **D.** Strategy used in family therapy to get consensus among those with divergent viewpoints

**106.** A social worker is seeing an elderly woman who has recently experienced declining health due to aging and loss due to the deaths of several close friends. She has missed several appointments due to illness and states that she is not participating in many of her of prior community activities as she is too tired to do so. In order to determine if the client is in crisis, the social worker should:

    **A.** Review her most recent physical evaluation to determine the severity of her health problems

    **B.** Refer her for neuropsychiatric testing to identify mental disorders which may be present

    **C.** Conduct an interview with her to gather subjective data on recent life events and changes

    **D.** Obtain information from collaterals to get a more comprehensive understanding of her current functioning

**107.** To be diagnosed with Cyclothymic Disorder, an adult must experience mood cycling over:

    **A.** 2 years

    **B.** 6 months

    **C.** 90 days

    **D.** 12 months

**108.** Emotional or psychological trauma is MOST significantly associated with events that:

    **A.** Occurred in adulthood

    **B.** Happened unexpectedly without warning

    **C.** Were anticipated due to existing antecedents

    **D.** Could have been prevented

**109.** A family seeks counseling as their adolescent daughter recently ran away from home. During the first session, the daughter states her parents do not care about her well-being and are overly concerned with meeting their job demands. She feels that all interactions with them are contentious and end in arguments. The mother admits to feeling overwhelmed by daily life and disconnected from both her husband and her daughter at times. The father feels that the root of the problem is that the daughter has been given too much control in the household. Using a structural family therapy approach, the social worker should:

A. Gather information on how the childhoods of both parents influenced their parenting styles

B. Assess whether the current state of the mother requires immediate attention due to a risk of self-harm

C. Instruct the daughter to discuss with her parents a current concern that she has that she feels they are not addressing

D. Determine when each family member's concerns began in an attempt to determine the etiology of the problem

**110.** When social workers engage in peer supervision, the PRIMARY method for learning is:

A. Modeling

B. Summative evaluation

C. Positive reinforcement

D. Formative feedback

**111.** A social worker is developing a contract with a client who has been mandated for treatment. All of the following actions by the social worker aim to promote the client's self-determination EXCEPT:

A. Explaining directives contained in the court order to the client

B. Advocating for clinically appropriate modifications to mandates based on client wishes

C. Eliciting input from the client about the methods of intervention to be used

D. Setting goals that the client wants to pursue

**112.** At the conclusion of the sixth session, a client states that her attorney would like to speak to the social worker. When the social worker asks about the nature of the request, the client states that she does not know and the social worker will need to contact the attorney to find out. The social worker should:

A. Contact the attorney immediately with the assurance that all legal matters will be discussed with the client in future sessions
B. Decline the request until the social worker's role is clarified and the client's expectations are better understood
C. Explore with the client why she is not being forthcoming about the reasons for the attorney request
D. Arrange a time for the client to be present during the social worker–attorney conversation to ensure that the client is aware of what is disclosed

113. During the first session, a client blames the recent termination from his job for many of his other problems. He reports that his girlfriend ended their relationship as she was angry that he was fired. He also had to move in with a relative as he could no longer afford his rent. He reports feeling like a failure and does not know "how things got so bad." The social worker should respond by:

A. Assisting him to find another job as his self-worth appears closely tied to his unemployment
B. Identifying which problem is the top priority so it can be targeted for immediate assistance
C. Assuring him that many people lose their jobs and experience similar feelings
D. Exploring the reasons for his termination in order to get at the root cause of the problem

114. A social worker, who is counseling a couple, learns that the husband has been recently diagnosed with a rare medical condition that is being treated with medication. The wife reports that this medication causes dramatic mood changes, which she has witnessed. Due to a lack of knowledge about this medical condition and the medication prescribed, the social worker contacts a physician for consultation. The social worker's action is based on which of the following concepts?

A. Interdisciplinary collaboration
B. Coordinated service delivery
C. Team building
D. Standard of care

115. Which of the following statements is TRUE about the blending and braiding of resources in human service programs?

    A. Federal categorical limitations make blending and braiding of resources difficult to administer.
    B. Blending of resources is preferred by funders over braiding due to administrative efficiencies.
    C. Braiding of resources is seen as advantageous by administrators due to ease of implementation.
    D. Blending and braiding of resources allows collective reporting on how monies are spent overall.

116. A client reports that she is very upset by her 17-year-old daughter's behavior. She has not been completing her homework and is showing up late for her classes. The client reports that she recently took away her daughter's cell phone until her behavior changes. Which of the following behavioral techniques is the mother using?

    A. Positive reinforcement
    B. Negative reinforcement
    C. Positive punishment
    D. Negative punishment

117. When an agency receives a single disbursement for services provided by two or more providers during a single episode of care or over a specific period of time, the payment methodology is known as:

    A. Capitation
    B. Fee-for-service
    C. Bundled payment
    D. Shared savings

118. A client who is planning on ending her marriage comes from a culture in which divorce is strictly prohibited. The client has a poor self-image due to years of feeling a duty to stay married despite being unhappy. In order to be most effective, the social worker should:

    A. Use universalization when speaking with the client about her situation
    B. Ensure that the client understands the consequences of her actions

C. Help the client identify the steps needed for her to achieve her goal

D. Explore why the client wants to end her marriage now

119. A social worker whose client engages in heavy alcohol consumption notices that he has confusion, problems with muscle coordination, drowsiness, and memory loss which persist even when he has not been drinking. These symptoms, which are associated with his alcoholism, are BEST treated with:

A. Thiamine injections
B. Cognitive rehabilitation
C. Physical therapy
D. Antipsychotic medications

120. A social worker is providing counseling to a client who is having trouble in her workplace. The client feels isolated as she does not have any meaningful collegial relationships in her job. The client, who is lesbian, feels that her support system is limited to her partner with whom she has been living for the past 2 years. At the end of a session, the client gives the social worker a hug while thanking her for understanding the situation. The social worker, who has a policy not to have physical contact with her clients, hesitates, which causes the client to accuse her of being homophobic. In this situation, the social worker should:

A. Ask the client why the action is being viewed as homophobic
B. Explain the reasons for the rule about not touching clients
C. Continue to hug the client after apologizing for the hesitation
D. Provide assurance that the response was not meant to be homophobic

121. A social worker is reviewing referral information for a new client which identifies him as xenophobic. In order to address this fear, services should focus on:

A. Exploring the benefits of his interaction with those who are younger
B. Educating him about the importance of injections, especially for required vaccinations
C. Managing the anxiety which results from his physical contact with others

**D.** Understanding his aversion to those from other countries and their cultures

**122.** Which is the sole condition listed in a new category on behavioral addictions in the *DSM-5*?

**A.** Sexual Addiction

**B.** Compulsive Shopping

**C.** Gambling Disorder

**D.** Internet Gaming Disorder

**123.** In the provision of mental health counseling, the primary purpose of social workers' case notes is to:

**A.** Serve as documentation by which supervisors can evaluate worker performance and skill

**B.** Provide evidence of service receipt for reimbursement by third-party insurers

**C.** Ensure continuity of care as well as a means by which to evaluate client progress

**D.** Comply with agency and regulatory requirements which exist to ensure service quality

**124.** The goal of a client with terminal cancer is to receive hospice services at home. Her health has deteriorated rapidly, but the social worker is having difficulty finding an appropriate provider due to the complexity of the client's medical condition and her current living situation. In order to meet the needs of the client, which social work value is most critical when intervening?

**A.** Dignity and worth of the person

**B.** Competence

**C.** Integrity

**D.** Social justice

**125.** A social worker at an outpatient treatment program observes a court-mandated client who is being treated for Alcohol Use Disorder become outraged during a group session when leniency for those arrested for addiction-related offenses is discussed. The client states that severe punishment, as opposed to treatment options, must be required. This behavior surprises the social worker as the client has repeatedly expressed his appreciation for being offered treatment in lieu of imprisonment. Based on this behavior, the social worker feels that the client is MOST likely using which of the following defense mechanisms?

A. Denial
B. Projection
C. Displacement
D. Reaction formation

126. When evaluating the effectiveness of treatment, which technique statistically controls, on a post hoc basis, for differences between nonequivalent groups on outcomes of interest?

A. Random sampling
B. Case-mix adjustment
C. Inter-rater reliability
D. Descriptive analyses

127. A social worker is working with a client who is attending an adult medical day program. Staff report that her hygiene has deteriorated and she is increasingly disoriented. She has a visiting nurse coming to her home to administer her medications on the evenings when her adult son, with whom she lives, works. After a stroke several months ago, she began getting home-delivered meals. The client requires constant supervision while in the day program and the social worker is concerned about her current safety. Which collateral source will be MOST helpful in making this assessment?

A. The client's adult son
B. The client herself
C. The agency staff who are providing direct care and ancillary services
D. The client's physician who is prescribing her medications

128. Fee splitting is unethical in social work practice because it:

A. Represents a conflict of interest, which can adversely impact client care
B. Establishes rates, which do not consider what clients can afford to pay
C. Creates prohibited dual relationships, which are boundary violations
D. Occurs without client consent, which is mandatory for all treatment decisions

**129.** A mother and her adult son with developmental disabilities meet with a social worker for assistance in helping the young man move into his own apartment. While both the mother and son would like this move to occur, they have concerns as he will need support to meet his daily living needs, as well as attend to ongoing medical issues. The social worker recommends an interdisciplinary team approach to service planning. The FIRST step in this process would be to:

   **A.** Complete a biopsychosocial history so that team members have adequate background information for planning
   **B.** Determine whether there are professionals known to the family who would be good team members
   **C.** Develop a timeline for the problem-solving process to help structure the team's decision making
   **D.** Identify areas of anticipated support to ensure that individuals with needed skills and perspectives are identified for the team

**130.** A former client contacts a social worker and requests a copy of her record. The social worker asks about the reason for the request, but no explanation is provided. While the social worker is not worried about the client seeing the information in the record, the social worker is concerned about the client sharing it with others as it contains sensitive information about the client's history. The social worker should:

   **A.** Send a copy of the entire record to the client
   **B.** Meet with the client to assess why she has not explained how the record will be used
   **C.** Remove material that may be harmful to the client if shared and send the remaining information
   **D.** Ask the client to put her request and the reason for it in writing prior to making a decision

**131.** Which approach focuses on well-being and happiness through cultivation of meaningful experiences?

   **A.** Psychoanalysis
   **B.** Positive psychology
   **C.** Behaviorism
   **D.** Psychoeducation

**132.** Which statement BEST describes the difference between values and ethics?

   **A.** Values are unwritten personal belief systems while ethics are written rules or regulations that guide professional behavior.
   **B.** Values are principles which guide behavior while ethics dictate whether this behavior is appropriate based on a moral code of conduct.
   **C.** Values are customs that are considered desirable by individuals while ethics are collective practices embraced by larger groups or societies.
   **D.** Values are individual standards of conduct which are stable over time while ethics vary based on cultural changes and advances.

**133.** Magical thinking is a characteristic of which cognitive developmental stage?

   **A.** Concrete operations
   **B.** Preoperational
   **C.** Formal operations
   **D.** Sensorimotor

**134.** Which criteria must be present for a social worker to diagnose a child with Gender Dysphoria?

   **A.** Dislike of one's sexual anatomy
   **B.** Sexual interest in those of the same gender
   **C.** Desire to be the other gender or belief that one is the other gender
   **D.** Preference for clothing and playmates of the other gender

**135.** Which of the following statements is TRUE about the inclusion of assessment and service provision descriptions in client discharge plans?

   **A.** Reasons for admission should not be incorporated, but descriptions of treatment must be contained in client discharge plans.
   **B.** Both reasons for admission and services provided must be included in client discharge plans.
   **C.** Client discharge plans should include reasons for admission, but not descriptions of treatment provided.

D. Neither reasons for admission nor services provided should be included in client discharge plans.

136. Which nonverbal technique used in social work practice aims to primarily gain rapport at the unconscious level?

A. Questioning
B. Clarifying
C. Mirroring
D. Reframing

137. A counseling agency charges the same amount to all clients enrolled in its group treatment program. Given a recent bequest, the board of directors proposes providing a standard subsidy to all group therapy clients to reduce their fees by a set amount. A social worker in the agency advocates for these subsidies to be proportional, with clients having the lowest incomes receiving the highest subsidies. The social worker argues that some clients can afford to pay the actual cost while those who have lower incomes cannot and should receive the subsidies. The social worker's recommendation for resource allocation promotes:

A. Equity
B. Sustainability
C. Equality
D. Fidelity

138. A hospital social worker is meeting with a 54-year-old man who was admitted after police found him walking in the middle of the highway intoxicated. An assessment reveals that the client has tried unsuccessfully to reduce his drinking for many years, most recently after his wife left him. His marital problems stemmed from being fired from work due to excessive absenteeism related to his alcohol use. The client admits to spending most of his time drinking or thinking about drinking and often drinks more than he intends. According to the *DSM-5*, the client should be diagnosed with:

A. Alcohol Abuse
B. Alcohol Intoxication
C. Alcohol Dependence
D. Alcohol Use Disorder, severe

**139.** A social worker is interested in determining the impact of culture and race on self-image using an ethnographic approach. The BEST method for this inquiry would be:

A. Statistical regression
B. Participant observation
C. Experimental design
D. Self-administered questionnaires

**140.** Unconditional positive regard is supported by the social work core value of:

A. Importance of human relationships
B. Self-determination
C. Dignity and worth of the person
D. Integrity

**141.** Dyspareunia is defined as:

A. Pain that occurs during sexual intercourse
B. Short-term memory loss due to brain damage
C. Slurring speech that results from neurologic impairment
D. Urinary incontinence associated with age-related muscular changes

**142.** At which age does object permanence typically develop?

A. 18 months
B. 8 months
C. 3 years
D. 5 years

**143.** A social worker is providing counseling to a couple who are experiencing communication problems in their marriage. During a session, the wife becomes angry as she states that she never gets to speak or express her opinions. The social worker calls attention to an observation that the wife has done almost all of the talking during the weekly sessions to date. The social worker is using which of the following interviewing techniques?

A. Confrontation
B. Interpretation
C. Universalization
D. Clarification

**144.** A client tells a social worker that he needs help managing his anxiety as it is interfering with both his professional and personal lives. He states that he has had problems with anxiety throughout his life, but it has become worse lately. The client reports being overwhelmed and wanting to change, but not knowing where to start. The social worker should FIRST:

A. Explore options for treatment including relaxation techniques to provide immediate relief

B. Examine what informal or formal treatments have been tried in the past to address the symptoms

C. Provide cognitive behavioral therapy to replace unhelpful thoughts occurring in fearful situations

D. Determine any risk for self-harm due to the report of being overwhelmed

**145.** A social worker has been working with an 8-year-old girl for over a year. The client's mother, who is going through a divorce, states that she is going to ask if the social worker can be appointed to supervise visits with the father. The need for supervised visitation has already been determined by the court. The mother feels strongly that the social worker is the best choice given the presence of a strong relationship with the child. The social worker should:

A. Inform the mother that this additional role would not be possible

B. Determine the child's feelings about the mother's request since the child is the client

C. Request to meet with the father to determine if he feels comfortable with the arrangement

D. Explore with the mother the impacts of the divorce on the child

**146.** When engaging in reflective listening, it is critical for social workers to:

A. Think about what should be said next to move clients through the therapeutic process

B. Reconstruct what clients are thinking and feeling through verbal and nonverbal methods

C. Direct discussion toward nonthreatening topics when clients become emotional

D. Help clients understand social workers' responsibilities in the problem-solving process

**147.** The primary goal of interdisciplinary service collaboration is to:

  **A.** Reduce duplication in order to avoid wasting scarce resources
  **B.** Address the holistic needs of clients across life domains
  **C.** Develop innovative strategies for addressing social problems
  **D.** Increase the effectiveness of assistance provided to clients

**148.** A 22-year-old woman meets with a social worker due to her excessive fear of heights. During the assessment, the client states that she avoided climbing trees and other activities which raised her above the ground when she was a child. Recently, she has been unable to fly in planes and drive over bridges, causing her to be restricted in her travels. The client is very upset as she spends a great deal of time worrying about whether she will need to cross a bridge, causing her to sweat, breath heavily, and feel anxious throughout the day. During a recent visit with her physician, she was prescribed medication for this condition. Which medication was MOST likely recommended?

  **A.** Mellaril
  **B.** Ativan
  **C.** Risperdal
  **D.** Tegretol

**149.** A social worker formats client records into distinct sections representing all relevant information, issues to be addressed, and activities that need to be undertaken, respectively. Which model of recording is this social worker MOST likely using?

  **A.** Narrative
  **B.** SOAP
  **C.** DAP
  **D.** APIE

**150.** A social worker is approached by a group therapy client who is concerned about the confidentiality of information that he would like to share during the next session. The social worker should:

  **A.** Inform the client that information disclosed during meetings will be kept private unless it involves danger to himself or others
  **B.** Ask the client about the nature of the disclosure so that appropriate guidance can be given as to whether it should be shared

C. Advise the client not to disclose sensitive information as there may be repercussions associated with sharing it with others

D. Inform the client that confidentiality cannot be guaranteed as group members are not legally prohibited from disclosing information that is learned

151. A client has been approved for six sessions with a social worker by his insurance company. In formulating treatment goals, the client articulates changes which the social worker does not feel are achievable in the time frame approved. The social worker should:

A. Inform the client that more feasible goals must be developed

B. Advocate for the insurance company to authorize additional sessions

C. Respect the client's right to self-determination by working toward the client's desired changes

D. Identify other issues which may be of concern to the client

152. A social worker is working in a cultural community in which bartering is the accepted practice for obtaining goods and services. In order for the social worker to accept goods from clients for the provision of services, all of the following criteria have to be met EXCEPT:

A. Clients must demonstrate that these arrangements will not be detrimental.

B. Bartering must be essential for the provision of services.

C. Coercion must not be used in the negotiation of the arrangement.

D. Clients must initiate the request for bartering arrangements.

153. According to family systems theory, in what types of relationships does blame for the dynamics rest with specific individuals?

A. Parent–child

B. Polygamous

C. Abusive

D. Adulterous

154. A social worker who is seeing a client for the first time asks the client how she would like to be addressed. The social worker's action demonstrates:

A. Cultural sensitivity

B. Professional boundaries

    **C.** Practitioner objectivity

    **D.** Ethnocentrism

**155.** A social worker proposes a pilot program for youth with substance use problems in order to determine whether an intervention which has been highly effective with adults has similar results with children. The social worker wants to examine whether outcomes can be generalized to younger age groups before offering the service to all minors in the agency. The pilot program aims to address concerns about:

    **A.** Measurement error

    **B.** Internal validity

    **C.** Reliability

    **D.** External validity

**156.** Which of the following disorders is listed as an Anxiety Disorder in the *DSM-5*?

    **A.** Obsessive-Compulsive Disorder

    **B.** Acute Stress Disorder

    **C.** Posttraumatic Stress Disorder

    **D.** Separation Anxiety Disorder

**157.** A social worker is counseling a middle-aged client who regrets spending most of his time during his adult life building a business. He blames this decision for preventing him from getting married and having children. The client would like to spend more time focused on hobbies that he abandoned due to his work schedule, but does not know how to make this change. This client appears to be struggling with which stage of psychosocial development?

    **A.** Ego identity versus despair

    **B.** Generativity versus stagnation

    **C.** Industry versus inferiority

    **D.** Initiative versus guilt

**158.** After social workers determine that ethical dilemmas exist, they should NEXT:

    **A.** Seek supervision to determine which agency policies impact on the situation

B. Prioritize the ethical values which must be used to choose correct courses of action

C. Weigh the issues in light of key social work values and principles

D. Determine the root causes of the problems so that they can be eradicated

159. The most effective treatment for Alcohol Withdrawal is:

A. Psychopharmacology

B. Self-help group participation

C. Cognitive behavioral therapy

D. Family therapy

160. With regard to client privacy, privilege is BEST defined as the:

A. Legal rule that protects communications from compelled disclosure in court proceedings

B. Mandate to obtain written consent from clients when information is to be disclosed

C. Duty to report concerns of child abuse and neglect to appropriate authorities

D. Requirement to keep treatment information of minors confidential even from their parents

161. A purpose of a forensic interview with a child is to:

A. Identify emotional and psychological strengths to be used in successfully coping with abuse and trauma

B. Gather abuse or trauma histories when making sentencing recommendations for juvenile offenders

C. Determine the occurrence of abuse or trauma based on information that can be used for prosecution of perpetrators

D. Assess whether abuse or trauma has led to the perpetration of violent acts against others

162. Which of the following is NOT considered a deficiency need?

A. Self-actualization

B. Safety

C. Esteem

D. Physiological

**163.** Which of the following actions by a social worker is considered unethical according to the professional code of ethics?

   **A.** Charging rates which are significantly higher than those of other colleagues for the same services based on professional experience and training
   **B.** Bartering in limited circumstances when it is an accepted cultural practice and not detrimental to clients or professional relationships
   **C.** Soliciting private fees for providing services which are available through the social worker's employer or agency
   **D.** Terminating services to clients who are not paying overdue balances after financial contractual arrangements have been made clear

**164.** A social worker at an inpatient psychiatric unit is reviewing an intake assessment completed on a 21-year-old college student who was admitted the previous day due to bizarre behaviors. He was brought to the emergency department by the police who responded to student concerns about him yelling in an agitated voice, even though there was no one nearby. When asked about his actions, the client stated that he was being monitored by a deadly chip implanted in his brain by evil aliens. When contacted, his parents reported that they began to worry about him 8 months ago due to the presence of some unusual behaviors, but their concerns grew in the last 2 months when he stopped attending classes altogether. The social worker sees that the client was examined by the psychiatrist upon intake and medication was prescribed. Due to these symptoms, the client was MOST likely prescribed:

   **A.** Paxil
   **B.** Lithium
   **C.** Prozac
   **D.** Clozaril

**165.** A woman comes to see a social worker as she does not want to cause conflict in her marriage, but she is very unhappy. She has a preschool child and would like to return to working outside her home. The client reports that she misses working in the company that she left shortly before giving birth. She states that her husband's family comes from a culture which strictly forbids such employment. The social worker should view the problem as a:

A. Role conflict
B. Family issue
C. Cultural bias
D. Social injustice

166. "Doorknob disclosures" are MOST commonly caused by:

A. Premature closure of inquiry by social workers when doing biopsychosocial assessments
B. Fear and embarrassment by clients about information provided
C. Lack of empathetic responding by social workers during treatment
D. Perceived power imbalance by clients within therapeutic relationships

167. A mother comes with her 4-year-old daughter to a social worker as her husband is receiving hospice and she is worried about the child's reaction to his death in the coming weeks. The mother has many questions about the child's ability to comprehend what will happen. Based on developmental theories, the child is likely to view death as a:

A. Comforting experience which should not be feared
B. Temporary state which can be reversed at any time
C. Permanent condition which is caused by accidents and factors which cannot be controlled
D. Final part of the life course which inevitably happens to everyone

168. According to the professional code of ethics, social workers who need to report suspected abuse should:

A. Inform clients about the need to report and potential actions which may result *before* any disclosures are made
B. Seek supervision to determine that agency policies about informing clients are appropriately followed
C. Inform clients about the need to report and potential actions which may result *after* any disclosures are made
D. Refrain from telling clients about the need to report and reasons for reporting in order to protect the integrity of abuse investigations

169. A social worker employed in an agency setting receives a referral for a former girlfriend who he has not seen in 20 years. The

client is Spanish speaking and the social worker is the only staff linguistically competent to provide clinical services in Spanish. In order to act ethically in this situation, the social worker should:

A. Speak to his supervisor to disclose the prior relationship before meeting with the client
B. Inform agency personnel that he cannot provide services to the client
C. Meet with the client to determine the severity of the need in order to weigh the ethical options
D. Schedule an intake given the time that has passed since the prior relationship

170. For which diagnoses is brief cognitive behavioral therapy MOST appropriate?

A. Substance Use Disorders
B. Personality Disorders
C. Dissociative Disorders
D. Adjustment Disorders

# Answer Key

| | | | |
|---|---|---|---|
| 1. A | 18. D | 35. C | 52. A |
| 2. C | 19. D | 36. B | 53. B |
| 3. D | 20. B | 37. B | 54. A |
| 4. C | 21. A | 38. C | 55. C |
| 5. B | 22. D | 39. D | 56. C |
| 6. A | 23. A | 40. C | 57. B |
| 7. D | 24. B | 41. D | 58. C |
| 8. C | 25. B | 42. D | 59. D |
| 9. B | 26. D | 43. C | 60. B |
| 10. D | 27. B | 44. B | 61. B |
| 11. D | 28. C | 45. B | 62. D |
| 12. C | 29. D | 46. D | 63. B |
| 13. C | 30. B | 47. C | 64. B |
| 14. D | 31. D | 48. B | 65. C |
| 15. D | 32. C | 49. D | 66. B |
| 16. C | 33. C | 50. A | 67. C |
| 17. C | 34. A | 51. B | 68. A |

| | | | |
|---|---|---|---|
| 69. B | 95. D | 121. D | 147. B |
| 70. A | 96. A | 122. C | 148. B |
| 71. A | 97. C | 123. C | 149. C |
| 72. A | 98. A | 124. A | 150. D |
| 73. A | 99. C | 125. D | 151. A |
| 74. D | 100. C | 126. B | 152. A |
| 75. A | 101. D | 127. A | 153. C |
| 76. D | 102. C | 128. A | 154. A |
| 77. B | 103. B | 129. D | 155. D |
| 78. C | 104. C | 130. A | 156. D |
| 79. D | 105. C | 131. B | 157. B |
| 80. B | 106. C | 132. B | 158. C |
| 81. A | 107. A | 133. B | 159. A |
| 82. D | 108. B | 134. C | 160. A |
| 83. B | 109. C | 135. B | 161. C |
| 84. C | 110. D | 136. C | 162. A |
| 85. C | 111. A | 137. A | 163. C |
| 86. D | 112. B | 138. D | 164. D |
| 87. B | 113. C | 139. B | 165. A |
| 88. B | 114. D | 140. C | 166. B |
| 89. D | 115. A | 141. A | 167. B |
| 90. A | 116. D | 142. B | 168. A |
| 91. C | 117. C | 143. A | 169. B |
| 92. C | 118. A | 144. B | 170. D |
| 93. A | 119. A | 145. A | |
| 94. D | 120. B | 146. B | |

# Answers With Analytic Rationales

**1. A**

*Rationale*

A **flashback** is an **indicator of trauma** that is characterized as reexperiencing a previous traumatic experience as if it were actually happening in that moment. It includes reactions that often resemble the client's reactions during the trauma. Flashback experiences are very brief and typically last only a few seconds, but the emotional aftereffects linger for hours or longer. Flashbacks are commonly initiated by a trigger, but not necessarily. Sometimes, they occur out of the blue. Other times specific physical states increase vulnerability to reexperiencing a trauma (e.g., fatigue, high stress levels). Flashbacks can feel like a brief movie scene that intrudes on the client. For example, hearing a car backfire on a hot, sunny day may be enough to cause a veteran to respond as if he or she were back on military patrol. Other ways people reexperience trauma, besides flashbacks, are via nightmares and intrusive thoughts of the trauma.

During flashbacks, clients need to focus on what is happening in the here and now, which is accomplished using **grounding techniques**. Social workers should be prepared to help the client get regrounded so that he or she can distinguish between what is happening now versus what had happened in the past.

There are lots of grounding techniques, but the best are those that use the five senses (sound, touch, smell, taste, and sight) as they bring attention to the present moment; for example, turning on loud music (sound), feeling something cold or comforting (touch), sniffing a strong pleasant fragrance (smell), and so on.

Social workers should also offer education about the experience of triggers and flashbacks, and then normalize these events as common traumatic stress reactions. Afterward, some clients need to discuss the experience and understand why the flashback or trigger occurred. It is often helpful for a client to draw a connection between the trigger and the traumatic event(s). This can be a preventive strategy whereby the client can anticipate that a given situation places him or her at higher risk for retraumatization and requires use of coping strategies, including seeking support.

### Test-Taking Strategies Applied

The question contains a qualifying word—PRIMARILY—even though it is not capitalized. While all of the answers are helpful for survivors of trauma, the aim of grounding techniques is immediate assistance to get clients back to the "here and now." The incorrect answers involve "talk" or psychotherapy by discussing, understanding, and teaching. Several of them also do not address that clients are "experiencing flashbacks of past traumatic events," but instead deal with the impacts of or responses to trauma more broadly. Only the correct response choice deals with orienting the client to the present, which is necessary when flashbacks occur.

### Question Assesses

Content Area II—Assessment, Diagnosis, and Treatment Planning; Assessment and Diagnosis (Competency); The Indicators of Traumatic Stress and Violence (KSA)

## 2. C

### Rationale

Each culture has its own traditions, rituals, and ways of expressing grief and mourning. The **effects of culture, race, and ethnicity on behaviors, attitudes, and identity** must be considered. Almost every religion or culture has its own traditions involving mourning. Grief is the thoughts and feelings associated with loss, while mourning is the outward behaviors that represent a person's grief. Every culture has its own traditions regarding mourning, and it is important for people to realize that everyone mourns differently and that there is no right way to mourn. While social workers cannot be expected to know the mourning ceremonies and traditions of each client's culture, understanding some basics about how different cultures may prepare for and respond to death is important. Though difficult to ask, there are crucial questions that need to be part of conversations between social workers and clients. For example:

- What are the cultural rituals for coping with dying, the deceased person's body, the final arrangements for the body, and honoring the death?

- What are the family's beliefs about what happens after death?

- What does the client consider to be the roles of each family member in handling the death?

- Are certain types of death less acceptable (e.g., suicide) or are certain types of death especially hard to handle for that culture (e.g., the death of a child—in countries with high infant mortality, there may be different attitudes about the loss of children)?

*Clients should be viewed as a source of knowledge about their special/cultural needs and norms*—but social workers sometimes are at a loss about what to ask under such trying circumstances. While there are many similarities across cultures, such as wearing black as a sign of mourning, there are always exceptions. The mix of cultural/religious attitudes and behaviors surrounding death and dying can become very complex indeed. And when a death actually occurs, some clients break with tradition entirely, often creating chaos within families.

### Test-Taking Strategies Applied

The question contains a qualifying word—MOST. The client's behavior may be psychotic, placing her at risk for self-harm. It also may be typical given the client's cultural practices and religious beliefs. In order to best understand these actions, the social worker must ask the client about her mourning rituals. It will be important for the client to employ coping strategies to deal with her loss, but there is no indication that they are not already being utilized and such identification is not directly related to the behaviors described in the scenario.

### Question Assesses

Content Area I—Human Development, Diversity, and Behavior in the Environment; Diversity and Discrimination (Competency); The Effect of Culture, Race, and Ethnicity on Behaviors, Attitudes, and Identity (KSA)

### 3. D

### Rationale

**Human genetics** is the study of inheritance as it occurs in humans. **Genetic testing** can confirm or rule out suspected genetic conditions or help determine clients' chances of developing or passing on genetic disorders. This process can be very stressful for clients and it is important that social workers have knowledge about the benefits, as well as the limitations and risks, of genetic testing. Social workers can help clients weigh the pros and cons of the test and discuss the social and emotional aspects of testing.

Every person carries two copies of most genes (one copy from the mother and one from the father). A carrier is a person who has a change in one copy of a gene. The carrier does not have the genetic disease related to the abnormal gene. A carrier can pass this abnormal gene to a child. Carrier identification is a type of genetic testing that can determine whether clients who have a family history of a specific disease, or who are in a group that has a greater chance of having a disease, are likely to pass that disease to their children. Information from this type of testing can guide a couple's decision about having children.

For many genetic disorders, carrier testing can help determine how likely it is that a child will have the disease:

- If both parents carry the abnormal gene, there is a one-in-four (25%) chance that their child will have the disease and a two-in-four (50%) chance that their child will be a carrier of the disease (but will not have it). There is also a one-in-four (25%) chance that the child will not get the abnormal gene and so will not have the disease nor be a carrier.
- If only one parent carries the abnormal gene, the child has a one-in-two (50%) chance of being a carrier but almost no chance that he or she will have the disease.

### Test-Taking Strategies Applied

The question asks about an appropriate role for a social worker when a client has learned information through genetic testing. The client is a woman who was recently married. It would not be appropriate to meet with the husband as there is no indication, in the scenario, that the client wants a joint session to occur and the couple is not the client. Additionally, no medical issues have been raised by the client, making a referral to a physician unwarranted. While the client is anxious and upset, her feelings may result from not understanding that her children will not automatically contract the disease. The client needs information about the potential likelihood that her children would be carriers or have the disease. This information may alleviate some of her fears. Knowing whether the husband is also a carrier is critical information which may not yet be known and/or is not provided in the scenario. Anxiety and depression are the symptoms, not the root of the problem, which is a lack of understanding. Providing education is a critical social work task when clients are deciding to have genetic testing and interpreting its results.

## Question Assesses

Content Area I—Human Development, Diversity, and Behavior in the Environment; Human Growth and Development (Competency); Basic Principles of Human Genetics (KSA)

### 4. C

## Rationale

Therapy requires recognizing a client as part of a family system. Additionally, it focuses on studying the role that a client has in a **family dynamic**. Sometimes client problems arise due to dysfunctional communication within the family. Disturbed communication in families resulted in enormous pressure being felt by one or more members of that family system.

A **double bind** is a dilemma in communication in which an individual (or group) receives two or more conflicting messages, with one message negating the other; this is a situation in which successfully responding to one message means failing with the other and vice versa, so that the person will automatically be put in the wrong regardless of response. And the person can neither comment on the conflict, nor resolve it, nor opt out of the situation. Contradictory messages result in the "victim" feeling powerless and trapped in a "damned if you do and damned if you don't" double bind.

A **paradoxical directive** involves prescribing the very symptom the client wants to resolve. It is often equated with reverse psychology. The underlying principle is that a client engages in a behavior for a reason, which is typically to meet a need (rebellion, attention, a cry for help, etc.). In prescribing the symptom, a social worker helps a client understand this need and determine how much control (if any) he or she has over the symptom. By choosing to manifest the symptom, a client may recognize that he or she can create it, and therefore has the power to stop or change it.

A **negative feedback loop** is information that flows back into the family system to minimize deviation and continue functioning within prescribed limits. It helps to maintain homeostasis or keep things stable or the same over time.

A **metacommunication** is an implicit, nonverbal message that accompanies verbal communication.

### Test-Taking Strategies Applied

This is a recall question which relies on social workers understanding communication patterns within families so that they can assist in addressing them when they interfere with effective functioning. Often roles within family units can be identified through assessing both verbal and nonverbal communication. Much of social work intervention focuses on helping clients with enhancing their expressive and receptive communication skills.

### Question Assesses

Content Area III—Psychotherapy, Clinical Interventions, and Case Management; The Intervention Process (Competency); Family Therapy Models, Interventions, and Approaches (KSA)

### 5. B

### Rationale

When a client has experienced multiple, severe forms of trauma, the psychological results are often multiple and severe as well; this phenomenon is sometimes referred to as complex posttraumatic disturbance. **Complex trauma** can be defined as a combination of early and late-onset, multiple, and sometimes highly invasive traumatic events, usually of an ongoing, interpersonal nature. In most cases, such trauma includes exposure to repetitive childhood sexual, physical, and/or psychological abuse, often (although not always) in the context of concomitant emotional neglect and harmful social environments. Complex trauma has a dramatic impact on development and resulting emotional dysregulation and the loss of safety, direction, and the ability to detect or respond to danger cues—this often sets off a chain of events leading to subsequent or repeated trauma exposure in adolescence and adulthood.

The impact of complex trauma includes anxiety and depression; dissociation; relational, identity, and affect regulation disturbance; cognitive distortions; somatization; "externalizing" behaviors such as self-mutilation and violence; sexual disturbance; substance abuse; eating disorders; susceptibility to revictimization; and traumatic bereavement associated with loss of family members and other significant attachment figures.

Clients who have experienced complex trauma may be diagnosed with a range of disorders, and consequently treated with multiple medications and therapies that are ultimately ineffective because they fail to address the underlying problem and do not reflect a trauma-informed approach to assessment and treatment. It is essential that social workers perform comprehensive assessments that capture the broad range of reactions. Thorough assessments must also carefully date and track the various traumatic events so they can be linked with developmental derailments. Treatment approaches that are limited to a single modality (e.g., exposure therapy, cognitive therapy, or psychiatric medication) may be less helpful—especially if the intervention is not adapted to the specific psychological and cultural needs of a client.

Treatment should focus on:

- *Removal of and protection from the source of the trauma and/or abuse*
- *Acknowledgement that recovery from the trauma is not trivial and will require **significant time** and effort*
- *Separation of residual problems into those that clients can resolve (such as personal improvement goals) and those that clients cannot resolve (such as the behavior of disordered family members)*
- *Acknowledgment of the trauma as real, important, and undeserved*
- Acknowledgment that the trauma came from something that was stronger than clients and therefore could not be avoided
- Acknowledgment of the "complex" nature of trauma (trauma may have led to decisions that brought on additional, undeserved trauma)
- Mourning for what has been lost and cannot be recovered
- Identification of what has been lost and can be recovered
- Placement in a supportive environment where clients can discover they are not alone and can receive validation for their successes and support through their struggles

### Test-Taking Strategies Applied

The question contains a qualifying word—NOT—that requires social workers to select the response choice which is not a goal of treatment. When NOT is used as a qualifying word, it is often helpful to remove it from the question and eliminate the three response choices which are goals. This approach will leave the one response choice which is NOT a reason for conducting a needs assessment.

While recovery from complex trauma is possible, it will require significant time and effort. Thus, the correct answer is NOT a goal of treatment as it inaccurately indicates that recovery can occur quickly.

### Question Assesses

Content Area II—Assessment, Diagnosis, and Treatment Planning; Treatment Planning (Competency); Methods and Approaches to Trauma-Informed Care (KSA)

## 6. A

### Rationale

When evaluating agency programs, it is necessary to understand different types of assessment and the terms used to describe them. The resources organizations devote to particular programs are called **inputs**. Those resources can be financial or the time of staff or volunteers. Expertise, such as a consultant or a partner organization, can be considered an input as well.

Outputs, outcomes, and impacts are often used interchangeably, but are not the same.

**Outputs** are what are produced by programs. For instance, a training program provides graduates. A homeless shelter creates filled beds. Outputs are usually described with numbers. For instance, "96% of available beds were filled" or "the training program graduated 96 individuals." Outputs are measurable and readily determined. It is tempting to stop with outputs because they are easy to produce as they reflect the number of people served or meals distributed.

**Outcomes** are the effects programs produce on the people served or issues addressed. For instance, the result of a training program might be the number of graduates who get a job and keep it for a particular period. An outcome is a change that occurred because of a program. It is measurable and time limited, although it may take a while to determine its full effect. Measuring outcomes requires a bigger commitment of time and resources.

**Impacts** are the **long-term or indirect effects** of outcomes. Impacts are hard to measure since they may or may not happen. They are what is hoped that efforts will accomplish. For instance, graduating from a training program may eventually lead to a better quality of life for the individual.

*Test-Taking Strategies Applied*

This is a recall question about evaluation methods. Social workers are required to know terms, as well as key concepts, related to each of the KSAs. This scenario requires the ability to distinguish between an output and outcome, as input and impact are clearly the response choices which are more easily eliminated.

*Question Assesses*

Content Area III—Psychotherapy, Clinical Interventions, and Case Management; Service Delivery and Management of Cases (Competency); Methods to Evaluate Agency Programs (e.g., Needs Assessment, Formative/Summative Assessment, Cost-Effectiveness, Cost-Benefit Analysis, Outcomes Assessment) (KSA)

## 7. D

*Rationale*

**Benzodiazepines** are psychotropic medications that help relieve nervousness, tension, and other symptoms by slowing the central nervous system. Benzodiazepines are a type of *antianxiety drug*. While anxiety is a normal response to stressful situations, some clients have unusually high levels of anxiety that can interfere with everyday life. For them, benzodiazepines can help bring their feelings under control. The medicine can also relieve troubling symptoms of anxiety, such as pounding heartbeat, breathing problems, irritability, nausea, and faintness. They are also sometimes prescribed for other conditions, such as muscle spasms, epilepsy and other seizure disorders, phobias, Panic Disorder, withdrawal from alcohol, and sleeping problems. The family of antianxiety drugs known as benzodiazepines includes alprazolam (Xanax), chlordiazepoxide (Librium), diazepam (Valium), and **lorazepam (Ativan)**. These medicines take effect fairly quickly, starting to work within an hour after they are taken. Benzodiazepines are available only with a prescription and are available in tablet, capsule, liquid, or injectable forms.

 **Prolixin** is an *antipsychotic medication* used to treat hallucinations and delusions.

 **Lithium** is a *mood stabilizer* used for the treatment of Bipolar Disorder.

 **Prozac** is an *antidepressant medication* used to treat depression.

*Test-Taking Strategies Applied*

This is a recall question about benzodiazepines (commonly called "tranquilizers"), which are useful for treating anxiety. They are highly addictive, and their use is normally limited to a short-term, as-needed basis. They need to be carefully controlled by prescribing physicians.

The examination requires social workers to be aware of the four major types of psychotropic medications—antipsychotics, antidepressants, mood stabilizers, and antianxiety drugs—and be able to identify some common medications in each of these types. While it is possible to have no medication questions on the examination as other KSAs under assessment, diagnosis, and treatment planning are tested instead, it is important to have some knowledge about psychotropic drugs. For example, knowing which types of medications are commonly prescribed for various diagnoses can be helpful.

*Question Assesses*

Content Area II—Assessment, Diagnosis, and Treatment Planning; Assessment and Diagnosis (Competency); Common Psychotropic and Non-Psychotropic Prescriptions and Over-the-Counter Medications and Their Side Effects (KSA)

### 8. C

*Rationale*

There are two major forms of **Bipolar Disorder**—Bipolar I and Bipolar II (also known as Bipolar 1 and 2)—which are separate diagnoses with significant differences between them. To be diagnosed with Bipolar I, a client must have had at least one manic episode. The manic episode may be preceded by or followed by hypomanic or major depressive episodes. Mania symptoms cause significant impairment in life and may require hospitalization or trigger a break from reality (psychosis). To be diagnosed with Bipolar II Disorder, a client must have had at least one major depressive episode lasting at least 2 weeks and at least one hypomanic episode lasting at least 4 days, but never had a manic episode. Major depressive episodes or the unpredictable changes in mood and behavior can cause distress or difficulty in areas of your life.

The most important distinction between Bipolar I and II is that a client **with Bipolar I has manic episodes while a client with Bipolar II has hypomanic episodes.** The main difference between mania and hypomania is a matter of severity. In the hypomania of bipolar II, a client has a sustained mood that is elevated (heightened), expansive (grand, superior), or irritable. This mood has to be noticeably different from his or her normal mood when not depressed. In mania, that mood is extremely abnormal, and is also combined with increased activity or energy that is also abnormal. Examples of hypomania may include being exceptionally cheerful, needing only 3 hours of sleep instead of the usual 7, spending more money than can be afforded, and/or speaking far more rapidly than usual. Hypomanic behavior is *noticeably different* from a client's *own* mood, but not outside the range of possible behavior in general. Manic episodes may include being out-of-control happy even during serious events, which is atypical behavior for anyone.

Someone with Bipolar I Disorder may also have hypomanic episodes, but someone with Bipolar II cannot ever have had a manic episode. If a manic episode occurs in someone with Bipolar II, the diagnosis will be changed. However, the depressive episodes of Bipolar II Disorder are often longer-lasting and may be even more severe than in Bipolar I Disorder. Therefore, Bipolar II Disorder is not simply a "milder" overall form of Bipolar I Disorder.

*At least one of* the following conditions has to exist in mania, but can't be present in hypomania:

■ Mania may include psychotic symptoms—delusions or hallucinations. Hypomania does not have psychotic symptoms. (However, a client with bipolar II may experience hallucinations or delusions during depressive episodes without the diagnosis changing to Bipolar I.)

■ While hypomania may interfere to a degree with daily functioning, in mania day-to-day life is significantly impaired.

■ The manic person was hospitalized because of the severe symptoms.

### Test-Taking Strategies Applied

The question contains a qualifying word—MAIN—even though it is not capitalized. "Main" refers to the need to select an answer that is the primary distinction between Bipolar I and II. In this question, only one answer is an accurate statement and it is the primary difference between the disorders.

Rapid cycling is a pattern of frequent, distinct episodes in Bipolar Disorder. In rapid cycling, a client with Bipolar Disorder moves between mania/hypomania and depression frequently. It can occur at any point in the course of Bipolar Disorder, and can come and go, so it is not necessarily a "permanent" or indefinite pattern. It is not unique to Bipolar I as it can occur in Bipolar II. Bipolar II also does not include manic episodes, making the first response choice incorrect. Depressive episodes of Bipolar II Disorder are often longer-lasting and may be even more severe than in Bipolar I Disorder, making the second answer inaccurate. A client with Bipolar II may experience hallucinations or delusions during depressive episodes without the diagnosis changing to Bipolar I. Thus, the last response choice is not correct.

### Question Assesses

Content Area II—Assessment, Diagnosis, and Treatment Planning; Assessment and Diagnosis (Competency); The Use of the Diagnostic and Statistical Manual of the American Psychiatric Association (KSA)

### 9. B

### *Rationale*

Competently conducting **evaluations of practice** requires skill and knowledge. There are also many ethical considerations. Social workers engaged in evaluation should obtain voluntary and written informed consent from participants, when appropriate, without any implied or actual deprivation or penalty for refusal to participate; without undue inducement to participate; and with due regard for participants' well-being, privacy, and dignity. Informed consent should include information about the nature, extent, and duration of the participation requested and disclosure of the risks and benefits of participation in the research.

*When evaluation or research participants are incapable of giving informed consent (including due to being below the age of consent), social workers should provide an appropriate explanation to the participants, obtain the participants' assent to the extent they are able, and obtain written consent from those legally authorized to act on their behalf.*

### *Test-Taking Strategies Applied*

This is a recall question which relies on social workers being fully informed of ethical standards of evaluation and research. The correct answer is that which is required for "the social worker to ethically conduct the evaluation." When questions concern ethical behavior, the 2018 *NASW Code of Ethics* must be remembered. Written consent is necessary, but not sufficient, as the assent of the children is also needed. Assent is a willingness to participate even though a child is not legally able to provide authorization. Children are not able to provide written consent as consent indicates authority to make legal decisions, which those under the age of majority are not able to do unless emancipated. Lastly, separate informed consent procedures are needed for evaluation and research. Those given for service participation cannot be used to indicate that participation in evaluation and research are permissible.

Written permission from the agency is not sufficient as it is not legally authorized to act on behalf of the children or their guardians.

*Question Assesses*

Content Area IV—Professional Values and Ethics; Professional Values and Ethical Issues (Competency); Research Ethics (e.g., Institutional Review Boards, Use of Human Subjects, Informed Consent) (KSA)

## 10.  D

*Rationale*

Social workers must handle issues surrounding the **discharge and termination of services** very carefully. Clients whose services are discharged or terminated unethically may not receive needed supports.

Once services are provided, social workers have legal and ethical responsibilities to continue these services or properly refer clients to alternative providers. While social workers do not have to work with all those in need or requesting services, services cannot terminate abruptly once therapeutic relationships have been established. Social workers must take reasonable steps to avoid abandoning clients who are still in need of services. Social workers should withdraw services precipitously only under unusual circumstances, giving careful consideration to all factors in the situation and taking care to minimize possible adverse effects. Social workers should assist in making appropriate arrangements for continuation of services when necessary (*NASW Code of Ethics, 2018— 1.17 Termination of Services*). When it is necessary to terminate services, social workers should provide clients with names, addresses, and telephone numbers of at least three appropriate referrals. *When feasible, they should follow up with clients who have been terminated. If clients do not visit the referrals, clients should be contacted about the risks involved with the lack of follow.*

Clients who will be terminated should be given as much advance notice as possible. When clients announce their decision to terminate prematurely, social workers must explain the risks involved and provide suggestions for alternative care. All decisions and actions related to termination of services should be documented in letters and clients should be provided with clear written instructions to follow and telephone numbers to use in the event of an emergency. Clients should be asked to sign a copy of the documents, affirming that they received the instructions and that the instructions were explained to them.

In instances involving court-ordered clients, social workers should seek legal consultation and court approval before terminating services.

### Test-Taking Strategies Applied

The correct answer involves direct action by the social worker to assist with the referral and discharge process. Seeking consultation to review what has already occurred may be helpful for professional development after the situation has been resolved, but it will not directly help reengage the client. Additionally, sending a letter is very passive and there is no reason to believe that the client is not aware of the discharge plan and contact information of the new provider. This action should have been taken earlier in the referral process and will not be helpful now. Lastly, meeting with the client to discuss "new issues" is contraindicated as the social worker needs to discharge the client. The client should be discussing new problems with a provider who will be able to assist with assessing and treating them.

Contacting the client about not following through is an active response to address the situation in the scenario. Central to this contact can be an assessment of why the benefits of continuing treatment have not compelled the client to make contact.

### Question Assesses

Content Area II—Assessment, Diagnosis, and Treatment Planning; Treatment Planning (Competency); Discharge, Aftercare, and Follow-Up Planning (KSA)

## 11. D

### Rationale

Social workers must be aware of **models of supervision and consultation**, including those provided via contract. In situations in which an agency may not have a clinical supervisor who meets the qualifications of a supervisor, a social work supervisee may contract for supervision services outside the agency. Supervisees should contact the regulatory board in their jurisdictions in advance of contracting to confirm if such a practice is permitted and confirm the documentation required from the supervisor. The time frame required for the supervision period should also be verified. Contracting for "outside supervision" can be problematic and place a supervisor at risk. If the supervisee is paying for the services, he or she can dismiss the supervisor, especially if disagreements or conflicts arise. In addition, the supervisor may encounter conflicts between the supervisee and the agency.

*Development of a contractual agreement among the social worker, the supervisor, and the employing agency is essential* in preventing problems in the supervisory relationship. The agreement should clearly delineate the agency's authority and *grant permission for the supervisor to provide clinical supervision.* Evaluation responsibilities, periodic written reports, and issues of confidentiality should also be included in the agreement. Supervisors and supervisees should also sign a written contract that outlines the parameters of the supervisory relationship. *Monthly written progress reports prepared by the supervisor should be required* and, if appropriate, meet the standards established by licensing boards for supervision.

### Test-Taking Strategies Applied

The question contains a qualifying word—EXCEPT—that requires social workers to select the response choice which is not a requirement when supervision is contractual. While it is always good to understand the practice histories of supervisors, including actions taken by licensing boards against them, before hiring and entering into contractual relationships, it is not necessary. Social workers may still choose to be supervised by supervisors who have had licensing infractions. The other three response choices directly relate to the parameters of the contracted relationship and/or monitoring the actions of social workers through progress reporting in order to ensure that client services are not compromised by these arrangements.

### Question Assesses

Content Area III—Psychotherapy, Clinical Interventions, and Case Management; Consultation and Interdisciplinary Collaboration (Competency); Models of Supervision and Consultation (e.g., Individual, Peer, Group) (KSA)

### 12. C

### Rationale

Clients with mental health disorders are more likely than clients without mental health disorders to experience an alcohol or substance use disorder. **Co-occurring disorders** can be difficult to diagnose due to the complexity of symptoms, as both may vary in severity. In many cases, clients may receive treatment for one disorder while the other disorder remains untreated. This may occur because both mental and Substance Use Disorders can have biological, psychological, and social components. Other reasons may be inadequate training or screening by service providers, an overlap of symptoms, or that other health issues need to be addressed first. In any case, the consequences of undiagnosed, untreated, or undertreated co-occurring disorders can lead to a higher likelihood of experiencing homelessness, incarceration, medical illnesses, suicide, or even early death.

Clients with co-occurring disorders are best served through integrated treatment. With integrated treatment, social workers can address mental and Substance Use Disorders at the same time, often lowering costs and creating better outcomes. Increasing awareness and building capacity in service systems are important in helping identify and treat co-occurring disorders. Early detection and treatment can improve treatment outcomes and the quality of life for those who need these services.

*Prescribed medications play a key role in the treatment of co-occurring disorders.* They can reduce symptoms and prevent relapses of a psychiatric disorder. Medications can also help clients minimize cravings and maintain abstinence from addictive substances.

In order to get the most out of medication, clients must make an informed choice about taking medications and understand the potential benefits and costs associated with medication use. In addition, they must take the medication as prescribed.

Taking medication is not substance abuse. Clients in recovery for a Substance Use Disorder may think it is wrong to take any medications. However, a medication that manages clients' moods is very different from a drug that alters clients' moods.

### Test-Taking Strategies Applied

As co-occurring disorders are so prevalent, social workers must be versed in their treatment. While not all clients with psychiatric comorbidities need or receive psychotropic medications, the treatment of mental health symptoms with medications can be effective in reducing the severity of the symptomatology. Much research has been done in this area. Further, it might reduce the elevated risk of suicide attributed to each of the comorbid disorders and to their combined effect. Reducing risk of suicide is an important aim of treatment.

Psychotropic medications should only be prescribed after clients understand their side effects, but informed consent is not unique to only those with co-occurring mental health and Substance Use Disorders—which makes it an incorrect answer.

### Question Assesses

Content Area I—Human Development, Diversity, and Behavior in the Environment; Human Behavior in the Social Environment (Competency); Co-occurring Disorders and Conditions (KSA)

### 13. C

*Rationale*

There are many **models of supervision** described in the literature, ranging from traditional, authoritarian models to more collaborative models. Different models of supervision place emphasis, in varying degrees, on the client, the supervisor, the supervisee, or the context in which the supervision takes place. Ideally, the supervisor and the supervisee use a collaborative process when a supervision model is selected; however, *it is ultimately the responsibility of supervisors to select the model that works best for the professional development of supervisees.*

Supervision encompasses several interrelated functions and responsibilities. Each of these interrelated functions contributes to a larger responsibility or outcome that ensures clients are protected and that clients receive competent and ethical services. As a result, supervision services received by the client are evaluated and adjusted, as needed, to increase benefits. It is supervisors' responsibilities to ensure that supervisees provide competent, appropriate, and ethical services.

*Test-Taking Strategies Applied*

Social workers must be knowledgeable about supervision models. This question requires social workers to remember that supervisors are responsible for the quality of services delivered by supervisees and their ultimate benefit to clients. Ruling out administrators and funders leaves supervisees and supervisors as possible correct answers. As the question asks about "ultimate responsibility," supervisors are distinguished from the supervisees as they have authority in supervisory relationships. While administrators and funders have influence on service delivery, they are not direct parties in supervisory relationships and their directives should never be honored over those of supervisors.

*Question Assesses*

Content Area III—Psychotherapy, Clinical Interventions, and Case Management; Consultation and Interdisciplinary Collaboration (Competency); Models of Supervision and Consultation (e.g., Individual, Peer, Group) (KSA)

### 14. D

*Rationale*

Many programs use the ability to perform **activities of daily living** (ADLs) and **instrumental activities of daily living** (IADLs) as eligibility criteria to determine eligibility and/or **level of care**. Whether or not clients are capable of performing these activities on their own or if they rely on family caregivers to perform the ADLs can serve as a comparative measure of their independence. Assessments can help with determining assistance needed.

Measuring a client's ability to perform the ADLs and IADLs is important not just in determining the level of assistance required, but as a metric for a variety of services and programs related to caring for older adults and for those with disabilities.

Many state-funded, non-Medicaid programs use an inability to perform two or three ADLs as one of the eligibility criteria for participation in their assistance programs.

Medicaid often requires older adults to be qualified for nursing home care, and nursing home care qualification can be determined by how much assistance one requires with ADLs. Long-term care insurance often uses an inability to perform the ADLs as a trigger for paying out on a policy. Social Security Disability Insurance (SSDI) also considers ADLs as a qualification factor.

ADLs are activities in which clients engage on a day-to-day basis. These are everyday *personal care* activities that are fundamental to caring for oneself and maintaining independence.

There are many variations on the definition of the ADLs, but most organizations agree there are five basic categories.

- Personal hygiene—bathing, grooming, and oral care
- Dressing—the ability to make appropriate clothing decisions and physically dress oneself
- Eating—the ability to feed oneself though not necessarily to prepare food
- Maintaining continence—both the mental and physical ability to use a restroom
- Transferring—moving oneself from seated to standing and getting in and out of bed

IADLs are activities related to *independent living*. The instrumental activities are more subtle than ADLs. They can help determine with greater detail the level of assistance required. The IADLs include:

- Basic communication skills—such as using a regular phone, mobile phone, email, or the Internet

- Transportation—either by driving oneself, arranging rides, or the ability to use public transportation

- Meal preparation—meal planning, preparation, storage, and the ability to safely use kitchen equipment

- Shopping—the ability to make appropriate food and clothing purchase decisions

- Housework—doing laundry, cleaning dishes, and maintaining a hygienic place of residence

- Managing medications—taking accurate dosages at the appropriate times, managing refills, and avoiding conflicts

- Managing personal finances—operating within a budget, writing checks, paying bills, and avoiding scams

### *Test-Taking Strategies Applied*

The question contains a qualifying word—MOST. While it may be useful to assess all areas listed, level of care is primarily determined by the amount of help that the client needs to complete necessary personal assistance and independent living tasks.

Adapting to life changes may be important to the client's ability to adjust to his or her new home, but will not directly relate to "making a determination of the needed level of care." Managing medical problems may also need to be addressed. However, such assistance can be done by care management in any setting. Lastly, while cognition is related to self-care abilities, performing the tasks is also based on mobility or the ability to move upper or lower extremities in order to complete them. Thus, assessing cognitive tasks will not give a complete picture of assistance needed.

### *Question Assesses*

Content Area II—Assessment, Diagnosis, and Treatment Planning; Assessment and Diagnosis (Competency); Placement Options Based on Assessed Level of Care (KSA)

### 15. D

### *Rationale*

Clients engaged in **enmeshed interpersonal relationships** are nearly always the last to know. Often social workers work with adult children who are recovering from the pain and confusion caused by enmeshed relationships with parents.

There are many signs of enmeshed relationships including:

- Neglecting other relationships because of an obsession or concern about one relationship
- Happiness contingent upon a relationship
- Self-esteem contingent upon a relationship
- Excessive anxiety, fear, or a compulsion to fix the problem whenever there is a disagreement in a relationship
- Feeling of loneliness that overwhelms when not with the other person—often creating irrational desires to reconnect
- Symbiotic emotional connections which result in an individual becoming angry, upset, or depressed when another person is angry, upset, or depressed
- Strong desire to fix another person's situation and change his/her state of mind

When relationships are enmeshed, they are no longer able to grow. Social workers must work to establish healthy boundaries and respect for autonomous choices. This process can be painful for clients.

*Test-Taking Strategies Applied*

In order to select the correct answer, social workers must first diagnose the problem. The feelings and behaviors of the couple are indicative of enmeshment. Once the cause of the problem is known, the question can be simplified to picking out the treatment focus when working with enmeshed relationships. The wife is not the client as the couple sought treatment, so focusing on the wife's self-worth will not address the problem. Finding out more about past intimate relationships is an assessment—not a treatment—task. Understanding each other's feelings will not help each person develop boundaries and differentiate from one another, which is the root of the issue.

*Question Assesses*

Content Area I—Human Development, Diversity, and Behavior in the Environment; Human Behavior in the Social Environment (Competency); The Dynamics of Interpersonal Relationships (KSA)

### 16. C

*Rationale*

**Case notes** may be subject to a range of legislative processes and requirements during and following the conclusion of professional relationships. The nature of these requirements may differ greatly according to the jurisdiction or nature/context of practice. Social workers should use care to make sure that case notes are impartial, accurate, and complete. Information may need to be added to client records to ensure that they are not misleading and are comprehensive. Care should be taken at all times to avoid errors or omissions. If a change must be made to correct an error or omission, the change must be recorded as a new and separate case note. In addition to outlining the error or omission as part of new case notes, it is advisable to provide explanations for earlier absences or inaccuracies.

An existing case note should never be amended or changed in light of additional information obtained at a later date. This should always constitute a new case note.

### Test-Taking Strategies Applied

This scenario requires knowledge about documentation and the management of practice records.

Careful and diligent documentation enhances the quality of services provided to clients. Social workers should take reasonable steps to ensure that documentation in records is accurate and reflects the services provided. In addition, social workers should include sufficient and timely documentation in records to facilitate the delivery of services and to ensure continuity of services provided to clients in the future. Comprehensive records are necessary to assess clients' circumstances, as well as plan and deliver services.

Social workers should know the professional protocol for adding or making changes to client records, so asking for supervisory input is not needed, making the first answer incorrect. Material should never be added to existing case notes as they need to accurately reflect documentation of "the facts" that were known at the times of these entries. Thus, the second answer is not correct. Lastly, client records should be complete, so not recording information in client files is also unethical, eliminating the last response choice listed.

### Question Assesses

Content Area III—Psychotherapy, Clinical Interventions, and Case Management; Service Delivery and Management of Cases (Competency); The Principles of Case Recording, Documentation, and Management of Practice Records (KSA)

### 17. C

### Rationale

**Interviewing skills** are essential to ensuring that clients feel understood, problems are assessed, and effective treatment is delivered. A comprehensive social work interview includes conducting a multiple biopsychosocial–spiritual–cultural assessment in order to better understand the presenting problem. Questions asked and techniques used may promote or inhibit information gathering and other aspects of the problem-solving process. Skills and questioning techniques used include active listening, empathy, rapport building, open- and closed-ended inquiries, silence, and so on.

When interviewing clients, social workers should avoid "Why" questions in order to prevent clients from feeling as though they need to defend their choices and actions. Although it may be necessary to learn the reasoning behind clients' choices and actions, the wording used may impact responses. For example, if a social worker needs to know why a client is missing doses of medication, instead of asking "Why haven't you been able to take your medication as prescribed?" it is better to ask "What are some of the reasons for skipping your medication?" The difference may be subtle, but it can affect the way a client perceives the question. With the "Why" method, a client may be defensive, whereas the "What" method allows a client to reflect on action without feeling judged.

### Test-Taking Strategies Applied

The correct answer is the BEST question for the social worker to ask as part of the assessment. The use of the qualifying word, which is capitalized, indicates that other response choices may be appropriate, but are not as essential to identifying causes for the presenting problem, the primary aim of assessment. In the scenario, the social worker must find out the reasons for the medication noncompliance. There is no indication that the client is not taking the medication to become hospitalized. It is also premature to see how the social worker can assist as the reasons for missing the doses is not known.

The correct "What" question is preferred to the inaccurate "Why" question to avoid having the client feel judged. The "Why" response choice also implies that the client's actions are in direct violation of the doctor's orders as she has not been able to take her medication "as prescribed." Pointing out that she has done something other than what the doctor stated can cause defensiveness or shame.

### Question Assesses

Content Area III—Psychotherapy, Clinical Interventions, and Case Management; The Intervention Process (Competency); The Principles and Techniques of Interviewing (e.g., Supporting, Clarifying, Focusing, Confronting, Validating, Feedback, Reflecting, Language Differences, Use of Interpreters, Redirecting) (KSA)

## 18.  D

*Rationale*

**Family therapy** is based on the idea that a family is a system of different parts. A change in any part of the system will trigger changes in all the other parts, so when one member of a family is affected by a **Substance Use Disorder**, everyone is affected. As a result, family dynamics can change in unhealthy ways. Some family members may take on too much responsibility, other family members may act out, and some may just shut down. Often a family remains stuck in unhealthy patterns even after the family member with the behavioral health disorder moves into recovery. Even in the best circumstances, families can find it hard to adjust to the person in their midst who is recovering, who is behaving differently than before, and who needs support. *Family therapy can help the family as a whole recover and heal.*

*Family therapy is typically introduced after the individual in treatment for addiction has made progress in recovery.* This could be a few months after treatment starts, or a year or more later. Timing is important because people new to recovery have a lot to do. They are working to remain stable in their new patterns of behavior and ways of thinking. They are just beginning to face the many changes they must make to stay mentally healthy, as well as remain clean or sober. They are learning such things as how to deal with urges to fall into old patterns, how to resist triggers and cravings, and how to avoid temptations to rationalize and make excuses. For them to explore family issues at the same time can be too much. It can potentially contribute to relapse. *Family therapy tends to be most helpful once the person in treatment is fully committed to the recovery process and is ready to make more changes.*

*Test-Taking Strategies Applied*

Social workers must understand family roles in addiction and codependency. Addiction is a "family affair"; therapy with the entire family involves understanding the roles that members assume which are dysfunctional and support the addictive behavior. However, it is important that clients have made progress in their recovery before taking on additional stress, which comes with understanding family roles in families impacted by addiction. Clients' acknowledgement of their addictions and family dysfunction, as well as detoxification—if needed—would come prior to the onset of family therapy. Clients may not yet be stable in their new patterns of behavior.

This question contains a qualifying word—BEST—even though it is not capitalized. There may be reasons for engaging in family therapy earlier or later in the recovery process, but it is most beneficial after individual progress has been made by clients. Only the correct answer describes this progress.

*Question Assesses*

Content Area I—Human Development, Diversity, and Behavior in the Environment; Human Behavior in the Social Environment (Competency); Addiction Theories and Concepts (KSA)

### 19.  D

*Rationale*

**Ethical and legal issues regarding mandatory reporting** are very clear when victims are minors. There is both a legal and ethical obligation to report all child abuse to protective services. However, when the victim is a client who is now an adult, the required action becomes less clear. Laws vary by jurisdiction and it is important for social workers to be aware of their legal duties.

Social workers face ethical dilemmas in these situations as they may want perpetrators to be accountable for their actions. However, if clients disclose such abuse in strict confidence and do not want it reported, there is a need to respect their privacy. This abuse does not meet any of the exceptions for disclosure such as due to consent by clients, clear and immediate danger, and other requirements by law (such as duty to warn).

In these instances, social workers may provide clients with information and other support so they can consider their options more fully. For instance, they may not be familiar with what happens during abuse investigations, fearing that reports may lead to immediate notoriety and broad publication. Legal and procedural protections afforded to survivors of sex-related crimes may also not be known.

However, even with such information and support, adult clients may resist wanting their abuse reported. Thus, social workers must respect their right to self-determination and should avoid imposing their own beliefs on clients.

*Test-Taking Strategies Applied*

As the 2018 *NASW Code of Ethics* does not explicitly address the situation in the scenario, it is necessary to consider the ethical principles of beneficence (doing good), nonmaleficence (avoiding doing harm), justice, and respect. While reporting the abuse may help protect other minors from being abused, it may be experienced as harm by the client as she is not emotionally ready to confront her father about the abuse. Reporting the abuse also may have a negative impact on the social worker/client relationship as the client may feel betrayed by the disclosure. From a justice perspective, reporting the abuse may be a method of bringing the alleged perpetrator to justice, but justice could entail prioritizing the client's emotional well-being. Finally, respect involves honoring the client's rights to privacy and self-determination.

The scenario stated that there was no legal duty for social workers, in this jurisdiction, to report past abuse as the survivor is no longer a minor. If it were required, the correct response may have been different. The scenario also indicates that the father is not a danger to other children given his physical and/or mental status.

Meeting with the father is not appropriate as he is not the client and it is not the social worker's role to assess his risk. In addition, while supervision is always useful, the social worker should not be "passing the buck" and relying on the supervisor to make the decision. The social worker must be knowledgeable about the laws and issues regarding mandatory reporting.

### Question Assesses

Content Area IV—Professional Values and Ethics; Confidentiality (Competency); Ethical and/or Legal Issues Regarding Mandatory Reporting (e.g., Abuse, Threat of Harm, Impaired Professionals, etc.) (KSA)

### 20. B

### Rationale

In using **feedback** during the beginning phase of treatment, a social worker encourages clients to comment about service purpose, social worker–client roles, ethical factors, or any other aspect of the introductory sessions. An important part of communicating effectively involves checking whether clients have understood the messages being conveyed. Seeking feedback serves this function. Seeking feedback early in the problem-solving process is part of the informed consent process. Clients are forced to identify areas that are unclear, share thoughts that have occurred to them, or express disagreements. The use of feedback sends the message that treatment is a mutual and reciprocal process and that social workers are interested in what clients have to say. It sets the expectation that clients will continue to be active participants throughout the helping process.

### Test-Taking Strategies Applied

The question contains a qualifying word—EXCEPT—that requires social workers to select the response choice which is not a reason for seeking feedback. The question specifically asks about "the beginning phase of treatment." During the beginning phase, social workers introduce and identify themselves and seek introductions from clients. Following the exchange of introductions, social workers describe the initial purposes for meetings, identify professional roles that social workers might undertake, orient clients to the process, and identify relevant policy and ethical factors that might apply. Three of the response choices directly relate to this initial orientation and educating clients about the reciprocal nature of the work, as well as engaging them by showing interest. *The correct answer is important when actually intervening with clients, but is not appropriate for the beginning phase as the delivery of treatment occurs later in the process.*

## Question Assesses

Content Area III—Psychotherapy, Clinical Interventions, and Case Management; Therapeutic Relationship (Competency); Methods to Obtain and Provide Feedback (KSA)

### 21. A

*Rationale*

**Social stratification** refers to a system by which a society ranks categories of people in a hierarchy. By examining policies, procedures, regulations, and laws—as well as practices—it is perfectly clear that some groups have greater status, power, and wealth than other groups. Social stratification is based on four major principles:

1. Social stratification is a trait of society, not simply a reflection of individual differences.
2. Social stratification persists over generations.
3. Social stratification is universal, but takes different forms across different societies.
4. Social stratification involves both inequality and beliefs, as inequality is rooted in a society's philosophy.

*Test-Taking Strategies Applied*

This question requires social workers to understand the effects that policies, procedures, regulations, and laws have on practice, including perpetuating social stratification.

**Racial inequality** results from institutional discrimination in which policies and procedures do not treat all racial groups equally. While people of color often do not have the same opportunities, the question is broader, seeking the term which relates to differences in social status. These differences can also result from other attributes, such as gender.

**Institutional malfeasance** refers to wrongdoing by an organization or corporation.

**Cultural difference** involves the integrated and maintained system of socially acquired values, beliefs, and rules of conduct which impact the range of accepted behaviors distinguishable from one societal group to another. Cultural difference is not negative in nature, like social stratification.

### Question Assesses

Content Area I—Human Development, Diversity, and Behavior in the Environment; Diversity and Discrimination (Competency); Systemic (Institutionalized) Discrimination (e.g., Racism, Sexism, Ageism) (KSA)

### 22. D

### Rationale

**Supervision** is an essential and integral part of training and continuing education required for the skillful development of professional social workers. The knowledge base of the social work profession has expanded and the population it serves has become more complex. Supervision protects clients, supports practitioners, and ensures that professional standards and quality services are delivered by competent social workers. It is important to the profession to have assurance that all social workers are equipped with the necessary skills to deliver competent and ethical social work services. Equally important to the profession is the responsibility to protect clients.

Documentation is an important legal tool that verifies that services, including supervision, occurred. Supervisors should assist supervisees in learning how to properly document client services performed, regularly review their documentation, and hold them to high standards. When appropriate, supervisors should train the supervisees to document for reimbursement and claim submissions.

*Each supervisory session should be documented separately by supervisors and supervisees.* Documentation for supervised sessions should be available to both parties and provided to supervisees within a reasonable time after each session. Social work regulatory boards may request some form of supervision documentation when supervisees apply for licensure. Records should be safeguarded and kept confidential.

## Test-Taking Strategies Applied

The question contains a qualifying word—MOST. Supervisors are responsible for the actions of supervisees, but records should not only be kept by them. Failure to keep any documentation of supervision sessions is ill-advised as information used to make critical treatment decisions will not be recorded. It is true that licensing entities may require supervision notes, but the correct answer describes the "MOST appropriate" documentation practice, namely that both supervisees and supervisors should maintain separate records.

## Question Assesses

Content Area III—Psychotherapy, Clinical Interventions, and Case Management; Service Delivery and Management of Cases (Competency); Case Recording for Practice Evaluation or Supervision (KSA)

### 23. A

## Rationale

Social workers employed in agency settings may find that they are required to have **multiple supervisors**. In circumstances in which a social worker is being supervised simultaneously by more than one person, it is best practice to have a contractual agreement or memorandum of understanding delineating the role of each supervisor, including parameters of the relationships, information sharing, priorities, and how conflicts will be resolved. If no agreement exists, the immediate employment supervisor may have the final say. If the setting permits, a separate third-party may be brought in to help resolve the conflict.

## Test-Taking Strategies Applied

Only the correct answer results in *a written agreement* delineating the role of each supervisor. Written parameters are superior to meeting together, reviewing professional standards, or understanding personal values. When a social worker must answer to more than one supervisor, the likelihood of conflict is enhanced; therefore, guidelines which outline the agreed upon flow of information and how conflicts should be resolved are essential.

## Question Assesses

Content Area III—Psychotherapy, Clinical Interventions, and Case Management; Consultation and Interdisciplinary Collaboration

(Competency); Models of Supervision and Consultation (e.g., Individual, Peer, Group) (KSA)

### 24. B

*Rationale*

Social workers who do forensic work wrestle with professional ethical issues that emerge in determining **client mental fitness** to face prosecution. The process of evaluating whether clients are competent to stand trial involves two major areas. First, clients must understand the legal proceedings against them, what they have been charged with, what the roles of the different court personnel are, the difference between pleading guilty and not guilty, and what accepting a plea bargain means. The second factor is the clients' ability to assist in their own defense or their ability to work with their attorneys and take an active part in their own defense.

If a client's mental status is in question, the social worker tells the defense attorney, who then brings the issue to the judge. Alternately, the state's attorney or the judge could raise the issue. The judge then issues a court order mandating a formal evaluation of client **competency to stand trial**.

A formal evaluation may be done by a psychiatrist working alone or a team of mental health professionals, including a psychiatrist, psychologist, and/or forensic social worker.

After the formal evaluation of competence to stand trial, the next phase is often "restoration," in which a client is sent to a particular setting, most often a hospital, to be "restored to competence." A client is usually in the hospital for 60 to 90 days for the initial restoration, undergoing a full evaluation by psychologists, psychiatrists, and social workers and attending classes to learn about the court process to face charges as a competent defendant.

**Competency restoration** is a psychoeducational intervention in which clients who have been found incapable of proceeding in legal trials due to any combination of limited understanding, communication deficits, or impaired ability to conform their behaviors to the demands of the courtroom are rendered capable. It is generally a part of a multifaceted treatment strategy that may include anger management skills, relaxation training, and cognitive behavioral therapy (CBT) as adjunct interventions to education regarding general legal processes and specific aspects of the defendant's case. At the conclusion, clients should be able to discuss aspects of their cases with their attorneys, differentially weigh the risks and possible benefits of the different pleadings, strategize consideration of testimonials and evidence, testify, and conduct themselves in a manner suitable to the courtroom. Clients should understand the roles of the court officers, the responsibilities and limitations of judges and juries, and that their attorneys have their best interests in mind.

### Test-Taking Strategies Applied

The question contains a qualifying word—PRIMARY—even though it is not capitalized. Competency restoration processes occur before sentencing or restitution decisions. Social workers evaluate and deliver services focused on developing or regaining clients' abilities to participate in legal proceedings. It is not the clients' responsibility to identify legal standards that may apply to their conduct, which eliminates the last response choice.

### Question Assesses

Content Area IV—Professional Values and Ethics; Professional Development and Use of Self (Competency); Client/Client System Competence and Self-Determination (e.g., Financial Decisions, Treatment Decisions, Emancipation, Age of Consent, Permanency Planning) (KSA)

### 25. B

### Rationale

The right of **privileged communication**—which assumes that a professional cannot disclose confidential information without the client's consent—originated in British common law. The attorney–client privilege was the first professional relationship to gain the right of privileged communication. Over time, other groups of professionals have sought this right.

Social workers should understand the distinction between confidentiality and privileged communication. Confidentiality refers to the professional norm that information offered by or pertaining to clients will not be shared with third parties. Privilege refers to the disclosure of confidential information in court or during other legal proceedings.

Courts commonly cite the following four conditions that must be met for information to be considered privileged:

- The harm caused by disclosure of the confidential information would outweigh the benefits of disclosure during legal proceedings.
- The parties involved in the conversation assumed that it was confidential.

- Confidentiality is an important element in the relationship.
- The broader community recognizes the importance of this relationship.

A significant court decision for social workers concerning privileged communications was the landmark case of *Jaffe v. Redmond* (1996) in which the U.S. Supreme Court ruled that the clients of clinical social workers have the right to privileged communication in federal courts. Many states, though not all, now extend the right of privileged communication to clinical social workers' clients.

### Test-Taking Strategies Applied

The question contains a qualifying word—NOT—that requires social workers to select the condition which does not need to be met in order for information to be considered privileged. When NOT is used as a qualifying word, it is often helpful to remove it from the question and eliminate the three response choices which are legal effects. This approach will leave the one response choice which is NOT a decision-making variable.

While documentation is important in the provision of social work services, confidentiality and privilege do not only apply to written materials.

### Question Assesses

Content Area IV—Professional Values and Ethics; Confidentiality (Competency); Legal and/or Ethical Issues Regarding Confidentiality, Including Electronic Information Security (KSA)

### 26. D

### Rationale

There are four major **parenting styles** which reflect the skills and capabilities of clients.

**Permissive parenting**, sometimes referred to as indulgent parenting, has very few demands placed on children. Permissive parents rarely discipline their children because they have relatively low expectations of maturity and self-control. They are often nontraditional and lenient, not requiring mature behavior, allowing considerable self-regulation, and avoiding confrontation. Permissive parents are generally nurturing and communicative with their children, often taking on the status of a friend more than that of a parent.

**Authoritative parenting** establishes rules and guidelines that children are expected to follow. However, this parenting style is democratic.

Authoritative parents are responsive to their children and willing to listen to questions. When children fail to meet the expectations, these parents are nurturing and forgiving rather than punishing. These parents monitor and impart clear standards for their children's conduct. They are assertive, but not intrusive and restrictive. Their disciplinary methods are supportive, rather than punitive. They want their children to be assertive as well as socially responsible and self-regulated as well as cooperative.

In **authoritarian parenting**, children are expected to follow the strict rules established by the parents. Failure to follow such rules usually results in punishment. Authoritarian parents do not explain the reasoning behind these rules. If asked to explain, the parent might simply reply, "Because I said so." These parents have high demands but are not responsive to their children. These parents are obedience- and status-oriented, and expect their orders to be obeyed without explanation.

An **uninvolved parenting** style is characterized by few demands, low responsiveness, and little communication. While these parents fulfill the child's basic needs, they are generally detached from their child's life. In extreme cases, these parents may even reject or neglect the needs of their children.

### Test-Taking Strategies Applied

This is a recall question on parenting styles. Social workers should be knowledgeable about the impact that parenting styles have on child development outcomes. Authoritarian parenting styles generally lead to children who are obedient and proficient, but they rank lower in happiness, social competence, and self-esteem. Authoritative parenting styles tend to result in children who are happy, capable, and successful. Permissive parenting often results in children who rank low in happiness and self-regulation. These children are more likely to experience problems with authority and tend to perform poorly in school. Uninvolved parenting styles rank lowest across all life domains. These children tend to lack self-control, have low self-esteem, and are less competent than their peers.

### Question Assesses

Content Area I—Human Development, Diversity, and Behavior in the Environment; Human Growth and Development (Competency); Parenting Skills and Capacities (KSA)

### 27. B

### Rationale

**Dysfunctional family dynamics** are traits or behaviors that characterize unhealthy interactions between members. In dysfunctional families, members tend to communicate poorly and not listen to each other. **Triangulation** is a family therapy concept discussed most famously by multigenerational family systems theorist Murray Bowen. Bowen described dyads as being inherently unstable under stress, much like a two-legged stool. When in balance, the dyad is capable of functioning well and meeting the needs of both people in it. However, when thrown out of balance by conflict, stress, or transitions, the dyad will often pull in a third person, or "leg" of the stool, to help them stabilize the relationship.

According to Bowen, some triangulation is normal and even healthy in the course of family interactions. Because dyads are inherently unstable, the involvement of a third party can assist a two-person relationship in overcoming impasses, meeting needs, and coping through stressful times. This kind of triangulation occurs because both people in a dyad are looking for healthy and effective mediation. When the triangulated person gives input, it is accepted into the dyad and processed together in a way that moves the original dyad forward in their relationship. Healthy triangulation can also occur in the context of parents (or other family caregivers) who come together to meet the needs of a third member, such as a child.

Triangulation can become unhealthy in families when it causes undue stress on the third party and/or when it prevents, rather than invites, resolution of the dyad's conflict. In the scenario, the triangulation is being sought by only one of the spouses. Furthermore, the input provided is not being brought back into the marriage for joint processing by both spouses. It is being withheld by the husband for his own individual purposes. The husband's conversations with his mother are essentially taking the place of the emotional process that needs to be occurring within the marriage itself in order to return the marriage to healthy functioning.

**Role reversal** is a situation in which two people have chosen or been forced to exchange their duties and responsibilities, so that each is now doing what the other used to do. This scenario is not a role reversal as the mother has taken on being an emotional confidant, a function usually assumed by a spouse. However, the wife has not taken on the mother's duties or responsibilities.

**Entropy**, based in systems theory, is characteristic of randomness and disintegration within a structure.

The **Oedipal complex**, also known as the **Oedipus complex**, is a term used by Sigmund Freud in his theory of psychosexual stages of development to describe a boy's feelings of desire for his mother and jealousy and anger toward his father. This answer is not correct given the age of the man. It also does not address the "family dynamic," which includes the wife.

### Test-Taking Strategies Applied

This is a recall question related to family systems. Even when the names of theories are not mentioned, social workers are often asked about their key terms and concepts. When proper names are listed as answers, it is useful to look at them first, before reading the question. Often a response choice will look correct after reading the question simply due to the words used. However, the one that looks the best is often not correct. Defining the terms in your head first helps you remember them without distraction or having the question's wording inappropriately influence your answer.

### Question Assesses

Content Area III—Psychotherapy, Clinical Interventions, and Case Management; The Intervention Process (Competency); Family Therapy Models, Interventions, and Approaches (KSA)

### 28. C

### Rationale

**Delusions** are false beliefs which clients hold with a strong amount of conviction. These beliefs are not typical of their culture or religion, and clients adhere to the erroneous beliefs despite evidence and proof which totally contradict them. **Delusions of reference** are perceptions that stimuli in the environment are directed toward clients themselves and referencing them specifically even though they are not. It is the belief that simple coincidences are relevant and specific to clients even though they are not connected to them in any way; for example, clients thinking people they do not know are talking about them or thinking that newscasters are speaking directly to them.

Clients with delusions of reference may think that things written in newspapers or stated in newscasts, passages found in a book, or the words in a song are about them directly. Thus, neutral events are believed to have special and personal meaning; for example, clients might believe billboards or celebrities are sending messages meant specifically for them.

These ideas and connections are delusions as they are thought to be true, though they are not. This can be a sign of mental illness such as Schizophrenia Spectrum and Other Psychotic Disorders.

*Test-Taking Strategies Applied*

The question requires knowledge about basic terminology associated with psychopathology or the study of mental illness or the manifestation of behaviors that may be indicative of mental illness or psychological impairment. There are also common delusions such as delusions of grandeur, control, guilt, persecution, jealousy, or paranoia. Social workers must be aware of the presence of delusional thoughts by clients and the diagnostic methods/tools that can be used to identify them.

The first response choice provides an accurate statement about delusions generally; for example, they are false, fixed beliefs despite evidence to the contrary, but it is incorrect as it does not provide information specifically about delusions of reference. The qualifying word—BEST—indicates that more than one listed answer may apply, but the most suitable definition is the one that illustrates the key attributes of this delusional type. Thus, the correct response choice is the one which indicates that neutral events are believed to have special and personal meaning.

*Question Assesses*

Content Area II—Assessment, Diagnosis, and Treatment Planning; Assessment and Diagnosis (Competency); The Indicators of Mental and Emotional Illness Throughout the Lifespan (KSA)

**29. D**

*Rationale*

**Client-centered therapy**, also known as **person-centered therapy**, is a nondirective form of talk therapy that was developed by humanist psychologist Carl Rogers during the 1940s and 1950s. Client-centered therapy operates according to three basic principles that reflect the attitude of the therapist to the client:

1. The social worker is **congruent** with the client.
2. The social worker provides the client with **unconditional positive regard**.
3. The social worker shows **empathetic** understanding to the client.

Congruence is also called genuineness. Congruence is the most important attribute in counseling, according to Rogers. This means that, unlike the psychodynamic practitioner who generally maintains a "blank screen" and reveals little of his or her own personality in therapy, the Rogerian is keen to allow the client to experience the social worker as he or she really is. A social worker does not have a façade (like psychoanalysis); that is, a social worker's internal and external experiences are one in the same. In short, a social worker is authentic.

The next Rogerian core condition is **unconditional positive regard**. Rogers believed that it is important that clients are valued as themselves so they can grow and fulfill their potential. A social worker must have a deep and genuine caring for a client. A social worker may not approve of some of a client's actions, but a social worker does approve of a client. In short, a social worker needs an attitude of "I'll accept you as you are." The person-centered social worker is thus careful to always maintain a positive attitude to a client, even when disgusted by a client's actions.

**Empathy** is the ability to understand what a client is feeling by having the ability to understand sensitively and accurately a client's experience and feelings in the here-and-now.

### Test-Taking Strategies Applied

The question contains a qualifying word—NOT—that requires social workers to select the response choice which is not a core condition "in client-centered therapy." When NOT is used as a qualifying word, it is often helpful to remove it from the question and eliminate the three response choices which are core conditions. This approach will leave the one response choice which is NOT an important social work quality according to Rogers. While cultural awareness is essential for working with diverse client groups, it is not specifically related to client-centered therapy, which is the focus of the question.

### Question Assesses

Content Area III—Psychotherapy, Clinical Interventions, and Case Management; Therapeutic Relationship (Competency); The Concept of Congruence in Communication (KSA)

### 30. B

### Rationale

Social workers must be knowledgeable about **legal documents** related to confidentiality of client information. **Confidentiality of mandated clients** is particularly tricky as documents may be subject to release without client consent.

Social workers have a duty to claim privilege on behalf of their clients when asked to release any information without client permission. **Privilege** is a right owned by clients to prevent their confidential information from being used in legal proceedings. The *NASW Code of Ethics* requires social workers to wait until *ordered by the court before disclosing information* in legal proceedings, absent client consent or an imminent threat of harm. A **subpoena** is a mandate to provide evidence or testimony—but is not a final ruling or order by a court on the legal requirement to provide information or admissibility of the evidence. A subpoena is not a **court order**. Most subpoenas are issued by attorneys.

The *NASW Code of Ethics* provides that *when a court-ordered disclosure could cause harm to the client, the social worker should request that the court withdraw or limit the order or keep the records under seal*. It is not clear how a social worker can meaningfully implement this provision. The social worker could refuse to obey a court's order as a matter of conscience, but this should be done only if he or she is prepared to be found in contempt of court and face time in jail, a fine, or both.

The need to be aware of court or legal mandates is the cost of doing business in a profession where clients can be involved in legal disputes or matters.

### Test-Taking Strategies Applied

Clients who are mandated to receive services may also be referred to as involuntary or court-ordered clients. All of these terms indicate that clients did not voluntarily choose or consent to receipt of services. There is legal authorization to mandate the receipt of treatment. Thus, there may also be a similar mandate to get access to documentation related to the receipt of services. The extent of what will need to be disclosed can vary and social workers are advised to be aware of these limits before the onset of treatment and review them with clients in their initial meetings.

In the scenario, it is the social worker's responsibility to understand the extent to which documentation is privileged, so there is no need to have the client see a lawyer. The social worker should be aware of any specific limits to confidentiality before the onset of services, so seeking supervision and/or consultation to understand them is problematic. Documentation associated with treatment needs to be generated according to practice standards. It would not be appropriate to forgo keeping notes which are essential to continuity of care just because they may be released. Also, promising the client that he or she will be able to consent to information release when mandated by the court can be misleading.

The court order and any relevant legal documents should be obtained by the social worker and consulted whenever there are questions related to the service provision and/or reporting. Social workers have legal mandates to comply with court orders once they are appointed to be providers of services and agree to the terms. If there is concern about mandates in court orders, social workers should try to get them changed or be removed as treating professionals by the appointing courts.

## Question Assesses

Content Area IV—Professional Values and Ethics; Confidentiality (Competency); Legal and/or Ethical Issues Regarding Confidentiality, Including Electronic Information Security (KSA)

## 31. D

### Rationale

When **addiction and substance abuse** occur during pregnancy, it can have effects not only on the pregnant mother, but also on the unborn child. **Opioid use** in pregnancy is associated with an increased risk of adverse outcomes. *The current standard of care for pregnant women with opioid dependence is referral for opioid-assisted therapy with methadone.* Medically supervised tapered doses of opioids during pregnancy often result in relapse to former use. Abrupt discontinuation of opioids in an opioid-dependent pregnant woman can result in preterm labor, fetal distress, or fetal demise. After birth, special considerations are needed for women who are opioid-dependent to ensure appropriate pain management, to prevent postpartum relapse and a risk of overdose, and to ensure adequate contraception to prevent unintended pregnancies. Stabilization with opioid-assisted therapy is compatible with breastfeeding. Neonatal abstinence syndrome is an expected and treatable condition that follows prenatal exposure to opioid agonists.

The rationale for opioid-assisted therapy during pregnancy is to prevent complications of illicit opioid use and narcotic withdrawal, encourage prenatal care and drug treatment, reduce criminal activity, and avoid risks to a client of associating with a drug culture. Methadone maintenance, as prescribed and dispensed on a daily basis by a registered substance abuse treatment program, is part of a comprehensive package of prenatal care, chemical dependency counseling, family therapy, nutritional education, and other medical and psychosocial services as indicated for pregnant women with opioid dependence.

### Test-Taking Strategies Applied

This is a recall question which assesses social workers' awareness of the effects of addiction and appropriate treatment protocols. Medically supervised withdrawal from opioids in opioid-dependent women is not recommended during pregnancy because the withdrawal is associated with high relapse rates. During pregnancy, chronic untreated heroin use is associated with an increased risk of fetal growth restriction, fetal death, preterm labor, and other adverse outcomes. Additionally, the lifestyle issues associated with illicit drug use put the pregnant woman at risk of engaging in activities, such as prostitution, theft, and violence, to support herself or her addiction.

Methadone is an opioid used to treat pain and as maintenance therapy or to help with tapering in clients with opioid dependence. Thus, discontinuation of all opioids is an incorrect answer. Intensive therapy and social support are beneficial, but not sufficient for treating heroin. Best practice includes medication-assisted treatment for all clients, including pregnant women.

*Question Assesses*

Content Area I—Human Development, Diversity, and Behavior in the Environment; Human Behavior in the Social Environment (Competency); The Effects of Addiction and Substance Abuse on Individuals, Families, Groups, Organizations, and Communities (KSA)

### 32. C

*Rationale*

**Older adulthood** is a time of continued growth. Clients in the later stages of life contribute significantly to their families, communities, and society. At the same time, clients face multiple biopsychosocial–spiritual–cultural challenges as they age: changes in health and physical abilities; difficulty in accessing comprehensive, affordable, and high-quality health and behavioral health care; decreased economic security; increased vulnerability to abuse and exploitation; and loss of meaningful social roles and opportunities to remain engaged in society. Social workers must understand the needs of older adults and issues that may be facing them.

**Sundowning** is a term used to refer to behavioral changes that often occur in the late afternoon or evening in people with Alzheimer's disease and similar conditions. The behavioral changes may take the form of aggression, agitation, delusions, hallucinations, paranoia, increased disorientation, or wandering and pacing about. Sundowning is not a disease, but a group of symptoms that occur at a specific time of the day that may affect people with dementia. The exact cause of this behavior is unknown. Factors that may aggravate late-day confusion include fatigue, low lighting, increased shadows, disruption of the body's "internal clock," and/or difficulty separating reality from dreams. Reducing sundowning can be assisted by maintaining a predictable routine for bedtime, waking, meals and activities, and limiting daytime napping.

When sundowning occurs in a nursing home, it may be related to the flurry of activity during staff shift changes or the lack of structured activities in the late afternoon and evening. Staff arriving and leaving may cue clients with Alzheimer's to want to go home or to check on their children—or other behaviors that were appropriate in the late afternoon in their past. It may help to occupy their time with another activity during that period.

**Folie à deux**, or shared psychosis, is when symptoms of a delusional belief and hallucinations are transmitted from one individual to another. While not listed in the *DSM-5*, recent psychiatric classifications refer to the syndrome as shared psychotic disorder.

**Dementia** is a chronic or persistent disorder of the mental processes caused by brain disease or injury and marked by memory disorders, personality changes, and impaired reasoning.

**Neurodegeneration** is an umbrella term for the progressive loss of structure or function of neurons. Many neurodegenerative diseases including amyotrophic lateral sclerosis, Parkinson's, Alzheimer's, and Huntington's occur as a result of neurodegenerative processes. Such diseases are incurable.

*Test-Taking Strategies Applied*

This is a recall question which relies on social workers being able to recognize and understand terms associated with neurogenerative diseases, such as Alzheimer's. Such diseases cause changes in client behavior. One of the response choices, folie à deux, is used to describe shared psychosis, which is not associated with neurogenerative disease. Social workers must be well-versed in actions associated with typical human development, as well as those which indicate the presence of disease or disturbance.

*Question Assesses*

Content Area II—Assessment, Diagnosis, and Treatment Planning; Biopsychosocial History and Collateral Data (Competency); Symptoms of Neurologic and Organic Disorders (KSA)

33. C

*Rationale*

There is tremendous importance placed on social relationships, which consist of interactions between clients and their family and friends.

Thus, social workers often rely on the **use of collaterals to obtain relevant information** to assist clients. Unfortunately, while the 2018 *NASW Code of Ethics* advises social workers of their ethical obligations to clients, it is silent on what obligations, if any, social workers owe to clients' family members, friends, and other collaterals who may be brought into the helping process. Thus, social workers must adhere to broad professional values when interacting with collaterals regardless of whether a particular situation is explicitly covered by the code of ethics.

In the absence of ethical standards, it is helpful for social workers to have agency policies and contracts that fill these gaps. For instance, before meeting with collaterals, there should be an agreement regarding the meeting's purpose, what information will be shared, and how that information may be used. Although contracts have traditionally been used with clients, they can also be used with collaterals to clarify expectations, to preempt conflicts, and to provide clients, collaterals, and social workers with legal safeguards. Service contracts with collaterals could include, but not be limited to, explaining the roles of social workers, their primary commitments to clients, any commitments to collaterals, the roles of collaterals, the nature of collateral involvement, benefits and risks to collaterals, and/or confidentiality issues.

### Test-Taking Strategies Applied

The scenario relates to the client's request to have his daughter come to the next session. Using other family members or friends as collaterals may be helpful, but does not address the suggestion at hand. Confidentiality is a client right, so a social worker can share information with others when requested by the client. It is allowed and appropriate to discuss client information with collaterals as long as the social worker ensures that the sharing is done at the client's wishes and there is a clear understanding about what will be discussed. Including his daughter in discussions about the extent of the client's current problems was suggested by the client. Thus, it is not appropriate for the social worker to identify them without addressing the desire to use her as a collateral informant to obtain relevant information.

The correct response choice ensures that there is a mutual understanding about key ethical issues which may arise when using the daughter as a collateral informant.

### Question Assesses

Content Area II—Assessment, Diagnosis, and Treatment Planning; Assessment and Diagnosis (Competency); Methods of Involving Clients/

Client Systems in Problem Identification (e.g., Gathering Collateral Information) (KSA)

### 34. A

*Rationale*

With the increasing focus on **interdisciplinary practice** in recent years, social workers may be supervised by a professional of a different discipline. Although this may be appropriate within the team or unit context, social workers should seek supervision or consultation from another social worker with regard to specific social work practices and issues. Similarly, a social worker providing supervision to a member of another discipline should refer that supervisee to a member of his or her own profession for practice-specific supervision or consultation.

*Test-Taking Strategies Applied*

While a qualifying word is not used in the scenario, a social worker should review the response choices and select the one that best assists in resolving a social work practice issue. It is unlikely that another supervisor will be assigned, and requesting one will not necessarily mean that a new supervisor will be familiar with social work practice. Self-help resources may be helpful, but should have already been consulted. The social work profession has a unique set of values and practice standards, so it is essential that the social worker seek supervision or consultation from another social worker. The hospital supervisor should be aware that such supervision is being sought and involved clients must be informed of the need for "outside" supervision or consultation if applicable.

*Question Assesses*

Content Area III—Psychotherapy, Clinical Interventions, and Case Management; Consultation and Interdisciplinary Collaboration (Competency); The Process of Interdisciplinary and Intradisciplinary Team Collaboration (KSA)

### 35. C

*Rationale*

**Performance monitoring** is used to provide information on (a) key aspects of how programs are operating; (b) whether, and to what extent, program objectives are being attained (e.g., numbers of clients served compared to target goals, reductions in target behaviors); and (c) identification of failures to produce program outputs, for use in managing or redesigning program operations. Performance indicators can also be developed to (d) monitor service quality by collecting data on the satisfaction of those served and (e) report on program efficiency, effectiveness, and productivity by assessing the relationship between the resources used (program inputs) and the outcome indicators.

If conducted frequently enough and in a timely way, performance monitoring can provide social workers with regular feedback that will allow them to identify problems, take timely action, and subsequently assess whether their actions have led to the improvements sought.

Performance monitoring involves identification and collection of specific data on program outputs, outcomes, and accomplishments. Although they may measure subjective factors such as client satisfaction, data is often numeric, consisting of frequency counts, statistical averages, ratios, or percentages.

## Test-Taking Strategies Applied

The question contains a qualifying word—NOT—that requires social workers to select the response choice which is not an aim of performance monitoring. When NOT is used as a qualifying word, it is often helpful to remove it from the question and eliminate the three response choices which are aims. This approach will leave the one response choice which is NOT a reason for doing performance monitoring.

Justification of the need for a service is not the aim of performance monitoring. Performance monitoring occurs during implementation of services while identification of needs happens before they are designed or planned. Needs assessments are conducted to determine the scope and severity of problems. Performance monitoring should not be approached as a perfunctory task to justify ongoing operations or delivery or it will not lead to quality evaluations of what is working and what is not.

## Question Assesses

Content Area III—Psychotherapy, Clinical Interventions, and Case Management; Service Delivery and Management of Cases (Competency); Quality Assurance, Including Program Reviews and Audits by External Sources (KSA)

### 36. B

## Rationale

Clients who suffer from severe depression may be at **risk of suicide**. Although suicide cannot be predicted or prevented with certainty, knowing the warning signs can help recognize when clients are at risk. The most effective way to try to prevent suicide is to recognize the warning signs, respond immediately, and treat underlying causes of suicide such as depression.

Some warning signs of suicide include the following behaviors:

- Talking about suicide or death
- Feeling hopeless, helpless, or worthless and saying things like, "It would be better if I wasn't here" or "I want out"
- Exhibiting deep sadness, loss of interest in pleasurable activities, trouble sleeping and eating
- *Having abrupt change of mood, from extreme sadness to happiness or calm*
- Engaging in risk-taking behavior such as driving too fast and recklessly
- Calling or visiting people to say goodbye
- Putting affairs in order such as making changes to a will

Along with these behaviors, clients who are depressed have a higher risk of attempting suicide if they have ever previously made attempts, have chronic or terminal illnesses, are separated or divorced, are underemployed or unemployed, or have family histories of suicide.

### Test-Taking Strategies Applied

The question contains a qualifying word—FIRST. There may be more than one appropriate response choice, but the order in which they are to occur is critical. In this situation, the social worker must immediately find out more information about the reasons for the change in mood. Improvement in depressive symptoms can be an indication of upcoming suicide attempts. Clients who have put plans in place to end their lives often appear to be calmer or happier. The knowledge that they will be ending their lives soon appears to bring with it peace or happiness for clients plagued by depression.

Asking about changes which have recently taken place in the client's life is too vague and does not contain the questions needed to do a proper suicide risk assessment. Documentation and praise will not assist the social worker in understanding the client's current mental status. The need for a suicide risk assessment is most immediate when warning signs are present, such as those described in the scenario.

### Question Assesses

Content Area II—Assessment, Diagnosis, and Treatment Planning; Assessment and Diagnosis (Competency); The Indicators and

Risk Factors of the Client's/Client System's Danger to Self and Others (KSA)

### 37. B

*Rationale*

There are many methods that social workers use to **facilitate communication**. For example, within the teaching of dialectical behavior therapy (DBT), **conscious validation** is often called upon to help clients improve interpersonal effectiveness and mindfulness skills. DBT has six levels of validation, with each "level" offering a different tactic for validating a client.

*Six Levels of Validation*

1. *Mindful engagement*—listening as a way of showing presence and interest—communicating understanding by way of nodding, making eye contact, and asking appropriate questions. ("I hear you! What'd you do after she told you that?")

2. *Accurate reflection*—repeating to ensure that the message is being received accurately. ("I just heard you say that your boss really likes you, but you don't think you're doing a good job.")

3. *Reading cues*—using nonverbal and other cues to determine current feelings. The social worker may need some guesswork and should seek correction from a client if misunderstood. ("You look unhappy. Is something bothering you?")

4. *Historical perspective*—drawing on knowledge of a client's prior experiences to lend perspective to current feelings. ("Maybe you don't trust your new girlfriend because your previous girlfriend cheated on you?")

5. *Assuring reasonableness*—letting a client know that his or her thoughts, feelings, or behaviors are normal and quite reasonable. This provides reassurance, comfort, and healthy perspective. ("I see your frustration. Most people would be annoyed.")

6. *Respectful honesty*—providing feedback that lets a client know that you respect him or her enough to "keep it real." This level of validation is best delivered with an accompaniment of *radical acceptance/genuineness*, along with a nonjudgmental stance—taking into account that everyone has his or her strengths and limitations. ("I understand why you said that,

but I think you could have had a better result if you used a softer tone.")

### Test-Taking Strategies Applied

The correct answer is the one that demonstrates "a higher level of validation." In the scenario, the social worker has already reflected the client's nervousness (Level 2). Suggesting that the client's feelings may result from his prior job loss—information that was deliberately provided in the scenario—draws on knowledge of the client's prior experience to lend perspective to his current feelings (Level 4).

Listening to him is the first level of validation—*prior to* reflection. Helping the client examine behavioral cues may be helpful, but is not a validation tool aimed at acknowledging and accepting his feelings. Similarly, explaining to the client that his firing is unlikely given his recent promotion discounts the client's feelings, which are real whether supported by external factors or not.

While this question does not mention DBT, social workers are often called upon to apply practice modalities and techniques to scenarios on the examination. Social workers should never answer based on their own opinions of what they think is best. Correct answers are grounded in social work theories, models, and perspectives that were learned in graduate coursework.

### Question Assesses

Content Area III—Psychotherapy, Clinical Interventions, and Case Management; The Intervention Process (Competency); The Principles and Techniques of Interviewing (e.g., Supporting, Clarifying, Focusing, Confronting, Validating, Feedback, Reflecting, Language Differences, Use of Interpreters, Redirecting) (KSA)

### 38. C

### Rationale

Preparing a **case presentation** can be a daunting task for a social worker. While there is no standard format, there are key sections which should be included. Sections include:

- **Demographics**: Age, gender, ethnicity, living situation, social work involvement, and so on
- **Background**: Relevant history
- **Presenting Problem/Key Findings**: Details of the presenting problem and current situation—signs and symptoms of illness,

environmental factors that impinge on the situation, and actual or potential resources

- **Formulation**: Understanding of why things are as they are—including one or more theoretical perspectives and any uncertainty or ambivalence about the situation

- **Interventions and Plans**: What has been done and what plans exist to address the situation

- **Reason for Presentation**: Explanation of why this situation is being discussed—unique challenges? unusual problems?

More detailed case presentations may include additional sections including legal/ethical, crisis/safety, diversity, and so on.

### Test-Taking Strategies Applied

The supervisor is used in this question to determine if all the necessary elements of a case presentation were included. The goal of supervision is to ensure that clients receive the most effective and efficient services possible. Thus, the supervisor will appear in many questions throughout the examination to provide quality assurance, ensuring that a social worker is meeting acceptable standards.

The case presentation described only contains some of the required elements. Even a brief case presentation must contain information on the presenting problem. The presenting problem was not mentioned, making the case presentation incomplete.

### Question Assesses

Content Area III—Psychotherapy, Clinical Interventions, and Case Management; Consultation and Interdisciplinary Collaboration (Competency); The Elements of a Case Presentation (KSA)

### 39. D

### Rationale

Social workers must be well versed in **techniques and instruments used to assess client problems**. There is evidence that early identification of problematic alcohol or drug use can save lives and reduce costs related to health care and behavioral health care, crime and incarceration, and overall loss of productivity. Thus, Screening, Brief Intervention, and Referral for Treatment (SBIRT) is reimbursable service by the Centers for Medicare and Medicaid Services. SBIRT has been identified as an evidence-based practice by the Substance Abuse and Mental Health

Services Administration (SAMHSA) as it matches clients with the appropriate type and amount of services they require, avoiding under- or overtreatment.

**Screening** is the first step in the SBIRT process. Screening is a universal process, meaning that an entire population group is screened for an illness or disease. Screening is different from assessment. Screening is brief, time limited, and intended to simply identify clients with problem alcohol or drug use. In contrast, assessment is a deeper, more thorough process that may take several sessions. Assessment interviews are conducted by substance abuse specialists who consider multiple domains of a client's alcohol or drug use, including risk for withdrawal, medical complications, emotional/behavioral complications, stage of change, relapse potential, recovery environment, legal complications, family system, and employment history.

*The result of the screening dictates one of three clinical responses: no intervention, brief intervention, or referral to treatment.*

- **No Intervention**: A screening interview with negative results requires no further action specific to substance abuse intervention or treatment.

- **Brief Intervention**: A screening interview that indicates moderate risk requires a brief intervention, or a discussion aimed at raising an individual's awareness of his or her risky behavior and motivating the individual to change his or her behavior. Brief interventions are conducted in the community sector, often at the same time and by the same clinician who conducted the screening interview. A key component of brief interventions is to educate clients on safe drinking behavior, as well as the physical, social, and familial consequences of alcohol and drug abuse.

- **Referral to Treatment**: A screening interview that indicates severe risk of dependence requires a referral to a specialized alcohol and drug treatment program for comprehensive assessment and treatment. It is insufficient to simply give a client the name and number of an alcohol and drug treatment program. Instead, it is best for social workers to make an appointment with the client and follow up to be sure the client follows through. Recommendations from a substance abuse assessment may include one or more of the following interventions: detoxification, short-term residential treatment, long-term residential treatment (such as a half way house or therapeutic community), outpatient treatment, day or evening treatment, medications, and/or group treatment.

*Test-Taking Strategies Applied*

The question contains a qualifying word—NOT—that requires social workers to select the response choice, which is not "the resulting action taken from screening." When NOT is used as a qualifying word, it is often helpful to remove it from the question and eliminate the three response choices which are resulting actions. This approach will leave the one response choice which would NOT result from screening.

Social workers need to be aware of screening models used in public health which identify people in large populations who need further assessment. It would be unlikely that clients would receive long-term treatment directly after being screened. Further information about the scope and severity of the problem would be needed if issues were detected. Short-term intervention and referrals to treatment would yield data to justify long-term treatment if needed. Social workers seek to serve clients in the least restrictive and intensive environments possible.

*Question Assesses*

Content Area II—Assessment, Diagnosis, and Treatment Planning; Biopsychosocial History and Collateral Data (Competency); Techniques and Instruments Used to Assess Clients/Client Systems (KSA)

**40. C**

*Rationale*

**Attending** is a term frequently used to describe the process of nonverbally communicating to clients that social workers are open, nonjudgmental, accepting of them as people, and interested in what they say. The purpose of attending is to encourage clients to express themselves as fully and freely as possible. During the beginning of the problem-solving process, especially, nonverbal presentation is equally important to verbal communication as clients are usually doing most of the talking.

Many of the guidelines available may be useful, but they tend to reflect nonverbal characteristics of majority-member, middle- and upper-class adults. Good attending behavior is usually described as follows.

- **Eye Contact**: Looking at clients is one way of showing interest. However, social workers can make clients feel uncomfortable if they stare at them too intensely. The best way of showing that social workers are listening is by looking at clients naturally.

- **Posture**: This is a natural response of interest. It is best to lean slightly toward clients in a relaxed manner. Relaxation is important, since social workers want to shift focus from themselves so they are better able to listen to clients.

- **Gesture**: Social workers communicate a great deal with body movements. If hands are flailed, arms are crossed, or chest/shoulders are hunched, then messages, whether intentional or unintentional, will be communicated.

- **Facial Expressions**: Facial expressions, such as smiling, eyebrow raising, and frowning, indicate responsiveness.

### Test-Taking Strategies Applied

Social workers must be aware of verbal and nonverbal communication techniques. This question requires recall of the name of a nonverbal technique. Determining the scope and severity of client problems, as well as the barriers which impede progress, are assessing tasks. Identifying alternatives which will result in change is a planning or intervening action. Attending behavior is heavily used in engaging, though it continues throughout the problem-solving process. The correct answer is much broader than the other response choices and is the aim of attending behavior.

### Question Assesses

Content Area III—Psychotherapy, Clinical Interventions, and Case Management; Therapeutic Relationship (Competency); Verbal and Nonverbal Communication Techniques (KSA)

### 41. D

### Rationale

**Effective interventions** depend on using the most appropriate theory and practice strategies for a given problem or situation. *Different theories/interventions are best suited for different problems.* Evidence-based practices (EBPs) are treatments that have been proven effective (to some degree) through outcome evaluations. EBPs are interventions that have strong scientific proof that they produce positive outcomes for certain types of disorders. *Clearly defining problems will help rationalize the implementation of EBPs and help inform the selection process.*

Other interventions—sometimes labeled promising practices—may also produce good outcomes, but research has not been conducted at a level to say that there is strong evidence for those practices. As such, EBPs are treatments that are likely to be effective in changing target behaviors if implemented with integrity.

The selection of an EBP depends on client problems, the outcomes desired, and treatment preferences. For example, both antidepressant medications and psychotherapy interventions are effective in the treatment of depression in older adults. The choice of one of these interventions over the other may vary with respect to the nature and severity of depression, the presence of other health conditions or medications, tolerability of side effects or required effort, and the preferences and personal values of older adults regarding these treatment characteristics.

### Test-Taking Strategies Applied

The question contains a qualifying word—MOST—that indicates that all response choices may be considered, but the correct answer is the factor which must drive this decision. Treatment modalities differ depending upon presenting problems. Social workers should not limit available options to clients based on available resources, past history, and/or setting. EBPs which have demonstrated that they are effective for problems at hand must be used. Social workers can advocate for additional resources or refer clients to settings which provide the appropriate treatment if it is not available in the current setting. In addition, treatment decisions should not be based predominantly on what has been done in the past. Interventions can be very effective to address some problems and useless in helping others. Thus, matching EBPs/interventions to presenting problems is vital to ensuring that change will occur.

### Question Assesses

Content Area II—Assessment, Diagnosis, and Treatment Planning; Treatment Planning (Competency); The Criteria Used in the Selection of Intervention/Treatment Modalities (e.g., Client/Client System Abilities, Culture, Life Stage) (KSA)

### 42. D

### Rationale

The 2018 *NASW Code of Ethics* provides standards with regard to **confidentiality**, including the process for disclosing information as a result of **mandatory reporting**. Social workers should respect clients' right to privacy. Social workers should not solicit private information from clients unless it is essential to providing services or conducting social work evaluation or research. Once private information is shared, standards of confidentiality apply. Social workers may disclose confidential information when appropriate with valid consent from a client or a person legally authorized to consent on behalf of a client. Social workers should protect the confidentiality of all information obtained in the course of professional service, except for compelling professional reasons. The general expectation that social workers will keep information confidential does not apply when disclosure is necessary to prevent serious, foreseeable, and imminent harm to a client or others. In all instances, social workers should disclose the least amount of confidential information necessary to achieve the desired purpose; only information that is directly relevant to the purpose for which the disclosure is made should be revealed. *Social workers should inform clients, to the extent possible, about the disclosure of confidential information and the potential consequences, when feasible before the disclosure is made. This applies whether social workers disclose confidential information on the basis of a legal requirement or client consent.*

### Test-Taking Strategies Applied

The scenario calls for reporting the suspicions to the child protection agency (referred to as the authorities in this question). The social worker does not need to prove that the abuse is occurring or identify the perpetrator. The child protection agency is responsible for doing the investigation. While two answers include reporting the suspicions, only the correct one involves informing the clients about the disclosure and the information which needs to be legally released without the clients' consent. Informing clients—or even involving them in the process—is required, when feasible, according to the 2018 *NASW Code of Ethics*.

### Question Assesses

Content Area IV—Professional Values and Ethics; Confidentiality (Competency); Ethical and/or Legal Issues Regarding Mandatory Reporting (e.g., Abuse, Threat of Harm, Impaired Professionals, etc.) (KSA)

### 43. C

### Rationale

A social worker's own **values and beliefs** can greatly influence the social worker–client relationship. Culture, race, and ethnicity are strongly linked to values. *Social workers must have self-awareness about their own attitudes, values, and beliefs and a willingness to acknowledge that they may be different than those served.* Differences in values and beliefs are very common when working with diverse populations. A social worker is responsible for bringing up and addressing issues of cultural difference with a client and is also ethically responsible for being culturally competent by obtaining the appropriate knowledge, skills, and experience.

Social workers should:

1. Move from being culturally unaware to aware of one's own heritage and the heritage of others
2. Value and celebrate differences of others rather than maintaining an ethnocentric stance
3. Have an awareness of personal values and biases and how they may influence relationships with clients
4. Demonstrate comfort with racial and cultural differences between themselves and clients
5. Have an awareness of personal and professional limitations
6. Acknowledge their own attitudes, beliefs, and feelings

### Test-Taking Strategies Applied

The question acknowledges that "both school officials and the social worker feel that the student is making a mistake." Thus, it is critical for the social worker to acknowledge the differences in values between the professionals involved and the student as she is choosing family responsibilities over pursuit of her education. This choice is based on the personal principles and tenets that are important to her.

The incorrect answers may be useful, but the correct one is essential for the formation of a social worker–client relationship built on the core values of the profession, including the student's right to self-determination. Despite the extent of the existing responsibilities, her career goals, and/or the supports available, the student may value the needs of her family over furthering her own education.

### Question Assesses

Content Area IV—Professional Values and Ethics; Professional Development and Use of Self (Competency); The Influence of the Social Worker's Own Values and Beliefs on the Social Worker–Client/Client System Relationship (KSA)

### 44. B

### Rationale

Many believe that **Gender Identity Disorder**, **Gender Incongruence**, and **Gender Dysphoria** should be viewed and approached from the perspective of a **medical model** rather than that of a **mental health model**. Many anatomical inconsistencies can now be corrected surgically or chemically to align with the experienced true self. A medical diagnosis for individuals who are transgender, whose self-experienced gender does not match the sex assigned at birth and who require medical services to align the body with the experienced self, is considered more appropriate and consistent with research and best practices.

Those with the aforementioned diagnoses already are stigmatized by society due to myths and misunderstandings, and victimized by intolerance and prejudice. The effects of this stigma are profound and long-standing, resulting in increased risks for negative health, mental health, educational, professional, and social outcomes. Continuing to include these diagnoses in the *DSM* contributes to sustained oppression of those who receive them.

Labeling individuals with Gender Identity Disorder, Gender Incongruence and Gender Dysphoria views these conditions as aberrant and is harmful. Considering medical diagnoses instead is more appropriate and addresses intolerance, discrimination, and oppression related to considering these diagnoses as psychological problems needing to be fixed.

### Test-Taking Strategies Applied

This question requires knowledge about "using a medical model." A **medical model** is based on the assumption that abnormal behavior is the result of physical problems and should be treated medically. Providing therapy as mentioned in the first response choice implies that a mental health model is being used. Also, treatment may involve corrective surgery—not just medication. Exploring the mind-body connection and screening for physical conditions may help in considering biological or medical issues, but are not directly related to gender identity. The question contains a qualifying word—BEST— that requires selecting a response choice that is essential if these diagnoses are viewed using a medical model or resulting from physical problems—not psychological ones.

### Question Assesses

Content Area I—Human Development, Diversity, and Behavior in the Environment; Diversity and Discrimination (Competency); Gender and Gender Identity Concepts (KSA)

## 45. B

*Rationale*

Despite the high prevalence of alcohol and substance use problems, many go without treatment—in part because their disorders go undiagnosed. Regular screenings enable earlier identification. Screenings should be provided to people of all ages, even the young and the elderly.

The Alcohol Use Disorders Identification Test (**AUDIT**) is a 10-item questionnaire that screens for hazardous or harmful alcohol consumption. Developed by the World Health Organization (WHO), the test correctly classifies 95% of people into either alcoholics or non-alcoholics. The AUDIT is particularly suitable for use in primary care settings and has been used with a variety of populations and cultural groups. It should be administered by a health professional or paraprofessional

The **SCOFF** Questionnaire is a five-question screening tool designed to clarify suspicion that an *eating disorder* might exist rather than to make a diagnosis. The questions can be delivered either verbally or in written form.

The **CAGE** Tool consists of five commonly used questions to screen for drug and alcohol use. The CAGE is a quick questionnaire to help determine if an alcohol assessment is needed. If a client answers "yes" to two or more questions, a complete assessment is advised.

The Severity of Dependence Scale (**SDS**) was devised to provide a short, easily administered scale which can be used to measure the degree of dependence experienced by users of different types of drugs. The SDS contains five items, all of which are explicitly concerned with psychological components of dependence. These items are specifically concerned with impaired control over drug taking and with preoccupation and anxieties about drug use.

*Test-Taking Strategies Applied*

The question contains a qualifying word—NOT—that requires social workers to select the response choice which is not a screening tool for an alcohol or substance use problem. When NOT is used as a qualifying word, it is often helpful to remove it from the question and eliminate the three response choices which are such screening tools. This approach will leave the one response choice which is NOT a tool for alcohol or substance use, but may detect the potential presence of other disorders.

While most questions on the examination will not be this specific, there are always a few that require very specific knowledge related to a KSA. In these instances, it is helpful to try to eliminate any incorrect answers to increase the chances of selecting the correct ones. It is important not to get nervous when such questions arise as these select few can be missed and still get a passing score.

## Question Assesses

Content Area II—Assessment, Diagnosis, and Treatment Planning; Biopsychosocial History and Collateral Data (Competency); Techniques and Instruments Used to Assess Clients/Client Systems (KSA)

### 46. D

## Rationale

**Defense mechanisms** are *unconscious* mechanisms which are activated in times of anxiety, stress, and distress without any choice or conscious intentionality. They are a necessary tool of protection and in moderate use contribute to successful adaptation. Defense mechanisms are a part of normal functioning, but they can be considered as pathological in some instances.

**Coping,** on the other hand, includes *conscious* strategies that enable clients to attain realistic goals by using available resources and past experiences while acting within society's rules of conduct. While defense mechanisms are unconscious processes whereas coping methods are conscious, in reality, sometimes clients exhibit rational coping simultaneously with unconscious defenses.

Coping mechanisms are often confused and interchanged with defense mechanisms due to their similarities. Both processes are activated in times of adversity. Defense mechanisms and coping strategies reduce arousal of negative emotions. Furthermore, both processes aim at achieving adaptation; only the means to the end differ. Defenses help the individual by distorting reality and coping strategies attempt to solve the problem, thus changing the reality. Coping behaviors involve conscious modification of cognitive and emotional appraisals, which eventually modify the reactions to the stressful event rather than distort the perception of the event. Clients have full control of coping strategies used. They can choose to stop certain coping styles and choose others.

Defense mechanisms, on the other hand, operate outside consciousness and awareness. Clients cannot intentionally choose to use other defense mechanisms.

Coping involves flexibility, and defenses are more rigid. The choice of coping mechanisms is perceived more as dependent on timing, situation, and personality factors. Different situations lead to different coping strategies. Defense mechanisms are more stable and habitual.

The idea regarding whether defense mechanisms produce adaptive and functional behaviors is still controversial. In the long term, defense mechanisms do contribute to the development of severe pathology, yet the fact that they seem to help individuals to cope in the short term should not be ignored or dismissed. Defenses are efficient mechanisms that help deal with threatening and, at times, traumatic stressors. Pathology probably does not originate from the actual use of defense mechanisms; it is caused by a continuous reliance on defenses, instead of actually attempting to solve the core problems that cause their necessity in the first place.

### Test-Taking Strategies Applied

The question contains a qualifying word—PRIMARY—that indicates that there may be more than one distinction between defense and coping mechanisms. However, the correct response choice is the one which contains the most fundamental or important difference. Defense mechanisms and coping strategies describe distinct psychological processes, namely those which are unconscious and unintentional versus those which are not.

In addition, the first three response choices are not accurate statements. Coping mechanisms are not "unconscious actions" as stated in the first answer. Additionally, defense mechanisms are rigid and do not fluctuate like coping skills, contrary to what is stated in the second response choice. Lastly, defense mechanisms can be adaptive and functional ways to deal with stress, making the third answer incorrect as well.

### Question Assesses

Content Area I—Human Development, Diversity, and Behavior in the Environment; Human Behavior in the Social Environment (Competency); Psychological Defense Mechanisms and Their Effects on Behavior and Relationships (KSA)

### 47. C

### Rationale

**Feedback** during engagement in the problem-solving process encourages clients to comment about treatment purpose, social worker/client roles, policy or ethical factors, and so on. An important part of communicating effectively involves checking to see whether clients have understood social workers' messages. Seeking feedback serves this function. In addition, seeking feedback is essential for informed consent by inviting clients to identify areas that are unclear, share thoughts that have occurred to them, introduce new topics, or express disagreement. *By seeking feedback, social workers effectively send messages that treatment is a mutual and reciprocal process. Social workers convey that they are genuinely interested in what clients have to say and there is a desire to have them actively participate in the process.*

Social workers routinely seek feedback throughout the problem-solving process by asking, "How does that sound to you?" Other feedback can be elicited by inquiring, "What do you think about what we have talked about so far?" It is also good to find out about client questions or comments.

### Test-Taking Strategies Applied

When provided with a scenario, it is necessary to determine when it is taking place within the problem-solving process. In this question, the social worker is "in an initial meeting with a man," indicating that engagement is occurring. During engagement, a social worker must begin to form a working alliance with a client. A client must feel respected and understand that a social worker can be a valuable resource toward making change, but cannot solve a client's problems and is not there to tell him or her what to do.

In this scenario, the social worker's question demonstrates to the client that his opinions about treatment matter despite the involuntary nature of the service. It aims to get the client talking about his feelings, which is the first step in forming a therapeutic relationship. While the client may reveal some resistance when answering, the question is not aimed to do so. It also does not seek to determine if denial is present or identify whether the client is aware of his legal mandates. All of these are assessment tasks which will occur later. Assessment follows engagement in the problem-solving process. In addition, a social worker should not make assumptions about the presence of resistance or denial just because a client is mandated into services.

Universal among involuntary clients is that other entities have the power to influence terms of their treatment, which may make them feel that they have less control in the process. Social workers can address this issue by eliciting their feedback, sending the message that their input is essential.

*Question Assesses*

Content Area III—Psychotherapy, Clinical Interventions, and Case Management; Therapeutic Relationship (Competency); Methods to Obtain and Provide Feedback (KSA)

### 48.  B

*Rationale*

**Symbolic interactionism** sees clients as active in shaping their world, rather than as entities who are acted upon by society. With symbolic interactionism, reality is seen as social, developed interaction with others. Symbolic interactionists believe physical reality exists based upon clients' social definitions, and that social definitions develop in part or in relation to something "real." Thus, clients do not respond to this reality directly, but rather to the social understanding of reality; that is, they respond to this reality indirectly through a kind of filter which consists of clients' different perspectives. This perspective is based on three premises:

- Clients act toward things on the basis of the meanings they ascribe to those things.

- The meaning of such things is derived from, or arises out of, the social interaction that they have with others and society.

- These meanings are handled in, and modified through, an interpretative process used by clients in dealing with the things encountered.

Essentially, clients behave toward objects and others based on the personal meanings that they have already given these items. The second premise explains the meaning of such things is derived from, or arises out of, the social interaction that one has with other humans. Lastly, clients interact with each other by interpreting or defining each other's actions instead of merely reacting to each other's actions. Therefore, responses are not made directly to the actions of one another, but instead are based on the meaning which clients attach to such actions.

Thus, the interaction of intimate couples involves shared understandings of their situations. Wives and husbands have different styles of communication, and social class affects the expectations that spouses have of their marriages and of each other. Marital problems stem from different understandings and expectations that spouses have of their marriage.

In **conflict theory**, the family is viewed as contributing to social inequality by reinforcing economic inequality and by reinforcing patriarchy. Family problems stem from economic inequality and from patriarchal ideology. The family can also be a source of conflict, including physical violence and emotional cruelty, for its own members.

In **functionalism**, marriage performs several essential functions for society. It socializes children, it provides emotional and practical support for its members, it helps regulate sexual activity and sexual reproduction, and it provides its members with a social identity. Marital problems stem from sudden or far-reaching changes in the structure or processes; these problems threaten the marital stability and weaken society.

**Psychodynamic models** focus on the dynamic relations between the conscious and unconscious mind and explore how these psychological forces might relate to early childhood experiences.

### Test-Taking Strategies Applied

This is a recall question which requires knowledge of various theories, perspectives, and treatment approaches. When response choices consist of proper names in recall questions, it is often wise to look at the answers first and ruminate about the theories, perspectives, and treatment approaches before reading the questions. Getting the question correct requires some basic knowledge about each of the four answers so they can be appropriately selected or eliminated.

### Question Assesses

Content Area I—Human Development, Diversity, and Behavior in the Environment; Human Behavior in the Social Environment (Competency); Theories of Couples Development (KSA)

### 49. D

### Rationale

Social workers' commitment to **informed consent** is based on clients' right to self-determination. The informed consent process is one of the clearest expressions of social workers' respect for clients' dignity and worth as individuals to make choices which are best suited to meet their needs.

A client must have the right to refuse or withdraw consent. Social workers should be prepared for the possibility that clients will exercise these rights. Social workers should inform clients of their rights and help clients make thoughtful and informed decisions based on all available facts and information about potential benefits and risks.

Social workers must be familiar with informed consent requirements concerning clients' right to consent, especially when working with those who are incarcerated, children, individuals with cognitive impairments, and so on.

While laws and regulations vary in interpretations and applications of informed consent standards, there are essential standards in all processes which are needed for their validity. First, coercion and undue influence must not have played a role in clients' decisions. As social workers often maintain control over approving benefits, admission into programs, and the termination of services, they must ensure that clients do not feel pressured to grant consent based upon this control.

Second, social workers must not present clients with general, broadly-worded consent forms that may violate clients' right to be informed and may be considered invalid if challenged in a court of law. The use of broad or blank consent forms cannot possibly constitute informed consent. Social workers should include details that refer to specific activities, information to be released, or interventions. Typical elements include details of the nature and purpose of a service or disclosure of information; advantages and disadvantages of an intervention; substantial or possible risks to clients, if any; potential effects on clients' families, jobs, social activities, and other important aspects of their lives; alternatives to the proposed intervention or disclosure; and anticipated costs for clients. This information should be presented to clients in clear, understandable language. Consent forms should be dated and include a reasonable expiration date.

Third, clients must be mentally capable of providing legal consent. Clearly, clients with significant permanent cognitive deficits may be unable to comprehend the consent procedure. Social workers should assess clients' ability to reason and make informed choices, comprehend relevant facts and retain this information, appreciate current circumstances, and communicate wishes. *Some clients may be only temporarily unable to consent, such as individuals who are under the influence of alcohol or other drugs or are experiencing transient cognitive symptoms at the time consent is sought. Clients who are unable to consent at a given moment may be able to consent in the future if the incapacity is temporary.*

### Test-Taking Strategies Applied

The scenario described a man who is using drugs which interfered with his ability to give informed consent. It is not appropriate to waive consent procedures or have the man sign a form which he does not understand.

Verbal consent procedures are also problematic as "the social worker questions his ability to understand what she is asking." Thus, he cannot give consent if he is unable to understand parameters of the information to be gathered or the services to be delivered (the nature and purpose of the service; the advantages and disadvantages of an intervention; substantial or possible risks; anticipated costs; and so on).

His impairment may be temporary as he admits to using drugs which interfered with his reasoning prior to the meeting. Arranging to meet him at a later time may result in him being in a mental state in which he can make informed choices and comprehend relevant facts, which are necessary elements for informed consent.

### Question Assesses

Content Area IV—Professional Values and Ethics; Professional Values and Ethical Issues (Competency); The Principles and Processes of Obtaining Informed Consent (KSA)

## 50. A

### Rationale

Developing goals, objectives, and interventions is critical to alleviating client problems. The document that contains the problem statement, goals, objectives, and methods is the **intervention, treatment, or service plan** (contract). It is a road map that outlines the journey from problems that are identified through assessment to life when those issues have been successfully addressed.

The first step in any helping process is to identify the solvable problem and why a client is seeking help now. Once the problem is identified, goals and objectives can be specified that will help toward a solution. *Goals are long-term, general, and often the opposite of the problem.* The most basic goal should be for a client to be able to function at the level of functioning before the current problem started. This baseline is referred to as premorbid functioning.

The specific steps taken to achieve the goal are called objectives. *Objectives are short term and specify who does the action, for how long, and how often to achieve the desired outcome (who will do what by when).* Because the goals and objectives derive from the assessment, the frequency of the desired outcome should not be made up out of thin air. Using the frequency before the problem starts and working backwards is helpful. Being realistic and precise in targets will assist in achieving success. Considering premorbid functioning ensures that goals and objectives are not set too high.

*Strategies are the means by which treatment goals are achieved.* Each objective can have more than one intervention. Interventions are typically specific to varying theoretical approaches.

### Test-Taking Strategies Applied

In the scenario, since the client is feeling worthless—specifically that she is not important to anyone—the goal or solution is to help her see that she is important to someone. This is obviously not the only problem in her life, but it is the one identified to be worked on. The identified objective was to meet friends, which is not happening now. If she met friends weekly in the past, prior to her feelings of worthlessness, the objective would be to engage in that behavior again. The objective has a baseline (zero times a week) as well as a target (once a week). It will also need a time frame for achievement.

The incorrect response choices do not relate to the stated objective of seeing her friends or are a method needed to achieve the objective (such as identifying accessible transportation) of establishing "the measurable target."

### Question Assesses

Content Area III—Psychotherapy, Clinical Interventions, and Case Management; The Intervention Process (Competency); Methods to Develop and Evaluate Measurable Objectives for Client/Client System Intervention, Treatment, and/or Service Plans (KSA)

### 51. B

### Rationale

In addition to the typical diagnosis of Bipolar I Disorder, further information about the mood can be denoted with a **"specifier."** *A specifier is an extension to the diagnosis that further clarifies the course, severity, or special features of the disorder or illness.* Two new specifiers in the *DSM-5* are: with mixed features and with anxious distress.

- **With Mixed Features**: The "with mixed features" specifier means that something is abnormal or uncommon about the manic and depressive episodes. There will be symptoms that do not fit with other symptoms. For example, if clients are in the midst of a manic episode, but their mood is still depressed or they feel slowed down rather than sped up, this specifier may be appropriate. Similarly, if they are in a depressed episode, but their mood is really good and they are more talkative than normal, the "with mixed features" specifier may be used.

- **With Anxious Distress**: The "with anxious distress" specifier means that during periods of mania, hypomania, or depression, clients also have anxiety symptoms. The symptoms include feeling tense, feeling especially restless, problems concentrating due to worry, fear that something terrible will happen, and feeling a loss of control. The intensity ranges from mild to severe, depending on how many symptoms are present.

The difference between this specifier and having an Anxiety Disorder, such as Generalized Anxiety Disorder or a Panic Disorder, is that these symptoms are only present during mood episodes related to Bipolar Disorders. When a client's mood is normal, the anxiety will be gone.

Having Bipolar Disorder With Anxious Distress means clients have Bipolar Disorder, plus anxiety that interferes with life, but do not meet the diagnostic criteria of an Anxiety Disorder.

*High levels of anxiety have been associated with higher suicide risk, longer duration of illness, and greater likelihood of treatment nonresponse. As a result, it is clinically useful to specify accurately the presence and severity levels of anxious distress for treatment planning and monitoring of response to treatment.*

In order to add the specifier "with anxious distress," at least two of these symptoms should be present:

- Feeling tense or keyed up
- Unusual restlessness
- Worry that makes it difficult to concentrate
- Fear that something terrible may happen
- Feeling that clients might lose control

The symptoms have to be present most days of the current or most recent bipolar episode, regardless of whether the episode involved manic, hypomanic, or depressive symptoms.

The severity of the condition is determined by the number of symptoms present: two symptoms means the condition is mild, three symptoms means it is moderate, four to five symptoms means it is moderate to severe, and four to five symptoms with psychomotor agitation means it is severe.

Clients with Bipolar Disorder with anxious distress also can be diagnosed with other Anxiety Disorders. For example, if they get panic attacks, they can be diagnosed with Panic Disorder, and if they are acutely afraid of a specific object or situation (e.g., spiders or flying), then they could be diagnosed with Specific Phobia.

When two or more illnesses not related to each other are diagnosed in a single client, they are called "comorbid," which simply means they occur together.

Anxiety Disorders that frequently have been diagnosed together with bipolar Disorder include:

- Panic Disorder
- Generalized Anxiety Disorder
- Obsessive Compulsive Disorders
- Social Anxiety Disorder (Social Phobia)
- Agoraphobia
- Specific Phobia

Other specifiers for Bipolar Disorder include:

- With rapid cycling
- With melancholic features
- With atypical features
- With mood-congruent psychotic features or with mood-incongruent psychotic features
- With Catatonia
- With peripartum onset
- With seasonal pattern

### Test-Taking Strategies Applied

This is a recall question about the use of specifiers with diagnosed mental disorders. Social workers must be familiar with the criteria associated with their use and know when they are to be appropriately added.

### Question Assesses

Content Area II—Assessment, Diagnosis, and Treatment Planning; Assessment and Diagnosis (Competency); The Use of the Diagnostic and Statistical Manual of the American Psychiatric Association (KSA)

### 52. A

### Rationale

Understanding **the impact of caregiving** includes understanding transitions into and out of caregiving.

There is much evidence on the health effects of caregiving. Providing assistance with basic ADLs has resulted in increased depression and psychological distress, impaired self-care, and poorer self-reported health.

Also studied are the effects of making the transition out of the caregiving role because individuals improve, enter institutions, or die. Improved functioning of care recipients is associated with reductions in caregiver distress. The death of the care recipient has been found to reduce caregiver depression, and caregivers are often able to return to normal levels of functioning within a year. However, the effects of a transition to a nursing home are less positive, with caregivers continuing to exhibit the same level of psychiatric morbidity after placement.

### Test-Taking Strategies Applied

The question contains a qualifying word—NOT—that requires social workers to select the response choice which is not associated with reduced emotional distress due to caregiving. When NOT is used as a qualifying word, it is often helpful to remove it from the question and eliminate the three response choices which do result in reduced distress for caregivers. This approach will leave the one response choice which does not alleviate some of the caregiving stress.

The incorrect response choices, even the death of the person requiring care, alleviate responsibilities associated with care. While nursing home placements may reduce the strain associated with physical assistance, family members often still have responsibilities associated with caregiving, including the added financial burden of paying for out-of-home care and/or losing complete control over the delivery of services.

### Question Assesses

Content Area I—Human Development, Diversity, and Behavior in the Environment; Human Behavior in the Social Environment (Competency); The Impact of Caregiving on Families (KSA)

### 53. B

### Rationale

A chapter on **Obsessive-Compulsive and Related Disorders**, which is new in the *DSM-5*, reflects the increasing evidence that these disorders are related to one another in terms of a range of diagnostic validators, as well as the clinical utility of grouping these disorders in the same chapter. New disorders include Hoarding Disorder, Excoriation (Skin-Picking)

Disorder, Substance-/Medication-Induced Obsessive-Compulsive and Related Disorder, and Obsessive-Compulsive and Related Disorder Due to Another Medical Condition. The *DSM-IV* diagnosis of Trichotillomania is now termed Trichotillomania (Hair-Pulling Disorder) and has been moved from a *DSM-IV* classification of Impulse-Control Disorders Not Elsewhere Classified to Obsessive-Compulsive and Related Disorders in the *DSM-5*.

*There are a number of specifiers for Obsessive-Compulsive and Related Disorders.* Specifiers are extensions to a diagnosis that further clarify its course, severity, or special features. The "with poor insight" specifier for Obsessive-Compulsive Disorder (OCD) has been refined in *DSM-5* to allow a distinction between individuals with "good or fair insight," "poor insight," and "absent insight/delusional" OCD beliefs (i.e., complete conviction that OCD beliefs are true). Analogous "insight" specifiers have been included for Body Dysmorphic Disorder (BDD) and Hoarding Disorder. These specifiers are intended to improve differential diagnosis by emphasizing that individuals with these two disorders may present with a range of insight into their disorder-related beliefs, including absent insight/delusional symptoms. This change also emphasizes that the presence of absent insight/delusional beliefs warrants a diagnosis of the relevant Obsessive-Compulsive or Related Disorder, rather than a Schizophrenia Spectrum and Other Psychotic Disorder. There is one more specifier, a "tic-related" specifier, for OCD that reflects the growing literature on the diagnostic validity and clinical utility of identifying individuals with a current or past comorbid Tic Disorder, because this comorbidity may have important clinical implications.

### Test-Taking Strategies Applied

This is a recall question about specifiers which are appropriate for diagnoses contained in the *DSM-5*.

According to the *DSM-5*, one of the diagnostic criteria for OCD is that the person at some point in time has recognized that the obsessions or compulsions they experience are "excessive or unreasonable." This acknowledgment of the irrational nature of the OCD symptoms has been coined "insight."

However, social workers who treat clients with OCD observe that they do not always seem to recognize or agree that their obsessions and compulsions do not make sense. In reality, it seems that insight into OCD symptoms exists on a continuum, with some clients completely acknowledging that their symptoms do not make sense, and others having a very strong belief in the validity of their obsessions and compulsions. For this reason, the *DSM-5* has been modified to include distinctions in levels of OCD insight, including "good or fair insight," "poor insight," and "absent/insight delusional," which means clients perceive their OCD symptoms as completely rational and true.

Although there is some disagreement, poor or absent insight into OCD symptoms is generally thought to predict a worse response to both psychological and medical treatments for OCD. Poor or absent insight may make it difficult for the client to get up the motivation to do the hard work that therapy requires or to stick with taking a medication daily, especially if there are initial side effects that are unpleasant. Clients with less insight may also be less likely to attend regular appointments or to contact social workers in the first place.

### Question Assesses

Content Area II—Assessment, Diagnosis, and Treatment Planning; Assessment and Diagnosis (Competency); The Use of the Diagnostic and Statistical Manual of the American Psychiatric Association (KSA)

### 54. A

### Rationale

**Autism Spectrum Disorder** (ASD) is a Neurodevelopmental Disorder, characterized by severe and pervasive impairments in reciprocal social communication and social interaction (verbal and nonverbal), and by restricted, repetitive patterns of behavior, interests, and activities. There are many changes between the *DSM-IV* and the *DSM-5* regarding this Neurodevelopmental Disorder.

The *DSM-IV* described Pervasive Developmental Disorder (PDD) as the diagnostic umbrella, with five subtypes. The first change is that there is a single category of ASD instead of five subtypes. The second change is that the three domains are combined into two: (a) deficits in social communication and social interaction, and (b) restricted, repetitive patterns of behavior, interests, or activities. The third change is that there must be five out of seven criteria to make the diagnosis of ASD. The fourth change is that "restricted, repetitive patterns of behavior, interests, or activities" expanded to include "abnormalities in sensory processing." The fifth change is the broadened age of onset criteria—symptoms must be present in the early developmental period. The sixth change is the addition of "specifiers" to describe features such as "with or without intellectual impairment," "with or without language impairment," "associated with known medical or genetic condition or environmental factor," "associated with another neurodevelopmental, mental, or behavioral disorder," and "with Catatonia." The seventh change is the addition of Level 1, 2, or 3 as severity specifiers requiring supports.

### Test-Taking Strategies Applied

This is a recall question which relies on social workers understanding the use of specifiers and subtypes when making diagnoses using the *DSM-5*. Specifiers and subtypes delineate phenomenological variants of a disorder indicative of specific subgroupings. The numbers of specifiers and subtypes in the *DSM-5* have been expanded from the *DSM-IV*.

The question contains a qualifying word—NOT—that requires social workers to select the response choice that is not a specifier for ASD. When NOT is used as a qualifying word, it is often helpful to remove it from the question and eliminate the three response choices which are specifiers. This approach will leave the one response choice that is NOT a recognized variation of ASD.

### Question Assesses

Content Area II—Assessment, Diagnosis, and Treatment Planning; Assessment and Diagnosis (Competency); The Use of the Diagnostic and Statistical Manual of the American Psychiatric Association (KSA)

### 55. C

### Rationale

Despite advances in human rights and acceptance, stigma, both internal and external, continues to be the greatest problem facing **sexual and gender minorities**. Internally, many people who are lesbian, gay, bisexual, transgender, queer, or intersex (LQBTQI) develop an internalized homophobia that can contribute to problems with self-acceptance, anxiety, depression, difficulty forming intimate relationships, and being open about what sexual orientation or gender identity one actually has. Externally, stigma may be exhibited by the surrounding society and even from within the LGBTQI community. For example, some people who are gay or lesbian may have difficulty accepting those who are bisexual. People who are transgender also have historically been excluded from some gay organizations.

In addition, most people who are LGBTQI are not raised by people who identify as LGBTQI. Accordingly, they might not have the ability to seek support from parents or peers who may understand these struggles.

Lastly, those who are LGBTQI struggle with higher rates of anxiety, depression, and Substance Use Disorders. Many have struggled with stigma and the self-acceptance process. Alarmingly, those who are LGBTQI have higher rates of suicide or suicidal behavior.

They are also at greater risk for discrimination, verbal abuse, physical assaults and violence, and so on. Though legal protections have been increasing, fear of potential discrimination contributes to not seeking needed help.

Appropriately, in 1973, the American Psychiatric Association voted to remove "Homosexuality" from the second edition of the *DSM* (*DSM-II*), which meant that homosexuality was officially no longer considered a disorder. However, the diagnosis of homosexuality was immediately replaced by "Sexual Orientation Disturbance," renamed "Ego-Dystonic Homosexuality" in the *DSM-III*, which was released in 1980. **Ego-Dystonic Homosexuality** was specifically aimed at clients who expressed ongoing distress or sadness about their sexual orientation, even if homosexuality could no longer be considered a mental illness. Many used the diagnosis of Ego-Dystonic Homosexuality as an excuse to legitimize reparative therapy. Although the diagnosis was removed from the *DSM* in 1987, it remains today as Ego-Dystonic Sexual Orientation in the 10th edition of the WHO's *International Classification of Diseases*. The diagnosis of "Gender Dysphoria" in the *DSM-5*, released in May 2013, also bears a strong resemblance, framing the distress commonly associated with gender variance as an individual rather than social problem.

### Test-Taking Strategies Applied

In the scenario, the distress experienced by the client is an issue which can result from oppression and discrimination. It is critical for the client to understand that his lack of self-worth comes from societal problems and should not be associated with his sexual feelings or preferences. Treatment is directed toward decreasing shame over the homosexual orientation and integrating the client's social role and personal identity.

The scenario also asks about appropriate actions "in assisting the client to formulate treatment goals," which is part of planning in the problem-solving process. While those who are LGBTQI are at higher suicide risk, there are no immediate risk factors mentioned; being distraught does not mean suicidal. In addition, the question is asking about treatment goals. Suicide risk would have been assessed earlier, and nothing in the scenario indicates the presence of new signs or feelings. Exploring familial relationships is an assessment task which would have happened prior to planning. Lastly, role modeling can be effective, but it does not help address the feelings which are the basis of the client's concerns.

## Question Assesses

Content Area I—Human Development, Diversity, and Behavior in the Environment; Diversity and Discrimination (Competency); The Influence of Sexual Orientation on Behaviors, Attitudes, and Identity (KSA)

### 56. C

## Rationale

Many ethical standards speak to the **professional boundaries** that social workers should maintain with clients. Social workers must ensure that they do not engage in dual or multiple relationships that may impact on the treatment of clients. Social workers should be alert to and avoid conflicts of interest that interfere with the exercise of professional discretion and impartial judgment. Social workers should avoid potential or real conflicts of interest. Dual relationships can be simultaneous or consecutive.

## Test-Taking Strategies Applied

In this scenario, the social worker cannot commence a relationship with the student given the presence of a dual relationship. The student may not be able to be honest with the social worker if therapy were to begin, given a belief that what would be disclosed may impact his or her standing in the social work program. Contrarily, the social worker may receive information that would otherwise not be known by a faculty member, calling into question the ability of the student to competently practice. Even though the social worker did not have the student in class, there is a conflict of interest as the social worker is a faculty member in the program.

The means by which the student learned about the social worker does not impact the decision to treat the student. Meeting with the student is inappropriate given the presence of an existing relationship. Lastly, referring the student is also inappropriate. Social workers should refer clients to other professionals when the other professionals' specialized knowledge or expertise is needed to serve clients fully or when social workers believe that they are not being effective or making reasonable progress with clients and additional service is required. *When making a referral, it is critical that a social worker refers to a competent provider, someone with expertise in the problem that a client is experiencing.*

In the scenario, the social worker is unaware of the student's problem, so it is impossible to ensure that the provider is competent in this issue. In addition, the student may feel pressured to go to this provider as he or she was selected by a social worker who is a faculty member in his or her program. "Inform the student that services cannot be provided given the potential for a conflict of interest" is the correct method "in order to handle the situation ethically."

### Question Assesses

Content Area IV—Professional Values and Ethics; Professional Values and Ethical Issues (Competency); Ethical Issues Related to Dual Relationships (KSA)

### 57. B

### Rationale

**Schizophrenia** is a brain disorder that affects how clients think, feel, and perceive. The hallmark symptom of Schizophrenia is psychosis, such as experiencing auditory hallucinations (voices) and delusions (fixed false beliefs).

Clients with the disorder may hear voices or see things that are not there. They may believe other people are reading their minds, controlling their thoughts, or plotting to harm them. This can be scary and upsetting to clients with the illness and make them withdrawn or extremely agitated. It can also be scary and upsetting to others around them.

Clients with Schizophrenia may sometimes talk about strange or unusual ideas, which can make it difficult to carry on a conversation. They may sit for hours without moving or talking. Sometimes clients with Schizophrenia seem perfectly fine until they talk about what they are really thinking.

The symptoms of Schizophrenia fall into three broad categories: positive, negative, and cognitive symptoms.

**Positive symptoms** are psychotic behaviors not generally seen in healthy people. Clients with positive symptoms may "lose touch" with some aspects of reality. For some, these symptoms come and go. For others, they stay stable over time. Sometimes they are severe, and at other times they are hardly noticeable. The severity of positive symptoms may depend on whether a client is receiving treatment. Positive symptoms include the following:

*Hallucinations* are sensory experiences that occur in the absence of a stimulus. These can occur in any of the five senses (vision, hearing, smell, taste, or touch). "Voices" (auditory hallucinations) are the most common type of hallucination in Schizophrenia. Many clients with the disorder hear voices. The voices can either be internal, seeming to come from within one's own mind, or they can be external, in which case they can seem to be as real as another person speaking. Sometimes clients with Schizophrenia talk to the voices that they hear. Clients with Schizophrenia may hear voices for a long time before family and friends notice the problem.

Other types of hallucinations include seeing people or objects that are not there, smelling odors that no one else detects, and feeling things like invisible fingers touching their bodies when no one is near.

*Delusions* are strongly held false beliefs that are not consistent with a client's culture. Delusions persist even when there is evidence that the beliefs are not true or logical. Clients with Schizophrenia can have delusions that seem bizarre, such as believing that neighbors can control their behavior with magnetic waves. They may also believe that people on television are directing special messages to them, or that radio stations are broadcasting their thoughts aloud to others.

*Thought disorders* are unusual or dysfunctional ways of thinking. One form is called "disorganized thinking." This is when a client has trouble organizing his or her thoughts or connecting them logically. He or she may talk in a garbled way that is hard to understand.

*Movement disorders* may appear as agitated body movements. A client with a movement disorder may repeat certain motions over and over. In the other extreme, a client may become catatonic. Catatonia is a state in which a client does not move and does not respond to others.

*Negative symptoms* are associated with disruptions to normal emotions and behaviors. These symptoms are harder to recognize as part of the disorder and can be mistaken for depression or other conditions.

These symptoms include the following:

- "Flat affect" (reduced expression of emotions via facial expression or voice tone)
- *Diminished feelings of pleasure in everyday life*
- *Difficulty beginning and sustaining activities*
- *Reduced speaking*

Clients with negative symptoms may need help with everyday tasks. They may neglect basic personal hygiene. This may make them seem lazy or unwilling to help themselves, but the problems are symptoms caused by Schizophrenia.

For some, the **cognitive symptoms** of Schizophrenia are subtle, but for others, they are more severe; clients may notice changes in their memory or other aspects of thinking. Similar to negative symptoms, cognitive symptoms may be difficult to recognize as part of the disorder. Often, they are detected only when specific tests are performed.

Cognitive symptoms include the following:

■ Poor "executive functioning" (the ability to understand information and use it to make decisions)

■ Trouble focusing or paying attention

■ Problems with "working memory" (the ability to use information immediately after learning it)

Poor cognition is related to worse employment and social outcomes and can be distressing to clients with Schizophrenia.

*Test-Taking Strategies Applied*

The question contains a qualifying word—NOT—that requires social workers to select the response choice that does not contain a negative symptom of Schizophrenia. When NOT is used as a qualifying word, it is often helpful to remove it from the question and eliminate the three response choices which are negative symptoms. This approach will leave the one response choice which is NOT a negative symptom.

This question is particularly tricky as all the response choices are, in fact, symptoms of Schizophrenia. However, the correct answer is a *positive* symptom—not a negative one. It is necessary to know the difference between negative, positive, and cognitive symptoms of Schizophrenia in order to answer correctly. Experiencing sensory experiences in the absence of a stimulus is referred to as hallucinating and is classified as positive as it is "added on" to a client's experience as a result of having the illness.

*Question Assesses*

Content Area II—Assessment, Diagnosis, and Treatment Planning; Assessment and Diagnosis (Competency); The Use of the Diagnostic and Statistical Manual of the American Psychiatric Association (KSA)

### 58. C

*Rationale*

**Engagement with mandated clients** takes skill and patience. Most therapeutic models are based on the assumption that the process of therapy will be a voluntary endeavor in which both clients and social workers will engage in therapeutic relationships through mutual consent. While clients often seek mental health services because they feel the need to, many may also be referred involuntarily to mental health professionals for treatment. Mandated clients are individuals who are sent or brought by someone else for treatment, including courts, protective service agencies, employment assistance programs, schools, and so on. Clients mandated for therapy may indicate the insistence of others as their reasons for coming to therapy, present themselves as not needing help, or demonstrate little willingness to establish a relationship with social workers. The involuntary nature of the relationship could present hurdles early on in the therapeutic process, making it exasperating both for social workers and their involuntary clients. *Clients mandated into therapy may view the process of therapy as being forced upon them, with social workers representing yet another part of the legal system.* On the other hand, social workers may anticipate certain attitudes in mandated clients and label them as resistant, unmotivated, uncooperative, involuntary, defiant, reluctant, difficult, or noncompliant.

### Test-Taking Strategies Applied

The question contains a qualifying word—MOST. While the apprehension by the client to speak to the social worker in the scenario may be an indication of more than one of the response choices listed, it is likely related to the involuntary nature of the relationship. Only two answers are directly related to being court-ordered to receive services— the correct one and an incorrect response choice which attributes the apprehension to fear of having the information shared. The client would be correct in realizing that not all shared information is confidential. However, it is unlikely that the client would be providing information in the first session that would be highly sensitive. The question also states that the client is apprehensive to discuss mandated services—not current problems. The discussion of mandated services would not likely be personal in nature.

The first session focuses on engagement and the formation of a therapeutic alliance. It is likely that the client will be upset about being told that he or she has to see the social worker, regardless of a willingness to make changes. The assumption that legally mandated clients will not contemplate change and voluntary clients are open to modifying behavior is not supported by research. Those who are court-ordered into treatment often have made decisions that changes are needed. However, they must learn to trust social workers who they did not choose to see. Acknowledging clients' lack of choice during the first meeting can often be common ground upon which to build relationships in the future.

### Question Assesses

Content Area III—Psychotherapy, Clinical Interventions, and Case Management; The Intervention Process (Competency); Methods to Engage and Work With Involuntary Clients/Client Systems (KSA)

### 59. D

### Rationale

**Narrative therapy** is a method of therapy that separates a client from a problem and encourages clients to rely on their own skill sets to minimize problems that exist in their everyday lives. Throughout life, personal experiences are transformed into personal stories that are given meaning and help shape a client's identity; narrative therapy utilizes the power of clients' personal stories to discover their life purpose.

Narrative therapy was created as a nonpathologizing, empowering, and collaborative form of therapy that recognizes that clients possess natural competencies, skills, and expertise that can help guide change in their lives. *Clients are viewed as separate from their problems, and in this way, social workers can help externalize sensitive issues.* This objectification dissipates resistance and defenses and allows a client to address this issue in a more productive manner. *By externalizing a problem, a client sees that a problem can be separated from his or her identity or sense of self (ego) and therefore can be removed or changed. It can be very empowering for a client to see that he or she is separate from, and has a degree of control over, the "problem."*

Rather than transforming a client, narrative therapy aims to transform the effects of a problem. The objective is to get some distance from the issue; in this way, it is possible to see how a particular concern is serving a client, rather than harming him or her. For example, posttraumatic stress might help protect a client from the difficult emotions associated with a particular event, although it also contributes a host of new troubling symptoms, such as anxiety. This process of externalization can help a client develop greater self-compassion, which, in turn, can help him or her to feel more capable of change. Social workers using narrative therapy help clients view their problems within the context of social, political, and cultural storylines that influence the way they view themselves and their personal stories.

Social workers who use narrative therapy believe that simply telling one's story of a problem is a form of action toward change. *They help to objectify problems, frame them within a larger sociocultural context, and make room for other stories.* Together, a social worker and client identify and build upon "alternative" or "preferred" storylines that exist beyond the problem story; these provide contrast to the problem, reflect a client's true nature, and offer opportunities to rewrite the story. In this way, clients move from what is known (problem stories) to what is as of yet unknown.

By exploring the impact of a problem, it is possible to identify what is truly important and valuable to a client in a broader context beyond the problem. This can help a client identify a common thread to connect his or her actions and choices throughout life.

### Test-Taking Strategies Applied

Knowledge of various intervention techniques is needed to answer questions successfully. The underlying premise of, as well as key terms associated with, social work models and approaches should be studied as they are often required to get the correct answer. Material to be studied should be "an inch deep, but a mile wide." It does not need to cover the material in great depth. However, basic understanding of social work paradigms will assist with selecting answers which contain important concepts or terms.

For example, knowing that narrative therapy is a collaborative approach which does not view problems as pathological and sees clients as the experts of their own lives is critical. By viewing problems as separate from people, it assumes clients have many skills, abilities, values, commitments, beliefs, and competencies that will assist them to change their relationship with the problems influencing their lives.

### Question Assesses

Content Area III—Psychotherapy, Clinical Interventions, and Case Management; The Intervention Process (Competency); Psychotherapies (KSA)

### 60. B

### Rationale

**Self-monitoring** is a key feature of cognitive behavioral therapy (CBT) for Feeding and Eating Disorders. It provides a detailed measure of eating problems and the circumstances under which they occur. It indexes the progress of treatment and helps guide the focus of each therapy session. Food diaries are self-monitoring tools.

One of the reasons self-monitoring is so helpful is that it can be very difficult to recall thoughts, feelings, or behaviors after some time has passed. In the moment, self-monitoring makes it possible to get an accurate picture of what is really going on with eating behavior. This can be an important tool when clients are working to change behaviors or problems.

CBT focuses on the relationship between thoughts, feelings, and behaviors. Social workers assist clients in identifying patterns of irrational and self-destructive thoughts and behaviors that influence emotions.

Task-centered practice is a short-term treatment where clients establish specific, measurable goals. Social workers and clients collaborate together and create specific strategies and steps to begin reaching those goals.

Narrative therapy externalizes a person's problem by examining the story of the person's life. In the story, the client is not defined by the problem, and the problem exists as a separate entity. Instead of focusing on a client's depression, in this social work practice model, a client would be encouraged to fight against the depression by looking at the skills and abilities that may have previously been taken for granted.

Crisis intervention is used when someone is dealing with an acute crisis. The model includes seven stages: assess safety and lethality, rapport building, problem identification, address feelings, generate alternatives, develop an action plan, and follow up. This social work practice model is commonly used with clients who are expressing suicidal ideation.

### Test-Taking Strategies Applied

The question contains a qualifying word—MOST. While self-monitoring may be used in various social work practice models, it is a common cognitive behavioral technique with Socratic questioning, homework, behavioral experiments, systematic desensitization, and so on. CBT is also effectively used with Feeding and Eating Disorders, which may be an additional clue as to the correct answer.

### Question Assesses

Content Area III—Psychotherapy, Clinical Interventions, and Case Management; The Intervention Process (Competency); Client/Client System Self-Monitoring Techniques (KSA)

### 61. B

### Rationale

**Hegemony** refers to the leadership, dominance, or great influence that one entity or group of people has over others. Historically, this term often referred to a country that exerted power over other countries indirectly rather than through military force. Modern uses often refer to a group in a society having power over others within that society. For example, the wealthy class might be said to have hegemony over the poor because of its ability to use its money to influence many aspects of society and government. Wealthy individuals can contribute the most money to the campaigns of certain political candidates, political parties, or causes. To ensure reelection or continued contributions, government officials who use those funds might then pass laws or create policies that favor those who contributed to the campaigns. People who don't have the money to contribute, however, are unable to influence the government in the same way.

This word is derived from the Greek verb *hegeisthai*, which translates as "to lead." Early leaders who were able to exert control and influence over a group of people might be referred to as hegemons. A hegemon had to have the support from at least one dominant class of people to keep the population as a whole from rebelling against the leadership. A single country might also be considered to be hegemonical if it has enough power to influence the way that other countries behave.

### Test-Taking Strategies Applied

The question contains a qualifying word—BEST. While all of the answers relate to diversity among groups and/or its impact on values, only the correct response choice speaks to the power to "lead" or dominate, which is the essence of hegemony. Social workers must be familiar with key concepts and terms related to the KSAs, including those related to morals and beliefs that are consistent with and antithetical to the social work profession.

### Question Assesses

Content Area I—Human Development, Diversity, and Behavior in the Environment; Diversity and Discrimination (Competency); Systemic (Institutionalized) Discrimination (e.g., Racism, Sexism, Ageism) (KSA)

### 62. D

### Rationale

**Borderline Personality Disorder (BPD)** is characterized by emotional instability, distress, and neurosis. Clients with this disorder tend to experience difficulty in forming stable relationships. A paranoid fear of being abandoned haunts these clients, and this fear frequently becomes a self-fulfilling prophecy. Angry outbursts are common. Clients with

BPD tend to view people in black and white, idealizing someone one day and devaluing that person the next.

Clients with BPD have an increased incidence of childhood neglect and abuse. They are also at greater risk of suicide, but the risk is greatest in early adulthood and decreases with age. Many clients who have been diagnosed with BPD are told that their chronic disorder is not treatable. However, BPD can have a good prognosis if properly treated. Specialized psychotherapy can significantly improve the lives of individuals with this debilitating disorder. A majority of clients with BPD attain greater stability in their relationships and vocational functioning in their 30s and 40s.

Major research has been conducted on the prognosis of clients with BPD, namely two long-term studies called the Collaborative Longitudinal Personality Disorders Study (CLPS) and the McLean Study of Adult Development (MSAD). These studies examined the course of BPD in those seeking treatment for the disorder.

One major finding was that the remission rate went from about 30% to 50% by the second year follow-up, and up to about 80% by the 10th year. Thus, remission of symptoms is more frequent than what researchers and clinicians previously believed.

### Test-Taking Strategies Applied

The question contains a qualifying word—TRUE. It is even capitalized to assist with identifying the distinguishing factor of the correct response from the rest. Each statement must be read carefully and evaluated as to its accuracy. The correct answer is identified through the process of elimination, with each false assertion being excluded.

### Question Assesses

Content Area II—Assessment, Diagnosis, and Treatment Planning; Assessment and Diagnosis (Competency); The Use of the Diagnostic and Statistical Manual of the American Psychiatric Association (KSA)

### 63. B

### Rationale

Several hundred **screening instruments** are available today to aid social workers and others in identifying clients with alcohol problems. One instrument in particular, the **CAGE assessment**, is useful in a variety of settings and with a range of target populations. CAGE is an acronym for its four questions; the instrument is a widely used screening test for problem drinking and potential alcohol problems. Instrument administration takes less than 1 minute, and is often used in primary care or other general settings as a quick screening tool rather than as an in-depth interview for those who have alcoholism. The CAGE instrument does not have a specific intended population, and it is meant to find those who drink excessively and need treatment. The CAGE questionnaire is reliable and valid; however, it is not valid for diagnosis of other Substance Use Disorders, although somewhat modified versions of the CAGE questionnaire have been frequently implemented for such a purpose.

The CAGE is designed as a self-report questionnaire. Because talking about drinking behavior can be uncomfortable or stigmatized, client responses may be subject to social desirability bias. The honesty and accuracy of responses may improve if clients trust social workers doing the interviews. Responses also may be more honest when the form is completed online, on a computer, or in other anonymous formats.

The CAGE assessment can identify alcohol problems over the lifetime. Two positive responses to the questions are considered a positive test and indicate further assessment is warranted.

**C**: Have you ever felt you should *cut down* on your drinking?

**A**: Have people *annoyed* you by criticizing your drinking?

**G**: Have you ever felt bad or *guilty* about your drinking?

**E**: *Eye opener*: Have you ever had a drink first thing in the morning to steady your nerves or to get rid of a hangover?

Addiction—or compulsive alcohol or drug use despite harmful consequences—is characterized by an inability to stop using alcohol or drugs; failure to meet work, social, or family obligations; and, sometimes (depending on the drug), tolerance and withdrawal. The latter reflect physical dependence in which the body adapts to the drug, requiring more of it to achieve a certain effect (tolerance) and eliciting drug-specific physical or mental symptoms if drug use is abruptly ceased (withdrawal). Physical dependence can happen with the chronic use of many drugs—including many prescription drugs, even if taken as instructed. Thus, physical dependence in and of itself does not constitute addiction, but it often accompanies addiction.

### Test-Taking Strategies Applied

While this question appears to be a scenario, it really assesses social workers' use of standardized instruments in practice. The correct answer is the missing question needed to complete the CAGE assessment, which is a screening tool to detect alcohol problems. Just because the name of a theory, perspective, practice model, or—in this case—assessment tool is not explicitly stated, it does not mean that the answers should not be selected based upon their application to the question. In all instances, an answer should be based upon material in the social work literature, not just opinion of what is best or what would seem reasonable in practice.

### Question Assesses

Content Area II—Assessment, Diagnosis, and Treatment Planning; Biopsychosocial History and Collateral Data (Competency); Techniques and Instruments Used to Assess Clients/Client Systems (KSA)

### 64. B

### Rationale

Resisting disclosure of privileged information is required to protect the **confidentiality of clients**. Social workers must employ varying methods to protect the confidentiality of clients during legal proceedings to the extent permitted by law. *When a court of law or other legally authorized body orders social workers to disclose confidential or privileged information without a client's consent and such disclosure could cause harm to the client, social workers should request that the court withdraw the order or limit the order as narrowly as possible or maintain the records under seal, unavailable for public inspection.*

Social workers can use several additional strategies to protect clients' confidentiality during legal proceedings. If social workers believe a subpoena is unwarranted or without merit, they can arrange for a lawyer to file a motion asking the court to rule that the request is inappropriate. In addition, social workers may request that a judge review clinical notes and records in chambers to protect confidentiality and then rule on whether the information should be revealed in open court and made a matter of public record. A judge may issue a protective order explicitly limiting the disclosure of specific privileged information to certain portions of a social worker's clinical notes or certain aspects of his or her interpersonal communications.

Social workers are instinctively inclined to protect clients' confidentiality. Clients' legal right to privileged communication strengthens social workers' ability to protect clients. To fulfill their ethical duty, social workers should be familiar with the concept of privileged communication, practical steps they can take to protect clients, and exceptions to clients' right to privileged information.

### Test-Taking Strategies Applied

The question contains a qualifying word—EXCEPT—that requires social workers to select the response choice which is not specified in the 2018 *NASW Code of Ethics*. When EXCEPT is used as a qualifying word, it is often helpful to remove it from the question and eliminate the three response choices which must be done as per ethical standards. This approach will leave the one response choice which is not required.

Redacting information is not recommended when a social worker receives a court order which mandates release of information which can be harmful without client consent. This action is probably prohibited by law as the court has requested the information in its entirety. In addition, if a social worker is successful in getting the court to withdraw an order, it would be better to not submit any documentation even if the most sensitive parts have been redacted.

### Question Assesses

Content Area IV—Professional Values and Ethics; Confidentiality (Competency); Legal and/or Ethical Issues Regarding Confidentiality, Including Electronic Information Security (KSA)

### 65. C

### Rationale

**Professional development** ensures that social workers continue to strengthen their skills and learn throughout their career. The most effective professional development engages social workers to focus on meeting the needs of their clients. Social workers learn new skills and competencies to ensure clients receive the most effective and efficient services possible.

Professional development refers to many types of educational experiences. Social workers participate in professional development to learn and apply new knowledge and skills that will improve service delivery.

Effective professional development enables social workers to develop the knowledge and skills they need to address complex client problems. To be effective, professional development requires thoughtful planning followed by careful implementation with feedback to ensure it responds to social workers' needs. Social workers who participate in professional development then must put their new knowledge and skills to work. Professional development is not effective unless it causes social workers to learn new theory and techniques aimed at helping clients reach their goals.

### Test-Taking Strategies Applied

This question contains a qualifying word—BEST. While the incorrect answers may be reasons that social workers engage in professional development, the correct one focuses on its benefits for improved practice. Correct answers on the examination are always ones that focus on the delivery of effective services and place client needs above agency policy, regulatory requirements, and employment considerations.

## Question Assesses

Content Area IV—Professional Values and Ethics; Professional Development and Use of Self (Competency); Professional Development Activities to Improve Practice and Maintain Current Professional Knowledge (e.g., In-Service Training, Licensing Requirements, Reviews of Literature, Workshops) (KSA)

### 66. B

## Rationale

Interaction of people, organizations, and governments is the process of **globalization**. The process is determined by trade between the nations, investments in their businesses, and data gathered through information technology and has some effects on the cultural, environmental, political, and economic development of the countries. Globalization can have both negative and positive effects on quality of life.

**Cultural convergence** means bringing together different cultural groups, which results in these cultures becoming more alike in terms of technology, sports, language, and even politics.

Globalization and culture are interdependent. Globalization lies at the heart of modern cultural; culture practices lie at the heart of globalization. Their relationship is reciprocal.

History shows that contact between different cultures leads to trade of products between them or globalization. Travelers and merchants from one culture to another culture bring products with them which allow people to know about the other culture and its products. Technology has made nations know about other nations and even adopt their customs if they like them.

Globalization is resulting in greater homogeneity around the globe, but it is also said that globalization is demolishing local cultures and traditions. Thus, there are positive and negative impacts of globalization.

## Test-Taking Strategies Applied

The question contains a qualifying word—MOST—even though it is not capitalized. Though some of the incorrect responses can lead to cultural convergence, globalization is the greatest or most significant contributor. Globalization causes the greatest interaction between people, which results in cultural convergence. Social workers must be familiar with how human behavior changes as a result of the interactions of those from different societies and parts of the world.

## Question Assesses

Content Area I—Human Development, Diversity, and Behavior in the Environment; Human Behavior in the Social Environment (Competency); The Impact of Globalization on Clients/Client Systems (e.g., Interrelatedness of Systems, International Integration, Technology, Environmental or Financial Crises, Epidemics) (KSA)

### 67. C

## Rationale

**Gender identity** is an individual sense of femaleness or maleness or neither. It is also, to some degree, a social construction that categorizes certain behaviors into primarily binary, male and female, roles. Gender identity conflicts can stem from gender identity not matching an individual's biological sex, gender identity being neither completely male nor female, or biological sex not being uniquely male or female. The use of Latinx began more than a decade ago and is the gender-neutral alternative to Latino or Latina. The use of Latinx is gaining popularity as part of an effort to move beyond gender binary and be inclusive of the intersecting identities of Latin American descendants.

Latinx makes room for people who are trans, queer, agender, nonbinary, gender nonconforming, or gender fluid. In Spanish, the masculinized version of words is considered gender neutral, but that does not work for some who think it is inappropriate to assign masculinity as gender neutral. The use of "x" is a way of rejecting the gendering of words and recognition that language changes in order to accommodate the times in which it is used.

Though people may not identify as Latinx for various reasons, it is important to respect others who do and who want to be referred to as such. Latinx is a way to be more inclusive of identities that go beyond gender norms that are rapidly shifting and being redefined in today's culture. It is seen by some as vital to expressing who they are and being able to explain it to others.

## Test-Taking Strategies Applied

This question requires knowledge of a specific term related to gender identity. There are always several questions on every version of the examination which include very unique and specific knowledge. While this term may be unfamiliar, it is possible to use reasoning to get to the correct answer with some familiarity that most nouns (not all) are assigned a gender—masculine or feminine—in the Spanish language. The endings of words often indicate whether they are masculine or feminine. As "Latinx" does not end in the traditional "a" or "o" for this word, it may be possible to reason that the substitution concerns the assignment of gender.

When a question asks about a term that is unknown, it is best to use any information or reasoning available and select the answer which appears logical (even if it is just a guess). Failing the exam will not occur just because there are a handful of unfamiliar names or concepts.

*Question Assesses*

Content Area I—Human Development, Diversity, and Behavior in the Environment; Diversity and Discrimination (Competency); Gender and Gender Identity Concepts (KSA)

### 68. A

*Rationale*

**Termination** is an important part of the problem-solving process as there is a beginning, middle, and end to all clinical relationships. Most social work focuses on engaging clients in services, followed by helping them obtain stability. Too often, references to the inevitable end of client–social worker relationships are absent during all steps in the treatment process. Yet, clinical relationships have an end point. Some have clearly defined time limits, while others use assessment of clinical outcomes to determine when clients are ready for discharge. Even long-term programs serving chronic populations such as those with mental illness, persons with developmental disabilities, or persons with chronic medical conditions still experience staff turnover requiring termination issues to be broached.

The final stages of treatment with clients can be met with a range of emotion from jubilation to deep sorrow. Nevertheless, if work has been done during the initial and maintenance phases of treatment, transition and termination discussion should not be a surprise and should actually be expected.

During termination, greater independence should be encouraged. As it is important that clients not feel cast aside or abandoned, in-depth conversation about clients' reactions to the end of their clinical relationships should take place in order to let them voice their fears. In addition, progress must be reviewed and appropriate actions if problems reappear should be identified.

*Test-Taking Strategies Applied*

In the scenario, the social worker is in the last step in the problem-solving process, termination. However, new information about the client's situation has been revealed. This information appears to be directly related to the problem which originally brought her into treatment. While her anxiety has improved in recent months, a change in her environment, such as going to a new school, may serve as a stressor. Thus, termination may be premature as the client could require additional support. *Assessment is an ongoing activity which can take place during any step in the problem-solving process.* Thus, the social worker should determine whether termination is still appropriate through a thorough assessment.

Acknowledging progress made during treatment and identifying needed follow-up services are standard activities which occur during termination. However, they are incorrect answers as they do not consider the third sentence in the scenario, which presents the social worker with new information about the client's situation. Identifying relaxation techniques appears to be an intervention which should have been done prior to termination, making it incorrect.

*Question Assesses*

Content Area III—Psychotherapy, Clinical Interventions, and Case Management; The Intervention Process (Competency); The Indicators of Client/Client System Readiness for Termination (KSA)

### 69. B

*Rationale*

The Health Insurance Portability and Accessibility Act of 1996 Medical Privacy Regulations (known as the HIPAA Privacy Rule) has important implications for the **confidentiality of psychotherapy notes**. The HIPAA Privacy Rule recognizes the unique characteristics of "psychotherapy notes" and defines them as notes that are:

- Recorded (in any medium) by a mental health professional documenting or analyzing the contents of conversation during a private counseling session or a group, joint, or family counseling session; and

- Separated from the rest of the individual's medical or clinical record.

Thus, any additional privacy protection that may be available to clients' psychotherapy notes depends on whether the notes are maintained separately from the rest of the clinical file. This has been interpreted to mean in a separate file (paper or electronic), rather than a subsection of a file. The underlying rationale is that the notes are intended primarily for use by social workers. Access to the notes should be limited to primary clinicians.

Under the Privacy Rule, the definition of "psychotherapy notes" does not include session start and stop times, modalities and frequency of treatment, medication monitoring, clinical tests, or summaries of diagnosis, prognosis, treatment plan, or progress.

If a social work practice decides to maintain separate psychotherapy notes, all of the previously listed excluded material would be maintained in the primary client file or "medical record," while the psychotherapy notes would be kept elsewhere. Thus, the primary client chart would include, as applicable:

- Medication prescription and monitoring
- Counseling sessions' start and stop times
- The modalities and frequencies of treatment furnished
- Results of clinical tests
- Any summary of diagnosis, functional status, treatment plan, symptoms, prognosis, and progress to date
- Intake information
- Billing information
- Formal evaluations
- Notes of collateral contacts
- Records obtained from other providers

The previous information would be considered the "medical record" for HIPAA purposes and subject to disclosure with a general consent or authorization to release information, as required by the 2018 *NASW Code of Ethics*.

Under the Privacy Rule, in order for separately maintained psychotherapy notes to be released, the client must sign a separate authorization form. This means clients will be more aware as to when such a specific request has been made, and clinicians can provide clients an opportunity to consider whether or not they wish to sign a separate authorization for release of psychotherapy notes. Thus, if a clinician receives a request for "all records" or the "complete medical record," along with a signed authorization, this is not sufficient to release separately maintained psychotherapy notes. A separate signed authorization, specific to the psychotherapy notes, is required. This provides additional protection from routine disclosure of the notes to third parties, such as insurers.

### Test-Taking Strategies Applied

This is a recall question which relies on social workers understanding confidentiality standards concerning psychotherapy notes.

Storing them in a section of a client's file does not afford them "the greatest confidentiality protections" under HIPAA. Social workers should never take client information home where there is a greater likelihood of confidentiality breaches. Additionally, such actions violate trust as clients are unlikely to think that their personal information is leaving the security of professional offices. Lastly, agency policy will not provide additional protections if separate files are not maintained for psychotherapy notes.

### Question Assesses

Content Area IV—Professional Values and Ethics; Confidentiality (Competency); Legal and/or Ethical Issues Regarding Confidentiality, Including Electronic Information Security (KSA)

### 70. A

### Rationale

**Cannabis-Related Disorders** are a group of mental health conditions that stem from the use of THC-containing marijuana or hashish. The American Psychiatric Association (APA) classifies these conditions as specific examples of a more comprehensive category of problems called Substance-Related Disorders.

The *DSM-5* contains definitions for four Cannabis-Related Disorders: Cannabis Intoxication, Cannabis Use Disorder, Cannabis Withdrawal, and Other Cannabis-Induced Disorders.

Cannabis Intoxication is the only one of these disorders that appears in the *DSM-5* in essentially the same form as it appeared in the *DSM-IV*. Cannabis Use Disorder replaces both Cannabis Abuse and Cannabis Dependence. Cannabis Withdrawal was created for *DSM-5* in recognition of the possible effects of suddenly stopping or heavily reducing habitual marijuana or hashish intake. The Other Cannabis-Induced Disorders listing replaces several different *DSM-IV* disorders, including

Cannabis-Induced Anxiety Disorder, Cannabis-Induced Psychotic Disorder With Hallucinations, and Cannabis-Induced Psychotic Disorder With Delusions.

People affected by **Cannabis Intoxication** have typically smoked or ingested marijuana or hashish within roughly 2 hours of the onset of their symptoms. Specific symptoms that indicate the presence of intoxication include a significant spike in the normal heart rate, mouth dryness, appetite elevation, and unusual fluid accumulation in the eyelids (a condition known as conjunctival injection). In addition to at least two of these cannabis-related alterations, all diagnosed clients must experience substantial psychological or behavioral impairments as a result of marijuana or hashish use. They must also lack other conditions that provide a more reasonable basis for their mental/physical state.

Under the criteria listed in the *DSM-IV*, clients with significant problems related to their cannabis use who show no signs of physical/mental dependence could receive a diagnosis of Cannabis Abuse. Examples of problems that qualified as significant include a frequent inability to meet any essential duties or responsibilities, frequent participation in dangerous activities while under the influence of cannabis, and an insistence on continuing cannabis use despite its known harmful life impact. The *DSM-IV* criteria also allowed for a separate diagnosis of Cannabis Dependence in people who do show signs of physical/mental dependence on marijuana or hashish.

However, modern scientific thinking indicates that the difference between Substance Abuse and Substance Dependence is not definitive. Social workers do not address abuse and dependence as separate issues. For this reason, *DSM-5* includes combined listings for specific Substance Use Disorders instead of listings for various forms of abuse and dependence. This means that Cannabis Abuse and Cannabis Dependence are now addressed together under the **Cannabis Use Disorder** heading.

Substance withdrawal qualifies as a mental health concern when it produces symptoms that significantly degrade participation in a functional routine or trigger troublesome states of mind. Prior to the publication of the *DSM-5*, there was not enough scientific evidence to ascribe these types of effects to withdrawal from the use of marijuana or hashish. However, the APA now officially recognizes the fact that at least some of the people who withdraw from these substances meet the mental health criteria for substance withdrawal. Social workers can now use the **Cannabis Withdrawal** diagnosis to identify these people.

Criteria for Cannabis Withdrawal include:

- Cessation of cannabis use that has been heavy and prolonged (i.e., usually daily or almost daily use over a period of at least a few months).

- *Three or more of the following signs and symptoms* develop within approximately 1 week after cessation of heavy, prolonged use:
  - Irritability, anger, or aggression
  - *Nervousness or anxiety*
  - Sleep difficulty (insomnia, disturbing dreams)
  - Decreased appetite or weight loss
  - *Restlessness*
  - *Depressed mood*
  - At least one of the following physical symptoms causing significant discomfort: abdominal pain, shakiness/tremors, sweating, fever, chills, or headache
- The signs or symptoms cause clinically significant distress or impairment in social, occupational, or other important areas of functioning.

- The signs or symptoms are not attributable to another medical condition and are not better explained by another mental disorder, including intoxication or withdrawal from another substance.

Cannabis is known for its ability to produce symptoms in some users that strongly resemble the symptoms of certain diagnosable mental conditions. *DSM-IV* identified two such conditions: anxiety—which produces unreasonable worry, fear, or dread—and psychosis, which classically involves the onset of either sensory hallucinations or fixed, irrational beliefs known as delusions. *DSM-5* still allows social workers to diagnose these conditions in cannabis users; however, it also acknowledges the fact the cannabis users can potentially develop other mental health problems directly related to their marijuana or hashish use. **Other Cannabis-Induced Disorders** was created in order to provide social workers with the freedom to specify exactly which issues they uncover in their cannabis-using clients.

### Test-Taking Strategies Applied

This is a recall question which relies on social workers knowing the signs of substance withdrawal and whether the withdrawal meets the diagnostic criteria for a mental health concern because they significantly degrade participation in a functional routine or trigger a troublesome state of mind.

Withdrawal of cannabis often produces decreased appetite or weight loss—not hunger. Hallucinations are not a sign of withdrawal, but may be an indication of an Other Cannabis-Induced Disorder when associated with use. Denial is often associated with drug use, but it is not a diagnostic criterion for withdrawal.

Depressed mood is the only withdrawal symptom listed that appears in the *DSM-5* as one of three or more that must be present within a week of stopping cannabis in order to be diagnosed with Cannabis Withdrawal.

*Question Assesses*

Content Area II—Assessment, Diagnosis, and Treatment Planning; Assessment and Diagnosis (Competency); The Use of the Diagnostic and Statistical Manual of the American Psychiatric Association (KSA)

## 71. A

*Rationale*

The **Neurodevelopmental Disorders** are a group of conditions with onset often before the child enters grade school, and are characterized by developmental deficits that produce impairments of personal, social, academic, or occupational functioning. Diagnosing them involves understanding strong knowledge of **child development** and its milestones.

The range of developmental deficits varies from very specific limitations of learning or control of executive functions to global impairments of social skills or intelligence. The Neurodevelopmental Disorders frequently co-occur, with individuals with Autism Spectrum Disorder often having Intellectual Disability (Intellectual Developmental Disorder), and many children with Attention-Deficit/ Hyperactivity Disorder also having a Specific Learning Disorder. For some disorders, the clinical presentation includes symptoms of excess as well as deficits and delays in achieving expected milestones.

*Test-Taking Strategies Applied*

The scenario requires that the correct answer be one that is needed "to effectively work with this child." The first sentence is critical as it indicates that the child has a Neurodevelopmental Disorder characterized by deficits in typical functioning. As the social worker is charged with developing learning opportunities to address these delays, it is essential that these activities be developmentally appropriate and targeted at areas needing growth.

While the scenario does not contain a qualifying word, there is a need to pick out the most salient or relevant answer. School policy and family supports may be useful when developing an intervention plan, but they do not directly speak to the child's area of need, addressing areas of delay. Past academic performance will not be needed to effectively work with the child as it is likely poor, hence the reason for the current referral.

## Question Assesses

Content Area II—Assessment, Diagnosis, and Treatment Planning; Assessment and Diagnosis (Competency); The Use of the Diagnostic and Statistical Manual of the American Psychiatric Association (KSA)

### 72. A

*Rationale*

A **sociogram** is a graphic representation which serves to reveal and analyze the relationships of a person with his or her family or social circle, or to visualize the relationships within the family or of certain members of the family with their external environment such as health and education services, leisure time activities, work, friends, or place in the extended family.

A **genogram** gives information about the composition of families and the interactions and influences between generations, but it does not show the nature of the relationships within a family nor those with the exterior environment, which may be very useful in certain situations. Sociograms are used to illustrate human resources and networks that can be mobilized to support clients.

A client is born within a family, with parents who protect him or her, a family circle, and a specific environment. This is known as the **belonging group**, with which, in one way or another, a client maintains a lifelong tie. A human group, whatever its nature, always presents a particular character, with specific values, distinct cultural tastes, a dynamic, and an ideology, which make it unique. The persons, groups, or organizations which serve as role models for a client's moral, religious, or political conduct is the **reference group**. The sociogram can target either one or the other of these groups.

In this graphic representation, as in the genogram, the **intensity of the ties is indicated by a code of lines**: a dotted line indicates a weak relationship, and as the dots get weaker, the relationship is weaker.

**Arrows pointing one or both ways** show whether a relationship is reciprocal or only one-way, where one person is providing support and the other person is not allowed/able to give back.

**Circles** with names inside, big or small, represent the different members of a family based on the importance they have in the family.

The shading of circles or shapes of diagrams do not have any intrinsic meaning.

### Test-Taking Strategies Applied

This is a recall question which relies on social workers understanding techniques and instruments used in assessment. While knowledge about sociograms may not be as robust as that about genograms, many of the features are the same. Usually relationships are depicted as lines. Intensity does not directly relate to direction, so arrows can be eliminated. Shapes and shading do not also intuitively have to do with connections, which are the essence of relationships. Often the correct answer in recall questions happens through the process of elimination.

### Question Assesses

Content Area II—Assessment, Diagnosis, and Treatment Planning; Biopsychosocial History and Collateral Data (Competency); Techniques and Instruments Used to Assess Clients/Client Systems (KSA)

### 73. A

### Rationale

Social workers respect and promote the right of clients to **self-determination** and assist clients in their efforts to identify and clarify their goals. Social workers may only limit clients' right to self-determination when, in the social workers' professional judgment, clients' actions or potential actions pose a serious, foreseeable, and imminent risk to themselves or others. Limitation should not be made when social workers feel that clients are simply making poor choices or the actions could have negative ramifications for their well-being, but these consequences are not serious, foreseeable, and imminent.

### Test-Taking Strategies Applied

The question contains a qualifying word—FIRST. There may be more than one appropriate action by the social worker to the scenario, but each must be done after recognition that this decision is ultimately to be made by the client. Despite the social worker's belief that the decision is a poor one, the client must not be judged and instead should be supported throughout the process.

The decision by the client to leave her employment does not meet the threshold of causing serious, foreseeable, and imminent harm. The social worker may assess whether changes in the client's life have influenced this decision, help the client to understand the consequences of her decision, and assist the client with locating new employment. However, these actions should occur after the right of the client to make such a choice is acknowledged.

*Question Assesses*

Content Area IV—Professional Values and Ethics; Professional Development and Use of Self (Competency); Client/Client System Competence and Self-Determination (e.g., Financial Decisions, Treatment Decisions, Emancipation, Age of Consent, Permanency Planning) (KSA)

## 74. D

*Rationale*

The **effects of substance abuse and/or dependence** can be detrimental to client functioning. **Wernicke's encephalopathy** and **Korsakoff syndrome** are different conditions that often occur together. Both are due to *brain damage* caused by a lack of vitamin $B_1$. Korsakoff syndrome is most commonly caused by alcohol misuse, but can also be associated with certain other conditions. Korsakoff syndrome is often, but not always, preceded by an episode of Wernicke's encephalopathy, which is an acute brain reaction to severe lack of thiamine. Wernicke's encephalopathy is a medical emergency that causes confusion, staggering and stumbling, lack of coordination, and abnormal involuntary eye movements. Symptoms of Korsakoff syndrome include inability to form new memories, loss of memory, making up stories (confabulation), and seeing or hearing things that are not really there (hallucinations).

**Confabulation** is defined as the spontaneous production of false memories: either memories for events which never occurred, or memories of actual events which are displaced in space or time. These memories may be elaborate and detailed. The exact causes of confabulation are unknown, but basal forebrain damage may lead to memory impairments, while frontal damage may lead to problems in self-awareness. Thus, a client may have a memory deficit, but be unaware of this deficit.

Confabulators are not lying. They are not deliberately trying to mislead. In fact, clients are generally quite unaware that their memories are inaccurate, and they may argue strenuously that they have been telling the truth.

## Test-Taking Strategies Applied

The correct answer must be the name of a disorder which is characterized by telling stories based on false memories due to brain damage. Hallucinations are hearing, seeing, smelling, or touching things that are not there. While **hallucinations** can be associated with Korsakoff syndrome, the creation of false memories is not characteristic of hallucinations. **Denial** is the refusal to accept reality—not creating false memories. Lastly, confabulation should not be confused with false memory syndrome, the phenomenon whereby otherwise typical clients suddenly "remember" repressed incidents of childhood abuse or other trauma. Confabulation is a clinical syndrome resulting from injury to the brain, whereas false memory syndrome is not.

## Question Assesses

Content Area I—Human Development, Diversity, and Behavior in the Environment; Human Behavior in the Social Environment (Competency); Addiction Theories and Concepts (KSA)

### 75.  A

## Rationale

Many **ethical issues in social work**—although certainly not all—require some **legal knowledge**. In addition, the 2018 *NASW Code of Ethics* requires social workers to consult laws that are relevant to ethical decisions. In the United States, three branches of government create laws: legislative, executive, and judicial. Statutory laws, regulatory laws, case laws, the U.S. Constitution, and executive orders often have profound implications when social workers make ethical decisions. **Statutory law** is enacted by Congress (federal) and legislatures (state). Statutes govern social workers' obligation to report suspected abuse and neglect of children, elders, and other vulnerable people; minors' right to consent to mental health counseling and to drug and alcohol abuse treatment; protection of school social workers' confidential records; and federal Health Insurance Portability and Accountability Act of 1996 (HIPAA) laws. **Regulatory law** is promulgated by federal and state government agencies, such as the U.S. Department of Health and Human Services and state human service, child welfare, and mental health agencies. Under our system of law, federal and state agencies have the authority to establish enforceable regulations. Public agencies must follow strict procedures when they create regulations (e.g., providing public notice and opportunity for public comment about drafts of regulations). Once enacted, federal and state regulations have the force of law. **Case law** is created in the context of litigation and judicial rulings. For example, a judge may need to interpret the meaning or application of existing law, resolve conflicts between laws, or fill gaps in existing laws. Such rulings by appellate courts become legal precedent or case law. **Constitutional law** is dictated by the Constitution and includes numerous provisions that pertain to social work practice. Examples concern Fourth Amendment guidelines concerning citizens' right to privacy and protections against improper search and seizure (important in residential treatment programs) and Eighth Amendment protections against cruel and unusual punishment (important in juvenile and adult correctional facilities). **Executive orders** may be issued by chief executives in federal, state, and local governments. This authority usually is based in federal and state statute. Executive orders resemble regulations.

### Test-Taking Strategies Applied

This question requires social workers to be familiar with a landmark California court case related to duty to warn. Current guidelines concerning social workers' duty to disclose confidential information without client consent to protect third parties from harm were initially established by *Tarasoff v. Board of Regents of the University of California*. In 1976, the California Supreme Court ruled that mental health clinicians have a duty to protect potential victims if their clients make threats or otherwise behaved as if they presented a "serious danger of violence to another." In its ruling, the court determined that the need for mental health clinicians to protect the public was more important than protecting client confidentiality.

### Question Assesses

Content Area IV—Professional Values and Ethics; Confidentiality (Competency); Legal and/or Ethical Issues Regarding Confidentiality, Including Electronic Information Security (KSA)

## 76. D

### Rationale

Social workers must be mindful of **value differences** which often arise with clients. Social workers' own values and beliefs can greatly influence social worker–client relationships. Culture, race, and ethnicity are strongly linked to values. *A social worker's self-awareness about his or her own attitudes, values, and beliefs and a willingness to acknowledge value differences are critical factors in working with clients.* A social worker is responsible for bringing up and addressing issues of cultural or other differences with clients.

Social workers should value and celebrate differences of others rather than ignoring or minimizing them. Social workers must have an awareness of personal values and biases and how they may influence relationships with clients. They must also understand their own personal and professional limitations, as well as acknowledge their own stereotypes and prejudices.

### Test-Taking Strategies Applied

All the response choices are plausible, but the correct one is most appropriate and relevant in this situation. Even though a qualifying word is not used, it is necessary to select the best action when value conflicts with clients arise. Referring clients to other practitioners implies that such conflicts cannot be successfully managed. It is common for social workers to have different beliefs and attitudes than their clients. Clients should not be penalized by having to reengage with other providers simply because their views differ. It is the responsibility of social workers to acknowledge and manage these conflicts.

Seeking supervision can be helpful in practice, but social workers should be able to address this situation independently. Supervision is not required in every instance in which social workers have value conflicts with clients, whereas the correct response choice is always needed.

Social workers should always respect clients' rights to self-determination. Self-determination relates to the differences in values between social workers and clients. These differences can impact all steps in the problem-solving process—engagement, assessment, planning, intervention, evaluation, and termination. Self-determination concerns clients' rights to make decisions and take actions in their lives. Role conflicts can also impact social workers' abilities to form therapeutic alliances and gather all relevant information during assessment—problems that will persist unless the impacts of these conflicts are examined.

### Question Assesses

Content Area IV—Professional Values and Ethics; Professional Development and Use of Self (Competency); The Influence of the Social Worker's Own Values and Beliefs on the Social Worker–Client/Client System Relationship (KSA)

### 77. B

### Rationale

The **impacts of mental illness on family dynamics** can be devastating. Impaired awareness of illness (**anosognosia**) is a major problem because it is the single largest reason why individuals with Schizophrenia and Bipolar Disorder do not take their medications. It is caused by damage to specific parts of the brain, especially the right hemisphere. It affects about half of individuals with Schizophrenia and about 40% of individuals with Bipolar Disorder. Impaired awareness of illness is a relative, not an absolute, problem. Some may also fluctuate in their awareness, being more aware at times and less at others. When taking medications, awareness of illness can improve for some.

It is difficult to understand how a person who is ill would not know it. Impaired awareness of illness is very difficult for family members to comprehend. Psychiatric symptoms seem so obvious that it is hard to believe that those exhibiting them are not aware. The term comes from the Greek word for disease (nosos) and knowledge (gnosis). It literally means "to not know a disease."

### Test-Taking Strategies Applied

Social workers need to understand the complex nature of mental illness, especially on members of families. While side effects of antipsychotics for the treatment of Schizophrenia can be both dangerous and annoying, the son would have to have taken medication to be bothered by its effects. Also, side effects associated with a particular medication can be overcome by using a different antipsychotic drug instead.

The comorbidity of a physical condition would not impact on the ability to take medication. A physical condition is different than a medical condition, with the former impacting mobility or coordination. A medical condition may need to be considered when taking an antipsychotic medication, but not a physical one.

Lastly, denial is a psychological defense mechanism while impaired awareness of illness has a biological basis and is caused by damage to the brain, especially the right brain hemisphere. The specific brain areas which appear to be most involved are the frontal lobe and part of the parietal lobe. Anosognosia differs from denial. Often those with Schizophrenia who refuse medication do not see themselves as ill as they do not recognize their symptoms (anosognosia); rather, they are using a strategy to minimize the signs of their illness as they do not want to address it (denial).

### Question Assesses

Content Area II—Assessment, Diagnosis, and Treatment Planning; Assessment and Diagnosis (Competency); The Indicators of Mental and Emotional Illness Throughout the Lifespan (KSA)

### 78. C

*Rationale*

**Intersectionality** is the intersecting systems of privilege and oppression. **Privilege** is when people do not have to face an institutionalized form of oppression, and **oppression** is when they do have to face it. Just because one person has one form of privilege does not mean he or she only has privilege.

People can be oppressed and privileged in many different ways, such as due to their genders, sexual orientations, races, and so on. While a straight, white cisgender man has privilege, he may have a lower socioeconomic status and be oppressed for economic status. He also may have a physical or mental disability which results in oppression. This is an example of intersectionality.

Race, gender, gender expression, sexual orientation, socioeconomic status, physical and mental ability, religion, language, age, physical attractiveness, occupation, and education are just some of the categories of intersectionality.

*Test-Taking Strategies Applied*

Social workers must be aware of privilege and oppression, which are shaped by racism, homophobia, ableism, and other institutionalized discrimination. This recall question requires knowledge that inequities are never the result of single, distinct factors. Rather, they are the outcome of intersections of different social locations, power relations, and experiences. While some of the incorrect response choices are true or contain important points, they are not the BEST (which is a qualifying word) definitions of intersectionality, which is the criteria used to select the correct answer.

*Question Assesses*

Content Area I—Human Development, Diversity, and Behavior in the Environment; Diversity and Discrimination (Competency); Systemic (Institutionalized) Discrimination (e.g., Racism, Sexism, Ageism) (KSA)

### 79. D

*Rationale*

**Dissociation** is a mental process that severs connections among a person's thoughts, memories, feelings, actions, and/or sense of identity. Dissociation—losing the ability to recall or track a particular action (e.g., arriving at work but not remembering the last minutes of the drive)—is common and happens because the person is engaged in an automatic activity and is not paying attention to his or her immediate environment. However, dissociation can also be an **impact of trauma** as it serves as a protective element whereby the victim incurs distortion of time, space, or identity.

Dissociation helps distance the experience from the individual. People who have experienced severe or developmental trauma may have learned to separate themselves from distress to survive. At times, dissociation can be very pervasive and symptomatic of a mental disorder, such as Dissociative Identity Disorder (DID; formerly known as Multiple Personality Disorder). Diagnoses of Dissociative Disorders are closely associated with histories of severe childhood trauma.

There are many signs of dissociation including fixed or "glazed" eyes, sudden flattening of affect, long periods of silence, monotonous voice, stereotyped or repetitive movements, responses not congruent with situations, and/or excessive intellectualization.

**Excessive guilt** is another response to trauma. It attempts to make sense cognitively and gain control over a traumatic experience by assuming responsibility.

**Intrusive thoughts and memories** can also occur as a result of trauma. Experiencing, without warning or desire, thoughts and memories associated with the trauma can easily trigger strong emotional and behavioral reactions, as if the trauma was recurring in the present. The intrusive thoughts and memories can come rapidly, referred to as flooding, and can be disruptive at the time of their occurrence.

**Depression** can also result from guilty feelings associated with the trauma. Survivors often believe that others will not fully understand their experiences, leading to isolation and depression.

### Test-Taking Strategies Applied

In the scenario, there are many responses to trauma—substance use, aggression (perhaps tied to underlying anger), and memory gaps. However, no indicators of guilt or depression, such as crying, self-blaming, and lethargy, are mentioned. In addition, the scenario does not describe the presence of intrusive thoughts, such as flashbacks. It is likely that the client would exhibit strong emotional or behavioral reactions to such memories. Instead, the client is unemotional, denying the impact of the abuse. This reaction is typical of dissociation.

### Question Assesses

Content Area I—Human Development, Diversity, and Behavior in the Environment; Human Behavior in the Social Environment (Competency); The Impact of Stress, Trauma, and Violence (KSA)

### 80.  B

*Rationale*

Schizoid Personality Disorder is characterized by eccentricity; clients with this disorder often appear odd or peculiar. They tend to be distant, detached, and indifferent to social relationships. They generally are loners who prefer solitary activities and rarely express strong emotion. Many people with Schizoid Personality Disorder are able to function fairly well, although they tend to choose jobs that allow them to work alone, such as night security officers, library workers, or lab workers.

Clients with Schizoid Personality Disorder often are reclusive, organizing their lives to avoid contact with other people. Many never marry or may continue to live with their parents as adults. Other common traits of people with this disorder include:

- No desire or enjoyment in close relationships, even with family members
- Choice of solitary jobs and activities
- Pleasure in few activities, including sex
- Difficulty relating to others
- Indifferent to praise or criticism
- Aloof with little emotion
- Daydreaming and/or creating vivid fantasies of complex inner lives

*Test-Taking Strategies Applied*

The question contains a qualifying word—ATYPICAL—even though it is not capitalized. The correct answer must list behaviors which are unlikely given the defining characteristics of this disorder. Clients with Schizoid Personality Disorder do not enjoy relationships and have no close friends. They desire solitude. Thus, clients would avoid sexual activities and social events with no desire to leave their family home to marry or be independent.

As clients with Schizoid Personality Disorder rarely express emotion, it would be unlikely that they would express anger when criticized.

*Question Assesses*

Content Area II—Assessment, Diagnosis, and Treatment Planning; Assessment and Diagnosis (Competency); The Use of the

Diagnostic and Statistical Manual of the American Psychiatric Association (KSA)

## 81. A

*Rationale*

There are a number of contraindications to **family-centered social work practice**. These include, but are not limited to, when:

- There is an unstable member or members and the risk of stimulating intense affect in a session might lead to decompensation or other adverse effects.
- There is violence in the family (elder abuse, domestic violence, and child abuse).
- Family members are physically or emotionally destructive toward one another.
- Essential members of the family cannot or refuse to be included.
- Detoxification of a family member or the stabilization of a family member with psychosis is the goal.
- There is not a commitment to address issues by all family members or one member is being deceptive (e.g., one partner has not disclosed his or her plan to leave the relationship).

*Test-Taking Strategies Applied*

This question is focused on choosing appropriate treatment modalities for client problems. Family-centered social work practice recognizes that people do not exist in a vacuum and it is important, at times, to look at families as a whole, not just their members.

Three of the four response choices are contraindications of family therapy, making them incorrect. Only the first answer, the correct one, illustrates a reason to treat a family as a whole.

Boundaries occur at every level of a system. They influence the flow of information into and within a system. Using family systems theory, social workers can assist with establishing healthy structures in situations where they do not exist or are continually violated.

*Question Assesses*

Content Area II—Assessment, Diagnosis, and Treatment Planning; Treatment Planning (Competency); The Criteria Used in the Selection of Intervention/Treatment Modalities (e.g., Client/Client System Abilities, Culture, Life Stage) (KSA)

### 82. D

*Rationale*

The *DSM-5* has created a new chapter for a cluster of disorders that involve obsessional thoughts and/or compulsive behaviors. These include Obsessive-Compulsive Disorder (OCD), Body Dysmorphic Disorder (BDD), Hoarding Disorder, Trichotillomania (Hair-Pulling Disorder), and Excoriation (Skin-Picking) Disorder.

Motor tics are often comorbid in clients with OCD. Both OCD and Tic Disorders are best treated with medication and **behavior modification. Matching interventions to client problems** is paramount.

One behavior technique, **habit reversal training**, is extremely effective in reducing tics. Habit reversal training has four main components: awareness training, development of a competing response, building motivation, and generalization of skills. Awareness training is used to bring greater attention to tics and other behaviors so that a client can gain better self-control. Awareness training usually involves describing in detail each time the behavior occurs and identifying the earliest warning that a tic or impulsive behavior is about to take place. These warning signs can be urges, sensations, or thoughts. Once a client has developed a good awareness of his or her tic or impulsive behavior, the next step is to develop a competing response that replaces the old tic or impulsive behavior. Usually, the competing response is opposite to that of the tic or impulsive behavior and is something that can be carried out for longer than just a couple of minutes. Choosing a response that will be more or less unnoticeable by others is best. To keep the tics and impulsive behaviors from coming back, a client is encouraged to make a list of all of the problems that were caused by their behavior. The last step is to encourage new skills in a range of different contexts, not just those that clients mastered to date.

The treatment of OCD has also been well established in the roots of behavior therapy. Exposing clients to the feared stimuli and blocking the conditioned response helps reduce both the onset and severity of symptoms.

**Solution-focused brief therapy (SFBT)** places focus on a client's present and future circumstances and goals rather than past experiences. In this goal-oriented therapy, the symptoms or issues bringing a client to therapy are typically not targeted.

**Existential psychotherapy** is based upon the fundamental belief that a client experiences intrapsychic conflict due to his or her interaction with certain conditions inherent in human existence called givens (such as freedom and associated responsibility, death, isolation, and meaninglessness). A confrontation with any of the aforementioned conditions fills a client with a type of dread commonly referred to as existential anxiety. This anxiety is thought to reduce physical, psychological, social, and spiritual awareness, which may lead to significant long-term consequences.

**Psychoanalytic psychotherapy** is a form of clinical practice which is based on psychoanalytic theory and principles and focuses on increasing self-understanding and deepening insight into emotional issues and conflicts which underlie the presenting difficulties. Treatment includes exploring unconscious thoughts and feelings and understanding aspects of the relationship between a social worker and client, which may relate to underlying emotional conflicts, interpretation of defensive processes which obstruct emotional awareness, and consideration of issues related to sense of self.

*Test-Taking Strategies Applied*

Social workers must be aware of interventions which have empirically been found to be effective with client problems or diagnoses. This is a recall question, testing knowledge of therapeutic models. In order to answer correctly, familiarity with the approaches listed as response choices is needed. In the scenario, the client would like to reduce the compulsive behavior which results from his obsessive thoughts. Existential and psychodynamic psychotherapy are based on the belief that client problems are caused by conditions or conflicts in human life. OCD and Tic Disorder are neuropsychiatric, making these two approaches not correct.

SFBT is based on the belief that problems do not happen all the time and studying the times when problems are less severe or absent can assist clients to see what life will be like when the goal is accomplished and the problem is gone. *It requires clients to take control of their situation* and focuses on developing greater awareness and repeating the successful things they do when the problem is less severe. OCD and Tic Disorders are pervasive, with behaviors seen as uncontrollable to clients. Behavior management, as opposed to insight-oriented or brief therapy, is much more effective.

*Question Assesses*

Content Area II—Assessment, Diagnosis, and Treatment Planning; Treatment Planning (Competency); The Criteria Used in the Selection of

Intervention/Treatment Modalities (e.g., Client/Client System Abilities, Culture, Life Stage) (KSA)

### 83. B

*Rationale*

Prevention includes a wide range of activities—known as "interventions"—aimed at reducing risks or threats. **Primary, secondary, and tertiary prevention** are three terms that describe the range of possibilities.

**Primary prevention** aims to prevent disease or injury before it ever occurs. This is done by preventing exposures to hazards that cause disease or injury, altering unhealthy or unsafe behaviors that can lead to disease or injury, and increasing resistance to disease or injury should exposure occur.

**Secondary prevention** aims to reduce the impact of a disease or injury that has already occurred. This is done by detecting and treating disease or injury as soon as possible to halt or slow its progress, encouraging personal strategies to prevent reinjury or recurrence, and implementing programs to return clients to their original health and function to prevent long-term problems.

**Tertiary prevention** aims to soften the impact of an ongoing illness or injury that has lasting effects. This is done by helping clients manage long-term, often-complex health problems and injuries (e.g., chronic diseases, permanent impairments) in order to improve as much as possible their ability to function, their quality of life, and their life expectancy.

*Test-Taking Strategies Applied*

The question contains a qualifying word—BEST. In the scenario, the client "is very worried about ensuring that the drug administration does not adversely affect her current routine." Her concern is the presenting problem and the social worker can assist the client to better understand what will be required by ensuring that she receives accurate and complete information about what is required. Psychoeducation is often used to help clients learn how to slow the progression of a disease or limit its long-term impacts through diet, medication, or exercise. She is in need of a tertiary prevention intervention.

The client may be worrying unnecessarily. Thus, providing information is the most effective strategy for determining whether there will be any impact to her current daily routine.

There is nothing in the scenario that indicates that the client needs help navigating multiple service delivery systems, thereby making the provision of case management futile at this point. The client also does not need to make behavioral changes, so interventions aimed at such are not warranted. Lastly, psychotherapy aims to facilitate change and confront barriers that interfere with emotional and mental well-being. Support may be needed to assist the client while she understands changes in her medication regimen, but there is no indication that she needs psychotherapy due to her most pressing concern.

*Question Assesses*

Content Area III—Psychotherapy, Clinical Interventions, and Case Management; The Intervention Process (Competency); Primary, Secondary, and Tertiary Prevention Strategies (KSA)

### 84. C

*Rationale*

Social workers often serve as consultants for problems related to clients, services, organizations, and/or policies. **Consultation** is the utilization of an "expert" in a specific area to assist with developing a solution to the issue. Consultation is usually time limited and the advice of consultants can be used or not used by those who have formal decision-making power. *Although consultants do not have formal authority within agencies, they have informal authority as "experts" based upon their expertise and skill.* Formal authority comes from one's official position with agencies, with those at the top of organizational structures having more formal authority than those at the bottom.

*Test-Taking Strategies Applied*

As the social worker in the scenario is a consultant, the source of his or her authority comes from professional expertise. This knowledge base evolves from both education and experience in the field. The incorrect answers are not sources of authority based on the social worker's role. The social worker is not an employee of the agency. There is no evidence that the consultation was mandated by the funder, just that funding data was used to illuminate the problem. Lastly, a consultant has no official position within an organizational structure. Thus, consultants usually do not appear on organizational charts or are depicted with dotted lines to show that they are advisory and not within the hierarchical structures.

*Question Assesses*

Content Area III—Psychotherapy, Clinical Interventions, and Case Management; Consultation and Interdisciplinary Collaboration

(Competency); Consultation Approaches (e.g., Referrals to Specialists) (KSA)

### 85. C

*Rationale*

Separation anxiety is normal in very young children (those between 8 and 14 months old). When this fear occurs in a child over age 6 years, is excessive, and lasts longer than 4 weeks, the child may have Separation Anxiety Disorder.

**Separation Anxiety Disorder** is a condition in which a child becomes fearful and nervous when away from home or separated from a parent or other caregiver. Some children also develop physical symptoms, such as headaches or stomachaches, at the thought of being separated. The fear of separation causes great distress to the child and may interfere with the child's normal activities, such as going to school or playing with other children.

Most mild cases of Separation Anxiety Disorder do not need medical treatment. In more severe cases, or when the child refuses to go to school, treatment may be needed. The **goals of treatment** include reducing anxiety in the child and developing a sense of security in the child and the caregivers. Treatment options include psychotherapy to help the child tolerate being separated from the caregiver without the separation causing distress or interfering with function. A type of therapy called **cognitive behavioral therapy** works to reshape the child's thinking (cognition) so that the child's behavior becomes more appropriate. Family therapy also may help teach the family about the disorder and help family members better support the child during periods of anxiety. Antidepressant or other antianxiety medications may be used to treat severe cases of Separation Anxiety Disorder.

There is no known way to prevent Separation Anxiety Disorder, but recognizing and acting on symptoms when they appear can minimize distress and prevent problems associated with not going to school. In addition, reinforcing a child's independence and self-esteem through support and approval may help prevent future episodes of anxiety.

*Test-Taking Strategies Applied*

The root cause of the problems experienced by the mother is her daughter's separation anxiety. Thus, appropriate intervention must focus on assisting the child to return to normal developmental functioning. A child with separation anxiety needs to be able to tolerate normal separation from caregivers without distress or impairment of functioning. A child with concomitant school refusal should return to school as quickly as possible. As the mother is the client, intervention should focus on helping her deal with the child's symptoms while seeking treatment for the daughter.

Suggesting that the woman tell her employer about her situation will not help to address the underlying problem. Job performance will continue to be impacted until the child's anxiety is managed. It is helpful for the woman not to feel isolated and understand that her emotional reaction is typical. However, this acknowledgment will also not address the problem. Placing the child on homebound instruction is contraindicated because it may prolong the child's symptoms and increase the severity of symptoms.

The question uses a qualifying word—MOST—to highlight that some of the response choices may be helpful to the client, but the correct answer is the one focused on addressing the presenting problem.

### Question Assesses

Content Area II—Assessment, Diagnosis, and Treatment Planning; Treatment Planning (Competency); The Criteria Used in the Selection of Intervention/Treatment Modalities (e.g., Client/Client System Abilities, Culture, Life Stage) (KSA)

### 86. D

### Rationale

Child development literature draws attention to the **importance of peer relationships in social development**, especially in adolescence, when peers may facilitate each other's antisocial behavior. It has often been assumed that peers are less important in early childhood, when relationships with family members are more influential. However, research shows clearly that even infants spend time with peers, and that some 3- and 4-year-olds are already having trouble being accepted by their peers.

Most infants and toddlers meet peers on a regular basis, and some experience long-lasting relationships with particular peers that start at birth. By 6 months of age, infants can communicate with other infants by smiling, touching, and babbling. In the second year of life, they show both prosocial and aggressive behavior with peers, with some toddlers clearly being more aggressive than others.

Although many investigators have described early peer relations, relatively little attention has been paid to the emotional, cognitive, and behavioral skills that underlie the ability to interact harmoniously with peers. Early peer relations depend on the following skills that develop during the first 2 years of life: (a) managing joint attention, (b) regulating emotions, (c) inhibiting impulses, (d) imitating another's actions, (e) understanding cause-and-effect relationships, and (f) linguistic competence.

Peer acceptance is affected by relationships at home with parents and siblings, the parents' own relationships, and families' levels of social support. However, peer acceptance is most directly affected by children's own behavior. Studies show that highly aggressive children are not accepted by their peers, but this may depend on gender.

There are clear links between very early peer relations and those that occur later in childhood. Peer acceptance in early childhood is a predictor of later peer relations. Children who were without friends in kindergarten were still having difficulties dealing with peers at the age of 10.

Thus, peers play important roles in children's lives. In fact, experiences in the first 2 or 3 years of life have implications for children's acceptance by their classmates in nursery school and the later school years. Children who are competent with peers at an early age, and those who show prosocial behavior, are particularly likely to be accepted by their peers.

## Test-Taking Strategies Applied

Answering the question correctly requires knowledge of the policy mandate to mainstream as per the Individuals with Disabilities Education Act (IDEA). Mainstreaming means that schools put children with unique learning needs into classrooms with peers who do not have special needs. Students who are mainstreamed have higher self-esteem and develop better social skills. Their nondisability peers also become more tolerant and accepting.

Understanding that the goal of mainstreaming is to increase peer interactions with nondisabled peers will assist with selecting the correct answer. The age at which peer interactions start and the influences of peer relationships are not directly related to the aims of mainstreaming.

Family support, parental interactions, and sibling relationships are also not directly related to greater exposure with nondisabled peers in school settings. The idea that interactions lead to peer friendships which have positive effects is the most salient reason for inclusion of those with unique learning needs into classrooms with other students who are classified as disabled.

## Question Assesses

Content Area I—Human Development, Diversity, and Behavior in the Environment; Human Growth and Development (Competency);

Theories of Human Development Throughout the Lifespan (e.g., Physical, Social, Emotional, Cognitive, Behavioral) (KSA)

### 87. B

*Rationale*

Selective serotonin reuptake inhibitors and other second-generation antidepressants have become common therapeutic options for the management of depression. Although these medications are effective, they frequently cause sexual adverse effects that can impact clients' quality of life, thus ultimately leading to nonadherence in many cases.

Clients must be educated about these possible adverse effects. Assessments of sexual functioning before the medication (baseline) and during its administration (treatment) should occur to monitor for these effects. Management strategies include watchful waiting, dosage reduction, drug holidays, switching antidepressants, and use of add-on medications.

*Test-Taking Strategies Applied*

The question contains a qualifying word—MOST—that requires social workers to select the response choice which is likely the cause. When MOST is used as a qualifying word, other appropriate and possible answers will be listed. It is necessary to take all the information provided and pick the probable cause of the sexual dysfunction.

There is no indication of relationship problems between the client and his wife in the scenario. While sexual dysfunction can occur due to physical changes associated with age, his erectile dysfunction coincided with his taking of antidepressant medication. Antidepressants are known to cause sexual problems, so his issue is likely a side effect of his medication.

The last response choice does not relate to the problem presented and is not a cause of his dysfunction.

*Question Assesses*

Content Area II—Assessment, Diagnosis, and Treatment Planning; Biopsychosocial History and Collateral Data (Competency); The Indicators of Sexual Dysfunction (KSA)

### 88. B

*Rationale*

**Observation** is probably the most common and the simplest method of data collection. It does not require much technical knowledge. Although scientific controlled observation requires some technical skill, it is still often easier than other methods.

There are many advantages and disadvantages to observation. With other data collection methods like interviewing and surveying, information is provided by clients so there is no means to examine the accuracy of the data supplied. But in observation, social workers can directly check the accuracy by seeing it happening. Thus, data collected through observation is often more reliable than that collected through interviewing or surveying. Observation can also be useful in learning about phenomena that occur for persons who are not capable of giving verbal information about their behavior, feelings, and activities simply for the reason that they cannot speak, such as infants. Observation is indispensable in finding out information on infants who can neither understand questions by social workers nor express themselves verbally.

However, some occurrences may not be open to observation. Personal behaviors are usually done when others are not present. In addition, much can occur when observers are not present. One is also not sure that what is observed is the same as it appears to others. Two persons may judge the same phenomena differently. Lastly, observation is a time-intensive process, making it costly.

### Test-Taking Strategies Applied

The question contains a qualifying word—MOST. While there is more than one concern, the correct answer is most significant about "using this approach." Observations are costly, but the expense does not appear to be prohibitive as the social worker is doing the data collection. No additional costs are incurred.

Behavior frequency is being collected. As the behavior was modified using operant conditioning, there is likely a well-defined behavior which can be directly observed. There can be ethical issues in the choice of any therapeutic technique. However, there is no indication that unethical practices were used. There are many punishments which are not aversive, such as time out. Also, the question is asking about "this approach"—observation—not the behavioral strategy.

The scenario states that the behavior has a "high rate" or occurs frequently. It is likely that many behaviors will be occurring when the social worker is not present. The social worker will need to get information on what is happening when the client is alone or not with the social worker as the client may be acting differently in these situations. Self-monitoring or self-reports—not direct observation—can be helpful in these instances.

*Question Assesses*

Content Area II—Assessment, Diagnosis, and Treatment Planning; Biopsychosocial History and Collateral Data (Competency); The Principles of Active Listening and Observation (KSA)

## 89. D

*Rationale*

Erik Erikson maintained that personality develops in a predetermined order. He was interested in how children socialize and how this affects their sense of self. He saw personality as developing throughout the life course and looked at identity crises as the focal point for each stage of human development.

According to Erikson, there are eight stages of **psychosocial development**, with two possible outcomes. Successful completion of each stage results in a healthy personality and successful interactions with others. Failure to successfully complete a stage can result in a reduced ability to complete further stages and, therefore, a more unhealthy personality and sense of self. These stages, however, can be resolved successfully at a later time.

Industry versus inferiority occurs during childhood between the ages of 6 and 11 and is the fourth stage of psychosocial development. School and social interaction play an important role during this time of a child's life. Through social interactions, children begin to develop a sense of pride in their accomplishments and abilities. During the earlier stages, a child's interactions centered primarily on caregivers, family members, and others in their immediate household. As the school years begin, the realm of social influence increases dramatically. Friends and classmates play a role in how children progress through the industry versus inferiority stage.

At earlier stages of development, children were largely able to engage in activities for fun and to receive praise and attention. Once school begins, actual performance and skill are evaluated. Grades and feedback from educators encourage kids to pay more attention to the actual quality of their work.

During the **industry versus inferiority** stage, children become capable of performing increasingly complex tasks. As a result, they strive to master new skills. Children who are encouraged and commended by parents and teachers develop a **feeling of competence** and belief in their skills. Those who receive little or no encouragement from parents, teachers, or peers will doubt their ability to be successful.

According to Erikson, this stage is vital in developing self-confidence. During school and other social activities, children receive praise and attention for performing various tasks such as reading, writing, drawing, and solving problems. *Kids who do well in school are more likely to develop a sense of competence and confidence. They feel good about themselves and their ability to succeed.*

*Children who struggle with schoolwork may have a harder time developing these feelings of sureness. Instead, they may be left with feelings of inadequacy and inferiority.*

At this stage, it is important for both parents and teachers to offer support and encouragement. However, adults should be careful not to equate achievement with acceptance and love. Unconditional love and support from adults can help all children through this stage, but particularly those who may struggle with feelings of inferiority.

Children who are overpraised, on the other hand, might develop a sense of arrogance. Clearly, balance plays a major role at this point in development. Parents can help kids develop a sense of realistic competence by avoiding excessive praise and rewards, encouraging efforts, and helping kids develop a growth mindset. Even if children struggle in some areas of school, encouraging kids in areas in which they excel can help foster feelings of competence and achievement.

### Test-Taking Strategies Applied

The question contains a qualifying word—MOST. In order to select the correct answer, it is necessary to recall Erikson's stages of psychosocial development. The incorrect answers reflect problems associated with other psychosocial crises throughout the life course. **Trust versus mistrust** occurs in the first year of life and is the first stage. **Intimacy versus isolation** happens in young adulthood when there is a longing for long-term relationships with others. Lastly, **initiative versus guilt** begins at age 3 until age 6. In the scenario, the boy is in third grade, making him too old for this stage and appropriate for struggles associated with industry versus inferiority.

When age is included in a question, it is usually critical to selecting the correct answer. In addition, even though Erikson is not explicitly mentioned, the question asks about a "psychosocial problem." Erikson is a well-known theorist in this area and all the answers are associated with negative outcomes of his stages. Thus, his work should be used to distinguish the correct answer from the incorrect ones. Often the names of theorists are not mentioned in questions. However, reasoning using their work is essential to successfully selecting the correct answers.

*Question Assesses*

Content Area I—Human Development, Diversity, and Behavior in the Environment; Human Growth and Development (Competency); Theories of Human Development Throughout the Lifespan (e.g., Physical, Social, Emotional, Cognitive, Behavioral) (KSA)

### 90. A

*Rationale*

**Informed consent** is most often thought of in the context of the contracting stage with a client, which comes at the beginning of the professional relationship. *To be effective, informed consent should be seen as an ongoing process. Informed consent can be integrated into each session with a client, or at regular/periodic intervals throughout a professional relationship. As the goals of the relationship change, informed consent should be revisited.*

Informed consent is the process through which social workers discuss with clients the nature of the social worker/client relationship. Through informed consent, the social worker and client outline what the client can expect from the professional relationship, as well as what the social worker expects from the client's participation. Informed consent often includes a discussion of basic protocols, such as how to make or cancel appointments or the best way to contact the social worker. The process should also involve outlining what work will be done with and for the client and what expectations there are for client involvement. Integral to the informed consent process is a discussion of client confidentiality.

*Using simple language, appropriate to the developmental and language needs of the client, the social worker needs to explain to the client that he or she will generally keep information private, but there are specific instances when the social worker is required to break client confidentiality.* It is at this point that the social worker should highlight that if he or she suspects child maltreatment based on information received from the client, the social worker must break client confidentiality to make a report of the suspicion to child protective services.

In some agencies or practice settings, informed consent involves the client signing a form that acknowledges receipt of certain information. Although a written tool is a good idea, it is important that there be additional methods for ensuring informed consent. In all cases, with or without written informed consent tools, the social worker and client should discuss, face-to-face, expectations for confidentiality and when confidentiality will be breached. The social worker should use language the client can understand. As with other forms of communication with clients, it is important to ensure that the client understands what is said with regard to informed consent.

### Test-Taking Strategies Applied

The qualifying word—BEST—indicates that more than one listed answer may be informative or useful, but the correct one is that which most effectively "informs clients of the nature and expectations of the social worker/client relationship."

None of the incorrect answers speak to exchanges between social workers and clients about consent policies. They simply provide clients with, or have clients sign, written materials, which is not sufficient for informed consent. Clients should have the opportunity to ask questions and have policies explained in clear, concise ways which are easy to understand. The correct answer also acknowledges that informed consent is an ongoing process and does not just occur at intake.

### Question Assesses

Content Area IV—Professional Values and Ethics; Professional Values and Ethical Issues (Competency); The Principles and Processes of Obtaining Informed Consent (KSA)

## 91. C

### Rationale

**Object relations** is a variation of psychoanalytic theory that diverges from Sigmund Freud's belief that humans are motivated by sexual and aggressive drives, suggesting instead that humans are primarily motivated by the need for contact with others—the need to form relationships. The aim of a clinical social worker using object relations theory is to help a client in therapy uncover early mental images that may contribute to any present difficulties in relationships with others and adjust them in ways that may improve interpersonal functioning. In the context of object relations theory, the term "objects" refers not to inanimate entities but to significant others with whom a client relates, usually a mother, father, or primary caregiver. In some cases, an object may also be used to refer to a part of a person, such as a mother's breast, or to the mental representations of significant others.

Object relations theorists stress the importance of early family interactions, primarily the mother–infant relationship, in personality development. It is believed that infants form mental representations of themselves in relation to others and that these internal images significantly influence interpersonal relationships later in life. Since relationships are at the center of object relations theory, the client–social worker alliance is important to the success of therapy.

Internal objects are formed during infancy through repeated experiences with one's caregiver. The images do not necessarily reflect reality but are subjectively constructed by an infant's limited cognitive abilities. In healthy development, these mental representations evolve over time; in unhealthy development, they remain at an immature level. The internal images have enduring qualities and serve as templates for future relationships.

Central to object relations theory is the notion of **splitting**, which can be described as *the mental separation of objects into "good" and "bad" parts. This is a process of "psychic economy" whereby a complex situation is simplified by separation rather than resolution.*

Infants first experience splitting in their relationship with the primary caregiver: The caregiver is "good" when all the infant's needs are satisfied and "bad" when they are not. Initially, these two aspects of the object (the caregiver) are separated in the mind of the infant, and a similar process occurs as the infant comes to perceive good and bad parts of the self. If the mother is able to satisfactorily meet the needs of the infant or—in the language of object relations—if the mother is "good enough," then the child begins to merge both aspects of the mother, and by extension the self, into an integrated whole.

**Isolation** is a state of separation from others. Intimacy versus isolation is one of Erikson's psychosocial stages of development which occurs in early adulthood.

**Resistance** is an attempt to prevent action or refuse to accept something new. Clients often display resistance during the problem-solving process as they are not ready to change or are fearful about addressing long-standing issues in their lives.

**Rapprochement** is broadly defined as the reestablishment of happy relationships. It is also the name of a subphase in object relations theory which occurs when a child is about 15 months old and once again becomes close to the primary caregiver (usually the mother), though he or she is beginning to differentiate oneself. Physical mobility demonstrates psychic separateness, but the toddler may become tentative, wanting the caregiver to be in sight so that exploration can occur.

### Test-Taking Strategies Applied

This is a recall question which relies on social workers understanding object relations theory. Questions on the examination may focus on general underlying principles of theories, as well as key terms. It is not necessary to memorize terms, but being able to identify them when they are listed is essential. Often ones that look correct, just based on their wording, are not. For example, in this question, "isolation" may seem to fit as it implies separation. However, it is not the correct answer as "splitting" is the formal name of this process. Thus, social workers must know specific terms associated with all the major theories studied.

*Question Assesses*

Content Area III—Psychotherapy, Clinical Interventions, and Case Management; The Intervention Process (Competency); Psychoanalytic and Psychodynamic Approaches (KSA)

### 92. C

*Rationale*

When there is **addiction in a family system**, members typically adapt to the person with the substance use problem by taking on roles that help reduce stress, deal with uncertainty, and allow the family to function. There is a problem with taking on these roles. While they tend to reduce stress, they allow the member with the addiction to continue his or her behavior. The following are roles that family members often take on in these relationships.

**The Enabler:** The enabler is a family member who steps in and protects the addict from the consequences of his or her behavior. The motivation for this may not be just to protect the addict, but to prevent embarrassment, reduce anxiety, avoid conflict, or maintain some control over a difficult situation. The enabler may try to clean up the messes caused by the addict and make excuses for him or her, thus minimizing the consequences of addiction.

**The Mascot:** The mascot attempts to use humor as a means to escape from the pain of the problems caused by addiction. He or she will often act out by "clowning around," cracking jokes or making light of serious situations. While the mascot can certainly help lighten up a desperate situation, the real intent is to ease tension in order to keep the peace. Many comedians come from dysfunctional homes.

**The Scapegoat:** *The scapegoat is a family member who creates other problems and concerns in order to deflect attention away from the real issue.* This can be through misbehavior, bad grades, or his/her own substance abuse. Oftentimes, the scapegoat is very successful at distracting the family and others from the addiction.

**The Lost Child:** The lost child is a family member who appears to be ignoring the problem completely. There could be a fight, with yelling and screaming, and the lost child will be absent or secluded from the situation. He or she is often perceived as the "good" child because much time is spent alone with books or involved in isolated activities. While the lost child will not be successful at drawing attention away from the family problem, he or she is able to avoid stress personally.

**The Hero:** The hero is a family member who attempts to draw attention away from the addict by excelling, performing well, and generally being "too good to be true." The hero has a hope that somehow his or her behavior will help the addict to stop using. Additionally, the hero's performance-based behavior helps to block emotional pain and disappointment.

### Test-Taking Strategies Applied

This is a recall question about "survival" roles in families with members who have addictions. Families are organized around roles, rules, rituals, boundaries, and hierarchies. Structure serves to promote their well-being and the happiness of their members. But addiction in families distorts their structure, and family members assume roles that naturally do not belong to them. Members abandon their identities and needs and become enmeshed in the lives of those who are addicted. Each of the roles listed as response choices aims to release stress related to addiction.

The hero, like the scapegoat, attempts to draw attention away from the problem, with the former role doing so by excelling and the latter one distracting through misbehavior. The hero is not a provided response choice, so the scapegoat is the correct answer.

### Question Assesses

Content Area I—Human Development, Diversity, and Behavior in the Environment; Human Behavior in the Social Environment (Competency); Addiction Theories and Concepts (KSA)

### 93. A

### Rationale

**Disruptive Mood Dysregulation Disorder (DMDD)** is a childhood condition of extreme irritability, anger, and frequent, intense temper outbursts. DMDD symptoms go beyond being "moody" child—children with DMDD experience severe impairment that requires clinical attention. DMDD, a new diagnosis in the *DSM-5*, is characterized by severe and recurrent temper outbursts that are grossly out of proportion in intensity or duration to the situation. These occur, on average, three or more times each week for 1 year or more.

A child with DMDD experiences:

- Irritable or angry mood most of the day, nearly every day
- Severe temper outbursts (verbal or behavioral) at an average of three or more times per week that are out of keeping with the situation and the child's developmental level
- Trouble functioning due to irritability in more than one place (e.g., home, school, with peers)

To be diagnosed with DMDD, a child must have these symptoms steadily for 12 or more months.

Between outbursts, children with DMDD display a persistently irritable or angry mood, most of the day and nearly every day, that is observable by parents, teachers, or peers. A diagnosis requires the previous symptoms to be present in at least two settings (at home, at school, or with peers) for 12 or more months, and symptoms must be severe in at least one of these settings. During this period, the child must not have gone 3 or more consecutive months without symptoms.

The onset of symptoms must be before age 10, and a DMDD diagnosis should not be made for the first time before age 6 or after age 18.

While the *DSM-5* does include two diagnoses with related symptoms to DMDD, Oppositional Defiant Disorder And Bipolar Disorder, the symptoms described in DMDD are significantly different than these two diagnoses.

Oppositional Defiant Disorder is an ongoing pattern of anger-guided disobedience and hostilely defiant behavior toward authority figures that goes beyond the bounds of normal childhood behavior. While the symptoms may overlap with the criteria for DMDD, the symptom threshold for DMDD is higher since the condition is considered more severe. Thus, while most children who meet the criteria for DMDD will also meet the criteria for Oppositional Defiant Disorder, the reverse is not the case. *To avoid any artificial comorbidity of the two disorders, it is recommended that children who meet the criteria for both should only be diagnosed with DMDD.*

Bipolar Disorder also has similar symptoms. While a social worker may have been assigning a diagnosis of Bipolar Disorder to these severely irritable youth to ensure their access to treatment resources and services, these children's behaviors may not present in an *episodic way* as is the case with Bipolar Disorder. In an effort to address this issue, research was conducted comparing youth with severe nonepisodic symptoms to those with the classic presentations of Bipolar Disorder as defined in *DSM-IV*. Results of that extensive research showed that children diagnosed with Bipolar Disorder who experience constant, rather than episodic, irritability often are at risk for Major Depressive Disorder or Generalized Anxiety Disorder later in life, but not lifelong Bipolar Disorder. This finding pointed to the need for a new diagnosis for children suffering from constant, debilitating irritability. The hope is that by defining this condition more accurately, social workers will be able to improve diagnosis and care.

### Test-Taking Strategies Applied

This is a recall question which relies on social workers understanding new diagnoses in the *DSM-5*, as well as the justification for their creation. Social workers must be able to differentially diagnose, choosing one disorder over another based on the presence or severity of beliefs, attitudes, and/or behaviors.

### Question Assesses

Content Area II—Assessment, Diagnosis, and Treatment Planning; Assessment and Diagnosis (Competency); The Use of the Diagnostic and Statistical Manual of the American Psychiatric Association (KSA)

### 94. D

### Rationale

The Individuals with Disabilities Education Act (IDEA) requires that all children with disabilities be educated in the least restrictive environment (LRE) that is appropriate. The spirit of this requirement is to ensure that children are not unnecessarily removed from the regular classroom or isolated from other nondisabled children of their age.

To the maximum extent appropriate, children with disabilities, including children in public or private institutions or other care facilities, must be educated with children who are not disabled. Thus, special classes, separate schooling, or other removal of children with disabilities from the regular educational environment can only occur when the nature or severity of the disability of a child is such that education in regular classes with the use of supplementary aids and services cannot be achieved satisfactorily.

The IDEA mandates that every student with a disability should be given the opportunity to start out in a general education classroom;

if that environment does not allow for success and a more restrictive environment is deemed appropriate, then good reason must be given as to why the LRE is not working. This decision should be a main topic of discussion in Individual Education Planning (IEP) meetings.

LRE decisions are made based on children's learning needs and vary from child to child. IDEA also requires that schools provide a full continuum of services ranging from regular classrooms with support to special classes and special school placements, as needed.

### Test-Taking Strategies Applied

The scenario describes a situation where a school official has an opinion contrary to the student's legal right under IDEA. The student's needs "can be adequately met in either the regular classroom with additional supports or a separate resource room for students who require special assistance." The right to be served in the LRE should be the guiding principle in making decisions about needed level of care.

The child's preferences do not take precedent over the legal right to obtain supports in the regular classroom, so meeting with the child is not needed to resolve the presenting conflict. The guidance counselor's feelings also do not negate the rights of the child, as his or her academic needs can be met in the regular classroom with additional supports. Thus, understanding the guidance counselor's recommendations is not necessary. Lastly, suggesting ways to maintain friendships assumes that the child will be receiving instruction in a resource room, which is in violation of the IDEA.

Social workers must advocate for client rights when they are threatened or violated by others. Being knowledgeable about laws which must be followed when assessing and deciding needed level of care is critical.

### Question Assesses

Content Area II—Assessment, Diagnosis, and Treatment Planning; Assessment and Diagnosis (Competency); Placement Options Based on Assessed Level of Care (KSA)

### 95. D

### Rationale

The *DSM-5* introduces important changes in the diagnostic system for **Feeding and Eating Disorders** that improves the ability for social workers to arrive at accurate diagnoses. Perhaps the most significant improvement with the *DSM-5* is that **Binge Eating Disorder** (BED) has been moved from an appendix in the *DSM-IV* to being designated in the *DSM-5* as a full-fledged diagnosis that parallels the other main eating disorders of Anorexia and Bulimia Nervosa. In the *DSM-IV*, clients with BED would have been diagnosed with an Eating Disorder Not Otherwise Specified.

BED is defined as recurring episodes of eating significantly more food in a short period of time than most people would eat under similar circumstances, with episodes marked by feelings of lack of control. A client with BED may eat too quickly, even when he or she is not hungry. The client may have feelings of guilt, embarrassment, or disgust and may binge eat alone to hide the behavior. This disorder is associated with marked distress and occurs, on average, at least once a week over 3 months.

With this diagnosis and others, social workers must be able to understand the **differential use of therapeutic techniques**, including those which are evidence-based practices. Cognitive behavioral therapy **(CBT)**—alone or in combination with **medication**—is effective in reducing binge eating. It is unclear which medications provide the greatest benefit in terms of binge eating remission; however, they do facilitate short-term weight loss in clients who are overweight due to BED. In addition to reducing binge eating, CBT can improve related psychological comorbidities.

*Test-Taking Strategies Applied*

This is a recall question about different intervention techniques and their appropriate usage. The incorrect response choices contain legitimate social work treatments, but are not best suited for the diagnosed problem.

**Psychoanalysis** is a form of psychotherapy to treat clients who have a range of mild to moderate chronic life problems. It is related to a specific body of theories about the relationships between conscious and unconscious mental processes. The purpose is to bring unconscious mental material and processes into full consciousness so that clients can gain more control over their lives.

**Ego psychology** is psychoanalysis that attempts to hypothesize how the ego functions and can cause harm to psychopathology. It is rooted in the belief that healthy ego is independent of any mental divergence and is inclusive of autonomous ego functions like reality-testing and memory. Thus, it should function without any interruption of any emotional conflict. Ego psychology aims at increasing the conflict-free circle of ego functioning. This work will bring about better adaptation and also an effective regulation of environment and ego.

**Task-centered treatment** involves working closely with clients to establish distinct and achievable goals based on an agreed-upon presenting problem(s). Clients and social workers collaborate on devising tasks to work on those target problems which are memorialized in contracts that contain the target problems, tasks to be implemented by both clients and social workers to address the target problems, and overall goals of the treatment. Task-centered treatment emphasizes client preferences by asking clients what they most want to work on to address their problems. This approach involves working briefly with clients, typically for 8 to 12 sessions over the course of a 6-month period.

*Question Assesses*

Content Area II—Assessment, Diagnosis, and Treatment Planning; Treatment Planning (Competency); The Criteria Used in the Selection of Intervention/Treatment Modalities (e.g., Client/Client System Abilities, Culture, Life Stage) (KSA)

### 96. A

*Rationale*

**Major Neurocognitive Disorder (formerly called Dementia)** and **Delirium** are prevalent mental disorders in those who are elderly. While Major Neurocognitive Disorder is prevalent in the community, hospitals, and nursing homes, Delirium is seen most often in acute care hospitals. It is imperative that social workers be adept at recognizing, evaluating, and managing clients with these syndromes.

The differential diagnosis hinges on a careful clinical evaluation. The first step is to recognize which of the syndromes is present. Major Neurocognitive Disorder is defined by a chronic loss of intellectual or cognitive function of sufficient severity to interfere with social or occupational function. Delirium is an acute disturbance of consciousness marked by an attention deficit and a change in cognitive function. It is important to recognize that these syndromes are not mutually exclusive, as Major Neurocognitive Disorder can coexist with Delirium and other disorders, such as Major Depressive Disorder.

When a client presents with new cognitive complaints, the first consideration is whether this condition represents Major Neurocognitive Disorder or Delirium. Generally, a major difference between Delirium and Major Neurocognitive Disorder is the rapidity of onset: Progression of symptoms is usually acute in Delirium, rather than insidious and slowly progressive as in Major Neurocognitive Disorder. Additionally, Delirium may cause disturbance in the level of consciousness, attention, and vital signs, whereas Major Neurocognitive Disorder should not. The *DSM-5* defines Delirium as a disturbance from baseline in attention, awareness, and cognition over a short period of time, with fluctuation in severity throughout the day. These changes must not be explained by another Neurocognitive Disorder, and there must be evidence that the condition is not explained by another condition such as infection or Substance Intoxication and Withdrawal.

### Test-Taking Strategies Applied

This is a recall question about the differences between Delirium and Major Neurocognitive Disorder. Social workers must be able to make differential diagnoses as many of the response choices related to the competency of assessment and diagnosis have similar symptoms. Picking among them will require knowing how disorders differ from one another.

A significant difference that is used to diagnose Delirium is the rapid onset of symptoms. Major Neurocognitive Disorder causes a more gradual progression of impairment. Alertness and orientation also fluctuate and are variable throughout the day when a client has Delirium. In Major Neurocognitive Disorder, a client may have issues with alertness or orientation, but his or her symptomology should be stable throughout the day.

The severity of the memory loss, family history, and the impact of the symptoms are not the best methods "to differentiate" between these diagnoses.

### Question Assesses

Content Area II—Assessment, Diagnosis, and Treatment Planning; Biopsychosocial History and Collateral Data (Competency); Symptoms of Neurologic and Organic Disorders (KSA)

### 97. C

### Rationale

A **functional behavior assessment** is a comprehensive and individualized strategy to identify the purpose or function of a client's problem behavior(s), develop and implement a plan to modify variables that maintain the problem behavior, and teach appropriate replacement behaviors using positive interventions. While there are a variety of techniques available to conduct a functional behavioral assessment, the first step in the process, regardless of technique, is to define the behavior in concrete terms.

Before a functional behavioral plan can be implemented, it is necessary to pinpoint the behavior causing problems and to define that behavior in concrete terms that are easy to communicate and simple to measure and record. Behavior must be in specific, observable, and measurable terms. Simply stating that a client is aggressive is too vague.

Instead, for example, a social worker should specify that a client pokes, hits, and kicks other students with her feet or hands during lunch period.

It may be necessary to carefully and objectively observe client behavior in different settings and during different types of activities, and to conduct interviews with others in order to pinpoint the specific characteristics of a behavior. Once a problem behavior has been defined concretely, it is possible to devise a strategy for determining the functions of this behavior.

### Test-Taking Strategies Applied

The question contains a qualifying word—FIRST. While there may be more than one appropriate action by a social worker listed, the correct answer is the initial step in conducting a functional behavioral assessment. Determining why intervention is needed now and explaining the limits of confidentiality occur during engagement with a client. Engagement occurs prior to assessment in the problem-solving process. However, the question is asking about the first action taken "when completing a functional behavioral assessment"—not ever with a client. When doing a functional behavioral assessment, a problem behavior is defined in measurable terms; data is collected and analyzed; a hypothesis is formulated; and an intervention plan is developed, implemented, and monitored, respectively. Thus, the first action taken by a social worker is to define a problem behavior in measurable terms. Identifying antecedents may be important if an operant approach is being used, but this action would occur after the behavior has been defined and data has been collected.

### Question Assesses

Content Area II—Assessment, Diagnosis, and Treatment Planning; Biopsychosocial History and Collateral Data (Competency); Techniques and Instruments Used to Assess Clients/Client Systems (KSA)

### 98. A

### Rationale

**Shared power** views clients as experts on their lives, cultures, dreams, experiences, and goals. This perspective mandates that social workers assume power only over the limited activities in which they are trained while clients retain power to direct the work.

Often shifting views on expertise and interest in sharing power do not come easily. In the United States, there is a strong socialization to value expertise. Thus, social workers' values and contributions are seen through the lens of expertise. Social workers are educated and socialized in professional programs to become respected members of a profession. They are often pushed to adopt "expert" roles.

Additionally, some clients may want social workers to be experts on their lives and relationships—just as they want doctors to dictate their medical care. Adopting the "expert" role can obscure client ownership or participation in the work.

Most social work services are delivered in agency settings. These settings, which are traditionally operated with "top down" approaches, place service recipients at the bottom of hierarchies with little say in many decisions.

Social workers must recognize that the only experts on experiences are those who have lived them. Social workers honor this wisdom by sharing power within therapeutic relationships. Systems that rely on expertise can be humiliating, insulting, or patronizing and inspire disillusionment in those served.

### Test-Taking Strategies Applied

The question contains a qualifying word—NOT—that requires social workers to select the response choice which is not a threat to shared power. When NOT is used as a qualifying word, it is often helpful to remove it from the question and eliminate the three response choices which are threats. This approach will leave the one response choice which is NOT a threat to having shared power with clients.

While objectivity is important in social work practice, it is not directly related to shared power which views clients as experts in their lives. Objectivity should not be used to justify beliefs that clients cannot solve their own problems.

### Question Assesses

Content Area III—Psychotherapy, Clinical Interventions, and Case Management; Therapeutic Relationship (Competency); The Dynamics of Power and Transparency in the Social Worker–Client/Client System Relationship (KSA)

### 99. C

### Rationale

**Behavior modification** is the generic term given to any process derived from **learning theory** where the goal is to change client behavior. To understand behavior modification, it is necessary to understand the two main concepts that it is based on: classical and operant conditioning.

**Classical conditioning** refers to the pairing of naturally occurring stimulus-response chains with other stimuli in order to produce a similar response. **Operant conditioning** is recognition that behaviors have antecedents and consequences—and are increased or decreased by reinforcement or punishment, respectively.

**Biofeedback** is the process of learning to voluntarily influence physiological processes by making changes in cognition. It provides a visible and experiential demonstration of the mind–body connection. Biofeedback is also a therapeutic tool to facilitate learning self-regulation of autonomic functions for improving health.

**Modeling** is learning by observing or imitating. There are different types of modeling techniques to assist learners.

**Shaping** refers to the reinforcement of behaviors that approximate or come close to desired new behaviors. The steps involved are often called successive approximations because they successively approximate or get closer and closer to desired behaviors. This technique works well for phobias and anxiety-related disorders as the process of shaping can involve the creation of a hierarchy ranging from the least feared situation to the most feared situation. Rewards to greater incremental exposure are provided as a means to confront fears.

**Flooding** is a form of behavior therapy based on the principles of respondent conditioning. It is sometimes referred to as exposure therapy or prolonged exposure therapy. As a psychotherapeutic technique, it is used to treat phobia and Anxiety Disorders including Posttraumatic Stress Disorder. It works by exposing clients to their painful memories, with the goal of reintegrating their repressed emotions with their current awareness.

### Test-Taking Strategies Applied

The question requires recall knowledge about behavioral techniques. Shaping is used when it may be, or has been, difficult to achieve a goal or demonstrate a behavior. Shaping allows the goal or behavior to be achieved in steps, each reinforced positively. After a client achieves each successive step of the behavior or goal, a reward is received and the next one is presented until the desired end result is reached. If there is difficulty in a client reaching the steps, they should be broken down into smaller increments.

While behaviors may be broken down when they are modeled, there is no mention of the social worker demonstrating them or the client observing or imitating the social worker in the scenario presented.

*Question Assesses*

Content Area I—Human Development, Diversity, and Behavior in the Environment; Human Growth and Development (Competency); Theories of Human Development Throughout the Lifespan (e.g., Physical, Social, Emotional, Cognitive, Behavioral) (KSA)

### 100. C

*Rationale*

The **dynamics of loss, separation, and grief** are different for all who experience them. However, the needs of those who are grieving are universal. Unlike "stages of grief," these needs of mourning are not orderly or predictable. Clients will address each need when ready to do so, sometimes working on more than one need at a time. These needs include:

- *Accepting the reality of the death*
  Whether the death was sudden or anticipated, acknowledging the full reality of the loss can take weeks, months, and even years.

- *Feeling the pain of the loss*
  It is easier to avoid or deny the pain of grief than to confront it. Yet, it is only reconciled through feeling the pain associated with the loss.

- *Remembering the person who died*
  Mourning involves allowing the pursuit of the relationship, instead of trying to take memories away.

- *Developing a new self-identity*
  Part of self-identity comes from relationships with others. When someone dies, the self-identity of those involved in these relationships naturally changes.

- *Searching for meaning*
  When someone dies, it is natural to question the meaning of life as death is a reminder of one's lack of control.

- *Receiving ongoing support from others*
  The quality and quantity of support obtained from others has a major influence on the capacity to heal. Drawing on the experiences and encouragement of others is not a weakness but a healthy human need.

*Test-Taking Strategies Applied*

This question requires knowledge about the dynamics of loss, separation, and grief. Even if the correct answer is not readily apparent, it can be identified by eliminating the incorrect answers. Individuals do not sequentially move through stages of grieving, making the first response choice incorrect. Often people think that they are helpful by removing pictures of those who have died or not speaking about them. They try to keep those grieving busy. However, it is important to keep memories alive while embracing the reality of the death by talking to others, making the second answer incorrect. The last response choice does not recognize that death will likely require the adoption of new roles, leading to identity change. Many people find positive aspects of their changed self-identities and a renewed self-confidence which results in their new roles.

*Question Assesses*

Content Area I—Human Development, Diversity, and Behavior in the Environment; Human Growth and Development (Competency); The Dynamics and Effects of Loss, Separation, and Grief (KSA)

### 101. D

*Rationale*

Social workers must ensure that they do not engage in **dual or multiple relationships** that may impact on the treatment of clients. *Dual or multiple relationships occur when social workers relate to clients in more than one relationship, whether professional, social, or business. Dual or multiple relationships can occur simultaneously or consecutively.*

Social workers should be alert to, and avoid, conflicts of interest that interfere with the exercise of professional discretion and impartial judgment. Social workers should inform clients when a real or potential conflict of interest arises and take reasonable steps to resolve the issue in a manner that makes clients' interests primary and protects clients' interests to the greatest extent possible. In some cases, protecting clients' interests may require termination of the professional relationship with proper referral of clients. Social workers should not take unfair advantage of any professional relationship or exploit others to further their personal, religious, political, or business interests.

Social workers should not engage in dual or multiple relationships with clients or former clients in which there is a risk of exploitation or potential harm to a client. In instances when dual or multiple relationships are unavoidable, social workers should take steps to protect clients and are responsible for setting clear, appropriate, and culturally sensitive boundaries.

*Test-Taking Strategies Applied*

The scenario suggests that a former client would like to enter into a new relationship with a social worker. While this new relationship is professional in nature, it still reflects the existence of a dual relationship. While perhaps not readily apparent, the former client may be harmed by this relationship with the social worker. For example, the client may need treatment again in the future. Being a co-facilitator with the social worker would preclude him or her from providing services, thereby eliminating the availability of a clinical support for the former client if needed. In addition, the client may personalize or feel that examples provided by the social worker during group sessions relate to her own service provision. While the former client is not currently receiving services from the social worker, dual or multiple relationships can occur consecutively such as described in the scenario.

Co-facilitating, even for a short time, would be inappropriate. In addition, assisting the former client in preparing for the group is also problematic. The former client may experience anxiety during this process and confuse the social worker's support with a therapeutic alliance. It is best for the social worker to keep involvement, even encouragement, to a minimum.

*Question Assesses*

Content Area IV—Professional Values and Ethics; Professional Values and Ethical Issues (Competency); Ethical Issues Related to Dual Relationships (KSA)

### 102. C

*Rationale*

The function of **silence**, like its meaning, is culturally defined. There are vast **differences in culture, race, and/or ethnicity** with regard to its use. It has a "linkage" function in that it can bind people together as well as isolate. Being silent with others can indicate rapport, respect, and comfort as it acknowledges solidarity or that no conversation is needed. Silence can also have an "affecting" function, meaning that it has the power to affect others for both good and ill. Silence can be interpreted as indifference, causing negative feelings by others who observe it. Conversely, it can also be seen as a sign of respect, viewed positively.

Assumptions should not be made that those who are silent are not benefitting from others' participation or not actively engaged. For some, silence is seen as an opportunity given to others to speak or express their ideas. This dialogue by others mutually benefits those who do not verbalize. Silence also can indicate assent—there may be no need to verbally affirm what is said as remaining quiet is seen as having the same effect. Silence may be viewed as a way to retain harmony among the group.

Silence can be seen as a way to agree with others without vocalizing. This indirect form of communication is more common among some cultures, including those who are Asian. In addition, some cultures are more collectivist, placing the views of larger groups as more important than those of individual members. Thus, remaining silent is seen as a sign of respect even when having an opposing view. Dissenting opinions are viewed as having possible negative repercussions for the work of the overall group, which is prioritized.

### Test-Taking Strategies Applied

In the scenario, there is no indication of the race, culture, and/or ethnicity of other group members. However, the recent immigration of the youth may have been mentioned as an indication that her participation may be influenced by different cultural, racial, and/or ethnic norms. Some races, cultures, and/or ethnicities are more dominant and pervasive than others. This influences how people in both dominant and minority cultures interact; this, in turn, can impact on a group's interactions. It is the social worker's job as facilitator to encourage participation and challenge behavior which inhibits it. The facilitator is not responsible for what a member chooses to say or withhold in a group—clients should not be forced to participate. *What a social worker can and must do is create an environment in the group where clients can choose to contribute and where it is safe for them to do so.* Thus, a social worker must challenge and dilute any negative impacts of prejudice which may arise in the group due to differences in communication styles. Ensuring that any negative effects of social prejudice are not tolerated will create a "safe space" where group members can choose to express their opinions if they wish.

### Question Assesses

Content Area I—Human Development, Diversity, and Behavior in the Environment; Diversity and Discrimination (Competency); The Effect of Culture, Race, and Ethnicity on Behaviors, Attitudes, and Identity (KSA)

### 103. B

*Rationale*

**Engagement** within the context of **building and maintaining helping relationships** is defined as a point at which clients view treatment as a meaningful and important process. It involves developing agreement with social workers on the goals and tasks of treatment. Engagement can also be described as the time when the therapeutic relationship or therapeutic alliance forms between social workers and clients. The engagement process is sometimes described using words like *cooperation*, *collaboration*, *participation*, or *buy in*. During the engagement process, clients' worldviews including their values, core beliefs, and ways of life are challenged in order to facilitate substantive change.

As clients realize the need to change, resistance can occur. **Resistance** to change can occur throughout the problem-solving process as it helps clients to protect the status quo. Closely related to resistance is **ambivalence**, which is a condition of both wanting and not wanting a particular change. Social workers must be alert to the forces of ambivalence and, when necessary, assist clients in working through these blocks to decision making and action. Such work involves various interviewing and therapeutic techniques, but initially it is critical that clients feel that social workers are there to help and will not be judging or giving advice.

*Test-Taking Strategies Applied*

Material in quotation marks deserves particular attention and usually relates to the answer. The client's comment may result from apprehension about the ability to make change or fear of the therapeutic process. Being reluctant to tell others about problems is typical and should not be viewed as a therapeutic issue. The client is in the beginning phase of treatment (engagement) where the goal is to build a strong helping relationship with the social worker. Ignoring the comment may send a message to the client that the articulated feelings are not important and asking about other situations distracts from the situation at hand. The best way to deal with any resistance or apprehension is by educating the client about what will happen in the future.

*Question Assesses*

Content Area III—Psychotherapy, Clinical Interventions, and Case Management; Therapeutic Relationship (Competency); The Principles and Techniques for Building and Maintaining a Helping Relationship (KSA)

### 104. C

*Rationale*

**Defense mechanisms** are psychological mechanisms aimed at reducing anxiety. They were first discussed by Sigmund Freud as part of his psychoanalytic theory and further developed by his daughter, Anna Freud. Often unconscious, defense mechanisms are used to protect clients from psychological pain or anxiety. While such mechanisms may be helpful in the short term, alleviating suffering that might otherwise incapacitate, they can easily become a substitute for addressing the underlying cause and so lead to additional problems. The solution, therefore, is to address the underlying causes of the pain these mechanisms are used to defray.

**Sublimation** is a mature type of defense mechanism where socially unacceptable impulses or idealizations are unconsciously transformed into socially acceptable actions or behavior. It causes "id" impulses to be channeled into refined and civilized behavior. Alfred Adler called sublimation "the healthy defense mechanism" because it produced socially beneficial outcomes for humanity.

*Test-Taking Strategies Applied*

This is a recall question on the defense mechanisms. It is not necessary to memorize the definitions of the defense mechanisms, but their meanings should be familiar.

Often questions on defense mechanisms include scenarios which describe clients' behavior. Thus, social workers must be able to distinguish between the defense mechanisms based on client verbalizations and actions using the situational contexts as clues.

*Question Assesses*

Content Area I—Human Development, Diversity, and Behavior in the Environment; Human Behavior in the Social Environment (Competency); Psychological Defense Mechanisms and Their Effects on Behavior and Relationships (KSA)

### 105. C

*Rationale*

**Defense mechanisms** are psychological mechanisms aimed at reducing anxiety. They were first discussed by Sigmund Freud as part of his psychoanalytic theory and further developed by his daughter, Anna Freud. Often unconscious, defense mechanisms are used to protect clients from psychological pain or anxiety. While such mechanisms may be helpful in the short term, alleviating suffering that might otherwise incapacitate, they can easily become a substitute for addressing the underlying cause and so lead to additional problems. The solution, therefore, is to address the underlying causes of the pain these mechanisms are used to defray.

**Conversion** is a defense mechanism which occurs when cognitive tensions manifest themselves in physical symptoms. The symptom may be symbolic and dramatic and often acts as a communication about the situation. Extreme symptoms may include paralysis, blindness, deafness, becoming mute, or having a seizure. Lesser symptoms include tiredness, headaches, and twitches. For example, a client's arm becomes suddenly paralyzed after he or she has been threatening to hit someone else.

Conversion is different from psychosomatic disorders where real health changes are seen (such as the appearance of ulcers). It also is more than malingering, where conscious exaggeration of reported symptoms is used to gain attention. With time, symptoms will go away, especially if clients' stress is reduced, such as by taking them away from the initial, anxiety-provoking situations.

## Test-Taking Strategies Applied

This is a recall question on the defense mechanisms. It is not necessary to memorize the definitions of the defense mechanisms, but their names should be familiar. The correct answer could have been obtained simply by recognizing that conversion was a defense mechanism.

Often questions on defense mechanisms include scenarios which describe clients' behavior. Thus, social workers must be able to distinguish between the defense mechanisms based on client verbalizations and actions using the situational contexts as clues.

## Question Assesses

Content Area I—Human Development, Diversity, and Behavior in the Environment; Human Behavior in the Social Environment (Competency); Psychological Defense Mechanisms and Their Effects on Behavior and Relationships (KSA)

## 106. C

### Rationale

**Crises** are defined as an acute disruption of psychological homeostasis in which a client's usual coping mechanisms fail and there exists evidence of distress and functional impairment. The *subjective reaction* to life experiences dictates clients' abilities to cope or function. The main cause of a crisis is a stressful, traumatic, or hazardous event, but two other conditions must be present—(a) a client's perception of the event causes considerable upset or disruption and (b) a client is unable to resolve the disruption by previously used coping skills. Thus, it is a client's subjective experience that signals whether a crisis exists as it is the way that these experiences are perceived by a client that cause a crisis. Clients can encounter life stressors (deaths, health issues, etc.), but it is only if these events are perceived as threats or beyond coping abilities that crises occur.

### Test-Taking Strategies Applied

The question requires knowledge about the **difference between subjective and objective data** in assessment and treatment planning. While all of the response choices may be helpful in gathering information relevant to a client's state, a crisis is a subjective experience. Many clients experience adversity and cope. Only the correct response choice involves speaking with the client directly to understand her feelings about recent events. Two incorrect answers involve reviewing or obtaining objective, not subjective, information related to her physical/neurological condition. The remaining incorrect response choice relies on speaking to collaterals whose views about the current happenings may be different, and are less relevant, than the client's.

### Question Assesses

Content Area II—Assessment, Diagnosis, and Treatment Planning; Assessment and Diagnosis (Competency); Biopsychosocial Responses to Illness and Disability (KSA)

### 107. A

### Rationale

**Cyclothymic Disorder** is a rare mood disorder which describes clients who experience mood cycling over a 2-year period, but have not met the diagnostic criteria for Bipolar I, Bipolar II, or Depressive Disorder. There is debate if Cyclothymic Disorder is a discrete disease process, a temperamental variation, or a premorbid syndrome for Bipolar I or II, as many clients with Cyclothymic Disorder will develop one of these conditions.

According to the *DSM-5*, there are six diagnostic criteria, with one specifier:

**A.** For at least a 2-year period, there have been episodes of hypomanic and depressive experiences that do not meet the full *DSM-5* diagnostic criteria for Hypomania or Major Depressive Disorder.

**B.** The previous criteria had been present at least half the time during a 2-year period, with not more than 2 months of symptom remission.

**C.** There is no history of diagnoses for manic, hypomanic, or depressive episodes.

**D.** The symptoms in criterion A cannot be accounted for by a Psychotic Disorder such as Schizophrenia, Schizoaffective Disorder, Schizophreniform Disorder, or Delusional Disorder.

**E.** The symptoms cannot be accounted for by substance use or a medical condition.

**F.** The symptoms cause distress or significant impairment in social or occupational functioning.

A specifier is "with anxious distress."

The disorder can also be diagnosed in children or adolescents, but the observational period for symptoms is 1 year rather than 2. However, diagnosing in younger children should be considered with clinical skepticism, as they are prone to moodiness, emotional dysregulation, and overreacting to minor stressors as they do not yet have adult coping skills. It is a fallacy to project adult behavioral norms onto children and adolescents and pathologize age-appropriate and typical behaviors.

### Test-Taking Strategies Applied

This question requires recall about the *DSM-5* and its disorders, specifically Cyclothymic Disorder. Social workers must be aware of diagnostic criteria, including those for Bipolar and Related Disorders. The mention that the time frame is associated with the observational period for adults provides a clue that it is different for children. It may also be assumed that the observational period for adults would be longer than that required for children. Such an inference may help to eliminate some of the response choices with shorter time frames.

*Question Assesses*

Content Area II—Assessment, Diagnosis, and Treatment Planning; Assessment and Diagnosis (Competency); The Use of the Diagnostic and Statistical Manual of the American Psychiatric Association (KSA)

### 108.  B

*Rationale*

**Emotional and psychological trauma** result from extraordinarily stressful events that destroy a sense of security, making a client feel helpless and vulnerable in a dangerous world.

Traumatic experiences often involve a threat to life or safety, but any situation that leaves a client feeling overwhelmed and alone can be traumatic, even if it does not involve physical harm. It is not the objective facts that determine whether an event is traumatic, but a subjective emotional experience of the event.

A number of risk factors make clients susceptible to emotional and psychological trauma. Clients are more likely to be traumatized by a stressful experience if they are already under a heavy stress load or have recently suffered a series of losses.

Emotional and psychological trauma can be caused by one-time events or ongoing, relentless stress.

Not all potentially traumatic events lead to lasting emotional and psychological damage. Some clients rebound quickly from even the most tragic and shocking experiences. Others are devastated by experiences that, on the surface, appear to be less upsetting.

Clients are also more likely to be traumatized by a new situation if they have been traumatized before—especially if the earlier trauma occurred in childhood. Experiencing trauma in childhood can have a severe and long-lasting effect. Children who have been traumatized see the world as a frightening and dangerous place. When childhood trauma is not resolved, this fundamental sense of fear and helplessness carries over into adulthood, setting the stage for further trauma.

An event will most likely lead to emotional or psychological trauma if it happened unexpectedly; there was no preparation for it; there is a feeling of having been powerless to prevent it; it happened repeatedly; someone was intentionally cruel; and/or it happened in childhood.

*Test-Taking Strategies Applied*

The question contains a qualifying word—MOST. Emotional or psychological trauma may occur as a result of events in adulthood or those which were anticipated/preventable. However, events which happen unexpectedly with no preparation or warning are those which are associated with the greatest negative impacts. Clients who feel that there is no way to prevent these traumatic circumstances are likely to feel ongoing danger or that they are vulnerable for repeated incidents in the future.

### Question Assesses

Content Area I—Human Development, Diversity, and Behavior in the Environment; Human Behavior in the Social Environment (Competency); The Impact of Stress, Trauma, and Violence (KSA)

### 109. C

### Rationale

**Structural family therapy (SFT)** is similar to other types of family therapies that view the family unit as a system that lives and operates within larger systems, such as a culture, the community, and organizations. This system—ideally—grows and changes over time. But sometimes a family gets "stuck," often resulting from behavioral or mental health issues of one of its family members.

Rather than focus on the individual's pathology, however, SFT considers problems in the family's structure—a dysfunction in the way the family interacts or operates. SFT does not maintain that the family's interactions, or "transactions," cause the pathology, but rather that the family's transactions support or encourage the symptoms. Transactions are simply patterns of how family members routinely interact with each other. Through its transactions, a family establishes a set of rules for its daily functioning, and these rules form its "structure." A social worker employing SFT must first assess a family's interactions, figuring out a family's hierarchy and alliances within a family. The social worker composes a map or flow chart describing the process that a family unconsciously follows.

Ultimately, the social worker's goal is to change or modify the family map or structure—to get it "unstuck" from its harmful transactions that are supporting and amplifying certain issues or problems.

They delineate proper "boundaries" between family members and their transactions or interactions.

When boundaries are crossed, ignored, and distorted, the family's structure becomes dysfunctional.

Social workers using SFT identify a wide range of dysfunctional communication and interaction patterns. Unlike more traditional approaches that prescribe a supportive, empathetic-listening approach to therapy, social workers using SFT get involved with a family's transactions. In this unique role, and in the context of the therapeutic setting, a social worker will provoke the family members to interact and speak about the problem or issue. The therapist asks questions, points out harmful transactions, and uncovers not only dysfunctional patterns, but positive behaviors or personal qualities that are ignored or overlooked by a family.

During interactions that take place in therapy, hidden conflicts become apparent, inappropriate or counterproductive transactional patterns are observed, and, finally, ways to help a family change or restructure interactions are made.

To assist with understanding the family system, social workers will ask for "live" displays of concerns called *enactments*. The family will be encouraged to engage in a difficult communication so that social workers can best identify the current problematic patterns and dynamics. SFT focuses on family interaction in the "here and now." It is less concerned with how their interactional styles evolved.

### Test-Taking Strategies Applied

While several response choices may appear appropriate, the correct one is most closely associated with SFT. This approach focuses on the boundaries, communication patterns, and interactions between family members. Obtaining information about childhood events or past feelings is not viewed as being as helpful as "enactments" or observing current relational communication between members. Using this technique, a social worker takes a very active role to provoke conflict and point out maladaptive behavior.

While the mother's current mental status may be a concern and requires assessment, it is not the correct answer as it does not most directly relate to a SFT approach.

### Question Assesses

Content Area III—Psychotherapy, Clinical Interventions, and Case Management; The Intervention Process (Competency); Family Therapy Models, Interventions, and Approaches (KSA)

### 110. D

### Rationale

**Peer supervision** enables social workers to go beyond individual limitations and to expand on their knowledge, skills, and experiences. It involves groups of social workers with the same knowledge, skill levels, and statuses meeting regularly to discuss challenges in the profession, self-exploration, diversity and culture, new interventions and solutions, and ethical dilemmas or situations in the workplace. Peer supervision groups do not have defined leaders. As a result of peer supervision, social workers may feel validated, discuss difficult situations, self-explore, and learn different interventions and perspectives. Peer supervision counteracts burnout and social isolation as members are supported and feel group cohesion.

Members also learn to practice supervisory skills for when they become supervisors in the field. They are able to do this because they practice *giving and receiving feedback* as well as boundary management. Peer groups serve as trusting environments where social workers talk about their mistakes and feelings in the field.

### Test-Taking Strategies Applied

The question contains a qualifying word—PRIMARY—that requires identification of the main way in which social workers "learn" in peer supervision. **Modeling** is demonstration of a skill or task which may occur in peer supervision, but is not the primary method for learning. **Summative evaluation** focuses on assessing outcomes, which is not the aim of peer supervision. Peer supervision is not evaluative in nature. **Positive reinforcement** is a technique to increase behavior frequency by adding a desirable stimulus. For example, praising actions can be very rewarding, making it likely that social workers will do them again. While peer supervision can be supportive, it is not the "PRIMARY method for learning" within these venues.

Feedback, specifically **formative feedback**, which is characterized as nonevaluative and supportive, is regarded as crucial to improving knowledge and skill acquisition in peer supervision. Formative feedback represents information communicated to social workers by peers that is intended to modify thinking or behavior. Formative indicates that it is occurring while social workers are experiencing difficulties with client situations, not after treatment has ended. It is instructional rather than evaluative. Feedback from others who have had similar experiences is the main method through which social workers gain new knowledge and develop their skills in peer supervision.

### Question Assesses

Content Area III—Psychotherapy, Clinical Interventions, and Case Management; Consultation and Interdisciplinary Collaboration (Competency); Models of Supervision and Consultation (e.g., Individual, Peer, Group) (KSA)

## 111.  A

*Rationale*

**Self-determination** is a cornerstone of the social work profession. Self-determination is built on the values of autonomy and respect for the dignity and worth of all people. So, given the primacy of self-determination, it is necessary to examine how its mandate can be met when working with clients who are mandated to receive services.

Social workers respect and promote the right of clients to self-determination and assist clients in their efforts to identify and clarify their goals. Social workers may limit clients' right to self-determination when, in the social workers' professional judgment, clients' actions or potential actions pose a serious, foreseeable, and imminent risk to themselves or others (*NASW Code of Ethics, 2018—1.02 Self-Determination*).

Posing "a serious, foreseeable, and imminent risk to themselves or others" typically applies to situations of suicidal or homicidal ideation. Thus, the *NASW Code of Ethics* is giving priority to the principle of protecting life over the principle of respecting self-determination. This could include initiating processes that may result in involuntary admission for psychiatric treatment as a last resort.

This ethical standard does not say social workers may ignore self-determination. It says they may limit self-determination. Implicit in this language is the notion of the "least intrusive" course of action. In instances when clients are receiving services involuntarily, social workers should provide information about the nature and extent of services and about the extent of clients' right to refuse service (*NASW Code of Ethics, 2018—1.03 Informed Consent*).

This standard recognizes that, even though involuntary clients are being pressured into services, they still have certain rights. First, social workers need to inform clients about the services being offered. For instance, social workers should inform them about the purpose and goals of the services, models of intervention used, research about benefits and risks, and expectations as participants in services. Social workers should inform clients about the extent of their right to refuse services. Social workers should also help clarify the consequences if clients do not fulfill what has been mandated.

Self-determination is not simply an either/or situation. Honoring self-determination as much as possible may be more difficult with some clients than with others. Although social workers should recognize that self-determination may be imperfect for involuntary clients, workers are able to enhance self-determination through various intervention strategies:

- Social workers can empower clients by helping them set goals and objectives that they genuinely want to pursue—even if they did not initially choose to participate in services.

- Social workers may be able to offer clients a range of choices about which methods of intervention will be used (e.g., individual vs. family counseling).

- Social workers may be able to have clients pick their choice of practice modality (cognitive vs. narrative therapy).

In addition, social workers must engage clients by empathizing and acknowledging pressures placed on them, building trust, and validating concerns, so clients are more willing to participate in services. In appropriate instances, social workers can advocate with authorities to honor client wishes and revise court orders or other mandates in attempts to promote self-determination.

### Test-Taking Strategies Applied

The question contains a qualifying word—EXCEPT—that requires social workers to select the response choice which would not promote client self-determination during planning in the problem-solving process. When EXCEPT is used as a qualifying word, it is often helpful to remove it from the question and eliminate the three response choices which must be done as per ethical standards. This approach will leave the one response choice which is not required.

In the scenario, the social worker is "developing a contract." A contract is another name for an intervention or service plan and outlines goals, objectives, time frames for completion, and so on. It is done during the planning step of the problem-solving process, following engagement. While it is important for a mandated client to understand the contents of a court order related to treatment, such a review usually occurs prior to planning, such as part of the informed consent process at the onset of the therapeutic relationship. In addition, explaining directives contained in the order to the client does not "promote self-determination," which is the lens through which each response choice must be evaluated.

### Question Assesses

Content Area IV—Professional Values and Ethics; Professional Development and Use of Self (Competency); Client/Client System

Competence and Self-Determination (e.g., Financial Decisions, Treatment Decisions, Emancipation, Age of Consent, Permanency Planning) (KSA)

## 112.  B

*Rationale*

**Policies, procedures, regulations, and laws** can have a profound impact on social work practice. Social workers who treat clients involved with the legal system must be aware of problems that can arise prior, during, and after the delivery of services. Many of these issues can be avoided by clarifying and defining the nature of a social worker's role. For example, some clients may be uncertain about what to expect from psychotherapy or have unrealistic hopes. Ethically, a social worker is expected to work jointly with clients in the development of treatment plans. By discussing what can and cannot be provided, clients are offered realistic portrayals of what may be expected from therapy, which may assist in deciding whether to work with a particular social worker.

*Test-Taking Strategies Applied*

In this scenario, the client appears to be directing the social worker and her behavior suggests that she believes the social worker is obligated to contact the attorney. In fact, the social worker would have no such obligation and would be wise to decline the client's request, in order to clarify the social worker's role and to better understand the client's expectations. If the social worker elects to contact the attorney prior to discussing the specifics and implications with the client, there is a risk that the client may interpret the social worker's action as an implied agreement to become involved in the legal matter. If the social worker and client ultimately determined that the client's expectations were inconsistent with the social worker's understanding of his or her role, there may be a need for a referral to another professional who is better suited to the client's needs.

The incorrect answers all focus on contacting the attorney or viewing the client's lack of information as resistance to discussing the legal matter. There is no indication that the client is being resistant and to assume so is adding material to the question.

*Question Assesses*

Content Area IV—Professional Values and Ethics; Professional Values and Ethical Issues (Competency); Legal and/or Ethical Issues Related to the Practice of Social Work, Including Responsibility to Clients/Client Systems, Colleagues, the Profession, and Society (KSA)

113. C

*Rationale*

In order to facilitate change through the problem-solving process, a social worker must use various **verbal and nonverbal communication techniques** to assist clients to understand their behavior and feelings. In addition, critical to ensuring that clients are honest and forthcoming during this process, social workers must build trusting relationships with clients. These relationships develop through effective verbal and nonverbal communication. Social workers must be adept at using both forms of communication successfully, as well as understanding them, because verbal and nonverbal cues will be used by clients throughout the problem-solving process. Insight into their meaning will produce a higher degree of sensitivity to clients' experiences and a deeper understanding of their problems.

A social worker should also display *genuineness* in order to build trust. Genuineness is needed in order to establish a therapeutic relationship. It involves listening to and communicating with clients without distorting their messages and being clear and concrete in communications.

Another method is the use of *positive regard*, which is the ability to view a client as being worthy of being cared about and as someone who has strengths and achievement potential. It is built on respect and is usually communicated nonverbally.

Communication is also facilitated by *listening, attending, suspending value judgments*, and helping clients develop their own resources. A social worker should always be aware of *culturally appropriate communication* behaviors. It is also essential to be clear to establish *boundaries* with clients to facilitate a safe environment for change.

*Test-Taking Strategies Applied*

Material in quotation marks deserves particular attention and usually relates to the answer. The client–social worker interaction in the scenario is occurring in the first session. The first session focuses on engagement or building a therapeutic alliance. The correct response choice is the one which addresses the client's belief that he is a failure and his comment about not understanding "how things got so bad." The incorrect response choices may be actions that will be taken at some time during the problem-solving process, but do not make him feel that the social worker understands his situation. The question asks for the social worker's response to his statements. Central to the formation of a therapeutic alliance is displaying *empathy*, which the social worker is doing in the correct answer.

### Question Assesses

Content Area III—Psychotherapy, Clinical Interventions, and Case Management; The Intervention Process (Competency); The Principles and Techniques of Interviewing (e.g., Supporting, Clarifying, Focusing, Confronting, Validating, Feedback, Reflecting, Language Differences, Use of Interpreters, Redirecting) (KSA)

### 114. D

### Rationale

Relying on the **expertise of other professions** when needed can reduce major liability risks for social workers. For example, in situations which require medical or other expertise, social workers should look to obtain appropriate guidance from others or else clients may be harmed. If such consultation does not occur, social workers breach **standards of care** through acts of omission (not acting when they should have done so).

Under the common law doctrine of standard of care, courts usually seek to determine what a typical, reasonable, and prudent (careful) social worker with the same or similar education and training would have done under the same or similar conditions. In many instances, establishing the standard of care is easy. But in other instances, it is not easy to establish what constitutes ordinary, reasonable, and prudent practice. Well-educated, skilled, thoughtful, and careful social workers may disagree with colleagues about the best course of action in complex circumstances, perhaps because of their different schools of thought, training, and experience.

### Test-Taking Strategies Applied

In the scenario, the social worker has "a lack of knowledge about this medical condition and the medication prescribed," which is causing dramatic mood changes in the client. Thus, the social worker has an ethical responsibility to learn more through consultation with an appropriate medical professional. Failure to seek consultation may adversely affect the client.

The reason for the contact is for the social worker to learn more about the medical condition and medication. The social worker is not collaborating, which is defined as working with another to produce or create something. Joint work by both the social worker and physician is not occurring. There is also no indication that the physician is the treating medical professional of the husband, so the social worker's action is not an effort to enhance coordination of services. Similarly, the social worker and physician are not part of a team, so the action is not aimed at team building.

*Question Assesses*

Content Area III—Psychotherapy, Clinical Interventions, and Case Management; Consultation and Interdisciplinary Collaboration (Competency); Consultation Approaches (e.g., Referrals to Specialists) (KSA)

### 115. A

*Rationale*

Enhanced **coordination of client services** can be achieved through the use of alternative funding approaches. Blending or braiding funding across related programs and across multiple agencies is a basic way that state and local agencies can more effectively serve the holistic needs of clients, more efficiently target high-priority performance goals, and streamline administrative requirements. *Blending and braiding of fiscal resources aim to enhance service coordination to meet the holistic needs of clients.*

Some jurisdictions, particularly at the local level, have successfully used blended and braided funding, but *federal categorical limitations make taking this concept to a larger scale difficult.* The terms "blending" and "braiding" are used frequently, often together, and generally with little definition. However, they refer to two very different approaches to fiscal coordination.

**Blending funding** involves comingling the funds into one "pot" where social workers can draw down service dollars, personnel expenses can be paid, or other program needs can be met. When funding is blended, it goes into the "pot," and when it is pulled back out to pay for an expense, there is no means for the fiscal manager to report which funding stream paid for exactly which expense. Blending funding is politically challenging. Some funding streams cannot be blended. Other funding streams will require the funder to allow an exception to how the reporting normally functions. Instead of usual reporting, funders can opt to accept reports on services and outcomes across the population being served, rather than exactly which children, youth, and families received services with their dollars. To blend funding, social workers need to work closely with funders and ensure that reporting requirements are met. Though it is challenging politically, once funders are on board, blended funding is less challenging to implement than braided funding. There is significantly less workload, as the tracking and accountability happens across all of the funding streams. *Rather than reporting to funders on their funding stream alone, reporting is done on how the collective funds are used. Blended funding can allow you to pay for services that may not be allowable with more categorical funding approaches. However, for many funders, the flexibility associated with blending makes it seem too "risky" as it often looks like supplanting, and they end up with less detailed information about how each of their dollars have been spent.*

**Braided funding** involves multiple funding streams utilized to pay for all of the services needed by a given population, with careful accounting of how every dollar from each funding stream is spent. The term "braiding" is used because multiple funding streams are initially separate, brought together to pay for more than any one funding stream can support, and then carefully pulled back apart to report to funders on how the money was spent. Braided funding is often the only option. Federal funding streams require careful tracking of staff time and expenses to ensure that a federal funding stream only pays for those things directly associated with the intent of the funding. *Consequently, when multiple funding streams are paying for a single program or system, the system will need to be carefully designed to allow for sufficient reporting to ensure each funding stream is only paying for activities eligible under that funding stream. Braided funding requires significant effort to create the systems for tracking how funding is utilized.*

The design of a braided funding system that can respond to the individualized needs of many types of clients will require social workers to decide which services will be paid for by which funding streams. Ideally, this decision happens after the needs of the individual or family being served is identified, so that the funding does not drive the services being provided. This type of braided model requires a clear understanding of the eligible populations and the eligible services, so that decisions on how to fund the services can be made post hoc, rather than prior to discussing service needs with the families. The design of a braided funding program is simpler than the design of a braided funding system. Programs typically have clearly defined services that are provided and sometimes have very defined populations who are eligible for services.

## Test-Taking Strategies Applied

The question contains a qualifying word—TRUE. It is even capitalized to assist with identifying the distinguishing factor of the correct response from the rest. Each statement must be read carefully and evaluated as to its accuracy. The correct answer is identified through the process of elimination, with each false assertion being excluded.

Blending is often not preferred by funders as they receive less detail about how monies are spent, while braiding is frequently not seen as possible due to the burden of the tracking associated with its implementation. It requires detailed reporting to ensure each funding stream is only paying for eligible activities. Thus, only the first statement is true as both blending and braiding are difficult to administer due to federal categorical limitations.

*Question Assesses*

Content Area III—Psychotherapy, Clinical Interventions, and Case Management; Service Delivery and Management of Cases (Competency); Methods of Service Delivery (KSA)

### 116. D

*Rationale*

**Operant conditioning** attempts to understand complex human behavior without studying the internal mental thoughts and motivations.
B. F. Skinner based his theory of conditioning on the preexistent theory called "Law of Effect," or the belief that responses that produce satisfying effects become more likely to occur again and responses that produce discomforting effects become less likely to occur again.

**Punishment** has as its objective to decrease the rate of certain undesired behavior from occurring again. Punishment can be further classified into two major parts—positive and negative.

**Positive punishment** focuses on decreasing the undesired behavior by presenting negative consequences once undesired behavior has been exhibited. When subjected to negative consequences, individuals are less likely to repeat the same behavior in the future.

**Negative punishment** focuses undesired behavior by removing favorite or desired items. When desired stimuli are removed, there is less chance of the behavior occurring again in the future.

**Reinforcement** aims to strengthen or increase behavior frequency.

**Positive reinforcement** increases the likelihood that behavior will occur again in the future by pairing it with desirable stimuli (reinforcers).

**Negative reinforcement** increases the probability that behavior will occur again in the future by removing negative stimuli.

*Test-Taking Strategies Applied*

This is a recall question which relies on social workers understanding various operant conditioning techniques. Negative punishment is when a desirable stimulus is removed following an undesirable behavior for the purpose of decreasing or eliminating the behavior. In the scenario, the client takes away her daughter's cell phone (a desirable stimulus) with the desire to decrease her homework incompletion and tardiness (targeted behaviors).

*Question Assesses*

Content Area I—Human Development, Diversity, and Behavior in the Environment; Human Growth and Development (Competency); Theories of Human Development Throughout the Lifespan (e.g., Physical, Social, Emotional, Cognitive, Behavioral) (KSA)

117. **C**

*Rationale*

**Reimbursement methodologies** can have a dramatic impact on the delivery of services. Social workers must be aware of different payment policies and the implications of each.

**Capitation** is based on a payment per person, rather than a payment per service provided. There are several different types of capitation, ranging from relatively modest per-person per-month case management payments to assist with care coordination to per-person per-month payments covering all professional services (professional, facility, pharmaceutical, clinical laboratory, durable medical equipment, etc.). There may also be particular services that are "carved out" of such payments. These may be handled on either a fee-for-service basis or by delegation to a separate benefit management company. Capitation is often used as a means of controlling growth in the cost of care.

**Fee-for-service** is a payment model where services are unbundled and paid for separately. It gives an incentive to provide more treatments because payment is dependent on the quantity of care, rather than quality of care. Similarly, when clients are shielded from paying (cost-sharing) by health insurance coverage, they are incentivized to welcome any medical service that might do some good. Fee-for-service is the dominant physician payment method in the United States.

In a **bundled payment** methodology, a single, "bundled" payment covers services delivered by two or more providers during a single episode of care or over a specific period of time. For example, if a client has cardiac bypass surgery, rather than making one payment to the hospital, a second payment to the surgeon, and a third payment to the anesthesiologist, the payer would combine these payments for the specific episode of care (i.e., cardiac bypass surgery). In some cases, one entity (for instance, an accountable care organization) may receive the bundled payment and subsequently apportion the payment among participating providers. In other cases, the payer may pay participating providers independently, but adjust each payment according to negotiated, predefined rules in order to ensure that the total payments to all of the providers for all of the defined services do not exceed the total bundled payment amount. This latter type of payment methodology is frequently referred to as "virtual" bundling. Bundled payment arrangements are a type of risk-contracting. If the cost of services is less than the bundled payment, participating providers retain the difference. But if the costs exceed the bundled payment, providers are not compensated for the difference.

**Shared savings** models can be roughly divided into two categories. In the first category, if the actual total costs of all care received by clients is lower than budgeted costs, the entities responsible for their care receive a percentage of the difference between the actual and budgeted costs (i.e., a "share of the savings"). However, if actual total cost exceeds the budgeted costs, the entities are not on the hook for any portion of the difference. Because the entities are only at risk for additional revenue, shared savings arrangements are sometimes said to involve only "upside" risk.

### Test-Taking Strategies Applied

This is a recall question which relies on social workers understanding the effects that policies, procedures, regulations, and laws have on practice. Reimbursement methodologies can dramatically impact the ways in which services are coordinated and delivered. The question focuses on a single payment for multiple services. Fee-for-service would be excluded as it represents a separate reimbursement for each service provided. There is no mention of savings in the question, eliminating the last response choice.

Capitation should not be confused with bundled payments. Capitation is an actuarially determined payment per client who may or may not use services. The distinction between capitation and bundled payment is that capitation pays the same amount regardless of what clients need clinically or receive. The calculation of the capitation amount derives from actuarial principles of insurance. The big risk in capitation is incidence risk. The question asks about "services provided," making bundled payment the correct answer over capitation.

*Question Assesses*

Content Area III—Psychotherapy, Clinical Interventions, and Case Management; Service Delivery and Management of Cases (Competency); Methods of Service Delivery (KSA)

### 118. A

*Rationale*

**Cultural identity** is often defined as the identity of a group, culture, or an individual, influenced by one's belonging to a group or culture. Certain ethnic and racial identities may also have privilege.

Cultural, racial, and ethnic identities are important, particularly for those who are members of minority groups. They may instill feelings of belonging to a particular group or groups and identification with that group (i.e., shared commitment and values). Cultural, racial, and ethnic identities are passed from one generation to the next through customs, traditions, language, religious practice, and cultural values. Cultural, racial, and ethnic identities are also influenced by the popular media, literature, and current events.

Self-esteem or image can be negatively impacted by cultural issues, especially when practices interfere with childhood development, such as being subject to criticism or abuse; missing out on experiences that would foster a sense of confidence and purpose; and/or receiving little or no positive reinforcement for accomplishments. In adulthood, cultural beliefs may compound life changes by further stigmatizing losing a job or changing jobs, ending an intimate relationship, having legal or financial troubles, struggling with addiction or substance abuse, having children with emotional troubles, developing physical health concerns, and so on.

People with poor self-image may work with social workers on becoming more assertive, confident, and self-aware. Finding a sense of accomplishment is a huge boost to self-esteem, and therapy can help clients identify specific activities that boost confidence and competence. In addition, many social workers focus on helping people develop self-compassion so that they can develop more realistic, achievable goals for themselves and treat themselves with kindness and encouragement.

**Universalization** is a supportive intervention used by social workers to reassure and encourage clients. Universalization places client experiences in the context of other individuals who are experiencing the same or similar challenges, and it seeks to help clients grasp that their feelings and experiences are not uncommon given the circumstances. A social worker using this supportive intervention intends to "normalize" client experiences, emotions, and reactions to presenting challenges. By normalizing client experiences, social workers attempt to help avert the client's natural feelings of shame due to feeling alone or judged.

### Test-Taking Strategies Applied

The scenario requires the correct answer to be chosen as it is "most effective." As the poor self-image of the client is presented as a problem, it is necessary to select a response which will help the client see that she is not alone or to blame for her situation. The incorrect answers may be actions that the social worker will take, but they are not the most critical. The woman has not felt that she had any other choice than to stay married. She may have been skeptical and cautious about seeking help for fear of being mistreated or misunderstood. Thus, trust is an important element in establishing a therapeutic alliance. The client needs to know that the social worker can be trusted and is competent to help her. Only the correct answer helps build trust and rapport by helping her to see that the social worker accepts and understands her situation.

### Question Assesses

Content Area I—Human Development, Diversity, and Behavior in the Environment; Diversity and Discrimination (Competency); The Effect of Culture, Race, and Ethnicity on Behaviors, Attitudes, and Identity (KSA)

## 119. A

### Rationale

Long-term **alcohol dependence** leads to a variety of moderate to severe health problems. The longer and heavier the consumption, the worse the physical results become. "**Wet brain**" is another way of describing a condition called Wernicke-Korsakoff syndrome. It is caused by a deficiency in vitamin $B_1$ (thiamine). If "wet brain" is allowed to progress too far, it will not be possible to recover from it.

Wernicke-Korsakoff syndrome is actually a combination of two separate conditions: **Wernicke's encephalopathy** and **Korsakoff psychosis**. These two disorders combine to produce a variety of symptoms including confusion, changes to vision, loss of muscle coordination, difficulty swallowing, and speech problems.

Hallucinations, loss of memory, confabulation (occurs as clients make up stories to compensate for their memory loss), inability to form new memories, inability to make sense when talking, and apathy are due to Korsakoff psychosis. It is possible for clients who are alcoholic to develop either Korsakoff psychosis or Wernicke's encephalopathy independently.

It is usual for the effects of Wernicke's encephalopathy to become noticeable first of all. These symptoms tend to come on suddenly. The first sign that something is wrong will be that a client appears confused. This can be hard to diagnose in a client who is habitually intoxicated. This confusion differs from drunken confusion because it lasts even when a client has not been drinking. Later, the symptoms of Korsakoff psychosis will also become noticeable. In the beginning, only the ability to form new memories will be damaged, so a client can still appear quite lucid.

Clients who are alcoholic have poor dietary habits; over a long time, this will lead to nutritional deficiencies. Lack of thiamine in the diet interferes with glucose metabolism, which can then lead to atrophy in the brain. Wernicke's encephalopathy occurs due to damage to the thalamus and hypothalamus. Korsakoff psychosis occurs because of damage to those parts of the brain where memories are managed.

If wet brain syndrome has been allowed to progress too far, there may be little that can be done to reverse the effects. *Thiamine injections can improve things greatly and may restore a client back to full recovery.* Those who have developed the chronic form of wet brain will be far less likely to recover. In some cases, the best that can be done is prevention of any further deterioration.

The only possible cure for wet brain syndrome is complete abstinence from alcohol. Most of those who do find their way into recovery will be able to regain all functioning that was lost due to Wernicke-Korsakoff syndrome. Other clients will have to deal with lingering effects of the damage, but they should be able to adapt and find a good life away from alcohol.

### Test-Taking Strategies Applied

The question contains a qualifying word—BEST—that requires social workers to select the response choice which will optimally treat the root cause of the symptoms listed. While some of the incorrect response choices may be helpful to the client, only the correct answer addresses the reason for the wet brain symptoms. Cognitive rehabilitation and physical therapy address the manifestations of the vitamin B$_1$ (thiamine) deficiency, but not the underlying problem. There is also no justification for antipsychotic medications as delusion or hallucinations by the client were not mentioned in the question.

*Question Assesses*

Content Area I—Human Development, Diversity, and Behavior in the Environment; Human Behavior in the Social Environment (Competency); Addiction Theories and Concepts (KSA)

### 120. B

*Rationale*

There are many ethical standards, including those on touching clients, that speak to **professional boundary issues** that social workers face in practice. Often the maintenance of appropriate boundaries can be challenging for social workers. Social workers should not engage in physical contact with clients when there is a possibility of psychological harm to the client as a result of the contact (such as cradling or caressing clients). Social workers who engage in appropriate physical contact with clients are responsible for setting clear, appropriate, and culturally sensitive boundaries that govern such physical contact. The 2018 *NASW Code of Ethics* leaves the door open, but cautions social workers that they bear responsibility for ensuring that no negative consequences ensue.

The language leaves open the possibility that, when used responsibly, touch might occasionally make clinical sense, perhaps by helping a client stay grounded or feel less isolated or overwhelmed.

However, social workers using touch within the context of a therapeutic alliance must always carefully consider clients' factors, such as presenting problems and symptoms, personal touch and sexual history, ability to differentiate types of touch, and clients' ability to assertively identify and protect their boundaries, as well as the gender and cultural influences of both clients and social workers.

Social workers should have clear policies about touching, self-disclosure, and other boundary areas which are applied consistently to client situations. One of the most effective ways to establish clear professional boundaries is for a social worker's behavior to set the standard for meetings with clients. Appropriate dress and behavior should be displayed and talk should not include a social worker discussing his or her personal life.

*Test-Taking Strategies Applied*

The scenario describes a client's reaction to a hesitation by a social worker to a hug *at the end of a session*. There is no indication that physical touch has been discussed between the client and social worker in this or any prior interaction. The client may be accusing the social worker of being homophobic due to an exchange with someone else in the past. In the scenario, it is necessary for the social worker to explain her policy on physical touch, as well other boundary issues. Educating clients about the 2018 *NASW Code of Ethics* is essential so they can better understand therapeutic or helping alliances and not confuse them with friendships or romantic relationships. None of the incorrect responses include this critical education.

It would not be appropriate to explore the client's belief about being rejected based on her sexual orientation when the session is ending. In addition, there is no indication that the client's statement is anything other than a misunderstanding about professional boundaries between the social worker and client. The client may not realize that the social worker has a policy which is applied to all clients.

Continuing to hug the client would be contraindicated, especially given the accusation. It violates the social worker's policy on physical contact and treats this client differently than others.

Simply telling the client that the social worker is not homophobic does not provide an explanation for the hesitation. It also misses the opportunity to educate the client about the importance of maintaining professional boundaries and differentiating the therapeutic alliance from other personal relationships.

*Question Assesses*

Content Area IV—Professional Values and Ethics; Professional Values and Ethical Issues (Competency); Professional Boundaries in the Social Worker–Client/Client System Relationship (e.g., Power Differences and Conflicts of Interest) (KSA)

### 121. D

*Rationale*

**Xenophobia** is a severe aversion to foreigners, strangers, their politics, and their cultures. Often, the term "xenophobia" is used interchangeably with racism, yet the two are actually different. While racism defines prejudice based solely on ethnicity, ancestry, or race, xenophobia covers any kind of fear related to **differences in culture, race, and/or ethnicity**, as well as other ways of being different. Those with xenophobia do not understand or accept that their condition is based in fear, yet it is the perceived threat of losing one's own identity, culture, and imagined superiority or purity that is the cause.

If left untreated, xenophobia can have seriously detrimental effects. An individual who is xenophobic is liable to pass along his or her highly generalized and ungrounded perceptions to children and family members. Some symptoms of a xenophobic person include:

- Feelings of fear or dread when exposed to people or cultural items perceived to be different

- Apparent hostility toward people or cultures perceived to be different

- Distrust aimed specifically toward cultures perceived to be different

- Rash generalizations and stereotypes aimed at a set of people based on superficial qualities

Like all phobias, there is no universally specific cause that leads to the development of xenophobia. It can be caused by unique experiences or can simply be the result of alienation from people and cultures different from one's own.

Like many phobias, treatment focuses on first targeting the initial inciting factor that caused the irrational and extreme fear. Therapy includes talking about why the fear was unfounded and addressing any traumatic experiences that caused the phobia, as well as identifying ways to deal with symptoms. Sometimes behavioral techniques are used to systematically and gradually confront the source of fear and learning to control the physical and mental reactions to it. By facing the phobia directly, it is possible to realize that fears are not grounded in real or imminent danger.

### Test-Taking Strategies Applied

This is a recall question which relies on social workers understanding terminology related to cultural awareness and its barriers. Social workers should promote conditions that encourage respect for cultural, racial, and/or ethnic diversity and promote policies and practices that demonstrate respect for difference; support the expansion of relevant knowledge and resources; advocate for programs and institutions that demonstrate cultural, racial, and/or ethnic competence; and promote policies that safeguard the rights of all people.

If the definition of xenophobia is not known, it may be possible to narrow the choices through eliminating other answers.

**Ephebiphobia**, also known as hebephobia, is the fear of young people or teenagers.

**Trypanophobia** is the fear of needles which can lead to potential health issues, especially when important vaccines and medications that require injections are refused.

**Mysophobia**, also known as germophobia, is a common fear of general contamination which can lead to extreme anxiety about contact with others.

*Question Assesses*

Content Area II—Assessment, Diagnosis, and Treatment Planning; Treatment Planning (Competency); The Criteria Used in the Selection of Intervention/Treatment Modalities (e.g., Client/Client System Abilities, Culture, Life Stage) (KSA)

### 122. C

*Rationale*

In the *DSM-5*, the chapter on **Substance-Related and Addictive Disorders** also includes Gambling Disorder as the sole condition in a new category on behavioral addictions. *DSM-IV* listed Pathological Gambling, but in a different chapter. This new term and its location in the new manual reflect research findings that Gambling Disorder is similar to Substance-Related Disorders in clinical expression, brain origin, comorbidity, physiology, and treatment. Recognition of these commonalities will help people with Gambling Disorder get the treatment and services they need, and others may better understand the challenges that individuals face in overcoming this disorder.

While Gambling Disorder is the only addictive disorder included in *DSM-5* as a diagnosable condition, Internet Gaming Disorder is included in Section III of the *DSM-5*. Disorders listed there require further research before their consideration as formal disorders. This condition is included to reflect the scientific literature that persistent and recurrent use of Internet games, and a preoccupation with them, can result in clinically significant impairment or distress. Other repetitive behavior, such as that related to exercise, sex, or shopping, are not included because there is insufficient peer-reviewed evidence to establish the diagnostic criteria to identify these behaviors as mental disorders at this time.

## Test-Taking Strategies Applied

This is a recall question which relies on social workers understanding that empirical evidence supports treating other addictions, such as gambling, like Substance-Related Disorders since gambling behaviors activate reward systems similar to those activated when abusing drugs. In addition, Gambling Disorder produces behavioral symptoms that are comparable to those produced by Substance Use Disorders. Knowing which other addictions are included in the *DSM-5* is essential when social workers are working with clients who are experiencing impairment due to excessive or repetitive behaviors.

## Question Assesses

Content Area II—Assessment, Diagnosis, and Treatment Planning; Assessment and Diagnosis (Competency); The Use of the Diagnostic and Statistical Manual of the American Psychiatric Association (KSA)

### 123.  C

## Rationale

Central to required **social work documentation** are case notes. Case notes are an integral and important part of practice. Record-keeping practices have an impact on client outcomes such that poor case notes can result in poor decision making and adverse client outcomes. *A case note is a chronological record of interactions, observations, and actions relating to a particular client.*

The guiding principle for deciding what information should be included in case notes is whether it is relevant to the service or support being provided. Case notes can include, but are not limited to:

- Biopsychosocial, environmental, and systemic factors
- Considerations of culture, religion, and spirituality
- Risk and resilience present
- Facts, theories, or research underpinnings that impact on assessments and/or treatment
- Summaries or all discussions and interactions
- Persons/services involved in the provision of supports including referral information, telephone contacts, and email/written correspondence
- Attendance/nonattendance at scheduled sessions

- Discussions of legal and ethical responsibilities (client rights, responsibilities, and complaints processes; parameters of the service and support being offered and agreed to; issues relating to informed consent, information sharing, confidentiality, and privacy; efforts to promote and support client self-determination and autonomy)

- Details of reasons for and outcomes leading up to or following the termination or interruption of a service or support

### Test-Taking Strategies Applied

The question contains a qualifying word—PRIMARY. Unlike other questions, the qualifying word in this question is not capitalized. Qualifying words may be capitalized or not, so it is important to read questions carefully.

While case notes may have multiple functions, the correct answer is the one that highlights their usefulness in ensuring efficient and effective client care. Using case records for worker development, reimbursement, and/or regulatory compliance is not the main reason that social workers keep case or progress notes. These notes are used mainly by social workers to help them recall what was done in prior meetings or sessions so that future work can pick up there. It helps to ensure that time is not wasted talking about issues that were already resolved. Additionally, by reviewing case notes prior to sessions, social workers reduce the likelihood that important next steps in discussions take place and therapeutic gaps do not emerge. Case notes also help social workers look back to initial and other past sessions to see progress made. This progress should be regularly reviewed with clients.

### Question Assesses

Content Area III—Psychotherapy, Clinical Interventions, and Case Management; Service Delivery and Management of Cases (Competency); The Principles of Case Recording, Documentation, and Management of Practice Records (KSA)

### 124. A

### Rationale

The mission of the social work profession is rooted in a set of **professional values**. These core values—service, social justice, dignity and worth of the person, importance of human relationships, integrity, and competence—are the foundation of social work's unique purpose and perspective.

These core values reflect what is unique to the social work profession. Core values, and the principles that flow from them, must be balanced within the context and complexity of the human experience.

When providing **service**, social workers' primary goal is to help people in need and to address social problems. *Social workers elevate service to others above self-interest.* Social workers are encouraged to volunteer some portion of their professional skills with no expectation of significant financial return (pro bono service).

Social workers value **social justice**, challenging social inequities on behalf of vulnerable and oppressed individuals and groups of people. *Social workers' social change efforts are focused primarily on issues of poverty, unemployment, discrimination, and other forms of social injustice.*

Social workers respect the inherent **dignity and worth of the person**, treating each person in a caring and respectful fashion, mindful of individual differences and cultural and ethnic diversity. Social workers promote clients' socially responsible self-determination. *Social workers seek to enhance clients' capacity and opportunity to change and to address their own needs.*

Social workers recognize the central **importance of human relationships**, as relationships between and among people are an important vehicle for change. Social workers engage people as partners in the helping process. *Social workers seek to strengthen relationships among people in a purposeful effort to promote, restore, maintain, and enhance the well-being of individuals, families, social groups, organizations, and communities.*

**Integrity** means that social workers behave in a trustworthy manner. *Social workers act honestly and responsibly and promote ethical practices on the part of the organizations with which they are affiliated.*

Social workers practice within their areas of **competence** and develop and enhance their professional expertise. *Social workers continually strive to increase their professional knowledge and skills and to apply them in practice.*

## Test-Taking Strategies Applied

Social workers should uphold all social work values. However, this scenario contains a qualifying word—MOST—which is not capitalized. The problem of finding an appropriate provider presents a barrier to fulfilling the client's wish to die at home. Thus, the social worker must focus on developing creative solutions to promoting the client's need for self-determination.

Competence involves practicing within one's expertise and developing as a professional, which are not prevailing issues in this scenario. Integrity, being honest or trustworthy, is also not directly related to the situation presented. Lastly, pursuing social change or justice for those who are oppressed and disenfranchised does not apply as there is no indication that the barrier encountered results from oppression or unequal treatment.

*Question Assesses*

Content Area IV—Professional Values and Ethics; Professional Values and Ethical Issues (Competency); Legal and/or Ethical Issues Related to Death and Dying (KSA)

### 125.  D

*Rationale*

**Defense mechanisms** are unconscious processes that protect clients from unacceptable or painful ideas or impulses.

**Denial** involves blocking external events from awareness. If some situation is just too much to handle, a client may refuse to experience it. It is a primitive defense, operating by itself or, more commonly, in combination with other, more subtle mechanisms that support it.

**Projection** involves clients attributing their own thoughts, feelings, and motives to others. Thoughts most commonly projected onto another are the ones that would cause guilt. For instance, a client might hate someone, but his or her superego tells him or her that such hatred is unacceptable. Thus, the client solves the problem by believing that the other person hates him or her.

**Displacement** is the redirection of an impulse (usually aggression) onto a powerless substitute target. The target can be a person or an object that can serve as a symbolic substitute. A client who is frustrated by his or her superiors on the job may go home and kick the dog or yell at a family member.

**Reaction formation** is actually a mental process, transforming anxiety-producing thoughts into their opposites in consciousness. A client goes beyond denial and behaves in the opposite way to which he or she thinks or feels. By using reaction formation, the id is satisfied while keeping the ego in ignorance of the true motives. In short, reaction formation means expressing the opposite of inner feelings in outward behavior.

*Test-Taking Strategies Applied*

The question contains a qualifying word—MOST. While the client may be using more than one of the defense mechanisms listed, it is likely the behavior constitutes reaction formation. There is no evidence that the client denies having an Alcohol Use Disorder or fails to recognize the implications of this disorder, which are both indications of denial. The client's actions go beyond denial as the client is engaging in actions, outrage, and advocacy, which are counter to his inner beliefs of appreciation for his own mandated services.

*Question Assesses*

Content Area I—Human Development, Diversity, and Behavior in the Environment; Human Behavior in the Social Environment (Competency); Psychological Defense Mechanisms and Their Effects on Behavior and Relationships (KSA)

### 126. B

*Rationale*

Social workers must be familiar with various **research techniques** which are applied to practice. **Case-mix adjustment** is the process of statistically controlling for group differences when comparing nonequivalent groups on outcomes of interest. It is done on a post hoc basis, after the treatment groups have been formed and the performance measures collected. The groups may be treatment agencies, consumers, providers, programs, regions, or states/jurisdictions. Any time these groups are to be compared on performance indicators, case-mix adjustment must be considered.

For example, mental health authorities and providers in both the public and private sectors are increasingly interested in measuring outcomes of mental health care. Performance measurement is mandated by some public mental health systems and managed care organizations. By using comparative performance indicators, mental health systems can track the effects of changes within their systems and the effectiveness of routine care provision across sites. They can identify sites providing the highest quality care and sites that may need to improve the quality of care they provide.

However, populations of mental health consumers served by different behavioral health care agencies can be vastly different. Agencies serving individuals with severe and comorbid impairment cannot equitably be compared using raw outcome scores to agencies serving individuals with less challenging mental health concerns. The outcomes that providers or agencies strive for, and for which they are held accountable, are only partly under their control; many individual and environmental variables affect outcomes independently of care. These critical case-mix variables are not evenly distributed across groups.

Case-mix adjustment attempts to identify the individual and environmental variables that influence outcomes, measure those variables, correct for their influence through post hoc statistical methods, and display the case-mix adjusted results in ways that allow for ease of interpretation and use.

Case-mix adjustment is a partial correction that cannot create perfectly equivalent groups or duplicate the rigor of experimental assignment. In a true experiment, the researcher assigns people randomly to different treatment groups, controls the administration of the treatment, and measures the outcome or dependent variable. Statistical laws tell us that, with enough people, the average characteristics will be equal in all groups; the only systematic variation is the treatment. So if the results show that the groups are unequal on the dependent variable, one concludes that the treatment caused the difference. Case-mix adjustment is a post hoc effort to correct for differences among the groups served by the agencies since random selection does not take place.

Case-mix adjustment has an additional function in setting appropriate reimbursement rates in capitation contracts. Adequately and fairly compensating providers on the basis of how much service will be needed, as indicated by case-mix adjustment, removes the incentive for providers to attract only those who are relatively healthy and avoid those with more severe conditions that will require more services.

There may be situations where case-mix adjustment is unnecessary. This situation will occur when the case-mix adjusted results lead to the same conclusions as the unadjusted results regarding group level performance. It may also occur when the gain from doing case-mix adjustment is considered to be small relative to the costs, or when the potential case-mix indicators that are available in a limited dataset do not correlate with the outcome. In the latter case, it is important to recognize that any results to be compared among groups are unadjusted and therefore potentially misleading.

**Random sampling** assists with creating equivalent treatment and control groups prior to the delivery of interventions.

**Inter-rater or interobserver reliability** assesses the degree to which different raters/observers give consistent estimates of the same phenomenon.

**Descriptive statistics** describe the basic features of data in a study. They provide simple summaries and form the basis of virtually every quantitative analysis of data.

### Test-Taking Strategies Applied

This is a recall question which relies on social workers being able to apply research principles to practice. Social workers should be able to correctly interpret empirical findings. Understanding whether outcomes are related to differences in sample selection or client characteristics rather than interventions is critical as social workers may inappropriately conclude that services are effective or ineffective when they are not.

### Question Assesses

Content Area III—Psychotherapy, Clinical Interventions, and Case Management; Service Delivery and Management of Cases (Competency); The Effects of Program Evaluation Findings on Services (KSA)

### 127. A

### Rationale

A valuable source for data is **collateral contacts or informants**—relatives, friends, teachers, physicians, and others who possess insight into clients' lives. Collateral sources are particularly important when, because of developmental capacity or functioning, clients' ability to generate information may be limited or distorted. For example, assessments of clients with memory or cognitive limitations will be enhanced with data that collaterals (family members and friends) can provide.

Social workers must exercise discretion when deciding that such information is needed and in obtaining it. Clients can assist in this effort by suggesting collateral contacts who may provide useful information. Social workers must weigh the validity of information obtained from collateral sources. It is important to consider the nature of their relationships with clients and the ways in which that might influence these contacts' perspectives. Family members may be emotionally involved in client difficulties, skewing their perceptions. Other service providers may have limited contact with clients, with narrow views of their situations. As with other sources of information, input from collateral contacts must be critically viewed and weighed against other information.

### Test-Taking Strategies Applied

The question contains a qualifying word—MOST. While all of the sources listed may provide some useful information, it is likely that the client's adult son will be able to provide the most detailed and accurate information as he lives with her. The scenario states that the client is disoriented. Additionally, clients often overrate their functioning. Therefore, the client herself is not the best person to provide information on her safety. While she is getting visiting nurse services and home delivered meals, agency staff involvement in the home is limited to medication administration and delivery of meals. The social worker's concern about her safety does not focus on her day program as she is constantly supervised there. The client's functioning at the day program may also be different than at home. Staff in the home will not be able to comment on her ability to perform activities of daily living (ADLs) like bathing, toileting, and cooking. Similarly, her physician will only be familiar with her medical status.

Collateral contacts who live with clients—in this scenario, her adult son—are usually very good sources of information about clients' functioning as they have the opportunity to observe them for extended periods while performing all tasks which are required for safe, daily living.

### Question Assesses

Content Area II—Assessment, Diagnosis, and Treatment Planning; Assessment and Diagnosis (Competency); Methods of Involving Clients/Client Systems in Problem Identification (e.g., Gathering Collateral Information) (KSA)

### 128. A

### Rationale

Social workers must be familiar with **ethical standards related to payment for services**. There are many practices which are not ethical such as setting unreasonable fees, bartering in most instances, and soliciting extra fees from clients when services can be provided by agencies at no additional cost. In addition, an arrangement where social workers accept a percentage of other independent providers' fees for professional services that they have not directly provided is not ethical. Receiving money for referrals made to other professionals constitutes "fee splitting" and is strictly prohibited. Costs of social work services should be established at market value and paid per agreement or contract with clients for services actually received.

"Fee splitting" represents a conflict of interest which may adversely affect client care and well-being. For example, clients may not necessarily be referred to the most appropriate professionals, but instead those with whom referring social workers have "fee splitting" or commission payment type arrangements.

Fee splitting is not only prohibited for social workers, but other professionals as well.

*Test-Taking Strategies Applied*

This is a recall question which relies on social workers understanding the ethical issues regarding payment for services, and specifically the term "fee splitting."

*Question Assesses*

Content Area IV—Professional Values and Ethics; Professional Values and Ethical Issues (Competency); Legal and/or Ethical Issues Related to the Practice of Social Work, Including Responsibility to Clients/Client Systems, Colleagues, the Profession, and Society (KSA)

### 129. D

*Rationale*

An **interdisciplinary team** is a group of individuals from different disciplines, each with unique skills and perspectives, who work together toward a common purpose or goal. The benefits of this approach are well documented. Interdisciplinary teams are often seen as advantageous to clients because they do not have the burden of navigating multiple service systems and communicating to multiple providers who are involved in their care.

*Test-Taking Strategies Applied*

The question contains a qualifying word—FIRST. While more than one response choice may be helpful throughout the process, the order in which they are to occur is critical. The first answer is incorrect as the team should be involved in determining what assessment information is needed and helping to gather it. Additionally, a biopsychosocial history may not be needed or appropriate as the goal is to determine the current and future needs of the young man. The second response choice is also incorrect. While it may be useful to have professionals who have treated the client in the past on the team, identifying actual individuals comes after the unique skills and perspectives needed have been articulated. It is also premature to outline the timeline for moving as the specific goals and objectives which need to be accomplished before the move have not been set. Thus, the third response choice is incorrect.

The initial action must be to identify the requisite skills needed. Without knowing what other disciplines need to be represented, a social worker will be unable to understand his or her role, as well as those of others, on interdisciplinary teams. Central to effective interdisciplinary team approaches is the seeking to establish common ground with other professionals, including commonalities in goals. Professionals should also acknowledge the differences within the field and across other disciplines.

### Question Assesses

Content Area III—Psychotherapy, Clinical Interventions, and Case Management; Consultation and Interdisciplinary Collaboration (Competency); The Process of Interdisciplinary and Intradisciplinary Team Collaboration (KSA)

### 130. A

### Rationale

Social workers should respect clients' right to privacy or **confidentiality**. In addition, social workers may only disclose confidential information when appropriate with valid consent from a client or a person legally authorized to consent on behalf of a client. Social workers should protect the confidentiality of all information obtained in the course of professional service, except for compelling professional reasons. The general expectation that social workers will keep information confidential does not apply when disclosure is necessary to prevent serious, foreseeable, and imminent harm to a client or others.

Social workers should also provide clients with reasonable **access to records**. Social workers who are concerned that clients' access to their records could cause serious misunderstanding or harm to a client should provide assistance in interpreting the records and consult with a client regarding the records. *Social workers should limit clients' access to their records, or portions of their records, only in exceptional circumstances when there is compelling evidence that such access would cause serious harm to a client.* Both clients' requests and the rationale for withholding some or all of the record should be documented in clients' files. When providing clients with access to their records, social workers should take steps to protect the confidentiality of other individuals identified or discussed in such records.

### Test-Taking Strategies Applied

The scenario clearly states that "the social worker is not worried about the client seeing the information in the record." Thus, there is no compelling reason to limit the client's access to her record. The client's lack of explanation about what will be done with the information does not change the social worker's duty to send a copy of the entire record to the client.

It is inappropriate for the social worker to meet with the former client to do an assessment. Termination has already occurred and the former client has the right to withhold the reason for the request. The social worker also should not remove information from the record as there is no concern with having the client see it. The client can decide whether she will share all, some, or none of the information with others once she receives and reviews it. It is always good to have requests put in writing, but the reason for the request is not needed. In addition, this response is incorrect as it is concerned more with administrative procedure than the issues of record access.

### Question Assesses

Content Area III—Psychotherapy, Clinical Interventions, and Case Management; Service Delivery and Management of Cases (Competency); The Principles of Case Recording, Documentation, and Management of Practice Records (KSA)

### 131. B

### Rationale

**Positive psychology** is the scientific study of the strengths that enable individuals, families, and communities to thrive. The field is founded on the belief that people want to lead meaningful and fulfilling lives, to cultivate what is best within themselves, and to enhance their experiences of love, work, and play.

It is a reaction against psychoanalysis and behavioral analysis, which focus on negative thinking and emphasize maladaptive behavior. It builds further on the humanistic movement, which encouraged an emphasis on happiness, well-being, and positivity, thus creating the foundation for what is now known as positive psychology.

Positive psychology is concerned with eudaimonia, "the good life," or flourishing, living according to what holds the greatest value in life—the factors that contribute the most to a well-lived and fulfilling life. While not attempting a strict definition of the good life, positive psychologists agree that one must live a happy, engaged, and meaningful life in order to experience "the good life" or use signature strengths every day to produce authentic happiness and abundant gratification.

**Psychoanalysis** refers both to a theory of how the mind works and a treatment modality. It is based on the belief that people could be cured by making conscious their unconscious thoughts and motivations, thus gaining insight. The aim is to release repressed emotions and experiences (i.e., make the unconscious conscious).

**Behaviorism** is an approach to the understanding of human and animal behavior. It assumes that all behaviors are either reflexes produced by a response to certain stimuli in the environment or a consequence to antecedents. Thus, behaviorists focus primarily on environmental factors which serve as reinforcers or punishers of behavior.

**Psychoeducation** refers to the process of providing education and information to those seeking or receiving services and their family members.

### Test-Taking Strategies Applied

This is a recall question which requires social workers to be familiar with a type of psychology which is rooted in the humanistic movement and has many similarities to the strengths perspective used by social workers. Positive psychology is a strengths-based approach to working with clients.

When the names of diagnoses, theories, or approaches are listed as response choices, it is often wise to think about each of the answers listed *before* looking at the question. Getting the question correct relies on knowing about all four of the answers. Whenever there is a gap in knowledge about one of the diagnoses, theories, or approaches listed, the likelihood of getting the question wrong increases. Knowledge should be used to try to narrow down the possibilities by eliminating incorrect answers, leaving response choices that are candidates for selection.

### Question Assesses

Content Area I—Human Development, Diversity, and Behavior in the Environment; Human Growth and Development (Competency); Strengths-Based and Resilience Theories (KSA)

### 132. B

### Rationale

Often **values** and **ethics** are terms that are used interchangeably. Though different, together they form the basis for making decisions. *Values are beliefs that a person holds about aspects of life and serve as guiding principles that influence behavior.* Every individual has a set of values through which he or she looks at all things and also at the world.

*Ethics refers to the guidelines for conduct or a system of moral principles.* For example, killing and rape are acts which violate a code of conduct which dictates what is wrong and what is right. When these ethics were not in place, no human behavior could be categorized as good or bad, which is what led to the development of these standards to guide human behavior in a society.

### Test-Taking Strategies Applied

The question contains a qualifying word—BEST. While the incorrect answers contain some true assertions about values and/or ethics, they do not contain the basic distinction that values are principles held by people to help guide behaviors while ethics are moral codes of conduct that decide what is wrong and what is right about these behaviors.

There is incomplete or inaccurate information contained in many of the incorrect answers. For example, ethics can be unwritten and do not only apply to professional behavior. Values can be customs, beliefs, standards of conduct, and principles considered by a culture, a group of people, or an individual. Thus, they are not only customs of individuals. In addition, values and ethical beliefs can both change over time, though such changes often occur slowly.

### Question Assesses

Content Area IV—Professional Values and Ethics; Professional Development and Use of Self (Competency); Professional Values and Principles (e.g., Competence, Social Justice, Integrity, and Dignity and Worth of the Person) (KSA)

### 133.  B

### Rationale

According to psychologist Jean Piaget, children progress through a series of four critical stages of **cognitive development**. Each stage is marked by shifts in how kids understand the world.

- The sensorimotor stage, from birth to age 2
- The preoperational stage, from age 2 to about age 7
- The concrete operational stage, from age 7 to age 11
- The formal operational stage, which begins at age 11 and spans into adulthood

According to Piaget, children in the preoperational stage of cognitive growth (ages 2–7) use magical thinking until they learn the properties of physics and reality—a trial and error process that takes years. Little children do indeed have a hard time drawing the distinction between what is real and what is not, and they sometimes get confused and think that what occurs in their heads is happening in the outside world.

Children do not make these errors because they are delusional or confused about the rules of the physical world. The more likely reason that imagination and fact can blend together is that little kids have acute powers of perception—they are experts at seeing, hearing, feeling, thinking, and imagining—but they cannot reflect on those perceptions. In other words, they think a lot, but they do not yet think about thinking. When adults wake up from a scary dream, the primitive brain feels the emotion, but advanced reasoning puts it in context. Kids, on the other hand, operate more from the gut, with less contemplation or insight about what they have experienced.

Around the age of 4, kids turn a corner and become more aware of their own perceptions and more astute about distinguishing appearance and reality, even though it is a process that takes time to truly sink in. One theory for why this happens is that the right brain, which processes perceptions, and the left brain, which analyzes them, start to communicate better with each other, leading to a higher level of insight for kids in the later preschool years.

### Test-Taking Strategies Applied

This is a recall question which relies on social workers understanding stages of cognitive development. Even when theorists are not explicitly stated in questions, correct answers require knowledge of their specific work. For example, being familiar with the work of Kohlberg on moral reasoning, Piaget on cognitive development, and Erikson on psychosocial development can assist with narrowing down response choices to identify the correct answers to questions in their areas.

### Question Assesses

Content Area I—Human Development, Diversity, and Behavior in the Environment; Human Growth and Development (Competency); Theories of Human Development Throughout the Lifespan (e.g., Physical, Social, Emotional, Cognitive, Behavioral) (KSA)

### 134. C

### Rationale

The diagnosis formerly known as Gender Identity Disorder was changed in the *DSM-5* to **Gender Dysphoria**.

In order for a client to be diagnosed with Gender Dysphoria, he or she must exhibit a strong and persistent cross-gender identification (not merely a desire for any perceived cultural advantages of being the other sex).

In children, the disturbance is manifested by six (or more) of the following for at least 6 months:

- Repeatedly stated desire to be, or insistence that he or she is, the other sex (*must be present*)

- In boys, preference for cross-dressing or simulating female attire; in girls, insistence on wearing only stereotypical masculine clothing

- Strong and persistent preferences for cross-gender roles in make-believe play or persistent fantasies of being the other gender

- A strong rejection of toys/games typically played by one's gender

- Intense desire to participate in the stereotypical games and pastimes of the other gender

- Strong preference for playmates of the other gender

- A strong dislike of one's sexual anatomy

- A strong desire for the primary (e.g., penis, vagina) or secondary (e.g., menstruation) characteristics of the other gender

In adolescents and adults, the disturbance is manifested by symptoms such as a stated desire to be the other gender, frequently passing as the other gender, desire to live or be treated as the other gender, or the conviction that he or she has the typical feelings and reactions of the other gender.

Gender Dysphoria causes clinically significant distress or impairment in social, occupational, or other important areas of functioning.

Gender Dysphoria is not concurrent with a physical intersex condition.

There is a specifier for gender Dysphoria in the *DSM-5*—post-transition, that is, the client has transitioned to full-time living in the desired gender (with or without legalization of gender change) and has undergone (or is undergoing) at least one medical procedure or treatment regimen, namely—hormone treatment or gender reassignment surgery—confirming the desired gender.

### Test-Taking Strategies Applied

The question contains a qualifying word—MUST—even though it is not capitalized. Dislike of one's sexual anatomy and preference for clothing and playmates of the other gender are indicators of Gender Dysphoria, but do not have to be present. The only criterion that must be present is that the client must want to be the other gender or believe that he or she is the other gender.

"Gender nonconforming" is a broader term that can include clients with Gender Dysphoria, but it can also describe those who feel that they are neither only male nor only female. "Transgender" is an umbrella term for clients whose gender identity and/or expression is different from cultural expectations based on the gender they were assigned at birth. Being transgender does not imply any specific sexual orientation. Clients may be straight, gay, lesbian, bisexual, and so on.

### Question Assesses

Content Area II—Assessment, Diagnosis, and Treatment Planning; Assessment and Diagnosis (Competency); The Use of the Diagnostic and Statistical Manual of the American Psychiatric Association (KSA)

### 135. B

### Rationale

Effective **discharge planning** and appropriate post-discharge care are key for client well-being. Discharge planning usually begins early in treatment or clients' inpatient stays. In general, discharge planning is conceptualized as having four steps: (a) assessment; (b) development of plans; (c) provision of service, including providing education and making service referrals; and (d) follow-up/evaluation.

Discharge summaries serve as the primary documents communicating clients' care plans. Often discharge summaries are the only communication with subsequent client care settings. High-quality discharge summaries are generally thought to be essential for promoting client safety when returning home or going to other settings.

While the format of discharge summaries varies across settings, there are some *required components*:

1. Reason for admission
2. Significant findings
3. Procedures and treatment provided
4. Discharge condition and prognosis
5. Client and family instructions (as appropriate)—including needed follow-up services by other providers

Discharge summaries also should be signed by medical or other treating professionals.

## Test-Taking Strategies Applied

The question contains a qualifying word—TRUE. It is even capitalized to assist with identifying the distinguishing factor of the correct response from the rest. Each statement must be read carefully and evaluated as to its accuracy. The correct answer is identified through the process of elimination, with each false assertion being excluded.

## Question Assesses

Content Area II—Assessment, Diagnosis, and Treatment Planning; Treatment Planning (Competency); Discharge, Aftercare, and Follow-Up Planning (KSA)

### 136. C

## Rationale

**Mirroring** is a technique used to gain rapport at the unconscious level. Mirroring, as the name suggests, means copying another person's gestures, tone of voice, or even catchphrases. Mirroring has numerous benefits provided social workers carry it out properly.

One reason that spiders are hated, but other mammals are not, is that mammals look much more similar to people than insects. Individuals are hard-wired to like and feel comfortable around other humans.

When mirroring, social workers try to convince the subconscious mind of clients that they are similar to them. If it works, clients feel comfortable without knowing why. In mirroring, social workers copy the gestures of clients consciously with the goal of making them feel comfortable, even if they didn't feel that way initially. Mirroring requires copying their gestures, using the same tone, or talking about common interests in a manner that is slow enough to make it unnoticeable to their conscious mind. There are other features that can be mirrored using neurolinguistic programming such as blinking rate, facial expressions, or tension in the muscles of the person. Even repeating words can lead to successful mirroring. For instance, if clients say "yes" social workers say "yes," they say "no" social workers say "no," and so on. The key is to do it very moderately and occasionally, without making clients suspicious.

If social workers want to make sure that mirroring was successful and clients are feeling comfortable, they can assume a new gesture. If clients unconsciously copy, then mirroring has been successful.

There are other verbal communication techniques.

**Questioning** includes open- and closed-ended formats to *get relevant information in a nonjudgmental manner.*

**Clarifying** uses questioning, paraphrasing, and restating to *ensure full understanding of clients' ideas and thoughts*, including formulation of the existing problem.

**Reframing** shows clients that there are different perspectives and ideas that can *help to change negative thinking patterns and promote change.*

### Test-Taking Strategies Applied

Selecting the correct answer requires knowledge of the verbal and nonverbal communication techniques listed. The question is asking about a "nonverbal technique." Mirroring is the only nonverbal technique provided. In addition, the sole function of mirroring is rapport building while the other techniques focus more on gathering information, ensuring understanding of information provided, or challenging negative thinking.

### Question Assesses

Content Area III—Psychotherapy, Clinical Interventions, and Case Management; Therapeutic Relationship (Competency); Verbal and Nonverbal Communication Techniques (KSA)

### 137.  A

### *Rationale*

Social workers must be aware of the effects **policies, procedures, regulations, and laws** have on practice. Many of these impacts concern choices made based on equality and equity. While there is a common misconception that equity and equality mean the same thing and that they can be used interchangeably, they cannot as there is an important distinction between them. The idea of **equality** is that everyone should receive the same treatment and opportunities, a notion that is fundamental to democracy and the belief that everyone should benefit from the fruits of a good society.

However, when a society is stratified into poles of advantage and disadvantage, with the inevitable consequences of privilege and exclusion, the notion of equal access is just an ideal and does not exist in reality. Fair access, then, may take on a different meaning than equal access and opportunity. Rather than fairness occurring from uniform distribution (equality), where there is an entitlement to the same amount, there may be a need to level the playing field. In other words, **equity** is concerned with fairness by remedying historic injustices that have prevented or diminished access in the first place.

Policies aimed at ensuring that everyone can have access to the same opportunities (equity) provide more resources to those who need them.

**Sustainability** is the ability to continue over time.

**Fidelity** is the quality of being loyal or faithful.

### Test-Taking Strategies Applied

This is a recall question which relies on social workers understanding the values used in making decisions about policies, procedures, regulations, and laws. It requires knowing the definitions of each of the words listed as response choices.

### Question Assesses

Content Area III—Psychotherapy, Clinical Interventions, and Case Management; Service Delivery and Management of Cases (Competency); The Effects of Policies, Procedures, Regulations, and Legislation on Social Work Practice and Service Delivery (KSA)

### 138. D

### Rationale

In the *DSM-5*, there were some important changes with regard to **Substance-Related and Addictive Disorders**, including the use of alcohol. *DSM–IV* described two distinct disorders, Alcohol Abuse and Alcohol Dependence, with specific criteria for each. The *DSM–5* integrates the two *DSM–IV* disorders, Alcohol Abuse and Alcohol Dependence, into a single disorder called **Alcohol Use Disorder** with mild, moderate, and severe subclassifications. Under *DSM–IV*, the diagnostic criteria for Abuse and Dependence were distinct: Clients meeting one or more of the "Abuse" criteria within a 12-month period would receive the "Abuse" diagnosis. Clients with three or more of the "Dependence" criteria during the same 12-month period would receive a "Dependence" diagnosis. Under *DSM–5*, clients meeting any two of the 11 criteria during the same 12-month period would receive a diagnosis of Alcohol Use Disorder.

*The severity of an Alcohol Use Disorder is based on the number of criteria met.* The severity of the Alcohol Use Disorder is defined as: mild (presence of two to three symptoms), moderate (presence of four to five symptoms), or severe (presence of six or more symptoms). The *DSM–5* eliminates legal problems and adds craving as a criterion for Alcohol Use Disorder.

### Test-Taking Strategies Applied

This is a recall question which relies on social workers understanding the severity of the impairment due to Alcohol Use Disorder. In the scenario, the client has six or more signs, indicating severe impairment. Alcohol Abuse and Alcohol Dependence have been removed from the *DSM-5* and are reflected in the severity classification of the Alcohol Use Disorder.

The following six criteria were explicitly described:

1. Drank more than intended
2. Wanted to cut down drinking, but could not
3. Spent a lot of time drinking
4. Had employment troubles due to drinking
5. Continued to drink even though it caused marital breakup
6. Engaged in risky behavior (walking in the street) when drinking

**Alcohol intoxication** is a harmful physical condition caused when more alcohol than the body can handle is ingested. It includes alcohol poisoning or being drunk.

*Question Assesses*

Content Area II—Assessment, Diagnosis, and Treatment Planning; Assessment and Diagnosis (Competency); The Use of the Diagnostic and Statistical Manual of the American Psychiatric Association (KSA)

### 139. B

*Rationale*

**Ethnography** affords social workers a powerful and unique vehicle for obtaining an in-depth, contextualized understanding of clients' perspectives and experiences necessary for effective social work practice and advocacy. Unlike other forms of social inquiry such as surveys, interviews, and analysis of administrative databases, a hallmark of ethnographic research is sustained engagement in clients' lives. **Participant observation** is a qualitative method with roots in traditional ethnographic research, in which the objective is to help social workers learn the perspectives held by clients. As qualitative researchers, social workers presume that there will be multiple perspectives within any given community. They are interested both in knowing what those diverse perspectives are and in understanding the interplay among them. Qualitative researchers accomplish this through observing and participating, to varying degrees, in a community's daily activities. Participant observation always takes place in community settings, in locations believed to have some relevance to the issues at hand. The method is distinctive because social workers approach participants in their own environment. Generally speaking, social workers who engage in participant observation try to learn what life is like for "insiders" while remaining, inevitably, as "outsiders."

While in these community settings, social workers make careful, objective notes about what they see, recording all accounts and observations as field notes in a field notebook. Informal conversation and interaction with members of the study population are also important components of the method and should be recorded in the field notes, in as much detail as possible. Information and messages communicated through mass media such as radio or television may also be pertinent and thus desirable to document.

### Test-Taking Strategies Applied

The question contains a qualifying word—BEST. The question asks for the method which is used with "an ethnographic approach." Social workers need to know the meaning of "ethnographic," including basic research methods which would be consistent with this inquiry. Participant observation approaches have historically been important components of ethnographic research.

The incorrect answers are all research terms, but do not relate to ethnography in any way.

**Statistical regression** is a statistical process for estimating the relationships among variables. It includes many techniques for modeling and analyzing several variables, when the focus is on the relationships between dependent variables and one or more independent variables (or predictors).

**Experimental design** is a blueprint that enables the testing of hypotheses by reaching valid conclusions about relationships between independent and dependent variables. It refers to the conceptual frameworks within which experiments are conducted.

**Self-administered questionnaires** are data collection instruments, either in paper or electronic form, which respondents complete on their own.

### Question Assesses

Content Area II—Assessment, Diagnosis, and Treatment Planning; Assessment and Diagnosis (Competency); Data Collection and Analysis Methods (KSA)

### 140. C

*Rationale*

The mission of the profession is rooted in a set of **social work core values**. These core values, embraced by social workers throughout the profession's history, are the foundation of social work's unique purpose and perspective and include:

- Service—providing help and resources to help others achieve their maximum potential
- Social justice—ensuring equal rights, protections, and opportunities for all
- Dignity and worth of the person—believing everyone is valuable
- Importance of human relationships—understanding how interactions can be used
- Integrity—being trustworthy
- Competence—providing services within skills and abilities

This constellation of core values reflects what is unique to the social work profession.

**Unconditional positive regard** is a term used by humanist psychologist Carl Rogers to describe a technique used in his nondirective, client-centered therapy. According to Rogers, unconditional positive regard involves showing complete support and acceptance of a client no matter what that person says or does. It is the ability to view a client as being worthy of being cared about and as someone who has strengths and achievement potential. It is built on respect and is usually communicated nonverbally.

Social workers accept and support clients, no matter what they say or do, placing no conditions on this acceptance. It means caring for clients as separate people, with permission to have their own feelings and experiences. Rogers firmly believed every person was born with the potential to develop in positive, loving ways. Through the provision of services, social workers become clients' next chance, maybe their last chance, to be welcomed, understood, and accepted. Acceptance creates the conditions needed for change.

*Test-Taking Strategies Applied*

This is a recall question which relies on social workers knowing both the core social work values and the meaning of unconditional positive regard. Self-determination is not a core social work value, so it must be eliminated as a possible correct response. The correct answer distinguishes itself from the other choices as the dignity and worth of an individual are directly related to the notion of unconditional acceptance and support. Social workers must accept and support clients, no matter what they say or do, placing no conditions on this acceptance. This goal can only be accomplished if there is true belief in the dignity and worth of all humans.

*Question Assesses*

Content Area IV—Professional Values and Ethics; Professional Development and Use of Self (Competency); Professional Values and Principles (e.g., Competence, Social Justice, Integrity, and Dignity and Worth of the Person) (KSA)

### 141. A

*Rationale*

**Dyspareunia** is **sexual dysfunction** characterized by pain that occurs during sexual intercourse. It is not a disease but rather a symptom of an underlying physical or psychological disorder. The pain, which can be mild or severe, may occur in the genitals, the pelvic region, or the lower back. The condition is much more common among women than among men. Treatment for dyspareunia is aimed at identifying and properly treating the underlying disorder.

There are many potential causes of dyspareunia including vaginismus (a condition characterized by involuntary spasms of the vaginal muscles), insufficient vaginal lubrication, scars from an episiotomy (an incision made to facilitate childbirth), thinning and dryness of the vaginal wall due to estrogen deficiencies accompanying menopause or breastfeeding, and inadequate foreplay. Conditions that may cause pain upon vaginal penetration include, but are not limited to, pelvic inflammatory disease, ovarian cysts, and endometriosis. Other causes include infections, such as sexually transmitted diseases, which may irritate the vaginal walls; bladder or other urinary tract disorders such as cystitis or urethritis; cancer in the sex organs or the pelvic region; arthritis (especially in the lower back); and allergic reaction to clothes, spermicides or latex in condoms, and diaphragms.

For men, dyspareunia can result from such disorders as irritation of the skin of the penis due to an allergic rash; sexually transmitted diseases, which may irritate the skin of the penis; physical abnormalities of the penis; and infections of the prostate gland or testes.

*Test-Taking Strategies Applied*

This is a recall question about sexual dysfunction. It is necessary to know both general key concepts and specific terms associated with all of the KSAs. Terms do not need to be recalled from memory, but there should be a general familiarity with them as a result of studying so that they can be matched to definitions. All of the response choices, except the correct one, are not associated with sexual dysfunction. Thus, knowing that this is a term to describe a sexual issue would be sufficient to select the correct answer even if its exact meaning is unknown.

*Question Assesses*

Content Area II—Assessment, Diagnosis, and Treatment Planning; Biopsychosocial History and Collateral Data (Competency); The Indicators of Sexual Dysfunction (KSA)

### 142. B

*Rationale*

**Object permanence** is the understanding that objects continue to exist even when they cannot be observed (seen, heard, touched, smelled, or sensed in any way). Object permanence occurs during the first of Piaget's four stages, the sensorimotor stage.

Piaget assumed that a child could only search for a hidden toy if she or he had a mental representation of it. Piaget found that infants searched for hidden toys when they were around 8 months old.

Object permanence typically starts to develop between 4 and 7 months of age and involves a baby's understanding that when things disappear, they are not gone forever. Before a baby understands this concept, things that leave his view are gone, completely gone. Developing object permanence is an important milestone. It is a precursor to symbolic understanding (which a baby needs to develop language, pretend play, and exploration) and helps children work through separation anxiety.

*Test-Taking Strategies Applied*

The question requires knowledge of cognitive development, including key milestones. Understanding that object permanence is part of Piaget's sensorimotor stage can assist with narrowing down possible correct answers as this stage ends at age 2, thereby eliminating two incorrect choices. Recent research suggests that development of object permanence may begin before 4 months and be in place earlier than

Piaget originally hypothesized. However, 8 months is the best answer as object permanence is clearly developed by 18 months and "typically" associated with infancy, rather than toddlerhood.

## Question Assesses

Content Area I—Human Development, Diversity, and Behavior in the Environment; Human Growth and Development (Competency); Theories of Human Development Throughout the Lifespan (e.g., Physical, Social, Emotional, Cognitive, Behavioral) (KSA)

### 143. A

*Rationale*

**Techniques of interviewing** should be tailored to the specifics of a client, not generic, "one size fits all" inquiries. The focus is on the uniqueness of a client and his or her unique situation.

The purpose of the social work interview can be informational, diagnostic, or therapeutic. The same interview may serve more than one purpose.

Communication during a social work interview is interactive and interrelational. A social worker's questions will result in specific responses by a client that, in turn, lead to other inquiries. The message is formulated by a client, encoded, transmitted, received, processed, and decoded. The importance of words and messages may be implicit (implied) or explicit (evident).

There are a number of techniques that a social worker may use during an interview to assist clients.

**Confrontation** occurs when social workers *call attention to clients' feelings, attitudes, or behaviors*, often when there is inconsistency in them. Confrontation can be very effective when there is a need to highlight feelings, attitudes, or behaviors which may be useful to the therapeutic process.

**Interpretation** occurs when social workers pull together patterns of behavior to *get a new understanding* of client situations or problems.

**Universalization** helps social workers reassure clients about the "normality" of their feelings regarding their own situation. This technique is used to demonstrate that client *feelings and experiences are shared by others*.

**Clarification** uses questioning, paraphrasing, and restating to *ensure full understanding of clients' ideas and thoughts*, including formulation of the existing problem.

*Test-Taking Strategies Applied*

This is a recall question that relies on social workers knowing techniques of interviewing. The question contains part of the definition of confrontation by stating that the social worker "calls attention to an observation."

In the scenario, there is a lack of congruence between the wife's beliefs and actions. Congruence is the matching of awareness and experience with communication. It is essential that a client is able to express himself or herself and that this communication is reflective of his or her feelings. Congruence is essential for the vitality of a relationship and to facilitate true helping as part of the problem-solving process.

In the scenario, confrontation of the wife's actions by the social worker may assist her in seeing that her perceptions are not supported by the observed interactions during the sessions.

*Question Assesses*

Content Area III—Psychotherapy, Clinical Interventions, and Case Management; The Intervention Process (Competency); The Principles and Techniques of Interviewing (e.g., Supporting, Clarifying, Focusing, Confronting, Validating, Feedback, Reflecting, Language Differences, Use of Interpreters, Redirecting) (KSA)

### 144. B

*Rationale*

The **problem-solving model** is based on the belief that an inability to cope with a problem is due to some lack of motivation, capacity, or opportunity to solve problems in an appropriate way. Clients' problem-solving capacities or resources are maladaptive or impaired.

The goal of the problem-solving process is to enhance the client's mental, emotional, and action capacities for coping with problems and/or making accessible the opportunities and resources necessary to generate solutions to problems.

A social worker engages in the problem-solving process via the following steps—engaging, assessing, planning, intervening, evaluating, and terminating.

*Test-Taking Strategies Applied*

The question contains a qualifying word—FIRST—that is capitalized to stress the importance of the order in which the actions should occur. When answers represent actions that social workers would take throughout the helping process, using the problem-solving model (also called the planned change or helping process) can be extremely helpful in determining their order.

Exploring options for treatment is a task which occurs during planning, and providing therapy is an intervention. The correct answer, determining what has been done before to address the problem, takes place during engagement and assessment—both of which precede planning and intervention. Anxiety Disorders do not go away and require psychotherapy, medication, or both. It is likely that the client in the scenario has a treatment history that can be useful in learning about what has worked and not worked in the past.

There is no indication of risk for self-harm as the client states that he wants to change and is relying on the social worker to help him start the process.

### Question Assesses

Content Area III—Psychotherapy, Clinical Interventions, and Case Management; The Intervention Process (Competency); Problem-Solving Models and Approaches (e.g., Brief, Solution-Focused Methods or Techniques) (KSA)

### 145. A

### Rationale

**Professional objectivity** in social worker–client relationships is critical. This objectivity can be compromised if there is a conflict of interest in relationships with clients. A conflict of interest is a situation where regard for one duty may lead to disregard of another. When faced with potential or actual conflicts of interest, it is important that social workers consider the perceptions of others (clients, colleagues, the community, employers, etc.). It is important, therefore, that social workers are proactive in avoiding conflicts of interest and discuss any actual conflicts of interests with supervisors or employers so that they can be resolved. Dual relationships should never be entered into knowingly even if social workers feel that they can manage the potential conflicts or feel that there are no significant issues.

### Test-Taking Strategies Applied

While the mother in this scenario has considerable confidence in the child's social worker, there is an apparent conflict of interest for the social worker in supervising the child's visits with the father. The social worker will be expected to provide feedback to the court concerning the need for ongoing supervision of the dad's contact with his daughter.

The objectivity in writing the report may actually be or could be perceived as being impaired by virtue of the preexisting treatment role with the child.

Thus, even if the child and father are comfortable with the social worker taking on this additional role, it is inadvisable for legal and ethical reasons. The divorce may have a profound impact on the child, but exploring the effects is not related to the request at hand, so the last answer is a distractor.

*Question Assesses*

Content Area IV—Professional Values and Ethics; Professional Development and Use of Self (Competency); Professional Objectivity in the Social Worker–Client/Client System Relationship (KSA)

### 146. B

*Rationale*

**Reflective listening** is a valuable **method used to facilitate communication**. Reflective listening is at times used interchangeably with active or empathic listening. It is a way of listening and responding to clients that improves mutual understanding and trust. It is an essential skill and critical to the therapeutic process. Empathic listening builds trust and respect with clients by enabling them to share their emotions and reduce tensions. It encourages the surfacing of information and creates "safe" environments that are conducive to collaborative problem solving. When engaging in empathic listening, social workers should:

- **Concentrate on not talking** and pay attention while looking directly at clients
- **Prepare their replies**
- **Ask for time to respond** if needed
- **Pay attention** to how the person is behaving nonverbally (e.g., yelling or screaming and not making eye contact)
- **Demonstrate listening** by nodding or shaking head
- **Paraphrase** or translate what is said; reflect it back
- **Recognize client feelings** ("you seem to be frustrated," "you sound angry," "you seem to be upset")
- **Be attentive**, interested, nonjudgmental, and noncritical
- **Avoid interrupting**, changing the subject, interrogating, teaching, and giving advice

*Test-Taking Strategies Applied*

Selecting the correct answer requires knowledge that reflective listening is a communication strategy involving two key steps: seeking to understand client ideas and then offering the ideas back to them to confirm they have been understood correctly. It attempts to reconstruct what clients are thinking and feeling and to relay this understanding back. While used interchangeably at times with active listening, reflective listening is a more specific strategy than the more general methods of active listening. It arose from Carl Rogers' school of client-centered therapy in counseling theory.

The incorrect answers either do not reflect good listening skills (thinking about what should be said next or directing discussion toward other topics) or are not related to listening at all (helping clients to understand social workers' roles).

*Question Assesses*

Content Area III—Psychotherapy, Clinical Interventions, and Case Management; Therapeutic Relationship (Competency); The Principles and Techniques for Building and Maintaining a Helping Relationship (KSA)

### 147. B

*Rationale*

**Interdisciplinary collaboration** is a necessary, yet challenging social work activity. When multiple agencies which work with clients act independently of each other, the result is that clients are subject to fragmented services, none of which address clients as whole individuals. A shared vision among collaborators facilitates strategies to achieve common goals. The biggest benefit of collaboration among agencies is the improved well-being of clients.

Collaboration among agencies is the key to preventing fragmentation. In addition to reducing the likelihood of clients falling through the cracks between disparate and unconnected agencies, collaboration fosters a more holistic view of clients. With effective collaboration, service providers recognize differing viewpoints through their contact with professionals with expertise in different areas. In addition to decreasing paperwork and minimizing fragmentation, this process could help to strengthen linkages and communication among various agencies providing different services to meet clients' varying needs.

### Test-Taking Strategies Applied

The question contains a qualifying word—PRIMARY—though it is not capitalized. While the benefits listed in the incorrect response choices may result from collaborations between service providers, the correct answer to any question on the examination is always the one which speaks to enhancing the well-being of clients.

Interdisciplinary service collaborations can reduce duplication, foster innovation, and lead to enhanced effectiveness. However, they predominantly exist to bring together professionals from different professions or disciplines. The multifaceted training and experience of these providers helps to ensure that all client needs are addressed. The correct answer is the only one that references the needs of clients across life domains, which is the principal reason for taking an interdisciplinary approach.

### Question Assesses

Content Area III—Psychotherapy, Clinical Interventions, and Case Management; Consultation and Interdisciplinary Collaboration (Competency); The Process of Interdisciplinary and Intradisciplinary Team Collaboration (KSA)

### 148. B

### Rationale

A **phobia** is an Anxiety Disorder involving a persistent fear of an object, place, or situation disproportional to the threat or danger posed by the object of the fear. The person who has the phobia will go to great lengths to avoid the object of the fear and experience great distress if it is encountered. These irrational fears and reactions must result in interference with social and work life to meet the *DSM-5* criteria. There are five subtypes of Specific Phobia: animal (including the fear of snakes, spiders, rodents, and dogs), natural environment (including the fear of heights, storms, water, and the dark), blood-injection-injury (including the fear of blood, injury, needles, and medical procedures), situational (including the fear of enclosed spaces, flying, driving, tunnels, and bridges), and other. Social Phobia, involving fear of social situations, is a separate disorder.

Under *DSM-5*, several changes have been made to prevent the over-diagnosis of Specific Phobias based on the overestimation of danger or occasional fears. A client no longer has to demonstrate excessive or unreasonable anxiety for a diagnosis of Specific Phobia. Instead, the anxiety must be "out of proportion" to the threat, considering the environment and situation.

A client who has a **Specific Phobia Disorder** experiences significant and persistent fear when in the presence of, or anticipating the presence of, the object of fear, which may be an object, place, or situation.

The *DSM-5* criteria for a Specific Phobia are:

■ There is a marked and out-of-proportion fear within an environmental or situational context to the presence or anticipation of a specific object or situation.

■ Exposure to the phobic stimulus provokes an immediate anxiety response, which may take the form of a situationally bound or situationally predisposed panic attack.

■ There is recognition that the fear is out of proportion.

■ The phobic situation(s) is avoided or else is endured with intense anxiety or distress.

■ The avoidance, anxious anticipation, or distress in the feared situation(s) interferes significantly with the person's normal routine, occupational (or academic) functioning, or social activities or relationships, or there is marked distress about having the phobia.

The new *DSM-5* criteria state that the symptoms for all ages must have a duration of at least 6 months.

The anxiety, panic attack, or phobic avoidance associated with the specific object or situation must not be better accounted for by another mental disorder.

Many different types of medications are used in the treatment of Anxiety Disorders, including traditional **antianxiety drugs** such as benzodiazepines. Because they work quickly—typically bringing relief within 30 minutes to an hour—they are very effective when taken during a panic attack or another overwhelming anxiety episode. However, they can be physically addictive and need to be closely monitored.

*Test-Taking Strategies Applied*

This question requires determining the correct diagnosis for the client in the scenario. Based on the information provided, it appears that the client has a Specific Phobia, natural environment type. This diagnosis, which is an Anxiety Disorder, is best treated with antianxiety medications. Thus, the response choices must be reviewed and the drugs must next be classified into one of four major types—antipsychotics, mood stabilizers, antidepressants, or antianxiety medications. Ativan is the only antianxiety drug listed, making it the correct response choice.

Mellaril and Risperdal are antipsychotic medications which are used to control hallucinations and delusions. Tegretol is a mood stabilizer used for the treatment of Bipolar Disorder.

## Question Assesses

Content Area II—Assessment, Diagnosis, and Treatment Planning; Assessment and Diagnosis (Competency); Common Psychotropic and Non-Psychotropic Prescriptions and Over-the-Counter Medications and Their Side Effects (KSA)

### 149. C

## Rationale

There are many formats for the recording of **case notes**. Case notes document activity and client progress. They help social workers identify effective and ineffective treatment strategies. In addition, if auditors, advocates, or supervisors look at files, they need to be able to get clear pictures of clients and learn what has been done, what is working, and what areas need attention. In addition, without good, clear case notes, it can be next to impossible for successful client transition to other professionals should it be needed.

**Narrative** notes are summaries about client interactions which provide an overview of what occurred during meetings or conversations. There are no means for organizing these notes and they may vary in specificity and topic, depending upon the pressing issues. While they are open-ended, social workers should make sure that they contain all relevant information, summarizing what has occurred and what will be the focus of treatment in the future.

Subjective, objective, assessment, plan **(SOAP)** is a format used predominantly in health care facilities. The subjective section includes clients' reported symptoms and the objective section contains test and exam results. The assessment section includes conclusions and impressions based on the first two sections. The plan section explains the next steps, including the need for treatment, medication, and/or further testing.

Another format is referred to as **DAP**. This format is similar to SOAP except that both subjective and objective data are included in the same section. DAP is an acronym that stands for data, assessment, and plan. The data section includes contact information for clients, subjective and objective data, and observational notes. Subjective data is a summary of information given by clients and may include direct quotes. Objective data includes information often gleaned from direct observation or other sources, including body movements, facial expressions, test results, and so on. The assessment is a summary based on subjective and objective information collected. The last section is the treatment plan, including any referrals or interventions that have been completed or are recommended.

Another popular problem-based case recording format is assessed information, problem addressed, interventions provided, and evaluation (**APIE**). The first section includes documentation of assessed information with regard to clients' problems while the second is an explanation of problems that are to be addressed. These sections are followed by intervention descriptions and plans and evaluations of problems once interventions are complete, respectively.

### Test-Taking Strategies Applied

The question contains a qualifying word—MOST. While the client may be using another model, the scenario only describes three distinct sections, making DAP the probable model.

Narrative recording does not have distinct sections, but it is an overall summary of the details which are thought to be important. SOAP includes both the assessment and plan as separate sections, but it also separates the subjective information from the objective data. Therefore, there are four separate components of a case record. APIE contains information on evaluation findings, which are not mentioned in the social worker's notes in this question.

### Question Assesses

Content Area III—Psychotherapy, Clinical Interventions, and Case Management; Service Delivery and Management of Cases (Competency); The Principles of Case Recording, Documentation, and Management of Practice Records (KSA)

### 150. D

### Rationale

**Confidentiality** is a cornerstone of healthy therapeutic relationships and effective treatment and is based upon the ethical principles of autonomy and fidelity and, to a lesser degree, beneficence and nonmaleficence. Autonomy assumes clients have the right to decide to whom they will reveal information, and confidentiality is based upon respect for clients' ability to choose what they disclose. Fidelity refers to social workers' faithfulness and loyalty to keep promises to clients, including not revealing information clients disclose. Social workers are also honest about limits of confidentiality so clients are able to make informed decisions about self-disclosure. Beneficence and nonmaleficence have an important role in confidentiality. Clients benefit when information is kept confidential and trusting relationships can be achieved. The disclosure of private information without client consent can do harm to therapeutic relationships even when such disclosures are mandated by law.

Issues of confidentiality are often complex, especially when group therapy is provided. Group psychotherapy is a powerful and curative method of psychological treatment, but issues of confidentiality are magnified at least as many times as there are group members. Not only is information revealed to social workers, it is also revealed to other group members, and there is no guarantee that other group members will maintain confidentiality. However, group members expect complete confidentiality and do not fully understand how confidentiality in group settings differs from confidentiality in individual therapy.

Informed consent is the process whereby clients learn about confidentiality. When group treatment is being provided, education regarding confidentiality should begin prior to entering the group. Potential group members should be informed that social workers may have to break confidentiality in certain circumstances, and those circumstances should be fully explained. They should also be informed that social workers can assure confidentiality on their part (within the constraints of the law), but cannot promise that other group members will maintain confidentiality. Another important issue to discuss is the probable lack of privileged communication. Privileged communication does not usually exist in group settings due to the third-party rule, which states that information revealed in front of a third party was not intended to be private and is not privileged. Therefore, group members may be called to testify against their peers regarding information obtained in group sessions.

Confidentiality should be discussed openly, thoroughly, and often among group members. Maintaining confidentiality should be the goal for group members, and consequences for participation for those who breach confidentiality should be openly discussed. A common phrase used in group therapy is, "What is said in group—stays in group." However, absolute confidentiality in groups is difficult and often unrealistic.

### Test-Taking Strategies Applied

This is a recall question which relies on social workers understanding the ethical standards related to the provision of group versus individual therapy. In order for clients to make informed choices about what they disclose, it is critical that they understand the confidentiality standards which apply.

The social worker cannot assure the client in this scenario that information disclosed will be kept confidential as there are no legal mandates which prohibit group members from sharing it with others. The client is participating in group therapy, not individual treatment, so it is not appropriate for the social worker to ask about the nature of the information and provide "guidance" to the client. The group is the helping agent and concerns should be shared with all members, not the social worker individually. The client should also not be discouraged from sharing sensitive information with others as doing so is the basis of group therapy.

The correct answer provides the client with accurate information about confidentiality in group treatment and lets him make the decision on his own about whether to share it during the next session.

### Question Assesses

Content Area III—Psychotherapy, Clinical Interventions, and Case Management; The Intervention Process (Competency); Group Work Techniques and Approaches (e.g., Developing and Managing Group Processes and Cohesion) (KSA)

## 151. A

### Rationale

**Contracts** in social work specify goals to be accomplished and tasks to be performed to achieve these aims. They also set **time frames for interventions** and deadlines for completion of goals. They are agreements between social workers and clients and essential for positive outcomes.

It is essential that goals contained in contracts be feasible. Unachievable goals set clients up for failure, which can lead to continued disappointment, disillusionment, and defeat. Chosen goals must be able to be accomplished. In instances where clients may have unrealistic expectations, social workers must assist them in realizing what is realistic.

### Test-Taking Strategies Applied

There are many reasons that desired goals need to be examined and revised in order to be realistically achievable. In the scenario, the client has a limited number of sessions which will be paid by insurance coverage. It is premature for the social worker to advocate for additional sessions as there is no new information which would cause the insurance company to alter its decision. It is unfair for the client to think that the changes desired will occur in the time frame allotted. The client may become increasingly discouraged when goals are not achieved, jeopardizing motivation to reach desired outcomes. Lastly, making progress toward the target problem should not be abandoned completely as it was identified and prioritized through the assessment process. Instead, the social worker must tactfully work with the client to temper expectations about the amount of change that is possible in the fixed time frame.

### Question Assesses

Content Area II—Assessment, Diagnosis, and Treatment Planning; Treatment Planning (Competency); The Criteria Used in the Selection of Intervention/Treatment Modalities (e.g., Client/Client System Abilities, Culture, Life Stage) (KSA)

## 152. A

### Rationale

**Bartering arrangements**, particularly involving services, create the potential for conflicts of interest, exploitation, and inappropriate boundaries in social workers' relationships with clients. Social workers should avoid accepting goods or services from clients as payment for professional services. *Social workers should explore and may participate in bartering only in very limited circumstances* when it can be demonstrated that such arrangements are an accepted practice among professionals in the local community, considered to be essential for the provision of services, negotiated without coercion, and entered into at the client's initiative and with the client's informed consent. *Social workers who accept goods or services from clients as payment for professional services assume the full burden of demonstrating that this arrangement will not be detrimental to the client or the professional relationship.*

### Test-Taking Strategies Applied

While bartering in social work is extremely rare, the 2018 *NASW Code of Ethics* provides specific guidance about the criteria which must be met in order for it to occur. While these standards are located in provisions about payment for services, they speak to the potential that such financial arrangements have for inappropriate professional boundaries between social workers and clients.

The question contains a qualifying word—EXCEPT—that requires social workers to select the response choice which is not specified in the 2018 *NASW Code of Ethics* with regard to bartering. When EXCEPT is used as a qualifying word, it is often helpful to remove it from the question and eliminate the three response choices which must be done as per ethical standards. This approach will leave the one response choice which is not required.

Social workers—not clients—must demonstrate that bartering relationships are not detrimental.

## Question Assesses

Content Area IV—Professional Values and Ethics; Professional Values and Ethical Issues (Competency); Legal and/or Ethical Issues Related to the Practice of Social Work, Including Responsibility to Clients/Client Systems, Colleagues, the Profession, and Society (KSA)

### 153. C

## Rationale

**Family systems theory** views issues and problems within a circular fashion, using what is described as a systemic perspective; this means that the event and the problem exist within the context of the relationship, where each influences the other. Family systems theory aims to assess these patterns of interactions and look at why things may be happening instead of why they happened.

Family systems theory considers the nature of relationships to be bidirectional, and moves away from seeking blame of one person for the dynamic of the relationship. *The exception to this theory is within abusive relationships, where the responsibility and blame lay clearly with the perpetrator of the abuse.*

Within family systems theory, behaviors are believed to arise due to the interrelated nature and connectedness of various family members. For example, to seek understanding of children in distress, their behavior would be viewed through the lens of their **family (parent–child) behaviors** and family systems rather than looking at young persons in isolation.

**Polygamy** or the act of having more than one spouse at a time is based on cultural beliefs or traditions. There is no blame associated with polygamy.

**Adultery** or infidelity, using a family systems approach, is seen as a "family affair" that must be understood and treated within the marital system rather than from an individual perspective. Social workers use marital therapy to understand the relational dynamics that led to and/or sustain affairs. They shy away from blame and focus on issues of intimacy, communication, expectations, agreements, and conflict management in the marriage.

### Test-Taking Strategies Applied

This is a recall question about family dynamics and functioning. Social workers must understand family systems theory, as well as the dynamics of abuse. *Victims should never be seen as contributing to or responsible for their abuse.* As the question asks about "blame for the dynamics" resting with specific individuals as opposed to resulting from the action of all parties, a belief contrary to a family systems approach, the correct answer must involve abuse of one person by another.

### Question Assesses

Content Area I—Human Development, Diversity, and Behavior in the Environment; Human Behavior in the Social Environment (Competency); Family Dynamics and Functioning and the Effects on Individuals, Families, Groups, Organizations, and Communities (KSA)

### 154. A

### Rationale

**Cultural sensitivity** refers to a set of skills used in social work practice that facilitates learning about and understanding clients whose cultural background may not be the same. Social workers must operate with the awareness that cultural differences exist between them and clients without assigning these differences a value. These differences are positive—not better or worse, right or wrong.

Being culturally sensitive does not mean being an expert in each culture's values. It simply means a willingness to ask honest questions, seek understanding, and demonstrate empathy rather than judging. It also means that, when knowingly entering spaces in which there will be cultural differences at play, social workers should do a bit of homework beforehand and avoid jumping to conclusions.

The most important thing when being culturally sensitive is remembering to ground interactions in the understanding that clients' background, experiences, and values naturally vary from those of social workers. These differences should lead to understanding and empathy, rather than judgment.

*Test-Taking Strategies Applied*

This is a recall question which relies on social workers understanding the effect of culture, race, and ethnicity on behaviors, attitudes, and identity. In the scenario, the social worker is demonstrating respect and not assuming that the client would like to be called by his or her first name. Such action is an example of cultural sensitivity. Professional boundaries are the invisible structures which are imposed in therapeutic relationships. The question to the client is not indicative of a limit placed on the interactions between the client and social worker. Objectivity concerns examining issues truthfully and impartially. The social worker is not examining or viewing information—he or she is simply asking a question. Ethnocentrism is viewing others' cultures solely by the values and standards of one's own culture. The social worker is doing the opposite in the scenario.

*Question Assesses*

Content Area I—Human Development, Diversity, and Behavior in the Environment; Diversity and Discrimination (Competency); The Effect of Culture, Race, and Ethnicity on Behaviors, Attitudes, and Identity (KSA)

## 155. D

*Rationale*

Social workers must have basic **research knowledge** in order to evaluate the appropriateness of interventions and assist in decision making. The promotion of evidence-based research within social work is widespread. Evidence-based research gathers evidence that may be informative for clinical practice or clinical decision making. It also involves the process of gathering and synthesizing scientific evidence from various sources and translating it to be applied to practice.

The use of evidence-based practice places the well-being of clients at the forefront, desiring to discover and use the best practices available. The use of evidence-based practices (EBPs) requires social workers to only use services and techniques that were found effective by rigorous, scientific, empirical studies—that is, outcome research.

Social workers must be willing and able to locate and use evidence-based interventions. In areas in which evidence-based interventions are not available, social workers must still use research to guide practice. Applying knowledge gleaned from research findings will assist social workers in providing services informed by scientific investigation and lead to new interventions that can be evaluated as EBPs.

When reading and interpreting experimental research findings, social workers must be able to identify **independent variables** (or those that are believed to be causes) and **dependent variables** (which are the impacts or results). In many studies, the independent variable is the treatment provided and the dependent variable is the target behavior that is trying to be changed. The **reliability** and **validity** of research findings should also be assessed. Reliability is concerned with obtaining the same findings repeatedly when conditions are not altered. Validity focuses on accuracy. There are two types of validity—internal validity and external validity. **Internal validity** is the confidence that exists that the independent variable is the cause of the dependent variable and not extraneous factors. **External validity** is the extent to which the same results will be produced if the context or population is altered. It determines to what extent an intervention can be generalized.

    **Measurement error** is the difference between what assessments indicate and actual constructs (knowledge and abilities). These errors are often introduced when collecting data.

### Test-Taking Strategies Applied

This is a recall question which relies on social workers understanding key research terms and concepts. Such knowledge is essential to having a sufficient understanding of KSAs related to the use of measurable objectives, subjective and objective data, applying research to practice, and so on. In addition to being able to understand and explain the meaning of important research terminology, social workers must be versed in experimental and single-subject research designs.

### Question Assesses

Content Area II—Assessment, Diagnosis, and Treatment Planning; Treatment Planning (Competency); Methods to Assess Reliability and Validity in Social Work Research (KSA)

### 156. D

### Rationale

**Anxiety Disorders** include disorders that share features of excessive fear and anxiety and related behavioral disturbances. Fear is the emotional response to real or perceived imminent threat, whereas anxiety is anticipation of future threat. Fear is more often associated with surges of autonomic arousal necessary for fight or flight, thoughts of immediate danger, and escape behaviors, and anxiety is more often associated with muscle tension and vigilance in preparation for future danger and cautious or avoidant behaviors. *Panic attacks* are a type of fear response. Panic attacks are not limited to Anxiety Disorders, but rather can be seen in other mental disorders as well.

In the *DSM-5*, changes were made to the chapter on Anxiety Disorders, representing both additions and deletions. Obsessive-Compulsive Disorder (OCD), which was listed as an Anxiety Disorder in the *DSM-IV*, was moved into its own chapter with Hoarding Disorder (a new disorder), Trichotillomania (Hair-Pulling), and so on. Acute Stress Disorder was also moved—into a chapter with Trauma- and Stressor-Related Disorders, which includes Post-Traumatic Stress Disorder. Such removals resulted from a scientific review that concluded that these disorders were not characterized by the presence of anxiety.

In the *DSM-IV*, Separation Anxiety Disorder was included in a chapter with other disorders that are first diagnosed in infancy, childhood, or adolescence. However, its listing as an Anxiety Disorder in the *DSM-5* is based on scientific evidence that links it with other disorders, such as Selective Mutism, Specific Phobia, Social Anxiety Disorder, Agoraphobia, and so on.

### Test-Taking Strategies Applied

This is a recall question which relies on social workers knowing the *DSM-5* and its diagnoses. Social workers should expect to get as many as eight or so such questions.

When studying for the examination, social workers do not need to memorize all of the diagnostic criteria, but should know the defining or distinguishing feelings, thoughts, and behaviors associated with each disorder. Also, questions may ask about groupings of disorders—such as those which are Neurodevelopmental, Psychotic, Depressive, and so on. Thus, being able to recall in which chapter particular disorders are listed can be helpful, such as is the case in this question.

### Question Assesses

Content Area II—Assessment, Diagnosis, and Treatment Planning; Assessment and Diagnosis (Competency); The Current Diagnostic and Statistical Manual of the American Psychiatric Association (KSA)

### 157. B

### Rationale

Erikson's psychosocial theory of development considers the impact of various "crises" **on personality development** from childhood to adulthood. According to Erikson's theory, everyone must pass through a series of eight interrelated stages over the entire life cycle.

1. **Infancy**

   *Basic Trust Versus Mistrust*

   During the first or second year of life, the major emphasis is on nurturing, especially in terms of visual contact and touch. A child will develop optimism, trust, confidence, and security if properly cared for and handled. If a child does not experience trust, he or she may develop insecurity, worthlessness, and general mistrust of the world.

2. **Toddler/Early Childhood Years**

   *Autonomy Versus Shame and Doubt*

   At this point, a child has an opportunity to build self-esteem and autonomy as he or she learns new skills and right from wrong. The well-cared-for child is sure of himself or herself, carrying himself or herself with pride rather than shame. Children tend to be vulnerable during this stage, sometimes feeling shame and low self-esteem during an inability to learn certain skills.

3. **Preschooler**

   *Initiative Versus Guilt*

   During this period, a child experiences a desire to copy adults and take initiative in creating play situations. A child also begins to use that wonderful word for exploring the world—"Why?" If a child is frustrated over natural desires and goals, he or she easily experiences guilt. The most significant relationship is with the basic family.

4. **School-Age Child**

   *Industry Versus Inferiority*

   During this stage, a child is capable of learning, creating, and accomplishing numerous new skills and knowledge, thus developing a sense of industry. This is also a very social stage of development; if there are unresolved feelings of inadequacy and inferiority, there can be serious problems in terms of competence and self-esteem. As the world expands a bit, the most significant relationship is with the school and neighborhood. Parents are no longer the complete authorities they once were, although they are still important.

5. **Adolescence**

   *Identity Versus Role Confusion*

   An adolescent must struggle to discover and find his or her own identity, while negotiating and struggling with social interactions and "fitting in," as well as develop a sense of morality and right from wrong. Some adolescents attempt to delay entrance to adulthood and withdraw from responsibilities. Those unsuccessful with this stage tend to experience role confusion and upheaval. Adolescents begin to develop a strong affiliation and devotion to ideals, causes, and friends.

6. **Young Adulthood**
*Intimacy Versus Isolation*
At the young adult stage, people tend to seek companionship and love. Young adults seek deep intimacy and satisfying relationships, but if they are unsuccessful, isolation may occur. Significant relationships at this stage are with marital partners and friends.

7. **Middle Adulthood**
*Generativity Versus Stagnation*
During this time, adults strive to create or nurture things that will outlast them, often by parenting children or contributing to positive changes that benefit other people. Contributing to society and doing things to benefit future generations are important. **Generativity** refers to "making a mark" on the world through caring for others, as well as creating and accomplishing things that make the world a better place. **Stagnation** refers to the failure to find a way to contribute. Those who are successful during this phase will feel that they are contributing to the world by being active in their homes and communities. Others may feel disconnected or uninvolved. Some characteristics of stagnation include being self-centered, failing to get involved with others, not taking an interest in productivity, exerting no efforts to improve the self, and placing one's concerns over above all else. It is at this point in life that some experience what is often referred to as a "midlife crisis" and feel regret. This might involve regretting missed opportunities such as going to school, pursuing a career, or having children. In some cases, this crisis is an opportunity to make adjustments that will lead to greater fulfillment.

8. **Late Adulthood**
*Integrity Versus Despair—Wisdom*
The last stage involves much reflection. Some older adults look back with a feeling of *integrity*—that is, contentment and fulfillment—having led a meaningful life and made a valuable

contribution to society. Others have a sense of despair during this stage, reflecting upon their experiences and failures. They may fear death as they struggle to find a purpose to their lives, wondering "What was the point of life? Was it worth it?"

### Test-Taking Strategies Applied

This is a recall question which relies on social workers understanding the stages of psychosocial development. The scenario provides the age of the client, as well as his struggles—both of which can assist with distinguishing the correct answer from the incorrect ones.

### Question Assesses

Content Area I—Human Development, Diversity, and Behavior in the Environment; Human Growth and Development (Competency); Theories of Human Development Throughout the Lifespan (e.g., Physical, Social, Emotional, Cognitive, Behavioral) (KSA)

## 158. C

### Rationale

An **ethical dilemma** is a predicament when a social worker must decide between two viable solutions that seem to have similar ethical value. Sometimes two viable ethical solutions can conflict with each other. Social workers should be aware of any conflicts between personal and professional values and deal with them responsibly. In instances where social workers' ethical obligations conflict with agency policies or relevant laws or regulations, they should make a responsible effort to resolve the conflict in a manner that is consistent with the values, principles, and standards expressed in the 2018 *NASW Code of Ethics*.

In order to resolve this conflict, ethical problem solving is needed. There are six essential steps in ethical problem solving:

1. Identify ethical standards, as defined by the professional code of ethics, that are being compromised (always go to the code of ethics first—do not rely on a supervisor or coworkers).

2. Determine whether there is an ethical issue or dilemma.

3. Weigh ethical issues in light of key social work values and principles as defined by the code of ethics.

4. Suggest modifications in light of the prioritized ethical values and principles that are central to the dilemma.

5. Implement modifications in light of prioritized ethical values and principles.

6. Monitor for new ethical issues or dilemmas.

### Test-Taking Strategies Applied

The question contains a qualifying word—NEXT. Its use indicates that the order in which the response choices should occur is critical. Knowledge of the sequential steps in the ethical problem-solving process is needed. The question states that there is already a realization that an ethical dilemma exists. Once the issue has been identified, social workers must next weigh ethical issues in light of key social work values and principles.

Seeking supervision is a practical answer which is incorrect as it does not represent a step in the ethical problem solving model. Social workers often seek supervision when they are not sure of the correct course of action. The examination expects social workers to have knowledge about the proper actions to take based on best practices in the field.

Social workers cannot choose a correct course of action based on prioritized ethical values until they have been weighed in light of existing principles. Thus, this action will occur after the one specified in the correct answer.

Determining the root cause of problems is critical, but the question is asking for the sequential steps in ethical problem solving. The issues cannot be eradicated until all steps have been taken, making this answer also incorrect.

### Question Assesses

Content Area IV—Professional Values and Ethics; Professional Values and Ethical Issues (Competency); Techniques to Identify and Resolve Ethical Dilemmas (KSA)

### 159. A

### Rationale

**Alcohol Withdrawal** is a potentially life-threatening condition that can occur in clients who have been drinking heavily for weeks, months, or years and then either stop or significantly reduce their alcohol consumption. Alcohol Withdrawal symptoms can begin as early as 2 hours after the last drink, persist for weeks, and range from mild anxiety and shakiness to severe complications, such as seizures and **delirium**

tremens (DTs). DTs are characterized by confusion, rapid heartbeat, and fever.

Because Alcohol Withdrawal symptoms can rapidly worsen, it is important for clients to seek medical attention even if symptoms are seemingly mild. Appropriate Alcohol Withdrawal treatments can reduce the risk of developing withdrawal seizures or DTs.

Prescription drugs of choice include benzodiazepines, such as diazepam (Valium), chlordiazepoxide (Librium), lorazepam (Ativan), and so on. Such medications can help control the shakiness, anxiety, and confusion associated with alcohol withdrawal and reduce the risk of withdrawal seizures and DTs. In clients with mild to moderate symptoms, anticonvulsant drugs may be an effective alternative to benzodiazepines, because they are not sedating and have low potential for abuse.

*Because successful treatment of Alcohol Withdrawal does not address the underlying disease of addiction, it should be followed by treatment for alcohol abuse.* Relatively brief outpatient interventions can be effective, but more intensive therapy may be required. Services range from 12-step groups—such as Alcoholics Anonymous and Narcotics Anonymous—to residential treatment that offers a combination of cognitive behavioral and family therapy.

### Test-Taking Strategies Applied

The question is asking about Alcohol Withdrawal—not the treatment of the underlying disorder. Alcohol Withdrawal focuses on reducing the effects of the symptoms and medically monitoring them for serious health implications. Medications are used to help shakiness, anxiety, and confusion. Thus, psychopharmacology is the treatment of choice to address them. The incorrect response choices are effective treatments for the underlying disease and relapse prevention, which occur after withdrawal symptoms have been addressed.

### Question Assesses

Content Area II—Assessment, Diagnosis, and Treatment Planning; Treatment Planning (Competency); The Criteria Used in the Selection of Intervention/Treatment Modalities (e.g., Client/Client System Abilities, Culture, Life Stage) (KSA)

### 160. A

### Rationale

**Privileged communication** is a legal right, existing by statute or common law, that protects the client from having his or her confidences revealed publicly from the witness stand during legal proceedings. Certain professionals, including social workers, cannot legally be compelled to reveal confidential information they received from their clients. The privilege protects clients, and the right to exercise privilege belongs to clients, not to professionals.

There are four conditions that are generally accepted as being necessary for a communication to be considered privileged:

1. The communication must originate in the confidence that it will not be disclosed.

2. The element of confidentiality must be essential to the full and satisfactory maintenance of the relationship between the parties.

3. The relationship must be one that in the opinion of the community ought to be fostered.

4. The injury to the relationship caused by disclosure must be greater than the benefit gained through disclosure for the correct disposal of litigation.

The landmark Supreme Court decision on the protection of psychotherapist–client privilege is *Jaffee v. Redmond*, 518 U.S. 1 (1996). The case created by common law the right for federal litigants and witnesses to keep their private psychotherapy records out of the courtroom, rejecting an approach that would have permitted federal judges to review and weigh the value of the potential evidence excluded under the privilege.

The *Jaffee* decision is notable in several respects. For social workers, it is a landmark ruling recognizing the professionalism and relevance of social workers providing psychotherapy in today's mental health treatment milieu. For trial lawyers and their clients, *Jaffee* presented a new rule of evidence, drawing a bright line around a certain type of evidence that is inaccessible for legal probing. For mental health clients, the case bolsters the wall of protection afforded to the intimacy of the therapeutic relationship. *Jaffee* has also contributed to the treatment of health privacy in the Health Insurance Portability and Accountability Act of 1996 (HIPAA) regulations.

Although *Jaffee* is only directly applicable to cases filed in federal court, many states have had occasion to review the *Jaffee* decision as they decide similar matters under their jurisdiction.

### Test-Taking Strategies Applied

The question contains a qualifying word—BEST. While all of the response choices relate to client privacy, only the correct answer mentions privilege being a legal term which aims to keep communication from being disclosed in court proceedings.

It is best practice for social workers to get clients' written consent when releasing information, though verbal consent is acceptable in certain situations. Social workers must report suspected child abuse and neglect, but such a mandate is not related to the definition of privilege, making the third answer listed incorrect. Lastly, often treatment information of minors cannot be withheld from parents, though laws vary across states/jurisdictions given the ages of minors and types of treatment received. This answer is also incorrect as it is not related to privilege, but concerns instead another important privacy topic.

### Question Assesses

Content Area IV—Professional Values and Ethics; Confidentiality (Competency); Legal and/or Ethical Issues Regarding Confidentiality, Including Electronic Information Security (KSA)

### 161. C

### Rationale

A **forensic interview** of a child is a developmentally sensitive and legally sound method of gathering factual information regarding allegations of abuse or exposure to violence. This interview is conducted by a competently trained, neutral professional, such as a social worker, utilizing research and practice.

The forensic interview is one component of a comprehensive child abuse investigation, which includes, but is not limited to, the following disciplines: law enforcement and child protection investigators, prosecutors, child protection attorneys, victim advocates, and medical and mental health practitioners. *Forensic interviewing is a first step in most child protective services investigations, one in which a professional interviews a child to find out if he or she has been maltreated.*

*In addition to yielding the information needed to make a determination about whether abuse or neglect has occurred, this approach produces evidence that will stand up in court if the investigation leads to criminal prosecution.* Properly conducted forensic interviews are legally sound in part because they ensure the interviewer's objectivity, employ nonleading techniques, and emphasize careful documentation of the interview.

A fuller understanding of forensic interviewing and its role in child welfare can be gained by comparing it with social work interviewing, another type of interviewing commonly used by child welfare workers. The social work interview allows social workers to assess and identify a family's strengths and needs and develop a service plan with the family. This broad, versatile approach incorporates the use of a variety of interviewing techniques. Social work interviewing is used at every step of child welfare, from intake through closure; it is used with individuals and groups, children and adults.

Although it employs some of the same techniques as the social work interview, such as open-ended and forced-choice questions, the forensic interview is much more focused. Generally, it is used only during the assessment portion of an investigation, and involves only the children who are the subject of the investigation.

### Test-Taking Strategies Applied

Forensic denotes the scientific methods and techniques used in the investigation of crime. Its use relates to the collection of evidence used for prosecution. This question requires social workers to be knowledgeable about legal terms and the distinction between forensic and social work interviewing.

### Question Assesses

Content Area IV—Professional Values and Ethics; Confidentiality (Competency); Legal and/or Ethical Issues Regarding Mandatory Reporting (e.g., Abuse, Threat of Harm, Impaired Professionals, etc.) (KSA)

### 162. A

### Rationale

**Maslow's hierarchy of needs** is a motivational theory comprising a five-tier model of human needs, often depicted as hierarchical levels within a pyramid.

Maslow stated that people are motivated to achieve certain needs and that some needs take precedence over others. The most basic need is for physical survival, which will be the first thing that motivates behavior.

This five-tier model can be divided into **deficiency needs** and **growth needs**. The first four levels are often referred to as deficiency needs and the top level is known as growth needs. Growth needs can never be satisfied completely. They consist of the need to know and understand. They are linked to **self-actualization.**

Deficiency needs are said to motivate people when they are unmet. Also, the need to fulfill such needs will become stronger the longer the duration they are denied.

Lower level deficit needs must be satisfied before progressing on to meet higher level growth needs. When a deficit need has been satisfied it will go away, and our activities become habitually directed toward meeting the next set of needs that we have yet to satisfy. These then become our salient needs. However, growth needs continue to be felt and may even become stronger once they have been engaged.

### Test-Taking Strategies Applied

Often the names of theorists are not mentioned in questions. However, reasoning using their work is essential to successfully select the correct answers. Maslow's hierarchy of needs can be divided into basic (or deficiency) needs (i.e., physiological, safety, social, and esteem) and growth needs (i.e., self-actualization). "Deficiency needs" arise due to deprivation, according to Maslow.

The question contains a qualifying word—NOT—that requires social workers to select the response choice which is not a deficiency need. When NOT is used as a qualifying word, it is often helpful to remove it from the question and eliminate the three response choices which are deficiency needs. This approach will leave the one response choice which is NOT a deficiency need, but instead a growth need.

### Question Assesses

Content Area I—Human Development, Diversity, and Behavior in the Environment; Human Growth and Development (Competency); Basic Human Needs (KSA)

### 163. C

### Rationale

Social workers' **ethical responsibilities** include those related to payment for services.

When setting fees, social workers should ensure that the fees are fair, reasonable, and commensurate with the services performed. Consideration should be given to clients' ability to pay.

Social workers should avoid accepting goods or services from clients as payment for professional services. Bartering arrangements, particularly involving services, create the potential for conflicts of interest, exploitation, and inappropriate boundaries in social workers' relationships with clients. Social workers should explore and may participate in bartering only in very limited circumstances when it can be demonstrated that such arrangements are an accepted practice among professionals in the local community, considered to be essential for the provision of services, negotiated without coercion, and entered into at the client's initiative and with the client's informed consent. Social workers who accept goods or services from clients as payment for professional services assume the full burden of demonstrating that this arrangement will not be detrimental to the client or the professional relationship.

Social workers in fee-for-service settings may terminate services to clients who are not paying an overdue balance if the financial contractual arrangements have been made clear to the client, if the client does not pose an imminent danger to self or others, and if the clinical and other consequences of the current nonpayment have been addressed and discussed with the client. Social workers should not terminate services to pursue a social, financial, or sexual relationship with a client.

*Social workers should not solicit a private fee or other remuneration for providing services to clients who are entitled to such available services through the social workers' employer or agency.*

### Test-Taking Strategies Applied

This is a recall question which requires social workers to select the unethical action "according to the professional code of ethics." While the examination will never refer directly to the 2018 *NASW Code of Ethics* as there are other professional organizations with ethical mandates, it is helpful to read the 2018 *NASW Code of Ethics* and remember its standards when choosing between answers. Most questions on the examination will focus on the first section, which addresses social workers' ethical responsibilities to clients. The correct answer is always the one which most closely mirrors the standard which is explicitly stated in the 2018 *NASW Code of Ethics*.

### Question Assesses

Content Area IV—Professional Values and Ethics; Professional Values and Ethical Issues (Competency); Legal and/or Ethical Issues Related to the Practice of Social Work, Including Responsibility to Clients/Client Systems, Colleagues, the Profession, and Society (KSA)

### 164. D

### Rationale

According to the *Diagnostic and Statistical Manual of Mental Disorders* (5th ed.; *DSM-5*), to meet the criteria for diagnosis of **Schizophrenia**, a client must have experienced at least two of the following symptoms:

- Delusions
- Hallucinations
- Disorganized speech

- Disorganized or catatonic behavior
- Negative symptoms

At least one of the symptoms must be the presence of delusions, hallucinations, or disorganized speech.

Continuous signs of the disturbance must persist for at least 6 months, during which the client must experience at least 1 month of active symptoms (or less if successfully treated), with social or occupational deterioration problems occurring over a significant amount of time. These problems must not be attributable to another condition.

The American Psychiatric Association (APA) removed Schizophrenia subtypes from the *DSM-5* because they did not appear to be helpful for providing better-targeted treatment or predicting treatment response.

Treatments for Schizophrenia are aimed at reducing or eliminating symptoms of Schizophrenia, including hallucinations, delusions, and jumbled speech. There is, however, no cure for Schizophrenia. Most clients will require both medications and psychotherapy. **Antipsychotics** are a class of psychiatric medication primarily used to manage psychosis (including delusions, hallucinations, paranoia, or disordered thought), principally in Schizophrenia. However, their long-term use is associated with significant side effects such as involuntary movement disorders and metabolic syndrome.

### Test-Taking Strategies Applied

This question requires determining the correct diagnosis for the client in the scenario. Based on the information provided, it appears that the client has Schizophrenia. This diagnosis is listed in the *DSM-5* with Schizophrenia Spectrum and Other Disorders, such as Delusional Disorder, Brief Psychotic Disorder, Schizophreniform Disorder, Schizoaffective Disorder, and so on. These disorders are generally treated with antipsychotic medications. Thus, the response choices must be reviewed and the drugs must next be classified into one of four major types—antipsychotics, mood stabilizers, antidepressants, or antianxiety medications. Clozaril is the only antipsychotic drug listed, making it the correct response choice.

Paxil and Prozac are antidepressant medications while Lithium is a mood stabilizer used for the treatment of Bipolar Disorder.

### Question Assesses

Content Area II—Assessment, Diagnosis, and Treatment Planning; Assessment and Diagnosis (Competency); Common Psychotropic and

Non-Psychotropic Prescriptions and Over-the-Counter Medications and Their Side Effects (KSA)

### 165. A

*Rationale*

From the structural perspective, **roles** are the culturally defined norms—rights, duties, expectations, and standards for behavior—associated with a given social position. In other words, social position is seen as influencing behaviors. In addition, statuses such as gender, ethnicity, sexual orientation, and social class also shape roles.

For example, as a mother, a woman is expected to place the care of her child above all other concerns. However, this normative expectation varies across cultures, with some cultures expecting mothers to be paid workers as well. Many cultures believe that women with preschool-age children should not work outside of the home and that their children will suffer if they do.

The actual enactment of role behavior, however, may not correspond to the **role expectations**. **Role competence**, or success in carrying out a role, can vary depending on social contexts and resources. In countries with strong normative expectations for women to be full-time mothers, single mothers and low-income mothers often have to violate these role expectations and have been criticized as less competent mothers as a result.

Indeed, there is pressure to conform successfully to roles. Sanctions are used as tools of enforcement. Punishments for not following the role of mother can range from informal sanctions, such as rebukes from family members, to formal sanctions, such as divorce.

*Test-Taking Strategies Applied*

Social workers must be aware of social role theory and view problems as emerging from interactions between clients and their environments. Person-in-environment perspectives are sensitive to role conflicts experienced by clients.

In the scenario, the client is facing conflicting demands and expectations—as a mother, wife, professional, and so on. The client is the woman and the problem should not be viewed as a family issue. Family problems are best resolved by family therapy in which the interactions of members are the focus of intervention.

Cultural bias involves a prejudice or highlighted distinction in viewpoint that suggests a preference of one culture over another. There are cultural differences in views between the client and her husband's family, but the problem does not stem from cultural bias. If cultural bias existed, intervention would focus on education of the client about diverse perspectives. The client recognizes the views of her husband's family and does not appear to see her views as superior. However, she is unhappy due to the conflict that exists between the fulfillment of the various roles.

Social injustice is an unfair practice that results in violation of human rights. Her problem is a personal one and not an indicator of social injustice.

## Question Assesses

Content Area I—Human Development, Diversity, and Behavior in the Environment; Human Behavior in the Social Environment (Competency); Role Theories (KSA)

### 166. B

## Rationale

A **doorknob disclosure** is an uncomfortable, painful, or embarrassing revelation offered at the end of a session, usually by a client who is leaving. Social workers often see clients reveal their most painful conflicts during the last 30 seconds of sessions, just when they are ready to leave. Often they already have their hands on the door knobs. These revelations may be new issues or other aspects of problems already discussed.

The two main reasons for doorknob disclosures are (a) the need to gauge reactions because of fear, rejection, or judgment about the disclosed material; and (b) the need to prolong the helping relationship by extending the session or number of sessions due to fear of not being able to cope without support.

Doorknob disclosures are often a form of resistance. Bringing up important material or intense emotions at the end of sessions, rather than earlier, ensures that there will not be enough time to deal with it.

Social workers must be skilled in the principles of communication—encouraging clients to raise all issues early in the session and therapeutic process. Social workers should also help manage the time in sessions—giving clients ample notice of when sessions are drawing to an end, which is an inappropriate time to bring up new concerns or topics.

Immediate responses to doorknob disclosures need to be to reassure clients that they will get to discuss material at the next sessions (once ruling out that there is an immediate safety issue that requires immediate attention). If the disclosure comes from a fear of coping alone or ending the therapeutic relationship, time should be spent discussing this issue—rather than the disclosure itself.

## Test-Taking Strategies Applied

The question contains a qualifying word—MOST. While clients may use doorknob disclosures for more than one purpose, revealing information in this manner clearly stems from fear. Clients want the safety of gauging social workers' reactions to the material and/or lack time to discuss revelations more fully. It can be comforting to clients to bring up painful or sensitive topics in this manner as they have the knowledge that they will not have to explore them in more depth until the next session, giving them time to feel content with even saying the information out loud.

## Question Assesses

Content Area III—Psychotherapy, Clinical Interventions, and Case Management; Therapeutic Relationship (Competency); Verbal and Nonverbal Communication Techniques (KSA)

### 167. B

## Rationale

Death is just one **life event or crisis** which impacts families. When deaths of family members occur, children go through a series of stages in trying to understand its meaning. For example, preschool children usually see death as reversible, temporary, and impersonal. Watching cartoon characters on television miraculously rise up whole again after having been crushed or blown apart tends to reinforce this notion. In order to identify when death is truly understood by children, it is necessary to outline the complex concepts associated with death, including:

- Irreversibility or finality, the understanding that the dead cannot come back to life
- Universality or applicability, the understanding that all living things (and only living things) die
- Personal mortality, the understanding that death applies to oneself
- Inevitability, the understanding that all living things must die eventually
- Cessation or nonfunctionality, the understanding that bodily and mental functions cease after death
- Causality, the understanding that death is ultimately caused by a breakdown of bodily functions

■ Unpredictability, the understanding that the timing of (natural) death is not known in advance

Piaget's cognitive developmental stages indicate that these death concepts cannot really be understood by someone until age 7 years at the absolute earliest. Using Piaget's model, child understanding emerges as follows:

■ First stage—Preoperational (2–7 years)—Children think of death as a temporary or reversible state, and tend to characterize death with respect to concrete behaviors such as being still or having closed eyes or departing.

■ Second stage—Concrete operational (7–11 years)—Children recognize that all living things must die and that death is irreversible; however, they consider death to be caused by concrete elements originating from outside the body and do not recognize death as an intrinsic and natural part of the life cycle.

■ Final stage—Formal operational (11 years and older)—Children hold an adult view of death as an inevitable, universal final stage in the life cycle of all living things, characterized by the cessation of bodily functions.

Thus, children's understanding of death is truly linked to cognitive developmental maturation.

### Test-Taking Strategies Applied

If the age of a client is mentioned in a scenario, it is usually relevant in selecting the correct response choice. The age is a useful hint of where a client is in the life course and what might be expected with regard to his or her cognitive, emotional, and/or social development.

This scenario requires knowledge about the complex concepts associated with death as well as child development. Most questions, like this one, require an integration of several knowledge areas. Memorization is not needed when studying, but instead the ability to apply knowledge learned.

All of the response choices listed, except the first one, concern the child's ability to comprehend death. As the child is only 4 years old, each answer must be evaluated based on the theoretical knowledge about cognition at this age. As the beginning of abstract thought does not occur until age 7, the child would see death as a temporary or reversible state, like being asleep.

The first answer is incorrect as children find death to be an emotionally charged issue, reacting with sadness, anxiety, and fear over separation.

### Question Assesses

Content Area I—Human Development, Diversity, and Behavior in the Environment; Human Growth and Development (Competency); Theories of Human Development Throughout the Lifespan (e.g., Physical, Social, Emotional, Cognitive, Behavioral) (KSA)

### 168. A

### Rationale

Social workers should respect clients' right to **privacy and confidentiality**. Social workers may disclose confidential information when appropriate with valid consent from a client or a person legally authorized to consent on behalf of a client. Social workers should protect the confidentiality of all information obtained in the course of professional service, except for compelling professional reasons. The general expectation that social workers will keep information confidential does not apply when disclosure is necessary to prevent serious, foreseeable, and imminent harm to a client or others such as duty to warn, child abuse, and so on.

In these instances, social workers should inform clients, to the extent possible, about the disclosure of confidential information and the potential consequences, when feasible *before* the disclosure is made (*NASW Code of Ethics, 2018—1.07 Privacy and Confidentiality*). This applies whether social workers disclose confidential information on the basis of a legal requirement or client consent.

In all instances, social workers should disclose the least amount of confidential information necessary to achieve the desired purpose; only information that is directly relevant to the purpose for which the disclosure is made should be revealed.

### Test-Taking Strategies Applied

The 2018 *NASW Code of Ethics* explicitly acknowledges social workers' ethical obligation to inform clients, to the extent possible, of the need to make mandatory reports due to suspected child maltreatment. This obligation should not result in delays in reporting. Additionally, informing clients does not mean that social workers should be deterred in any way from reporting based upon clients' reactions. Social workers must be honest with clients throughout the problem-solving process.

Clients should be aware of social workers' obligations for mandatory reporting since it is to be discussed as soon as possible in social worker–client relationships and as needed throughout the course of these relationships.

### Question Assesses

Content Area IV—Professional Values and Ethics; Confidentiality (Competency); Legal and/or Ethical Issues Regarding Mandatory Reporting (e.g., Abuse, Threat of Harm, Impaired Professionals, etc.) (KSA)

### 169. B

### Rationale

The 2018 *NASW Code of Ethics* explicitly acknowledges that social workers should not provide clinical services to individuals with whom they have had a prior sexual relationship. Providing clinical services to a former sexual partner has the potential to be harmful to the individual and is likely to make it difficult for a social worker and individual to maintain **appropriate professional boundaries**. In addition, social workers should not engage in sexual activities or sexual contact with current or former clients or clients' relatives or other individuals with whom clients maintain a close personal relationship when there is a risk of exploitation or potential harm to a client (*NASW Code of Ethics, 2018—1.09 Sexual Relationships*).

### Test-Taking Strategies Applied

In the scenario, the social worker is aware that the referral is for a woman with whom he had a prior intimate relationship. According to the 2018 *NASW Code of Ethics*, it is unethical to provide clinical services to this client. Since there should be no therapeutic relationship between them, meeting with the client to discuss her problem or scheduling an intake are both inappropriate. Informing a supervisor is advisable, but not a sufficient action to properly "act ethically in this situation." The social worker must decline the referral even if he is the only Spanish-speaking clinician. Services may need to be located for the client at another agency if there is no one linguistically competent to counsel her at the existing one.

### Question Assesses

Content Area IV—Professional Values and Ethics; Professional Values and Ethical Issues (Competency); Professional Boundaries in the Social Worker–Client/Client System Relationship (e.g., Power Differences Conflicts of Interest, etc.) (KSA)

## 170. D

*Rationale*

Cognitive behavioral therapy (CBT) combines cognitive and behavioral therapies. The basic premise of CBT is that emotions are difficult to change directly, so CBT targets emotions by changing thoughts and behaviors that are contributing to the distressing emotions. CBT builds a set of skills that enables an individual to be aware of thoughts and emotions; identify how situations, thoughts, and behaviors influence emotions; and improve feelings by changing dysfunctional thoughts and behaviors. The process of CBT skill acquisition is collaborative. Skill acquisition and homework assignments are what set CBT apart from "talk therapies." Brief CBT is the compression of CBT material and the reduction of the average 12 to 20 sessions into four to eight sessions. In brief CBT, the concentration is on specific treatments for a limited number of client problems. Specificity of the treatment is required because of the limited number of sessions and because a client is required to be diligent in using extra reading materials and homework to assist in his or her therapeutic growth. Brief CBT can range in duration from client to client and provider to provider.

*Certain problems are more appropriate for brief therapy than others.* Problems amenable to brief CBT include, but are not limited to, Adjustment, Anxiety, and Depressive Disorders. Therapy also may be useful for problems that target specific symptoms (e.g., depressive thinking) or lifestyle changes (e.g., problem solving, relaxation), whether or not these issues are part of a formal psychiatric diagnosis. Brief CBT is particularly useful in a primary care setting for clients with anxiety and depression associated with a medical condition. Because these clients often face acute rather than chronic mental health issues and have many coping strategies already in place, brief CBT can be used to enhance adjustment. Issues that may be addressed in primary care include, but are not limited to, diet, exercise, medication compliance, mental health issues associated with a medical condition, and coping with a chronic illness or new diagnosis.

Other problems may not be suitable for the use of, or may complicate, a straightforward application of brief CBT. Borderline Personality Disorder or Antisocial Personality Disorder typically are not appropriate for a shortened therapeutic experience because of the pervasive social, psychological, and relational problems individuals with these disorders experience. Long-standing interpersonal issues often require longer treatment durations. Clients exhibiting comorbid conditions or problems also may not be appropriate because the presence of a second issue may impede progress in therapy. For example, a client with a Substance Use Disorder comorbid with Major Depressive Disorder may not be appropriate because the substance use requires a higher level of care and more comprehensive treatment than is available in a brief format. However, brief CBT could be used with Personality Disorders and comorbid clients in dealing with specific negative behaviors or in conjunction with more intensive treatment. Lastly, conditions such as serious mental illness require focused and more intensive interventions.

### Test-Taking Strategies Applied

Central to selecting the correct response choice is recognizing that the intervention modality mentioned in the question is brief therapy. Brief therapy is a systematic, focused process that relies on assessment, client engagement, and rapid implementation of change strategies. Brief therapy providers can effect important changes in client behavior within a relatively short period.

**Substance Use Disorders** are chronic, requiring long-term support. Brief therapy for substance abuse treatment can be a valuable, but limited, approach and it should not be considered a standard of care.

**Personality Disorders** form a class of mental disorders that are characterized by long-lasting, rigid patterns of thought and behavior.

Personality Disorders are seen as an enduring pattern of inner experience and behavior that deviates markedly from the expectations of the culture of the individual who exhibits it. These patterns are inflexible and *pervasive* across many situations. Thus, they are not optimally treated by brief therapy.

Dissociative Identity Disorder (DID), formerly called Multiple Personality Disorder, is a condition that is characterized by the presence of at least two clear personality states, called alters, which may have different reactions, emotions, and body functioning. While there's no "cure" for DID, long-term treatment is very successful. Effective treatment includes talk therapy or psychotherapy, medications, hypnotherapy, and adjunctive therapies to help clients with DID improve their relationships with others, prevent crises, and experience uncomfortable feelings. Because oftentimes the symptoms of Dissociative Disorders occur with other disorders, such as anxiety and depression, Dissociative Disorders may be treated using the same drugs prescribed for those disorders.

### Question Assesses

Content Area II—Assessment, Diagnosis, and Treatment Planning; Treatment Planning (Competency); The Criteria Used in the Selection of Intervention/Treatment Modalities (e.g., Client/Client System Abilities, Culture, Life Stage) (KSA)

# Evaluation of Results

These tables assist in identifying the content areas and competencies needing further study. Within each of the competencies, there are specific Knowledge, Skills, and Abilities (KSAs) that social workers should reference to assist with locating appropriate study resources. As there is tremendous overlap in the material that could be contained across the KSAs within a given competency, all KSAs for the competency should be reviewed to make sure of an adequate breadth of knowledge in the content area. A listing of the KSAs for each content area and competency can be found in Appendix A.

The results of this evaluation should be the basis of the development of a study plan. Social workers should get to a level of comfort with the material so that they can summarize relevant content, including key concepts and terms. Social workers do not need to be experts in all of the KSAs, but should understand their relevancy to social work practice. They should be able to describe how each of the KSAs specifically impact assessment, as well as decisions about client care.

Appendix B provides useful information on learning styles that can assist when determining the best ways to study and retain material. Success on the Association of Social Work Board (ASWB®) examination does not require a lot of memorization of material, but rather the ability to recall terms and integrate multiple concepts to select the best course of action in hypothetical scenarios. Thus, time is best spent really understanding the KSAs and not just being able to recite definitions.

**Analysis of Clinical Practice Test**
Content Area I: Human Development, Diversity, and Behavior in
the Environment (24%)

| Competency | Question Numbers | Number of Questions | Number Correct | Percentage Correct | Area Requiring Further Study? |
|---|---|---|---|---|---|
| 1. Human Growth and Development | 3, 26, 48, 86, 89, 99, 100, 116, 131, 133, 142, 157, 162, 167 | 14 | __/14 | __% | |
| 2. Human Behavior in the Social Environment | 12, 15, 18, 31, 46, 52, 66, 74, 79, 92, 104, 105, 108, 119, 125, 153, 165 | 17 | __/17 | __% | |
| 3. Diversity and Discrimination | 2, 21, 44, 55, 61, 67, 78, 102, 118, 154 | 10 | __/10 | __% | |

### Analysis of Clinical Practice Test
#### Content Area II: Assessment, Diagnosis, and Treatment Planning (30%)

| Competency | Question Numbers | Number of Questions | Number Correct | Percentage Correct | Area Requiring Further Study? |
|---|---|---|---|---|---|
| 4. Biopsychosocial History and Collateral Data | 32, 39, 45, 63, 72, 87, 88, 96, 97, 141 | 10 | —/10 | —% | |
| 5. Assessment and Diagnosis | 1, 7, 8, 14, 28, 33, 36, 51, 53, 54, 57, 62, 70, 71, 77, 80, 93, 94, 106, 107, 122, 127, 134, 138, 139, 148, 156, 164 | 28 | —/28 | —% | |
| 6. Treatment Planning | 5, 10, 41, 81, 82, 85, 95, 121, 135, 151, 155, 159, 170 | 13 | —/13 | —% | |

| Analysis of Clinical Practice Test<br>Content Area III: Psychotherapy, Clinical Interventions,<br>and Case Management (27%) | | | | | |
|---|---|---|---|---|---|
| Competency | Question Numbers | Number of Questions | Number Correct | Percentage Correct | Area Requiring Further Study? |
| 7. Therapeutic Relationship | 20, 29, 40, 47, 98, 103, 136, 146, 166 | 9 | —/9 | —% | |
| 8. The Intervention Processes | 4, 17, 27, 37, 50, 58, 59, 60, 68, 83, 91, 109, 113, 143, 144, 150 | 16 | —/16 | —% | |
| 9. Service Delivery and Management of Cases | 6, 16, 22, 35, 115, 117, 123, 126, 130, 137, 149 | 11 | —/11 | —% | |
| 10. Consultation and Interdisciplinary Collaboration | 11, 13, 23, 34, 38, 84, 110, 114, 129, 147 | 10 | —/10 | —% | |

### Analysis of Clinical Practice Test
Content Area IV: Professional Values and Ethics (19%)

| Competency | Question Numbers | Number of Questions | Number Correct | Percentage Correct | Area Requiring Further Study? |
|---|---|---|---|---|---|
| 11. Professional Values and Ethical Issues | 9, 49, 56, 90, 101, 112, 120, 124, 128, 152, 158, 163, 169 | 13 | —/13 | —% | |
| 12. Confidentiality | 19, 25, 30, 42, 64, 69, 75, 160, 161, 168 | 10 | —/10 | —% | |
| 13. Professional Development and Use of Self | 24, 43, 65, 73, 76, 111, 132, 140, 145 | 9 | —/9 | —% | |

| Overall Results of Clinical Practice Test | | | |
|---|---|---|---|
| **Content Area** | **Number of Questions** | **Number Correct** | **Percentage Correct** |
| Human Development, Diversity, and Behavior in the Environment (24%) | 41 | __/41 | __% |
| Assessment, Diagnosis, and Treatment Planning (30%) | 51 | __/51 | __% |
| Psychotherapy, Clinical Interventions, and Case Management (27%) | 46 | __/46 | __% |
| Professional Values and Ethics (19%) | 32 | __/32 | __% |
| Overall Clinical Examination Knowledge | 170 | __/170 | __% |

# Appendix A

## Content Areas, Competencies, and KSAs for the ASWB® Clinical Examination

**Human Development, Diversity, and Behavior in the Environment (Content Area)**

1. Human Growth and Development (Competency)

KSAs

Theories of human development throughout the lifespan (e.g., physical, social, emotional, cognitive, behavioral)

The indicators of normal and abnormal physical, cognitive, emotional, and sexual development throughout the lifespan

Theories of sexual development throughout the lifespan

Theories of spiritual development throughout the lifespan

Theories of racial, ethnic, and cultural development throughout the lifespan

The effects of physical, mental, and cognitive disabilities throughout the lifespan

The interplay of biological, psychological, social, and spiritual factors

Basic human needs

The principles of attachment and bonding

The effect of aging on biopsychosocial functioning

Gerontology

Personality theories

Factors influencing self-image (e.g., culture, race, religion/spirituality, age, disability, trauma)

Body image and its impact (e.g., identity, self-esteem, relationships, habits)

Parenting skills and capacities

Basic principles of human genetics

The family life cycle

Models of family life education in social work practice

The impact of aging parents on adult children

Systems and ecological perspectives and theories

Strengths-based and resilience theories

The dynamics and effects of loss, separation, and grief

2. Human Behavior in the Social Environment (Competency)

KSAs

Person-in-environment (PIE) theory

Family dynamics and functioning and the effects on individuals, families, groups, organizations, and communities

The dynamics of interpersonal relationships

Indicators and dynamics of abuse and neglect throughout the lifespan

The effects of physical, sexual, and psychological abuse on individuals, families, groups, organizations, and communities

The characteristics of perpetrators of abuse, neglect, and exploitation

The effects of life events, stressors, and crises on individuals, families, groups, organizations, and communities

The impact of stress, trauma, and violence

Crisis intervention theories

The effect of poverty on individuals, families, groups, organizations, and communities

The impact of the environment (e.g., social, physical, cultural, political, economic) on individuals, families, groups, organizations, and communities

Social and economic justice

Theories of social change and community development

The impact of social institutions on society

The impact of globalization on clients/client systems (e.g., interrelatedness of systems, international integration, technology, environmental or financial crises, epidemics)

Criminal justice systems

The impact of out-of-home placement (e.g., hospitalization, foster care, residential care, criminal justice system) on clients/client systems

Theories of couples development

The impact of physical and mental illness on family dynamics

Co-occurring disorders and conditions

The impact of caregiving on families

Psychological defense mechanisms and their effects on behavior and relationships

Addiction theories and concepts

The effects of addiction and substance abuse on individuals, families, groups, organizations, and communities

The indicators of addiction and substance abuse

Role theories

Feminist theory

Theories of group development and functioning

Communication theories and styles

Theories of conflict

3. Diversity and Discrimination (Competency)

KSAs

The effect of disability on biopsychosocial functioning throughout the lifespan

The effect of culture, race, and ethnicity on behaviors, attitudes, and identity

The effects of discrimination and stereotypes on behaviors, attitudes, and identity

The influence of sexual orientation on behaviors, attitudes, and identity

The impact of transgender and transitioning process on behaviors, attitudes, identity, and relationships

Systemic (institutionalized) discrimination (e.g., racism, sexism, ageism)

The principles of culturally competent social work practice

Sexual orientation concepts

Gender and gender identity concepts

**Assessment, Diagnosis, and Treatment Planning (Content Area)**

4. Biopsychosocial History and Collateral Data (Competency)

KSAs

The components of a biopsychosocial assessment

Techniques and instruments used to assess clients/client systems

The types of information available from other sources (e.g., agency, employment, medical, psychological, legal, or school records)

Components of a sexual history

Components of a family history

Methods to obtain sensitive information (e.g., substance abuse, sexual abuse)

The principles of active listening and observation

The indicators of sexual dysfunction

Symptoms of neurologic and organic disorders

5. Assessment and Diagnosis (Competency)

KSAs

The factors and processes used in problem formulation

Methods of involving clients/client systems in problem identification (e.g., gathering collateral information)

The components and function of the mental status examination

Methods to incorporate the results of psychological and educational tests into assessment

The indicators of psychosocial stress

The indicators, dynamics, and impact of exploitation across the lifespan (e.g., financial, immigration status, sexual trafficking)

The indicators of traumatic stress and violence

Methods used to assess trauma

Risk assessment methods

The indicators and risk factors of the client's/client system's danger to self and others

Methods to assess the client's/client system's strengths, resources, and challenges (e.g., individual, family, group, organization, community)

The indicators of motivation, resistance, and readiness to change

Methods to assess motivation, resistance, and readiness to change

Methods to assess the client's/client system's communication skills

Methods to assess the client's/client system's coping abilities

The indicators of client's/client system's strengths and challenges

Methods to assess ego strengths

The use of the Diagnostic and Statistical Manual of the American Psychiatric Association

The indicators of mental and emotional illness throughout the lifespan

Biopsychosocial factors related to mental health

Biopsychosocial responses to illness and disability

Common psychotropic and nonpsychotropic prescriptions and over-the-counter medications and their side effects

The indicators of somatization

The indicators of feigning illness

Basic medical terminology

The indicators of behavioral dysfunction

Placement options based on assessed level of care

Methods to assess organizational functioning (e.g., agency assessments)

Data collection and analysis methods

## 6. Treatment Planning (Competency)

KSAs

Methods to involve clients/client systems in intervention planning

Cultural considerations in the creation of an intervention plan

The criteria used in the selection of intervention/treatment modalities (e.g., client/client system abilities, culture, life stage)

The components of intervention, treatment, and service plans

Theories of trauma-informed care

Methods and approaches to trauma-informed care

The impact of immigration, refugee, or undocumented status on service delivery

Methods to develop, review, and implement crisis plans

Discharge, aftercare, and follow-up planning

Techniques used to evaluate a client's/client system's progress

Methods, techniques, and instruments used to evaluate social work practice

The principles and features of objective and subjective data

Basic and applied research design and methods

Methods to assess reliability and validity in social work research

## Psychotherapy, Clinical Interventions, and Case Management (Content Area)

## 7. Therapeutic Relationship (Competency)

KSAs

The components of the social worker–client/client system relationship

The principles and techniques for building and maintaining a helping relationship

The dynamics of power and transparency in the social worker–client/client system relationship

The social worker's role in the problem-solving process

Methods to clarify the roles and responsibilities of the social worker and client/client system in the intervention process

The concept of acceptance and empathy in the social worker–client/client system relationship

The dynamics of diversity in the social worker–client/client system relationship

The effect of the client's developmental level on the social worker–client relationship

The impact of domestic, intimate partner, and other violence on the helping relationship

Verbal and nonverbal communication techniques

The concept of congruence in communication

Methods to obtain and provide feedback

8. The Intervention Process (Competency)

KSAs

The principles and techniques of interviewing (e.g., supporting, clarifying, focusing, confronting, validating, feedback, reflecting, language differences, use of interpreters, redirecting)

The phases of intervention and treatment

Problem-solving models and approaches (e.g., brief, solution-focused methods or techniques)

The client's/client system's role in the problem-solving process

Methods to engage and motivate clients/client systems

Methods to engage and work with involuntary clients/client systems

Limit setting techniques

The technique of role play

Role modeling techniques

Techniques for harm reduction for self and others

Methods to teach coping and other self-care skills to clients/client systems

Client/client system self-monitoring techniques

Methods of conflict resolution

Crisis intervention and treatment approaches

Anger management techniques

Stress management techniques

The impact of out-of-home displacement (e.g., natural disaster, homelessness, immigration) on clients/client systems

Methods to create, implement, and evaluate policies and procedures that minimize risk for individuals, families, groups, organizations, and communities

Psychotherapies

Psychoanalytic and psychodynamic approaches

Cognitive and behavioral interventions

Strengths-based and empowerment strategies and interventions

Client/client system contracting and goal-setting techniques

Partializing techniques

Assertiveness training

Task-centered approaches

Psychoeducation methods (e.g., acknowledging, supporting, normalizing)

Group work techniques and approaches (e.g., developing and managing group processes and cohesion)

Family therapy models, interventions, and approaches

Couples interventions and treatment approaches

Permanency planning

Mindfulness and complementary therapeutic approaches

Techniques used for follow-up

Time management approaches

Community organizing and social planning methods

Methods to develop and evaluate measurable objectives for client/client system intervention, treatment, and/or service plans

Primary, secondary, and tertiary prevention strategies

The indicators of client/client system readiness for termination

9. Service Delivery and Management of Cases (Competency)

KSAs

The effects of policies, procedures, regulations, and legislation on social work practice and service delivery

The impact of the political environment on policy-making

Theories and methods of advocacy for policies, services, and resources to meet clients'/client systems' needs

Methods of service delivery

The components of case management

The principles of case recording, documentation, and management of practice records

Methods to establish service networks or community resources

Employee recruitment, training, retention, performance appraisal, evaluation, and discipline

Case recording for practice evaluation or supervision

Methods to evaluate agency programs (e.g., needs assessment, formative/summative assessment, cost-effectiveness, cost-benefit analysis, outcomes assessment)

The effects of program evaluation findings on services

Quality assurance, including program reviews and audits by external sources

10. Consultation and Interdisciplinary Collaboration (Competency)

KSAs

Leadership and management techniques

Models of supervision and consultation (e.g., individual, peer, group)

Educational components, techniques, and methods of supervision

The supervisee's role in supervision (e.g., identifying learning needs, self-assessment, prioritizing, etc.)

Methods to identify learning needs and develop learning objectives for supervisees

The elements of client/client system reports

The elements of a case presentation

The principles and processes for developing formal documents (e.g., proposals, letters, brochures, pamphlets, reports, evaluations)

Consultation approaches (e.g., referrals to specialists)

Methods of networking

The process of interdisciplinary and intradisciplinary team collaboration

The basic terminology of professions other than social work (e.g., legal, educational)

Techniques to inform and influence organizational and social policy

Methods to assess the availability of community resources

Techniques for mobilizing community participation

Methods to establish program objectives and outcomes

Governance structures

The relationship between formal and informal power structures in decision making

Accreditation and/or licensing requirements

**Professional Values and Ethics (Content Area)**

11. Professional Values and Ethical Issues (Competency)

KSAs

Legal and/or ethical issues related to the practice of social work, including responsibility to clients/client systems, colleagues, the profession, and society

Techniques to identify and resolve ethical dilemmas

The client's/client system's right to refuse services (e.g., medication, medical treatment, counseling, placement, etc.)

Professional boundaries in the social worker–client/client system relationship (e.g., power differences, conflicts of interest, etc.)

Ethical issues related to dual relationships

Self-disclosure principles and applications

The principles and processes of obtaining informed consent

Legal and/or ethical issues regarding documentation

Legal and/or ethical issues regarding termination

Legal and/or ethical issues related to death and dying

Research ethics (e.g., institutional review boards, use of human subjects, informed consent)

Ethical issues in supervision and management

Methods to create, implement, and evaluate policies and procedures for social worker safety

## 12. Confidentiality (Competency)

KSAs

The use of client/client system records

Legal and/or ethical issues regarding confidentiality, including electronic information security

Legal and/or ethical issues regarding mandatory reporting (e.g., abuse, threat of harm, impaired professionals, etc.)

## 13. Professional Development and Use of Self (Competency)

KSAs

Professional values and principles (e.g., competence, social justice, integrity, and dignity and worth of the person)

Professional objectivity in the social worker–client/client system relationship

Techniques for protecting and enhancing client/client system self-determination

Client/client system competence and self-determination (e.g., financial decisions, treatment decisions, emancipation, age of consent, permanency planning)

The influence of the social worker's own values and beliefs on the social worker–client/client system relationship

The influence of the social worker's own values and beliefs on interdisciplinary collaboration

The impact of transference and countertransference in the social worker–client/client system relationship

The impact of transference and countertransference within supervisory relationships

The components of a safe and positive work environment

Social worker self-care principles and techniques

Burnout, secondary trauma, and compassion fatigue

Evidence-based practice

Professional development activities to improve practice and maintain current professional knowledge (e.g., in-service training, licensing requirements, reviews of literature, workshops)

# Appendix B
## Learning Styles

The following are some suggested techniques for each learning style that can help to fill in content gaps that may exist.

## VISUAL LEARNERS

**Visual learners learn best through what they see. Although lectures can be boring for visual learners, they benefit from the use of diagrams, PowerPoint slides, and charts.**

- Use colored highlighters to draw attention to key terms
- Develop outlines or take notes on the concepts
- Write talking points for each of the Knowledge, Skills, and Abilities (KSAs) on separate white index cards
- Create a coding schema of symbols and write them next to material and terms that require further study
- Study in an environment that is away from visual distractions such as television, people moving around, or clutter

## AUDITORY LEARNERS

**Auditory learners learn best through what they hear. They may have difficulty remembering material, but can easily recall it if it is read to them.**

- Tape-record yourself summarizing the material as you are studying it—listen to your notes as a way to reinforce what you read

- Have a study partner explain the relevant concepts and terms related to the KSAs

- Read the text aloud if you are having trouble remembering it

- Find free podcasts or YouTube videos on the Internet on the content areas that are short and easy to understand to assist with learning

- Talk to yourself about the content as you study, emphasizing what is important to remember related to each KSA

## KINESTHETIC OR HANDS-ON LEARNERS

**Kinesthetic learners learn through tactile approaches aimed at experiencing or doing. They need physical activities as a foundation for instruction.**

- Make flashcards on material because writing it down will assist with remembering the content

- Use as many different senses as possible when studying—read material when you are on your treadmill, use highlighters, talk aloud about content, and/or listen to a study partner

- Develop mnemonic devices to aid in information retention (e.g., EAPIET or *EAt PIE T*oday is a great way to remember the social work problem-solving process [Engaging, Assessing, Planning, Intervening, Evaluating, and Terminating])

- Write notes and important terms in the margins

- Ask a study partner to quiz you on material—turn it into a game and see how many KSAs you can discuss or how long you can talk about a content area before running out of material